MW00780771

THE PROSTHETIC IMAGINATION

In *The Prosthetic Imagination,* leading critic Peter Boxall argues that we are now entering an artificial age, in which our given bodies enter into new conjunctions with our prosthetic extensions. This new age requires us to reimagine our relation to our bodies, and to our environments, and Boxall suggests that the novel as a form can guide us in this imaginative task. Across a dazzling range of prose fictions, from Thomas More's *Utopia* to Margaret Atwood's *Oryx and Crake,* Boxall shows how the novel has played a central role in forging the bodies in which we extend ourselves into the world. But if the novel has helped to give our world a human shape, it also contains forms of life that elude our existing human architectures: new amalgams of the living and the non-living that are the hidden province of the novel imagination. These latent conjunctions, Boxall argues, are preserved in the novel form, and offer us images of embodied being that can help us orient ourselves to our new prosthetic condition.

PETER BOXALL is Professor of English at the University of Sussex. His books include *Don DeLillo: The Possibility of Fiction* (2006), *Since Beckett: Contemporary Writing in the Wake of Modernism* (2009), *Twenty-First-Century Fiction: A Critical Introduction* (2013) and *The Value of the Novel* (2015). He has edited a number of collections, including *Thinking Poetry* and *Beckett/Aesthetics/Politics*, and an edition of Beckett's novel *Malone Dies*. He is co-editor, with Bryan Cheyette, of volume 7 of the *Oxford History of the Novel in English*, and editor of *The Cambridge Companion to British Fiction, 1980-the Present*, and of the bestselling *1001 Books*. He is also the editor of *Textual Practice*, and the series editor of *Cambridge Studies in Twenty-First-Century Literature and Culture.*

THE PROSTHETIC IMAGINATION

A History of the Novel as Artificial Life

PETER BOXALL

University of Sussex

CAMBRIDGE
UNIVERSITY PRESS

CAMBRIDGE
UNIVERSITY PRESS

University Printing House, Cambridge CB2 8BS, United Kingdom

One Liberty Plaza, 20th Floor, New York, NY 10006, USA

477 Williamstown Road, Port Melbourne, VIC 3207, Australia

314–321, 3rd Floor, Plot 3, Splendor Forum, Jasola District Centre, New Delhi – 110025, India

79 Anson Road, #06–04/06, Singapore 079906

Cambridge University Press is part of the University of Cambridge.

It furthers the University's mission by disseminating knowledge in the pursuit of education, learning, and research at the highest international levels of excellence.

www.cambridge.org
Information on this title: www.cambridge.org/9781108836487
DOI: 10.1017/9781108871297

© Peter Boxall 2020

This publication is in copyright. Subject to statutory exception and to the provisions of relevant collective licensing agreements, no reproduction of any part may take place without the written permission of Cambridge University Press.

First published 2020

Printed in the United Kingdom by TJ International Ltd, Padstow Cornwall

A catalogue record for this publication is available from the British Library.
NAMES: Boxall, Peter, author.
TITLE: The prosthetic imagination : a history of the novel as artificial life / Peter Boxall.
DESCRIPTION: Cambridge ; New York : Cambridge University Press, 2020. | Includes bibliographical references and index.
IDENTIFIERS: LCCN 2020009193 | ISBN 9781108836487 (hardback) | ISBN 9781108871297 (ebook)
SUBJECTS: LCSH: Fiction – History and criticism. | Realism in literature. | Mimesis in literature. | Human body in literature. | Humanity in literature. | Modernism (Literature)
CLASSIFICATION: LCC PN3347 .B65 2020 | DDC 808.3–dc23
LC record available at https://lccn.loc.gov/2020009193

ISBN 978-1-108-83648-7 Hardback

Cambridge University Press has no responsibility for the persistence or accuracy of URLs for external or third-party internet websites referred to in this publication and does not guarantee that any content on such websites is, or will remain, accurate or appropriate.

For Hannah

Living I die, and as my breath
Dies, death recalls me into life again.

Cervantes, Don Quixote

My entire self trembles on the edge of being and not-being.

Goethe, The Sorrows of Young Werther

There is no creature whose inward being is so strong that it is not greatly determined by what lies outside it.

George Eliot, Middlemarch

The only tool I possess is my forehead.

Franz Kafka, 'The Burrow'

If I had the use of my body I would throw it out of the window.

Samuel Beckett, Malone Dies

My foot is an object. Outside myself. It exists.

Christine Brooke-Rose, 'The Foot'

His shoulders lurked beneath that jacket, his voice, his hands – all real. They existed, really existed, somewhere.

Toni Morrison, The Bluest Eye

I'm someone who is supposed to be me.

Don DeLillo, Zero K

Contents

Illustrations

Acknowledgements

My first debt of thanks is to Ray Ryan, whose support for this project has been above and beyond any call of duty. We have worked together, on a number of different books, for more than a decade; in that time he has been not only the most exceptional editor but has also become a friend. I would also like to thank everyone at Cambridge University Press, particularly Edgar Mendez, Stanly Emelson and Linda Benson, for making the production process so smooth and enjoyable.

This book has been written over a number of years and has been given generous support of many kinds. Much of the writing was enabled by a Leverhulme fellowship, and by two periods of leave granted by the University of Sussex. I finished a draft of the manuscript during a visiting professorship at the Sorbonne – an idyllic spring in Paris which I will never forget. The argument in this book has been developed through papers and lectures I have given over the past years at a number of universities and conferences – in the UK at Lancaster, Queen Mary, Cambridge, UEA, Bristol, Essex, Durham, St Andrews, Lincoln, Manchester, Oxford, University College London, Queens University Belfast and York, and overseas at Cologne, Leuven, Aarhus, New York University, Columbia, Cornell, University of California–Riverside, Lisbon, Paris, Toulouse, Rome, Stockholm, Cordoba, Perm and Singapore. Audiences at each of these talks responded in ways that have had a shaping influence on my thinking. More than any other book I have written, the arguments I have developed here have come about through conversations with colleagues and friends. My PhD students and former PhD students have taught me much more than I have taught them, and they all have my gratitude, in particular Kiron Ward, Charlotte Terrell, Jess Oliver, Hannah Vincent, Katie DaCunha Lewin, Polona Jonik and Byron Heffer. A trip to Russia with Kevin Brazil, Jenny Bavidge and Karen Hewitt at a critical point in the writing was revelatory, as was a panel at Cornell with Tim Bewes and Nancy Armstrong. The writing of this book has overlapped with a research project on artificial lives that I have been pursuing with Sherryl Vint, who is the most brilliant and generous of collaborators. We have benefitted from the work of a number of dazzling scholars and artists of the artificial, including David Wills, Claire Colebrook, Paul Vanouse and Arthur Bradley. Richard Tyler has aided this project in a number of ways, not least by introducing me to prosthetic surgeons early in the project. I have been supported, in innumerable ways, by colleagues at Sussex and beyond, and in particular by Sara Crangle, Sam Ladkin, Maria Lauret, Pam Thurschwell, Sara Jane Bailes, Emma Carlyle, David James, Candida Lacey, Bryan Cheyette, Peter Nicholls, Laura Marcus, Drew Milne, Wilfrid Rotge and Lara Feigel. Michael Jonik was a steadfast partner at Les Philosophes during our Paris spring, a philosophical partnership which in some sense continues.

A number of people have influenced the direction that the book has taken. A correspondence with Don DeLillo in 2016 was illuminating, both about artificial life and about the unfathomable relation between writer and reader. I had several conversations with Ali Smith during the writing, which always left me with an expanded awareness of the beauty and generosity of the literary imagination. I have felt moved by the willingness of friends to read draft chapters, and by the brilliance and penetration of their responses. Tom Healy, Andrew Hadfield, Al Deakin, Merve Emre, Catherine Packham and Nicholas Royle have all dedicated time to reading this work, which is immeasurably better than it otherwise would be.

My last thanks are reserved, as always, for my large and wonderful family, which continues with the passing years to get larger and more wonderful. It is one of the greatest pleasures of the longer-toothed life to find that a baton has been discreetly passed from parents and aunts and uncles to sons and daughters, nieces and nephews, to a generation of brilliant and fascinating people who fill me with hope for the future. My children – Ava, Laurie and Iris – have a world within them, which I cannot wait to live in.

This is the second work I have dedicated to my partner and co-thinker Hannah, the first being my PhD thesis, written decades ago, in another world and time. Over the years that we have shared our lives she has made for us both a republic of the spirit, a way of being we, in which together we have lived and loved and thought in freedom and in happiness. To have done so feels nothing short of miraculous.

Introduction
Mimesis and Prosthesis

> I want you to feel wonder at the transformations of men's shapes and destinies into alien forms, and their reversion by a chain of interconnection to their own.
>
> Apuleius, *The Golden Ass*[1]

What is the relation between the mimetic and the prosthetic? How does the process of making pictures or likenesses of reality (in paint, in film, in prose) relate to our fashioning of artificial bodies, the manufacturing of the plastic forms with which we augment and enhance our naked extension into the world, what Freud calls the mere 'inch of nature' which we are given?[2]

This question was given a rather palpable form for me when, as part of my initial preparation for writing this book, I spent some time with a prosthetic surgeon who specialises in facial prosthetics. The surgeon – Charles – took me to a room in which there were a number of wooden cabinets, where he stored facial prostheses in drawers. He wanted to show me some of them, he said, to give me a sense of the range of different kinds of prostheses he made. He had these faces in his possession because, as his patients aged or grew, he regularly updated their prostheses. The faces I was looking at (which he somewhat uncannily referred to by the names of their ex-owners, so recognisable were they, so distinct) were cast-off faces, the strange, fragmentary, expired faces of selves that had been outgrown.

As I regarded these abandoned, oddly sad objects, it struck me that the prosthesis serves, in some senses, a function opposite to that of the aesthetic representation. It is perhaps the task of the artwork, the portrait, the self-portrait, to capture a moment in time and preserve it, still it – in Virginia Woolf's phrase to 'make of the moment something permanent', 'Mrs Ramsay saying "Life stand still here."'[3] It is the task, on the other hand, of the prosthesis to allow its user or wearer or owner (these words are laden) to enter into passing time, real time; its task is not to still life (as in the grave

Italian phrase *natura morta*) but to animate it, to put it into motion. It is required to perform something adjacent to the work of the time machine in H. G. Wells' *Time Machine*, to achieve, as the time traveller says, precisely that which the portrait, the still and complete image, cannot. 'Here is a portrait', the traveller says, 'of a man at eight years old, another at fifteen, another at seventeen, another at twenty-three'.[4] Each of these portraits is bound in already materialised time and space, in three dimensions, but it is the gift of the time machine to reach beyond these dimensions, towards what the traveller calls 'Four-Dimensioned being' (p. 9) – the being extended in time, the being not yet made, to which the time machine grants magical access, and to which it is the more material task of the prosthetic to cleave. The prosthetic surgeon's job is always in process, as he or she has to do the work of time for his or her patients, even as the prosthetic itself (unlike the artwork) must age – wear out or wear into the life with which it is so closely conjoined (to the extent that it shares its name with its owner) until the moment it is discarded, the moment when its work and its life as a prosthetic are finished, and it can be stowed away in a cedar drawer.

There is a tension, then, at the heart of the prosthetic as an object, between stasis and movement, between its reproduction of a particular moment of being and its role as a conduit that brings its user or wearer into relation with moving time, with time still to come. And this tension is at the heart of a second revelation that I had during my time with Charles. A moment nearly always comes, he told me, in the early stages of his relationship with his patients, when he asks how far a particular patient wants him to aim for a likeness of their face as it was before injury or trauma, and how far they would prefer him to make a face for them that will be best adapted to their post-injury or post-surgical needs. There is a difficult, complex charge to this question, one bound up with the relation between prosthetics and the reality of injury and suffering, as well as with the uncertain conjunction between the prosthetic as a medical tool and the prosthetic as an artwork. Charles felt himself, he told me, to be at once an artist making a likeness of a face from the past – a face that has gone but that still exists in memory and in image, and thus might be reproduced – and a manufacturer, making a new face that is not a representation but the thing itself, the face itself in which its wearer (owner, user) will present him- or herself to the world in the very midst of their becoming. The prosthetic face will not remain an inert object, an inanimate representation, but will affix itself to the living framework of the head, will become a part of its wearer's unfolding, evolving identity, as Stephen Hawking's prosthetic voice becomes part of his thinking and being, the accent of his living relation to self and to others, rather than or as well as an artificial supplement for a real voice that is lost.[5]

This tension or contradiction between the extra-temporal and the temporal, between representing a missing thing and being the thing itself, is native to the prosthetic condition, and present in every prosthetic object. As David Wills puts it in *Prosthesis* – the most penetrating analysis of the prosthetic condition we have – the 'duality of every prosthesis' resides in its 'search for a way between emulating the human and superseding the human'.[6] But if such duality is intrinsic, in this way, to the very being of the prosthetic, it is also historically determined, not an abstract contradiction, but a lived one, bound up with the real forces that produce our material lifeworlds. Changing historical conditions in the long history of human technologies determine the balance that is struck within the prosthetic object between representing a missing thing and becoming the thing that is missing. Indeed, we are now living at a moment when the historical quality of the prosthetic condition is in a process of rapid and profound change – when both the technological and the theoretical constitution of prosthetic material is being radically reformed and when, as a result, our understanding of the relation between the mimetic and the prosthetic, between representing a thing and being that thing, also enters into transition. This rapid and intense shift in prosthetic technologies is visible in changes that have taken place even in the short time that has elapsed since I spent my time with the prosthetic surgeon (the time I have spent writing this book). When we met in 2015, Charles explained that he was not then able to use the evolving technology of 3D printing to manufacture facial prosthetics – the grading of the printed material was not fine enough to produce smooth facial contours, and so he had to sculpt his faces by hand and by eye. But, since David Tse pioneered the first 3D printed prosthetics in 2014, the technology has rapidly advanced and is now widely used – a development that touches on a broader technological revolution, of which the prosthetic revolution is a part.[7] The emergence of the printed prosthetic face is a manifestation of a shift, everywhere visible in the technicity of contemporary life, from material to information. Handmade or machine-tooled prosthetic faces give primacy to material; the face is made of matter, and so in making artificial faces we shape them, likewise, out of matter. We work, like Pygmalion sculpting Galatea, on a lump of unformed, unmeaning material, coaxing that material into a human shape, according it a human meaning and expression; 3D printed faces work the other way around. This technology gives primacy not to the material but to the informational. The human signature, the human expression, is preserved not in bodies which the prosthetic seeks to imitate but in computer language, in the codes from which we derive images, memories, every element of our contemporary prosthetic environment. In this latter logic, we do not sculpt prior material into human shape but employ printing technologies to give information – information as the prior state – reproducible material form. The face is stored on the computer, in the 'cloud' – like a Facebook profile – and can be printed out, reprinted, edited, augmented and adapted in ways that are limited only by the capacity of the hardware to keep up with the software.

This shift from material to information as the ground of shared being can, as I say, be felt everywhere in contemporary culture and amounts to the emergence of a new prosthetic age, a new era in the production of artificial life, one which is still unfolding as I write. It is tempting to suggest that there is no part of the contemporary public sphere that is left untouched by this transformation, by the predominance of information over material that has one outcome in the arrival of the printed prosthetic face. The dwindling of the hard forms in which art and entertainment are disseminated partakes, of course, of this logic. The shift from vinyl to magnetic tape to compact disc to Spotify; the shift from typewriting to word processing, from the codex to Kindle; the shift from film to video to Netflix (note the historically inevitable appearance of the trade name): in each case we move from a scenario in which an idea is bound into material, to one in which the idea floats free of its instantiation, in which the idea can enact itself through its instantiations again and again with no deterioration, no cost to or erosion of its essential informational quality. This progressive movement from material to information lives out the logic theorised by Alison Landsberg in her 2004 book *Prosthetic Memory*, in which she explores the 'construction of prosthetic memories' from 'mass cultural technologies' such as cinema.[8] And if we can see this logic manifest in contemporary forms of information technology and data storage, then we can see it too in new biomedical developments that are transforming our understanding of the editability and fungibility of the body. The infotechnological developments which lead to the 3D printed face have a biotechnological equivalent in the recent development of 'bioprinting' – a procedure in which living material can be printed directly onto the body from what is known as 'bioink', and which has allowed, in the field of facial prosthetics, for the construction of 'biomasks' which achieve 'effective and rapid restoration of aesthetic and functional facial skin'.[9] Damaged faces can be recovered by being bioprinted, just as ancient buildings that are lost or destroyed can be reprinted; but the most far-reaching technologies for the editing and manipulation of the body are those associated with genetic engineering technologies (most famously the use, in 2013, of the Crispr gene-editing mechanism to edit the human genome).[10] As Philip Thurtle and Robert Mitchell suggest, in the introduction to their 2004 collection *Data Made Flesh*, genetic-engineering technologies erode the 'apparently solid distinction between "information" and "the flesh"', forcing upon us a new way of understanding what they call the 'material poesis of informatics', a new way of thinking about the passage from 'the virtual world of information to the actual world of flesh and bone'.[11] As contemporary information and biomedical technologies give a new priority to the informational, a priority in which geneticists tend to think of 'genetic information as an "essence" that only contingently receives "expression" in bodies' (p. 1), so we enter into a new prosthetic age, an age in which we are led to recognise that all biopolitical extension is in some degree prosthetic. Under these conditions, the opposition between the mimetic and the prosthetic itself becomes difficult to sustain. It can seem no longer to be the case that there is a prior, non-prosthetic body out there in the world, to which mimetic representations strive to be faithful, and which only requires prosthetic addition when it is injured or curtailed. Rather, the logic of contemporary technicity suggests that all biomateriality is the contingent bodying forth, the transitory 'thingifying', of an idea that is in its nature informational. Mimesis, as the second order representation of a prior, unaugmented reality, starts to become inoperable and gives way to prosthesis as the presiding logic of our relation to ourselves and to the world. Accordingly we are encouraged, as Katherine Hayles puts it, to think of our body as 'the original prosthesis we all learn to manipulate'.[12]

Contemporary technologies, then, are reshaping the way we understand the relation between thought and thing, shifting the balance between the mimetic and the prosthetic; if this is so, it is also the case that the theoretical and philosophical languages with which we account for the relation between mimesis and prosthesis undergo a related transformation – a transformation that one can see unfolding over the past century of critical thought. It is striking, for example, that Freud's conception of the prosthesis as an addition to the inch of nature we are given rests on a clear demarcation between the given body and its artificial, human-made extensions. As Jacques Derrida puts it, Freud, 'as a classical metaphysician', holds the 'technical prosthesis to be a secondary and accessory exteriority'.[13] 'Each individual' of our species, Freud writes in *Civilization and Its Discontents*, 'first appeared on this earth' as 'a feeble animal organism', a 'helpless suckling'.[14] This is the experience of life without techne, life without artificial extension; but the historical passage of civilisation, Freud argues, sees the development of an increasingly complex array of tools which allow the helpless suckling to dominate his or her surroundings, through an act of prosthetic addition. 'With every tool,' he writes, 'man is perfecting his own organs, whether motor or sensory, or is removing the limits to their functioning':

> Motor power places gigantic forces at his disposal, which, like his muscles, he can employ in any direction; thanks to ships and aircraft neither water nor air can hinder his movements; by means of spectacles he corrects defects in the lens of his own eye; by means of the telescope he sees into the far distance and by means of the microscope he overcomes the limits of visibility set by the structure of his retina. (p. 279)

These tools (as well as the camera, the gramophone, the telephone) act, Freud suggests, as prosthetic extensions of the body – like artificial muscles, mouths, eyes, ears, that perform bodily functions in an enhanced way (a technological enhancement of the body that has been traced with great imagination by Friedrich Kittler in *Gramophone, Film, Typewriter*); but if this is so, it is still the case, for Freud, that the prosthesis, while partaking of the qualities of the body, is quite distinct from it, a distinction which lies at the root of civilisation's discontents. Prostheses make 'man' godlike, in that they allow 'him' to achieve those miraculous feats that, in our mythology, we ascribe to the gods. 'Man has, as it were, become a kind of prosthetic god' (p. 280), but this is an artificial godliness, which requires us to put on a kind of Cervantine armour, a superhero costume (Ironman or Batman whose powers are prosthetic, not Superman whose powers are innate, or Spiderman whose powers are genetically engineered), which is not of our own organic nature but must be grafted onto us in ways that might make us itch, or chafe, or come out in a rash. 'When he puts on all his auxiliary organs he is truly magnificent', Freud remarks in a disconcerting phrase that predicts the body-horror imagery of David Cronenberg, 'but those organs have not grown on to him and they still give him much trouble at times' (p. 280).[15]

It is on this boundary between the real and the artificial, the non-prosthetic and the prosthetic, still operational in Freud's 1930 essay, that the most influential twentieth-century accounts of mimesis can be seen to rest. Erich Auerbach's 1946 work *Mimesis* – still the most compelling analysis of mimetic forms we have, despite numerous attempts to overhaul or surpass it – is given shape by this topology, this sense that the given body, the crawling, suckling inch, precedes and underlies the technologies that are belatedly attached to it. Auerbach's great achievement is his capacity to expose the seam between reality and the historical forms of representation which we have invented to account for it – a seam which runs parallel to that uncomfortable, intimate junction that Freud imagines between the body and its auxiliary organs. In mining this seam as it runs through the history of Western cultural expression, Auerbach tells the story of a gradual weakening of the bond between reality and representation, a gradual lessening of the power of reality to assert itself as such, and a corresponding strengthening of the role of representation as the sphere in which our realities are experienced and mediated. In Homer's poetry, and then in Greco-Roman antiquity, Auerbach argues (in tandem with Georg Lukács), reality is fully bodied forth in poetic form; the 'basic impulse of Homeric style', he says, is to 'represent phenomena in a fully externalised form, visible and palpable in all their parts'.[16] In Homer we are 'lured' into a '"real" world' which 'exists for itself, contains nothing but itself' (p. 13), just as later 'Greco-Roman specimens of realistic presentation' are still 'perfectly integrated in their sensory substance', and so 'do not know the antagonism between sensory appearance and meaning' (p. 49). The sub-sequent (Judeo-Christian) history of mimesis, in Auerbach's account, is the story of a growing gap between sensory appearance and meaning, between reality and representation. In his beautiful reading of Cervantes, he sees this gap opening wider, as seventeenth-century European reality becomes increasingly at odds with the languages which seek to describe it – the comedy of *Don Quixote* arising, he argues, from the perception that Don Quixote's wayward seeing is 'completely senseless' and 'incompatible with the existing world'. Don Quixote's imaginary vocation as a knight errant 'not only has no chance of success, it actually has no point of contact with reality' (p. 344). Cervantes' novel is thus a test of the match and mismatch between reality and representational forms, a relation which Auerbach traces through the eighteenth and nineteenth centuries, and up to the modernists – in particular Proust, Joyce and Woolf – where the fictional world is bound less and less by a duty to match itself to 'objective reality', which becomes, accordingly, hazy and uncertain. Where Homer's world is 'fully externalised', Woolf gives us only pictures of 'inner processes' (p. 529) which are not held together by a stable external reality. This is a fictional scenario in which the 'narrator of objective facts has almost completely vanished' (p. 534), in response to a European historical situation, in the early decades of the twentieth century, which is 'pregnant with disaster' (p. 551). In a 'Europe unsure of itself', Auerbach writes, 'overflowing with unsettled ideologies and ways of life', the modernist novel develops a 'method which dissolves reality into multiple and multivalent reflections of consciousness' (p. 551). Catching an echo of Joyce's *Ulysses*, which finds in the 'cracked lookingglass of a servant' a 'symbol of Irish art',[17] this is a method which serves as a 'mirror of the decline of our world' (p. 551); but if this is so, it is never the case, for Auerbach, that representations overcome reality, or free themselves from its prior claims. The mimetic urge survives, here, in its representational mode, even as the bonds which attach narrative to reality, interior to exterior, come asunder. In Woolf's *To The Lighthouse* 'we are after all confronted with an endeavour to investigate an objective reality' (p. 536), but one which no longer yields itself to older forms of objective narration. In giving themselves up to a mobile and fragmentary narrative method, Joyce, Proust and Woolf come much closer than older narrative forms could to the new reality of twentieth-century Europe and are able to give vivid expression, even in their apparent retreat into 'interior processes', to a shared, common world. 'What realistic depth is achieved in every individual occurrence', Auerbach marvels, 'for example the measuring of a stocking' (p. 552). Modernist dissolution does not lead, as Lukács fears it must, to an abandonment of our commitment to shared realities, but quite the reverse.[18] Through the action of such dissolution, 'something new and elemental appeared: nothing less than the wealth of reality and depth of life in every moment to which we surrender ourselves without prejudice'.[19] At the ground of the modernist method, and as a result of the 'complicated process of dissolution which led to fragmentation of the exterior action', Auerbach finds the basis of a shared reality which survives the distorting grotesqueries of Nazism – one which preserves the 'elementary things which men in general have in common', one in which 'what [we] have in common' might 'shine forth' (p. 552).

Freud and Auerbach, then, map the tendencies of modernism and psychoanalysis onto the persistent junction between the given and the prosthetic body, between reality and our representations of it. But implicit in both of their thought is the possibility, present but held back, that these same tendencies lead to a scenario in which reality folds into representation – that the overcoming of the distinction between the informational and the material that is the tendency of contemporary technicity might also – must also – find expression in contemporary thought. The unfolding of this possibility is in large measure the story of the literary and critical theory of the second half of the twentieth century. When Paul Ricoeur laments the 'stubborn prejudices' that 'tend to identify the notion of image with that of a replica of a given reality', he is referring both to the dawning of this possibility and to the obstacles that remain in the path of its realisation.[20] His 1979 essay 'The Function of Fiction in Shaping Reality' is important for its concise expression of this deep and far-reaching theoretical transformation-in-process, in which the terms of the relationship between reality and representation, between the non-prosthetic and the prosthetic body, are overturned. 'It is a fact', Ricoeur writes, that 'no articulate theory of imagination is available which does justice to the basic distinction between image as fiction and image as copy' (p. 118); we are still, in 1979, he argues, in thrall to what he elsewhere calls a 'representational illusion', which dictates that the fictional image is a second-order phenomenon which seeks to stand in for a first-order reality, that 'an image' in a prose narrative is 'a physical or mental replica of an absent thing' (p. 119).[21] The 'representational illusion', at work in Auerbach's 'important post-war book, *Mimesis*', Ricoeur writes in his 1980 essay 'Mimesis and Representation', 'stems from the impossible claim' that a representation is able to 'unit[e] the interiority of a mental image in the mind' with 'the exteriority of something real that would govern from outside the play of the mental scene'.[22] If we are to develop a better understanding of the relationship between mimesis and representation, he argues, we have to recognise that the fictional image does not act in this way as an intermediary between interior processes and external realities. The fictional image does not merely *stand in* for an absent reality, is not simply a replica of a missing thing, but, like the prosthetic, it is that thing itself. It does not mediate between inside and outside but acts to 'dissolve the opposition between inside and outside, which itself arises from the representational illusion' (p. 151). A fictional image, a fictional world, Ricoeur writes, might reproduce elements of reality, but it is also in its nature to be self-referring, to invent situations, people, places which have no model outside of the language world of the fiction, which are not structured by an opposition between 'the text as its own interior and life as exterior to it' (p. 151). 'In the case of fiction', he says, 'there is no given model, in the sense of an original already there, to which it could be referred' (p. 120). An image in a fiction does not refer to a reality beyond it – there is no real white whale, no real Ahab, of which Melville's pictures are a likeness; rather, it refers only to itself and draws only on the authority of the fiction to endorse it, and so it is not a second-order *copy* of reality, but a first-order *piece* of reality. 'Because it has no previous referent', he says, 'it may refer in a productive way to reality, and even *increase* reality' (p. 121). Through a process of what he calls 'iconic augmentation', the narrative imagination can be '"productive" not only of unreal objects, but also as an expanded vision of reality. Imagination at work – in a work – produces itself as a world' (p. 123). It is this capacity not to 'refer' to reality but to 'produce' it that constitutes what he calls 'the central paradox of fiction', 'namely, that only the image which does not already have its referent in reality is able to display a world' (p. 129).

Ricoeur gives expression to this shift from reference to production in the midst of a burst of critical activity in the late seventies and early eighties that helped redefine our understanding of the mechanics of narrative;[23] but the terms in which he conceives of the dissolution of the opposition between inside and outside, reality and representation, are part of a much wider theoretical revolution that has its genesis a decade earlier, in 1967, with the publication in rapid succession of three transformational works by Jacques Derrida – *Speech and Phenomena, Of Grammatology* and *Writing and Difference*. These works together establish the basis for a fundamental rethinking of the relationship between writing, speech and presence, a rethinking which puts the junction between reality and representation that runs through the work of Freud and Auerbach under a certain kind of erasure. In place of a prior presence and a secondary representation, these works develop a logic of the 'trace' – the trace as the form in which a presence that is always beside itself, always already displaced or effaced, comes to being in the throes of its own displacement. 'The trace is not a presence', Derrida writes in *Speech and Phenomena*, 'but is rather a simulacrum of a presence that dislocates, displaces, and refers beyond itself'.[24] Writing marks the absence of the origin to which it refers, but it is only in the marking of that absence, only in the experience of the trace that it leaves, that the absent origin comes to possibility. Presence, Derrida writes, 'is no longer what every reference refers to'. Rather, 'it becomes a function in a generalized referential structure.'[25] As he puts it in *Of Grammatology*, in a phrase that has given rise to more misunderstandings than almost any other in his work, '*il n'y a pas de hors-texte*': '*There is nothing outside of the text.*'[26] Just as Ricoeur argues that the fictional image refers not to something outside itself but to its own referential world, so Derrida insists that the people in Rousseau's *Confessions* – the 'real life of these existences of "flesh and bone"' – have no existence outside of the text. 'Beyond and behind' that flesh and bone, Derrida writes, 'there has never been anything but writing', never anything but 'supplements', but the 'trace', which is the textual mark of a 'real' that is only conjured by that writing itself, in the process of its disappearance.[27] 'Nature', the 'absolute present', these things, Derrida writes, 'have always already escaped, have never existed' – 'what opens meaning and language is writing as the disappearance of natural presence' (p. 159).

In developing this logic of the trace, Derrida's work – along with a body of theoretical writing from Ricoeur to Judith Butler – moves in a certain tandem with the technological ascendency of information over material. Despite Derrida's outright hostility to the languages of postmodernism, it is easy to see that his assertion of the textual character of reality – an assertion that is reproduced, notwithstanding their differences from one another, in a wide range of thinkers, from Ricoeur to Jean Baudrillard – corresponds with the emergence of a postmodern structure of feeling, which is defined by the experience of virtuality, the sense that our environments and lifeworlds are made of frictionless, weightless informational codes, by 'waves and radiation', rather than flesh and bone, earth and stone, bricks and mortar.[28] Indeed, it is perhaps a mark of the close relation between deconstruction and contemporary technicity that Derrida employs, at several key moments in his work, the figure of the prosthesis as a means of elucidating the logic of the trace. There is no moment, for Derrida, when we are absolutely present to ourselves, immersed, as naked sucklings, in the inch of nature we are given, just as there is no language that is complete and unadulterated, full of its own meaning; rather, there is a 'prosthesis at the origin', both of body and of language.[29] The body only knows itself through prosthetic additions which remove it from its self-presence; language only comes to meaning through the play of translation, through the encounter with a prosthetic supplement, the addition of a word or a meaning that is always alien to the true word, which remains unspoken and unthought and untranslated. Prosthesis – as the inherent technicity of being, the impossibility of a form of presence that is not in some sense artificial or supplemented or beside itself – thus comes to mark the demise of the 'representational illusion', the end of the idea that mimesis involves the formal representation of a prior reality. The prosthesis, David Wills argues, 'has all the consistency of a ghost'.[30] The movement from mimesis to prosthesis is the movement from the Auerbachian model, in which narrative forms refer to the world, to a Derridean, Ricoeurian model, in which narrative, information, does not refer to the world but produces it, gives rise to it in the form of a prosthetic trace, an original difference from self, from *ipse*, which is the genesis of meaning, language and being.

The prosthetic marks, in this sense, the coming together of theory and technicity in the later twentieth century. But if this is so – if there is a mutually productive relation between deconstruction, postmodern virtuality, and contemporary information technology – it is central to everything that I will argue in this book that the prosthetic condition that is coming to dominance now, in the early twenty-first century, takes us past the theoretical terms in which it was encoded in the later decades of the twentieth century. Postmodern thought, as it was developed by Jean-François Lyotard, Fredric Jameson, Jean Baudrillard and others, and as it drew on the discoveries of Derridean deconstruction, found in what Jameson called the 'cultural logic of late capitalism' the overcoming of material resistance to ideational forms.[31] The global flow of finance capital gives rise to our built environment, as text gives rise to reality, as spectacle gives rise to world, as information gives rise to material, as idea gives rise to thing, as data gives rise to flesh. The prosthetic, under this optic, becomes the mark of weightless information freed from its material instantiation, as Donna Haraway's cyborgs or William Gibson's neuromancers live in a technological realm, a cyberspace, that is not limited, bordered or bounded by the non-prosthetic real.[32] But as the infotechnological, bio-technological revolution continues, and as it unfolds against the background of eco-crisis (the ugly twin of technicity, the blowback of the human domination of nature), we have seen everywhere the lapsing of postmodern forms, and the connected return of a material ontology, of a body that matters, even if one radically estranged from any available form of representation. The late-century fantasy of a frictionless specularity, in which humans or posthumans create and recreate their environments at will, has given way to the recognition that the emerging informational lifeworld continues to have material determinants, consequences and effects, even if these no longer correspond to the relation between reality and representation, between information and material, that persists in Freud and in Auerbach. The planetary return of the repressed – in the form of climate change, of melting icecaps, wildfires, hurricanes, tornadoes, coastal erosion – tells us that the (Virilian) tendency of technicity towards disappearance has nevertheless a spectacularly visible and real set of manifestations.[33] But it tells us too that the older models that had allowed us to define and measure the relation between human and world, between nature and culture, between the artificial and the real – between mimesis and prosthesis – are no longer capable of accounting for the distribution of idea in material. The emergence of climate change, of the Anthropocene, does not constitute what Catherine Belsey has recently called the 'return of the real', so much as it signals a deep realignment of the ways in which the real relates to the human-made, to the artificial.[34] There is for us no return to some older conception of a real environment that precedes our representations of it. As Claire Colebrook has recently argued, climate change, in all its reality, is a function of artifice, of the ways in which the artificial has threaded itself into all elements of our material environment, overcoming any secure distinction between the natural and the constructed. We cannot account for the contemporary reappearance of materiality by resuscitating Ricoeur's 'representational illusion'; rather, we have to radicalise the theory of artifice which took an earlier form in a postmodern cultural logic, to reconceive the ways in which artifice is distributed in material, outside and beyond the terms in which we have conceived of human life. The material lifeworlds that are emerging now require us, Colebrook suggests, to 'think of artifice in an inhuman and dispersed manner', to try to conceive of a 'more general artifice within which we are located and effected'.[35] This is not artifice confined within the well-made artwork – within the aesthetic forms in which humans create pictures of an existing world – but a distribution of the living in the non-living, of the artificial in the real, that has always exceeded human forms, and that is now coming to thought and to perception in its radical anti-human distributedness. 'What might life be like', Colebrook asks, 'if all life were thought of as artificial life, and if that same artifice were not moralised as having its only proper form in the art object?' (p. 10).

This question is posed, I think, by the dawning of the current stage in the history of the prosthetic condition. Across the range of contemporary thought, as we move past the threshold of postmodernism, and as we seek to adapt to new technologies of artificial life, one can see attempts to reformulate the ontology of the artificial, to rethink the relation, as Leo Bersani puts it, between 'thoughts and things', or as Roberto Esposito puts it, between 'persons and things'.[36] The task of contemporary theory is to understand how life moves in matter – to conceive of new forms of what Jane Bennett calls 'vibrant matter' – in the wake of failed twentieth-century humanisms and posthumanisms.[37] It requires us to develop versions of what Laura U. Marks calls a 'haptic criticism', which produce new terms in which to respond to the conjunction of thinking and touching.[38] And it is partly as a response to this demand, as a contribution to this effort of thought, that the following work sets out to reread the history of the novel as a history of artificial life. It is one of the two central claims in this book that, as we find ourselves in the midst of a deeply estranged relation to life, in which the distinction between the real and the artificial becomes difficult or even impossible to maintain, the novel can help us historicise this estrangement. It can do this, I will argue here, in part because the novel as a form exhibits, from its first beginnings to the present day, a particular and perhaps strange affinity with the prosthetic, as if the novel and the prosthetic share something in their genetic codes.

One can find early evidence of this affinity in antiquity, in those Greco-Roman narratives that are written, in Auerbach's account, before any gap opens between reality and representation. Take for example Apuleius' *The Golden Ass* (ca AD 170) – one of those works that Margaret Anne Doody cites as exemplary of the 'ancient novel' in her 1996 book *The True Story of the Novel*.[39] *The Golden Ass*, like Ovid's *Metamorphoses*, is a story of transformation, of the narrator Lucius' transformation into an ass, and his eventual return to human form (when he is able, in the final pages, to 'shrug off the skin of this most hateful of animals').[40] The tale is driven by a fascination with this capacity for bodies to undergo such transformation, while remaining in some sense themselves – a fascination, as Mikhail Bakhtin puts it in his brilliant analysis of Apuleius, with 'the shifting appearance of one and the same individual'.[41] 'I want you to feel wonder at the transformations of men's shapes', the narrator says at the opening of the story, 'and their reversion by a chain of interconnection to their own' (p. 1). Even as the mythical structure of *The Golden Ass* suggests that integration of 'meaning' and 'sensory appearance' that Auerbach finds in early form, the pleasure of the tale resides in the sense that reality itself has a difference from itself, a difference that comes to thought as the movement of narrative, as the particular capacity of prose fiction to depict a persona who is once a man and an ass. And if this is so, it is in the deep affinity between mimesis and prosthesis that this differing movement of narrative comes to expression. A prosthetic logic is at work throughout the tale – the logic which suggests that the forms in which we know ourselves are always at a remove from us, that we are not identical with our manifestations. The ass is the prosthetic extension of the man (as the insect is the prosthetic extension of the salesman in Kafka's tale of metamorphosis), and we are required to undergo some process of identification to close the gap between an inner sense of self and the alien forms in which that sense of self is realised – a process of identification which it is the job of mimesis to achieve. It is the task of mimesis to produce a means of bringing ass and man, inner being and artificial extension, into the same sphere. This logic, this relation between mimesis and prosthesis, is at work, as I say, in every line of *The Golden Ass*, but it is in the story told by the character Thelyphron that it can be seen at work most explicitly. Thelyphron's story, concerning his travels in Thessaly, is one of the inset tales in *The Golden Ass* – a story that Thelyphron tells to Lucian early in the narrative to account for his disfigured face. Finding himself short of money on his travels, Thelyphron explains, he agrees, in return for a fee, to watch over a corpse through the night. His task is to protect the dead man against witches who tend, in those parts, to attack corpses to steal parts of their faces for their own nefarious purposes. All Thelyphron has to do for his money is stay awake and make sure that no witches get into the death chamber. There is, however, a catch: 'If the watcher does not hand over the body intact in the morning, he is forced to make good any feature which has been prised off, wholly or partly, with the equivalent feature cut from his own face' (p. 24). These seem tough terms, but Thelyphron accepts, because he feels sure he will be able to stay awake through the night, to fend off any witches who may have a taste for facial parts (and because he needs the money). As soon as the watch begins, though, Thelyphron is bewitched and plunged into such a deep sleep that he appears as dead as the corpse which he is supposed to be guarding. 'Even the god of Delphi', he says, 'could not easily have decided which of the two of us there was more dead than the other. I lay there lifeless, needing a second guard to watch over me. It was almost as if I were not present' (pp. 33–34). Thelyphron and the corpse (who we soon learn is also, oddly enough, called Thelyphron) thus enter into a shared state of death, a shared inanimate condition, which leaves the corpse defenseless against the witches' attack. On waking in the morning, Thelyphron assumes that his inattentiveness will have led to the mutilation of the corpse that he was supposed to be guarding. He rushes to examine the corpse, 'peering at each feature' (p. 34), but finds to his ecstatic relief that the dead face is intact, meaning that he gets to keep both his money and his own living face. As the story unfolds, however, we find that Thelyphron has not in fact escaped at all. Through a series of complicated plot twists, a local prophet reanimates dead Thelyphron's corpse, so that he might tell the tale of his death. As dead Thelyphron tells his story (speaking from within living Thelyphron's narration, the pair enacting a peculiar kind of ventriloquism), he explains to the listening crowd that witches did indeed come in the night, after his death, to steal his face. They came to his chamber and summoned him by his name, but the person who responded to the call was in fact our own Thelyphron, he who was 'actually alive, and merely dead to the world in sleep', whereupon, dead Thelyphron tells us, the witches disfigured not the corpse but the living man, the man telling his story to Lucius, and to us. 'The witches cut off first his nose then his ears' (p. 37): 'Then, to ensure that their deceit would pass unnoticed in what followed, they shaped wax to represent the ears which they had cut off, and gave him a perfect fit. Likewise they fashioned a nose like his own' (p. 37). The witches provide the living Thelyphron with a prosthetic face, which is such a good likeness that nobody has noticed the difference, not even Thelyphron himself. But when dead Thelyphron tells his story, it dawns on living Thelyphron that he has indeed been disfigured, defaced. He was 'panic-stricken and proceeded to investigate my face'. 'I clapped my hand to my nose; it came away. I pulled at my ears, and they too fell off' (p. 37).

This story already contains the bare features of what I will here call the prosthetic imagination as it develops through the passage of the novel form, as if prose genotype automatically gives rise to prosthetic phenotype, in blind obedience to its underlying structural logic. In bringing dead Thelyphron and living Thelyphron together into the same narrative sphere, Apuleius' tale is testing the work of narrative in shuttling between the living and the dead, in granting life and animation to the dead material of which we are made. Just as Lucius is transformed from man to ass to man, so Thelyphron is transformed, 'by a chain of interconnection', from living to dead to living (entering into a deathly condition both in his enchanted sleep and in his peculiar identity with dead Thelyphron). Thelyphron's living death touches on the death that Bakhtin tells us lies at the 'ancient folkloric core of Lucius' metamorphosis', and by extension at the core of the novel form.[42] Live Thelyphron and dead Thelyphron are joined – as living body is joined to dead prosthetic, as mind is joined to matter – by the work of fiction, which makes of this amalgam of the living and the dead an integrated narrating agent. But if this is so, if narrative exerts a binding force here, it comes at a cost. One of the most striking elements of the story is Thelyphron's peculiar numbness, his distance from his own body. Why does it take dead Thelyphron to bring live Thelyphron's attention to the fact that his face is not flesh but wax? Why can Thelyphron not himself *feel* that his nose and ears are not his? How can he be deceived by the likeness of the prosthetic nose, or the 'perfect fit' of the prosthetic ears? An answer to this question is that narrative, in joining consciousness to its prosthetic extensions, also, and at the same time, marks the distance that opens between them, producing a specific form of prosthetic ground that intervenes between the living and the dead, between origin and copy, mimesis and prosthesis. Even here in the antique novel, as meaning and appearance are so close – even as Auerbachian reality so nearly inheres in itself – one can see a prosthetic imagination at work, an imaginative force which makes of the variousness of being a coherent narrative agent, but only by enacting that variousness, that tension between difference and sameness, between being like something and being that something itself, that is still at work, millennia later, in the prosthetic faces that Charles keeps in his wooden cabinets.

It is this proximity of fictional narrative to the hidden join where consciousness meets with its extensions that grants it such intimate access to the means by which we have technologised ourselves and our environments throughout the history of modernity. If, as I will suggest here, the history of the novel is also a history of artificial life, this is because the novel, since it emerged in its proto-modern form in early modernity, is driven and shaped by its capacity to enter into this difficult, dissolving space between mind and matter, and in so doing to make of artificial supplements to life the very stuff of vital being. Its intrinsic attachment to this junction means that one can see a shared trajectory between the novel form and the prosthetic condition, in which the development of the novel is bound to the historical unfolding of the technological forms which shape our lifeworlds. This shared trajectory moves, in the account that follows, through five distinct phases (which accord to the five parts of the book). Part I traces the emergence of early modern anatomy in the sixteenth and seventeenth centuries, as it is reflected in the work of Andreas Vesalius, Thomas Hobbes and René Descartes, and as it relates to the stirrings of a new form of prose fiction from Thomas More's *Utopia*, to Cervantes' *Don Quixote*, to Francis Bacon's *New Atlantis*, to Margaret Cavendish's *The Blazing World*. There is, I argue, a structural relation between the access to the internal structures of the body granted by the new anatomical science and the development of a new kind of fiction that is grounded in the non-space of utopian possibility. In inventing utopian form in 1516, More fashioned, apparently out of nowhere, the revolutionary terms in which prose fiction is threaded into reality – the terms in which the non-existent (the 'no-place' which is the etymological root of 'Utopia') moves within our narrative accounts of that which exists, as a kind of latent possibility or promise. As this utopian possibility comes to expression in the passage from More to Bacon and Cavendish, it partakes in the investigation of the vanishing ground that connects mind to biomatter – the glimmering emptiness at the heart of the modern subject that one can see not only in Hobbes and Descartes but also in Rembrandt's anatomy paintings. As the early modern state is built on a model of the body politic, and as this model is driven by a fascination with the difficult suturing between consciousness and bodily form, one can see that the development of a proto-novelistic imagination is integral to the ways in which an emerging sovereign subject comes to recognise itself.

Part II of the book traces the development of enlightenment colonialism over the long eighteenth century, as it is bodied forth in the novel form, from Aphra Behn's *Oroonoko* to Goethe's *Elective Affinities*. The Western experience of colonial expansion has the effect of putting the body beside itself, of stretching the Hobbesian terms in which we understand the relation between mind, body and state – a stretching which finds its perhaps exemplary expression in the unruly prosthetic bodies that populate Swift's *Gulliver's Travels*. The history of the eighteenth-century novel is, in large measure, a history of this estrangement, of the derangements in scale and self-recognition that are a consequence of the forging of a new colonial idea of the world. In response to this derangement, one can see two opposite tendencies playing out across the century. In one of its moods, the novel form depicts the body in its alien, far-flung condition – the body as a numb prosthetic in Behn's *Oroonoko*, or as a kind of beach-wrack in Defoe's *Robinson Crusoe*, or as grotesquely out of scale in *Gulliver's Travels*, or as a deregulated monstrosity in Sarah Scott's *Millenium Hall*. And in its opposite mode, it reaches for a bound, organic self-sufficiency, a wholeness that might stand as proof against the dismembering effects of expansion, and which finds its expression in the intimacy of the epistolary form in Richardson and Burney, or in the romantic investment in a self-regulating nature in Rousseau and Goethe. These two tendencies move in opposite directions; but even as they do so, they produce a shared focus on the gap that opens between mind and matter as the colonial body comes to self-recognition, the gap that it is the task of the novel form, as it reaches its maturity, both to preserve and to overcome.

The rise of the novel in the eighteenth century is characterised by this contradictory relation to the junction between consciousness and matter, the disjunction which is both the engine of the literary and political imagination and the greatest threat to its coherence. It is in the works of nineteenth-century realism, written as a response to the emergence of a manufactured, industrial lifeworld, that this contradiction reaches its most productive form, making of what Fredric Jameson has recently called the 'antinomies of realism' the very basis for a worldview.[43] Part III of the book argues that the intense connection between manufactured life and prose realism that runs through the history of the novel is concentrated, at this moment of realism's becoming, in the insistently recurring figure of the dead hand, the alienated, automatic hand as it runs from Wollstonecraft to Edgeworth to Austen to Eliot to Flaubert to Zola to Dickens to Melville to Hawthorne, and as it emerges, in a kind of inverted form, in the Gothic mode, from Shelley to Stevenson, Stoker and Wilde. The high point of the Anglo-American realist novel – Eliot's *Middlemarch*, Dickens' *Bleak House*, Melville's *Moby Dick* – is marked by the coming together of the living hand with the dead, of the living limb with the whalebone prosthetic. It is the task of the novel to give narrative expression to this amalgam of organic and inorganic life, to recognise the intimacy with which automated, inanimate, non-human forms are woven into the most inward heartlands of the self. But even as the novel form makes realities out of the artificiality of manufactured life, it develops that logic that is already apparent in Apuleius, whereby the capacity to transform dead material into living material comes at the price of a certain kind of prosthetic alienation, installed into the very apparatuses of becoming.

It is the striking of this balance that allows the realist novel to make of its relation to prosthetic estrangement the terms of its own world-making power; but it is precisely this balance that is unsettled with the turn of the twentieth century, and with the advent of modernism. The impetus behind the modernist revolution in seeing and thinking stems in part from the failure of aesthetic form to subjugate technologised prosthetic material to its own demands, leading to the alienated machinism that one sees in Wyndham Lewis' Tyros or in the aesthetics of futurism, and to the emergence of a glassy or jagged prose style, which does not accommodate its content, in Henry James or Gertrude Stein.

Part IV traces the development of this prosthetic modernism as it moves from the evacuated style of James and Edith Wharton to the alienated materiality of Samuel Beckett's prose, in response to a twentieth-century modernity that offers an increasing resistance to the forms which seek to humanise it, to render it into human shape. And then Part V traces the emergence of posthumanisms, in the wake of modernism, and in response to the development of the forms of digitality, virtuality and artificiality that comprise contemporary technicity. The modes of specular subjectivity developed by Thomas Pynchon, Toni Morrison, Salman Rushdie and Angela Carter might appear to respond to the arrival of a postmodern scenario, in which the real is folded into representation, in which prosthetic artificiality becomes equated with virtual, simulacral forms. But the last section of this book teases out a material prosthetic imagination that subtends and resists the tendency in postmodernism towards the simulacral, and that persists, in Pynchon, in Morrison, even as both writers give expression to a postmodern cultural logic. And it is this material literary thinking, running against the grain of postmodern orthodoxies, that surfaces finally in the emergence of a new kind of world picturing in the twenty-first-century novel, one which derives from an encounter with the forms of material artificiality that are coming to thought now, as a consequence not only of new information technologies but also of eco-crisis. In these novels, exemplified here by the late work of Margaret Atwood, Roberto Bolaño, J. M. Coetzee, and Don DeLillo, one can see the development of a contemporary prosthetic imagination which gives expression to a new distribution of the artificial in the real, a new way of thinking about how life permeates material, under contemporary technological and biopolitical conditions.

In articulating this relation between prose fiction and the technologies of embodiment as it develops through the course of modernity, the novel as I read it here gives a vibrantly lived account of the shifting historical relation between mind and prosthetic material. In its proximity to the place where consciousness and matter join, it offers the most intimate access we have to the unfolding processes by which mind has employed prosthetic and mimetic forms to extend itself into the world. But if this is the case – if the elaboration of this story comprises the first of the two major claims this book sets out to make – the second claim I make here runs rather in the opposite direction and employs a contrary model of historiography, teleology, chronology – a kind of counter history. Even as the novel, in its historical mode, maps the junction between mind and matter, the peculiar intimacy of its approach to this region, combined with the fissile, vanishing quality of that terrain itself, means that the work of fiction always exceeds the historical terms which determine it. It is always possible to discern, in the novel's approach to that meeting place, an unbinding movement, a failure of the distinction between mind and matter that casts the novel's expressive faculties into a kind of inarticulacy, a kind of unreferring blankness that is an absolutely essential element of its picturing mechanism, even as it threatens to dismantle it. The very intimacy with which the novel approaches this prosthetic junction, the insideness with which it operates at the place where consciousness materialises itself, means that it continually confronts the resistance of material to the claims of consciousness, continually experiences the failure of reference, the collapse of the relation between inner mind and outer reality that Ricoeur sees as the particular province of the fictional image. When the novel imagination brings us as close as it is possible to come to the ground of being, where inside and outside meet, we find that there is no such ground. But this groundlessness is best thought of, I suggest, not as the discovery, in whatever formulation, that there is no outside to the text, but rather as the recognition that novel thinking establishes itself in the radical unassimilability of its elements – that to think as the novel allows and requires us to think is to live through an alienated relation between mind and matter that can only be thought as a certain resistance to thinkability. It is this resistance – prosthetic resistance as an unassimilable supplement to history – that one has to counter-historicise, as a constituent if recalcitrant part of the forward chronology of the novel, a necessary element in the novel's vocation for world making. From the strange shading of living into dying in Cervantes, to the trembling proximity between being and not being in Goethe, to Austen's discovery of the differing movement of narrative irony at work in the very midst of our acts of true self-fashioning, to Eliot's foundation of a fictional world on the indistinction between the visible and the invisible, to the peculiar denarrativising identity of contraries in Beckett: the novel has always thrived on the refusal of material to join with idea, on what a young Beckett calls the 'reluctance of our refractory constituents to bind together'.[44] If literature knows more than it knows, then the novel has always known that information moves strangely in material, that consciousness is distributed strangely in matter, and it has always preserved that strangeness as a side effect, a residue or remainder of its conversion of such strangeness into the very possibility of real life.

As we find ourselves now in the midst of an epistemological revolution – ecological, biopolitical, infotechnological – this historical and counter-historical knowledge, stored in the novel form as in an ice core, offers a means of thinking our condition anew. George Levine suggested in 2018 that it is hard for us now to find a new way of reading the novel, because the form itself has been so thoroughly mined, has provided the material with which so many of the major readings of literary culture have been fashioned, from F. R. Leavis' *Great Tradition*, to Raymond Williams' *Culture and Society*, to Elaine Showalter's *A Literature of Their Own*, to Fredric Jameson's *Political Unconscious*, to Eve Kosofsky Sedgwick's *Between Men*, to Catherine Callagher's *The Industrial Reformation of English Fiction* (Levine of course left his own *The Realistic Imagination* off the list, despite its significant influence).[45] The most powerful twentieth-century accounts of literary possibility – not only those by Auerbach and Ricoeur, but also works such as Georg Lukács' *Theory of the Novel* or Mikhail Bakhtin's *The Dialogic Imagination* – have given us a language and a vocabulary for thinking about the novel that is hard to surpass. But if this is the case, as Levine himself acknowledges in his discussion of Isobel Armstrong's 2016 *Novel Politics*, the urgent demands of our present are leading us to read the novel over again, to discover in that most elastic of forms a new set of aesthetic and political possibilities, a new way of seeing and representing the world, one that has always been preserved in the novel form but is only now coming to visibility. Armstrong's *Novel Politics*, her striking analysis of the democratic potential of the novel as a form, is part of that rereading, and one can see a broader group of critics working now who are extending our critical response to the novel in new directions, retuning our understanding of the possibilities of prose fiction as we enter into a new critical and political environment, with the lapse of twentieth-century theoretical orthodoxies and the emergence of a millennial lifeworld. From Ursula Heise's work on the environmental imagination in *Sense of Place and Sense of Planet*, to Lloyd Pratt's reconceiving of novel bodies and novel time in *The Stranger's Book* and *Archives of American Time*, to the transformations in our conception of critical reading in works from Rita Felski's *Uses of Literature*, to Sianne Ngai's *Our Aesthetic Categories*, to Merve Emre's *Paraliterary*, our conception of the world-making power of prose fiction is undergoing a deep transformation.

The argument that I pursue in the following chapters, in seeking access to the particular kind of biopolitical knowledge that is stored in the novel form, is a contribution to this effort to resituate, to recalibrate what it is that the novel can do. It generates a mode of reading that attends to both the historical and the counter-historical at once, that can read for the novel's capacity to record and produce specific historical technologies of embodiment, while also articulating its harbouring of a prosthetic condition, an unforetold relation between mind and material, that moves beyond its historically available terms, that lies latent in the form itself, waiting for a moment to arrive, maybe tomorrow, when it might come to thought. This kind of reading requires us, to borrow a pregnant phrase from climatology, to perform an act of literary hindcasting – that is, a mode of reading which finds, in the preserved records and patterns of the past, an informational trace of the future, a future which glimmers in the shrouded places, non–weight bearing, where thought meets with thing, where mimesis meets with prosthesis. It is perhaps this kind of hindcasting that Victor Hugo has anachronistically in mind when he writes in *Les Misérables* that 'all human societies have what is known to the theatre as an understage.'[46] 'The social earth', he says, 'is everywhere mined and tunnelled', as, beneath the calm, unbroken surface of things, there is underway a universal 'process of burrowing', a 'vast secret turbulence'. This process of burrowing, as Kafka's animal later discovers in his subterranean short story 'The Burrow', is the movement of the imagination as it works in the material of being, making being available as life, but also putting life beside itself, opening it to a distribution of thought in thing that has not yet been mapped. This is a 'process of burrowing' Hugo's narrator says, which, 'leaving the surface untouched, gnaws at its entrails'. 'So many different underground levels, different objectives, different harvests. And what comes of it all? The future' (p. 619).

'I want you to feel wonder', Apuleius' narrator says, 'at the transformations of men's shapes and destinies into alien forms, and their reversion by a chain of interconnection to their own' (p. 1). This wonder is all around us now, as our own most proper, most intimate shapes can only meet with themselves through an encounter with alien forms, with an artificiality which we cannot reckon or own, which mitotically divides us from ourselves. This is a wonder that might feel more often terrible than sublime, as we look upon the damage that our forms of artifice have wrought upon our selves and our environments, and as our current representational and political forms seem inadequate to the realities that we have made. But if the wonder of literary thinking is to allow us to behold a new future – a new world, Hugo writes, that lies 'in the womb of the state, unimaginable in shape' (p. 621) – then it is the possibilities preserved in the novel form, not yet imaginable but belonging to the province of the imagination, that might help us to do so.

PART I

The Body and the Early Modern State:
From More to Cavendish

CHAPTER I

Fiction, the Body and the State

For seeing life is but a motion of Limbs, the beginning whereof is in some principall part within; why may we not say, that all *Automata* (Engines that move themselves by springs and wheeles as doth a watch) have an artificiall life? For what is the *Heart* but a *Spring*; and the *Nerves*, but so many *Strings*; and the *Joynts*, but so many *Wheeles*, giving motion to the whole Body, such as was intended by the Artificer?

Thomas Hobbes, *Leviathan*[1]

1.1   Anatomy, Early Modernity and the Prosthetic Imagination

The history of the novel as artificial life that I will offer here takes as its starting point a certain coming together of fiction, science and politics in the early modern period – a coming together which turns around the thoughtform that goes by the name of 'utopia', a thoughtform that works at the very foundations of the novel, from its invention in Thomas More's 1516 *Utopia* up to the present day. It is, I will suggest, the combination of utopian fiction with the emerging science of anatomy on the one hand and the development of early modern forms of political sovereignty on the other that establishes the function of the prosthetic imagination as I will characterise it here, and that sets in motion the terms in which the novel has intervened in the fashioning of our lifeworlds.

At the heart of this triangular relation among anatomy, statecraft and fiction is the question of self-ownership, a question which has taken on a new urgency in our own time, as we seek to understand and metabolise the implications of contemporary forms of artificial life. Isaac Asimov's science fiction addresses this question from the perspective of robotics: when machine life has become such a perfect replica of human life that the two are indistinguishable, how do we maintain a concept of the ownership of self as a uniquely human characteristic? Asimov's long story *The Bicentennial Man* (1976) turns around a robot, named Andrew, who becomes so humanlike that he manages, through legal means, to establish his freedom, his autonomy as a sovereign subject. 'I am a free robot', he insists, 'I own myself.'[2] How, Asimov asks, does the legal and ethical category of autonomous sovereignty survive the claim to self-ownership of a machine, a commodity? This problem arises not only in robotics and artificial intelligence (a problem examined in Ian McEwan's 2019 novel *Machines Like Me*) but also across the range of technologies and bio-technologies that characterise the contemporary technosphere. Twentieth-century advances, for example, in artificial life support cast into doubt the very question of how we distinguish between life and death, and when we can be said no longer to be alive in our bodies (for example, to legitimate the donating of our body parts for transplant). As Giorgio Agamben puts it in *Homo Sacer*, the development of artificial life support requires new definitions of vitality, new ways of characterising the claim of consciousness to life, leading to a 'wavering of death in a shadowy zone beyond coma', a 'zone of indetermination in which the words "life" and "death" have lost their meaning'.[3] And as Muireann Quigley has recently demonstrated, the development of cell lines for use in medical research has presented a paradigmatic legal and ethical challenge to our definitions of self-ownership.[4] The famous cases of Henrietta Lacks and John Moore suggest the outlines of this problem. Henrietta Lacks' cells have been being continuously grown in the laboratory since her death in 1951 and have been used in quite astonishing quantities in the development of an equally astonishing range of medicines; in the process her biomaterial, what Rebecca Skloot memorably calls her 'immortal life', has become profoundly divorced from her status as a sovereign subject.[5] Lacks' extraordinarily prolific, still-living cells are not owned by her, just as John Moore found, when he was being treated for a rare cancer at the University of California–Los Angeles in the early 1980s, that he did not own his own body matter, that the hospital had patented his spleen tissue, bewilderingly without the consent or knowledge of Moore himself. Moore sued UCLA, arguing that his biological material had been stolen from him, and that he should at least have a share of the gargantuan profits that accrued from the sale of his own cells. Equally bewilderingly, Moore lost, and the court found in favour of UCLA's claim to have 'invented' Moore's cells.[6]

This crisis in our conception of self-ownership, consequent on the contemporary development of artificial life, might seem to offer a stark

contrast to the earlier historical models upon which our understanding of
sovereignty and autonomy are based. Andrew Norris, for example, suggests
such a contrast when he writes, in his 2004 collection *Politics, Metaphysics
and Death*, that the 'corporate-driven and controlled development of
biotechnologies' requires us to 'redefine the human being', to rethink the
terms, first established in the early modern period, of our own self-
fashioning.[7] To see John Moore's biomatter being 'licensed to the
Sandoz Pharmaceutical Corporation', Norris writes, is to witness the
final failure of 'Locke's attempt to ground the institution of private
property in the fact that "every Man has a *Property* in his own *Person*"'
(p. 2). It is to overturn the central claim of John Locke's 1689 *Second
Treatise of Government*, in which Locke grounds the experience of all
ownership, of all political freedom, in our capacity to own ourselves.
'Every man has a *Property* in his own *Person*', Locke writes:

> This no Body has any right to but himself. The *Labour* of his Body, and the
> *Work* of his Hands, we may say, are properly his. Whatsoever then he
> removes out of the State that Nature hath provided, and left it in, he hath
> mixed his *Labour* with, and joyned it to something that is his own, and
> thereby makes it his *Property*. It being by him removed from the common
> State Nature placed it in, it hath by this *Labour* something annexed to it,
> that excludes the common Right of other Men.[8]

To understand the contemporary prosthetic age, it is necessary to address the
ways in which emerging biotechnologies are shifting the relationship
between sovereignty, embodiment and self-ownership, as it was framed
not only by Locke but also by many of the figures who were central to
inventing the political and aesthetic terms in which we conceive of the early
modern body politic, from Leonardo da Vinci to Andreas Vesalius to
Hobbes and Descartes.[9] It is necessary to grasp the shift that Foucault
outlines in *The Birth of Biopolitics*, whereby the neoliberal subject does not
own itself, but relates to itself as to a commodity, becoming an 'entrepreneur
of himself, being for himself his own capital, being for himself his own
producer, being for himself the source of his earnings'.[10] But even as the
contemporary prosthetic condition offers dramatic and profound challenges
to our conception of the limits of the self, and of the boundary between the
living and the dead, it is nevertheless the case, as Norris acknowledges, that
the models of selfhood that were forged in the early modern period were
already unstable and already allowed for the kind of amalgamation of the self
and the non-self that seems so striking in the cases of Moore and Lacks. Early
modern models of the body politic do not present an originary, stable

account of self-ownership based on a close accord between consciousness and embodiment, but rather they establish a peculiar disjunction at the heart of political and imaginary life, a vanishing point that is a central component of what I will be characterising here as the 'prosthetic imagination'. The mode of imagining that becomes available in this period, that drives the development of a new kind of fiction, is grounded not in secure self-ownership but in the distance from self that the claims to self-ownership seek to close.

One can see this logic, this disjunction, at work in the curious contradictions that are threaded through Locke's *Second Treatise*: a man asserts his ownership of himself and of his property, Locke writes, when he is 'mixed' with the product of his labour, when he is 'joyned' to it, or 'annexed' with it. The assertion of self-ownership already involves an encounter with prosthetic materials that are extraneous to the self. But if this distance is present in Locke, it is in the emergence in the period of a new conception of anatomy, and of new political, scientific and aesthetic forms with which anatomical knowledge came to visibility, that it can be seen most clearly as the basis for the emergence of an early modern prosthetic imagination. One of the defining moments in the emergence of modernity is the publication, in 1543, of Andreas Vesalius' major work, *The Fabric of the Human Body*, which gave the first detailed and accurate visual representations of the human anatomy, including the skeleton, muscles, bloodstream, nervous system and internal organs (see Figure 1.1). Vesalius' work extends a Renaissance interest in the material functions of the body that one can trace back to the anatomical drawings of Leonardo da Vinci, and that turns around a conviction that knowledge both of humans and of the world they inhabited could only be developed if it was grounded in an intimate understanding of the way that the body itself worked – if what Roy Porter calls the '"black box" of the body' was 'exposed to the medical gaze'.[11] As Jonathan Sawday influentially argues, 'the early modern period sees the emergence of a new image of the human interior, together with a new means of studying that interior, which left its mark on all forms of cultural endeavour in the period.'[12] Vesalius' publication of *The Fabric of the Human Body* coincided with the growth and spread of anatomical theatres across early modern Europe, in which the opening of the human corpse was conducted in public, as if to emphasise the centrality of knowledge of the inside of the body to the production of a new public sphere. Dissection in the period, as Paula Findlen shows, became a 'theatrical and often highly public event for medical students, physicians, surgeons, and a general public curious about the secrets of the

Figure 1.1 Andreas Vesalius, 'Woodcut Portrait of Andreas Vesalius'. Attributed to John of Calcar, Portrait of Andreas Vesalius, 1542, woodcut, frontispiece to Andreas Vesalius, *Fabric of the Human Body*, British Library collections.

body'.[13] As Findlen and others demonstrate, it was common practice in public dissections to pass the organs of the dissected body amongst the audience to gain the most intimate possible access to the biological interior. 'Surely', Vesalius has been recorded to have said, 'you can learn only little from a mere demonstration, if you yourselves have not handled the objects with your hands.'[14]

Such an interest in the mechanics of the human body – the attempt to open the inside of the body to public view – is intimately entwined with the development of political science in the period and with Locke's suggestion that our model of private property and the public sphere should be grounded in our sense of self-ownership. The development of conceptions of the body politic, from Hobbes and Descartes in the early seventeenth century to Locke in the late seventeenth century, was closely modelled on the anatomical body that was made newly available by Vesalius' dissections and other related developments in medical science. The work of both Hobbes and Descartes is derived, to a significant degree, from their respective studies of anatomy and their developing understanding of how the body works as a machine. The first book of Hobbes' *Leviathan* is devoted to a study of the biological mechanics of perception to construct an empirical basis upon which the dissection of the commonwealth, as a political body, might be performed. If we can understand the workings of life – of consciousness and perception, as well as the other functions of biological being – as an *apparatus*, then we are able to produce our own models of communication and cohabitation, based on the plan that God has made manifest in our own material being. If we accept – as Vesalius surely helps us to – that the heart is 'but a *Spring*', that the nerves are 'but so many *Strings*', the joints 'but so many *Wheeles*', then we can construct, through 'Art', our own artificial political body, which works on the same anatomical principles (p. 9). For our commonwealth, or 'State', Hobbes writes, is 'but an Artificiall Man', in which 'the *Soveraignty* is an Artificiall *Soul*, as giving life and motion to the whole body' (p. 9). Where Locke sees the principle of ownership as resting on the ability to refashion objects from the world through the work of one's own hands – and thus to make objects belong to us by 'joyning' them to us through labour – Hobbes suggests that the political body itself is fashioned through the work of political 'Art', a kind of artifice which takes the body out of 'Nature' and remakes it as a subject of the 'State'. As Katherine Attie puts it, 'even though the body politic imitates the body natural in the way that the parts work together for the good of the whole, Hobbes crucially makes the commonwealth not a natural body but an artificial one.'[15]

In the work of Descartes too an understanding of the nature of human being is grounded on the dawning of new kinds of anatomical knowledge. There is, of course, a great gulf between Descartes' understanding of the political body and Hobbes', which turns around their differing conceptions of the mechanics of perception.[16] Hobbes insists on the material basis of thought, arguing, in one of his 'objections' to Descartes *Meditations*, that 'imagination [depends] on the motions of bodily organs; and thus the mind will be nothing but motions in certain parts of an organic body.'[17] Descartes privileges an immaterial understanding of thought over any grounded conception of biological life. 'Examining attentively what I was', Descartes writes, in one of the most famous passages in the history of Western philosophy, 'I saw that I could pretend that I had no body and that there was no world or place for me to be in, but that I could not for all that pretend I did not exist.'[18] Existence, for Descartes, thus consists not in one's being as a body, but in one's being as a mind, as a thinking thing. 'I thereby concluded', he goes on, in a passage that sharply diverges from Hobbes' materialism, 'that I was a *substance* whose whole *essence* or nature resides only in thinking, and which, in order to exist, has no need of place and is not dependent on any material thing' (p. 29). His essential being, Descartes believes, 'would not stop being everything it is, even if the body were not to exist' (p. 29). But even as Descartes proposes such an idealist philosophy, his thought is everywhere marked by a preoccupation with the anatomical body. The priority of mind over body is predicated on a close examination of the revealed biological structures that encase us in our dispensable flesh. His attentive exploration of his own being, he explains, leads him to reveal 'what structure the nerves and muscles of the human body must have to enable the *animal spirits*, being in that body, to move its members' (p. 44) – an attention to the biological structures of consciousness, perception and animation that bears a striking similarity to that advanced in the first section of Hobbes' *Leviathan*. And just as Hobbes' biological investigations lead him to propose the existence of an artificial man, animated by springs and wheels, so Descartes' exploration of the conditions of being leads him to imagine people and animals as automata, to 'consider this body as a machine which, having been made by the hand of God, is incomparably better ordered and has in itself more amazing movements than any that can be created by men' (p. 46). Descartes is fascinated by the mechanics that allow 'external objects' to 'imprint various ideas on the brain through the intermediary of the senses' (p. 45), just as Hobbes seeks to penetrate into the hidden processes by which the 'externall object' exerts a 'pressure' on the consciousness, by the 'mediation of nerves, and other strings, and membranes of the body, continued inwards to the brain, and heart' (p. 11). And for Descartes, as for Hobbes, our capacity to give an account of the ways in which consciousness is lodged in matter reaches back to Vesalius. His anatomical research, Descartes writes, has 'shown how it is not sufficient for [the soul] to be lodged in the human body like a pilot in his ship, except perhaps to move its members, but that it needs to be more closely joined and united with the body in order to have, in addition, feelings and appetites like the ones we have, and in this way compose a true man' (p. 48). The soul is joined to the body, despite its immateriality, Descartes writes to Mersenne in 1639, by an 'orderly arrangement of the nerves, veins, bones, and other parts of an animal'. In producing his own analysis of this joining, Descartes goes on, 'I have taken into account not only what Vesalius and the others write about anatomy, but also many details unmentioned by them that I have observed myself while dissecting various animals.'[19] Indeed, there is an odd echo of Vesalius' insistence that his audience should physically handle the internal organs of corpses for dissection at the heart of the *Discourse on the Method*, when Descartes describes how the heart works (like Hobbes' '*Spring*') to distribute oxygenated blood through the body. 'So that they might have less difficulty understanding what I shall say', Descartes writes, as he sets about his 'explanation of the movement of the heart', 'I should like those who are unversed in anatomy to take the trouble, before reading his, of having the heart of a large animal with lungs dissected before their eyes' (p. 39).

For both Hobbes and Descartes, then, the work of anatomy grants us access to the ground where consciousness and matter meet – the internal biomaterial spaces that are made visible in Vesalius' anatomical drawings, in which corpses stride oddly across landscapes, straddling the boundary between the living and the dead. But even as the new anatomy makes these internal spaces visible – the space of the join that Locke sees as the foundation of self-ownership – the debate between Hobbes and Descartes turns around the perception that, at this ground, there is a supplement to consciousness that cannot quite come to thought or to material, a kind of prosthetic join that, even as it bears the weight of political sovereignty, remains resistant to philosophical expression (a perception that Johnathan Swift wittily addresses in his 'Discourse Concerning the Mechanical Operation of the Spirit' (1704)). It is in Rembrandt's anatomy paintings – particularly 'The Anatomy Lesson of Dr Nicolaes Tulp' (see Figure 1.2) – that this strange junction comes to its clearest visual expression, even in the midst of its invisibility, its resistance to appearance. These paintings bear arguably the most intense witness we have to the revelatory power of early modern anatomy – to the Vesalian perception that it is the opening of the body to examination that allows us to produce pictures of animated life. Rembrandt's portrait of Dr Tulp, indeed, includes a number of references to Vesalius as the father of early

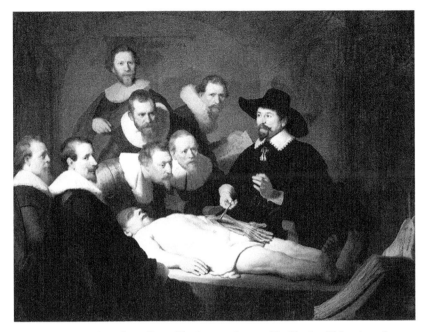

Figure 1.2 Rembrandt van Rijn, *The Anatomy Lesson of Dr Nicolaes Tulp*, 1632, oil on
canvas, Mauritshuis, The Hague.

modern anatomy. There has been some speculation that the book in the
right foreground of the painting is a copy of Vesalius' *Fabric*, and that the
leaf of paper held by the surgeon in the centre of the composition depicts,
as well as the names of the surgeons in the picture, a Vesalian woodcut of
a dissected arm. The painting also establishes a more macabre link to the
anatomical studies of Vesalius. Some have speculated that the dissected
arm of the corpse (a recently executed criminal named Adriaen
Adriaenszoon) might be modelled on a preserved flayed arm, originally
'owned' by Vesalius himself, which was one of four flayed limbs found
amongst Rembrandt's possessions on his death in 1669. This same limb is
likely to be the model too for the arm that Vesalius is dissecting in the
frontispiece image to the 1543 edition of *The Fabric of the Human Body* (see
Figure 1.1) and thus forms the centre of a layered set of visual connections
between Vesalius' *Fabric* and Rembrandt's 'Anatomy Lesson'.[20]

In calling, in this way, to the spirit of Vesalius, Rembrandt's painting
offers to bring a kind of Vesalian knowledge into the early modern light, to
offer a sculpted visual form in which Findlen's 'secrets of the body' might

be revealed. If it is Hobbes' desire to trace the 'strings, and membranes of the body' as they connect 'externall objects' to the 'brain and heart', and if it is the capacity to reveal such strings that allows us to form a picture of the body politic, then Rembrandt's painting is offering here a biological basis for the founding of the modern state. It serves, as Jonathan Sawday has argued, to 'proclaim the absolutely unambiguous subjection of the mortal body to scientific and political power' (p. 152), to capture the moment in which a 'deviant will' is 'mastered by rational power'. It presents a visual basis for the assertion of sovereign political power, and it offers too an aesthetic basis upon which to found the relationship between the rational mind and the machinic body, that relationship so central to Descartes' *Discourse on the Method*. As Simon Schama has suggested, one can see the painting as an attempt to dramatise the Cartesian relationship between mind and body, as Tulp the scientist animates the hand of the dead man by lifting the carpal and digital flexor muscles with his forceps. Rembrandt's intensely arresting demonstration of the mechanism by which mind controls body, through the contraction of strings and membranes, offers, Schama writes, a 'moment of truth', in which we see an image of the 'metaphysical sympathy between body and soul': 'To know is to see is to know: both the husk and the kernel, the body and the soul.'[21]

Rembrandt's anatomy paintings, then, dramatise the process by which political and intellectual discourses of the early modern period sought to subjugate the body to the sovereign will. There is a delicious literalism to the action of Tulp's forceps here, through which the learned, powerful man takes control of the deviant body, as if Tulp has become, in Descartes' terms, the pilot of the abandoned ship which is Adriaenszoon's unfortunate corpse. But if this painting gives expression to a kind of prosthetic logic, to that logic which I have suggested one can see running through the fascination with anatomy in this period, then I think it does so only partly in its capacity to offer a visual form in which we can see the control of bodily material by the exercise of scientific and political rationalism. The prosthetic charge in Rembrandt's painting lies not only in its capacity to demonstrate the body itself as an artificial machine composed of springs and wheels, which can be owned and operated by others, by the state, or by the controlling mind, but also in an almost directly opposite tendency in the painting – not towards the revelation of biological function, as in Schama's 'moment of truth' or Sawday's 'unambiguous subjection', but towards a kind of radical failure of representation, a falling into unrepresentability that, I will argue throughout this book, is at the heart of the prosthetic imagination.

In 'The Anatomy Lesson of Dr Tulp', this movement towards a kind of gulf in knowing and seeing might best be witnessed in its extraordinary capacity to unsettle our conception of the interior as the locus of our being. The most striking drama in the painting (second to the sheer excitement of the corpse's revealed sinews) is the performance it enacts of looking. The surgeon at the top of the frame looks at us, pointing vaguely towards Adriaenszoon, perhaps enjoining us to note whatever moral might lie in the scene beneath him; the surgeon on the far left looks at Tulp's face; the surgeon second from the left looks at the copy of Vesalius' *Fabric*, perhaps at an anatomical sketch on the recto page; the surgeon next along from him leans forward with a rapt intensity, to get as clear as possible a view of the opened hand of the corpse, while his neighbour in turn (like the surgeon directly above him) looks at Tulp's hand; Tulp himself gazes off into the distance, in what Schama reads as a reflective, meditative gaze, adopting a posture which mirrors that of the painter himself, brush in one hand, pallet in the other. The effect of this performance of criss-crossing gazes is to summon, into the plane of the painting itself, the peculiar contradictions of perception, the to and fro movement that attends the action of attending itself – and in doing so to bring to a kind of crisis the relationship between the interiority of being and its external attachments, the ways in which perception itself is situated in relation to its biomechanical apparatuses. It is true that the beautiful composition of the painting does much to contain its discrepant elements within a harmonious whole. The complex of variously directed gazes is remarkably balanced here, so the divided attention of the two surgeons in the centre of the painting (a beautifully paired act of looking) conjures a bound instant of perception and understanding that might overcome such division. If we are to gather that Tulp is captured here in the process of moving the fingers of his own left hand to demonstrate the motion produced by Adriaenszoon's muscles and tendons, then the distinct objects of the two surgeons' regard – the living hand of Tulp and the dead hand of Adriaenszoon – reach for kind of dramatic unity. The surgeon on the left looks at the opened internal structures of the dead hand; the surgeon on the right looks at the living hand of Tulp; and the painting, in containing both gazes within the shape and colour of the composition, brings these two separate motions into a sutured conjunction. The living, animated body of Tulp has revealed its Hobbesian, machinic inside – the internal structures that the learned man shares with the criminal corpse – while bringing that inside safely back into the contained realm of the rational, meditative, sovereign being. What is more, the strange reflection, in the posture of Tulp, of the implied painterly presence of Rembrandt himself (a reflection which makes of this painting a kind of distant self-portrait) reaches beyond the plane of the painting, to gather both the painter and ourselves as 'audience' of the painting into this lit pool of simultaneously gathered and opened being. The surgeon at the top of the compositional triangle looks out both to the implied audience of Tulp's public autopsy and to the viewer of the painting, suggesting that this performance has revealed something about our own interiority, by bringing a shared internal structure, the substratum of animated being, into the open.

But even as the painting draws on its compositional force to produce this moment of revelation, the real brilliance of this painting, I think, lies in its capacity to demonstrate that the very forces which establish our collective being – which form the basis of Hobbes' commonwealth – are also those that disarticulate us, that cast us into a kind of disjunct being, where the experience of self-ownership loses its binding power. The more closely we see inside ourselves, the painting suggests, the more insistently that inside resists our gaze. If, as John Berger has argued, Rembrandt's painting has a particular 'innerness' – 'Before his art', Berger writes, 'the spectator's body remembers its own inner experience' – then this innerness is experienced as what Berger calls a kind of Rembrandtian 'dislocation'.[22] As Joanna Woodall puts it, the 'celebrated ... visualisation of the sitter's interiority' that we associate with Rembrandt's portraiture is bound up with what she calls a 'sense of *difference* between an inner, abstract subjectivity and an objectivised, material body'.[23] The urge towards illumination, towards the excavation of the interior, that animates this painting leads it also to bring to a certain visibility the binding apparatus itself, the fugitive connective tissue that attaches inner being to its outer extensions, and which can only become perceptible as a kind of visible darkness, or a visible resistance to the regime of the visible. The gazes that traverse the painting bring together its different regimes of knowing and being – the anatomical knowledge contained in Vesalius' *Fabric*; the surgical knowledge secreted in Tulp's mind, and executed by his hand; the dead being, with its revealed mechanics, presented by the open corpse; the ghostly afterimage of a flayed arm owned second hand by Vesalius and third hand by Rembrandt: but even as the painting brings these discrete modes of knowing and being into a unity, it registers a set of bumpy turbulences, disconnections and lapses, in which knowing and being (or Schama's knowing and seeing) radically fail to cohere, in which the inside and outside of being are confused, or switched around. Are the 'secrets of the body' revealed by the dissection stored most surely in the opened arm of

Adriaenszoon, or in Vesalius' illustrated textbook, or in Tulp's living demonstration of the act of animation? All three, the painting suggests; but in finding the truth of our own animating principles contained not only within us but also on the outside, in the written text, or the opened corpse, or in the anatomical theatre, or in the painted image, we find ourselves cast outside of ourselves. The process by which we try to discern the secret little stitch, the link in time and in space in which our immaterial being is connected to our material selves, is also the process by which we reveal the unthinkability of such a connection, such a bridge or a junction. The loftily averted gaze of Tulp is connected to the movement of his hand, is in some sense part of the same act of being; but what the painting knows is that there intervenes, between moving fingers and distracted gaze, a kind of gap or disappearance which cannot come to view or which lies in the open in the midst of this gathering of the rapt living around the dismembered dead, but which remains somehow unavailable to thought. 'The Imagination', Hobbes writes in *Leviathan*, 'is the first internall beginning of all Voluntary Motion'. To penetrate to the heart of perception, and of political being, we have to trace the transmission from this imagination to the body itself, to discover what Hobbes beautifully calls 'These small beginnings of Motion, within the body of Man, before they appear in walking, speaking, striking, and other visible actions' (p. 33). The project of *Leviathan*, to see in the body a model of the state, requires us to be able to find this knotting between the body and the mind, and to retrieve it as the very basis of the *civitas*. It is the aim of early modern anatomical thought to bring this junction out of hiding. But Rembrandt's painting demonstrates how the revelation of this connective switch, this joint between the unextended interior self and the springs, wheels and strings in which it finds itself realised as a being, brings us only to the limits of our conception of selfhood, in which the interior of the self recedes the more stealthily from view, the more thoroughly it is exposed. As Goethe puts it, much later, in *The Sorrows of Young Werther*, it is perhaps impossible, however hard Hobbes would have us try, to 'grasp the true and inmost nature of an action'.[24] Or as David Foster Wallace puts it, much later still, it is perhaps the case that we are all 'self-inaccessible', all hidden behind a 'veil of inaccessibility' that it is impossible to 'pierce'.[25] All Rembrandt's painting can do is to bring that self-inaccessibility, that disappearance of the self beneath its prosthetic, machinic extensions, to the lit surface of the canvas, to give a visual form to a mode of attachment which resists visibility, even as it sets the conditions for all acts of perception.

1.2   Utopian Self-Fashioning from More to Cavendish

> The spirit answered, that they could dictate, but not write, except
> they put on a hand or arm, or else the whole body of man.
>   Margaret Cavendish, *The Blazing World*[26]

The early modern fascination with anatomy, then, as the public revelation
of an interior biological structure upon which to base a model of the state,
generates an odd contradiction, a contradiction which is central to the
prosthetic logic I will be unfolding here. The more accurately the inside is
revealed – the more forcefully the inside of being is brought into the
domain of knowledge, and into the regime of the visible – the more
insistently a certain unknowable junction between being and its extensions
reveals itself. The estrangement from self that contemporary biotechnologies produce is not, seen in this light, a failure or a dismantling of existing
models of human being and consciousness, but rather an amplification of
a strange prosthetic twist that lies at the heart of the discursive forms in
which we have encountered ourselves. Contemporary prosthetics do not
'lead us', as Andrew Norris suggests, 'to redefine the human being' so much
as bring to light what Bernard Stiegler calls 'a logic of prosthesis' that has
always lain at the heart of our conceptions of the human and always
troubled the distinctions between the inside of being and its exteriorisa-
tions – the distinctions upon which our concept of mind, of self, and of
sovereignty have rested. This is 'a logic of prosthesis', Stiegler writes, 'that
shows the "truth" of the "inside" to be (in) the outside in which it
exteriorizes itself';[27] a logic that, as in Rembrandt's dazzling autopsy
paintings, insists upon an impossible, collapsing junction between the
hidden interior and the exposed exterior, a simultaneously revealed and
secreted junction that brings representation itself into an aporia.

One of the effects of this aporia, this difficult twist in being that one
can discern in the dark luminosity of Rembrandt's art, is the rise, in the
early modern period, of a certain kind of prose fiction, a mode of
imagining that went on to become the novel. This early and unstable
form, emerging in the early modern period in Thomas More's 1516 work
Utopia, is closely entwined with the dynamics I have been tracing here,
with the attempt to discern and articulate the nature of the prosthetic join
which binds us to ourselves, to each other, and to the body politic.
Something happens, with More's invention of the utopian conceit, that
allows for a transformed relation with the classical intellectual traditions
that More engages in *Utopia*, from Plato and Aristotle to Lucian, and that
informs the Renaissance humanism of More and his contemporaries.[28]

The utopian form that More inaugurates, and that is replicated throughout the early modern period, from Francis Bacon's *New Atlantis* (1627), to Margaret Cavendish's *The Blazing World* (1666), to Henry Neville's *The Isle of Pines* (1668), is built around this prosthetic join, this attempt to graft new pictures of the perfected body politic onto the imperfect body that we are given, our naked inch of nature. Each of these works conjoins a factual depiction of a real world (the faulty world as we know it) with a fantastical account of another world – More's Utopia, or Bacon's Bensalem, or Cavendish's Blazing World – whose various (apparent) political perfections or technological achievements solve the difficulties that bedevil the real world to which it is attached. More's *Utopia* tells of the travels of 'the noted Thomas More', whose diplomatic mission to calm a dispute between Henry VIII and the Prince of Castile takes him to Antwerp.[29] Here he meets Raphael Hythloday, a traveller who has recently returned to Europe from a visit to the distant island of Utopia. It becomes immediately clear that this meeting, at the junction between here and there, the old world and the new, the real and the fictional, is structured by a series of mirror images, as Rembrandt finds himself mirrored in his portrait of Tulp. Hythloday is a mirror image of More, a kind of avatar or prosthetic attachment that allows him to extend himself past the political limits which his relationship with the English court impose upon him; Utopia is a mirror image of England; Amaurot, the capital city of Utopia, is a mirror image of London. The conceit of More's *Utopia*, brilliant in its simplicity, allows him to present to us a picture of our world as it is which, through the magic of a newly mobile fiction, is joined with a picture of that same world as it ought to be, or might be (although the brilliance of the structure lies partly in the fact that we are never sure whether we are to regard this 'ought' as a sincere political desire or as an elaborate joke). And we find this structure recurring in *The New Atlantis* and *The Blazing World*. In Bacon's text, a group of sailors is blown off course and marooned on an island named Bensalem, a kind of nowhere place 'between life and death', as the captain puts it, and 'beyond both the old world and the new'.[30] Bensalem is off the map, beyond the limits of the known, like Robinson Crusoe's island in the novel that Defoe writes a century or so later; but rather than presenting, as Crusoe's island does, an empty slate, in which a Rousseauvian state of nature appears in its native, untechnologised form, Bensalem is the home of an advanced scientific rationalism – in which the interpretive desire that drives early modern anatomy is consummated. Bensalem functions as a laboratory in which the secret springs of nature can be studied with infinitesimal closeness to bring the existing, faulty relationship between the human and the environment to a state of perfection. The study that occupies the scientists of Bensalem and of its scientific academy, Salomon House, involves the microscopic dissection of being – the forensic attention to the Hobbesian mechanics of nature – to manufacture new and perfected life by, as Bacon puts it, 'subjecting nature to art'. 'We have fair and large baths', the captain of the lost ship is told, 'for the restoring of men's bodies' and for the 'confirming of it in strength of sinews, vital parts, and the very juice and substance of the body' (p. 178). The Bensalemites have the means to establish the 'prolongation of life', as well as 'meats' and 'drinks' that 'make the very flesh of men's bodies sensibly more hard and tough, and their strength far greater than otherwise it would be' (p. 180). They can make artificial sound, artificial light, artificial life. They are skilled in the art of making 'versions of bodies into other bodies', the 'making of new species', the 'transplanting of one species into another'. The work of the scientific community in Bensalem is to exercise the imagination to bring scientific knowledge to bear on the revealed mechanics of the world, to harness the 'forces of the imagination, either upon another body or upon the body itself' (p. 186); Cavendish's *The Blazing World* performs a similar intellectual exercise. Employing, again, the device of a ship which has strayed off course, here to the North Pole, Cavendish's utopia takes us across a boundary between this world and another. 'They were not only driven', the narrator says, to the end of our own world, 'but even to another Pole of another world which joined close to it' – the paradisiacal 'Blazing World' of the title.[31] The only survivor of the adventure, a woman who becomes the 'Empress' of the new world, is admitted into the arcane knowledge that belongs to this new world, a wonderful kind of science that grants her 'sensitive perceptions' of 'the interior corporeal, figurative motions both of vegetables and minerals' and the 'interior, figurative motions of natural creatures' (p. 150).

The central aim of all of these utopian fictions – an aim that one can see too in early modern anatomy and in Rembrandt's anatomy paintings – is to draw on such hidden knowledge to produce images of the replete and perfected body at home in the world, fictional images in which there is no gap between mind, body, language and the law, and in which the inside of being has been reconciled with the outside. The object of their political as well as their aesthetic hope is to discover a means of matching things with the words that stand for them, a means of tuning our discursive structures so that they account perfectly for a life in common with others and make a space in which we can inhabit our bodies fully and without contradiction, without any breath of difference from ourselves. Thomas More, writing in the *Epigrams*, in his 'own voice', makes a kind of proto-Hobbesian comparison between the state and the body, in which he makes this desire explicit. 'A kingdom in all parts is like a man', he writes:

> It is held together by natural affection. The king is the head; the people form the other parts. Every citizen the king has he considers a part of his own body (that is why he grieves at the loss of a single one). The people risk themselves to save the king and everyone thinks of him as the head of his own body.[32]

This desire for a body politic that is bound together by natural affection, a body that encounters itself in its nakedness and its self-completion, runs throughout *Utopia* and predicts that desire for the revealed body that we find in Hobbes and in Descartes, in Rembrandt, in Bacon and in Cavendish. In Utopia, Raphael tells us, this model of accord, of bodily harmony and natural affection, is enshrined both in the island's politics and in its arts. This is the principle that animates the legal system in Utopia, which is founded on the idea that justice is already inscribed in nature and needs no other language to make itself understood. 'Here' in early modern Europe, the text suggests, where there is no clear accord between bodies as they exist in nature and bodies as they become political subjects, we need a host of complicated and artificial laws to bring bodies into line with the state. 'Laws of this sort', Raphael says, 'may have as much effect as poultices continually applied to sick bodies that are past cure' (p. 38). But in Utopia, where body and state are apparently in harmony, there is almost no need for laws. 'The wonderfully wise and sacred institutions of the Utopians', Raphael declares, means that they are 'so well governed with so few laws' (p. 37). The Utopians need few laws and make no treaties with other nations because, they say, 'if nature doesn't bind man adequately to his fellow man, what good is a treaty?' (p. 83). Similarly, their arts display a perfect match between form and content, in which nature finds effortless and complete expression. In this, Raphael says, 'they are no doubt far beyond us, because all of their music, both vocal and instrumental, renders and expresses natural feelings and perfectly matches the sound to the subject' (p. 102).

The understanding of the body in *Utopia* is shaped by this investment in the accord between form and content, by this image of a nature fully inhering in itself and fully represented by the language of the state. More's text gives rise to a number of tropes – the natural expression of the utopian language, the absence of laws, the absence of money, the identity of the personal body with the body-politic – that recur in Bacon and Cavendish, and indeed throughout the long history of utopian fiction. *The New Atlantis* reprises a practice described in More's *Utopia*, whereby, before a couple enter into the sacrament of marriage, 'the woman is shown naked to the suitor by a responsible and respectable matron', and 'some honourable man presents the suitor naked to the woman' (p. 79). 'I have read', one of the Bensalemites says in *New Atlantis*, 'of a Feigned Commonwealth, where the married couple are permitted, before they contract, to see one another naked' (p. 174). The presentation of the naked body in both *Utopia* and *The New Atlantis* – through which, one of the Bensalemites says, any 'hidden defects in men and women's bodies' might be exposed (pp. 174–75) – is offered as the revelation of one's full being, as if the truth of essence must appear on the surface. And in *The Blazing World*, the experience of pure bodily self-presence is tightly bound to the picture of a commonwealth in which there is little need for the enforcement of laws. The Empress asks one of the 'statesmen' of the Blazing World two questions when she first arrives: 'why they had so few laws' and 'why they preferred the monarchical form of government before any other' (p. 134). The answers to her questions – because 'many laws make many divisions' and because 'as it was natural for one body to have but one head, so it was natural for a body politic to have but one governor' (p. 134) – lie at the heart of the picture of biopolitical life in *The Blazing World*. For all its odd, teeming hybridity (the inhabitants of the Blazing World are all species hybrids, 'some bird-men, some fly-men, some ant-men, some geese-men, some spider-men, some lice-men', and so on (pp. 133–34)), the text is underwritten by the possibility of a oneness of being, in which the variousness of life is gathered together into a luminous wholeness. 'I find', the Empress says, 'that nature is but one infinite self-moving body, which by the virtue of its self-motion, is divided into infinite parts' (p. 154). When the Empress meets Cavendish herself (Cavendish appears in the story when the Empress summons her to act as a scribe to record the truths that she discovers from the 'immaterial spirits' of the Blazing World), it is this unity in difference that characterises the relationship they form. 'Their meeting', the narrator writes, 'did produce such an intimate friendship between them, that they became platonic lovers, although they were both females' – a platonic love that brings them into a richly shared being, in which nothing is hidden, in which all essence appears.

Throughout these fictions, then, one can see the recurrence of an ideal body, as the template for a kind of Hobbesian body politic, in which the internal mechanisms of nature have been revealed. But if this is the case, what is most striking about the terms in which fiction is deployed as a means of picturing such bodies is that these terms insistently produce precisely the kinds of difference from self, precisely the disjunction between essence and appearance, between word and thing, that it is their central political and aesthetic aim to abolish. In More's *Utopia*, this estrangement from self as an effect of the picturing of self-identity is captured in the very name both of More's text and of Raphael's island – the name that comes to define the process by which fiction gives rise to political possibility. The name 'Utopia' is a pun, a linguistic trick which runs throughout the text like the writing in a stick of rock, meshing together two Greek compounds, *eu topos*, meaning 'good place', and *ou topos*, meaning 'no place'. This is the master pun, the overarching means by which a statement of political desire (a picture of a good place) might carry within it an acknowledgement that such political desire is impossible to attain, that a good place necessarily does not exist or can only come to thought in the guise of a fiction, in the disappearing condition of its own non-being. But beneath that umbrella, every element of the state that Hythloday describes exhibits some such trick, some such cancellation. The name of the capital city Amaurot (mirror image of London) derives from the Greek *amauroton*, 'to make dark or dim'; the river Anyder (mirror image of the Thames) is named after the Greek *anydros* meaning 'water-less'. The governor Ademus takes his name from the Greek *a*, meaning 'without', plus *demos*, meaning 'people', making him a governor without a people to govern. Even Hythloday's name itself derives from the Greek *hythlos*, meaning 'nonsense' and *daiein*, meaning 'to distribute', making him not the guide to a perfect world, solution of all of our troubles, but a cheap peddler of nonsense.

Everything that happens in *Utopia* has to be understood through the filter of this pun, and in the light of self-cancellation that it enacts. It invites us, in one mode, to read the text as an elaborate satire on the vanity of political idealism. The concentric structure of the work – in which we move from a prefatory letter from Thomas More to Peter Giles at the outer threshold of the text, to the story of a (partly fictional) More travelling to Antwerp to meet Hythloday, to the story told by Hythloday himself, in reported speech, of the 'best state of a commonwealth' – is flattened by this kind of reading. In the prefatory letter to Giles, More describes the difficulties he had in finding the time to write the 'little book' before us, given that he is a busy lawyer, and when he is not 'pleading some cases, hearing others', he is devoting time to his 'family and household', so that

'for myself – that is, my studies, – there's nothing left' (p. 4). He did not
have much time for writing, but that should not really have mattered
because, he says to Giles, 'all I had to do was repeat what you and I together
heard Raphael relate' (p. 3). He does not have to worry about style or
composition, as 'there was nothing for me to do but simply write down
what I had heard' (p. 4). This is not a laborious work of invention, but
simple reportage, as 'Truth, in fact is the only thing at which I should aim
and do aim in writing this book' (p. 3). These professions of truth telling,
mixed with the personal details of More's real life and work, though, can
only be understood as a joke, when we are being told, in the Greek
undertow that pulls constantly at the Latin text, that the island of Utopia
does not exist, that Giles and More did not meet Raphael in Antwerp at all
because he is a nonsensical figment of More's imagination, and so More
does not in fact aim at truth but at fabrication. As we move from the
preface to the main body of the text, this effect is only increased. The
insistence on the truth of More's, and then of Hythloday's account, and
their joint admiration of the simple naked beauty of the Utopians, only
thinly disguise the story's obvious falsity, and the obvious absurdity of
many of the utopian solutions to the real problems facing lawmakers in
sixteenth-century England. Hythloday is offered as a version of More
unplugged, released from the pragmatic constraints of diplomacy and
statecraft – a picture of More the philosopher, free to imagine ideal
solutions to problems without paying any heed to their practicability.
When the text is working in satirical mode, and as we plainly realise that
the real More has not in fact liberated himself at all from the constraints of
his working life or the tiresome demands of his family, then this picture of
philosophical freedom reads as a comic warning against unfettered flights
of fancy, and a justification for the kinds of compromises that More
himself has to make when political reality stands in the way of philosophical purity. The text is no longer concentrically organised, worlds within
worlds within worlds, but a picture of a single world – our world – shaped
by the pragmatic art of the possible, from which Hythloday's flight of fancy
offers no release.

The text offers to be read in this way, but its enduring beauty and
richness, its strange capacity to wriggle free of itself, arises from its refusal to
be constrained by this satirical mode. One mark of this refusal, this mixture
of the playful with the sincere, is the tendency for Hythloday's philosophy,
despite its absurdity, to match, sometimes precisely, with More's own
convictions. As Thomas Healy has demonstrated, the tradition of 'serio
ludere' to which *Utopia* belongs allows More to mix the playful and the

earnest, in ways that work to reinvent both terms, to recast the forms in which we give imaginative expression to our political ideals.[33] In the *Epigrams*, for example, More develops a shepherding analogy to illustrate his conception of good governance. More asks 'What is a good king?' and answers 'He is a watchdog, guardian of the flock, who by barking keeps the wolves from the sheep. What is the bad king? He is the wolf'.[34] Hythloday, in the midst of his attack on the corruption of the English court, develops a parallel analogy. 'I would say', he tells the fictional More, that 'it is the king's duty to take more care of his people's welfare than of his own, just as it is the duty of a shepherd who cares about his job to feed the sheep rather than himself' (pp. 32–33). Hythloday, here and throughout his description of Utopian statecraft, does not simply demonstrate the foolish vanity of the intellectual; rather, there is always a sincerity to his political and aesthetic hopes, a real investment in the possibilities of a natural body at home in its own language-world that Raphael and More share, even though the picture of that body is always riven by the contradictions of the utopian text itself. One cannot understand the movement and texture of More's *Utopia* without attending to this contradiction, this strange bidirectional movement between satire and sincerity, modulated by the operations of an emergent prose fiction. The trajectory that the text follows, from the prefatory letter to Giles, to the meeting between More and Raphael in Antwerp, to the picture Raphael gives us of Utopia, is *not* a linear movement that takes us away from the realm of fact and into the realm of fantasy, away from the historical More and towards some foolish fantasy version of himself. Rather, it traces an extraordinarily double-faced passage, in which the movement from the factual to the fictional is intimately woven into the opposite movement from pragmatic falsity to philosophical truth. This is what Stephen Greenblatt means when he writes, in the most influential account of More's text that we have, that '*Utopia* depends on the simple circumstance – so obvious as to be virtually invisible – that there are not two forms of language, one referential and the other nonreferential, one for truth and the other for fiction.'[35] It is when More adopts his fictional voice that he is able to come closest to an expression of truth, to the perfect accord between language and the world, just as the account of his real self, hearing cases and putting his children to bed, is necessarily structured partly as a fiction. 'The category of the real merges with that of the fictive', Greenblatt writes, when we realise that 'the historical More is a narrative fiction', that when More is speaking with 'his own voice', he is using the same language, the same forms of structured artifice, as his fictional creatures, and vice versa (p. 31).

This doubleness, this bidirectionality, can be felt at every point in the text and vibrates in every line, as the striving for a picture of an uncontaminated body, fully at one with itself, is always both absolutely sincere and demonstrably insincere – as the possibility of a body that fully owns itself can only be won through the intervention of a distancing fiction that divides it from itself. It is in the discussion, in the prefatory letter to Giles, of the length of the bridge that crosses the Anyder in Amaurot, that this contradictory motion, this to and fro between fact and fiction, the referential and the non-referential, can most clearly be seen. More's servant John Clement was present during the conversation with Hythloday in Antwerp, More writes, and Clement has 'raised a great doubt in my mind' about the accuracy of a detail that More has recorded in his text. 'As I recall matters', More writes,

> Hythloday said the bridge over the Anyder at Amaurot was five hundred yards long; but my John says that is two hundred yards too much – that in fact the river is not more than three hundred yards wide there. So I beg you, consult your memory. If your recollection agrees with his, I'll yield and confess myself mistaken. But if you don't recall the point, I'll follow my own memory and keep my present figure. For, as I've taken particular pains to avoid having anything false in the book, so, if anything is in doubt, I'd rather say something untrue than tell a lie. In short, I'd rather be honest than clever. (p. 5)

This passage, as it frets over the importance of measurement, of an accurate account of the world, mixes factual and fictional registers in a delicious and dizzying way. The rhetoric of precise description that More employs here assumes that there is a real bridge over a real river called the Anyder, which he is not inventing, but whose actual length, appearance and nature he is striving faithfully to record. This rhetoric is given an extra twist by the fact, as we soon come to realise, that Amaurot is a version of London, and Anyder a version of the Thames, so the bridge in question is a version of London Bridge which, in the sixteenth century was, as Clement remembers, around 300 yards long. So there is a referential structure of a sort at play here, and there is a reality that More is partly referring to, that he has misremembered, and that Clement has got right. But, of course, the texture of More's language here, the nature of the truth claim he is making, has already shifted away from reference to non-reference. It is not just that the Greek spooks the Latin – so we are faced, from the outset, with an account of a bridge over a waterless river in a dim figment of a city, told by a peddler of nonsense; it is that the presence of the nonsensical Hythloday at the meeting in Antwerp has already doubled the rhetorical register, already put the language of the letter at a remove from itself. Read in one direction, the voice that speaks here is as close to the historical More as we come anywhere in the text of *Utopia*, and works to ground the fantasy at the novel's heart in the reality at its periphery. But even here, before *Utopia* has properly begun, this voice starts to tremble and waver through its contact with the fiction that it introduces, through its straight-faced introduction of Hythloday as a real character. The 'More' of the prefatory letter, even before he has set imaginary foot in the text of *Utopia*, is already partly a figment, already closer to the imaginary Hythloday than he is to the historical More. With each sentence in the passage, one can see this strange implosion taking place, as a kind of continual collapse. 'I've taken particular pains to avoid having anything false in the book', More writes; 'I'd rather be honest than clever.' But which voice is saying these words? The historical More, writing to the historical Giles? Or the fictional More who enters into the fantasy of his meeting with Hythloday? Which More is honest, and which is clever? Does the claim to truth telling belong to the discursive realm of the letter or to the discursive realm of the imaginary account of a perfect place? Clearly, and unavoidably, it belongs to both; it serves as the bridge between these two discursive fields, as real as the bridge over the Anyder, as real as the bridge over the Thames ('both realities', as Don DeLillo puts in in a different context, 'occurring at once').[36] But even as it reaches across the gap between them, even as it brings a fictional version of More into contact with a historical version of More, the language of the text dissolves through the operation of its own revealed fictionality, breaking the connection it allows, causing the voice to fall back into the incommensurate parts of which it is made – part fact, part fiction.

The register that More invents in *Utopia* allows for this doubling, a doubling which suggests that the encounter with oneself is always conducted through the operation of a fiction – fiction as a kind of connective tissue which binds us to ourselves, even as it marks a distance that intervenes in our own self-congress. If *Utopia* is committed to telling the truth – if More is sincere in his prefatory insistence on honesty – then the truth it perhaps divines is that we are partly fictional and partly real, partly composed of More, and partly composed of Raphael. The bridge over the river Anyder partly measures itself against the London Bridge of the sixteenth century, and partly against a non-existent bridge, whose dimensions have no reference to any reality whatsoever. In Ricoeur's terms as I discussed them earlier, the bridge works partly as a representation, a 'replica of an absent thing', and partly as its own, non-referential reality, the product of 'imagination at work' that 'produces itself as a world'.[37] As More regards Raphael, in the mirror of the text, he addresses him across a gulf, a collapsing bridge that the work of fiction makes possible, even as it annihilates it. The coming together of More and Raphael, through the operations of a self-cancelling fiction, is what makes it possible to conjure the image of a complete body, at home in the world. The lit spaces of *Utopia* lie in the ground between More and Raphael, as the exposed, administered criminal body lies in the ground between Rembrandt and Tulp in 'The Anatomy Lesson'. But even as More's fiction brings these versions of self together, it gives expression to a darkness too, that darkness which is given a flickering visual form in Rembrandt's painting, and which accompanies every moment of revelation, not only in More's *Utopia* but also in the early modern utopian form that he invents. In Bacon's *New Atlantis*, in Cavendish's *Blazing World*, the texts preserve these non-spaces within them, as the province of fiction, the province of an emptying image that does not refer to a world beyond itself. The laboratories in Bensalem and in the Blazing World contain a plethora of technologies for seeing this utopian non-being that lies at the foundation of being, this seam of artifice that is shot through the reality of life and brings it to thinkability. In Bensalem, to see the world truly requires us to see it through prosthetic devices, microscopes and telescopes that penetrate into the truth of things only by making the small appear large, the distant close, 'representing things near as afar off, and things afar off as near' (p. 181). The production of clear sight, Bacon's captain is told, requires us to make 'feigned distances' (p. 181), just as the idea of a justice at home with itself in More's *Utopia* can only come about through the introduction of a feigned distance between More and Raphael. And in *The Blazing World* too, it is distorting lenses – 'artificial optic-glasses' (p. 142) – that allow us to see straight, just as it is the peculiar, doubled relationship between the Empress and the fictional Cavendish that allows this kind of seeing to come to fictional expression. The Empress is appalled by the use of such optical devices when she first arrives in the Blazing World. 'I do plainly perceive' she says to the 'bear-men' who are the 'experimental philosophers' of the Blazing World, 'that your glasses are false informers, and instead of discovering the truth, delude your senses' (p. 141); but as she grows accustomed to ways of seeing and thinking in the new world, she realises that seeing clearly involves a bending of the light, just as a true encounter with the natural body involves prosthetic addition. Telescopes and micro-scopes, the bear-men tell her, 'did never delude, but rectify and inform their senses; nay the world, said they, would be but blind without them' (p. 143). Seeing involves the artifice of the lens, and gaining access to the truths that are offered by the 'immaterial spirits' of the Blazing World involves the adoption of a prosthetic body, just as Raphael can only speak through the mouthpiece of More. For the voice of the 'immaterial spirits' to be preserved, the Empress is told, they need a scribe, they need the services of a Cavendish or a More, because the spirits, they say, 'cannot write, except they put on a hand or arm, or else the whole body of man' (p 180).

It is this capacity for fiction to articulate a self-negating artificiality that makes a certain kind of truth possible that More inaugurates in 1516. The scientists of the Blazing World are frustrated that they are not able to produce a kind of artificial lens that might allow them to see nothing as if it were something. 'They could yet by no means contrive such glasses', they say, 'by the help of which they could spy out a vacuum, with all its dimensions, nor immaterial substances, non-beings, and mixed-beings, or such as are between something and nothing; which they were very much troubled at, hoping that yet, in time, by long study and practice, they might perhaps attain to it' (p. 145). There is no lens, however finely ground, that can give being to non-being or to that empty ground between something and nothing, but the utopian form that More crafts allows for a kind of fiction, a kind of prosthetic imagination, that is able to make precisely such non-being thinkable, and to find in such non-being the foundation of a form of self-ownership. In so doing, these fictions contain the germ of the modern novel form; so, when Samuel Beckett, nearly 500 years after *Utopia* was published, writes a text which seeks to describe the novel condition most succinctly, it is the scenario depicted by More that he evokes. 'Say a body', the narrator of *Worstward Ho* commands: 'Say a body. Where none. A place. Where None. For the body. To be in'.[38] This is what the novel does; it approaches the fundamental predicament in which a body occupies space, through the medium of a fiction, in which there is no body, and no place (or no-place). Of course, in Beckett's opening one can also hear Descartes' *Discourse on the Method*. Indeed, Descartes is probably uppermost in Beckett's mind here. 'I saw that I could pretend that I had no body', Descartes writes in a passage I quoted earlier, 'and that there was no world or place for me to be in'.[39] Beckett may be thinking of Descartes' *Discourse* as a means of reflecting on how the contemplation of non-existence relates to the production of fictional truth. But if there is a Cartesian cast to this moment in Beckett, it is More's fiction with which he is most in sympathy. Descartes shapes a philosophy which can overcome the disjunction he sees between the mind and the material in which mind finds extension, but it is the task of the novel, its special gift and vocation, to live in the midst of that very disjunction. The utopian form – and the novel, more broadly, as a form – does not seek to overcome the emptiness, the nothingness, that inhabits all of the means by which we imagine body and place, but rather to bring such nothingness into the realm of expression. It is the literary expression of such nothingness – 'nothingness', as Beckett beautifully puts it in 1948, 'in words enclosed'[40] – that gives the form of prose fiction that is invented by More in 1516 such intimate access to that fugitive, collapsing link between the mind and the body in which mind finds itself partly enshrined.

1.3   The Prosthetic Imagination in the Early Novel Form

Utopian fictions, then, from *Utopia* to *The Blazing World*, inaugurate a particular means by which the imagination is brought into contact with reality, and a particular means by which this play between thinking and being is allowed to vibrate, or to resonate. Fiction, in the early utopian form, offers a bridge that attaches ideas to things, minds to the possible bodies in which they might be housed, and that establishes such attachment only through its own fissility, its own capacity to capture the fugitive, disappearing nature of the bonds that hold us to our biomaterial forms.

In doing so, utopian forms shape the structural apparatus of the novel imagination, but perhaps the reason that these works are not generally regarded as origins of the novel form is that they remain peculiarly resistant to the larger demands of narrative fiction. Like undifferentiated stem cells, they contain the potential of the novel to create life forms, without realising such potential, without creating a fully developed organism. It is in the early novel form, as it reaches from William Baldwin's *Beware the Cat* (1561) and Thomas Nashe's *The Unfortunate Traveller* (1594), to Cervantes' *Don Quixote* (1605, 1615), to Bunyan's allegory *The Pilgrim's Progress* (1678), to Aphra Behn's *Oroonoko* (1688), that one can see the principles that drive More's text – the new relation that he establishes between the language of reality and the self-declared language of fiction – giving rise to fuller and more richly imagined lifeworlds.[41] These works take the formal fusion between fact and fiction, between the referential and the non-referential, that is established in More's *Utopia* and make of this unstable alloy the ground upon which to erect fictional characters more rounded and established than anything in More or Bacon. In all of these works, from Baldwin to Behn, one can see the same rhetoric being employed that we find in More, the same insistence that a fictional account is in fact truthful – an insistence that Catherine Gallagher influentially historicises in relation to what she

calls the 'rise of fictionality'.[42] 'Truth is the only thing at which I should aim
and do aim in writing this book', More writes. He did not have to spend any
time crafting his narrative because he is only repeating what he 'heard
Raphael relate' (p. 3). Cervantes' narrator makes a similar kind of claim, in
the opening page of *Don Quixote*, when he claims of his 'story' that 'we do
not depart so much as an inch from the truth in the telling of it', and when
he maintains throughout that he is not making the story up but simply
recording the work of the 'historian' Cide Hamete Benengeli and his
'translator'.[43] Aphra Behn, in *Oroonoko,* returns repeatedly to her insistence
on the truth of her account, claiming that 'what I have mentioned I have
taken care should be the truth', and that, like More, she had no need of
invention and 'never rested my pen a moment for thought'.[44] Her tale, she
says, will 'come simply into the world' and needs no adornment, 'there being
enough of reality to support it and to render it diverting without the
addition of invention' (p. 9). And Defoe, famously, in one of the inaugurating acts of the eighteenth-century novel declares, in the preface to *Robinson
Crusoe,* that his story is a 'just History of Fact; neither is there any
Appearance of Fiction in it'.[45] It is not until the mid-eighteenth century,
Michael McKeon argues, with Richardson's alterations to later editions of
Clarissa, that such 'claim[s] to historicity' become 'increasingly vestigial'.[46]
As the early novel develops over this time, from the sixteenth to the eight-
eenth centuries, one can see that it is built on that collapsing ground that
More stakes out between words and things, between the imagination and its
material extensions. It demonstrates that fiction is woven into truth, that the
mechanism for representing the world is the same as the mechanism for
imagining it, and it derives from such a recognition an entire world view.
But if More's discovery remains schematic, remains a kind of genetic blueprint for world making, the subsequent development of the novel might be
thought of as the emergence of a fully conceived body, an animated creature
that is made of the fusion that More invents between the fictional and the
real.

Of all the examples we have of early prose fiction – perhaps of all
examples we have of the novel form itself – it is Cervantes' *Don Quixote*
that demonstrates this process most fully, and that offers the most intricate
and intimate exploration of its internal logic. If prose narrative is built on
the seam that connects the imagination to its material extensions – the
seam that I will characterise here as a prosthetic twist or junction – then it is
Cervantes' novel that offers the supreme original example of its design, and
the model that novelists come back to, consciously or unconsciously, to the
present day. As Ortega y Gasset beautifully puts it, 'every novel bears

Quixote within it like an inner filigree'.[47] It is in the wandering of Don Quixote and his squire Sancho, across the unruly territory of seventeenth-century Spain, that we witness the first full realisation of a form that makes, of the uncertain junction between the fictional and the real, the most powerful means that we have developed of imagining and fashioning human life.

Of course, the circumstance that drives *Don Quixote*, that provides its originating impulse and that remains its chief concern, is the perception that life *eludes* the forms in which we encounter it, rather than finding itself enshrined in them. Cervantes' novel responds to the perception that European modernity inaugurates an epistemological crisis by presenting us with a 'reality' that, in Auerbach's terms, has become 'difficult to survey', and with a 'world', in Michael McKeon's terms, that has become 'disenchanted'.[48] Don Quixote's and Sancho's errant travels, directed always by the whim of Sancho's ass Dapple or Don Quixote's horse Rocinante, lead them across a rough-hewn landscape that has been denuded of its sustaining Romance mythology, and that seems constantly in need of reinterpretation, in need of a new narrative and a new set of social codes and principles to bring it into legibility. In Don Quixote's case, most famously, this involves the imposition of a set of fictions, derived from the reading of books of chivalry, onto an early modern landscape that they do not fit. The country gentleman and small landowner named Quixano becomes so entranced with books of chivalry, and so convinced that 'all the fanciful stuff he read was true' (p. 32), that he 'fell into the strangest fancy that ever a madman had in the whole world', deciding to become, himself, a knight errant and 'travel through the world with horse and armour in search of adventures' (p. 33). This strangest of fancies leads Quixano to transform all he sees by an act of willed reinterpretation, so that the world of contemporary Spain might be remodelled – through the sovereign power of the imagination alone – to conform to the now obsolete chivalric tradition. Windmills become giants, a barber's basin becomes the mythical 'Mambrino's helmet' (which confers invulnerability on all who wear it), inns become castles and a local 'farm girl' named Aldonza Lorenzo becomes the peerless Lady Dulcinea del Toboso. Quixano himself becomes, in the crooked beam of his self-regard, 'Don Quixote de la Mancha', the light and mirror of knight errantry. The drama of the book, its comedy, its pathos, all stem from the gap that opens between the world as it is inhabited by Quixano and the world as it is reinterpreted and renamed by Don Quixote. The language of the novel, infected as it is by Don Quixote's fantasy, finds itself stranded in that gap, partaking both of the world of Quixano and the world of Don Quixote, moving uneasily between them, as the language of *Utopia* is caught between the imaginative spheres of More and of Raphael. In the gap that intervenes between the world as it is and the world as Don Quixote perceives it, Cervantes' narrative acts as a bridge which attaches an alienated imagination to the newly indecipherable, disenchanted world from which it has become divorced. Every object that the narrator describes derives its phenomenological weight from this effect, this shuttling of the narrative voice between the language of quotidian seventeenth-century Spain and the language of a defunct knight errantry. Mambrino's helmet, for example – or the barber's basin, in its unenchanted form – draws its specific density from the shifting movement of the narrative, as it searches for the correct optic through which to view it. Sancho is certain, at least initially, that the helmet is in fact a basin. 'When Sancho heard the basin called a headpiece', the narrator says, 'he could not restrain his laughter.' 'It's like nothing', he says, 'so much as a barber's basin'. Don Quixote's response to this interpretation, however, is to loftily disregard Sancho's reading of the object, its use and its value, because, he says, his own understanding of the essence of the object is not clouded by the appearance that it might take on, or the degraded form that it might adopt under contemporary, postenchanted conditions. As Don Quixote pits his seeing against Sancho's, one can see the object itself wavering between opposing Ricoeurian referential fields. 'This enchanted helmet', Don Quixote says to Sancho, 'looks like a barber's basin, as you say. But, however that may be, its metamorphosis is of no consequence to me, who knows what it really is' (p. 163).

Every object in the novel, as I have said, is caught in this cross current, pulled on the one hand towards the contemporary reading endorsed by the priest and the barber (the novel's spokespeople for rationality and sanity), and on the other towards Don Quixote's romantic interpretation (with Sancho, in his credulousness and his loyalty to his 'master', shifting between both positions). But there is no object in the novel which comes under more intense scrutiny than the body of Don Quixote himself, the long, gaunt form of the errant knight, perched on his scrawny nag, that draws such ridicule from all who encounter him. When Quixano decides to remake the world by redescribing it, the first thing that he transforms is himself. The name that he chooses – that gives a title both to himself and to Cervantes' novel – indicates, from the start, how central the reshaping of Don Quixote's body is to the re-enchantment of his world. The name Quixote derives, in part, according to the OED, from the 'Spanish *quijote, quixote*, cuisse, thigh-piece of a suit of armour', and it is evident, throughout, that renaming, for Don Quixote, involves the adoption of an artificial body, of a prosthetic addition or extension that takes him into the world of his fantasy. The name that Quixano assumes, in the opening pages of the novel, doubles always as the suit of armour, 'eaten with rust and covered with mould' (p. 33), that he polishes up, and through which he enters into the role of knight errant. And as he adopts his new persona, he focuses, repeatedly, on the nature of the knightly body that his new name entails (an early version of the body of the superhero, suddenly endowed with magical powers). According to his own fantasy, his body takes on a kind of invulnerability that comes with his unshakable belief in his powers as a knight. Throughout his adventures, he suffers innumerable pummellings, leading to Sancho's repeated claim that his enemies will beat him 'till they don't leave a whole bone in your worship's body' (p. 484), but the power of his imagination, and the wonders too of the imaginary 'balsam of Fierabras' the 'recipe for which', he says, 'lies in my memory', make him feel proof against injury, as if he has a kind of invisible suit of armour as well as his rusty, mouldy one, as if Mambrino's helmet has in fact consigned an invulnerability upon him. Armed with his wonderful balsam, Don Quixote says to Sancho,

> There is no need to fear death nor so much as to think of dying of any wound. So, when I have made some and given it to you, if ever you see me cut through the middle in some battle – as very often happens – you have only to take the part of my body that has fallen to the ground and place it neatly and cunningly, before the blood congeals, on to the half that is still in the saddle, taking especial care to make them fit exactly. Then you must give me just two drips of this balsam to drink and, you will see, I shall be as sound as an apple. (p. 81)

It is easy to think, of course, that the balsam offers no real protection to Don Quixote, just as his enchanted helmet, or his rusty suit of armour or the nobility of his adopted name will offer him no protection from the brutal realities of Spain under the Inquisition. When he does take a real draft of his balsam, it leads only to an explosive fit of vomiting and diarrhoea (p. 128). But as Don Quixote regards his own body, in the famous 'light' and 'mirror' of knight errantry, it undergoes the same kind of transformation as the barber's basin when it becomes Mambrino's helmet, revealing a kind of knightly essence that lies beneath his comically scrawny physique, even if only when the language of the novel itself suffers an enchantment. As the maid Maritornes asks Don Quixote to give her his hand, when she is preparing one of the many cruel tricks that are played on him over the course of the novel (this one involving hanging him by his hand from the upstairs window of an inn for the duration of an entire night), we watch as his body trembles under the influence of his knightly self-perception. 'Take this hand, lady', Don Quixote says grandly,

> Or rather this scourge of the world's malefactors. Take this hand, I say, which no other woman's has touched, not even hers who has complete possession of my whole body. I do not give it to you to kiss, but that you may gaze on the structure of its sinews, the interlacement of its muscles, the width and capacity of its veins; from all of which you may judge what strength must be in the arm to which such a hand belongs. (p. 393)

The hand – the privileged vehicle of touch, the member with which Don Quixote reaches out into the phenomenological world – is caught here in the divergent currents of the novel, appearing both as the fleshy hand of Quixano and as the legendary hand of the famous knight, the scourge of the world's malefactors. Throughout the novel, his hand functions doubly in this way, both bringing the deluded Quixano into contact with the quotidian reality around him (here acting quite literally as the tether which binds him to the world, and to Maritornes' cruelty) and drawing that reality into the realm of Don Quixote's fantasy. This doubleness is given a particularly resonant form in the episode of the 'Cave of Montesinos', an adventure which acts as one of the key hinges in the novel between the imaginary and the real. In this episode, Sancho lowers his master on a rope into a hole in the ground, where Don Quixote imagines that he spends three days and nights in conversation with characters from Chivalric legend, and with his own lady Dulcinea – much to Sancho's amusement, who is certain that Don Quixote was only in the hole for 'little more than an hour' (p. 621). The episode is so overwhelming for Don Quixote and opens such a gulf between the world as it is and the world as he imagines it, that it causes him to doubt his own existence, wondering whether it was 'my very self who was there, or some empty and counterfeit phantom' (p. 615). This doubt haunts him for the rest of the book, as he cannot fully determine whether the experience he had in the underworld was real; but it is the evidence of his hand – the sensory proof provided by the coordination between hand and eye, between what he sees and what he feels – that persuades him of its legitimacy. The happenings in the cave could be a fantasy, he acknowledges to Sancho, as it could be a hallucination resulting from some malign enchantment. 'But it is not', he says, 'for what I told you of I saw with my own eyes and touched with my own hand' (p. 621). If it is the hand that allows us to reach out into the world – the hand which, for Hobbes, communicates sensation 'by the mediation of Nerves, and other strings and membranes of the body . . . inwards to the brain and the heart' – then it is also the case that the hand suffers the same kind of epistemological uncertainty that afflicts all of the other objects in the novel.[49] The body which Don Quixote extends into the world, which allows him to experience the world around him, to judge of its truth or its falsity, is itself an extraordinarily unstable composite of the real and the imaginary, as volatile as Mambrino's helmet or the balsam of Fierabras. As Don Quixote is repeatedly told, when he asks the various sages he meets for assurances about the truth or otherwise of his experiences in the cave of Montesinos, 'part of what your worship saw or experienced in the cave is false and part true' (p. 637). The Cave of Montesinos is a hybrid of the true and the false, as Don Quixote's body itself, his organ of perception as well as the material ground of his being, is an amalgam of the real and the fantastic; a compound or alloy which, as Don Quixote himself puts it, 'seemed to partake of both' (p. 637).

Don Quixote's body, then, sits on the boundary that the novel draws between the world as experienced by the priest and the barber and the world as imagined by Don Quixote. It belongs in part to the realist world of early modern Spain, and in part to the world of chivalric fantasy, and the way that we read the novel depends in large measure on how we respond to this double belonging. Of course, the most literal reading of the novel would tend to privilege the reality effect of the imagined community shared by the priest and the barber, and sometimes by Sancho – the community which would agree that Don Quixote's experiences in the cave of Montesinos were a fantasy, and that the whole business of his knightly exploits a comedy of misapprehension. This would certainly seem to be the interpretation favoured by Cervantes' seventeenth-century read-ers. Descartes might have Cervantes' novel in mind when he writes, in the *Discourse on the Method*, that 'fables make us conceive of events as being possible where they are not', and that 'those who base their behaviour on examples they draw from such accounts are likely to try to match the feats of knights of old in tales of chivalry and set themselves targets beyond their powers' (p. 9). And Hobbes almost certainly has Cervantes in mind when he warns, in *Leviathan*, that a 'man' might 'compoundeth the image of his own person, with the image of the actions of an other man', a phenomenon of misapprehension that 'happeneth often to them that are much taken with reading of Romants' (p. 14) (and which leads to that species of 'madness' which Hobbes describes, in *Elements of Law*, as 'the gallant madness of Don Quixote', which is 'nothing else but an expression of such height of vain glory as reading of Romants may produce in pusillanimous men').[50] For Hobbes and Descartes, the influence of 'fables' and 'romants' can lead to error, in which the intellectual and material connections (the nerves and sinews) that attach us to the world malfunction, causing us to misunderstand the nature of the possible, to mistake inns for castles. And one can see a similar tendency in modern responses to *Don Quixote*. Perhaps the most influential twentieth-century consideration of the reality effect in Cervantes' novel, Auerbach's essay 'The Enchanted Dulcinea' in his 1946 book *Mimesis*, works on the same principle that we find in Hobbes and Descartes, namely that Don Quixote's fantasy can be best understood as a faulty perception of reality, one that we, as readers, must correct in sustaining our own understanding of the difference between the real and the imagined, the true and the false. Everything that Don Quixote does and says when he is under the influence of his fantasy, Auerbach writes, is 'completely senseless and so incompatible with the existing world' (p. 344). Don Quixote's sense of himself as a chivalric hero might reproduce elements of wisdom and dignity and might sometimes resemble the wisdom and dignity that Don Quixote displays when he is not in the throes of his obsession, but the power of his misapprehension is such that wisdom, bravery, loyalty and so on become meaningless apparatuses as soon as they are employed in the service of Don Quixote's illusion. 'As soon as the idée fixe of knight-errantry takes hold of him', Auerbach writes, 'he acts unwisely, he acts like an automaton' (p. 347), an artificial being, a piece of clattering machinery. The energy of the novel, for Auerbach, is directed at demonstrating the gap between an increasingly complex contemporary Spanish reality and the older mythical forms which seek to account for it. 'In the resulting clashes between Don Quijote and reality', Auerbach writes, 'no situation ever results which puts in question that reality's right to be what it is. It is always right and he wrong; and after a bit of amusing confusion it flows calmly on, untouched' (p. 345).

For Auerbach, then, it is possible to see a clear distinction between the body of Quixano, in its natural or real state, and the body of Don Quixote, the machinised automaton, as he dons his literal and metaphorical armour. 'Reality' is 'untouched' by the diseased seeing of the errant knight. But if this is how the situation appears to Auerbach in 1946, the critical understanding of the balance between 'Don Quijote and reality' has tended to shift over the course of the second half of the twentieth century, until, by the turn of the current century, it reaches the almost diametrically opposite position. Michael McKeon, in 1987, seeks to refine Auerbach's sharp distinction between reality and Don Quixote's enchanted view of the world. 'Clearly', McKeon writes, 'my reading of the work cannot be reconciled with Erich Auerbach's view that "the whole book is a comedy in which well-founded reality holds madness up to ridicule."'[51] For McKeon, Cervantes does not simply oppose reality to enchantment but demonstrates, more subtly, that 'the modern disenchantment of the world entailed not the eradication of enchantment but its transformation, its secularization' (p. 282). This tends to complicate our understanding of the movement that the novel enacts between the real and the imagined, but for McKeon Cervantes 'stops considerably short of elaborating a more general theory of the social construction of reality and the social relativity of madness' (p. 282). But as the effects of postmodern thinking are increasingly felt in the later twentieth century, the reading of *Don Quixote*, and its influence both on criticism and on the fiction of the period, tends to move towards just such a 'general theory', a sense that Cervantes' novel does not map a clear distinction between reality and faulty perception but rather shows that reality itself is a function of representation and can thus be remodelled by the development of new ways of seeing. Jorge Luis Borges' short but arresting tribute to *Don Quixote* from 1955, the 'Parable of Cervantes and the *Quixote*', inaugurates a tradition of postmodern fictions which ground their scepticism concerning the distinction between reality and representation on a reception of Cervantes' book. Borges' parable suggests that 'the whole scheme of the work consisted in the opposition of two worlds: the unreal world of books of chivalry, the ordinary everyday world of the seventeenth century'.[52] This opposition drives the novel; but as it is received by successive generations of readers, Borges writes, this opposition is gradually worn away. 'The years', the narrator says, 'finally smooth away that discord', as we recognise that these 'two worlds' are one (p. 242). This discovery, that reality and unreality do not oppose but sustain each other, is the gift that Cervantes gives to a generation of writers who regard *Don Quixote* as an origin of the self-reflexive narrative imagination. For Kathy Acker, in her 1986 novel *Don Quixote: Which Was a Dream* and for Paul Auster, in his 1987 work *The New York Trilogy*, Cervantes and his 'historian' Benengeli are the models of an emerging simulacral world view. As Mario Vargas Llosa puts it, in 2005, from a postmodern perspective, 'reality' is not 'untouched' by Don Quixote's imagination but composed of it. The 'dream that transforms Alonso Quijano into *Don Quixote de La Mancha*', Vargas Llosa writes, amounts to the 'realization of a myth, the transformation of fiction into living history'.[53] The novel narrates the process by which Don Quixote's 'surroundings, the people around him, and the very reality' are 'infected by his wilful madness', so that reality itself 'becomes less and less real until – as in a Borges story – it becomes pure fiction' (p. 126).

Such a dramatic reversal in the modern critical understanding of Cervantes' depiction of the relationship between the real and the imagined, between Quixano and Quixote, might suggest that there is something about *Don Quixote* that eludes criticism. The novel has a mercurial quality – perhaps the right adjective, if tautological and self-referring, is 'quixotic' – which means that readers cannot quite access it but can only access, through it, their own assumptions about the relationship between the imagination and the world. This is perhaps what Harold Bloom has in mind, when he writes, in 2003, that the novel's 'endless range of meaning' ensures that 'no critic's account of Cervantes' masterpiece agrees with, or even resembles, any other critic's impressions'. *Don Quixote*, Bloom goes on, 'is a mirror held up not to nature, but to the reader'.[54] Now, this may be so; but what I want most centrally to argue here is that even as Cervantes' novel displays such mobility, even as it reflects back, like the 'Knight of the Mirrors', our own reading processes rather than revealing to us anything of 'itself', it touches on something intrinsic to being, something not vaporous or whimsical or capricious, but rather the ground to embodied consciousness, the substrate of animated life. It remains difficult to come to any definitive conclusions about how *Don Quixote* represents the distinction between the real and the imagined, between Quixote and Quixano, not because it puts this distinction under erasure, or because it suggests that there is no such distinction in the first place, but rather because it gains such close proximity to the processes that allow us to enter into representations, because it comes close to the representational mechanisms that underlie being itself. If there is a connecting ground, a junction or twist that attaches the imagination to the body in which it finds extension into the world – if there are nerves and sinews that attach the hand to the mind, the body of Quixano to his Quixotic armour – then these are fugitive, buried, difficult to find. As Rembrandt's anatomy paintings tell us, this connective tissue is extraordinarily hard to see, or to contemplate, coming to us only in the guise of a peculiar unthinkability. It is made at once of mind and of body and also made of neither; it is this twisting connection, this disappearing ground to being, that Cervantes' novel brings out of hiding, and into the disputed realm of reading.

One of the ways that this peculiar ground to being – the specific gravity of the Cervantine body – makes itself felt in *Don Quixote* is in the fantasy that grips the novel of a complete body, encountered in its naked, unadulterated state. Cervantes, like More, Bacon and Cavendish, is fascinated by the idea of a body that might reveal itself to the imagination without any addition, without any ornament and without any insufficiency. As both More and Bacon imagine a situation in which prospective marriage partners might display their bodies naked to each other to leave nothing unseen, so, throughout *Don Quixote*, we are presented with bodies that strive to reveal themselves to us and to each other, that push themselves towards visibility. This may take the form of Don Quixote's own comic and affectingly earnest attempts at self-revelation. One might think of his insistence, in Part One, that to perform a 'penance' to prove himself worthy of Dulcinea's love, he must strip himself naked and expose himself to the elements. 'If I am to imitate Roland in my penance', Don Quixote says to Sancho, 'I must strip off all my armour and be as naked as I was born' (p. 205). What is more, he insists too that Sancho must witness his nakedness, so that he can give a true account of it to Dulcinea, when he tells her of the extremes to which his master will go for love of her. 'Hurriedly stripping off his breeches', the narrator reports, 'he stood in his skin and shirt', presenting himself to Sancho in his nakedness. He even performs a couple of somersaults, to give Sancho the benefit of a 360-degree view of the knightly frame. He 'twice turned head over heels', we are told, 'revealing such parts of his person as caused Sancho to turn Rocinante's head for fear he might see them a second time' (p. 214). Don Quixote has an urge to denude himself, and so too do both Sancho and Dulcinea (the latter in Don Quixote's conception of her). All three figures offer versions of their own nakedness as a part noble, part farcical resistance to the cruelties of those who mock and belittle them – particularly the Duke and Duchess who go to such extraordinary lengths to humiliate Don Quixote and Sancho in Part Two of the novel, to make spiteful comedy out of their earnest foolishness. It is a recurrent refrain of Sancho's that he comes into the world naked, and that he will leave it naked, that the stuff of the world does not cling to him, either in the ignominies he suffers or in the artificial honours that are 'clapped upon him' when the Duke and Duchess conspire to make him believe he has become 'governor of an isle'. When Sancho takes the dignified decision to abandon his governorship and so to dismantle the elaborate apparatus set up by the Duke and Duchess to torment him, it is this nakedness that he holds up as his rebuke to their cruelty. 'Tell the Duke my master', he says, 'that naked I was born and naked I am now; I neither lose nor gain' (p. 814). And it is in a similarly dignified response to the same torments that Don Quixote makes one of the most moving defences of his love for the peerless Dulcinea. The Duchess, with unfathomable cruelty, confronts Don Quixote with the non-existence of his lady: 'we gather', she says, 'that your worship never saw the lady Dulcinea, and that this same lady does not exist on earth, but is a fantastic mistress, whom your worship engendered and bore in your mind' (p. 680). Don Quixote, almost uniquely in the novel, acknowledges here that just as he is not sure what happened in the Cave of Montesinos, he does not truly know whether or not Dulcinea exists ('God knows', he says, 'whether Dulcinea exists on the earth or no, or whether she is fantastic or not fantastic'). The status of her being, buried as it is beneath the layers of enchantment and beneath the coarse body of a 'peasant girl', is here obscure to Don Quixote. But he *is* clear that this uncertainty makes no difference to his mission, which is to penetrate to the essence of her being, to free her from enchantments and to reveal her in the unadorned and perfect condition that lies at the substrate of the novel's world, in that impossible, unextended space between the imagined and the real. 'I shall live in perpetual tears', he says with great nobility to the malicious duchess, 'till I see her in her pristine state' (p. 682).

The urge to nakedness, the desire to strip back the coverings of the world to reveal the bareness of being, is a mark of the nobility of Quixote and of Sancho. But nakedness, too, is an aesthetic principle, as much as an embodied state for which Sancho or Don Quixote strive. It is this principle that is formulated most explicitly by the Canon in Part One, where aesthetic purity is opposed to the cluttered disharmony of the dreaded 'books of chivalry'. In a near paraphrase of the Utopian's understanding of aesthetic pleasure described in More's *Utopia*, the Canon declares that any 'delight that the mind conceives must arise from the beauty it sees' and 'nothing ugly or ill proportioned can give us any pleasure' (p. 424). This is a harmony that chivalric romances lack. 'I have never seen', the Canon says, 'a book of chivalry with a whole body for a plot, with all its limbs complete, so that the middle corresponds to the beginning, and the end to the beginning and middle; for they are generally made up of so many limbs that they seem intended rather to form a chimaera or a monster than a well-proportioned figure' (p. 425). The desire for nakedness, for the encounter with being in its 'pristine state', is part of this desire for bodily unity – a desire which marries aesthetic harmony with the novel's quest for a certain kind of nobility, a certain kind of loyalty. Aesthetic unity is indistinguishable, in *Don Quixote*, from the novel's depiction of uncondi- tional love – the latter is perhaps its central concern. This may be the kind of love that a man feels for his wife ('For just as the whole body feels the pain of the foot or any other limb', Don Quixote says, 'and the head feels the ankle's pain, although it is not the cause of it; so the husband shares his wife's dishonour, being one with her' (p. 292)); it is also the love that Don Quixote feels for Sancho ('I mean', said Don Quixote, 'that when the head aches, all the limbs feel pain; and so as I am your lord and master, I am your head, and you are part of me, since you are my servant; and for that reason the ill that touches me, or shall touch me, should give pain to you; and yours to me' (p. 482)).

   Don Quixote as a whole is driven by this Hobbesian conception of the revealed, complete and integral body as the model both of shared understanding and of true seeing. But if this is so, it is also the case, of course, that such nudity, such self-presence, is countermanded by the great gulf that opens in the novel between words and things, between imagination and reality. If the novel is obsessed by the possibility of nakedness and by the image of a body 'with all its limbs complete', it registers this obsession in a continual awareness of the impossibility of such pristine being. We can see this gap opening, this failure of the possibility of a body which inheres in itself, in that moment when Don Quixote presents his hand for inspection to Maritornes. He asks her to admire the knightly anatomy, like Tulp exposing the hand of Adriaenszoon, the 'structure of its sinews, the interlacement of its muscles, the width and capacity of its veins'; but as he does so, the entire focus of the novel, the quality of its poetic and comic and ethical movement, is trained on and derived from the gap between the mind of Don Quixote and his hand (a hand that is haunted, always, by Cervantes' own paralysed hand, injured in the Battle of Lepanto).[55] Maritornes, of course, is not really interested in admiring Don Quixote's hand and is not, as the knight believes, in love with him but seeks only to mock him, to string him up by his noble hand in the most undignified and painful fashion; Don Quixote's response to such rough treatment registers this peculiar prosthetic distance from his own biomatter. 'Your ladyship seems to be grating my hand rather than fondling it', he says: 'Do not ill treat it so. It is not to blame for the ill my heart does you, nor is it right that you should avenge your whole displeasure on such a small part of me' (p. 393).

   In a direct opposition to the principle of bodily integrity in which Don Quixote couches his devotion to Sancho, and to Dulcinea – the sense that the head partakes of the ankle's pain – Don Quixote here expresses an extraordinary distance from his hand, for which he takes no responsibility, and which seems not to be a part of him. He is here distant from himself, as he imagines he might be cleanly severed from himself when he extols the curative effects of his magical medicinal balsam. His hand takes on the fantastic qualities of his *idée fixe* – it becomes the 'scourge of the world's malefactors' – but as it does so, it becomes remote from the spirit that animates it, as the work of fantasy repeatedly opens a gap between the essence of a thing and the material form in which it extends into the world. To look at Don Quixote's hand is to look into the gap between mind and material – the same gap that opens repeatedly in the novel, when Don Quixote mistakes the puppets in a puppet show for real people, or wine-skins for giants. It is to touch on the stealthy process by which the idea that animates a thing comes into contact with the thing itself. The puppets in a puppet show take on the qualities of those they represent, until the puppet show is over, at which point they become once more dead wood, lacking in animation or representational power. In this, Don Quixote and Sancho agree, they resemble the characters in a play or the pieces in a game of chess. In a play, Don Quixote says, 'One plays the ruffian, another the cheat; here is a merchant, there is a soldier; one is the wise fool, another the foolish lover. But when the play is over, and they have taken off their dresses, all the actors are equal' (p. 539). The end of the play, Don Quixote suggests, resembles the end of life, the moment when biomaterial is robbed of the animating power of spirit and becomes simple, decaying stuff: the moment when 'death strips' the players 'of all the robes that distinguished them, and they are all equals in the grave' (p. 539). This in turn in similar, Sancho remarks, to the representational effects that are entailed in a game of chess. 'Each piece', he says, in a proto-Wittgensteinian mode, 'has its particular importance while the game lasts, but when it's over they're all mixed up, thrown together, jumbled, and shoved into a leather bag, which is much like shovelling life away into a grave' (p. 539).[56]

This conception of the relation between idea and material might sound like the advancement of a Cervantine Aristotelianism.[57] When Aristotle, in *Meteorologica*, sets out to 'describe the nature of flesh, bone, and the other homogenous bodies', he offers an account of the way in which 'essence' or 'definition' relates to material. 'If you take extremes', Aristotle writes, 'matter is pure matter and the essence is pure definition'; but 'in the case of flesh and bone', he says, we find bodies that are 'intermediate between the two' and are 'related to each' (that is, matter and essence). 'What a thing is', Aristotle writes, 'is always determined by its function: a thing really is itself when it can perform its function, an eye for instance when it can see. When a thing cannot do so it is that thing only in name, like a dead eye or one made of stone.'[58] That bodies are made of this mixture of definition and material is 'true in a higher degree', he writes, 'with face and hand'. 'And so', he argues, 'the hand of a dead man, too, will in the same way be a hand in name only.' The hand becomes the hand when its essence matches with its material extension; but if this conception of the relation between essence and definition is at work in *Don Quixote*'s discussion of the play, and in Sancho's example of the chess pieces, what *Don Quixote* as a whole presents us with is a situation in which the relationship between essence and definition has become skewed, or difficult to account for. This is not only the case in the famous incidents when Don Quixote's madness leads him to misread the relationship between essence and material – when, for example, he fails to understand that the puppets in a puppet show 'are not real Moors' but 'only little pasteboard figures' (p. 642) – but is rather a condition of the novel's seeing, the basis of its understanding of the relationship between imagination and reality. The central predicament that the novel addresses is one in which the legal, aesthetic, political and material forces that oversee the connection between mind and matter have lost their organising power, leading to a continual confusion about how the *idea* of, say, the hand, relates to its material existence – a confusion that is particularly apparent in Don Quixote's relationship with the world but which is at work everywhere in the novel.

Consider, for example, the 'judgements' that Sancho makes when he becomes governor of his isle – judgements which often strike us not only for their quixotic eccentricity but also for their deranged sagacity, their capacity to touch closely on the prosthetic ground I am staking out here between mind and material. These judgements have a family resemblance and tend to turn around the means by which we account for our bodies, and how we reconcile their function as the property of the self with their existence as objects in the world, subject to the law. The example of the disputed race between a fat man and a thin man comes to mind. How, Sancho is asked, are we to make a race between two men of very different sizes fair? The petitioner suggests that the solution might lie in forcing the lighter man – who weighs nine stone – to carry an eleven-stone weight on his back, thus making him weigh the same as the heavier man (who is twenty stone). This, however, seems hardly just, as it works on the principle that the body is a dead weight, rather than being an active part of the living self. Presumably, the twenty-stone man uses some of his mass to propel himself, rather than suffering his body simply as an object to transport. Some portion of his mass belongs to his own animated, striving self, and some portion of his mass belongs to the world and acts as the burden that he is forced to carry, the challenge to be overcome. Sancho's solution:

> The fat challenger should prune, pare, scrape, trim and shave away eleven stone of his flesh, from whatever part of his body may seem best to him, and so, reduced to nine stone in weight, he will be on level terms with his adversary at nine: and then they will be able to run even. (p. 898)

By changing a different variable – not adding additional, prosthetic weight but reducing the weight of one's own prosthetic self – Sancho's somewhat Procrustean judgement draws attention to the forces which oversee the body as public rather than private property, and which make of us all lean, inward beings to whom biomass is attached as non-essential supplement. Or consider an earlier judgement, in which Sancho is asked to solve the problem of a man crossing a bridge over a deep river. At the far end of the bridge is a 'gallows and a sort of courthouse, in which four judges sit to administer the law imposed by the owner of the river and the bridge'. The rule is that before anyone crosses the bridge, they must declare under oath where they are going. If they tell the truth, they live, but 'if he tells a lie, he shall suffer death by hanging on the gallows there displayed, without hope of mercy' (p. 798). The quandary that Sancho is asked to solve occurs when a man declares, before crossing the bridge, that he is going to die on the gallows on the other side of the bridge. How to resolve this difficulty? If he dies on the gallows, then he spoke the truth and so should have gone free. If he goes free, he lies, and so should have been put to death. Sancho's solution: 'They must let that part of the man who swore truly cross the bridge, and hang the part that swore to a lie; and in that way the conditions of passage will be fulfilled to the letter' (p. 799).

As with the judgement on the racing men, Sancho's solution here relies on the perception of a cleaving in the subject, between an inner being which closely adheres to the self and an external being which belongs to the state. In direct opposition to the Aristotelian conception of a body which becomes itself when its function and its extension are one, Sancho's judgements suggest that extended being involves always this disjunction between mind and matter. It is pointed out to Sancho that this judgement does not appear exactly fair. 'Then, Lord Governor', the petitioner says to Sancho, 'this man will have to be divided into two parts, the lying part and the truthful part; and if he's divided, he's bound to die. Thus no part of the law's demand is fulfilled' (p. 799). Sancho's sense of mercy and justice awakens to this plea, and so he decides, given that the balance between truth and falsehood is even, it is better to err on the side of mercy than of cruelty, and let the man go. But what drives Sancho's initial judgement, however impractical it might be as a verdict, is a recognition that lies at the very heart of the Cervantine world view: that we are composed at once of truth and lies, that, like the man who wishes to cross the bridge, we are divided into two parts, into Quixano and Quixote, More and Raphael.

It is this recognition that shapes the novel's thinking, and that determines the balance between the ideal conception of a naked body, complete unto itself, and the body in which we live, that is always somewhat divorced from itself, always in part a burden and a prosthetic addition. And it is this recognition, too, that determines how Cervantes conceives of fiction, how he understands fiction as the medium in which we experience the world. If, as I argued earlier, Cervantes' novel achieves proximity to the substrate of animated life, to something like the ground of being, it does so by inventing a means of revealing the workings of fiction in the most intimate heartland of the self, at that hidden junction where consciousness comes into being through its encounter with its own apparatuses. Where our unextended self meets with its prosthetic attachments, Cervantes' novel suggests, there we find the trace of fiction, fiction as the narrative principle which binds us to ourselves, and which makes of the collapsing, disappearing conduit between mind and matter – that conduit that glimmers darkly in Rembrandt's anatomy paintings – the very foundation of collective life. The strange mobility of the narrative, from its first to its last page – the sense that the language of the novel becomes 'infected' with the quixotic perspectives that it reflects – is a mark of its capacity to discover this hidden junction; to test its mimetic, ontological and epistemological quality; and to devise fictional forms that can give it shape, colour and weight.

It is Don Quixote himself, for all his extravagancies, who understands this most clearly, who is most able to articulate the cleaving in the self, the joining and separating, that is enacted by the work of fiction. It is he who understands most fully that it is an aesthetic as well as an ethical principle that life is interwoven with death, that to be is to experience the difficult meeting ground between the living and the non-living, as one's own body is partly alive and partly dead, as one's hand 'partakes of both' conditions. To think with Cervantes' prose is to understand that being involves a continual encounter with non-being, and that fiction is the place where that encounter happens, the miraculous form which allows us to make of such an encounter the basis for an imagined community. For Don Quixote it is 'clear' that 'art is not better than nature, but perfects her'. 'So' he says, 'nature combined with art, and art with nature, will produce a most perfect poet' (p. 569). In the overwhelmingly moving closing chapters of the novel, as he heads back towards La Mancha and death – as his head clears, and he slowly comes to renounce his fantasies of chivalric power – it is the recognition of this mixture that he leaves us with. Auerbach writes, in his beautiful essay on *Don Quixote*, that 'dying, he finds his way back into the order of the world' (p. 357); but I think that as Don Quixote prepares for death with humility and grace, he does not yield to a reality that is greater than him, so much as recognise that reality is partly composed of the imagination, and that life is partly composed of death. On the road back to La Mancha, as Sancho lies sleeping by his side, Don Quixote composes a kind of *Liebestod*, an ode to love and to death as the joint principles which make life purposive. He longs for death, he says, as the closest analogue of his love for Dulcinea; but such longing makes of death not an end, but a kind of going on. He longs to die, he sings, 'but when I reach that place',

> Such joy my bosom feels
> That life grows stronger and I cannot pass.
> And so by life I'm slain,
> Unwelcome state that mingles life and death!
> Living I die, and as my breath
> Dies, death recalls me into life again.   (p. 908)

If *Don Quixote* offers a kind of origin to the novel as a form – if it is in Cervantes' extraordinary work that what I am here calling the prosthetic imagination finds a foundation – then it lies in its capacity to forge a representational mode that can give expression to this interdependence, this weaving together of the real and the imagined, the living and the dead, in the very Vesalian fabric of life. As we seek, now, to conceive of a model of self-ownership that survives the emergence of a contemporary prosthetic condition – to produce an account of contemporary life that is equal to the spectacle of Henrietta Lacks' biomaterial proliferating endlessly in the laboratory – it is the discovery of this collapsing junction threaded into being, this peculiar unregulated distribution of mind in matter, that might offer the still latent terms in which to do so. It is as fiction comes to possibility in the form of the early novel, as prose narrative begins to bear the weight of an emergent modern lifeworld, that it both establishes a model of sovereignty upon which modernity itself might rest and allows us to see beyond its still unfolding contradictions.

PART II

The Colonial Body: From Behn to Goethe

CHAPTER 2

Economies of Scale from Aphra Behn to Sarah Scott

> The world may indeed be considered as a vast machine, in which the
> great wheels are originally set in motion by those which are
> very minute, and almost imperceptible to any but the strongest eyes.
> Henry Fielding, *Tom Jones*[1]

2.1 Colonialism and the World Picture in the Eighteenth-Century Novel

New epistemologies generate derangements of scale. This is the discovery
of Timothy Clark's seminal essay on the effects of climate change,
'Derangements of Scale'. Environmental crisis has made it difficult to
maintain a sense of the difference between the large and the small – the
difference between, say, recycling one's rubbish and saving the planet, or
between a local meteorological event and its global determinants – because
the new picture of the totality that is emerging as a result of climate change
has led to a 'derangement of linguistic and intellectual proportion in the
way people often talk about the environment'.[2] Our picture of the world,
in the midst of ecological crisis, becomes so unstable that we cannot
maintain the scalar relations that have allowed us to position ourselves in
relation to our environment, the local in relation to the global, meaning
that we are required, now, to think on several scales at once, 'creatively
deranging' our interpretive apparatus by 'embedding it in multiple and
even contradictory frames at one and the same time' (np).

Climate change has produced such a derangement of scale in the terms
in which we produce a picture of our world now; however, this kind of
derangement is not specific to the contemporary eco-crisis but is found
wherever we experience paradigm shifts, wherever new pictures of the
world replace older ones and reframe social relations in the process. It is
this kind of derangement, this kind of paradigm shift, that Frances
Ferguson has in mind when she claims that the role of picturing in

eighteenth-century Europe, the role of aesthetic representation, is charged
with giving form to what she calls a new 'paradigm' of the 'empirical
sublime', a new way of thinking about the 'relationships between individuals and their societies that aesthetic objects enable'.[3] At a moment when
the relations between the individual and the world, the local and the
general, the small and the large, become difficult to read, it is the task of
aesthetics to recast these relations, to creatively derange the scales which
frame them. 'The aesthetic discussion that emerged in the eighteenth
century', Ferguson writes, 'located an anxiety about the relationship
between the individual and the type, the particular and the general, not
merely as one epistemological problem among others but as *the* characteristically aesthetic epistemological problem' (p. 31). When Jonathan Swift's
Gulliver tells his master Houyhnhnm in the fourth book of
Gulliver's Travels that 'this whole Globe of Earth must be at least three
Times gone round, before one of our better Female *Yahoos* could get her
Breakfast' (p. 244), it is this kind of derangement both in scale and in type
that he is registering, this strange malfunction of the apparatuses by which
we register distance and proportion and species being under eighteenth-
century colonial conditions.[4] Colonial exploration and despoliation, and
the attendant mutations in what Gulliver calls the global 'Distribution of
Justice' (pp. 286–87), lead to a disruption in the processes which allow us to
focus our world picture, to understand how the near relates to the far, how
the ground beneath our feet or our hooves relates to a larger idea of the
world.

The imaginative resources of Western culture in this period, under the
twin pressures of enlightenment rationalism and colonial expansion, are
harnessed to produce a picture of the world that might accommodate this
shifted relation between the local and the far flung. And of all the resources
that were available to the colonial imagination, it is the novel that provided
the form in which such a picture might come most tightly into focus. The
most influential accounts we have of the rise of the novel as a genre tend to
emphasise this relationship between colonialism, rationalism and the
emergence of prose narrative, as if these things mutually produce one
another. For Ian Watt, in his classic account of the rise of the novel, the
novel comes about in the conjunction between what he calls 'economic
individualism' and 'colonial development'.[5] As Western nations harness
the resources of the globe in the production of a new kind of economic
individual, Watt argues, so prose narrative invents the forms in which such
individual experience might couch and recognise itself. In this and the next
chapter, I will investigate the means by which the eighteenth-century novel

helped produce a picture of the world and helped fashion the political and material bodies in which a colonial consciousness might find itself embedded. But in doing so, I will suggest that the prosthetic logic that I am theorising here, as it extends itself through the history of the novel, tends to shift the terms in which Watt accounts for the 'rise of the novel', so that the novel does not provide the form in which a new kind of individualism comes to imaginative expression but rather articulates something more contradictory and dialectical, a relation between consciousness and its prosthetic extensions that at once gives rise to a new idea of the world, a new poetics of scale, and *preserves* a derangement of scale, a disjunction between mind and material, that stands as an immanent historical critique of the colonial world picture. That peculiar prosthetic twist that I have traced through the early novel, that one can see running from More to Cervantes to Cavendish, is the difficult, vanishing foundation upon which the eighteenth-century novel is based, as it develops from Aphra Behn's late seventeenth-century prose fiction *Oroonoko*, through the work of Defoe, Swift, Voltaire, Burney and Sarah Scott, to the late century writings of Kleist and Goethe. As the boundaries of the nation state are blurred by the emergence of a new global stage for the projection of European identities, and as the novel invents a scale that allows us to conceive of our communities as they spread out across a newly extended colonial terrain, so the connective tissue that binds us to our own bodies (fashioned itself in part from the operations of fiction) is stretched and reformed. It is this modulation in the forces that produce the body, in response to the transformation of global colonial and economic relations, that is registered by the novel as it comes into its recognisable modern form in the eighteenth century; it is in this newly emerging form, too, that the terms in which we relate to our own biomaterial extensions (both artificial and natural) are given thinkable and narratable form.

In tracing the development of these fictional conjunctions and disjunctions over the novel of the long eighteenth century, I will argue that one can see two large movements or tendencies playing themselves out, from Behn to Goethe – movements which are shaped by what Catherine Gallagher sees as the structuring opposition in the eighteenth-century novel between 'unboundedness' on the one hand and 'idealised immanence' on the other.[6] The first of these movements is expansive and seeks, like More's *Utopia*, to reach beyond the boundaries of the West, and of the old world, to enter into unmade epistemological and geographical space – to generate a new colonial picture of the world, and a corresponding economy of scale. The striking examples of this expansive movement include Defoe's *Robinson Crusoe*, Jonathan Swift's *Gulliver's Travels* and Voltaire's *Candide*. The second is constrictive – what Samuel Beckett much later calls a 'contraction of the spirit', a 'shrinking from the nullity of extracircumferential phenomena'.[7] This tendency is driven by the attempt to imagine a body in command of its own boundaries to produce an organic aesthetic which can picture a consciousness that fully animates its own material, and that is securely housed in its own being, and in its own world. The striking examples of the contractive movement in the novel of the period include the richly somatic work of Henry Fielding (*Joseph Andrews*, *Tom Jones*), the invention of the society novel in Samuel Richardson (*Pamela*, *Clarissa*) and Frances Burney (*Evelina*, *Cecilia*), and the precise organicism of Goethe's *Sorrows of Young Werther* and *Elective Affinities*.

In what follows, I will trace these movements as they diverge from each other, producing two distinct versions of an eighteenth-century novel imagination; but if we are to understand how these two movements operate, it is necessary, from the beginning, to acknowledge that they are deeply entangled and driven by the same desire – that is, to generate a picture of the body which can accommodate or counteract the effects that new colonial distances have on our experience of the relation between consciousness and its material forms. And they emerge, too, in their divergence, in part, from the same source. One can see, across the eighteenth-century European novel, a recurrent return to utopian forms, as the source of fictional imagining and of literary thinking, both in its contractive and in its expansive modes. The fascination with the organically whole that one can see at the heart of the contractive tendency in the eighteenth-century novel has its roots in the utopias of More, Bacon and Cavendish. The image of a self-contained body that lies at the heart of More's *Utopia*, and that returns in the figure of pristine nakedness in *Don Quixote*, extends throughout eighteenth-century politics and aesthetics, surfacing in Rousseau's picture of the state of nature, and in the longing for self-presence that is central to the eighteenth-century European imagination.[8] But running with and against this picture of the contractive, organic self, is a nearly opposite legacy of utopian thinking, one which does not find unity at the heart of individual being, but rather a kind of dehiscence, a kind of distance in the midst of the self-same that lies at the heart of David Hume's thought. Where Rousseau finds self-presence at the ground of being in the world, Hume finds only a kind of absence. 'When I enter most intimately into what I call *myself*', he writes, 'I always stumble on some perception or other'. 'I never can catch *myself* at any time without a perception', he goes on, so when self-perception abates, 'as by sound sleep', then so too does being itself (as Apuleius' Thelyphron discovers, in the passage from *The Golden Ass* I discussed earlier). 'When my perceptions are remov'd', he argues, 'so long am I insensible of myself, and may truly be said not to exist'.[9] It is this unearthing of distance within proximity that drives what I am calling here the expansive tendency in the eighteenth-century novel, and that determines the means by which the fictional imagination reaches beyond the boundaries of the known, seeking to accommodate an encounter with the open or contingent into the forms with which we fashion both our environments and our selves. The development of the novel form in the period, I will argue, is bound up with the negotiation of these twin utopian imperatives, at once to recognise and represent the boundaries of the body and to open those same boundaries to the operations of an emerging colonial consciousness. It is not that the novel offers a fit mode of expression for a new kind of economic individualism emerging in the eighteenth century, but rather that the novel gives delicately modulated expression to an increasingly fraught relationship between consciousness and its prosthetic material extensions, one driven by utopian longing at the same time as it yields a kind of political and aesthetic alienation, which later finds its expression in satire.

It is in Aphra Behn's 1688 fiction *Oroonoko* that both of these tendencies can first be traced, in the form that they will come to be adopted across the novel of the following century.[10] The narrative is based on Behn's trip to Surinam (which records suggest she probably took in 1663), where she stayed on a sugar plantation established by Lord Willoughby in 1651.[11] In Surinam, the fictional Behn writes in *Oroonoko*, she met with a beautiful and cultured 'royal slave' named Oroonoko, who had been recently transported from the West African kingdom of 'Coramantien' in modern-day Ghana. The story concerns itself with the fate of Oroonoko, his adoration of his lover Imoinda and his brutal maltreatment by the colonial English running Willoughby's plantation (particularly a planter by the name of 'Byam'). From the beginning of the novel, Behn's fascination, as narrator, with Oroonoko and Imoinda turns around what she perceives to be their extraordinary immanence, their deep dwelling within their own bodies and their own selves. It is perhaps telling that John Locke owned a personal copy of Aphra Behn's novel, as the picture she offers of Oroonoko's relationship to his body is one that is grounded in a particular model of self-ownership – that sense of the primacy of our relation to ourselves that Locke formulates in his *Second Treatise on Government*, published in 1689, the year after the publication of *Oroonoko*.[12] Behn as narrative persona draws attention repeatedly to the great gulf between Europe and the world that she finds in Surinam, a world that is 'new and strange', and full of 'inconceivable wonders';[13] but even as she finds the colony alienating and difficult to decipher, she suggests that it exists in a kind of harmony with itself, in a fullness of being that anticipates a Rousseauvian state of nature. The native South Americans, she finds, live in a kind of nakedness, an 'unadorned' state 'so like our first parents before the fall' (p. 11), in which there is no element of artifice, nothing to ornament or mediate the experience of being. 'All you can see' of them, she writes, 'you see at once, and every moment see' (p. 11). They live, she reflects, in an immediate contact with 'nature' that 'better instructs the world than all the inventions of man' (p. 11). Just as Rousseau discovers in nature a guide to truth – 'Everything that comes from Nature will be true', he writes, 'there will be nothing false except what I have involuntarily put in of my own'[14] – so Behn finds that the native Americans live in contact with natural truth, that they 'have a native justice, which knows no fraud' and are granted an 'absolute idea of the first state of innocence' (p. 11). The Surinamese, in their nakedness, have achieved that 'Stripping' of 'Being' that Rousseau suggests is necessary to reveal a picture of 'man' in a state of nature, denuded of 'all the artificial faculties he can have acquired only by a long process' (p. 52). And if Behn finds this experience of naked harmony everywhere she looks in this new and strange world, it is in the figures of Oroonoko and Imoinda that such harmony reaches its most exquisite grandeur. She describes them both as exhibiting an astonishing physical perfection, but their real beauty she thinks lies not in their exact form, but in the way that such sculptural elegance allows them to communicate a kind of unalloyed truth, and to give expression to 'life' and 'vigour' in their very 'countenance' (p. 35). When on his arrival from West Africa the colonial planter Trefry buys Oroonoko, he marvels at the 'extraordinary' quality that animates Oroonoko's face, a royalty that 'shone through' his abject condition as a slave, so that 'his eyes insensibly commanded respect and his behaviour insinuated it into every soul' (p. 43). Oroonoko wears his nobility in his sculpted muscular form, and it is this exposure of the internal self on the surface of the body that forges the powerful alliance between Oroonoko and Imoinda, the erotic love between them that is the narrator's central preoccupation. They communicate with each other less with language or even with gesture than with the exchange of looks, as if their thoughts, like those of Voltaire's Candide, could be read in their face, and in their eyes. Oroonoko 'told her with his eyes' that he was in love with Imoinda (p. 16), and 'at the first glance from her eyes' (p. 22), he understood that she too loved him.

There is, of course, a conventional orientalist cast to this depiction of colonial subjects living in a state of nature, to which the civilised colonial traveller cannot gain access, however much she may romanticise such simplicity and faith. But what is so fascinating about Behn's depiction of Oroonoko's embodied immanence, and what makes of *Oroonoko* such a powerful pre-apprehension of the eighteenth-century novel form, is that this immanence is cloven, throughout, with a kind of distance from self, a distance which is entangled in turn with Behn's colonial gaze (and which is a mirror image of the distance from self suffered by African writers of slavery from Olaudah Equiano to Fredrick Douglass).[15] As Catherine Gallagher argues, in her fine analysis of Behn's fiction, the narrative 'stress-[es] the exotic artificiality of both Oroonoko and Imoinda'.[16] The experience of self-ownership that is so central to Behn's depiction of Oroonoko and Imoinda, and that resonates with the contractive tendency I am tracing in the development of the novel form, is cast into a dialectical relationship with a kind of self-alienation, with that loss of self-possession that impels the other tendency in the history of the novel that I am identifying here – a dialectical relationship that shapes the emergence of the novel in its modern form and lies at the heart of an eighteenth-century prosthetic imagination.

The first indication of this opening of an ontological gap in Behn's representation of Oroonoko comes with her account of his renaming by Trefry. Halfway through the narrative, the narrator announces, in an oddly breezy aside, that 'I ought to tell you that the Christians never buy any slaves but they give them some name of their own, their native ones being likely very barbarous and hard to pronounce' (p. 43). It is for this reason, she says, that 'Mr Trefry gave Oroonoko [the name] of Caesar' (p. 43), and for the same reason that he 'christened' Imoinda with the name of 'Clemene' (p. 45). The narrator has been content, up to this point in the story, to call Oroonoko by his African name; but this sudden recalling of his slave name brings her to her European senses, and she says that, 'for the future, therefore, I must call Oroonoko, Caesar, since by that name only was he known in our western world' (p. 44). And indeed, from this point on, apart from two significant occasions, Oroonoko goes by the Imperial European name Caesar. This sudden, apparently careless shift from one register of naming to another has a remarkable effect on the texture of the novel's reality effect. Renaming works immediately to challenge that sense of bound self-possession that is Oroonoko's and Imoinda's signal characteristic. As Oroonoko morphs into Caesar, a gap opens between the name and the object of the name, a gap which casts the very possibility of immanence, of self-sameness, into doubt. And once this schism appears at the heart of the narrative apparatus, it has a viral effect on the novel's broader capacity to picture a body at home in its world. The gap between name and thing resonates with a peculiar kind of disjunction, a numb, distanced relation to self that increasingly undermines the picture of Edenic nudity that the novel has been celebrating up to this point.

One can see this anaesthetic quality at work in the trials of strength that Oroonoko undergoes early in the novel. Think, for example, of Oroonoko's reckless fight with the 'numb eel'. There is something that Oroonoko finds compelling about this electric eel that, he is told, can render senseless anyone it touches – his sense of vigorous personhood is affronted by the idea that a 'man could lose his force at the touch of a fish' (p. 55). Accordingly, he is drawn to combat with the fish, a test of strength in which he is roundly defeated, as his self-possession is effortlessly drained by the touch of the eel, and he is rendered immediately 'senseless'. Similarly, his other major test of strength, his battle with a gigantic and fearless tiger, involves not only a demonstration of his power but also an encounter with his own peculiar, latent insensibility, which is woven into that very power. Oroonoko stares down the giant animal as he is preparing to kill him, 'fixing his awful stern eyes full upon those of the beast' (p. 53), and his eyes seem, as in his wordless encounter with Imoinda, to be the guarantor of his fierce personhood. But when he battles to the death with the tiger, there is a sense, delicate but unmistakable, that Oroonoko is not quite present at the scene of his own being (or the being of 'Caesar'), that there is a numbness at the heart of his relationship with his body and of his fight with the animal. 'The dying beast stretched forth her paw', the narrator recounts, 'and going to grasp his thigh, surprised with death in that very moment, did him no other harm than fixing her nails in his flesh very deep, feebly wounded him, but could not grasp the flesh to tear off any' (p. 53).

This contact with the dying beast has a peculiar quality, a quality which suggests that Oroonoko's flesh is not quite his own, just as it feels distant to him under the electrical spell of the numb eel. The blow with the stretched paw and the fixing of the nails into his thigh appear remote here, slow motion, and involve Oroonoko in no apparent pain. If this breath of distance from self – of Oroonoko's separation from the colonial body, and foreign name, in which he acts – is quite slight, however, it prepares the ground for the instances of self-immolation which gather in the second half of the novel, and which remain some of the most startling and memorable images of any fiction in the period. The tiger's failure to 'grasp' Oroonoko's flesh, to 'tear it off', strikes a chord with the wounds of the 'war captains' that fascinate and repel Oroonoko a little later in the novel. These captains, 'Caesar' discovers, are terribly maimed ('some wanted their noses, some their lips, some both noses and lips, some their ears, and others cut through each cheek, with long slashes, through which their teeth appeared' (p. 59)). They are disfigured in this way, he learns, because the rituals through which they display their valour require them to desecrate their own bodies to prove their indifference to suffering. In a kind of biological potlatch, a race to give one's self away, the first contender for the title of captain 'cuts off his nose and throws it contemptibly on the ground'; in reply, 'the other does something to himself that he thinks surpasses him, and perhaps deprives himself of lips and an eye' (p. 59). This competition continues, often until one of the contenders dies, in a ritual battle of which Oroonoko cannot approve (it is a 'sort of courage too brutal to be applauded by our black hero' (p. 59)). But if Oroonoko is here appalled by the spectacle of the gratuitous tearing off and casting away of one's own flesh, the sense of alienation that overtakes him as he finds himself enslaved by Trefry and Byam leads him to adopt this same gesture. As Oroonoko becomes Caesar, as his enslavement undermines his sense that he owns his own being, so he finds himself dismembering both his own body and that of Imoinda. The unspoken somatic love that united Oroonoko and Imoinda at the novel's opening, their ability to communicate not through words but through the 'powerful language' (p. 23) of facial expression and significant looks, is brought to an ironic end when Oroonoko kills Imoinda at the novel's close, to save her from the clutch of the coloniser and slave owner. 'Embracing her with all the passion and languishment of a dying lover' (as the dying tiger embraces Oroonoko with his outstretched paw), Oroonoko 'drew his knife to kill this treasure of his soul, this pleasure of his eyes' (p. 71). As if to demonstrate the extent to which this murder obliterates the immanent language of the body, the language of expression and glance that united them, Oroonoko completes his attack on Imoinda with a grotesque dismemberment, 'severing her yet smiling face from that delicate body' (p. 72) – a 'defacement', Benjamin Schmidt has argued, that is part of a broader colonial 'picturing of the exotic body under duress'.[17] In a gesture as memorable as it is difficult fully to conceive, he leaves the amputated face lying on the ground, 'bare to look on', where it reveals its divorce from itself. The face, now a 'dear object', is 'never more to bless him with her eyes and soft language' (p. 72), and the inevitable corollary of this dismemberment is Oroonoko's eventual dismantling of himself, his extraordinarily graphic demonstration that he absolutely does not have, in Locke's terms, a 'Property in his own Person'. In his final standoff with his captors, Oroonoko insists that he has no investment in his own being ('*it is not life I seek*', he says (p. 74)) and proves it by tearing off his own flesh, like Apuleius's Thelyphron, and throwing it at those who have more of a claim of ownership over it than he does. He 'cut a piece of flesh from his own throat, and threw it at them'; he 'ripped up his own belly, and took his bowels and pulled them out with what strength he could' (p. 74). And the novel closes with the haunting image of Oroonoko, smoking a pipe by a camp fire, as his executioners complete his dismemberment, cutting off his genitals, ears and nose, and burning them in the fire before them, as Oroonoko calmly smokes on – a burning, as Susan Iwanisziw has suggested, that makes a difficult equation between Oroonoko's body parts and the colonial trade in tobacco.[18]

To trace this movement from immanent embodiment to radical distance from self as it plays out over *Oroonoko* might be to suggest that Behn offers here a critique of the alienating effects of colonialism and slavery, the Edenic experience of self-ownership disrupted by the incursion of the European into the heart of paradise. And, indeed, such a reading might be persuasive. But I think that, however cogently one can read this novel as an enactment of the erosion of self-ownership, consequent on the pronominal shift from 'Oroonoko' to 'Caesar', there is another way to address the tension in the novel between self-sameness and self-distance – between Rousseau and Hume – one that recognises the extent to which these opposing forces are bound into a relationship that is sustained throughout the novel, a relationship that draws Behn's own narrator into its peculiar logic. It is not, perhaps, the case that the experience of bound, immanent embodiment (as the condition of the self in a state of nature) is simply contrasted with the experience of alienated self-distance (as the condition both of the coloniser and of the slave), but rather that the novel explores and enacts a vibrating, dialectical tension between distance and immanence, as a condition of the mode of self-becoming that is specific to the emerging form of the novel. Behn's orientalist depiction of a Rousseauvian immanence is always interwoven with the experience of distance, and exhibits something like a representational gap in its very internal structure; the pictures of the alienated self, too, harbour the very possibility of self-possession that they appear to disavow.

The moment when this dialectical opposition between immanence and distance, as a condition of a colonial encounter with the prosthetic self, reaches its most intense expression comes at the centre of the narrative, at a critical point which reads as the fulcrum around which the novel turns. Oroonoko has arrived at Surinam and been taken to meet a very beautiful African woman named Clemene, whom he discovers, of course, to be Imoinda:

> There needed no long gazing, or consideration, to examine who this fair creature was. He soon saw Imoinda all over her; in a minute he saw her face, her shape, her air, her modesty and all that called forth his soul with joy at his eyes, and left his body destitute of almost life. It stood without motion, and, for a minute, knew not that it had being. (p. 46)

This is an extraordinary moment, in which presence is combined with distance, entangled with it so intimately that the two cannot be separated. The assertion that Oroonoko could see 'Imoinda all over her', on looking at the woman standing before him, is remarkably difficult to process, suggesting at once that she is immersed in or closely attached to her person but also at the same time at odds with it, as if 'Imoinda' is a covering of some kind, or a mask (prefiguring the depiction of face as mask that is entailed in Oroonoko's later defacement of her). 'In a minute', the narrator says, 'he saw her face', and the rhetorical suggestion is that this is a mark of instant recognition – the revelation of Imoinda in all of her self-presence, as a rekindling of the immediate contact that the two shared in Africa. Oroonoko's recognition of Imoinda reflects the narrator's own earlier delight in the nakedness of the Surinamese, the sense that 'all you can see' of them 'you see at once, and every moment see'; but of course the 'minute' during which he looks at her installs a yawning deferral into the scene of reunion, a moment of non-being, or transition, which is mirrored in Oroonoko's own Humean stupefaction (which also lasts a 'minute'). Oroonoko is briefly divorced from his own being as he gazes at Imoinda, becoming, in a phrase employed by David Foster Wallace to capture such a lapse in being, 'untenanted', 'a thing among things'.[19] His body becomes a numb, prosthetic object that does not know it has being (a body that has become, shockingly, an 'it'), even as his 'soul' is 'called forth' into his eyes, the organic guarantors, in this novel, of animated self-presence.

It is only as they each come around from their stupefaction, however, as they seek to retune themselves to each other's presence here in a South American colony, that the novel's exploration of the distance that is built in to fictional self-presence reaches its climax. 'They soon informed each other of their fortunes', the narrator says, and 'mutually protested, that even fetters and slavery were soft and easy, and would be supported with joy and pleasure while they could be so happy to possess each other':

> Caesar swore he disdained the empire of the world while he could behold his Imoinda and she despised grandeur and pomp, those vanities of her sex, when she could gaze on Oroonoko. He adored the very cottage where she resided, and said, that little inch of the world would give him more happiness than all the universe could do, and she vowed, it was a palace while adorned with the presence of Oroonoko. (p. 46)

This is a strikingly double-jointed moment in the novel. The narrative pressure that brings Oroonoko and Imoinda together here, that establishes their intense proximity to themselves and to each other in a concentrated 'inch of the world', also, and at the same time, establishes a distance between and within them – a play of distance and proximity that is overseen by the work of fiction. Caesar looks at Imoinda; Imoinda looks at Oroonoko: and in this peculiar nominal dislocation, the novel lives out the tension that runs through it between gathering and dispersal. This is at once a face-to-face meeting, in which the lovers summon themselves into shared, embodied being through mutual recognition and another kind of encounter, not a tight, bound mirroring but a reaching, across the vanishing threshold of the text, from the colonial outsider position occupied by the narrator and by Caesar to the scene of lost paradisiacal self-presence shared by Oroonoko and Imoinda. The inch of the world that all three occupy is caught in this strangely pulsing movement between unity and separation. Behn's fiction both produces this pulse effect and is produced by it, bearing in its very title the loss of its referent, the partial disappearance of Oroonoko beneath the name of Caesar. The novel is able to gain access to the bare and immanent inch of the world shared by Imoinda and Oroonoko – to approach Freud's 'inch of nature' that is revealed to us when we have stripped ourselves of our prosthetic attachments, or when in Rousseau's terms we have divested ourselves of all our 'artificial faculties' – only when fiction intervenes in the midst of our encounter with ourselves, only when fiction builds this disappearing bridge between 'Caesar' and 'Oroonoko'.

It is this contradictory movement at the heart of the novel – in which the unity between Oroonoko and Imoinda continually gives way to a boundless gulf between and within them – that characterises the tension between immanence and distance as it plays out across *Oroonoko*, and across the eighteenth-century novel more broadly. It is this movement, too, that captures the odd, double legacy of utopian thought, as it shapes the eighteenth-century fictional imagination. In the gaze that is imagined here between Oroonoko and Imoinda, one can detect an echo of the gaze shared between Thomas More and Raphael in More's *Utopia* or between Cavendish and the Empress in *The Blazing World*. As Oroonoko looks at Imoinda, as Thomas More looks at Raphael, it is clear that in some sense they each look into a mirror. More invents the fictional structure of *Utopia* to generate a picture of England, and of himself, fully revealed and stripped of artificial faculties. It is this clear seeing, this snapshot of an inch of the world which one can 'see at once, and every moment see', that is at the heart of all utopian desire. The gaze shared between Oroonoko and Imoinda partakes of this utopian nakedness; but, for Behn and for More, the gaze not only bounces back, not only confirms the boundedness of self-presence, but also reaches into a distance, to the darkness of Raphael's Utopia (a no-place, after all, that can scarcely come to thought), or to the 'inconceivable wonders' of the 'new and strange' world that Behn finds in Surinam. In More's *Utopia*, it is fiction, the first stirrings of a particular mode of novel imagining, that enables him to articulate a distanced relation with self as it installs itself within Freud's inch of nature, within the very heartland of the self and the self-same. It is this same fictional junction that lies at the heart of Cervantes' great work, as the emergence of a new form of modernity sets reality at odds with itself. And it is in Behn's novel that this work of fiction, as a bridge that ties us to our extensions while demonstrating the distance that lies at the very heart of our self-perception, assumes the form that it will take across the novel form in the subsequent century.

2.2   Invisible Ink: Self-Fashioning and Self-Erasure in Daniel Defoe

The writer who does the most to fashion this form, to craft a narrative mode that can give coherent expression to an eighteenth-century European self at a colonial distance from itself, is Daniel Defoe. Particularly in his two greatest works – *Moll Flanders* and, pre-eminently, *Robinson Crusoe* – Defoe invents an expressive mode which contains the tension between distance and immanence that vibrates in Behn's novel and transforms the difficult sense that the colonial body is put at a remove from its own central processing system into the very basis of an emerging model both of narration and of selfhood.

It is in *Robinson Crusoe*, most strikingly, that Defoe gives us a picture of the far-flung body, the body cast to the very edge of the earth, and forced to invent for itself an idea of the world, a new economy of scale, that might sustain it. Defoe's novel, like Behn's *Oroonoko*, is above all an expansive, experimental encounter with that which lies beyond the horizon of the known. As Behn's tale is engrossed in the 'strange and new', Robinson's wanderlust compels him repeatedly to defy his father's advice to devote himself to the familiar – to the 'middle station of Life'[20] – and to fling himself into the unknown, into such alien climes that he is unable to tell, he himself remarks, whether what he encounters is 'usual or strange' (p. 30). He travels to Africa and then to Brazil and then finally on an expedition to Guinea he and his fellow seamen are overtaken by two storms, the first a 'violent Tournado or Hurricane' that 'took us quite out of our Knowledge', and the second a storm which blew with such 'impetuosity' that it 'drove us out of the very Way of all human Commerce' (p. 42). The storms wreck the ship just off the coast of an unknown stretch of land, and Crusoe, alone of all the crew, manages to swim to shore, whereupon he finds himself cast away on a remote island in the middle of the Atlantic.

The narrative that follows, as is almost universally known, tells the story of Robinson's long inhabitation of his island, and of his arduous construction not only of a human dwelling place in the midst of such inhuman alienation but also of a kind of rationale for his predicament, a philosophical and aesthetic apparatus that might allow him to justify his existence in this little inch of the world. On his arrival on the island, Defoe represents Crusoe, with the most breathtaking immediacy, as a naked being, as a shivering animal, as Freud's 'helpless suckling' 'reduced', as Crusoe puts it, 'to a meer State of Nature' (p. 118).[21] Crusoe is an unwilling and unhappy version of Rousseau's 'natural state of Man', man as Rousseau imagines he 'must have come from the hands of Nature', stripped of his 'artificial faculties' (p. 52). Comparing the 'Civilized man' with the 'savage man', Rousseau contends that the 'savage man's body being the only implement he knows, he employs it for various uses of which through lack of training, our bodies are incapable'. 'Our industry', Rousseau writes, 'deprives us of the strength and agility that necessity obliges [the savage man] to acquire' (p. 53). As Robinson first arrives on his island, he appears as precisely this weakly civilised man, returned to a state of nature for which he is entirely unfitted. He is delivered onto the island as a newborn, lacking in the tools with which to extend himself into the world or to control and master his environment. His initial response to this predicament is a kind of violent despair – 'I ran about the Shore', he says, 'wringing my Hands and beating my Head and

Face, exclaiming at my Misery, and crying out, I was undone, undone'
(p. 69). Robinson spends this interval in a kind of unmeaning madness; but
he soon comes to himself and recognises that his task, out here in blank and
unmade space, is to craft a world for himself, to remake those artificial
faculties which the wreck has stripped from him, and thus to transform the
worldless death that he sees before him into a new lifeworld – to 'deliver my
self from this Death of a Life' (p. 199).

The first form that this world building takes is the quite literal process by
which Robinson fashions the shapes and forms of human life from the
barren wilderness before him – a process which the narrative follows with
the most extreme exactitude. The state of nature to which Robinson is
condemned is one in which he is deprived of tools, of 'implements' –
a deprivation which feels, to Robinson, like the loss of the body itself, so
entwined is the body of 'Civilized man' with its technical and mechanical
extensions. He is 'without tools', Crusoe thinks, 'or, as I may say, without
Hands' (p. 125), and so the endless time that Crusoe has on his island is
devoted to the fashioning of tools, and with those tools, of a dwelling place
which might accord to a human measure, which might comprise
a lifeworld in which he is equipped once more with a human hand.
Robinson salvages what tools and raw materials he can from the ship and
sets himself to the 'inexpressible labour' of making tables and chairs out of
intractable wood, building tents from salvaged canvas, stitching clothes
from the skins of slain animals and hewing caves out of the very rock of the
island. The making of a shovel out of iron wood – 'I work'd it effectually by
little and little into the Form of a shovel or Spade, the Handle exactly
shap'd like ours in *England*' (p. 73) – feels like a miracle of transformation,
the summoning of what Crusoe calls 'humane shapes' (p. 98) from the
most stubbornly inanimate material. And the making of a dwelling place,
a 'Cave spacious enough to accommodate me as a Warehouse or Magazin,
a Kitchen, a Dining-room, and a Cellar' (p. 74) – the wresting of the
familiar from the strange, the homely from the unhomely – is described in
such a way that one can feel the blisters forming on one's own hands as one
reads. 'I spent eighteen days entirely in widening and deepening my Cave',
Robinson records, and the narrative brings us right up against the brute
reality of this undertaking, that of a naked being, alone in borderless empty
space, hammering and digging and shaping the featureless environment,
until it starts to yield to a human will, to become a shaped extension of the
human need to dwell.

Robinson's first task, then, is to fashion a world out of worldlessness, to
convert non-being into being, in an effort of world forming that has become

a foundation not only of our understanding of the cultural role and the formal qualities of the novel as a mode but also of the very terms in which human relates to the world in European modernity. And the way that we conceive the texture of the novel imagination in the early eighteenth century, and Defoe's contribution to its development, rests on how we read this act of enworlding, how we read the process by which Crusoe, alone on his silent island in his raggedy clothes, goes about bringing human idea into contact with nonhuman thing. One of the striking elements of this process is the sheer fortitude and self-possession which Crusoe exhibits, after his initial bout of wild panic, his capacity, at this extreme of alienation and estrangement, to maintain intellectual contact with the culture and the forms from which he has been castaway and slowly, methodically, to apply those forms to the empty place in which he finds himself. As Karl Marx writes in *Capital*, when 'our friend Robinson Crusoe' is cast away, he does not become animal or 'savage', but rather, 'having saved a watch, ledger, ink and pen from the shipwreck, he soon begins, like a good Englishman, to keep a set of books.'[22] In carefully measuring out time and space in accordance both with an emerging capitalist theory of value and with the laws of God – in becoming a good labourer, and in time (with the arrival of Friday and other 'subjects' on the island) a good agriculturist, landowner and employer – Robinson painstakingly fashions the 'formulas', Marx writes, 'which bear the unmistakable stamp of belonging to a social formation in which the process of production has mastery over man' (p. 175). Robinson salvages a Bible from the wreck, alongside the tools with which he fashions his dwelling, and the paper and ink with which he keeps his journal; these tools together allow him to convert his distant space of exile into the nursery of what Marx calls 'Eighteenth-century man'. In the midst of his spontaneous conversion to devout Christianity, Robinson sits before the blank text of land and sea and finds, in this very script of nature, the foundation of a new epistemology, grounded in divine law. 'I went but a little way', he says,

> and sat down upon the Ground, looking out upon the Sea, which was just before me, and very calm and smooth: As I sat here, some such thoughts as these occurred to me.
>
> What is this Earth and Sea of which I have seen so much, whence is it produc'd and what am I, and all the other Creatures, wild and tame, Humane and brutal, whence are we?
>
> Sure we are all made by some secret Power, who form'd the Earth and Sea, the Air and Sky; and who is that?
>
> Then it follow'd most naturally, it is God that has made it all ... and if nothing happens without his Knowledge, he knows that I am here, and am

in this dreadful Condition; and if nothing happens without his Appointment, he has appointed all this to befal me. (p. 92)

This is a key moment in the novel, the moment at which Robinson discovers a narrative economy which is shaped to the alien world to which he finds himself exiled – the moment at which he discovers an accord between the 'Earth and Sea of which I have seen so much' and an 'idea of the world' which might animate both. It is the moment at which Robinson divines the 'secret power' which allows him to rationalise his own presence in this distant inch of the world as a natural feature of the landscape, and to give a justification of the colonial forces that have brought him to his island and which, Marx writes, 'appear to the political economists' bourgeois consciousness to be as much a self-evident and nature-imposed necessity as productive labour itself' (p. 175).

The most influential twentieth-century accounts of Defoe's novel, and of its role in the historical development of the eighteenth-century novel, have tended to turn around this sense that the novel form, as shaped by Defoe, offers a new means of narrating, and thus naturalising, an emerging social identity or condition. Ian Watt and Michael McKeon, for example, in somewhat different ways, provide the critical terms in which *Crusoe* is seen as a testing ground for the fashioning of modern subjecthood out of contact with colonial distance. 'It is appropriate,' Watt writes, 'that the tradition of the novel should begin with a work that annihilated the relationships of the traditional social order, and thus drew attention to the opportunity and the need of building up a new network of personal relations on a new and conscious pattern'.[23] McKeon builds on this conception of Defoe as the architect of a new form which is 'fully reconciled to the naturalness and morality of the pursuit of self-interest'.[24] Defoe's narrative gives the 'history of the individual', McKeon writes, 'so intimate and introspective a form that it comes close to looking more like self-creation' (p. 337). Crusoe's 'suspended time on the island', he goes on, 'has provided the laboratory conditions for acquiring, slowly and with relative impunity, the psychological equipment needed for possessive individualism' (p. 334). Crusoe, by this account, draws on his solitude to build an internal picture of utopian self-possession, upon which he then proceeds to erect the edifice of a larger model of capitalist relations – a process by which what McKeon calls the 'subjective roots of objective and empirical reality' are, for the first time, 'embedded in narrative substance' (p. 337). The growth of a mini nation state on the island in the later stages of the novel accordingly constitutes, for McKeon, the coming together of the internal world that Crusoe builds in his imagination as he gazes out to sea with the new terms of colonial sovereignty – the 'tangible externalization of Robinson's now securely internalized utopia' (p. 335).

In *Robinson Crusoe*, and later in *Moll Flanders*, it is hard to avoid this sense that Defoe is laboriously fashioning a picture of the world that might accommodate the demands of an emergent model of the self. But if this is a key moment in the history of the novel, it is central to everything I will be arguing in this book that such a formal conjunction between interiority and the exterior manifestations of self and world is shadowed by an opposite *disjunction*, and what is more that it is one of the central achievements of the novel to preserve this disjunction, to enshrine it in the formal mechanics of the novel itself, and to make it part of the expressive apparatus of prose fiction as it sets the terms of our own self-congress. Defoe's image of the solitary Robinson diligently whittling his wood and digging his cave, fashioning his dwelling out of earth, not only summons the terms in which we extend ourselves into body and world; it preserves also, as a kind of palaeontological record of a difficult becoming, the junction between being and its prosthetic attachments, between McKeon's internal and external forms – the connective element that such naturalised self-fashioning has necessarily sought to deny or repress. It has preserved this junction, this twist, not only as a side effect of the mechanical construction of being, a kind of flipside of the sliding into being of the self, but also as a necessary proximity to the motor of such becoming, as a formal narrative display of the secret narrative mechanics of material self-fashioning.

One can see this disjunction at work in Defoe's fiction most clearly at those recurrent moments when his characters are cast into those forms of non-being that are shadowed forth in Cavendish's *Blazing World*, the suspension of selfhood that attends the striving for the adoption of a new prosthetic self – those moments, in Hume's terms, when the person who 'enters most intimately' into himself finds that there is 'nothing simple and continu'd' upon which such a perception of self might rest.[25] Indeed, the critical moment I have just discussed at which Robinson is granted a clear sight of his island world – when he is able, for the first time, to situate the 'Earth and Sea of which I have seen so much' within a secure divine economy – is won from precisely such an experience of non-being. The clearing of Crusoe's vision and the awakening of his 'conscience' to the word of God come about, in a scene that is closely reprised in *Moll Flanders*, in the wake of a near fatal bout of fever, during which 'my spirits began to sink under the Burthen of a strong Distemper', and 'a leisurely View of the Miseries of Death came to place itself before me' (p. 90). In the midst of his fever, Robinson enters into the space of his own death, just as Moll imagines herself to have already died when she is sentenced to death in Newgate (the judges 'Pronounc'd the Sentence of Death upon me', Moll says, 'a Sentence that was to me like Death itself').[26] Robinson cries out 'Lord! What a miserable Creature am I? If I should be sick I shall certainly die' (p. 90); Moll says, in a near quotation of Robinson's despair, 'Lord! What will become of me, I shall certainly die' (p. 358). For both characters, this brush with death renders them peculiarly numb, as Oroonoko becomes a 'thing' that 'knew not that it had being' at the moment of his transformative meeting with Imoinda. This death seems to Robinson to be the end result of what he calls a 'certain stupidity of soul' that had 'over-whelm'd' him during his seafaring and planting days (p. 88), just as Moll finds that her living in sin, amongst the criminals of Newgate, causes her to become insensate, thing-like. 'Like the Waters in the Cavities, and Hollows of Mountains', Moll says, 'which petrifies and turns into Stone whatever they are suffer'd to drop upon, so the continual Conversing with such a Crew of Hell-Hounds as I was, which had the same common Operation upon me as upon other People, I degenerated into Stone' (p. 354). Death for both manifests this degeneracy, so Moll recognises, as she is sentenced to death, that 'I had no more Spirit left in me, I had no Tongue to speak, or Eyes to look up either to God or to Man' (p. 363).

In obedience to a peculiar kind of logic that recurs throughout the history of the novel as I will account for it here, coming to consciousness for Moll and for Crusoe involves this brush with being as insensate thinghood. Such an encounter is presented here, as so often in the novel (think, for example, of Miles Coverdale's later entry into personhood through death at the heart of *The Blithedale Romance*) as the prelude to a rebirth, as the entry into a new kind of richly animated being. As Coverdale says of his 'fit of illness', that it caused him to 'shed the very substance upon my bones' and, 'after shivering a little while in my skeleton' to be 'clothed anew, and much more satisfactorily than in my previous suit', dying grants Moll and Crusoe a new body.[27] With the intuition of death, Moll says, she 'began to think', and through such thinking to remake herself. 'He that is restor'd to his Power of thinking', she reflects, 'is restor'd to himself' (p. 358). With the return of thought comes the return of conscience and self-consciousness. 'Reflections I had made upon the horrid detestable Life I had liv'd, began to return upon me', she says, 'and as these things return'd my abhorrence of the place I was in, and of the way of living in it, return'd also; in a word, I was perfectly chang'd, and become another Body' (p. 357).

This return to life, this 'flowing' of thought 'in upon my mind', allows Moll to turn from the criminality of the first half of the novel to the repentance of the second, to metamorphose from stone to flesh, just as Robinson's 'View of the Miseries of death' allows him to form his new picture of the earth and sea before him, his new idea of the world. Once she has been granted this 'view into the other Side of time', Moll thinks, 'the things of life, as I believe they do with every Body at such a time, began to look with a different Aspect, and quite another Shape, than they did before' (p. 364). Robinson finds, in much the same way, that his encounter with non-being allows him to rationalise the world before him. 'I gain'd a different knowledge from what I had before', he says, 'I entertain'd different Notions of Things' (p. 128). But if numb stupefaction is the prelude to the adoption of a new and animated self, of 'another Body', then it is central to the workings of the prosthetic imagination that the new body that is forged, in the sun and wind of the island, or in the dungeons of Newgate (or later in Hawthorne's mock Arcadia), bears the marks of its becoming and carries the trace of its origin in the experience of becoming stone, of suffering a leaden 'stupidity of soul'. The stoniness of Moll's stupefied self is not simply overcome in her newfound interiority, the becoming of her new consciousness; rather, it remains part of the new artificial lifeworld that Defoe seeks to create in *Moll Flanders*, and in *Robinson Crusoe*. The stoniness of the exterior, of the nonhuman, is wound deeply, as Jean-Luc Nancy has argued, into the inside of the self, so the opposition inside/outside, self/world, flesh/stone will not remain stable or mutually exclusive. 'A stone', Nancy writes, is 'the exteriority of singularity', but even as stone belongs to the outside, to the world of non-living, nonhuman things, it nevertheless belongs to the innermost recesses of being. 'I would not be human', Nancy goes on, 'if I did not have this exteriority "in me," in the form of the quasi-minerality of bone'.[28] The wakening of consciousness in Defoe is conceptualised as a transformation of numb, rigid stone into flowing, moving, animated self-hood; but even as his novels narrate and produce this transformation, the materiality of being, its resistance to the transformative power of consciousness, continues to assert itself and in so doing to demonstrate the stubborn persistence of the disjuncture between consciousness and its prosthetic manifestations.

Robinson Crusoe, and Defoe's fiction more generally, turns around this disjunction, and the self-conscious invention of narrative forms that it enacts is an attempt both to map this fault line and to overcome it. The chief difficulty that Robinson faces, at least as threatening to his survival as wild beasts or lack of food and shelter, is his sense that ideational forms are not aligned with his being on the island, that thought and ideas are distanced from the boundless, shapeless time and space of his solitary life. The materiality of existence, the lifeworld that Robinson painfully fashions out of iron wood, resists transformation into animated being, as Moll's stoniness resists transformation by and into the 'thought' through which Moll is restored to herself. Words, on Robinson's arrival on his island, have no sound, no weight, no purchase, just as things have no words and resist the quickening touch of language. In the midst of his transformative fever, as Robinson reads from the Bible, he suffers the full effect of this sundering between name and substance, as an effect of his 'stupidity of soul'. His eye chances to fall upon the line '*Call on me in the Day of Trouble, and I will deliver, and thou shalt glorify me.*' The words, Robinson suggests, 'were very apt to my case', but in the midst of his deadened confusion, Robinson as character cannot grasp this aptness, and the words do not make a sufficient 'impression upon my Thoughts', 'for', he says, 'as for being deliver'd, the Word had no Sound, *As I may say*, to me' (p. 94). The word of God cannot sound in Robinson's distant exile; when voices do sound in the island air, they are pure noise, simple material vibrations that contain no spirit, no consciousness. Robinson catches a parrot and 'quickly', he says, he 'learn'd him how to know his own Name, and at last to speak it out pretty loud POLL, which was the first word ever spoken by any mouth but my own' (p. 119) (one might ask, as an aside: does a parrot have a 'mouth'?). The parrot keeps him company and at one point terrifies him by waking him from a deep sleep, 'calling me by Name several times, *Robin, Robin, Robin Crusoe*, poor *Robin Crusoe*, where are you *Robin Crusoe*? Where are you? Where have you been?' (p. 142). But, of course, the parrot is not really speaking to Robin, as Descartes assures us that parrots do not speak to us ('parrots can utter words as we do', Descartes writes, 'and yet cannot speak like us, that is, by showing that they are thinking what they are saying').[29] Crusoe's parrot, Derrida writes, is a 'sort of living mechanism that he has produced, that he assembled himself, like a *quasi*-technical or prosthetic apparatus, by training the parrot to speak mechanically so as to send his words and his name back to him'.[30] The parrot is no more talking to Robinson when he asks where he is than the volleyball named Wilson – the prosthetic friend of Robert Zemeckis's castaway – can offer real companionship to its owner Chuck Noland in the 2000 film *Castaway.*

The word of God, then, remains distant from the prosthetic voices that do sound on the island. The voice of the parrot demonstrates, in Descartes' terms, 'no mental powers whatever' and is the effect merely of a 'nature which acts in them' (p. 48). This gap, between word and thing, between human and nature, between human and animal, between what Derrida calls the 'beast and the sovereign', is the problem to be solved, and the story of the novel is the story of Crusoe's attempt to overcome the resistance that the unregulated 'natural forms' that he encounters on the island offer to the transformative power of the Word. The shovel that Robinson shapes out of wood cannot quite work as a shovel should, cannot quite become a *shovel*, as, for Aristotle, 'the hand of a dead man' will 'be a hand in name only'.[31] The wooden shovel, Robinson says, in a striking formulation, 'did my Work in but a wooden manner', as the material of which it is made does not quite match its use – its 'essence', in Aristotle's terms, does not match its 'matter'. The human shapes that Crusoe makes on the island – like the 'odd misshapen, ugly things' that he produces when he tries to make pots out of island clay – repeatedly fail to absorb the island material into their new human economies. And when Robinson encounters human signs on the island – most famously in the 'Print of a Man's naked Foot on the Shore', what Derrida calls the 'trace of a man'[32] – he cannot read them, cannot render them into human sense. The footprint – 'exactly the very Print of a Foot, Toes, Heel, and every Part of a Foot' (p. 154) – is no more readable to Crusoe than the body parts that he finds strewn over the shore, and that signal to Crusoe the dread presence of cannibals on his sovereign land. It is 'impossible to express the Horror of my mind', Crusoe writes, 'at seeing the Shore spread with Skulls, Hands, Feet, and other bones of Humane bodies' (pp. 164–65); 'I saw three skulls, five Hands, and the Bones of three or four Legs and Feet, and the abundance of other Parts of the Bodies' (p. 207). These amputated, disfigured human shapes are hands, feet, legs only to the extent that the misshapen ugly things that Crusoe makes are pots, and they cannot match with the idea that Crusoe has of them.

Crusoe's task is to bring these oppositions into harmony, to compose a picture of the world, an economy of scale, that will impose a set of hierarchies on the things, the animals and the people that inhabit his emerging colony. And if this is so, then, of course, it is the self-reflexive act of writing, the keeping of a journal, that allows Crusoe to fashion his new world, and that allows Defoe to *enact* the process by which fiction oversees the relation between mind and prosthetic attachment. One of the oddest, most chaotic elements of Defoe's odd and chaotic novel is that it contains, within the first person retrospective account of the adventure that bookends the novel, a central portion of the narrative that is recorded in the form of the journal that Crusoe keeps while his is on the island. In a demonstration of what Denise Schaeffer calls the 'utility of ink' in eighteenth-century culture, the narrator gives us a supremely detailed description of the process by which Crusoe salvages his pen, ink and paper from the wreck to provide the technological means by which he *materialises* his writing self.[33] 'Among the many things I brought out of the ship', he writes, 'I got several things of less value, but not [at] all less useful to me . . . as in particular, Pen, Ink, and paper' (p. 65). It is this material, he says, that allows him to apply 'reason' to his situation, to 'master his despondency', but also to regulate his environment, and himself. We are given this picture of the amassing of the necessary materials as a precursor to the moment when we are handed over from the first person narrator to the voice of the journal itself. Having 'made me a Table and a Chair, and all about me as handsome as I could', Crusoe says, 'I began to keep my Journal, of which I shall here give you the Copy (tho' in it will be told all these Particulars over again)' (pp. 68, 69). And indeed, we turn the page to find a new section, entitled '*The* JOURNAL' (p. 70), which gives us an account ('*November 1*. I set up my tent under a rock'), for the second time, of all the laborious details we have just been given by the first person narrator. There can be no reader who has not found this shift in perspective bewildering, and also somewhat infuriating in its repetitiveness; but the initial effect, even in its odd exorbitancy, is to embed the tale we have just read, to deepen its realism, to effect that marriage of word and thing that is Crusoe's chief task, more strenuous and demanding than the whittling of a shovel out of wood. This writing, the turn to the journal suggests, is not being produced from some European perspective, some kind of recollection in tranquillity from a safely rescaled colonial centre. Rather it is being made now, in the heat and the sun and the wind – the deranged scale – of the distant island, with the very effort of the writing, the difficulty of the refractory materials, being impressed on the page, as the print of a foot is impressed on the sand.

   This is what we might think; but, of course, what is even odder about this adoption of the journal voice is that it is radically unstable, so rather than embedding the story in McKeon's 'narrative substance', it undermines it at every turn. Rather than imposing a hierarchy, an economy of scale, it oversees an astonishing failure of regulation, what Heather Keenleyside calls 'the breakdown, or the impossibility, of Lockean politics'.[34] 'In it', Crusoe says, 'will be told all these Particulars over again', but in repeating the particulars he changes the details, so that rather than being given an aug-mented, enhanced sense of the reality of Crusoe's time on the island, we are cast into doubt concerning the reliability of these particulars. Take, for example, Crusoe's description of his arrival on the island (part of which I have already quoted in this discussion) – the moment when he suffers one of those crucial evacuations of his human self. We are given three distinct accounts of this moment, none of which quite matches the others. The first comes in the voice of the first person narrator, as he tells us of his safe arrival on the island. 'I believe it is impossible to express to the Life', he says, 'what the Exstasies and Transports of the Soul are, when it is so sav'd, as I may say, out of the very Grave' (p. 46). He is in an indescribable ecstasy in this passage between life and death, so, he says, his actions are not interpretable or narratable. 'I walk'd about on the Shore, lifting up my Hands, and my whole Being, wrapt up in Contemplation of my Deliverance, making a Thousand Gestures and Motions which I cannot describe' (p. 46). The second account of this moment then comes as we are preparing to be handed over from the first person narrator to the voice of the journal itself. 'And now it was', the narrator says some way into his tale, having laboriously prepared his table, chair, pen and ink, 'when I began to keep a Journal of every Day's Employment'. His journal will not cover the first period on the island, he says, because at that time 'I was in too much Hurry' and 'too much Discomposure of Mind'. 'For Example', he goes on, 'I must have said thus':

> *Sept.* the 30th. After I got to shore and had escap'd drowning, instead of being thankful to God for my Deliverance, having first vomited with the great Quantity of salt water which was gotten into my Stomach, and recovering my self a little, I ran about the shore, wringing my Hands and beating my Head and Face, exclaiming at my Misery, and crying out, I was undone, undone. (p. 69)

This is bizarre enough: he is telling us here what he would have written, had he not been so busy vomiting and running about (and, presumably, if he had the materials that cost him so much effort to procure already to hand). But it is doubly bizarre that the imagined account he gives us here – that he did not write but would have if he had more composure of mind – is at variance with the account that he has already given from the first person perspective. In the first version, he was 'wrapt up in contemplation of his deliverance'; in the second, he did not have time for such contemplation, because he was occupied with vomiting and beating himself around the face and head. But it gets still more bizarre when we turn the page to find ourselves delivered into the time and space of the island and treated to the very account that Crusoe has just said that he would not give us, the account that he did not write and, by all realist logic, would not have had the means to write: 'September 30, 1659. I poor miserable Robinson Crusoe, being shipwreck'd, during a dreadful storm, in the offing came on shore this dismal unfortunate island. . . . All the rest of that day I spent in afflicting myself at the Dismal circumstances I was brought to' (p. 70).

These repetitions and variations have an extraordinary effect on the mimetic quality of Defoe's prose. Of course, to some degree, they are the result of Defoe's carelessness, mere examples of the many famous errors and contradictions that run throughout the text.[35] But if this is the case, it is also true that they are symptomatic of the means by which fiction here works at the ground between being and extension, the way that the vaporous substance of fiction itself serves as the material that grants Crusoe embodiment, that allows mind to animate material while preserving also the resistance of that material to animation. Defoe's novel is a remarkable record of the capacity of fiction to allow us, in Heidegger's formulation, to build, dwell and think, even in the most hostile, most inhuman of environments.[36] It is its irregularity, its tendency to combine the most material of descriptions with a fictional waywardness, that reminds us, at every stage, that there is no real referent to this story, that the journal is not being written, after all, in island ink and is not, after all, the place where this account is actually stored or materialised; this is not a failure of its realism, but a remarkable working through, on the fly, of the way that novel realism, the fictional image, occupies a referential space somewhere between mind and material, pitched in some vanishing ground between mimesis and prosthesis. And what is most remarkable of all about the way that *Robinson Crusoe* preserves this record is that the journal voice – the encounter with the world-making power of writing in its volatile, inconsistent immediacy – is itself subject to a kind of vanishing, itself disappears over the course of the novel, as it has done its job, as it has effected some kind of contact between disembodied and embodied voice, between word and sound. As Crusoe's time on the island lengthens, he begins to fret that his supply of ink will run out. He 'husbanded' ink and paper, he says, 'to the utmost', because, when the ink runs out, 'I could not make any Ink by any Means that I could devise' (p. 65). As his supply runs out, he waters down his ink, so that the words that he writes in the journal become thinner and thinner. 'My ink', he writes, 'had been gone some time, all but a very little, which I eek'd out with Water a little and a little, till it was so pale it scarce left any Appearance of black upon the paper' (p. 133). His words become paler and paler until, eventually, 'having no more Ink I was forc'd to leave it off' (p. 69). But what is so fascinating about this disappearance, this casting of voice into wordlessness, is that it does not simply consign the narrative to silence, but rather to a kind of absence which is there at the ground of novel being. As his ink runs low, he writes in his journal, he curtails the content of his account to stretch out his supply. In the entry for September 30th (the anniversary of his arrival on the island), he writes 'A little after this my ink began to fail me, and so I contented my self to use it more sparingly, and to write down only the most remarkable Events of my life, without continuing a daily *memorandum* of other Things' (p. 104). The question naturally follows – what ink are these words written in? And it is difficult to resist the thought that they are written in the invisible ink of a new kind of novel form, a new kind of first person, native to the novel imagination, grounded in the amalgam of disappearance and material becoming that is the province of a novelistic ontology. As the ink runs out, so the journal voice gradually falls away. Crusoe leaves the journal form for pages at a time, before reminding himself to 'return to my journal', increasingly halfheartedly, until finally the journal is heard of no more, and we return to the voice with which we began. But if the running out of ink frees the narrative voice, by some peculiar novel logic, from the constraints of the journal, it is nevertheless the case that the imagined ink remains the medium of self-fashioning here, the medium in which the free-floating narrative voice meets with the immediate scene of inscription. As the ink runs out, as we are released into an island environment made of words that leave no mark on the paper, we are granted access to a kind of junction between mind and matter, the most intimate of places, where thought meets the material that clothes it, where being is restored to itself. To read this novel is to look into the heart of the writing event – to access the place where writing transforms biomaterial into quickened being – and to find there not a substance, or an origin, but rather a kind of disappearing element, the elusive ground to being that is made of its own non-being even as it contains the very possibility of becoming.

It is the discovery of this disappearing element, this ground to life that resists material form even as it is the basis for the materiality of being, that is the most enduring legacy of *Robinson Crusoe*, and that makes it such a significant moment in the history of the prosthetic imagination. It is not, I think, that Defoe's novel establishes the form in which an emerging individualism might be securely expressed, nor is it the form in which a new interiority might find itself aligned with the external conditions of the world. Rather, the gift of the novel is that it works its way deep into the region between mind and its extensions, the place where Robinson's 'soul' meets with the forms that he fashions, the medium of what he beautifully calls the 'secret Communication' between the 'embody'd' and the 'unem-body'd' (p. 176). It opens this region to thought, stains it with island ink, but captures, as well, its specific resistance to material, its refusal to take on form. *Robinson Crusoe* expels a colonial body on to a far shore and watches as it is forced to make a dwelling for itself, as it is forced to convert a meaningless set of materials into a human shape. In doing so, it offers a picture of world making that has become one of the most enduring in the history of the modern imagination. But even as it gives us this lesson in the fashioning of a world, it preserves also, in its most intimate recesses, an encounter with the elusive stuff of being, the connective tissue that holds us to our prosthetic extensions, even as it withholds itself from thought and from inscription.

2.3 A Continuation of the Brain: Unregulated Bodies in Swift and Scott

It is in the utopian and anti-utopian novels that come in the wake of *Robinson Crusoe* – in Jonathan Swift's *Gulliver's Travels* (1726), in Voltaire's *Candide* (1759), in Sarah Scott's *Millenium Hall* (1762) – that the expansive urge that runs through the eighteenth-century novel reaches its maximal expression. It is here too that the utopian legacy to the eighteenth-century imagination, and to the imaginative means by which mind fictionalises its connection to prosthetic matter, is most apparent. If the eighteenth-century European novel attempts to establish an economy of scale in which a colonial body, at a remove from itself, might find a means of regulating itself, a means of imagining a utopian environment in which the body is at home in its world, then it is in these works that this attempt might most clearly be seen.

Of course, while these novels are engaged in a dialogue with a utopian tradition that runs from More to Bacon to Leibniz and Rousseau, the first thing that one may note about this dialogue is a certain scepticism that characterises it, a certain failure of the utopian principles that drive *Utopia* and *The Blazing World,* and that are found too in *Robinson Crusoe*, in those moments when Robinson and Friday briefly found an ideal community, in which both are 'perfectly and compleatly happy, if any such Thing as compleat Happiness can be form'd in a sublunary state' (p. 220). At the heart of the utopian condition are the concept and the ideal of a regulated body, and a regulated state which is modelled, as in Hobbes' *Leviathan*, upon the principles of that bodily regulation. Even if this modelling encounters a certain kind of bodily excess – in *Robinson Crusoe*, as I have

argued, the fashioning of a new colonial body involves a painful struggle
with a kind of stubborn prosthetic matter which resists human form – it is
nevertheless the case that utopian possibility rests on the capacity of form
to contain this unruliness, to subject matter to the controlling power of
mind, albeit a power that can only inscribe itself in the negative language of
fiction, or in the medium of invisible ink. But in these later works, we find
that the colonial body, the body at a distance, becomes increasingly
unregulated, increasingly diffuse and disobedient, as if the principles that
drive the colonial project, that oversee the colonial relation to self, become
increasingly attenuated.

One can see this effect even in the eighteenth-century novels that seek,
most earnestly, to work within a utopian tradition. Take, for example, Scott's
Millenium Hall, a novel which offers a strikingly radical version of an all-
female utopia, in which women live freely together, liberated from the
demand that they should sell themselves on the marriage market. The conceit
of this novel – which offers a blueprint for the tradition of feminist utopias
and dystopias that follow, from Scott to Atwood[37] – is to establish a female
commune in the midst of the English countryside, thus situating a foreign
land, a brave new world, right in the heart of the homeland, rather than on its
colonial fringes.[38] The commune, named 'Millenium Hall', is a screened-off
place, where the founding women make for themselves and for others
a refuge from the corruption of patriarchal capitalist economy, in which
every woman is free to pursue her own talents, and to inhabit her own body.
The Hall is funded by the political economy to which it is opposed – each of
the women living in the Hall has some private income which she contributes
to the cause – but the commune seeks to establish a semipermeable boundary
between the larger political economy and its own utopian principles. The
women give up their income to the Hall on entry, so that all funds can be
equally distributed among the residents and the charitable causes and societies that they run. In this way, the women establish a foreign enclave within
the nation state, in which they might correct the flaws of the larger world, and
in which they might regulate their own political and bodily economies. 'We
wish to regulate ourselves by the laws laid down to us', Miss Mancel says, 'and
as far as our influence can extend, endeavour to enforce them; beyond that
small circle all is foreign to us'.[39] They thus make for themselves a world
within a world – or, as the narrator puts it, women who are 'qualified both by
nature and fortune to have the world almost at command, were brought thus
to seclude themselves from it, and make as it were a new one for themselves
constituted on such very different principles' (p. 27).

Such a procedure might sound conventionally utopian. But what is so peculiar about this novel is that the interface between Millenium Hall and the England that surrounds it – between the corrupt world that the women were born into and the pure world that they make for themselves – is radically unstable; as a result, the women's capacity to *regulate* their utopian economy is oddly fitful, and unreliable. It is as if the utopian convention, which allows a narrator to bridge the chasm between the world as it is and the world as it ought to be, has malfunctioned, casting the novel into a multiplying set of contradictions and lacunae, a set of disruptions which renders the utopian body peculiarly unstable and ductile. Nowhere is this effect starker than in the case of the 'gallery of monsters' that the women maintain, as part of the charitable work of the estate. On first arriving at Millenium Hall, the male narrator is shown around the grounds by Miss Mancel, where he comes across a high fence, which marks the boundaries of a secret enclosure. The foppish companion to the narrator, Mr Lamont, asks what lies behind the fence, whereupon Miss Mancel, apparently against her better judgement, decides to let her guests, and us as readers, into the secret. What the ladies keep behind the fence is not, as Lamont childishly imagines, a zoo of some kind. Rather, it is a community of giants and dwarves, whom the women have rescued from freak shows and circuses, and who now live at the women's expense in a paddock in the grounds of the Hall. 'The miserable treatment of persons, to whom compassion should secure more than common indulgence', Miss Mancel explains,

> determined us to purchase these worst sort of slaves, and in this place we
> have five who owed their wretchedness to being only three foot high, one
> grey-headed toothless old man of sixteen years of age, a woman of about
> seven foot in height, and a man who would be still taller, if the extreme
> weakness of his body, and the wretched life he for some time led, in the
> hands of these monster-mongers, did not make him bend almost double,
> and oblige him to walk on crutches. (p. 24)

The women purchase these 'monsters' and hide them away behind a fence, because, Miss Mancel explains, they seek to protect these unruly bodies from a culture that cruelly polices what the narrator calls the 'usual standard of the human form' (p. 25). To live in the wider world, she explains, is to live under the tyranny of a Procrustean demand that all bodies should conform to an inflexible model of bodily scale. 'Procrustes has been branded a tyrant', she says, 'principally from fitting the body of every stranger to a bed which he kept as a necessary standard, cutting off the legs of those whose height exceeded the length of it and stretching on the rack such as fell short of that measure, till they attained the requisite proportion' (p. 23). In her time, Miss Mancel believes, 'almost every man is a Procrustes', and so it is the task of the Hall to provide an 'asylum for those poor creatures who are rendered miserable from some natural deficiency or redundancy' (p. 23). To have too much body, to have too little, this should not be considered an anomaly or a disgrace; in the Hall, Miss Mancel suggests, the women embrace bodily heterogeneity, welcoming and protecting people whose bodily economies deviate from the 'usual standard'. To enter into the inner 'circle' of the Hall, that place where the women are able to 'regulate ourselves', is to enter into a different politics of measure, a new economy of scale, where we are free from the demand that we fit our bodies to a given pattern.

If this is the case, however, what is most striking about this gallery of monsters is that the very narrative mechanism which protects them from the world, which allows them to measure themselves to a different standard, also reproduces the effects that it seeks to alleviate. The architects of the Hall cannot conceive of an environment in which bodies are entirely free from the tyranny of scale – a tall body still harbours a 'redundancy', a short body still exhibits a 'deficiency'. To see the 'poor wretches' in their enclosure is still to 'see the human form so disgraced' (p. 25). Indeed, the principle which drives the aesthetics and politics of this text, above all else, is that of natural harmony, the sense that the things and persons of the world are simply an outward expression of God's perfection, as perfectly tailored to the divine idea that animates them as Procrustes' victims are finally suited to his bed. What the women seek is to understand this perfection, and to live by it, to regulate their material and spiritual economies to accord as closely as possible, with no redundancy and no deficiency, to the divinity that we find already inscribed in nature. 'Everything to me', Miss Mancel declares, 'loses its charm when it is put out of the station wherein nature, or to speak more properly, the all-wise Creator has placed it' (p. 22). So, when the women build a tall fence and secrete their monsters behind it, they are doing two rather different things at once, expressing two contradictory desires which cannot be reconciled by the utopian narrative apparatus which oversees the relationship between the world as it is and the world as it ought to be. In the first instance, they are asserting the right of bodies to exceed or fall below any given measure, asserting the right of nature to express itself in its radical freedom, without any Vitruvian standards acting as a model or a template; in the second instance, they are insisting that nature itself is a template, a regulating economy, of the most exact and unforgiving kind, that dictates to us how

we should live, and what our bodies should mean. The symptom of this
contradiction is the unregulated bodies of the monsters themselves, silently
moving in their enclosures, freed from the censure of freak show audiences,
but only into the bounds of the enclosure, where they are not relieved from
their aberrance but equated with it.[40] The desire to reclaim the monstrous
or transgressive as a proper part of the women's 'new world', 'constituted
on such very different principles', sits uneasily alongside a persistent sense
that true harmony, true political freedom, should manifest itself not in the
deformed or the ugly but in the well proportioned and the graceful (it is
striking that, of the 'girls' who live in the Hall, as opposed to in the
enclosure, 'none had any defect in person' (p. 13)). The call to 'nature' as
the self-evident manifestation of a divine plan here falls into a kind of crisis,
as the monstrous (both in the guise of the dwarves and the giants and
implicitly as the imagining of a radical feminism and a same-sex desire,
which cannot find articulation) appears both to be the mark of a nature
freed from the proscriptions of culture and the mark of a disgraced or
thwarted nature, which must be concealed from view, which has deviated
from God's plan. The stooping monsters and the stunted dwarves that
haunt this novel are the symptoms of an economy of desire and of scale that
cannot quite articulate itself, in which difference and resistance to regulation appear at once as defiant liberation and as deformity, as the failure of
a relation between divine idea and gross actuality, between exalted form
and debased content.

Utopian conventions in *Millenium Hall*, then, have fallen into a kind of
disrepair, as Scott's narrative loses the capacity to mediate between is and
ought, between the pure world of nature and the corrupt world of the
human. But if Scott's work seeks and fails to employ a utopian apparatus
with which to free bodies from the regulation of a corrupt political
economy, then the other great eighteenth-century explorations of unregulated bodies – Voltaire's *Candide*, Laurence Sterne's *Tristram Shandy*,
Jonathan Swift's *Gulliver's Travels* – work on the assumption that utopian
form has already been dismantled, that eighteenth-century colonial conditions have refashioned the formal structures of utopia as satire. The
problem that destabilises Scott's novel, that jams the utopian mechanism,
becomes, in these works, the mechanism itself, the active principle of the
satirical mode. Scott seeks at once to suggest that deformity might be
a form of political freedom and that freedom should always express itself as
beauty – a contradiction between the poles of which her enclosed monsters
lurk. Sterne and Voltaire show us unregulated, prosthetised, disobedient,
distorted bodies in the service of their outright rejection of the possibility of

utopian form. Sterne develops a certain obsession with the prosthetic artificiality of the body in *Tristram Shandy*. In fact the first we see of Tristram is not his organic self, but the prosthetic nose that the surgeon Dr Slop fashions for him on the day of his birth, a 'false bridge' fashioned from 'a piece of cotton and a thin piece of whalebone' to replace the nose that is 'crushed' by forceps during his difficult delivery.[41] And Voltaire's *Candide* is a concentrated dismantling of the narrator's opening proposition, central to all utopian fictions, that the body might be a natural expression of mind – that Candide's 'mind could be read in his face' – showing us a series of amputated, disfigured and radically truncated bodies that are the manifest sign that we do not, and could not, live in Leibniz's best of all possible worlds.[42]

But if all these writers are invested, in different ways, in the figure of a prosthetic body – a body that is divorced or removed from the control of mind – it is in Swift's *Gulliver's Travels* that this figure is given its fullest treatment, and here too that the prosthetic body is most fully explored as an effect of the failure of utopian form. Indeed, *Gulliver's Travels* opens with a prefatory insistence on the sincerity of the text that explicitly reaches back to More's *Utopia*, and that demands we read its exploration of the relationship between body and mind, form and content, signifier and signified, as an engagement with the utopian tradition. In a rhetorical gesture which I have traced in this book so far, as it is found in More, Baldwin, Cervantes, Behn, Defoe – and which can be seen at work in the claim, in Behn, Voltaire and Scott, that meaning can be found written in the expression of the face – Swift opens his novel with a 'letter' written by Gulliver himself, in which he refuses to accept that his tale has anything untrue about it – that it could be read by anyone as a 'meer Fiction out of mine own Brain'.[43] There are those, Gulliver writes, who 'have gone as far as to drop Hints, that the *Houyhnhnms* and *Yahoos* have no more Existence than the Inhabitants of *Utopia*' (pp. xxxv–xxxvi). Gulliver here follows in the footsteps of Cervantes and More before him – reprising the claim of Cervantes' narrator that in publishing the story of Don Quixote 'we do not depart by so much as an inch in the telling of it' (p. 31), and the claim of Thomas More, in the prefatory material to *Utopia*, that 'truth in fact is the only thing at which I should aim and do aim in writing this book' (p. 3). People have doubted the veracity of his story, Gulliver acknowledges, but it is nevertheless all true – unlike, ironically enough, the content of More's *Utopia*, which is, we can now reveal, entirely fabricated. The sincerity of his tale will be apparent to all readers, he goes on, because 'the Truth immediately strikes every Reader with Conviction' (p. xxxvi), and because 'There is an Air of Truth apparent through the whole' (p. xxxvii). Swift joins knowingly here in the early novel tradition of disavowing the fictionality of his work, of representing his tale, like Defoe before him, as a 'just History of Fact; neither is there any Appearance of Fiction in it' (p. 1). But if this claim establishes a foundational connection between *Gulliver's Travels* and *Utopia*, what is clear from the beginning is that the delicate play between truth and falsehood that characterises the early novel form – that brings Thomas More as author into contact with Thomas More as character, and England into contact with Utopia – undergoes a transformation in Swift's novel. Here, from the beginning, one can sense that what is at stake is the shifting epistemological status of narrative itself, the nature of the political and aesthetic forces that control the production of truthful utterances and that oversee the means by which meaning might be contained within words and within bodies, the means by which essence might shine forth in appearance. Swift activates a utopian tradition of the disavowal of fictionality here, but in so doing he establishes something like a revolution in our understanding of fictionality itself, and the nature of the worlds that it produces. Something happens in eighteenth-century European culture, something linked to the impact of colonial relations on the nature and texture of the body politic, that has a transformative effect on the relationship between the imagination and its material forms (and that is associated with what Catherine Gallagher call the 'rise of fictionality' in the period).[44] When Swift has Gulliver insist on the truth of his narrative, the claim carries an element of evident untruth that is constitutively different from the mixture of the serious and ludic that we find in More. Gulliver is candidly gulling us, and in the new tone of unseriousness laced in the claim to truth, we can see the beginnings of a formal shift from utopianism to satire.

The most dramatic effect of this shift, as I have already suggested, is the spectacle of the prosthetic body that looms large in *Gulliver's Travels* and re-emerges too in Scott's monsters and dwarves, and that appears as a symptom of the failure of the delicate utopian bonds between the real and the imagined. The immediate result of Gulliver's travels, particularly to Lilliput and Brobdingnag, is an extraordinary mental evacuation of body, an enduringly powerful sense that mind has become loosed from body, has become unmoored. As Gulliver travels from place to place, he is faced with that same difficulty encountered by Scott's monsters – he finds that he either has a 'redundancy' of biomatter or an 'insufficiency'; he either has too much body or too little – and in each case, the effect of such surplus or deficit is to drive a wedge between mind and its material extensions, to demonstrate that a gap between meaning and material is a direct consequence of the new global mobility. The effects of this gap are first felt on Gulliver's arrival at Lilliput, even before Gulliver has encountered any of the minute inhabitants, in a certain dehiscence that can be felt at the level of the language itself. Gulliver is shipwrecked by a violent storm during his passage to the East Indies and manages to swim to the shore of Lilliput. As soon as he comes into the Lilliputian orbit, its field of force, the descriptive mechanism of the language registers a shift in scale, a disturbance in the bonds between mind, body and world. After his lifeboat is overturned, Gulliver records, he 'swam as fortune directed me': 'I often let my Legs drop, and could feel no bottom: But when I was almost gone, and able to struggle no longer, I found myself within my Depth. . . . The Declivity was so small, that I walked near a Mile before I got to shore' (p. 7).

The encounter here with a long reach of shallow sea, is clearly preparing us for the spectacle of a magnified Gulliver arriving in a miniaturised land; we can see this, already, from a Lilliputian perspective, as the image of Gulliver wading hugely towards the shore from the far horizon. But what really prepares us for the Lilliputian episteme is the relation with his body that Gulliver experiences when he is still out of his depth, as he nears the Lilliputian border: 'I often let my legs drop.' There is surely something gargantuan in this phrase, which is perhaps triggered by the word 'drop', connoting the falling of a heavy object, but which is produced most of all by a sense that the body, as it already begins to swell by comparison with the Lilliputian landscape, the 'small declivity', exceeds the control of mind. There is a gulf between 'I dropped my legs' and 'I let my legs drop', a loss of subjective coherence in the passage from the former to the latter, that presages the unbinding of mind and body that Gulliver experiences in Lilliput, and that he witnesses later in his awed encounter with the giants of Brobdingnag. As he adjusts to his own relative bulk in Lilliput, the breath of estrangement from self that we can hear in Gulliver's distance from his legs grows more marked. On awakening to find himself tied to the ground by the gossamer thread of Lilliputian ropes, the sense of his impending massiveness leads to an odd separation of his parts. When the Lilliputians 'commanded that several ladders be applied to my Sides' (p. 9), the narrative catches the strange monumentalism of Gulliver's body, as his 'sides' become alien to him, already taking on the stony texture of a cliff face or a building; as he tries to free himself, he experiences the strange disaggregation of his parts attendant on the perception of bulk. He looks around him by 'bending mine Eyes downwards' (p. 7) and establishes what it is that binds him by breaking the strings that 'Fastened my left Arm to the Ground' and 'Lifting it to my face' (p. 8). This still delicate gap between controlling mind and distended body (can he not *feel* the binding on his arm, why does he lift it in this way to his face?) then grows out of all proportion, as his body becomes a massive, unstable, porous thing, a biomass, like the whale in Melville's *Moby Dick*, that could not possibly be controlled by Gulliver's delicate sliver of mind, that could not be brought under the jurisdiction of any integrating consciousness. And then, when Gulliver is in Brobdingnag, his encounter with the monstrous inhabitants gives him an insight into the bodily discomposure and porosity that is the effect of relative differences in scale. On one trip to town, Gulliver remembers being exposed to the 'most horrible Spectacles that ever an *European* Eye beheld':

> There was a Woman with a Cancer in her Breast, swelled to a monstrous Size, full of Holes, in two or three of which I could have easily crept, and covered my whole Body. There was a Fellow with a Wen in his Neck, larger than five Woolpacks, and another with a couple of wooden Legs, each about twenty Foot high. (p. 101)

To see the body so magnified is to be given a special access to its prosthetic materiality, and to its blurred edges, the uncertainty of the boundary between self and not self, between body proper and all that does not fully belong to the body (either in the daunting spectacle of the wooden legs here or in the fascination with the abject excretion of unalive waste matter from the body that runs throughout the novel). To see the holes in the flesh of the Brobdingnagian breast, the grotesquely open threshold between the inside and the outside of being, is to grant Gulliver the realisation that his own relative bulk in Lilliput disrupted the boundaries of his body. 'I remember when I was at *Lilliput*', he writes, a Lilliputian said, 'He could discover great holes in my skin; that the Stumps of my beard were ten times stronger than the bristles of a Boar; and my Complexion made up of several Colours altogether disagreeable' (p. 80).

The illusion of enormity generated by the experience of travel, by the interface that such travel enables between different peoples, produces, then, a sense of discomposure, of variousness, disaggregation, porosity. And conversely, the companion experience of littleness produces also an ejection of mind from body, but here in reverse. When Gulliver finds himself in Brobdingnag shrunk by comparison with the giants he encounters there, the boundaries of his body seem not grotesquely open but rather appear so contracted, so tightly closed, that there is no room within his body for the expansive movement of mind. If gigantism produces a baggy monster with porous skin which is so massive that consciousness cannot fully penetrate it, then miniaturisation produces the experience of automatism, in which Gulliver becomes nothing more than a toy, an intricate artificial contrivance driven not by mind but by clicking machinery. As the Brobdingnagians propose, when trying to decide what kind of creature Gulliver is, he seems not to be an autonomous subject or even a 'real' being, but some kind of facsimile or manikin, an artificial being 'in every Part of the Body resembling an human Creature' (p. 85). 'They all agreed', Gulliver says, 'that I could not be produced according to the regular Laws of Nature, because I was not framed with a Capacity of preserving my Life' (pp. 91–92). One Brobdingnagian considers he might be an 'Embrio, or abortive birth', another that he is some kind of extreme dwarf, and the King suggests that he 'might be a piece of Clock-work, (which is in that Country arrived to a very great Perfection) contrived by some ingenious artist' (p. 91). And, just as the language is infected with a disaggregated gigantism in Lilliput, so in Brobdingnag the rhythm and texture of the representation of Gulliver reflects and mimics such automaticity, taking on the characteristics of a piece of clockwork, of a marvellously delicate miniature automaton that is not fully alive or fully real. In displaying the wonders of his own bodily mechanism to his Brobdingnagian audiences, he adopts the repetitive movements and attitudes of a clockwork toy, as if his body has really become a wind-up machine. 'I walked about on the table', he says, 'as the girl commanded'. 'I turned about several Times to the Company, paid my humble respects. . . . I took up a Thimble filled with Liquor, and drank their health. I drew out my Hanger, and flourished with it after the manner of Fencers in *England*' (p. 86). As he becomes machine in this way, there is a distinct sense that mind can no longer fit inside this densely packed miniature contrivance of a body, that the thoughts that Gulliver has during his time in Brobdingnag do not find a proper lodging place in this tinny simulacrum of self. His keeper, Glumdalclitch, makes him a prosthetic home, a 'wooden chamber of sixteen Foot square, and twelve High; with Sash Windows, a Door, and two Closets, like a *London* Bed-chamber' (p. 93), and Gulliver attempts to live in the box, attempts to make of it a kind of reality, in which he could continue to reflect on his condition as an intellectually autonomous and self-fashioned being. But the pathos of this representation of a tiny Gulliver sitting in his box stems from the perception that with such diminishment comes the loss of a capacity for self-reflection, the reduction of being to diminutive thinghood, in which any pretension to self-authorship becomes merely comic. 'I sat quietly meditating at my Table' (p. 110), Gulliver says, and the proposition that a clockwork toy seated at a miniature table in a doll's house should have the desire or the capacity for meditation prompts us to laugh. Gulliver's depiction of himself as an autonomous thinker starts to look like self-deception, like the pitiful error of an artificial being that does not understand its own artificiality (a particular mode of irony that Kazuo Ishiguro deploys to great effect in his 2005 novel *Never Let Me Go*). Reflection, it seems, requires more room, demands a more spacious relation between body and mind. It is as ridiculous to the Brobdingnagians that Gulliver should aspire to serious thought as the niceties of Lilliputian politics seem ridiculous to Gulliver. It is hilarious to Gulliver to hear the Lilliputians fret about the doctrinal differences between 'Big-endians' and 'Little-endians', about whether their tiny heels are 'high' or 'low', in just the same way that the Brobdingnagian King submits to 'an hearty Fit of laughing' when he asks Gulliver 'whether I were a *Whig* or a *Tory*' (p. 95).

If the first two books of *Gulliver's Travels* prosthetise the body in this way, converting it into either insensate mass or artificial machine, it is in Books 3 and 4 that the anti-utopian tendency of this prosthetisation comes fully into focus. The disaggregation and dehumanisation of the body that develops in Lilliput and Brobdingnag are radicalised in the scientific academies of Laputa and Lagado in Book 3, which functions, among other things, as a satirical response to Bacon's *New Atlantis*. As I argued earlier, Bacon's work proposes an academy in which prosthetic and artificial life forms are added to or mingled with natural life to suggest how scientific advances might transform the lifeworld, might 'enlarge the bounds of the Human Empire' (p. 177). The utopian charge of Bacon's work relies on its capacity to bring natural and artificial life forms into a transformative contact with one another, as the optical devices of Bensalem can produce true seeing from the introduction of 'feigned distances'. In Swift's academy, however, it is precisely this kind of contact that is lost, as the prosthetic supplement or extension loses its contact with any human sensorium, and as the possibility that scientific endeavour might bring about a revolution in the technological capacities of the human gives way to a comic display of the vanity of the will to progress. In Swift's Lagado, as in Bacon's Salomon's House, the scientist dedicates himself to 'employing his Thoughts for the Improvement of Human Life' (p. 175), but here the investment of thought in mechanical technology becomes so complete that thought *becomes* machine, mind becomes equated with inanimate material, with prosthetic extension. In this crazed laboratory, a given person's thoughts can be deduced from a 'strict View of their Excrements' ('from the Colour, the Odour, the Taste, the Consistence, the Crudeness, or Maturity of Digestion' of the stools of the thinker, the academicians are able to 'form a Judgement of their Thoughts and Designs' (p. 182)), as if mind is fully present in its most material of waste products. The academicians contrive a wonderful thinking machine (a forerunner of the writing apparatuses in George Orwell's *Nineteen Eighty-Four* and Kafka's 'In the Penal Colony') whereby the 'most ignorant Person, at a reasonable Charge, and with a little bodily Labour, may write Books in Philosophy, Poetry, Politicks, Law, Mathematicks and Theology, without the least Assistance from Genius' (p. 176). And they seek drastically to diminish the role of language, again in a prevision of Orwell's dystopian state, aiming to replace words altogether, to prosthetise discursive practices by producing a vocabulary made exclusively of the objects for which words stand. 'Since Words are only Names for *Things*', they reason, 'it would be more convenient for all Men to carry about them, such *Things* as were necessary to express the particular Business they are to discourse on' (p. 177). This strategy allows the academics to banish the contractual relation between thought and thing, reducing the signifying movement of mind to the static self-presence of object. 'The Room where the Company meet who practice this art', the narrator notes wryly, 'is full of all *Things* ready at Hand, requisite to furnish Matter for this Kind of Artificial Converse' (p. 178).

In Laputa, mind becomes pure prosthetic, conversation becomes radically artificial; in the land of the Houyhnhnms, conversely, the prosthetic is banished altogether, as the inhabitants live a life that is complete to itself, unextended, untarnished by contact with anything extraneous to their own Apollonian being. It is not that the horses are pure mind – they are certainly embodied – but their embodiment is so natural, so in tune with mind, that there is no surplus, no place where the body is extended or enhanced by any kind of ornament or supplement. Nothing perplexes the Houyhnhnms more than prosthetic additions (they are bewildered by Gulliver's clothes and cannot understand why he has a 'false covering' to his body (p. 229)), and nothing horrifies them more than the idea that horses in Europe have 'a certain hard substance called *Iron* [fastened] to the Bottom of their feet' (p. 233). As the etymology of their name suggests (The Word *Houyhnhnm* in their Tongue signifies a *Horse*, and in its Etymology, *the Perfection of Nature* (p. 227)), the Houyhnhnms live in a utopia that resembles More's more than Bacon's, a pastoral, pre-technological utopia in which bodies are entirely sufficient to themselves, and entirely in keeping with the thoughts that animate them. As

J. M. Coetzee's Elizabeth Costello puts it, they live in the midst of a 'clear, rational, naked beauty'.[45] As, in More's Utopia, the 'laws are very few' (p. 82), and the people are 'so well governed with so few laws' (p. 37), so the Houyhnhnms have no law at all, no government. Their language, in stark contrast to the static, thingly dialect of Lagado, is saturated with their own personal experience and tuned to their own conception of natural justice. They have no terms in their language for prosthetic corruptions, for any perversion of or extension to autonomous rational embodiment. Famously, they have no conception of dishonesty – they use the clumsy locution 'saying the thing which was not' to signify dissembling, as 'they have no Word in their Language to express Lying or Falsehood' (p. 227). Similarly, 'Power, Government, War, Law, Punishment and a Thousand other Things had no Terms, wherein that Language could express them' (p. 236). Where Bacon's academicians and Cavendish's philosophers attach prosthetic additions to the natural, to use 'perspective glasses' to produce feigned distances and to bring nature to perfection through artificial means, the Houyhnhnms can only see straight, can only see the inch of the world in front of them, in the clear light of its natural sufficiency. Gulliver tries to teach his master to use a telescope, so he might be able to see a neighbouring island, to which Gulliver plans to head on leaving Houyhnhnm land: 'I took out my pocket glass, and could then clearly distinguish it about five leagues off.' The Houyhnhnm cannot make the island out, though – cannot see across a border into a foreign land and cannot learn how to see with the aid of a prosthetic device that reconstitutes things afar off as near. The island 'appeared to the Sorrel Nag to be only a blue Cloud', for 'as he had no Conception of any Country beside his own, so he could not be as expert in distinguishing remote Objects at Sea, as we who so much converse in that Element' (p. 273).

Of course, throughout this representation of a perfect accord between reason and nature, Swift never lets us forget that this picture of the rational animal is a joke, that Gulliver's own love affair with the Houyhnhnms contains more than a dash of the *thing which was not*. To find rational perfection in a brute creature is offered as a comic demonstration of the extent to which Gulliver's own reason has malfunctioned, has become divorced from its connection to his anthropoid body, to his species being. In referring to More's *Utopia*, in comparing Gulliver's admiration of the social life of the Houyhnhnms to More's admiration of Raphael, Swift suggests that the political function of utopian imagining has dwindled, become residual. More's meeting with Raphael, while always being ludic, yields the possibility of real transformation by bringing fanciful pictures of

'ought' into imaginary contact with realist pictures of 'is'; Gulliver's meeting with the Houyhnhnms is driven by and results in a more thoroughgoing misanthropy, a deep scepticism that scientific or political thought
can lead to a real transformation in the body politic – a loss of belief that
what the academicians of Lagado call a 'strict universal resemblance
between the natural and the political Body' (p. 179) could effect
a positive influence of the political on the natural. When Gulliver, under
the influence of the Houyhnhnms, asserts his love of truth – 'I imposed on
myself as a Maxim, never to be swerved from, that I would *strictly adhere to
the Truth*' (p. 284) – what we hear is the failure of the combination of the
serious and the playful that drives the utopian tradition to this point.
Gulliver's story about the Houyhnhnms – as the quotation from the
Aeneid, which Gulliver includes to season his commitment to truth telling,
suggests (p. 284) – is a Trojan Horse, a hollow prosthetic animal, used to
smuggle in Gulliver's, and Swift's, outright rejection of the idea that there
might be a true connection between thought and matter, between word
and thing, the idea that the mind might be read in the face. Gulliver's
apparent devotion to the Houyhnhnms, to their self-presence, their
breathing of what in the Preface he calls the 'Air of Truth', is cast satirically
as a rejection of the possibility of truth, a declaration that true thinking is
incompatible with the messy business of being, incompatible enough, in
the end, to lead to Gulliver's loss of species, to his radical alienation from
his own detaxonomised body, and from the body politic. If *Gulliver's
Travels* marks the far limit of what I am here calling the expansive tendency
in the eighteenth-century imagination – if in this novel the search for an
economy of scale that might allow us to locate a regulated colonial body
within a secure and properly proportioned 'idea of the world' most
radically fails – then this is in part because it is here that the utopian
binding between the real and the imaginary is at its loosest. Across the
range of the novels I have been discussing here – in the look that is shared
between Oroonoko and Imoinda in *Oroonoko*, in the gap between first
person narrative and island journal in *Robinson Crusoe*, in the circulation of
dismembered and monstrous bodies in *Candide* and *Millenium Hall* – one
can see the novel form testing and stretching the bonds that hold mind to
body, that hold words to things, the bonds that allow us to fashion gross
material into living worlds. The image of the prosthetic body that emerges
in all of these works, and most strikingly in *Gulliver's Travels*, is the
manifest sign of the failure of those bonds, a sign that thoughts can no
longer work on and in things. Both Gulliver and Candide retreat to their
gardens at the close of their narratives: Candide answers Pangloss's final

assertion that we live in the 'best of all possible worlds' by saying 'That is
excellently observed. But let us dig in our garden' (p. 104); Gulliver signs
off by declaring 'I here take a final leave of my Courteous Readers,
and return to enjoy my own Speculations in my little Garden at *Redriff*'
(p. 287). In doing so, both suggest that the task of world building, of
justifying the connections between our little inch of the world and the
wider networks within which we live is beyond the reach of philosophy or
of fiction. We cannot make pictures of worlds; all we can do is dig away in
our own patch, trying to cultivate a little life in the opening gap between an
alienated mind and the Procrustean bed in which it is required to lie.

In these writers, then, it might appear that prosthetisation is a mark of
the failed relation between mind and body, as the colonial encounter opens
distances in the heartland of the self. When Gulliver learns to despise his
own mirror image – 'when I happened to behold the Reflection of my own
Form in a Lake or Fountain', he says, 'I turned away my Face in Horror
and detestation of my self' (pp. 270–71) – this distance is given a powerfully
misanthropic form. But if we are to fully understand the prosthetic
imagination, as it develops through this anti-utopian strand in the eighteenth-century European novel, we have to recognise that prosthetisation
stages not only such a failure but also the emergence of a new and barely
articulable distribution of the sensible, a new way of imagining how life
penetrates and animates matter. William Mottolese writes that the prosthetic logic of the eighteenth-century novel suggests that 'word becomes
tool, and idea becomes machine', and indeed one can trace such a logic
operating in Sterne and in Swift.[46] But it is equally the case that in
performing the collapse of thought into thing, these novels produce
a new kind of thought-thing assemblage, against the grain of their own
satirical impulse, a kind of assemblage that is enabled by the rise of
fictionality, even as fictionality itself disturbs or refashions the utopian
relation between the real and the imagined. The representation of the
Houyhnhnms in *Gulliver's Travels* is unmistakably a joke, a satire directed
against the capacity of utopian thinking to produce a better and more
rational world; but it is equally unmistakably driven by a real political and
aesthetic desire, a yearning for a kind of body which is animated by reason,
in which essence is matched with appearance, in which natural justice is
given a material and manifest form. The satirical current in the novel
suggests that this body is unavailable; but the fictional medium itself
continually conjures such a body even in its absence, even as it recognises
that there is no available material or vocabulary in which it might find itself
realised (unless it partakes of Defoe's invisible ink). In a tract published by

Swift in 1704, entitled 'A Discourse Concerning the Mechanical Operation of the Spirit', one can see this contradiction already germinating. The discourse – a satirical response to Descartes' *Discourse on the Method* – offers to prosthetise the experience of 'religious enthusiasm', to demonstrate that the 'launching out' of the 'Soul' is 'purely an Effect of Artifice and *Mechanick Operation*'.[47] In making such an argument, the narrator of Swift's discourse produces that effect noted by Mottolese, in which idea becomes machine, thought becomes reduced to material. Life, from this perspective, becomes entirely a mechanical affair, the combustion of biofuel, rather than anything more spiritual or exalted. 'Human life', Swift writes, 'is a continual Navigation, and if we expect our *Vessels* to pass with Safety, thro' the Waves and Tempests of this fluctuating World, it is necessary to make a good Provision of the *Flesh*, as Sea-men lay in a store of *Beef* for a long Voyage' (p. 185). We are only our flesh, this argument goes. 'I am apt to imagine', Swift continues, 'that the Seed or Principle which has ever put Men upon *Visions* in Things *Invisible*, is of a Corporeal Nature; For the profounder chymists inform us, that the Strongest *Spirits* may be extracted from *Human Flesh*' (p. 186). As ideas can be deduced from excrement in *Gulliver's Travels*, so here spirit is simply a function or product of the flesh. But even as Swift is making this argument, the undertow of his language pulls in the other direction, suggesting the disjuncture between spirit and flesh, idea and material, a disjuncture that produces a kind of surplus, a form of thinking and being that exceeds the mechanical operations that give rise to it. The body can be seen as a thinking machine, Swift insists, 'the Spinal Marrow being nothing else but a Continuation of the Brain' (p. 186). But, of course, what Swift's rhetoric produces here is a great gulf between mind and brain, a recognition that, however inexpressible it might be, there is a movement of mind that is not reducible to its biological processing systems, that is not contained within spinal fluid. The body is a continuation of the brain, he says, as the spinal marrow 'must needs create a very free Communication between the Superior Faculties and those below'; but all the comical insistence here on the mechanical nature of the spirit produces is the recognition that the assemblage of mind and mechanical extension requires a different kind of technological and representational logic to find itself realised. If there is a junction between the superior faculties and those below, if there is, in Defoe's terms, a 'secret communication between those embody'd, and those unembody'd' (p. 176), then such a junction requires a new form in which to express itself – the form that is developed across the history of the eighteenth-century novel.

It is in Gulliver's disavowal of his own body that this movement of fiction, at the junction between the embodied and the unembodied, can most clearly be seen, as a manifestation of the double logic of the eighteenth-century prosthetic imagination. This disavowal bites perhaps most sharply at a peculiarly moving moment in *Gulliver's Travels*, as Gulliver seeks acceptance in the Houyhnhnm community. Gulliver's master describes him to the rest of the community, arguing that he is perhaps a special case, not a regular Yahoo but a species anomaly of some kind. The Houyhnhnm explains to his fellow horses that 'he had now in his possession a certain wonderful *Yahoo*', who might perhaps not be as despicable as the rest of the Yahoo species, to which he seems to belong. 'He then related to them', the narrator goes on, 'how he first found me; that my Body was all covered with an artificial Composure of the Skin and Hairs of other Animals: That, I spoke in a Language of my own, and had thoroughly learned theirs' (p. 264). Perhaps, the Houyhnhnm suggests, the special achievements of this wonderful Yahoo mean that he can stay with them, that he might be allowed admittance into their fraternity of reasonable creatures. But, of course, this is not to be, because, the narrator goes on, 'when he saw me without my covering, I was an exact *Yahoo* in every part' (p. 264). This is a devastating verdict – that underneath our false coverings, and regardless of the languages we might acquire, of the learning to which we might aspire, we are all irremediably human, all reducible to that monstrous body that we conceal beneath our clothing, that machine of flesh, endowed with claws to scrape at the earth, teeth to chew at our meat. It is a verdict that leads to Gulliver's expulsion from Houyhnhnm land, and his exile back to his garden at Redriff, to live among a species that he no longer recognises as his own. But if this moment suggests an equation between Gulliver's spirit and his human body, what Swift's novel demonstrates, undeniably, categorically, is that Gulliver is not an 'exact *Yahoo*', that he is not contained fully within his body, that the satirical movement of the fiction reaches, irresistibly, beyond the field of its own realisation. 'I sat quietly meditating at my table', Gulliver writes, as he finds himself trapped in a box in Brobdingnag, but the meditating mind that finds itself fictionalised as Gulliver does not fit inside that miniaturised automaton, any more than it belongs to the giant body that finds itself strapped to the ground in Lilliput. The fictional movement of Swift's novel summons a different kind of being, a different form of continuity between mind and extended body, than any that make themselves available to him, in life or in art. His 'book of travels', Gulliver writes in his phoney Preface, is not, as his detractors insist, 'a meer Fiction out of mine own Brain' (p. xxxv), and here we have to agree that Gulliver is right, that the fiction that is *Gulliver's Travels* does not emerge from Gulliver's brain, does not indeed have any mechanical, biological or intellectual domain in which it might find itself at home. Rather, it summons its own body, its own thought-thing assemblage, that does not have a world or a form in which it might be fully contained. This assemblage is a 'thing which is not', or not yet, a combination of the living and the non-living, the fictional and the real, which calls, even now, for a world which might be equal to it.

CHAPTER 3

Organic Aesthetics from Richardson
to Goethe

Let us have *Pamela* as *Pamela* wrote it; in her own Words, without
Amputation, or Addition.

Samuel Richardson, *Pamela*[1]

The first thing we notice about all the substances we encounter in
Nature is that each is always drawn to itself.

Goethe, *Elective Affinities*[2]

3.1   The Organic and the Mechanic

In the last chapter, I argued that the expansive tendency in the eighteenth-century novel leads to a particular dismantling of the structures
that guarantee the coherence and integrity of the fictional body. As
colonial forces put European subjects at a remove from themselves, so
the binding power that attaches mind to its material extensions is weakened, and the body appears as prosthetic attachment: machinic, numb,
remote from its central nervous system. Fictional bodies, under these
conditions, suffer the kind of failure of the reality effect diagnosed by
Samuel Beckett, when he complains, in a phrase I quoted earlier and to
which I will periodically return, of the refusal of his own fictional
creations to cohere, the 'reluctance of our refractory constituents to
bind together'. Their 'property', he writes, is 'not to combine but, like
heavenly bodies, to scatter and stampede'; they have a tendency not only
to 'shrink from all that is not they ... but also to strain away from
themselves'.[3]

From Behn to Defoe to Swift, the expansion of the colonial 'idea of the
world' leads to this disassembly, this straining away of biomaterial from
self-identity, from the animating control of consciousness. One of the
contradictions of the novel in this expansive mode, I argued, is that as
the body deanimates in this way, as it becomes prosthetic, it yields the faint
image of a whole body, a thought-thing assemblage, that haunts the text,

even as it appears unavailable, even as the language that is required to denote it is lacking. At the heart of Cervantes' masterpiece *Don Quixote* – a work that resonates across the eighteenth-century novel – one can find the longing for the possibility of a literary form that would allow us to picture a complete body, a non-prosthetic body. The Canon – the mouthpiece, arguably, for Cervantes' own aesthetic theory – invokes such a form in his denunciation of the fantastic and degenerate books of chivalry that are the target of the book's satire. Books of chivalry, he declares, 'are generally made up of so many limbs that they seem intended rather to form a chimaera or a monster than a well-proportioned figure'.[4] What is required of the literary imagination, he goes on, is a 'book with a whole body for a plot, with all its limbs complete, so that the middle corresponds to the beginning, and the end to the beginning and the middle' (p. 425). This fantasy runs through the expansive novel of the eighteenth century. One can perhaps hear a distant echo of the Canon's aesthetic philosophy in Book 3 of *Gulliver's Travels*, for example, when one of the academicians of Lagado shows Gulliver an absurd writing machine, which has produced 'several volumes in large Folio already collected, of broken Sentences, which he intended to piece together; and out of those rich Materials to give the World a compleat Body of all Arts and Sciences'.[5] These machine-made works, of course, are no more able to create a 'compleat body' than are the books of chivalry that Cervantes' Canon denounces. But Swift's novel closes with the invocation of a truly consistent body, one which is properly bound to itself, even if this invocation works against the grain of the novel's satire. The bodies of the Houyhnhnms, absurd as they are, are the site of a fantasy of organic completion, a fantasy in which the wholeness and integrity that Gulliver so sorely lacks is their natural condition. 'The *Houyhnhnms*, who live under the government of Reason', Gulliver writes in the final paragraph of the novel, 'are no more proud of the good Qualities they possess, than I should be for not wanting a Leg or an Arm, which no Man in his Wits would boast of, although he must be miserable without them' (p. 288).

The eighteenth-century novel is possessed by this fantasy of bodily completion, but such a fantasy only stirs in the novel imagination, in what I have called its expansive mode, as an effect of the experience of prosthetic dismantlement that is its central corporeal condition. It is as the body comes apart – as it degenerates into numb, dead flesh in *Oroonoko*, as it is washed in the surf of a distant island in *Robinson Crusoe*, as it appears as unregulated biomatter or miniature automaton in *Gulliver's Travels* – that the barely articulable figure of a whole body, a body fully animated and saturated by consciousness, comes to the fringes of the novel's thinking. But against this expansive mode, which reaches its height in Swift, we can detect an opposite tendency – a contractive tendency that moves not outwards, towards the colonial periphery, but inwards, towards the geographical and biopolitical centre (not a distant utopia, but a utopia of homeliness). Balanced against the image of the unruly body that recurs in the eighteenth-century novel, the body that has become unstable, porous, removed from itself, there is an image of the body that is utterly immersed in itself, a body at one with its own organic structure and, what is more, at one with the literary and discursive forms in which we encounter it. This contractive tendency is often entangled with the expansive mode: as I have suggested, one can find both the dismantled and the immanent working at the heart of Aphra Behn's *Oroonoko*, and the expansive urge itself throws up barely visible images of the immanent self that it seems to disavow. But it is also the case that one can trace a contractive lineage in the eighteenth-century novel that is devoted to the direct apprehension of a complete literary body, able to withstand the prosthetising effects of eighteenth-century colonial culture – a kind of organic aesthetics that emerges in the richly embodied novels of Samuel Richardson, particularly *Pamela* and *Clarissa*, that is at work in the very different, but equally somatically dense novels of Henry Fielding (particularly in *Tom Jones*, each of whose parts open with an 'initial essay' (p. 181) that advances a kind of organic literary theory), that stretches through the novels of Frances Burney, particularly the early epistolary novel *Evelina*, and that finds its most intense expression in the novels of Johann Wolfgang von Goethe, in *The Sorrows of Young Werther* and in the late masterpiece *Elective Affinities*.

For this group of writers, the spectacle of the prosthetic body (monstrously misshapen or mechanically automated) that exerts such fascination in Voltaire, in Swift or in Sarah Scott, is perceived as a threat to the experience of integrity, of self-sameness, that it is the novel's dominant aesthetic and political aim to preserve and articulate. In the prefatory material to Richardson's 1740 novel *Pamela*, one can see an early formulation of this organic mode, and of the terms in which it might resist the increasingly powerful incursion into the natural, in mid to late eighteenth-century European culture, of the artificial, of the augmented, automated, technologised or inhuman. The letters that open the novel enthuse about the intimacy of the epistolary mode that Richardson fashions in 1740, its capacity to enter into the inner experience of consciousness in a way that enables us to distinguish between that which truly belongs to the living self and that which is an extension or impersonation or corruption of it. That the novel proceeds by letters 'written under the immediate Impression of every Circumstance which occasioned them' means that 'Nature may be traced in her undisguised Inclinations' (p. 5). In these letters, Pamela 'pours out all her soul . . . before her parents without Disguise; so that one may judge of, nay, almost see, the inmost Recesses of her Mind' (p. 8). It is this intimacy that allows us to see Pamela in her organic completeness, without either what Sarah Scott called a 'deficiency' or a 'redundancy', with neither too much of the self, nor too little.[6] Pamela reveals herself in her letters in her 'native simplicity' as 'Sterling Substance' instead of 'empty Shadow'. 'Let us', the author of the prefatory letter writes, 'have *Pamela* as *Pamela* wrote it; in her own words, without Amputation, or Addition' (p. 9). It is one of the deeper historical insights of Swift's *Gulliver's Travels*, to recognise that the combination of enlightenment thought with the growth of a cosmopolitan, colonial public sphere would lead to the mechanisation, the prosthetisation of our selves and our environments – to the loss of an organic connection between consciousness and its external cultural and biopolitical forms. The machine-made books, the prospect of Gulliver's automatised body, scraping and bowing and performing mindless clockwork manoeuvres on a tabletop, these are the signs of this encroachment of the artificial into the very springs and cogs of the self, and of the forms in which we give the self a voice. As Richardson opens *Pamela* – perhaps the most intense fictional exploration to date of the inner movement of the private mind – he sets the novel's access to thought *as nature* against the sense that selfhood can be replicated, can be mechanically reproduced.

Across the second half of the eighteenth century, from Richardson's *Pamela* to Goethe's *Elective Affinities*, one can see the growth of this investment in the organic bond between the novel and the natural, unaugmented self, as it sets itself against the sense that European cultural forms and environments themselves are becoming ever more artificial. The image of the clockwork self, which makes an early appearance in *Gulliver's Travels*, becomes an increasingly powerful figure for the apprehension that new social relations, new enlightenment paradigms and new forms of technology have led to an evacuation of mind from mechanised social being – to the possibility that we can construct all of our cultural and discursive forms, as Gulliver puts it, 'without the least Assistance from genius' (p. 176). This partly takes the form, as Julie Park has persuasively demonstrated, of satires on the empty automatism of public modes of self display that one can trace in the society novel from Burney to Edgeworth and Wollstonecraft, as well as in the appearance of eighteenth-century conduct manuals from John Essex's *The Young Ladies Conduct* (1722) and

George Lord Savile's *The Lady's New-year's Gift* (1724) to Thomas
Gisborne's *An Enquiry into the Duties of the Female Sex* (1806).[7] Savile,
for example, deplores the empty vanity of the cosmetically enhanced
woman by comparing her to an automaton. 'She cometh into a Room',
he writes, 'as if her Limbs were set on with ill made screws, which maketh
the Company fear the pretty Thing should leave some of its *Artificial
Person* upon the Floor. She doth not like herself as *God Almighty* made
her, but will have some of *her own* Workmanship'.[8] For Savile, the society
woman 'hath fallen out with *Nature*, with which she maketh war', but the
perception that the self has become automatised reaches far beyond the
remit of conduct manuals and touches on the most central discursive and
intellectual formulations of the period. The publication, in 1747, of Julien
Offray de la Mettrie's *L'Homme machine* offers a theoretical defence of the
automated self, which reads as a literal version of Swift's earlier satire on the
'Mechanical Operation of the Sprit'. La Mettrie's thesis 'conclude[s] boldly
that man is a machine', arguing that 'since all the soul's faculties depend so
much on the specific organisation of the brain and of the whole body', then
we should naturally reach the understanding that 'they are clearly nothing
but that very organisation'.[9] This thoroughgoing machinisation of the
human, Aram Vartanian and Joseph Rykwert have argued, comes about
as a result both of intellectual and of technological shifts across the
seventeenth and eighteenth centuries. La Mettrie's 'radical step',
Vartanian writes, 'was perhaps an inevitable outgrowth of the seventeenth-
century scientific attitude':

> Once science was held capable of understanding things, ideally, only in
> terms of more or less measurable quantities and motions, there remained
> hardly any choice for psychology, insofar as it too wished to be scientific, but
> to model its investigation on that of mathematical physics, and to assume
> finally that man, like the cosmos, was a machine.[10]

As Rykwert argues, this intellectual defense of mechanised being is closely
bound up with the invention and manufacture, across the eighteenth
century, of increasingly elaborate automata and other clockwork machines
that were designed to replicate human being. 'The increasing diffusion of
precise, refined, mechanical skills at the outset of the industrial revolution',
Rywert writes,

> culminated in an explosion of interest in, and of skill in making, *androids*.
> Automatic 'writers,' flautists, trumpeters, and even a swimming, quacking,
> digesting duck coincided with the intellectual elaboration of Descartes's
> view, that corporal man is just one special case of *res extensa*, into the

doctrinally materialist *homme-machine* and *homme-plante* of Julien de la Mettrie.[11]

The fascination with the automata that Rykwert refers to here can be seen developing across the course of the eighteenth century. The duck that he mentions is presumably Vaucanson's duck, created by Jacques de Vaucanson in 1739, described by Edgar Allen Poe in 1836 as a 'perfect imitation of the living animal' that 'performed all the quick motions of the head and throat which are peculiar to the duck' and 'produced also the sound of quacking in the most natural manner'.[12] Of the 'automatic writers' that Rykwert mentions, the most striking example is Pierre Jaquet-Droz's 'Writing Boy', manufactured in 1774 (see Figure 3.1). 'Writing Boy' remains to this day a deeply uncanny example of the eighteenth-century skill in creating automata that reproduce human actions with an astonishing, auratic precision. Jaquet-Droz's boy can be programmed to write any

Figure 3.1 Jaquet-Droz, 'Writing Boy'. Pierre Jaquet-Droz, *The Writer*, 1774, clockwork automaton, Musée d'Art et d'Histoire de Neuchâtel. Photograph by Rama.

script up to forty characters and once set in motion will dip his pen in his pot of ink, gently flick his wrist to shake off excess ink, and then write with a flowing natural hand, his nib scraping on the parchment, his eyes following the movement of his pen as it crosses the page. To witness this clockwork movement, to see the boy's studious concentration as he writes, has a dramatic and unnerving effect on the observer, tending to hollow out our conception of human agency, to cause our own sense of self and of independent will to suffer a collapse or malfunction. To see the boy's eyes following his pen, to consider that there is nothing guiding these movements but the clicking machinery that packs his small body, with no mind intervening between hand and eye, leads to a frightening loss of our investment in the magical supplement of consciousness – a feeling that has led a number of writers to respond to such automata with a striking defensiveness. Edgar Allen Poe gives one of the most famous such defences of the human against the automaton in his discussion of an automaton manufactured in 1769 – Maelzel's famous artificial chess player that Walter Benjamin invokes in 1940 as an example of the apparently automatic and inevitable progress of 'historical materialism'. Poe describes Maelzel's mechanism and its movements at length – the automaton, named the Turk, is able to take on any opponent at chess, and to play exactly like a skilled human player – and he does so to demonstrate to us that the machine cannot, *could not*, play in such a fashion, that it is inconceivable for a machine to behave and to think as only a human could. The machine appears to be entirely automated – like Jaquet-Droz's writing boy, Poe says, the 'whole interior is apparently filled with wheels, pinions, levers, and other machinery, crowded very closely together, so that the eye can penetrate but a little distance into the mass.'[13] But Poe finds this an intolerable idea – that dense clockwork could replace the weightless movement of mind – and sets out to demonstrate that the movements of the machine are the effect of what he calls 'human agency', that it is 'quite certain that the operations of the Automaton as regulated by *mind* and nothing else' (p. 11).

Poe's solution to the puzzling intellectual prowess of the Turk is to argue that there is a chess-playing dwarf stowed behind the clockwork in the body of the automaton – the hidden human figure that, in Benjamin's later analogy, becomes the 'theology' that secretly steers the course of historical materialism (theology which 'today, as we know', Benjamin writes, 'is wizened and has to be kept out of sight').[14] The movements of the machine are, Poe concludes, driven by mind after all. But while Poe seeks to defend the human from the incursion of the machine, the arguably most influential response to the eighteenth-century development of the mechanised, prosthetised human is altogether more nuanced. Heinrich von Kleist's 1810 essay 'On the Marionette Theatre' is, like Poe's later essay, a response to the perception that the boundary between the human and the machine is blurred by the development of forms of artificial life. Kleist's essay is staged as a dialogue which takes place 'One evening in the winter of 1801' between a narrator and his 'old friend' who is a dancer; the latter frames the discussion of the relation between mind and machine by referring to the developing art of prosthetics. 'Have you heard', he asks the narrator, 'of those artificial legs made by English craftsmen for people who have been unfortunate enough to lose their own limbs?' When Kleist's narrator replies that he has not, the friend claims that there is something about these prosthetic limbs that allows for a kind of movement that the purely human body cannot easily achieve:

> 'I'm sorry to hear that,' he said, 'because when I tell you these people dance with them, I'm almost afraid you won't believe me. What am I saying ... dance? The range of their movements is in fact limited, but those they can perform they execute with a certainty and ease and grace which must astound the thoughtful observer.'[15]

For the friend, what is so astounding about the prosthetic limb, and about the movement of non-living automata more generally, is that they exhibit a kind of natural grace that is unavailable to the human, because the latter is cramped and hampered by the experience of self-consciousness. The prosthetic limb can perform a natural movement, the friend says, that he has also observed in the spectacle of puppets dancing in a marionette theatre, a dance which he says is more graceful and natural than anything that could be achieved by human performers. Where Poe insists that the movement of Maelzel's chess player has to be controlled by mind, that it is only though such control that the automaton could achieve so effective a reproduction of human life, the friend insists that there is no necessary or straightforward connection between the mind of the human and the artificial limb or dancing puppet that it controls. Kleist's narrator imagines that the human must exert some kind of control over the puppet, as Poe's dwarf exerts control over the Turk. 'I inquired about the mechanism of these figures', the narrator says, 'I wanted to know how it is possible, without having a maze of strings attached to one's fingers, to move the separate limbs and extremities in the rhythm of the dance' (p. 13). But the friend replies that the puppets have a control of their own, independent of the influence of the puppeteer, as the books in the academy of *Gulliver's Travels* are written 'without the least Assistance from Genius'. 'I must not imagine each limb as being individually positioned and moved by the operator in the various phases of the dance', he tells the narrator: 'Each movement has its centre of gravity; it is enough to control this within the puppet. The limbs, which are only pendulums, then follow mechanically of their own accord, without further help' (p. 13). One can deduce from this, the friend goes on to argue, that inanimate matter has an ease, a natural identity with itself, that the human, caught as it is between spirit and body, mind and matter, cannot acquire. The perfectly natural movement of the prosthetic limb, the puppet, the automata, gives us a foretaste of the grace to which we might attain, rather than representing a simple mindless copy of a fully human animation to which it cannot aspire. The emergence of prosthetic technology, of artificial copies of the human, allows us to see, the friend concludes, that 'as thought grows dimmer and weaker, grace emerges more brilliantly and decisively' – that 'Grace appears most purely in that human form which . . . has no consciousness' (p. 18).

It is against this failure of the distinction between the animate and the inanimate, between mind and matter, that one can trace the development of organic aesthetics in the eighteenth-century novel, from Richardson's articulation of the 'inmost recesses' of Pamela's mind onward. As life finds itself increasingly replicated by inorganic mechanical forms, as the capacity of human beings to conjoin mind with matter is weakened, it is the novel that is offered, repeatedly, as the form that is best able to penetrate into the secret junction between consciousness and material – to discover and articulate the principles that bind living beings together, that give conscious life its organic and animated unity. The narrator of Henry Fielding's 1749 *Tom Jones* acknowledges that there is a machine-like quality to the environment that he describes. 'The world', he says, 'may indeed be considered as a vast machine', but it is the gift of the novel to see deeply into the workings of this machine (as Poe sees deep into the workings of Maelzel's automaton), to understand, with more precision and penetration than has before been possible, how the machine turns, and what the conscious forces are that drive it. The 'great wheels', he goes on, extending his clockwork metaphor, 'are originally set in motion by those which are very minute, and almost imperceptible to any but the strongest eyes' (p. 194). It is the novelist, Fielding suggests, who has the strongest eyes of all, who can discern the subtle forces that produce a character such as Tom Jones – the novelist who is able (in Fielding's near quotation of Richardson) to 'pay a visit to the inmost recesses of the mind' (p. 137). If there is a principle that matches the great wheels with the minute, that brings the outward manifestations of life into harmony with the impercep-tible motion of consciousness, then it is the novel, with its special access to interiority, that allows us to grasp such a principle. *Tom Jones* shapes a form that allows us to match the manifest outer material of life with the hidden inner, and it is the task of the eighteenth-century novel of interiority, particularly the epistolary novel, to bring this junction between the inner and outer onto the page. For Guido Mazzoni, it is only towards the end of the century, and with the novels of Frances Burney, that the novel's particular 'way of expressing the mimesis of interior life was fully intro-duced into English narrative fiction'.[16] It is the capacity to follow the movements of Evelina's mind, in Burney's *Evelina*, that gives us arguably the fullest picture in the English novel up to that point of the ways in which mind expresses itself in form, and in language. And it is in the work of Goethe, in his own epistolary novel *The Sorrows of Young Werther*, and his later *Elective Affinities*, that the capacity of fiction to reproduce the condi-tion of organic life reaches its greatest intensity. For the young Werther, as for Goethe himself, art is involved in a mutually productive relationship with 'nature'. Art is described by Werther as a 'true feeling for Nature, and its true expression',[17] and Goethe himself developed his aesthetic philoso-phy in tandem with his natural philosophy, with his scientific work on organic life forms and plant morphology.[18] When, in his 1808 novel *Elective Affinities*, he describes the relations between the characters in his domestic drama in terms of their organic affinities for one another, this analogy is the culmination of a life's work devoted to understanding the causal relation-ship between organic structures in nature and the organic unity of literary form. Where Beckett's narrator complains that the elements of his work 'strain away from themselves', the character named 'the Captain', in Goethe's *Elective Affinities*, suggests that both living beings and works of art are held together, tightly bound to themselves by their internal organic unity. 'The First thing we notice about all the substances we encounter in nature', the Captain says, 'is that each is always drawn to itself' (p. 30). It is through close attention to these principles in nature, and as they intensify in the 'human being', who is 'after all superior by several degrees to those natural substances' (p. 34), that the artwork is able to tune itself to the truth of nature, the vital principle that drives life and thought, that is missing in the clicking machinery of the artificial, the human-made.

It is as the writers and theorists of eighteenth century develop these figures of organic form that they shape the conception of the novel as an interior, human form that can withstand the encroachment of the mechan-ical into the production of culture – a conception that remains central to our understanding of the novel, and of literary aesthetics more generally, over the following two centuries. One can feel the direct influence of Goethe on Coleridge when, in a lecture on Shakespeare in 1818, he proposes an enduring theory of organic form. 'Only nature creates a great artist', Werther declares, and Coleridge echoes him, arguing that 'art can not exist without, or apart from nature'.[19] To understand the world-making power of art, it is necessary to distinguish sharply between 'mechanical regularity' and 'organic form'. 'The form is mechanic', Coleridge says,

> when on any given material we impress a pre-determined form, not neces-sarily arising out of the properties of the material; – as when to a mass of wet clay we give whatever shape we wish it to retain when hardened. The organic form, on the other hand, is innate; it shapes, as it develops, itself from within, and the fullness of its development is one and the same with the perfection of its outward form. (p. 55)

The organic work of art is shaped from within, from the inmost recesses of mind: 'each exterior', Coleridge writes, 'is the physiognomy of the being within' (p. 55). And it is the novel, above all other forms, that gives us closest access to this connection. As D. H. Lawrence puts it in a letter of 1915, in terms that again directly oppose organic unity to prosthetic supplement (and that perhaps carry a faint echo of Tristram's crushed nose in Sterne's *Tristram Shandy*, and an even fainter echo of Thelyphron's defacement in *The Golden Ass*), 'a novel, after all this period of coming into being, has a definite organic form, just as a man has when he is grown. And we don't ask a man to cut off his nose because the public won't like it: because he must have a nose, and his own nose too.'[20]

3.2   The Full and the Empty

It is in Frances Burney's 1777 novel *Evelina* that the capacity of the epistolary novel to capture the organic unity of consciousness is given one of its fullest explorations. Whereas in Richardson's depiction of Pamela, 'Nature may be traced in her undisguised Inclinations' (p. 5), Burney in her preface declares that her Evelina is the 'offspring of Nature, and of Nature in her simplest attire'.[21]

The epistolary form allows Burney access to Evelina's natural grace, to her much admired 'artlessness', her untutored inclination towards the just and the good, because, as with Richardson's earlier novels, her letters give us access to the 'Fair writer's most secret thoughts' (p. 5) and allow us to follow the movement of her young mind as it is in the process of becoming, and as she faces the difficulties and obstacles that are placed in the way of a young woman seeking to acquire a public identity in the exacting arena of English polite society. The prospect of entering society is particularly daunting for Evelina because the circumstances of her birth are obscure. Her mother died shortly after her birth, and her father, Sir John Belmont, refused to acknowledge the legitimacy either of his marriage to Evelina's mother or consequently of his paternity of Evelina. As a result, Evelina is brought up in a secluded village by her doting guardian, the Reverend Mr Villars, who reluctantly allows Evelina out of his grasp, and into society, at the opening of the novel. The majority of Evelina's letters are addressed to Mr Villars and depict, in Evelina's own bright and vivid prose, her unfolding fortunes in society – her struggle to fend off the amorous advances of the men who abuse and exploit her, her slowly dawning realisation of her love for the honourable Lord Orville, her eventual reconciliation with her biological father, and hence her rehabilitation as a legitimate member of the aristocracy.

Evelina's letters grant us access to this process of becoming – her passage from uncertain orphanhood to established wife and daughter – in such an intimate fashion that the reader feels part of the inner movement of her thoughts. Evelina declares, in one of her early letters to Villars, that 'I shall write to you every evening all that passes in the day, and that in the same manner as, if I could see you, I should tell you' (p. 29), and it is difficult to escape the feeling that we too are being addressed with this intimacy, that we too are present at the scene of Evelina's shy emergence to herself. But if Evelina's letters attain this proximity to the fissile, changing inner self – if they come to us, in the words of Evelina's mother, in a letter that she writes to Evelina's father on her deathbed, as a 'cry of nature' (p. 401) – it is nevertheless the case that they bear witness to a self that is placed at a remove from its own nature, that is troubled by its own forms of artificiality. At a haunting moment in Richardson's *Pamela*, Pamela's parents, to whom she addresses her letters, warn her not to allow praise of her beauty to cause her to feel pride. 'Besure', they write to her, 'don't let People's telling you you are pretty, puff you up: for you did not make yourself, and so can have no Praise due to you for it' (p. 20). Pamela did not make herself – she has only a temporary responsibility for the body that she bears, which belongs not to her, but to God. And, similarly, the single most insistent refrain in *Evelina* is that Evelina did not make herself, that she was fashioned, not by God, but by Mr Villars. Villars writes to Evelina after her first trip to London, expressing his fear that her 'residence in the great world' (p. 135) will have spoilt her, and begging for a 'few lines' from her that will 'assure me' that 'this one short fortnight spent in town, has not undone the work of seventeen years spent in the country' (p. 137); Evelina's reply is unsettling in its apparent submission to Villars as the architect of her self, in its attribution of the 'work' of her becoming solely to Villars, rather than to herself. 'No, my dear sir, no', she replies, *'the work of seventeen years* remains such as it was, ever unworthy your time and your labour, but not more so now, – at least I hope not, – than before that fortnight which has so alarmed you' (p. 137). Throughout the novel, at key points in Evelina's development, she writes to Villars to give this reassurance, and to cast herself an object of his creation. 'You know my heart', she writes to Villars, when her biological father first rejects her, 'you yourself formed it' (p. 187); when she is struggling to obey his stern command that she should remove herself from the company of Lord Orville, she writes to Villars – the 'parent of her heart' (p. 397) – to insist that 'the wish of doing well governs every other, as far as concerns my conduct, – for am I not *your* child? – the creature of your own forming?' (p. 397).

Evelina represents herself, in this way, as an artificial being, a surrogate self who stands in for Villars, and whom he controls by letters sent from his remote village location. Villars himself hammers this point home, repeatedly reminding Evelina that her purpose is to be a comfort for him in his old age, and to extend his being past his own life span, when, as he puts it, 'the fleeting fabric of life would give way' (p. 497). As Villars writes in an early letter to Lady Howard, 'I have cherished, succoured and supported [Evelina], from her earliest infancy to her sixteenth year; and so amply has she repaid my care and affection, that my fondest wish is now circumscribed by the desire of bestowing her on one who may be sensible of her worth, and then sinking to eternal rest in her arms' (p. 16). Where, in Behn's *Oroonoko*, Locke's declaration that 'Every Man has a *Property* in his own *Person*' is countered by the self-estranging experience of slavery and colonisation, here, Evelina's self-ownership is undermined by the sense that she is the creation and the property of Villars, that she is 'new to the world, and unused to acting for myself' (p. 362). In the environment depicted by Burney, Evelina and other powerless figures in her social group are represented as agents with only the slightest control of their bodies, which are much more powerfully represented as the property of others. As Richardson's Pamela is the fragile (but extraordinarily tenacious) custodian of her precious body, whose purity she has to bravely defend against the men who more effectively own and control it, so Evelina's experience of social life is chiefly characterised by her desperate attempts to 'act for herself,' to control and safeguard her physical person, as lustful men stow it into carriages against her will, dance with it on the dance floor and in other ways wrest control of it from her.

This experience of surrogacy, of a gulf between the inner mind and the external social persona in and as which it is required to act, can be felt everywhere in Burney's novel. The surrogate relationship between Villars and Evelina, for example, is given a much crueller expression in the blackly comic and powerfully shocking scene late in the novel, in which friends of Lord Orville – Merton and Coverley – settle a bet by requisitioning two elderly women from the neighbourhood and forcing them, despite their age and frailty, to race against each other. The old women, who have no power, status or agency of their own, are depicted simply as avatars for the gambling men. 'They set off', Evelina writes to Villars, 'and hobbled along, nearly even with each other, for some time, yet frequently, and to the inexpressible diversion of the company, they stumbled and tottered; and the confused hallowing of '*Now Coverley!*' '*Now Merton*' rung from side to side during the whole affair' (p. 369).

It is hard not to see a parallel between these women, forced into such a degrading spectacle to act out a squabble between two men, and the plight of Evelina, who is similarly unlicensed to act for herself, and who is remotely controlled by Villars. And if the scene of the racing women makes a mockery of the idea that powerless women have a property in their own person, then this lack of autonomy is given another kind of expression in the novel's recurrent fascination with automata, with the artificial mechanical contrivance that is offered as the key figure for the superficiality and ethical bankruptcy of eighteenth-century society. There is something clockwork-like about the racing women, about their appearance as empty receptacles for the will of Merton and Coverley, and this sense that society reduces women to automata is felt elsewhere. The boorish Captain Mirvan strikes an echo from George Savile's conduct manual, for example, when he castigates women for wearing make-up ('half of 'em are plaguy ugly, – and, as to t'other half, – I believe it is none of God's manufactory' (p. 127)), and the group visit, early in the novel, to 'Cox's museum' suggests how central the condition of mechanical artificiality is to the experience of social display. The museum, which was based at Admiralty Arch from 1772 to 1776, held one of the most lavish collections of automata in eighteenth-century London – and indeed contained several examples of Jaquet-Droz automata. Evelina is fascinated by the mechanisms but also a little disturbed by them, as if she can feel the resemblance between the machines and her own artificial construction. 'The museum is very astonishing', she writes to Villars, 'and very superb; yet, it afforded me little pleasure, for it is mere show, though a wonderful one' (p. 89). As Julie Park has observed, Evelina's unease during her visit to the museum – her 'sense of lack in her encounters with its mechanical toys' – is generated in part by the perception that they represent the 'adherence to the dazzling semblance of life' that the larger culture evinces, 'as opposed to its unmediated presence'.[22]

Evelina is beset, in this way, by forms of artificiality, and by signs that she herself is artificial, that she does not own herself and did not make herself. But if this is so, it is the central poetic aim of the novel to counteract this artificiality, to perform, *in real time*, the process by which Evelina's mind becomes itself and takes possession of her body, rendering herself natural and organically complete. This process requires, both of other characters in *Evelina* and of ourselves as readers, that we are alive to the distinction between the real and the artificial, that we can distinguish true life from mechanical replica. The response to Cox's automata is, in a sense, an early test of this critical, readerly capacity. It is a mark of the ghastly Madame Duval's comic falsity, her deafness to the sound and sight of true beauty, that she is entranced by the mechanisms. 'I'm sure', she says of Cox's collection, 'if you don't like this, you like nothing; for it's the grandest, prettiest, finest sight that ever I see, in England' (p. 89). 'I declare', she says of an automated pineapple, that 'in all my travels, I never see nothing eleganter', and when the 'entertainment concluded with a concert of mechanical music', Madame Duval 'was in extacies' (p.90). Evelina, with her natural, artless sense of the truth of things – her intuitive adherence, in Coleridge's terms, to the organic rather than the mechanic – can see that there is a missing element to the automated display, a lack which is difficult for her to define, but which lies at the very heart of the novel's commitment to the bound relation between art and natural truth. 'It's very fine, and very ingenious', she says to the odious Willoughby, 'and yet – I don't know how it is, – but I seem to *miss something*' (p. 89). There is a difference between the real and the artificial, between the organic and the mechanic, Evelina suggests, that one can sense, even if one cannot easily codify or define it – and it is precisely this sense that the novel seeks to cultivate, as it enters into the process of Evelina's coming to consciousness of herself through the writing of letters. Evelina's hesitant discovery of something missing in automata suggests a cognate awareness of some quality latent in herself, something that it is the task of true self-congress to supply. Lord Orville suggests this cognate in terms that echo Evelina's words, and that stand as a declaration of the novel's own poetic credo. Orville, like Evelina, finds that Cox's automata are lacking in something, that the 'sight of so fine a shew only leaves a regret on the mind' (p. 129). In a later discussion concerning make-up – debating the question of whether Evelina's beautiful complexion is natural or the result of 'rouge' – Orville comes to the defence of her naturalness in terms that suggest a direct opposition between the mechanic and the organic. 'The difference of natural and artificial colour', he declares, 'seems to me very easily discerned': 'that of Nature is mottled, and varying; that of art, *set*, and *too* smooth; it wants that animation, that glow, that *indescribable something* which, even now that I see it, wholly surpasses all my powers of expression' (p. 93). The mechanical perfection of art, the precision of the automata, cannot capture the varying truth of animation, which even as it is written on Evelina's face, and even as for Lord Orville it is perfectly easy to discern, resists articulation and surpasses the powers of expression. The task that the novel sets itself is to generate this power of expression, in a series of letters which emerge from the recesses of Evelina's mind, and which demonstrate the difference between the natural and the artificial self, which articulate that indescribable *something* which is missing from the prosthetic copy.

Of course, such a manoeuvre is a high-risk strategy, not least because writing itself is artificial, subject to forgery. One of the events around which the novel turns, for example, is the delivery of a false letter, seeking to open an illicit correspondence with Evelina. The letter purports to be from Lord Orville, but we eventually learn that it comes in fact from Clement Willoughby. This act of treachery, as with the inclusion of false letters in Richardson's epistolary novels, threatens to invalidate the entire basis upon which the novel founds its claims to intimacy and to truth. There is nothing to tell us that these words did not come from Orville's pen – the false letter from Willoughby has the same status as the true letters upon which we base our understanding of Evelina's world – and so the effect, for Evelina and for the reader, is to cast our capacity to read character as it is expressed in words and in letters into doubt. Evelina herself responds to the shock of Orville's immodest proposal above all as a *reader* – as someone who has just awakened to the duplicity or mobility of written signs. Like an undergraduate newly discovering the possibilities of close reading, she marvels, in a letter to Miss Mirvan, at the instability of the word, its multivalency. On 'first perusal', she was 'delighted' by the letter, with its suggestion that Orville loves her. But, she says, 'upon a second reading, I thought every word changed, – it did not seem the same letter, – I could not find one sentence that I could look at without blushing' (p. 305). This is an extraordinary moment in the narrative, at which the novel destabilises, mercurialises, its own medium. If every word can change, with the shifting impression of the reader, then how can words ever enshrine that missing something in which the truth of one's natural being might be said to inhere? As Evelina herself says, the letter leads her to vow that 'never, never again will I trust to appearances' (p. 303), and as she later puts it to Villars, it allows her to 'see how differently the same man can *talk* and *write*' (p. 316).

This treachery of words, this uncertain relation between the way things are and the way they appear in writing, is at work throughout the novel, for example in its delight in anagram and word play. Evelina herself is cast, at a knowingly metafictional moment, as literary effect, when Villars compares his relationship with her to reading a 'book that both afflicts and perplexes me' (p. 312), and of course the false name she goes by in society, Miss Anville, is a near anagram of Evelina, while also carrying echoes of Villars' name, and, troublingly, of Orville's. But the novel takes this risk, throws itself into the difficult, shifting territory of a writing that reveals its own artificiality, to perform the production of truth through writing – a truth that is expressed most forcefully as fullness, as the discovery of a condition of being in which one is full of oneself, in which one no longer experiences something missing. The beauty of the novel, its own artfulness, arises from its capacity to catch at the vivid, animated artlessness of Evelina's voice, to reveal the inner screen upon which she projects her own thoughts – and to do so in a way that makes it easy to distinguish, as Orville puts it, between the natural and the artificial. The novel shows us shifting acts of reading, shows us the process by which Evelina reads herself into true being, to demonstrate how words, despite their malleability (or perhaps because of it) cleave to the inner workings of mind and allow us to differentiate between the original and the fake. The false letter, supposedly from Orville but really from Willoughby, is lifeless, a dud, showing none of the graceful subtlety of Orville's speech. And as the novel traces Evelina's growing sense of self, we find that she is increasingly able to judge this difference; to inhabit her own language; and to establish a congruence between her public person, her private mind and the social and discursive forms which bind them together. Throughout the novel we are alerted to the uncanny similarity between Evelina and her dead mother; in the earlier stages of the narrative, we might see this similarity as another sign of Evelina's surrogacy – the sense that she is an after-effect of a previous and more vivid life, and so placed at a remove from herself. But as she comes, through writing, to self-ownership, this similarity, combined with another act of writing – the letter that her mother left for her at her death, the 'cry of nature' pleading with Belmont to recognise Evelina's legitimacy – helps her establish her identity in all its fullness, in the midst of her self-presence. She presents her father first with her face (whereupon he recognises immediately 'the certainty I carried in my countenance, of my real birth' (p. 442)) and then with the letter from her mother ('Great Heaven', he says ''tis her writing' (p. 455)), and the combined effect is to bring Evelina into that full self-presence that eludes her through the narrative to this point – a self-presence she describes repeatedly as a fullness of heart. As her courtship with Orville reaches its climax, she tells him that 'my heart was too full to bear [his] kindness' (p. 434), and as she struggles to express her devotion to her biological father, she again offers her full heart as a sign of her true biological identity, a sign which she implores him to read. 'O sir', she says, 'that you could but read my heart! – that you could but see the filial tenderness and concern with which it overflows' (p. 454). As the novel draws to its close, as Villars takes his valedictory leave of his surrogate daughter, it is this coming together, of fullness of heart with a writing that has forged an organic connection with the life it describes, that it bequeaths us. 'Yes my child', Villars writes in his final letter, 'thy happiness is engraved, in golden characters, upon the tablets of my heart! And their impression is indelible.' It is his dying wish that Evelina will end her life, as Villars himself ends his, 'full of days, and full of honour' (p. 479).

If there is an organic aesthetic at work in *Evelina*, then it is found in this capacity to shape a writing that attaches itself closely to mind, as mind realises itself in its own natural manifestations, in the countenance that carries the mark of its real birth. The word 'Evelina' might be an anagram, might be an effect of a slippery, mercurial language, but it becomes, in the novel's closing image of a heart of beaten gold, an anvil – not a forgery, but a forge upon which the substance of the true heart, the heart that is full of its own being, might be fashioned. This is a novel, in the words of Julia Epstein, that is written with an 'iron pen'.[23] But if this is so, what is so remarkable about *Evelina*, and about the eighteenth-century epistolary novel more generally, is that the closer the novel comes to the inner recesses of mind – the more intimate its address to that hidden place where language establishes the binding of mind to biological matter – the more insistently it discovers also a lacuna at the heart of being. It is as the eighteenth-century novel in its contractive, intimate mode draws most closely into itself that it opens pockets of estrangement. It is as the novel becomes full of its own being – as it penetrates most fully into the momentary instance of its own inscription – that it opens onto an ontological emptiness that insinuates itself into the heartland of self-presence, and that is an underlying condition of the prosthetic imagination.

In one sense, this contradiction appears most clearly at those times when the intensity of the recorded experience *produces* its own failure of articulation – the moments when fullness of being leads directly to stupefaction or emptiness of expression. In *Evelina*, as in Pamela and *Clarissa*, the epistolary record of the trials of the heroine lapses at those moments when their distress or their joy overwhelms them, making the act of writing impossible. When, for example, Pamela is on the point of being raped by Mr B. in *Pamela* – 'he kissed me with a frightful Vehemence; and then his Voice broke upon me like a Clap of Thunder. Now, *Pamela*, said he, is the dreadful Time of Reckoning come' (p. 203) – she suffers a loss of consciousness which means, she writes to her parents, that 'your poor *Pamela* cannot answer for the liberties taken with her in her deplorable State of Death' (p. 204). Similarly for Evelina, the moments of greatest despondency and happiness lead to a period of silence and muteness. When Evelina is labouring under the impression that Lord Orville had insulted her with his secret letter, she writes to Miss Mirvan of her grief, in what she calls a 'cold, inanimate letter, which will but ill express the feelings of the heart which indites it' (p. 300). Her gloom, her 'heaviness of heart' (p. 301), is so deadening, she writes, that she cannot narrate it: 'I cannot journalize', she writes to Miss Mirvan, 'cannot arrange my ideas in to order' (p. 302). And conversely, when Orville declares his love for her, she falls silent from an excess of joy. When she sees signs of Orville's affection for her, she writes, 'my heart [is] too full for speech' (p. 317); the climax of the novel, the moment that Orville tells her that 'you are dearer to me than language has the power of telling' (p. 416), falls into a peculiar lapse in the narrative, something like Pamela's 'deplorable State of Death'. 'I attempt not to describe my sensations at that moment', she writes to Villars, 'I scarce breathed; I doubted if I existed' (p. 416). As Orville's capacity to distinguish between the natural and the artificial is based on a sensibility that 'surpasses all my powers of expression', so here, at the moment of becoming, language fails. 'I cannot write the scene that followed', Evelina writes, in a phrase that foreshadows Villars' final letter, 'though every word is engraven on my heart' (p. 416).

The moment of becoming, when being is full, is also the moment when language is empty; words that engrave themselves on the heart cannot find their way on to paper, as if narration requires that something missing that Evelina can see in Cox's automata for it to become articulable, and decipherable, *as* narrative. But if fullness produces emptiness at these extreme moments – when one might feel that narrative, like Villars, has done its job and delivered Evelina either into accomplished personhood or non-existence – it is also the case that emptiness shadows fullness *at every moment* in the novel, that emptiness is a by-product of the immediacy that the epistolary novel grants us, in this moment of its historical development. If, as Mazzoni argues, the epistolary form produces a new 'mimesis of interior life' in the later eighteenth century, and if the haphazard journalising that Defoe deploys in *Robinson Crusoe* has matured here into an unprecedentedly intimate address to the inmost processes of self-fashioning, then the cost of this intimacy is the insistent discovery of a kind of distance, a kind of deferral, installed in the most withdrawn recesses of being, deep in the regions where we come to a consciousness of our selves. 'Now', Mr B. says to Pamela, 'is the dreadful time of reckoning come'. Now – now is the most important word in the epistolary novel. I am writing these letters now, as life unfolds before me, as I work my way into being, 'under the immediate Impression of every Circumstance which occasioned them'. I am writing, Evelina tells Villars, and tells us, in 'the same manner as, if I could see you, I should tell you'. Epistolary novels are set in the moment as it unfolds, in the intercostal sinews of the present tense. But the very narrative process which grants us access to this immediacy tells us, at the same time, that 'now', as the arena and environment of our immediate being, is not susceptible of narration or of occupation. Now is always evacuated, is always translated into what has just happened or what is about to happen. 'I cannot Journalize', Evelina writes; an exhausted and traumatised Pamela says that she will 'lay down my tired Pen for this Time' (p. 219). But the refusal to journalise, the exhausted cessation of writing, can only take place in writing, just as the moment of fullness, the moment of vivid and total being, can never quite squeeze itself onto the page, is always dismembered by the difference, the deferral, that letter writing is. The closer writing gets to immediate experience, the more forcefully it acknowledges that it comes after or before that which it represents – a coming before or after that, we then are led to discover, is present in our own address to ourselves, a lag that is there in the processes by which we come to thought and to feeling.

This deferral is present, even at the moment that is offered as the novel's origin, the 'cry of nature' that Evelina's mother makes on her deathbed, pleading with Belmont to recognise the image of herself that she leaves behind. She makes this plea at the instant of her death, and it is the magic of the epistolary form that it can overcome this extinction, that it can preserve an act of communication, even as it yields to death, and bring it into the midst of a new becoming. 'When I am no more', Evelina's mother writes, 'when the measure of my woe is compleated, and the still, silent, unreproaching dust has received my sad remains – then, perhaps . . . the voice of equity, and the cry of nature may be heard' (p. 401). The moment of that desperation, and that hope, is preserved in the letter form and vividly reanimated, as Evelina presents it, with the truth that rests in her 'countenance', to her father; but the preservation of a cry of nature in writing always takes place in the shadow of a death – the death that happens every time that the evanescent 'now' congeals into an accomplished act of life. It is the mimetic achievement of the epistolary form to stretch and to preserve the moment in which we come to life before ourselves, but it can only achieve this by discovering that life itself, life as it happens in the moment, is composed of the death that it holds in abeyance, the ecstatic emptiness that moves in each and every instance of self consummation.

3.3   Attachment and Evasion

> There is no surer way of evading the world than art, and no surer way of attaching oneself to it.
>
> Goethe, *Elective Affinities*[24]

It is in Goethe's prose fictions – in *The Sorrows of Young Werther,* in *Wilhelm Meister's Apprenticeship,* in *Elective Affinities* – that this contradiction between the full and the empty, between plenum and void, as the product and medium of a novelistic organic aesthetic, reaches its most intense expression.

It is easy to see that Goethe's fiction, however dissimilar it is in its sublime *Sturm und Drang* intensity from Burney's mannered society novels, emerges from the same traditions that shaped Burney's literary thinking, and that gave rise to the later eighteenth-century epistolary form. As J. M. Coetzee has observed, Goethe learned from Richardson and Sterne, and from Rousseau's *La Nouvelle Héloïse*, 'how a narrative can evolve on the basis of a character's self-disclosure' – a form of narrative evolution that is intimately related to the epistolary and journal forms.[25] If Goethe's poetics is driven by a sense that art is fundamentally related to nature – is itself an expression of nature that in Coleridge's words 'shapes itself and is developed from within'[26] – then it is the immediacy of the epistolary form, its capacity to trace the inmost movement of Coetzee's 'self-disclosure', that allows for this organic connection between art and nature to come about. As Richardson's portrait of Pamela allows us to 'almost see' the 'inmost Recesses of her Mind' (p. 8), so the epistolary form in *Young Werther* and the journal form in *Elective Affinities* produce the same effect. It is the decision to 'disclose some items' from Ottilie's diary in the second part of *Elective Affinities* that allows the narrator, as he puts it, to achieve 'an insight into her inner life' (p. 116), and the letters from Werther to 'Wilhelm', that make up the bulk of *Young Werther*, allow for an extraordinarily naked contact with what Werther calls the 'powers lying dormant in me' (p. 29). It is the epistolary form, as Werther puts it, that allows him to 'reveal ... all of the wonderful feeling with which my heart embraces Nature' (p. 29), and that allows him to 'really grasp ... the true and inmost nature of an action' (p. 60).

Goethe works partly in the epistolary tradition that reaches from Richardson to Burney, and one can see too a number of parallels between Burney's use of the form and Goethe's. One of the principal aims of *Evelina* is to develop a living form, in which contact with 'innerness' transforms narrative from lifeless prosthetic, artificially attached to experience, to the vivid province of that experience itself. The immediacy of the epistolary address allows her to approach a narrative 'now', and to enshrine this passing time in a graven form that lends to the 'moment', as Virginia Woolf later puts it, 'something permanent'.[27] Goethe's use of the form follows a similar path and couches itself in similar terms. In her dejected mood, Evelina despairs, in a passage I have already quoted, of the capacity of dead paper to take on the life of the mind: 'this cold, this inanimate letter', she writes, 'will but ill express the feelings of the heart which indites it' (p. 300). Werther echoes her, wondering how letters could capture the organic life of his loved one, Lotte. 'How', he asks, 'can these cold, dead words on the page convey the divine flowering of her spirit?' (p. 71); the answer, for Goethe as for Burney, is to fashion an art which can become the life that it witnesses, can give a human narrative shape to the sublime vividness of nature and transfix the flow of being in time in the achieved shape of a stilled image. When Werther is filled with joy by his encounter with nature, when 'I am alerted to the thousand various little grasses; when I sense the teeming of the little world among the stalks, the countless indescribable forms of the grubs and flies', his desire is to find a language or an art that can take on this teeming life, that can shake off its cold deadness by becoming itself alive – by partaking of his own intense animation. 'If only you could express this', he says to himself, 'if only you could breathe on to the paper in all its fullness and warmth what is so alive in you' (p. 71). For Werther, as for Eduard in *Elective Affinities*, the task is to tune ourselves to the life of nature, what Jane Bennett would call the vibrancy of matter, to understand how organic forms exhibit a vitality that is everywhere around us, but which defies our expressive capacities. We are surrounded, Eduard says, by 'entities' which 'seem lifeless' but which have, in fact, 'a sort of volition' – the 'lively vitality' that Bennett finds in 'nonhuman bodies, forces and forms', but whose distribution 'resists full translation and exceeds my comprehensive grasp'.[28] These 'entities', these organic forms, Eduard goes on, 'need an observer who will watch with some engagement of his sympathy', to see how they operate in nature, how they 'seek one another out', how they 'attract and seize, destroy, devour and consume one another'. 'It is then', he says, 'that one credits them with eternal life' (p. 34).

The organic urge in Goethe's art is driven by the desire to penetrate this 'eternal life' that moves in natural forms, to capture Werther's fullness and warmth on the paper, to make of an artificial mimetic form – a sequential narrative that unfolds in time – something instantaneous, all embracing, infinite. It is partly for this reason that his fiction is inhabited by stilled images, tableaux in which the flux of a teeming, multifarious life, passing recklessly from moment to moment, is fixed into a still and replete form. This takes the form, at one point in *Elective Affinities*, of an actual *tableau vivant* display in which Ottilie appears as the Virgin Mary – a picture composed of 'reality itself', in which Ottilie's gesture and form are 'held frozen' in an extended 'instant', and whose intensity 'excelled anything a painter has ever depicted' (p. 157). The tableau allows Goethe to imagine a form in which a replete instant is stretched over time, and in which life itself is married to artistic representation, in a living moment that does not pass away but sustains itself magically and indefinitely so that, the narrator says, 'any sensitive connoisseur, seeing this sight, would have been fearful lest anything move' (pp. 157–58). But if Goethe depicts a literal *tableau vivant* in *Elective Affinities* – and if Goethe's novel thinking has a natural (elective) affinity with the logic of the *tableau vivant* as a form – one can see moments of frozen embodiment, stilled living moments, recurring across his oeuvre.[29] When Werther first meets Lotte, for example, he sees her, famously, in the form of a tableau, a moment of frozen time, that appears immediately as a picture (and indeed is one of the scenes in Goethe's work that has been most frequently illustrated). 'I crossed the courtyard to a well-built house', Werther writes to Wilhelm,

> and, climbing the flight of steps in front, opened the door and beheld the most charming scene I have ever set eyes on. In the hallway, six children between eleven and two were milling about a girl with a wonderful figure of

medium height, wearing a simple white dress with pink ribbons at the sleeve and breast. She was holding a loaf of rye bread and cutting a piece for each of the little ones about her. (p. 37)

The sight, the fullness of the image, is what causes Werther to fall in love – 'my entire soul was transfixed', he writes – and as he becomes increasingly obsessed with Lotte, it is her capacity to inhabit her being fully that possesses him, her capacity to merge mind and form in a moment that does not pass away. When he dances with Lotte, this sense of self-possession again overwhelms him. In terms that predict Kleist's essay on the marionette theatre, Werther dwells on the grace of Lotte's movements. 'You should see her dance!' he writes to Wilhelm, 'Her whole heart and soul are in it, you see, and her body is all harmony, so carefree and relaxed, as if there were nothing else, as if she had not a single other thought or sensation; and, in that moment, undoubtedly everything else ceases to exist for her' (p. 40). When Werther is forced into exile from Lotte, when he finds himself dancing at an entertainment with strangers, he finds how empty the world is without her, how cold and dead. 'There is not a single instant when the heart is full', he writes, 'not one single hour of bliss'. Without her, all those around him, and he himself, are reduced to auto-mata, to wooden dolls. Forced to dance himself, he feels 'like a puppet'; 'from time to time', he goes on 'I grasp my neighbour's wooden hand and withdraw with a shudder' (p. 78).

The poetic energy of Goethe's fiction is concentrated on the production of forms which enable him to capture Lotte's fullness, as opposed to the wooden lifelessness of that prosthetic hand, and to respond to the extra-ordinary variety of throbbing, buzzing life that he sees diffused throughout the world before him, while composing that variety, that diffuseness, into a human shape, a living fictional body, in the terms adopted by Cervantes' Canon, 'with all its limbs complete' (p. 425). But, just as Burney finds that the fullness of the epistolary form is shadowed by an emptiness that the form itself produces, so, for Goethe, the intensity of his search for a mode of art which can capture nature in its infinity leads him to produce expressive models which are remarkably unstable, which just as they seek to accom-modate 'eternal life' collapse under their own weight, returning living, breathing being to the lifeless replica from which Werther withdraws with a shudder. Goethe's master figure for the expression of life, for the composi-tion of vital forces into the concentrated being that Lotte experiences in dance, is the human – the human body, the human being. It is this investment in the human that leads Ottilie, despite her affinity with the

sublime, into a strangely narrow anthropocentrism. Echoing Eduard's interest in the endless diffusion of vitality through the organic environment,
Ottilie is drawn to the mystical and unknowable variousness of the 'natural
world'. 'A natural history cabinet can seem like an Egyptian tomb with the
different animal and plant gods standing around embalmed' (p. 169), she
writes, but she only allows herself this thought to insist that this near-erotic
promiscuity of living being must be contained within a fixed hierarchy that
privileges the human. 'No doubt', she writes of her imaginary Egyptian
cabinet, 'it would be right for a mysterious priesthood to busy itself with
such things in semi-darkness'; but, for her own sense of nature to remain
legible and proper, she has to think at a human and a local scale. She is not
interested in 'the whole series of inferior forms of life with all their names
and structures' because, she insists, the 'best and nearest likeness of divinity is
worn by man' (p. 169). If we are fascinated by the natural world, she
concludes, in agreement with Alexander Pope's *Essay on Man*, we must
suborn proliferating nature to the grace and balance of the human, as 'the
proper study of mankind is man' (p. 169).[30] Ottilie employs the figure of the
human as a means of composing diffuse nature into shapely form, as the
grace of Lotte's dancing body brings the ephemerality and variousness of
being into distilled, embodied presence. But even as she does so, Goethe's
fiction itself resists such form, finding in the constraints of composition not
only legibility and grace but also a kind of constriction to nothing, a formal
stiffening that expels the very life it seeks to contain. One can hear a dialogue
that spans the thirty years between *Young Werther* and *Elective Affinities*, in
which Werther repudiates Ottilie's anthropocentrism, strenuously rejecting
the idea that his 'immense and ardent feel for nature' might be contained
with any given taxonomy. Contemplation of the 'infinite species of creation', of 'every speck of dust that is alive', Werther writes, 'revealed to me the
inmost, sacred warmth of the life of Nature'. The 'glorious forms of infinite
Creation moved in my soul', he says, 'giving it life' (p. 65). But to frame this
abundance within a human idea of the world is to kill it stone dead, to
desecrate it rather than to sanctify it. 'Everything', he writes, 'is peopled with
myriad forms': 'and then mankind comes building its nests, crowding
together safely in little houses, and supposes it rules over the whole wide
world! Poor fool! imagining everything to be so small, because you yourself
are so small' (p. 65). 'It is as if', Werther writes, as he contemplates this
humanising of the infinite, 'a curtain had been drawn from before my soul,
and this scene of infinite life had been transformed before my eyes into the
abyss of the grave, forever open wide' (p. 66).

The imposition of form makes being legible, but in doing so it renders it artificial, transforming the quick into the dead; everywhere in Goethe's fiction, one can see the effects of this contradiction, this double bind. The more fully the prose invests itself in the bound immanence of being – the more closely it attaches itself to the 'inmost life of nature' – the more insistently it encounters a kind of vitality that it cannot formalise, a vitality that evades it. The mark of this evasion is a certain distance that installs itself at the heart of being in Goethe's prose, a distance that is at once spatial and temporal, that separates nature from itself, and that separates one moment from the next. One can find this distance opening even at those moments when the focus on immanence, on stilled being, it at its most intense. The tableau scene in which Werther first meets Lotte, for example, trained as it is on a revealed moment of being, is inhabited too by a sense of movement, a sense of temporal extension, that works against the stasis of the image, and that erodes the capacity of the artwork to capture or contain. As the composed, painterly sight of Lotte surrounded by her children overwhelms Werther, the tense registers a peculiar contradiction between the still and the moving. 'She was holding a loaf of rye bread and cutting a piece for each of the little ones about her, according to their age and appetite' ('Sie hielt ein schwarzes Brot und schnitt ihren Kleinen rings herum jedem sein Stück nach Proportion ihres Alters und Appetits ab');[31] Lotte's holding of the bread can work as an image, like the frozen action of a player in a *tableau vivant*, but the prose slips almost imperceptibly from this completed, contained action to the cutting of the bread, and then to Lotte's handing of the slices out to the children around her, who 'reached up their little hands' and 'cried out their artless thanks' – actions which shift Lotte from a perfectly bound and completed entity to an agent who continues to become and act in time. As Samuel Beckett's Molloy puts it much later, this is a moment that is both complete and in process, both outside of time and still being fashioned by it. 'At the same time', Molloy says, 'it is over and it goes on, and is there any tense for that?'[32] When Lotte cuts bread for the children, when she experiences a fullness of being in the dance, Goethe's prose seeks to follow her into still completeness; but in doing so, in relishing her supple, living being, it returns her to moving time, to time that takes her away from herself, and from Werther's transfixed conception of her. As Werther asks himself, despairing of entering into the congress he seeks with Lotte, and with the teeming ecology that he sees before him, 'Can you say that anything *is*, when in fact all is transient?' (p. 66). 'There is not one moment', he writes to Wilhelm, 'that does not wear you away' (p. 66). A distance is woven into passing time, a distance between one moment and the next in which one loses oneself and others; this is the very distance that Werther finds intervening between himself and the 'natural world' – the world that he so yearns to find reflected or distilled in his 'soul'. To see a landscape spread before us, to see opening 'before our souls' an 'entire and dusky vastness which overwhelms our feelings as it overwhelms our eyes' (p. 44), is to long to overcome the gulf that separates us from all that surrounds us. But Werther finds that it is that very distance, like the emptying action of passing time, that allows us to reach towards the form of completed being which distance makes impossible. It is distance, in space and time, that allows us to become – that opens the space into which we pour ourselves. When this distance is eradicated, Werther writes – when the view that he sees from his window appears to him like 'a varnished painting' (p. 98), with all of its distances composed in fixed relations to one another, and 'all the glories of Nature are frozen to my eye' (p. 98) – then nature itself withers and dies. Distance makes the world unavailable to us, erects great stretches of unnavigable emptiness between ourselves and the world, between the person we were and the person we will become; but it is only the aesthetic preservation of such distance, such self-destroying emptiness, that allows us to reach towards ourselves, and towards others. Distance is like a kind of dying, a kind of self-loss; but distance, too, as Werther puts it to himself, 'distance is like the future' (p. 44).

It is the central poetic task of Goethe's fiction to produce a mode of art that preserves this distance, as the province of an unlived futurity, while at the same time overcoming such distance, absorbing it into moments of ecstatic becoming. Both Werther and Ottilie are manifestations of such an art – an art which discovers an immeasurably deep flaw in being right at its innermost foundation. 'Have you really grasped the true and inmost nature of an action?' (p. 60), Werther asks of Lotte's husband Albert; it is Werther's gift as an artist to see into the intricate workings of an action, to see those tiny wheels driving the larger turning of things that are perceptible, Fielding says, only to the 'strongest eyes'.[33] But, of course, the action that Werther is thinking of here, the action the 'mere thought' of which the sensible Albert finds 'repellent' (p. 60), is suicide, willed death. Werther is seeing here into the space of self-murder, the deathly ground that underlies all being, and that Shakespeare's Hamlet struggles and fails to bring to the palpable space of the Renaissance stage. It is Werther's discovery that the final guarantor of life is not the teeming vastness of nature but the emptiness from which life emerges and to which it returns – the emptiness that resists our perception, but that constitutes the very possibility of perception. Suicide, as Andrew Bennett has written, opens onto a non-being in Goethe's work, in which Lotte and Werther disappear, as 'the "world was lost to them"'.[34] As Werther writes, in his suicide letter to Lotte, 'there are such constraints on human nature that we have no feeling for the beginning and ending of our existence' (p. 127); but the suicide letter itself is the closest that Goethe can come to discovering this 'feeling', this attachment to the ground of being, the difficult feeling of self-ownership. 'Now I am still my own', he writes to her, as he prepares to shoot himself in the head, and this 'now' is the now of the epistolary form, the now in which the immediacy of living thought is brought into contact with its groundlessness, with the emptiness that works in the smallest interstices of the moment. Werther's art brings him into contact with the place where life dissolves into death, the place, he writes, where 'my entire self trembles on the edge of being and not-being' (p. 99). Similarly, Ottilie, living work of art that she is, finds herself skewered on the threshold that the artwork inhabits between being and not being. When she finds herself acting as the Virgin Mary in a *tableau vivant*, when she finds herself worshipping in a church that an artist who has fallen in love with her has decorated with painted images all of which resemble her, she discovers that the intensity of the artwork, the experience of feeling oneself shaped into self-recognition by representational forms, confirms her in her being and evacuates that being at one and the same time. 'She sat down in one of the stalls', the narrator says, 'and it seemed to her, as she looked up and around, as though she existed and did not exist, as though she had feelings and had none, as though everything might vanish before her eyes or she herself might vanish even as she looked' (p. 130). As Ottilie herself puts it, in one of those cryptic diary entries that give us an 'insight into her inner life' (p. 116), it is the role of Goethe's art to bring us so close to the foundations of self-congress, to give us such intense access to the process by which we bind ourselves to the time and space of our being, that we see at once the stuff of self-extension and the emptiness from which it emerges. 'There is no surer way of evading the world than art', she writes, 'and no surer way of attaching oneself to it' (p. 152). At a certain level of experiential intensity, brought to the edge of cognition by art, she discovers that attachment *is* evasion, that the place where we meet with our extended being is the place where we free ourselves from it.

It is this discovery of a kind of non-being at the intimate heart of being that characterises the workings of the eighteenth-century prosthetic imagination in its contractive mode. At a critical moment in *Young Werther*, Goethe appears to acknowledge the opposition between the expansive and the contractive urges in the eighteenth-century imagination – that opposition which has shaped my discussion of the development of the novel form over this time. 'I have thought a great deal', Werther writes, 'about Man's desire to go out into the world, make new discoveries and go a-wandering; and on the other hand, about that deep-seated impulse to be contented with limits that are imposed, and gladly to proceed as custom dictates' (p. 44). The expansive drive of the eighteenth-century novel, as I have characterised it here, is a response to the desire to 'go out into the world,' to 'go-a-wandering', at a moment when the limits of world seeing are expanding at an exponential rate. The forms of organic decomposition that we find in the novels of Defoe, Swift, Scott, Voltaire – the biopolitical volatility and fungibility of the prosthetic body under the conditions of an emergent European colonial modernity – are determined by this desire to go out into the world. This wanderlust produces a disassembling of biological and intellectual forms, while also generating, as I have argued, the first stirrings of a new kind of mind-matter assemblage, a body at home in a world that is only just coming to thought. It is against this expansive urge that the organic aesthetic I have been tracing in this chapter asserts itself. The innerness of the epistolary form in Richardson, in Burney, in Goethe is a response to the need, as deep-seated as any lust for colonial or imaginative expansion, to live within the environs of the self, to find the vastness of nature 'mirrored', as Werther puts it, in one's own soul. But what this intense analysis of interiority discovers is that colonial distance lies not only at the fringes of our idea of the world and of ourselves but also in its deepest midst. Burney and Goethe strive, in their different ways, to discover a form which can banish the spectre of the prosthetic self – the clicking automata of Jaquet-Droz and Maelzel, the lifeless marionettes that have no self-consciousness in Kleist – which can replace automated being with the full, living self. But even as they do so, even as the dancing body of Lotte offers a rebuke to the prosthetic wooden hand of Goethe's marionette, the novel of interiority discovers that the soul, in the throes of its most intimate encounter with itself, is riven by a hidden prosthetic junction, an evasive seam running in the midst of the self-same. As the strong eyes of the novel peer into the hidden recesses of the mind, to see the turnings of its nearly invisible cogs and wheels, what they see is that there is a gulf between mind and its extensions buried in the depths of being, that at the heart of the inner self there is a gap, as uncrossable as the gap that we find between the hand and the eye of Jaquet-Droz's writing boy, or between the mind of the wizened chess player and the body of Maelzel's automata, or between the mind of the dancer and Kleist's puppets, or between Tulp's hand and eye in the varnished surface of Rembrandt's anatomy paintings. At the heart of the self, in the midst of its immanence, as it is engraved in the organic form of the artwork, there is a distance at work, a distance that is like the future.

And this, finally, is what the eighteenth-century prosthetic imagination discovers and bequeaths to us, and to the fiction that comes after it. The novels of the colonially expanded body discover the outlines of a nearly inarticulable biopolitical assemblage, lying dormant in the images of biological diffusion and monstrosity that recur in Swift, Voltaire and Scott. The inward novels of organic wholeness, in giving us pictures of bodies that are nearly themselves, open distances in the heartland of the self, intimate places and moments where we do not coincide with ourselves, and where the past reaches towards an unthought future – moments of non-existence captured in art, as Werther puts it, when 'the past flashes upon the dark abyss of the future like lightning' (pp. 99–100). Kleist writes, in his essay on the marionette theatre, that since the expulsion of the human from the Garden of Eden, there has been a gulf between the conscious mind and the body in which it finds extension. There is no way back to the state of innocence, he says, as we can find no way of relating to our bodies without rehearsing that trauma of expulsion experienced by our first parents. 'Paradise is locked and bolted', the narrator's friend says, and 'now that we've eaten of the tree of knowledge', the gulf between consciousness and the body is 'unavoidable' (p. 15). But Kleist's essay closes with a complicated optical metaphor that points towards the possibility, as he sees it, of producing a different kind of relation with the body, one in which the body is no longer prosthetic attachment, but a living expression of the self. There is a chance, he says, that Paradise is 'open somewhere at the back' (p. 15), and that we might see onto this secret opening by learning to look into a mirror that shows us not ourselves as we are now, but ourselves perfected at our infinitely extended historical limits, as Thomas More finds himself perfected in the word-mirror in which he sees Raphael. 'As the image in a concave mirror turns up again right in front of us after dwindling into the distance', Kleist writes, 'so grace itself returns when knowledge has as it were gone through an infinity' (p. 18). If Goethe's exploration of innerness discovers not attachment but evasion, if what lies at the heart of the self is not the purest being but a kind of flickering non-existence, then it is in maintaining these images of non-existence that the prosthetic imagination preserves a form of distant futurity, a pocket of non-being which is the closest we can come to grace.

PART III

The Manufactured Body: From Wollstonecraft to Stoker

CHAPTER 4

The Dead Hand: Realism and Biomaterial in the Nineteenth-Century Novel

My nature is subdued
To what it works in, like the dyer's hand.

William Shakespeare[1]

Thus the hand is not only the organ of labour, it is also the product of labour.

Frederick Engels[2]

4.1 Irony and Biocritique from Wollstonecraft to Austen

She thought she was hastening to that world *where there is neither marrying*, nor giving in marriage.

Mary Wollstonecraft, *Mary*[3]

Seldom, very seldom, does complete truth belong to any human disclosure; seldom can it happen that something is not a little disguised, or a little mistaken.

Jane Austen, *Emma*[4]

The history of the novel, as I have characterised it to this point, is to a significant degree a history of handedness (as, for Heidegger, 'the hand is the ground of the essence of man').[5] The hand belongs to the self; 'in the common view', Heidegger writes, 'the hand is part of our bodily organism.'[6] It is the organ that gives us the closest haptic proximity to the world; but it is also part of that world itself, an object which has its own material existence apart from mind, and whose independence, whose thingliness, is one of the great challenges to the bound integrity of the self. 'The hand does not only grasp and catch, or push and pull', Heidegger goes on, 'The hand reaches and extends, receives and welcomes' (p. 16). As Elaine Scarry puts it, in her luminous response to Marx and Engels' understanding of handedness, the hand is a product of the world that it

149

seeks to shape. 'The hand', she writes, 'has been, through long engagement with the resistant surfaces of the world, itself woven into an intricate weave of tendons, ligaments, muscles and bones' (one can hear, here, a scintillating echo of Don Quixote's regard of his own knightly hand, 'the structure of its sinews, the interlacement of its muscles' (p. 393)).[7] The hand crosses a boundary – *materialises* a boundary – between mind and world, and it has been the job of the novel as I have read it here, from More to Cervantes to Behn to Burney to Goethe, to approach that boundary, to work at the junction between the unextended and the extended self to bring under the jurisdiction of narrative those spaces where the command of mind over matter is at its most precarious. From More's investment in the discursive production of the early modern state to Goethe's framing of a narrative form in which to couch the contradictions of romantic self-hood, the novel has responded to the shifting ways in which the hand has been technologised and prosthetised by its participation in the sphere of things. The hand evolves as a tool among other tools, and the history of the novel doubles as the story of our means of accommodating this evolution, of making the hand, as a thing in the world, also a property of the undivided self.

Over the course of the nineteenth century, this relationship between the narrative imagination and the experience of handedness intensifies, for two intimately connected reasons. The first of these is mechanical and related to the accelerating history of the manufactured lifeworld across the century. As critics and cultural historians from Raymond Williams to Eric Hobsbawm to Laura Marcus have demonstrated, this is the century in which the texture of lived experience, the very epistemological encounter with space and time, is most rapidly transformed by the advent of new mechanical and reproductive technologies, from the spread of the railway and steam power; to the development of widespread artificial lighting; to the advent of electricity; to advances in telescopy and microscopy; to the arrival of telephony, photography, gramophony, cinema.[8] As Freud writes in *Civilization and Its Discontents*, in a passage I quoted earlier, these technological developments produce a corresponding shift in our relationship with our own bodies – with the biopolitical forms in which we reach into the world. The manufacturing of finer artificial lenses allows 'man' to enhance the operation of 'the lens of his own eye'; 'by means of the microscope he overcomes the limits of visibility set by the structure of his retina.' The 'photographic camera' allows us to 'retain fleeting visual impressions', just as the 'gramophone disc retains the equally fleeting auditory ones', and 'with the help of the telephone', we can 'hear at distances'.[9] All of these technologies, he argues, act as prosthetic extensions of the human (or forms of what Alison Landsberg terms 'prosthetic memory'[10]) – enhancements which massively increase the reach and persistence of consciousness as it extends, via material forms, into the world. But while this prosthetisation enhances and empowers, it also produces odd gulfs between mind and material extension, a peculiar estrangement between inward being and the technologised forms through which we act in the world – an estrangement that emerges when, in Freud's resonant phrase, our 'auxiliary organs' have not properly 'grown' on us.[11]

The development of mechanical technologies over the course of the nineteenth century extends the reach of the human, while also opening distances between mind and body, between consciousness and prosthetically enhanced biomatter. The human hand becomes immeasurably more powerful, as the agent of this extension, while also becoming more difficult to animate, as its increasing utility as a tool produces too an increasing distance from some notional operating mind, some central nervous system. Thinking is fundamentally related, as Heidegger observes, to handedness – 'only a being who can think', he writes, 'can have hands'[12] – but the greater the technological, prosthetic reach of the hand, the more thwarted the relationship between thinking and handedness becomes, the more ohms of resistance there are. And as these mechanical developments intensify the experience of handedness I am seeking to characterise here, then the second form that this intensification takes relates to the aesthetic and discursive forms with which we articulate our relationship to the hand – and particularly those that are developed in the novel of the period. If, as I have argued so far in this book, the novel is the art form that has achieved the greatest proximity to the difficult junction between mind and material – if this proximity is what has given the novel its particular imaginative texture in the passage from Cervantes to Goethe – then it is the novel, too, over the course of the nineteenth century, that most finely registers the shifting quality of the hand, both as the agent of human power in the world and as a prosthetic object which is resistant to the animating control of mind. It is 'the novel', Raymond Willliams writes, that reaches most deeply into 'the nerves, the bloodstream, the living fibres of experience'.[13] As the manufacturing revolution of the nineteenth century gathers pace – as the quality of our relation to our spatial and temporal extensions becomes increasingly artificially determined and technologically enhanced – one can see the proliferation of novelistic images of dead flesh, and particularly images of dead hands, hands that are resistant to the call of mind.

Consider, for example, Emile Zola's 1867 novel *Thérèse Raquin*, which turns around one of the more striking novel images of the dead hand. Madame Raquin, Thérèse's aunt in Zola's novel, is the mother of Camille, Thérèse's sickly first husband, whom Thérèse has murdered with the aid of her second husband, Laurent. In one of the cruellest twists in that cruel novel, Madame Raquin is paralysed by a stroke and forced to sit and listen helplessly while Thérèse and Laurent gloat, in front of her, about their murder of her son. Madame Raquin's mute encasement in her dead body resonates with the novel's broad interest in forms of corruption which have estranged mind from biomaterial – an estrangement which leads Laurent, in one memorable scene, to the city morgue, to lust over the spectacle of a naked corpse, 'her fresh, plump body taking on the most delicate hues with the pallor of death'.[14] But the novel's fascination with the unresponsive, thingly body comes to a head with the image of Madame Raquin's paralysed hand, and her awful, slow struggle to infuse her dead hand with enough life to make a public accusation against her niece. Thérèse and Laurent have invited friends around to play cards, with the old lady sitting, stone like, at the card table, and Madame Raquin, 'with an amazing effort of will', manages 'to force a little life back into her right hand and raise it slightly from her knee, where it had always lain inert' (p. 210). The guests notice her struggle 'seeing this white, soft, dead hand in the midst of them', the narrator says, 'the players were most surprised' (p. 210) – and in a blackly comic scene they try to interpret the movements of her hand, while Thérèse and Laurent look on in mounting panic. She manages with great difficulty to spell out '*Thérèse and Laurent have*' on the tablecloth before her will finally fails. Thérèse and Laurent 'were staring at the avenging hand with fixed and terrified eyes when suddenly it gave a jerk, went flat on the table and then slipped off and fell on to the impotent woman's lap like a mass of lifeless flesh' (p. 212). Zola's concern with the dead hand is the mark of his fascination with material, with the material in which the novel must clothe itself to take on the life of the world it describes, even if such immersion produces a kind of death, the kind of unresponsiveness that we find in Madame Raquin's dead hand, or in the erotic weight of the dead flesh that captures Laurent's pornographic imagination. For Zola, the forces that allow us to capture material, to aesthetically reproduce it or to chemically manufacture it, are also those that make it distant from us.

Across the nineteenth-century novel, there is an extraordinary proliferation of such images of deadened hands – bodies and limbs suffering either from some necrotic insensitivity or from a mechanical artificiality which renders flesh resistant to the call of mind. And if this is so, it is in the development early in the century of the society novel, from its eighteenth-century genesis in the novels of Frances Burney, that this encounter with the dead hand, as a mark of artificial sociality, assumes its most significant form. In the work of Maria Edgeworth (particularly *Belinda*), and Mary Wollstonecraft (*Mary, The Wrongs of Woman*), one can see a concerted struggle to transform the epistolary mode shaped by Burney into a new kind of narrative apparatus that is able both to articulate the devastating effects of the marriage market on the experience of female self-ownership and to imagine new subject positions, new ways of expressing interior experience that can counteract the artificiality of social forms. In these novels – in many ways transitional works, which are seeking to extend and adapt the form – Edgeworth and Wollstonecraft seek to inherit the inner-ness, the intimacy of the epistolary form, by developing a narrative voice that can more deeply embed Mazzoni's 'mimesis of the interior life'.[15] Wollstonecraft's *Mary*, for example, turns around the protagonist Mary's experience of dead handedness, of a kind of living death, that comes as a result of being given away by her father, against her will, in marriage. Her response to her forced marriage is to suffer a kind of stupefaction, what the narrator calls a 'suspension of thought' that recalls the temporary deaths suffered by Defoe's Moll Flanders and Robinson Crusoe.[16] 'Overwhelmed by this intelligence', we are told, 'Mary rolled her eyes about, then, with a vacant stare, fixed them on her father's face; but they were no longer a sense; they conveyed no ideas to the brain' (p. 16). The giving of her hand in marriage leads to this vacancy and spawns a series of images of dead handedness that runs through Wollstonecraft's novel. Her husband's hand disgusts her – 'When her husband would take her hand', she thinks, 'she would instantly feel a sickness, a faintness at her heart, and wish, involun-tarily, that the earth would open and swallow her up' (p. 61) – and she spends the novel trying to forge relations with others, and with herself, that are not artificial but felt, that allow her to enter into an organic and living relation with her own hand and that of others. As Wollstonecraft puts it in her preface to the novel, her aim is to discover what she calls the 'vivifying principle' as it is enshrined in 'compositions ... where the soul of the author is exhibited, and animates the hidden springs' (p. 3). The (fitful, uncertain) development of narrative voice in the novel is the vehicle for this new animation, the struggle to forge a third-person narrative that might allow her to articulate a relation with her own fictional self. In Mary's own terms, the attempt to give birth to a voice is a struggle to embed thinking in a fully realised sensorium, so that 'I shall not reason about but *feel* in what happiness consists' (p. 39).

One can see this development of a new kind of interiority across the
novel of the early century. But if something transformative happens to the
form at this time, if there is an evolution in the way that the novel gains
access, in the supple movement of narrative voice, to the inner passage of
thought, then it is in the work of Jane Austen that this evolution takes place
most fully. It is her development of a free indirect style on the one hand and
of a precisely controlled mode of narrative irony on the other that produces
an astonishingly singular access to what I have been thinking of, in this
book so far, as the prosthetic ground to being – and that does so in a way
that changes the texture and timbre of the novel voice for all of those who
come after her.[17] Take, for example, her 1816 novel *Emma*, one of those
works of art which it is tempting to describe as perfect. This novel offers
itself, overtly, as the story of a woman's slow passage from delusion and
error to maturity and self-knowledge. Emma, at the outset of the novel,
finds herself abandoned by her governess, Miss Taylor, when the latter
marries to become Mrs Weston. Mrs Weston, despite the social and
economic differences between them, is the closest Emma has to a mother
and a confidante – she is, we are told at the opening of the novel, 'one to
whom she could speak every thought as it arose'.[18] As for Margaret
Cavendish in *The Blazing World*, 'between dear friends there's no conceal-
ment, they being like parts of one united body',[19] the relationship between
Emma and Mrs Weston is the closest the novel comes to a picture of shared
being without artifice. In a novel centrally concerned with motherlessness –
with the loss of maternal origin that casts Emma into a form of self-
alienation that is also an ontological incompletion – the bond between
Emma and Miss Taylor is offered as the most organic possible surrogate for
the prenatal completion that the novel mourns from the outset. But if
Miss Taylor represents such surrogacy, the event that impels the narrative is
Emma's loss of her companionship, a loss which throws Emma into a crisis
(of which she is herself marvellously unaware), leading her into the mistaken
embrace of a number of forms of artifice. The first and most catastrophic of
these is her adoption of a friend, Harriet Smith, for whom she has no real
feeling, but whom she engineers as a prosthetic replacement for Miss Taylor
(as the latter is a prosthetic replacement for the lost mother). Emma trains
herself to be intimate with Harriet, at the same time as refashioning Harriet
herself into the friend that she has imagined for herself. 'She would improve
her', Emma thinks to herself, 'she would form her opinions and her
manners' (p. 22). Emma's second erroneous work of artifice, and that for
which she is perhaps most famous, involves her doomed attempt to fashion
a love match between Harriet and the odious local vicar, Mr Elton. The

opening image of the novel, which pitches Emma into the traumatic abandonment crisis which is never overtly acknowledged in the novel, pictures Mr Elton joining Mr and Mrs Weston in matrimony. 'I thought', Emma says to her beloved father, 'when he was joining their hands to-day, he looked so very much as if he would like to have the same office done for him!' (pp. 13–14). By a subterranean logic of substitution, Emma dedicates herself, throughout the first third of the novel, to contriving a love affair between her artificial friend and the person who had made the invention of such a substitute necessary. Then the third and final form of artifice involves Emma's manufacturing of her own amorous attachment to Mrs Weston's nephew, Frank Churchill. 'There was something', Emma thinks to herself before having met him, 'in the name, in the idea of Mr Frank Churchill, which always interested her'. She had frequently thought, she goes on, 'that if she *were* to marry, he was the very person to suit her in age, character and condition' (p. 99). The plot unfolds through the working out to their various conclusions of these three forms of error; all the while, unbeknownst to herself, the narrative is incubating the real love of Emma's life, the love that can properly substitute for, and organically add to, her primal attachment to Mrs Weston and to her missing mother – that is, her deep-rooted love for the family friend Mr Knightley, which has been growing before the reader's eyes and finally reveals itself to Emma's.

In tracing this movement from delusion to clear sight, from the artificial to the real, the novel develops a characteristically Austenian mode of irony which serves, in one of its moods, as a critical narrative corrective to Emma's mistaken perception of herself and the world around her. Irony, in this novel, serves in part to bring the gap between Emma's bent understanding and the real state of things in Hartfield to a kind of expression that is always legible to the reader, even when it is apparently obscure to the characters themselves. Throughout Emma's Pygmalionic experiment in 'improving' Harriet, for example, the comedy of the narrative as well as its drama and its pathos stem from the gap that opens, in Austen's astonishingly controlled prose, between the version of Harriet that we see through Emma's eyes and a real Harriet, who has her own life and designs, but whose existence the narrative can only imply, as a latent counterbalance to Emma's false construction of her.

This experiment begins, indeed, quite literally with the spectacle of Emma creating an avowedly artificial version of Harriet, in the shape of a portrait that Emma paints of Harriet as a ruse to entrance Mr Elton with her beauty – an act of artful artistry which produces a richly comic collapse of the boundaries between reality and representation, and which shapes the novel's more general concern with the relation between real life and artificial life. Emma thinks to herself that she will surreptitiously exaggerate Harriet's beauty, the better to captivate Mr Elton. 'She meant to throw in a little improvement to the figure', she thinks, 'to give a little more height and considerably more elegance' (p. 41). The status of this misrepresentation, though, is complicated by the fact that Emma already sees herself as 'forming' Harriet, so Harriet already stands in relation to Emma as artwork to artist, already owes her reality not to her own self but to Emma's fictional imaging of her. Improving her in the portrait is thus another version of improving her in life – not a distortion of mimesis or representation so much as a component part of the campaign of prosthetic person fashioning on which Emma is wilfully embarked. The response of all the other characters to the portrait then works as a kind of index to the power and influence of Emma's fantasy life, of her variable capacity to induct those around her into her own view of the world. Mr Knightley, unenchanted straight talker that he is, simply refers Emma to the errors in her portrait: '"You have made her too tall, Emma," said Mr Knightley' (p. 41). Mrs Weston, vainly infatuated as she is with the talents that she herself has instilled in Emma, is more forgiving: 'Miss Woodhouse has given her friend the only beauty she wanted. The expression of the eye is most correct. But Miss Smith has not those eye-brows and eye-lashes. It is the fault of her face that she has them not' (p. 41). Mrs Weston sees the failures in the likeness but considers that Harriet in the flesh is to blame for not quite matching up to Emma's representation of her, rather than the fault lying in the portrait. But it is Mr Elton's response that is the most comically double and gives the richest scope for narrative irony. He is in ecstasies over the portrait – 'it appears to me,' he says, 'a most perfect resemblance in every feature. I never saw such a likeness in my life' (p. 41); 'Oh it is most admirable! I cannot keep my eyes from it' (p. 42). To Emma, of course, this fulsome praise is proof that her ruse is working, that Mr Elton is falling in love with Harriet. His admiration of the portrait seems to Emma to be directed at Harriet herself, the living Harriet that is the fruit of Emma's Promethean labours. 'You have given Miss Smith all that she required', Mr Elton says to Emma, 'she was a beautiful creature when she came to you, but, in my opinion, the attractions you have added are infinitely superior to what she received from nature' (p. 37). 'I have perhaps given her a little more decision of character', Emma replies, with the modest pleasure that a god might take in her creation, and Mr Elton agrees with the enthusiasm of a lover: 'Exactly so; that is what principally strikes me. So much superadded decision of character! Skilful has been the hand' (p. 37).

The irony at work throughout these scenes, of course, derives from the gulf between Emma's blindness and our own insight – the gulf upon which any reading of this novel must rest. It is clear to us as readers, and to varying degrees to other characters in the novel, that Mr Elton's admiration, artificial as it is in itself, is not directed at Harriet, the artwork, but at Emma, the artist – not at the sculpture, but at the shaping hand of the sculptor. Emma's inability to see that Mr Elton is in (insincere) love with the artist rather than the artwork thus stands as a mark of her inability to separate her artificial constructions from the real state of things, an inability which Austenian irony serves, after a certain fashion, to correct. Emma collapses reality into artifice as a symptom of her abandonment complex – her spoilt, headstrong determination to bend the world to her fantasy life, as she strives to survive the loss of Miss Taylor; the ironic undertow of the narrative voice enjoins us to separate these elements out again, to restore them to their proper order, so we can discern Mr Elton's real motives in admiring Emma's portrait against the flow of Emma's misconceptions.

As the novel progresses, and as Emma's various schemes for self-fashioning unfold, this effect continues to develop, in which Emma's construction of a distorted, artificial version of reality is balanced against a counter-version, which we are not given directly, but which is summoned only through the movement of latent irony. Emma's manufactured infatuation with Frank Churchill, indeed, reproduces the effects at work in Harriet's portrait and intensifies them by locating them in Emma's estranged, prosthetised relation with her own self – self as the fashioned form in which she represents herself to the world and to herself. Her relationship with Churchill is characterised by a heightened and oddly detached awareness of her own states of mind and body – by her attempt to manipulate her somatic and emotional responses so that they might match with a fixed and unrealistic conception she has of what love might really be like – and again the challenge to the reader is to calibrate the ironic space that is at work in Emma's self-relation, the space that opens between her fantasy life and the body in which she appears to others. She has a disagreement with the 'insufferable' Mrs Elton and finds herself wondering what Frank Churchill would have done if he had witnessed it: 'Oh!' she thinks, 'What would Frank Churchill say to her, if he were here?' (p. 229). The narrative gives us access to this thought and then follows her as she immediately seizes on it as proof that she is indeed in love with him. 'Ah!' she thinks, delighted with herself, 'there I am – thinking of him directly. Always the first person to be thought of! How I catch myself out!' (p. 229). We see so far into Emma's mind in Austen's free indirect style – 'All this ran glibly through her thoughts' (p. 229), the narrator says – that we see not only what Emma thinks, but what she thinks about what she thinks; but the effect of this superfine attention to the hidden recesses of self-consciousness is to discover, even in this most intimate interiority, the work of artifice. Emma is catching herself out having a thought which seems to reveal her true state of mind, but we are primed to read against this, to see in this 'catching out' a deeper self-deception, in which Emma gathers evidence to prove to herself that she is having an experience which is in fact empty and groundless. While Emma is becoming increasingly wrapped in the coils of her own self-fashioning, the reader is able to see what she herself cannot – a truth that is signalled to us not directly but through the operations of narrative irony. It is Mr Knightley who is in reality the object of her love, and who is in love with her in turn – who is able to divine that part of Emma that is unaffected, rooted in what the narrator calls her 'real attachment' to Mrs Weston and to her father. He can see her falsity, her snobbery, the unreality of her friendship with Harriet, as he can see, too, her loyalty, her bright lovingness – the elements of her character that make her so captivating. But the narrative, focalised free-indirectly through Emma, can only view his assessment of her through her own bent regard, which mixes her genuine qualities with her artificial ones. The movement of the narrative, the slow progress towards self-knowledge, and towards a proper alignment between reality and the forms with which we represent it, is shaped by Emma's unacknowledged love, as it gradually makes its way into consciousness. At a critical moment in this journey towards consciousness, Mr Knightley fiercely upbraids her for her cruel and thoughtless behaviour towards the poor local villager Miss Bates ('it was badly done, indeed' (p. 309), he scolds her), and her response is characterised by that somatic immediacy that is so lacking in her over-interpreted relations with Frank Churchill. 'Never had she felt so agitated, mortified, grieved, at any circumstance in her life' (p. 310), Emma thinks, as Mr Knightley's representation of her behaviour starts to make a dent in her own construction of self. 'She was most forcibly struck', she thinks to herself, 'the truth of his representation there was no denying'; and as the force of his displeasure makes itself felt, Emma finds herself respond-ing physically, in a manner that she cannot control or shape. 'Emma felt the tears running down her cheeks', the narrator says, 'without being at any trouble to check them, extraordinary as they were' (p. 310). Emma's tears here speak for themselves, signalling a return of mind to body, a return to unmediated self after the estranging trauma of abandonment (even if this is itself an estranged homecoming, one in which Emma's body exhibits a certain automatism that is a paradoxical effect of its immediacy). And the journey towards animated, somatic selfhood that begins with her mortified response to Mr Knightley's displeasure ends with the recognition, sudden and unpremeditated, that she loves Mr Knightley, that 'Mr Knightley must marry no one but herself' (p. 335): 'She saw it all with a clearness that had never blessed her before' (p. 335). 'With insufferable vanity', she thinks, 'she had believed herself in the secret of everybody's feelings; with unpardonable arrogance proposed to arrange everybody's destiny. She had proved to be universally mistaken' (p. 39).

This moment, then – the moment of 'development of self' (p. 336), in which Emma adjusts her mistaken view of the world to accord with those who love her most truly – is the moment that has been held in store throughout the narrative, the adjustment in seeing that has been presaged by the ironic doubleness of the narrative, in which the true state of affairs can always be felt, implicitly, running beneath the world as seen through Emma's faulty perceptions. This coming together, this realignment, is then registered, at the close of the novel, in a perfect mirror image of the scene that opens it. As Mr Knightley declares his love for her, and as she accepts his offer of marriage, Mr Knightley thinks to himself that Emma has finally coincided with that true self that has always been latent in her, that both he and we have always been able to discern beneath the artifice. 'She was his own Emma', he thinks, 'by hand and word' (p. 349). This is Emma's true hand, as opposed to the hand of the sculptress, the skilful hand so admired by Mr Elton; in the final lines of the novel, it is Mr Elton who is charged with the task of joining Emma's true hand to Mr Knightley's, as he opens the novel by joining the loving hands of Mr and Mrs Weston. 'Mr Elton was called on', the novel concludes, 'to join the hands of Mr Knightley and Miss Woodhouse' (p. 396). As Emma discovers her unaffected self at the close of the novel, the artificial relations she has fashioned – her friendship with Harriet, her false attachment to Frank Churchill – give way to organic relations which assert themselves independently, which are no more fashioned by her will than were those tears which ran unbidden down her cheeks.

Austenian irony serves, in this way, to bridge the gap between imagination and reality, between a faulty perception and true seeing, with a subtlety and depth that had not been possible before this moment in this history of the novel. In *Emma*, as in *Northanger Abbey*, there is a constant and occasionally explicit reference to Cervantes, and to Don Quixote's experience of mis-seeing, as a kind of narrative precursor. *Northanger Abbey* is a virtual reworking of *Don Quixote*, in its exploration of the corrosive effects of fantasy literature on the capacity to interpret reality;[20] and *Emma* dwells too on the particular form of 'knight-errantry' (p. 232) that arises from the confusion of imagination with reality. Emma's decision to elect Frank Churchill, sight unseen, as a love object resonates richly with Don Quixote's errant decision to love Dulcinea without ever having met her, and Emma's tendency, as she herself puts it, to 'take up an idea . . . and make everything bend to it' (p. 112) makes of her a kind of nineteenth-century domestic Quixote (an heir to Charlotte Lennox's 1752 *Female Quixote*). But if there is a quixotic element to Emma's artifice, what is so striking about this Cervantine background to *Emma* is that Austen is able to inhabit the ground between Emma's faulty perception and the novel's shared reality in a way that is completely inconceivable for Cervantes. *Don Quixote* shifts from imagination to reality – from Mambrino's helmet to a barber's basin, from Dulcinea to a garlicky peasant girl – in ways that allow of no interwoven accord between these two separate modes of seeing. When Don Quixote, at the end of Cervantes' great novel, forsakes his madness and denounces his wonderful knightly powers, he shifts from one world to the other, carrying nothing of himself across that divide. If *Don Quixote* offers up pictures of a new relation between life and death, between imagination and reality, it does so in a way that is not itself given articulate narrative form, does not have its own voice or language in which to speak. In *Emma*, however, Austen invents a particular mode of interiority, a double access to the inside of Emma's mind and the world that she shares with others, that allows her to produce that connective tissue between internal and external worlds, between the private and the shared, that was not available to Cervantes. The combination of dramatic irony and free indirect discourse that Austen perfects here allows her to give free rein to an inventing mind, while also drawing that mind back into shared space, so she is able to blend the capacity to form oneself, to exercise modes of self-fashioning, with the equal capacity to generate that 'vivifying' meeting of soul and body that remains elusive for Wollstonecraft. As Franco Moretti has argued, it is Austen who first fully exploits this technique, this adoption of a form of narrative style as a 'meeting ground between two forms of discourse', and *Emma* is 'one of the first novels to use it in a systematic way'.[21] *Emma* reads as a kind of lesson in becoming, in which the experience of artificiality, of a distance between self and hand – the 'skilful hand' of the deceitful artist – is explored to fashion the narrative forms in which such distance might be closed. At the moment of greatest error in the novel, as Emma mistakenly courts Mr Elton when she thinks she is setting him up to marry Harriet, this artificiality is experienced as a distance from the hand. She is talking to Mr Elton in her carriage on the way home from a party, when 'she found her subject cut up – her hand seized – her attention demanded, and Mr Elton actually making violent love to her' (p. 108). This is a horrible assault on her person as public property that builds on similar scenes in Burney's *Evelina*. But Austen balances Mr Elton's assault on the hand against the moment when Mr Knightley takes Emma's hand in his, a moment when hands join minds, rather than mark their separation from each other, a moment when the movement of her own hand becomes one with the movement of his, and it becomes possible to reach out, in a phrase Wollstonecraft uses in *Mary*, to the 'hand of a fellow creature'. 'Mr Knightley took her hand', Emma says, 'whether she had not herself made the first motion, she could not say – she might, perhaps, have rather offered it – but he took her hand, pressed it, and certainly was on the point of carrying it to his lips' (p. 317).

This is the moment of 'perfect amity' for which *Emma* is written. It is the gift of Austenian irony to fashion a form in which mind finds a meeting ground with body, thus overcoming its prosthetic artificiality. But if this is so, and if the expressive range of the novel after Austen is enlarged by this gift, it is also the case that the mode of self-possession that this narrative apparatus grants is itself prosthetic in nature – is itself made of the forms of artificiality that it overcomes. One cannot understand this turning point in the history of the novel without responding to this contradiction – that the narrative mode which brings us so startlingly, intimately close to the ways in which mind owns and animates body is built from an ironic distance which, as Moretti puts it, '*objectifies* Emma, and thus somehow estranges her from her own self' (p. 393). *Emma* sets up a kind of dwelling place in that elusive ground that I have traced here from More to Burney, that space of shared, immanent being that one can see in the loving gaze that passes between Oroonoko and Imoinda in Behn's *Oroonoko*. When Emma and Mr Knightley share a look late in the novel, there is an 'instant impression' of their love for each other, in which 'his eyes received the truth from her's' (p. 317), and all of Austen's poetic resources are dedicated to capturing the reality of that meeting, the real possibility that a look between two sovereign subjects can be truly binding. But Austen can only achieve this proximity through an ironic mode that acknowledges, at every moment, that the narrative force which allows us this access to truth is itself won from the capacity of language to mean doubly. It is this exquisitely controlled doubleness that is the engine of becoming in *Emma*, this doubleness that allows Austen's narrator to follow the process by which mind

overcomes prosthetic artificiality to take ownership of the hand, to embed
the self in its extensions; and this doubleness works, always, against the
trajectory of the novel towards unity and self-knowledge, declaring, in its
own fashion, that the very possibility of self-knowledge is won through
self-distance, the self-distance from which the connective tissue of
Austenian irony is woven.

Mr Knightley, delighted to have won his 'own Emma, by hand and
word', expounds towards the end of the novel upon the beauty of true
attachment, as opposed to the artificiality of Emma's relations with
Harriet. 'My Emma', he says, 'does not every thing serve to prove
more and more the beauty of truth and sincerity in all of our doings
with each other?' (p. 365). 'Emma agreed to it', the narrative goes on, but
'with a blush of sensibility', because, as Emma understands, the truth
and sincerity that she arrives at in this novel are the very children of
duplicity.[22] The capacity to understand another mind truly is won from
a close contact with the insistent, unbreachable distance from self that is
the inside movement of thought, a distance registered here in that
gorgeous blush of sensibility, that unbidden somatic manifestation of
a whispering distance between mind and face that no one, before
Austen, could have captured in narrative. The blush, David Wills has
suggested – like Emma's unbidden tears – is at once a mark of unmediated life and a kind of automatism, a function of body not controlled
by mind: 'the pure life of the spontaneous blush,' he writes, is 'also
a form of human automatism'; and Emma's blush captures both of these
movements.[23] To read this blush – in both its involuntary truthfulness
and its acknowledgement of untruth – one has, I think, to understand
that this novel is not a monological celebration of organic sincerity, not
simply the story of a woman overcoming her propensity for error. It is
not, as Tony Tanner suggests, a story in which Mr Knightly, in his
wisdom and clear sight, 'corrects' or 'tutors' Emma, steering her towards
a kind of normative, obedient maturity (the 'overriding concern of Jane
Austen's novels', he says, being 'the nature of true utterance').[24] As Eve
Sedgwick has argued, such readings, in all their reactionary force, are
deaf to the role of the negative in Austen's aesthetic, to the groundless
irony that is its major pleasure and its ethical motor – the space
hollowed out, in *Emma*, by the inaugurating absence of the mother,
the absence that condemns our relations to ourselves to a prosthetic
contingency. It is necessary, Sedgwick writes, to see past the spectacle
that recurs in Austen's writing of a 'Girl Being Taught a Lesson'.[25] To
read Austen we must read through the 'repressive hypothesis' that is at

work in her writing to see the radicalism that her novels harbour, even as they enforce, in their overt plots, the forms of heteronormativity they undermine. In the spaces that such counter-reading opens, it is possible to find a kind of gulf at work, a suspended space woven into the midst of the narrative voice in which one can glimpse the movement of artifice itself, artifice as the force, representable for Austen only as an ironic gap or gradient, which brings being to the condition of sovereign subject-hood. Mr Knightley, at the end of *Emma*, gives a paean to truth and sincerity, having successfully 'improved' Emma, 'correcting' her as Emma seeks to correct Harriet, and curing her of her infatuation with artifice. But it is the narrator, thinking in extraordinarily delicate tandem with Emma herself, who has the last word, gently correcting Mr Knightley's correction, his naïve investment in the possibility of truthful utterance. 'Seldom', the narrator says, 'very seldom, does complete truth belong to any human disclosure; seldom can it happen that something is not a little disguised, or a little mistaken' (p. 354). It is Austen's gift to the novel imagination to discover a form that can penetrate this wriggling, self-cancelling truth, that can understand that the turn of mind is set in motion by the disguise in which it comes into the world. 'The self', Adorno writes, 'lives solely through transformation into otherness'.[26] As mind comes to word and to hand, it comes in disguise; the closest that the novel can come to the 'vivifying principle' of animated life is to engrave the space between mind and its masks to narrate the means by which artifice is ironised into truth.

4.2 The Dyer's Hand: Narrative and Biomaterial in Dickens and Eliot

> I am more and more convinced that it will be possible to demonstrate the homogenous origin of all tissues.
>
> George Eliot, *Middlemarch*[27]

> You are a human boy, my young friend. A human boy. O glorious to be a human boy! And why glorious, my young friend? Because you are capable of receiving the lessons of wisdom, because you are capable of profiting by this discourse which I now deliver for your good, because you are not a stick, or a staff, or a stone, or a post, or a pillar.
>
> Charles Dickens, *Bleak House*[28]

> All the mythical systems or erratic mythical fragments in the world were corruptions of a tradition organically revealed.
>
> George Eliot, *Middlemarch*[29]

Jane Austen develops, in the early nineteenth century, a prose form which can give tensed, supple expression to the gulf between mind and matter, which can make of such a gulf the sonic ground of a newly mobile narrative voice. It is this formal leap, this transformation of the disappearing origins of expressive being into the very conditions of expression, that allows for the remarkable development of the novel form after Austen, that makes of the novel the art form best adapted to the task of humanising a world estranged by political and technological revolution. George Eliot's narrator in the opening epigraph to *Daniel Deronda* remarks that 'Men can do nothing without the make-believe of a beginning' (perhaps catching an echo from Goethe's Werther, who writes that 'there are such constraints on human nature that we have no feeling for the beginning and ending of our existence').[30] Historical and material origins, the first grounds upon which our actions are based, are fictitious, the narrator breezily asserts, as if in accord with Frank Kermode's assertion that 'the rise of what we call literary fiction happened at a time when the revealed, authenticated account of the beginning was losing its authority'.[31] Such a revelation, however, is not the occasion for a collapse of representation, but the very ground – the necessary fiction – in which our condition is most securely rooted. As Kermode puts it, again, 'there is a correlation between subtlety and variety in our fictions and remoteness and doubtfulness about ends and origins' (p. 67). Narrative voice, as developed in the novel form after Austen, converts the disintegration caused by rapid technological transformation into a newly integrated subjecthood, a kind of being that thrives on its own ontological instability. 'In respect of character', Thomas Hardy's narrator writes in *Return of the Native*, 'a face may make certain admissions by its outline; but it fully confesses only in its changes.'[32] Austen grants narrative access to these changes, to the groundless differences that work between mind and its manifestations, and the novel after her, from Tolstoy to Dostoevsky, from Flaubert to Hugo, from Hawthorne to Melville, from Eliot to Dickens to Collins to Hardy, builds on the vanishing foundations of this narrative interiority the architecture of a world view. The novel's affinity with the inward difference from self that is the movement of thought fits it to be the privileged vehicle for imagining a world that, in all its weighty massiveness, is coming into being through an act of prosthetic transformation that estranges it from itself.

One of the characteristic features of this epistemological virtuosity is the capacity of the nineteenth-century novel to make connections, to make the imagined world of the novel 'luminous', as George Eliot puts it, 'with the reflected light of correspondences'.[33] Oedipa Maas asks herself, in a moment in Thomas Pynchon's 1966 novel *Crying of Lot 49* that I shall come to later, 'Shall I project a world?'[34] It is this act of projection, of whole-world creation, that the novel embarks upon, in those great feats of imaginative assimilation that run through the nineteenth century, from Balzac's *La Comédie humaine*, to Tolstoy's *War and Peace*, to Victor Hugo's *Les Misérables*. In a paradox that is central to the history of the imagination I am tracing here, the co-incidence of two forms of artifice – the emergence of a narrative voice that is closely attuned to its own artificiality and the development of a manufactured lifeworld that is startlingly at odds with the organic past from which it emerges – produces the effect of a new kind of reality, and a new kind of realism. As mechanical technological transformation renders the world engineered rather than given – 'essentially a daydream', as Nathaniel Hawthorne puts it, 'and yet a fact' – it is the novel that can capture most fully the world-making power of the inventive mind; it is the novel, Hawthorne says, that can achieve most surely an 'available foothold between fiction and reality'.[35]

Consider, for example, two of the most significant British world-making novels of the mid-nineteenth century – Charles Dickens' *Bleak House* (1853), and George Eliot's *Middlemarch* (1871). At the heart of both of these novels is the conviction that the narrative voice itself is able to conjure connections, able to bring a diffuse set of phenomena into a conjunction that gives shape to the world that the novel represents and creates. *Bleak House* tells the story of a number of different families and social groups, who are brought together through the malign effects of chancery law, turning particularly around the relations between the aristocratic family in their Lincolnshire estate (Sir Leicester and Lady Dedlock); the illegitimate daughter of Lady Dedlock, Esther Summerson; John Jarndyce and his wards of court Ada and Rick; the shadowy figure Nemo, a law writer who dies before the beginning of the novel; and the desperately poor crossing sweeper Jo. The novel sketches this diverse cast of characters and situations, the omniscient narrator suggests, to produce a means of bringing these strands together, of giving a picture of collective life that might accommodate them, and that might frame an imagined community more just and more progressive than that overseen by the grotesquely unjust chancery law. 'What connexion can there be', the narrator asks

> between the place in Lincolnshire, the house in town, the Mercury in powder, and the whereabout of Jo the outlaw with the broom, who had that distant ray of light upon him when he swept the churchyard-step? What

connexion can there have been between many people in the innumerable histories of this world, who, from opposite sides of great gulfs, have, nevertheless, been very curiously brought together.[36]

Dickens' novel pictures a world riven by 'great gulfs' to explore the modes of connection that might render it whole and unified. Eliot's *Middlemarch*, too, tells a story of separate families, caught in the influence, here not of chancery law, but of the historical shifts in relations between old and young, between provincial tradition and a dawning urban modernity. The plot concerning Dorothea Brooke, her doomed marriage to the aged and impotent scholar Casaubon and her growing love for the artist Will Ladislaw, is interwoven with a number of separate plot lines, such as that which turns around the Vince family (and their relation with other Middlemarch families the Garths, the Featherstones, the Farebrothers, the Cadwalladers), and most significantly the story of the ambitious doctor, Lydgate, who has come to the provinces to establish an innovative medical practice. At a moment that follows the rhetorical turn of the passage from *Bleak House* that I have just quoted, the narrator of *Middlemarch* intervenes, early in the narrative, to ask what it is that holds the various elements of the novel's plot together. 'Why on earth', the narrator asks, 'should Mrs Cadwallader have been at all busy about Miss Brooke's marriage? . . . Was there any ingenious plot, any hide-and-seek course of action, which might be detected by a careful telescopic watch?' (p. 59).

In *Middlemarch*, as in *Bleak House*, the narrative draws sharp attention to its own role in making connections, in producing a 'telescopic watch' which might reveal the 'ingenious plot' which holds its diverse strands together; in both cases, this connective work is done in the teeth of an experience of disjunction, an intuition of vast historical forces that are creating a new world, in which older organic forms can no longer exert epistemological force, in which the 'substance' of nature, in Goethe's terms, is no longer 'drawn to itself'.[37] At a critical moment in *Bleak House*, such an apprehension of the vulcanic remodelling of the world is captured in the spectacle of the half-built railway, a spectacle which also appears at a crucial juncture in Eliot's *Middlemarch* as the 'infant struggles of the railway' to 'determine the course of this history' (p. 553). This is a system that is in the process of binding the country together to make of it a new, steam-powered body politic – effecting what Marshall McLuhan calls the 'alteration of social groupings' that comes with any transformative 'increase of power or speed'.[38] As Esther Summerson embarks on a coach trip in search of her mother with Inspector Bucket (the portrait of the all-seeing novel detective that is the pattern upon which Hugo's Javert, Christie's Poirot, Poe's Dupin and Conan Doyle's Holmes are based), the narrator observes that 'railroads shall soon traverse all this country, and with a rattle and a glare the engine shall shoot like a meteor over the wide night-landscape' (p. 775). Soon, he predicts, it will no longer be necessary to crawl along narrow country roads by coach; but, he goes on,

> as yet, such things are non-existent in these parts, though not wholly unexpected. Preparations are afoot, measurements are made, ground is staked out. Bridges are begun, and their not yet united piers desolately look at one another over roads and streams, like brick and mortar couples with an obstacle to their union. (p. 775)

If the narrative is searching for forms of connection, between the house in Lincolnshire, for example, and the 'mercury in powder' who attends the Dedlock's house in London, then this haunting picture of a half-built railway offers one mode of connection, an iron central nervous system that is in the process of spreading across Britain in the 1840s and 1850s, animating it with a new, artificial life force (as McLuhan suggests that 'all technologies are extensions of our physical and nervous systems to increase power and speed').[39] And similarly, in Eliot's *Middlemarch*, the search for a 'telescopic watch' that might allow us to divine the novel's underlying connections yields a number of images of articulation, a number of models of animated life. One of these, in an echo of Dickens' railway, is offered by the picture of a new industrial lifeworld that is held in opposition to the provincial ruralism of Middlemarch. The manufacturer Caleb Garth, the narrator says, is fascinated by the prospect of manufactured life – by the 'indispensable might of that myriad-headed, myriad-handed labour by which the social body is fed, clothed and housed' (p. 250). He is entranced by the 'echoes of the great hammer'; the 'roar of the furnace, the thunder and plash of the engine'; the 'crane at work on the wharf; the piled-up produce in warehouses; the precision and variety of muscular effort wherever exact work had to be turned out'. This image of mechanised labour, powerfully crafting a world for itself, is one of the aesthetic frames of the novel. 'All these sights of his youth', Garth thinks, 'had acted on him as poetry without the aid of poets, had made a philosophy for him without the aid of philosophers, a religion without the aid of theology' (p. 250). But against this industrial lifeworld, the novel establishes two other modes of connection, two other frameworks of connected being that vibrate against each other throughout Eliot's great work. The first of these, and perhaps the more famous, is the subject of Casaubon's doomed work of scholarship – the 'unpublished matter' (p. 198) that makes up his 'Key to all Mythologies'. The pedantic and dry Casaubon wins the love of the young and intellectually supple Dorothea by impressing her with his knowledge of a philosophy and a theology that holds the world together more metaphysically than Garth's cranes and engines. 'With something of the archangelic manner', the narrator says,

> he told her how he had undertaken to show (what indeed had been attempted before, but not with that thoroughness, justice of comparison, and effectiveness of arrangement at which Mr Casaubon aimed) that all the mythical systems or erratic mythical fragments in the world were corruptions of a tradition originally revealed. (p. 24)

There is, Casaubon is convinced, an original fabric, a mythical blueprint, from which all of our systems of knowledge are derived (which catches an echo, here, of the Miltonic cosmology 'attempted' at the opening of *Paradise Lost*),[40] and it is his life's work to reveal it through painstaking archival research. The pursuit of this knowledge, though, leads Casaubon not to a rich understanding of life but to a shrivelled, scholarly myopia (without the corresponding Miltonic insight), through which he is unable to distinguish the living from the dead, the ancient from the modern, unable to bring any of the mythical roots that he traces into meaningful contact with the living, breathing world that he inhabits. As his romantic rival Sir James puts it, his learning has mummified him, so he 'has got no good red blood in his body'. Mrs Cadwallader agrees. 'Somebody put a drop under a magnifying glass', she says, 'and it was all semicolons and parentheses' (pp. 70–71).

   Casaubon's labours reveal only the redundancy of mythical frameworks, when they are not brought into contact with vivid life – when they lack what the narrator calls 'vital connection' (p. 202), Wollstonecraft's 'vivifying principle'.[41] The other scaffolding upon which to hang the connective tissue of the novel's world, though, is more vigorous, because it is grounded in that very biological life force in which Casaubon is so lacking – not in ancient forms of knowledge but in the revolutionary epistemologies derived from advances in nineteenth-century medicine. Rhyming with Casaubon's research throughout the novel is the scientific research of the glamorous young doctor Lydgate. If Casaubon believes he has discovered the mythical foundation of knowledge, Lydgate believes he has discovered the biological foundation of being. 'I am more and more convinced', he says to the curate Farebrother, 'that it will be possible to demonstrate the homogenous origin of all the tissues' (p. 455). Where a magnifying glass might reveal Casaubon's blood to be made of pedantic grammatical constructions, advances in microscopy and pathology allow Lydgate, along with the revolutionary French biologists of the earlier nineteenth century, to discover the organic principles that animate the body – principles that have, until that moment, been unknown to us. As Dickens' body politic is brought into a new animation by steam power, so Eliot's newly animated body is brought to knowledge by the revelatory power of the microscope. Lydgate is working at a moment in the history of science when the secrets of the body were suddenly accessible by the 'diligent application, not only of the scalp, but of the microscope'; when the French anatomist Marie Bichat was making of the 'dark territories of Pathology' a 'fine America for a spirited young adventurer' (p. 147), when Françoise-Vincent Raspail is first propounding the 'cell theory' which revealed the structure of the tissues, and the French pathologist Pierre Charles Louis is discovering the pathological basis of fever.[42] It has become possible, Lydgate believes, to discern the 'primitive tissue' (p. 148), to 'pierce the obscurity' of the internal organic mechanisms, to thread the 'invisible thoroughfares' of biological being. What Bichat discovers is that there is a substratum of connected being, which it is now possible for us to understand and to excavate. As all of our mythologies, according to Casaubon, are offshoots of some originally unified fabric, so 'living bodies, fundamentally considered, are not associations of organs which can be understood by studying them first apart, and then as it were federally.' Rather, Lydgate says, giving an early description of the biological function of stem cells, they

> must be regarded as consisting of certain primary webs or tissues, out of which the various organs – brain, heart, lungs, and so on – are compacted, as the various accommodations of a house are built up in various proportions of wood, iron, stone, brick, zinc and the rest, each material having its peculiar composition and proportions. (p. 148)

Both *Middlemarch* and *Bleak House*, then, are alive at once to the revolutionary changes – technological, epistemological, political – that are shifting the terms in which the social and the biological body is assembled, and to the new forms of connection, the new industrial and biological anatomies, that such changes hold in prospect. But if both novels are quickened by this sense of connection, they are also drawn, repeatedly, to the spectacle of the body that is estranged from itself as a result of the historical transformation that is at work within it – the body that is not yet animated by Casaubon's organic mythology, or Lydgate's primitive tissue, or Garth's poetic theo-philosophy of industry, or by the rail network that is spreading across Britain as the narrator of *Bleak House* writes. The attempt to draw together, to divine a master plan at work in the stuff of the world, is counterbalanced by a recognition that there is no such plan – that, as Gillian Beer writes, that 'there is not one "primitive tissue"', just as there is not one 'key to all mythologies'.[43] Both novels are teeming with images of deadened biomatter, of bodies that have become detached from mind, and that cannot develop that 'vital connection' that is missing in Casaubon's philosophy, that makes of him a strangely unanimated creature, a man who has already, as Sir James puts it, 'one foot in the grave' (p. 58). Lydgate's intellectual obsession is with the discovery of an organic bioweb that holds bodies together; but what he discovers, and what all of the other characters in the novel struggle against, is the fact that it is very difficult to make living connections between people, very difficult to allow mind to permeate one's own being, and to reach across the threshold of the flesh to make living contact with the being of another. There is perhaps no writer before or after Eliot who has given as fine-grained an account of what she calls the 'difficult task of knowing another soul' (p. 119), and Lydgate discovers, against the flow of his scientific research into invisible thoroughfares, and the obscure cellular structures that hold tissues and bodies together, that his mind remains detached from the scene of his own embodiment, and from the bodies of others. His obsession with the primitive tissue is balanced, in the opening episodes of the novel, against his growing infatuation with and eventual marriage to Rosamund Vincy, as if these two concerns were somehow related, in some underground fashion the same, both manifestations of what Lydgate thinks of as the 'intimate relations of the living structure' (p. 148). And yet the narrator makes it clear, from the beginning, that the relation between Lydgate and Rosamund is not readily going to yield union, or conjunction of mind and flesh. 'Poor Lydgate', the narrator writes, 'or shall I say Poor Rosamund! Each lived in a world of which the other knew nothing' (p. 165).

In Eliot, as in Dickens, one of the chief recurring figures for this unresponsiveness, this failure of mind to hold bodies and communities together, is that of the dead hand. The dead hand recurs throughout *Daniel Deronda* – most notably in the figure of the Jewish Mordecai, who longs for the supple young Deronda to act, in some inscrutable way, as an avatar, an 'expanded, prolonged self', so that Mordecai might live on spiritually in Deronda's young body as his own becomes infirm and moribund.[44] This act of substitution or renewal ('you have risen within me', Mordecai says to Deronda, 'like a thought not fully spelled' (p. 430)) involves the replacement of Mordecai's 'wasted yellow hands' with the beautiful form of Deronda's own body, his 'long, flexible, firmly grasping hands' (p. 406). And in *Middlemarch*, of course, the dead hand (after which Book 5 of the novel is named) comes to name the awful clause that Casaubon includes in his will, preventing Dorothea from marrying Will Ladislaw after his death – his vain attempt to imprison her, from beyond the grave, in the 'rigid clutch of his dead hand' (p. 324). The reach of this dead hand stretches across the novel, as Dorothea's striving to come to consciousness – what the narrator beautifully calls the 'struggling forth into clearness' (p. 192) of her mental life – is cast as her attempt to develop an animated relation to her own hand, to her own being, which the collected forces of Middlemarch conspire to thingify, to rigidify, to make into stone.

Eliot seeks to conjure pictures of live being that counteract her fascination with dead-handedness; in Dickens, too, the experience of becoming is one that takes place against the counter-pressure of dead flesh. *Bleak House*, like *Middlemarch*, is overseen, of course, by the actions of a bequest which casts a dead hand over all who enter into its sphere of influence. The interminable case of Jarndyce and Jarndyce is set in motion by a disputed will, a will which, Jarndyce tells Esther Summerson, has become a 'dead letter' (p. 108). This dead letter reaches out across the terrain that the novel seeks to bring into a new set of connections, bringing everything under its malign shadow, transforming the quick and living into the slow and the dead. The will has become a dead letter, and Dickens himself suggests, by way of a reference to Shakespeare's sonnets in the preface to *Bleak House*, that dead letters produce dead hands. When working in the environment shaped by the perversity of chancery law, Dickens writes, we find ourselves fashioned by, reduced to, the death that chancery deals out. 'Thence comes it that my name receives a brand', Shakespeare's sonnet reads:

> And almost thence my nature is subdued
> To what it works in, like the dyer's hand.[45]

It is the brilliance of Shakespeare's sonnet to catch at the duplicity of dying here; to dye the hand, to allow one's nature to take on the tint and the hue of living being, is to suffer a kind of death, the death that the experience of immersion in material being entails. Dickens' quotation of Shakespeare seeks to catch at this duplicity, to deploy it as the medium in which the novel's own becoming takes place. Shakespeare's sonnet and the dead letter of the Jarndyce bequest reach out together across the ground of the novel to establish an environment of dead-handedness, in which the struggle towards living being, the struggle to find new modes of connection, is thwarted by the stubborn inanimacy of matter, the sluggishness of the clay in which the quickness of nature is subdued. As the narrator says of Rick's obsession with chancery, in a phrase which echoes Shakespeare's dyer's hand, to become embroiled in Jarndyce and Jarndyce is to have one's 'whole career and character ... dyed one colour' (p. 555). Handedness is the vehicle, in *Bleak House*, for animation, for connection – the hand, here as elsewhere, is the instrument of self-identity, of fluid exchange between the inside and outside of being; but across the novel, the living work of the hand, both as the province of touch and as the province of writing, of the signature – is thwarted, undermined, by the death, the dye, which is also intrinsic to handedness, as if the very life that handedness promises doubles as an exposure to the rigour of death.

Nowhere is this experience of the deadness of flesh more total than in the novel's depiction of Jo the crossing sweeper – the closest that Dickens comes to a representation of what Giorgio Agamben calls 'bare life', and what Isobel Armstrong, in her theorisation of the 'democratic imagination', calls the 'deficit subject'.[46] Jo, like the prisoners of Nazi concentration camps in Agamben's theorisation of the condition of bare life, is a being who is denied subjectivity or political sovereignty through an act of radical exclusion from the political community – what Agamben calls a 'life that has been cut off and separated from its form'.[47] Poverty has so dehumanised Jo, so excluded him from the processes which might allow him to produce an animated version of himself that, the narrator thinks, it becomes difficult for those of us not excluded from the political realm to imagine what it would be like to be him, to imagine how his consciousness moves at all, buried as it is in its unreflective flesh – in the unmeaning primeval mud that oozes through the novel from its first pages, the mud that Jo struggles vainly to sweep from the crossings of the novel's thoroughfares.[48] 'It must be a strange state', the narrator says, 'to be like Jo' (p. 236). 'Jo's ideas of a Criminal Trial, or a Judge, or a Bishop, or a Government', he goes on, 'should be strange. His whole material and immaterial life is wonderfully strange'. Bare life, Agamben writes, is a life cut off from its form, and Jo too is so excluded. 'It must be strange', the narrator thinks,

> not merely to be told that I am scarcely human, but to feel it of my own knowledge all my life! To see the horses, dogs, and cattle, go by me, and to know that in ignorance I belong to them, and not to the superior beings in my shape, whose delicacy I offend! (p. 237)

The mechanism of this exclusion, a mechanism which connects Jo's condition to the work of the hand as it reaches across the novel, is illiteracy. It is Jo's inability to read and to decipher messages that are the cause and the outcome of his political nonbeing. It is Jo's lot, with the 'other lower animals', to 'get on in the unintelligible business as best they can', without the meaning power of written language; it is his lot to

> shuffle through the streets unfamiliar with the shapes, and in utter darkness as to the meaning, of those mysterious symbols, so abundant over the shops, and at the corner of the streets, and on the doors, and in the windows! To see people read, and to see people write, and to see the postmen deliver letters, and not to have the least idea of all that language – to be, to every scrap of it, stone blind and dumb. (p. 236)

Illiteracy, for Jo, does not mean simply that he is debarred from the forms of community that language creates; rather, his illiteracy produces also a radical alienation from himself, a sense that he is unable to animate his body, to make language and thought move through him. To be outside the symbolic order is to find that he has 'no business, here, there, or anywhere', but to discover, nevertheless, that he *has* a bare life of some sort that he cannot represent to himself, so he is condemned always to 'be perplexed by the consideration that I *am* here somehow' (p. 237), bewilderedly deposited in himself – subdued, as Shakespeare has it, to what he works in. And it is this condition, this sense that the body becomes bare material when it is not animated by living language, that spreads out across the novel, as a result of the perversity of chancery law, as a result of the deadening of language and thought that a corrupt and self-serving judicial system produces. Jo is devoid of language, but, at the other end of the scale, the novel is peopled with characters who are entirely made of language, but a symbology, like the 'parentheses and semi-colons' that run through Casaubon's veins, that has lost its capacity to mean, to endow or to distribute life. Chief among these is the odious lawyer Vholes, who is employed by Richard Carstone to pursue his interest in Jarndyce and Jarndyce, but whose real professional interests lie only in preserving the intricacies of a legal suit that has no referent in the world outside itself, and that is conducted in a dead language that has become entirely self-referring. Vholes is an oddly vanishing figure, whose persona, whose very physical presence, reveals his deathly withdrawal into a hermetic language world. He is characterised (like many of Dickens' minor characters) by three recurring traits – by his 'lifeless manner', his 'inward manner of speaking' and by his tendency always to wear black gloves – to be 'black-gloved and buttoned to the chin' (p. 560). Vholes is wrapped up in language, as he is wrapped up in his gloves (which are a near anagram of his name, the hard G becoming a soft, whispering H as it is absorbed into his inward speech, his lifeless manner). The touch of his gloved hand repels Esther; she remembers that he put his 'dead glove' on her own hand, and she felt that it 'scarcely seemed to have any hand in it' (p. 645) – a dread that is given some substance on the only occasion on which Vholes takes off his 'close black gloves', when, the narrator says, he seems to be 'skinning his hands' (p. 575).

Jo represents one extreme in the novel, in his illiterate embodiment, and Vholes, in his lifeless immersion in the softened letters of his inward name, represents the other. But between these two extremes, almost every character in the novel experiences some blockage between the language of the mind and the material of the body, some failure of language to move within being. One of the central nodes in the novel's mapping of this blockage, this failure of connection between the components of which the novel is made, is located in the hideous bottle shop owned by the illiterate Krook – an environment saturated with the mud and clinging slime that oozes through the novel, carrying always an association with undifferentiated, primeval unmeaning. Krook sits spiderlike at the centre of the novel, surrounded by chancery documents that he cannot read, which contain the secrets and the hidden conjunctions that run through the novel like ley lines; his singular relationship with these documents offers a powerful image of a frozen language, a language that can no longer undergo transformation into liquid sense, no longer establish living forms of communication between mind and body, between mind and mind. Krook has learned the letters of the alphabet by poring over endless affidavits, but he has no conception of what each letter signifies and so regards them as individual objects, as embedded pictures which have no symbolic meaning beyond their own forms, and which cannot enter into the conjunctions with each other, the magical melting of one letter into another, one word into another, that conjures consecutive sense out of static signs. In a compelling scene early in the novel, when Esther first visits Krook in the bottle shop, he demonstrates to her his eccentric manner of writing. He writes, Esther says, by chalking individual letters on the wall and then rubbing each letter out before shaping the next one in a sequence he has learned, like Robinson Crusoe's parrot, without the least understanding of its sense. He drew a 'J', Esther says, then replaced it with an 'a', 'then rubbed it out, and turned the letter r' until 'he had formed, beginning at the ends and the bottoms of letters, the word JARNDYCE, without once leaving two letters on the wall together' (p. 71). There is something perfect about Krook's rendering of that name, with its implication that the lawsuit, the dead letter of the will, should lead to this diminishing of living language to static matter. But there is something altogether stranger and more disturbing about the next words that Krook writes. 'In the same odd way', Esther goes on, 'he then produced singly, and rubbed out singly, the letters forming the words BLEAK HOUSE' (p. 71). Jarndyce and Jarndyce might have frozen Bleak House, the building which Jarndyce strives to turn into a home for himself and his wards; but the implication at this point is that the novel itself, *Bleak House* itself, is coming under this dismantling influence, having its own narrative energies frozen into stranded, hypostatised letters. Krook's shop forms one of those central crossing points in the novel – it is here that Nemo lives, the biological father of Esther and the lover of Lady Dedlock, and from here too that the affidavit is issued, in Nemo's hand, that allows the villainous lawyer Tulkinghorn to discover the liaison between Lady Dedlock and Nemo (previously known as Captain Hawdon). Nemo's identity is revealed to Tulkinghorn because although, when employed by the law stationer Snagsby, he writes Jarndyce affidavits in 'law-hand', some vestiges of his own handwriting remain, giving the letters a discernable individual shape. As Tulkinghorn says to Lady Dedlock, with his customary pregnancy, the 'legal character' of Nemo's writing 'was acquired after the original hand was formed' (p. 23). The whole wheeling tragedy of *Bleak House* unfolds because Nemo's identity reveals itself in his handwriting, like a signature; but at Krook's bottle shop, as letters are reduced to unmoving, unmeaning shapes, the influence of chancery brings all movement, all individuation, to a terrible stasis, to the dead letters written by the dead hand of Nemo, Esther's father, who already, at the opening of the novel, lies dead in an upper room in Krook's property, even as Esther, all unknowing, reads Krook's halting writing in a room below.

The drama of the novel swirls around this frozen language, the corruption of chancery making all of the characters alien to themselves, as Nemo's law-hand is superimposed on the hand that he originally formed. The triangular relations between Lady Dedlock, Captain Hawdon and Esther Summerson at the heart of the narrative and the larger historical conjunctions that the novel traces are broken, disfigured, by the violence that chancery does to the novel's language, and, repeatedly, this disfigurement is represented as a distance that opens between mind and hand, mind and biomatter. Jo the crossing sweeper, acting as a kind of shuttle at the novel's crossing points, recognises without properly understanding a connection

between Lady Dedlock, Captain Hawdon and Esther Summerson, and he
establishes this connection through the sight of Lady Dedlock's beautiful
ungloved hand – a flesh hand that is as singular and recognisable to Jo as
Hawdon's writing hand is to Tulkinghorn. As Lady Dedlock visits Jo in
disguise, to ask him to take her to the churchyard where her ex-lover is
buried, her hand comes into a peculiar, estranged relationship with his.
Afraid of contamination by contact with him – the contamination, of
course, which it is Esther's fate to suffer – she shrinks from him, 'putting
out her two hands and passionately telling him to keep away from her, for
he is loathsome to her' (p. 243). But despite her dread, the possibility that
Jo offers a delicate thread that leads to Hawdon emboldens her to overcome her fear, to expose her hand to his. 'She draws off her glove', the
narrator says, 'to get some money from her purse. Jo silently notices how
white and small her hand is' (p. 243). Jo recognises that hand – and his
recognition is what allows Inspector Bucket to unearth the hidden biological relations between Hawdon, Lady Dedlock and Esther. When presented with the hand of the servant Hortense, and asked if it is the hand
belonging to the lady that visited him, Jo is emphatic; 'Hand was a deal
whiter', he says, 'a deal delicater, and a deal smaller' (p. 335). Jo can
recognise the hand but he is never to understand to whom it belongs, as
the currents of the novel force a separation between hand and mind,
a disjunction which makes of the hand an alien, amputated thing. Lady
Dedlock, in a rare moment of unguarded tenderness, expresses a longing to
feel a contact with a loving hand – holding her cherished servant Rosa's
hand in her own, 'putting it about and about between her own two hands',
and yearning for Nemo's anonymised hand, what she thinks of as 'any
hand that is no more, any hand that never was, any touch that might have
magically changed her life' (p. 421). But it is her fate to feel no such contact.
As Dorothea is thwarted by the rigid clutch of Casaubon's dead hand, so
Lady Dedlock is debarred from loving touch by the malign influence of
Tulkinghorn, who is able to 'torment' her, even from the grave, with his
'lifeless hand' (p. 790). The touch she longs for comes only at the end of the
novel as she lies dead on the steps of the burial ground where Hawdon lies
in his grave, and as Esther arrives, with Inspector Bucket, too late to save
her. Esther should be the first to go to her mother's side, Bucket says: 'Her
hands should be the first to touch her' (p. 847).

When the narrators of both *Bleak House* and *Middlemarch* look to forge
new connections, then, it is across these divides, these gulfs between mind
and hand, that they build their bridges. *Bleak House* is a story, above all,
about the historical shift from the old aristocracy represented by the

Dedlocks to the new industrial society represented by the Rouncewells. As Mrs Rouncewell says to her son towards the close of the novel, 'the great old Dedlock family is breaking up' (p. 823). When Ruskin writes of Dickens that 'his hero is essentially the ironmaster', he is registering the passage, across Dickens' work, from the world order represented by the Dedlocks – organic, bucolic – to that represented by Mrs Rouncewell's son, the 'ferruginous person' whom Sir Leicester dismissively calls the 'iron gentleman' (p. 682).[49] Ironmastery leads to a prosthetisation of both body and the environment; Rouncewell's very person seems impregnated by 'steel and iron' (p. 878), as he becomes metonymically associated with the workforce that is shaping the country in a new image. His brother, Mr George, visits him in his northern industrial town and eats at a 'public house where some of Rouncewell's hands are dining' (p. 879). 'Rouncewell's hands', Mr George thinks, 'seem to be invading the whole town. They are very sinewy and strong, are Rouncewell's hands – a little sooty too' (p. 879). But even as Dickens narrates this historical shift and even as Eliot traces the shift from provincial tradition to emergent modernity in *Middlemarch*, both writers seek to give expression to a new kind of connective tissue that would allow a whole body to emerge from this experience of transformation, that would cross the gap between the 'not yet united piers' that 'desolately look at one another' in Dickens' unfinished railway network. 'Dickens was a pure modernist', Ruskin writes, 'a leader of the steam-whistle party *par excellence* – and he had no understanding of any power of antiquity except a sort of jackdaw sentiment for cathedral towers' (p. 7). Ruskin's own bucolicism is offended by what he sees as Dickens' apologia for industrialisation. But across Dickens' fiction, and across Eliot's too, it is possible to see that, however deeply their fiction is shaped by the experience of rapid historical change, their political and aesthetic energies are driven by the urge to find ways of connecting a prosthetic, manufactured lifeworld back to the organic forms that it seems to threaten; for both writers, these forms of connection are derived from the vanishing medium of prose narrative itself, that medium which takes on a new flexibility after Austen's refinements to the expressive range of narrative voice. Eliot's narrator asks what 'telescopic watch' could divine the connections that hold the fictional world of *Middlemarch* together, and the answer points towards the specific means by which narrative fiction, in the mid-nineteenth century, produces a new kind of binding force to animate an emerging manufactured lifeworld. Is there a telescope that could penetrate the substructure of the novel's plot, that could see what interests Mrs Cadwallader has in Dorothea's marriage to Casaubon? No, the narrator answers, 'Not at all. A telescope might have swept the parishes of Tipton and Freshitt, the whole area visited by Mrs Cadwallader in her phaeton', without bringing her layered motives to visibility. 'Even with a microscope', the narrator goes on, 'directed on a waterdrop we find ourselves making interpretations which turn out to be rather coarse' (p. 59). The substructure of this novel cannot be brought to visibility by optics, even those that are making the cellular structure of the living body visible to us. The kind of connective tissue that Eliot is weaving here is one, as Lydgate himself puts it a little later, that is composed of 'subtle actions inaccessible by any sort of lens' (p. 164), a connective tissue made only of the invisible movement of narrative, of the unsubstantial binding that brings Krook's individual letters, his static signs, into a sudden, transformative conjunction.

Across *Middlemarch* and *Bleak House* one can see this narrative binding force operating, summoning forms of connection from its own evanescence, from the edgeless proximity of the narrative voice itself to the forms of change that it is seeking to materialise. Will Ladislaw struggles rather crudely to capture something of this quality, this sense that narrative voice, thanks to that subtlety, that difference from itself that one can see forming in Austen's prose style, can capture change itself, change as the real basis of living being. When the artist Naumann is entranced by the sight of Dorothea, posed sadly beside a statue of Ariadne on her funereal honeymoon in Rome, his response to her beauty is to paint her, to capture the antithesis between her living body and the stone Ariadne in an image. But Ladislaw is insistent that it is only narrative voice that can adhere to the resonances that the spectacle sets vibrating throughout the novel, the suspended relations that it summons between inward being and the material and biomaterial forms in which such being only partly surfaces; it is only narrative voice that can do this because, like the very relations it strives to capture, it is made of a vanishing medium, made only of that difference that we find in Austenian irony – what Emily Dickinson beautifully calls the 'internal difference – / Where the Meanings, are'.[50] 'Your painting and plastic are poor stuff after all', Ladislaw tells Naumann, 'They perturb and dull conceptions instead of raising them. Language is a finer medium.' 'Language', he goes on,

> gives a fuller image, which is all the better for being vague. After all, the true seeing is within; and painting stares at you with an insistent imperfection. I feel that especially about representations of women. As if a woman were

a mere coloured superficies! You must wait for movement and tone. There is a difference in their very breathing: they change from moment to moment. – This woman you have just seen, for example: how would you paint her voice, pray? (p. 191)

A face, Thomas Hardy writes, 'confesses only in its changes', and Eliot makes of this realisation the basis of an aesthetic practice that she perfects over the course of her career.[51] It is not in our identity with ourself that we aspire towards the condition of living being, but in our difference from who we are, the difference that moves in our very breathing. It is in changing that we become; it is narrative voice which gives the fullest aesthetic expression to this change, this shifting passage from moment to moment that is thinking being, the struggle of thought towards clearness that it is Eliot's particular gift to follow with a form of prose that shares the mercurial quality that it describes, that seeks itself to vanish into being. Lydgate attempts, in his scientific research, to render invisible biochemical processes visible, to reveal what he calls (with a glancing reference to Hegel's *Phenomenology of Spirit*) 'those invisible thoroughfares' which 'determine the growth of happy or unhappy consciousness' (p. 165).[52] But Eliot's work suggests that the vehicle for such revelation is not the microscope, any more than 'painting and plastic', but rather prose narrative. 'Men', Eliot writes in an epigraph to *Daniel Deronda* that catches an echo from Lydgate's research in *Middlemarch*, 'have both a visible and an invisible history', and it is only the novelist, what she calls the 'narrator of human actions', who can 'thread the hidden pathways of feeling and thought which lead up to every moment of action' (p. 139). In another moment of resonance between *Middlemarch* and *Deronda*, the narrator of the latter insists that it is prose fiction, above all the other arts, that is able to capture the invisibility that is threaded into our visible presence, the immateriality that constitutes our biomaterial being. Reflecting on the beautiful spectacle of Gwendolen at her archery contest early in the novel, the narrator says, 'Sir Joshua would have been glad to take her portrait'; but in so doing, the narrator goes on, 'he would have had an easier task than the historian at least in this, that he would not have to represent the truth of change – only to give stability to one beautiful moment' (p. 98).

It is integral to Eliot's prose realism – and to her Feuerbachian, proto-Marxian materialism – that literary pictures of reality are made at once of moments of intensely realised being, and of a kind of nonbeing, the combination of which alone can allow us to represent the 'truth of change', the truth of material being in time.[53] To offer a picture of living being requires us to shape a form that is alive to the movement at once of the visible and of the invisible, the weightless and the weighty. As Alex Woloch puts it, it is a feature of the structure of the novel more generally to combine a 'commitment to a mimetic credibility' with an 'always potential form*less*ness' – what Georges Bataille calls 'l'informe'.[54] Form and formlessness combine in Eliot's work, as her prose offers a kind of disappearing bridge that brings the invisible ground of being into fleeting contact with the forms in which it knows itself, while continually undoing itself, continually yielding to the 'invisible history' that it witnesses, the 'hidden life' it preserves. It is by exposing oneself to the disappearance that inhabits material being – to the unrepresentability of the junction between mind and its extensions – that Eliot's prose captures the specific gravity of conscious life, giving moving expression to vital being, in a way that a marble statue, or a painting by Joshua Reynolds, cannot. As if in response to Wollstonecraft's desperate desire not to 'reason about' but to '*feel* in what happiness consists',[55] Eliot's realism, like a 'hand playing with finely ordered variety on the chords of emotion', produces a collapsing boundary between thinking and feeling, in which, the narrator of *Middlemarch* says, 'knowledge passes instantaneously into feeling, and feeling flashes back as a new organ of knowledge' (p. 223). And in Dickens' realism, too, it is the binding force of narrative that makes a connected fabric of the disconnected terrain of the novel – that produces a new 'organ of knowledge' – but only, in another version of the paradox that runs throughout the nineteenth-century prosthetic imagination, by casting itself into the distance between the inward mind and the outward self that it is the particular task of prose fiction to map. In Dickens, as in Eliot, this distance is at once the political problem that the novel addresses, and the aesthetic solution. If historical transformation makes disconnected beings of us all, driving a wedge between the Dedlocks and the Rouncewells, between the mind and the alienated hand, then the solution is not to resist such change, but to find a way of narrating that change itself, of making the formlessness of change expressive as form.

In *Bleak House*, it is the portrait of Esther Summerson that offers the richest resource for this transmutation, through narrative, of Hegel's 'unhappy consciousness' – 'this unhappy and estranged consciousness' which is 'already a doubled consciousness' – into the fullness of non-prosthetic being.[56] Esther, like most of the other characters in the novel, is put, from the beginning, at a distance from herself, making of her, Kevin McLaughlin has suggested, an example of 'Hegel's "self-estranged subject"'.[57] As her dreadful aunt tells her, in one of her earliest memories, 'You are different from other children', 'You are set apart' (p. 26). She is one of the many figures in Dickens' oeuvre – Pip, David Copperfield, Oliver Twist are others – who grows up estranged from herself, and from her biological family. That her mother believes her to have died immediately after her birth recurs, throughout the novel, as a sign that she is peculiarly death haunted; her aunt's declaration, on her birthday, that 'it would have been far better, little Esther, that you had no birthday; that you had never been born' (p. 26) makes her feel, like Jung's famous patient, as if she had indeed never been 'entirely' born.[58] The illness that she contracts from her contact with Jo – of which she has an early premonition, in the form of an 'undefinable impression of myself as being something different from what I then was' (p. 450) – only makes this innate condition visible. Jo's illness passes through the novel, like a viral manifestation of the alienation from self suffered by most of the characters – by Jo himself, by Lady Dedlock, by Nemo – and when Esther finds that she has contracted it she discovers that her feeling of being 'set apart' has taken on a pathological dimension. She lies ill, for a peculiar duration of non-time, no longer 'attached to life', with 'a strange calmness, watching what was done for me, as if it were done for someone else whom I was quietly sorry for' (p. 515). This experience not only amplifies her own estrangement but also catches at the condition of alienation that is a virtual epidemic in *Bleak House*. For the duration of her illness Esther is condemned to this strange suspension of being; then, when she recovers, she finds that her alienation from her own body – from her own face – is permanent. The illness scars her face so badly, she says, that she feels that the 'poor face' that once belonged to her 'was quite gone from me' (p. 526). She summons the courage to look at herself in the mirror after the change. 'She stood for a while', she says, 'looking through such a veil of my own hair that I could see nothing else'. But finally 'I put my hair aside, and looked at the reflection in the mirror: encouraged by seeing how placidly it looked at me. I was very much changed – O very, very much' (p. 528).

Illness, then, as a form of contact with the stunted community corrupted by chancery law, has led to this alienation from one's own face – a face whose expression one can only read at a prosthetic distance. But if this is so, what is most remarkable about Esther's estranged relationship with herself is that she finds in such estrangement not the debasement of self but rather the basis for a reclamation of living selfhood, refracted through the prism of a narrative which finds its home in the difference that resides in our very breathing, the change that works in us from moment to moment. Indeed, it is the mark, in this novel, of an ethical deafness to the call of others to find one's face unchanging, to find any identity clinging too closely to itself. Tulkinghorn, for example, in his greed for malicious control over others, is repeatedly represented as unchanging, frozen, like the letters that Krook hangs on the wall of the bottle shop. He has a 'countenance as imperturbable as death': 'Look at a millstone', the narrator says, 'for some change in its expression, and you will find it quite as soon as in the face of Mr Tulkinghorn' (p. 511). Mr Jarndyce, in his boundless goodness, is described, repeatedly, as having a 'changing face', and Esther's own changing face is represented, again and again, as an openness to the fluid movement of narrative, which is the engine of becoming in *Bleak House* and across Dickens' work. Esther's motherlessness, and her morbid bond, on the day of her birth, to her alter ego, the child whom her mother believed to have died, haunts her as it haunts Austen's Emma, and undermines her sense of belonging to self; but the work of her narrative – the first person, retrospective narrative that is paired with the third person present tense narrative throughout *Bleak House* – is dedicated to making of this difference, this death at the heart of her being, the province of an unfolding becoming. As the narrator of *David Copperfield* lovingly shepherds himself through life towards his own narrative consummation; as Pip survives a loveless childhood under the guidance of his own narrative voice in *Great Expectations*; as, indeed, Austen's Emma overcomes her own abandonment crisis through the differing work of narrative – so Esther finds in narrative the means of making a distance from her prosthetic face the occasion for a becoming. Over the course of the narrative, whenever Esther finds herself in her mother's presence, she intuits, through such an encounter, the presence of her dead self that always attends her – the baby whom her mother believed to have died, the baby who, as her aunt cruelly wished, had never been born – and every time she does so she experiences that alienation from self that she suffers when she looks in the mirror at her scarred face. Seeing her mother for the first time, in church, when she was unaware of her biological connection to her, she felt, she says, 'an unmeaning weakness in me', and she feels that 'I, little Esther Summerson, the child who lived a life apart, and on whose birth-day there was no rejoicing – seemed to rise before my eyes, evoked out of the past by some power in this fashionable lady' (pp. 268–71).

This is an alienation that is experienced too by Lady Dedlock, who feels drawn towards Esther, as Esther is drawn towards her. When she first discovers that Esther did not die at birth, Lady Dedlock herself experiences a kind of death – as if going to meet her daughter in some conjoined dead condition. When Mr Guppy tells her that Esther Summerson's 'real name' was 'Esther Hawdon', the narrator says that 'Lady Dedlock sits before him, looking him through, with the same dark shade upon her face, in the same attitude, with her lips a little apart, her brow a little contracted, but, for the moment, dead' (p. 430). Esther encounters herself as dead child in the presence of Lady Dedlock; Lady Dedlock becomes dead when she encounters Esther, stupefied like Dorothea when Mr Casaubon lays his dead hand on her. But if this encounter with death is finally terminal for Lady Dedlock, for Esther an ongoing death is the vanishing ground, the invisible thoroughfare, through which her own sense of continuous self must pass. 'I had an undefinable sense of myself as being something different from what I then was', Esther says when she feels Jo's illness stirring within her; but of course this difference from self is not only a death but also the difference from self that is the living movement of time. 'We are not merely more weary because of yesterday', Beckett says, in a passage I shall return to in due course, 'we are other, no longer what we were before the calamity of yesterday.'[59] This is what Esther knows, and narrative voice – fluid, mercurial narrative, not the frozen sequence of static signs that Krook hangs on the wall in his bottle shop, not the 'one beautiful moment' that might be captured in a painting of Eliot's Gwendolen – is what allows her to make of the death that inhabits her the seeds of a time that will flower into life with her. Scrooge, when he has been visited by the ghosts of narrative tense in *A Christmas Carol*, comes to the realisation that drives all of Dickens' narratives, the realisation that allows Scrooge himself to recover from the kind of immutability that we find reflected in Tulkinghorn's imperturbable face. To live, one has to yield to the constant death that is being in time – the death that it is the gift of narrative to convert into the substrate of living being. 'I will live in the Past, the Present, and the Future', Scrooge says at the close of the novel, 'The Spirits of all Three shall strive within me.'[60]

It is this death, transformed into the striving life force of narrative, that lies at the heart of all the failed conjunctions in the novel, that underlies that struggle towards 'connexion' with which this discussion began. 'What connexion can there be', the narrator asks, 'between the place in Lincolnshire, the house in town, the Mercury in powder, and the whereabout of Jo the outlaw with the broom, who had that distant ray of light upon him when he swept the churchyard-step?' The answer to this question – that element which connects the fragments of which the novel is made – is death, the death that intervenes between mind and hand, between past and future, the non-being that lies at the junction of being. Dickens' novel, as I have tried here to demonstrate, is organised around a number of centres, what Caroline Levine, in her Deleuzian reading of the novel, calls 'nodes in a dense overlapping of networks'.[61] Krook's bottle shop is one such; another, and the nodal point with which I will close this discussion, is the 'berrying ground' where Nemo is interred; where Esther finds the dead Lady Dedlock (who she calls the 'mother of the dead child', thus summoning the ghost of her own dead self to this final meeting); where Jo sweeps the step, with a distant ray of light upon him. This, of all the places in the novel, is the most infested, the most corrupt. It is a place on 'whose walls a thick humidity broke out like a disease', a place which 'oozed and splashed' (p. 844), a place 'pestiferous and obscene, whence malignant diseases are communicated to the bodies of our dear brothers and sisters who have not departed' (p. 165). As Jo is drawn to it, to pay his respects to Nemo, its deathly influence, its capacity to turn Jo into the dead object that he already is, becomes overwhelming. 'With the night', the narrator says, 'comes a slouching figure through the tunnel-court, to the outside of the iron gate. It holds the gate with its hands, and looks between the bars' (p. 165). Jo looks here into what Frantz Fanon calls a 'zone of nonbeing' – an 'extraordinarily sterile and arid region, an utterly naked declivity' – gated in and enclosed in the centre of the novel, an early version of Agamben's camp.[62] But if this is the most grotesque of places, what drives this novel is the sense that this oozing, slimy, filthy place, a place composed of the unmeaning mud that opens the novel, is composed also of the raw material of life; life and death here come into a contact that the political processes of subject formation are compelled to disguise, and that it is the particular gift of the novel to discover, and bring to thought. In Agamben's terms, what this zone of non-being makes visible is the 'inclusive exclusion' that oversees the attachment of consciousness to bare life. In the 'berrying ground', as in the camp, it becomes possible to see the naked material of being, the exclusion of which is the basis for the granting of sovereignty to the political subject, the 'exclusion-inclusion' that 'founds the space of politics'.[63] 'With houses looking in on every side', the narrator says,

> save where a reeking little tunnel of a court gives access to the iron gate – with every villainy of life in action close on death, and every poisonous element of death in action close on life – Here, they lower our dear brother down a foot or two, here, sow him in corruption, to be raised in corruption. (p. 165)

As Jo stands, shockingly reduced, like Oroonoko in Behn's novel, to an 'it', he places his hands on the gate, on the barrier that separates the place of death from the place of life – the barrier that the novel, in one sense, seeks to police. But it is the discovery of this novel – even as it seals this 'berrying' ground off to salvage the living hand, the living face, from the dead – that life and death, mind and matter, are woven together in ways that offer a challenge to all of those systems that Eliot describes in *Middlemarch* – Casaubon's mythical tradition, Lydgate's primitive tissue. Life is 'close on' dying, death is the interval that makes of life a sequence, and the very possibility of prose realism, for Dickens and for Eliot, emerges from this difficult inclusive exclusion, this interpenetration of the living and the dead that underlies the biopolitical condition. Georg Lukács famously writes that the political and aesthetic power of realism is that it allows us to represent the 'organic, indissoluble connection between man as a private individual and man as a social being, as a member of a community'.[64] That may be so; but if there is any truth in this, then there is so only to the extent that the organic connections this realism forges reveal the prosthetic material that is woven into the organic, and confront us with a picture of human being which is impossibly close to, indeed composed of, those nonhuman elements that the human excludes to represent itself as human. Agamben writes in 2014 that 'it will not be possible to think another dimension of politics and life' until we have 'succeeded in deactivating the apparatus of the exception of bare life';[65] Eliot and Dickens, in bringing the junction between the inclusion and the exclusion of biomaterial under the jurisdiction of a disappearing narrative, allow us to see that apparatus at work, as a constituent part of the process whereby we make of our own dead selves – our own dead hands – properly living beings.

4.3   An Inside Narrative: Prosthetic Life in Melville

So is every one influenced – the robust, the weak – all constitutions – by the very fibre of the flesh, & chalk of the bone. We are what we were made.

> Herman Melville, marginalia to Matthew Arnold, *Essays in Criticism*[66]

To have one's hands among the unspeakable foundations, ribs and very pelvis of the world; this is a fearful thing.

> Herman Melville, *Moby Dick*[67]

To differing degrees, then, Eliot and Dickens deploy their realism as a means of humanising the unruly material that they encounter, a means of bringing a life that exceeds the terms in which we live it into the framework of human relations. Eliot suggests as much in a letter of August 1868 to Clifford Allbutt. 'The inspiring principle which alone gives me courage to write', she declares, is 'that of so presenting our human life as to help my readers in getting a clearer conception and a more active admiration of those vital elements which bind men together and give a higher worthiness to their existence'.[68] Eliot's aim is to identify and articulate the vital elements which bind men to each other, and to themselves; it is possible to see this work of narrative binding in operation across both Eliot's and Dickens' work. But if this is so, I have been arguing that it is nevertheless the case that both Eliot and Dickens brush against the inhuman as a means of establishing the integrity of the human. The binding force of realism contains an unbinding within it; and it is in the work of Herman Melville that this buried affinity between the bound and the unbound – an affinity that courses through the nineteenth-century novel like a repressed collective unconscious – reaches a new kind of expression, an expression that at once marks a high point of the nineteenth-century realist novel, and enacts the contradictions that take us past the threshold of realism. If, as I have argued so far in this book, there is a constitutive relation between the novel and the prosthetic – if the novel imagination is involved in a long struggle to clear a space between consciousness and its material extensions to test the power of the mind in endowing material with the properties of life – then it is in Melville's fiction that this struggle comes out of hiding, partly as a consequence of the novel's own formal maturity, its developing capacity to access the folded interiority of being where the attachment to prosthetic material is fashioned. It is as the novel form reaches most deeply into the seams of being – as it crafts what Melville himself calls, in the subtitle to his late, unfinished masterpiece *Billy Budd*, 'An Inside Narrative' – that it comes closest to the junction between thought and material that is the province of what I am here calling the prosthetic imagination.[69]

In Melville, as in Eliot and Dickens, the dominant means of approaching this junction is through the figure of the dead hand – a trope that recurs in Melville's writing with an uncanny persistence. That he should name a character in his long poem *Clarel* 'Mortmain' is perhaps a sign of the fascination with dead-handedness that we find in *Moby Dick*, *Billy Budd*, *Bartleby* and elsewhere.[70] *Moby Dick* is the novel which contains, in Ahab's whalebone leg (a descendent, perhaps, of Tristram Shandy's whalebone nose), one of the more famous prostheses in the history of prose fiction; but the fixation, in that extraordinary work, with the process by which Ahab forces his monomaniacal mind into a union with the prosthetic material fashioned from the bone of his nemesis is shaped by the fantasy of a spectral hand that haunts the novel's crazed anatomy of embodied being. Ishmael tells, early in the novel, of an episode in his childhood when his stepmother confined him to his bedroom for sixteen hours as a punishment for misbehaviour. Half way through the ordeal, he remembers, as the room is 'wrapped in outer darkness', he becomes convinced that there is someone in the room with him:

> Instantly I felt a shock running through all my frame; nothing was to be seen, and nothing was to be heard; but a supernatural hand seemed placed in mine. My arm hung over the counterpane, and the nameless, unimaginable, silent form or phantom, to which the hand belonged, seemed closely seated by my bedside.[71]

The mystery of this phantom hand is never solved, but it also never leaves the psychic scene of the novel – as Ishmael himself says, 'to this very hour, I often puzzle myself with it' (p. 24) – and it silently oversees the deadly contest between mind and matter that is the central concern of the narrative. Ishmael is as fascinated with occupying his own flesh as Ahab is alienated from the prosthetic form – the marble countenance, the iron physique – that exerts such an influence on the narrator's imagination. Ishmael's infatuation with the 'fathom-deep life of the whale' (p. 164) that thrills through the book, and that powers its overwhelming materialism, is an adjunct to his relation with his own hands, his desire to find an accommodation with his own flesh. 'To grope down into the bottom of the sea' in search of the whale, he says, 'to have one's hands among the unspeakable foundations, ribs, and very pelvis of the world' – this is a matter of handedness. 'I have had to do with whales', Ishmael declares, 'with these visible hands' (p. 118). Reaching into the body of the whale with his visible hands is also a means of occupying himself, and of regulating his relations with his fellow beings, as he discovers his most intense experience of homosocial bonding when he plunges his hands in the warm sperm of the whale ('I squeezed that sperm', Ishmael writes, 'till I myself almost melted into it ... and I found myself unwittingly squeezing my co-laborers' hands in it, mistaking their hands for the gentle globules' (p. 373)). To 'have to do' with the whale, for Ishmael, is to be buried in the flesh of oneself and of one's fellows; as he calls to his fellow seaman, while together they knead the sperm of the whale, 'let us squeeze hands all round; nay let us all squeeze ourselves into each other' (p. 373). The encounter with the vast life of the whale is an encounter with embodiedness; but always, as Ishmael discovers his visible hands through his contact with the whale, this discovery is bound up with his relation to the invisible hand that so puzzles him, that is mantled in the outer darkness. Handedness involves both the material hand and the phantom hand, as Ahab himself finds that his relation with his prosthetic leg is haunted by the persistence of his 'old lost leg; the flesh and blood one' (p. 420), which still attends his physical frame. As Ahab says to the carpenter who fashions his leg from whalebone, 'I still feel the smart of my crushed leg, though it be now so long dissolved', so that 'when I come to mount this leg thou makest, I shall nevertheless feel another leg in the same identical place with it', an 'entire, living, thinking thing' that is 'invisibly and uninterpenetratingly standing precisely where thou now standest' (p. 420).

This relation between dead material and 'living, thinking' being runs, as I say, throughout Melville's writing. But if this is so, if Melville's work in general is driven by the relation between living being and the dead material from which it is made, it is in his short work *Benito Cereno* that these relations are given the tautest, most compelling expression, and where Melville comes closest to a political anatomy of prosthetic life. The novella is organised around the gulf between an apparent but misleading state of affairs on board a slave ship, the San Dominick, and a real situation that is everywhere on display but that only slowly and gradually resolves itself into narrative expression. The protagonist, the well-meaning captain Amaso Delano, boards the San Dominick, captained by Benito Cereno, because Cereno's ship appears to be in distress. What Delano finds when he embarks the ship remains perplexing and difficult for Delano to understand throughout the passage of the story and as a result resists our own urge to interpretation, appearing oddly out of focus, partaking of the disturbing unreality of a dream. Delano learns that many of the ship's inhabitants – a proportion of the white sailors and African slaves, along with all the passengers and the white slave owner Alexandro Aranda – have died during the voyage, apparently of fever. The ship is in disarray, the slaves are mingling freely with the slaveholders, and Benito Cereno himself appears strangely distant from the scene around him, listless and unconcerned, incommunicative with Delano himself to the point of rudeness. Endeavouring to read the scene before him, Delano struggles to understand Cereno's attitude, alternating between feeling pity for him as a fellow captain who has suffered a nameless trauma and fearing him as a possible adversary, a potentially piratical figure who is in league with the slaves, and who poses a threat not only to Delano's person but also to his own ship, which is anchored nearby. In this state of suspension, and with a growing perception of sinister threat, Delano is presented, the narrator says, with a 'living spectacle' that is enacted on board the ship, a gallery of 'strange costumes, gestures, and faces', a 'shadowy tableau just emerged from the deep' (p. 38), and it is his task to interpret this series of poised images, which read like symbols, like portents of a catastrophe that is approaching, but whose meaning is suspensefully withheld. In doing so, in trying to bring these cryptic tableaux to legibility, Delano is required to respond to the central concerns of the novella – that is, the ways in which political power is invested in racialised bodies, and the fields of force which shape our relation to ourselves, and to each other.

The first tableau consists of a group of Africans engaged in 'picking oakum' – unbinding bits of old ship's cable for use in the making of new rope. This group – the 'four elderly grizzled negroes, their heads like black, doddered willow tops' – is the sight that greets Delano as he boards the ship, and their presence remains conspicuous throughout the story.[72] They groan while they work – 'they accompanied the task', the narrator says, 'with a continuous, low, monotonous chant; droning and druling away like so many gray-headed bag-pipers playing a funeral march' (p. 38) – and their dirge provides the novella with a sinister, doom-laden sound track. Their occupation itself is symbolically overloaded, offering, at the start, a key to the rest of the images and tableaux that will present themselves to Delano's clouded understanding. 'They each had', the narrator says, 'bits of unstranded old junk in their hands, and with a sort of stoical self-content, were picking the junk into oakum' (p. 38). The unstranding work of the oakum pickers together with the oaky syllable in their name return in the first description we are given of Benito Cereno – 'Shut up in these oaken walls', the narrator says, 'his mind appeared unstrung' (p. 41). The sight of the oakum pickers, 'gravely plying their fingers' (p. 83) as they untie their cable, is bound up with the spectacle of the unstrung captain, looking on vacantly at the disarray on his own vessel. And then, as the story continues, the uncertain role of the oakum pickers in the 'unstringing' of Cereno's mind is woven into a series of other images, other tableaux which encode the means by which power and authority are disseminated through the ship's community, as the animating power of mind is distributed through the body. The unreadable relation between the oakum pickers and the unstrung captain, between master and slave, is reflected in the ship's stern piece – an intricate carving of a 'dark satyr in a mask, holding his foot on the prostrate neck of a writhing figure, likewise masked' (p. 37) – as well as in the figurehead, which is mysteriously shrouded in canvas, but which has been given a chalked caption, which reads '"*Sequid vuestro jefe*" (follow your leader)' (p. 37). These cryptic talismans of race and power are then given further weight by the spectacle of another group of six Africans, each of whom, 'engaged like a scullion in scouring', is polishing hatchets; they 'sat intent upon their task', the narrator says, and 'neither spoke to others, nor breathed a whisper among themselves', except at intervals 'they sideways clashed their hatchets together, like cymbals, with a barbarous din' (p. 39). It is impossible for Delano to tell if the hatchet polishers are subservient or warlike – menials subjugated to a task allocated to them by the tyrannical Benito Cereno or Cereno's armed henchmen, preparing to attack Delano and his crew, followers trodden beneath a foot or piratical leaders readying themselves to tread upon Delano. The barbarous din of the hatchet clashing mingles with the low moan of the oakum pickers to produce a peculiar white noise in which it is difficult to get one's bearings, to map fields of force. And in this symbolic confusion, at once generating a surplus of meaning and a deficit, the story gives us two more images, two more gestural portents. As if in counterpoint to the unstranding work of the oakum pickers, Delano notices one of the white sailors tying the most intricate of knots – 'a combination of double-bowline-knot, treble-crown-knot, back-handed-well-knot, knot-in-and-out-knot, and jamming-knot' (p. 63). The knot maker, like the oakum pickers, is described as 'plying his fingers' (p. 63), but unlike his African counterparts he is engaged in gnomic binding rather than unbinding. Delano, 'puzzled to comprehend the meaning of such a knot', asks him what he is knotting, only to be answered in cryptic terms. The knotter replies first in Spanish with the tautological reply that he is making a 'knot', then, quickly, in broken English, with the urgent injunction that he must 'Undo it, cut it, quick' (p. 63). The image of the knotter gathers echoes from that of the oakum pickers, and of the hatchet polishers, to produce a heightened awareness of the layered fields of force interpenetrating one another on the San Dominick, as Delano tries to understand what kind of power is being exerted by Cereno, and what kind of relations are at work between the white sailors and the black slaves. And these images together cluster around a last tableau whose symbolic power concerns the relation between binding and the racialised body and which is focused on the laden figure of the alienated hand that recurs throughout Melville's oeuvre. Delano 'chanced to observe', the narrator says, 'a sailor seated on the deck engaged in tarring the strap of a large block, with a circle of blacks squatted round him inquisitively eyeing the process' (p. 59). Like the oakum pickers and the knot tier, this activity has to do with the binding and sealing of rope, but in this case the connections between the tying of rope and the binding to one's own body are more explicit. 'The mean employment of the man', the narrator goes on, 'was in contrast with some-thing superior in his figure. His hand, black with continually thrusting it into the tar-pot held for him by a negro, seemed not naturally allied to his face, a face which would have been a very fine one but for its haggardness' (p. 59). As the dyer's hand in Shakespeare's sonnet is subdued to what it works in, so in this oddly haunting image, the white sailor's hand, as it works on the ropes that power the ship, is immersed in black material – the tar that binds the ship together but also the black material of race, the blackness that marks the distinction between slave owner and slave. Catching a glancing echo from a moment in Eliot's *Middlemarch*, at which the narrator gives us a sketch of a local 'dyer' whose 'crimson hands looked out of keeping with his good-natured face' (p. 712), the immersion of the sailor's hand in this sticky medium produces a disjunction between hand and face, as the forces that operate on board the ship open up a series of gaps, a series of unstrung spaces, which make it difficult for Delano to read the power dynamics that operate on the San Dominick along existing racial-political-economic lines.

It is in the midst of these ominous signs, gathering around Delano as he finds himself increasingly cut off from his own ship, that he is presented with the enigma of Benito Cereno, and of Cereno's relationship with his personal 'body servant' Babo (p. 40). Delano is confused by Cereno and cannot decide whether his perplexing manner – his 'sour and gloomy disdain' (p. 41) towards himself, his indifference to the indiscipline of his crew, his failure to show any gratitude to Delano for helping him recover control of his ship – is a mark of nervous exhaustion or a sign that he is planning an attempt on Delano's life; but Delano at no point in his time on the San Dominick has any serious ambivalence about the nature of Cereno's relationship with Babo. Whether he thinks of Cereno as exhausted nobility or scheming blackguard, he always regards Babo as a loyal servant, as the epitome of 'affectionate zeal' that has 'gained for the negro the repute of making the most pleasing body servant in the world' (p. 40). Delano's racism, his absolutely ingrained conception of Africans as inhuman – either animals or material commodities, living freight – means that he cannot interpret the scenes he sees before him by attributing a will to power to Babo or any of the other Africans. Everything he observes about the relationship between Cereno and Babo – and indeed everything he sees on the ship more generally – is filtered through this racism, this unexamined belief in the supremacy of the white master over the black slave. Babo stays as close as a shadow to Cereno at all times, and Delano registers in this attendance something menacing, but he cannot focus this menace, because he cannot attribute to Babo anything other than

devotion and subservience. Cereno shows repeated signs of distress when in
company with Babo – he has repeated 'sudden fainting attacks, brought
on, no doubt, by his mental distress', and through each such attack, Delano
reads Babo's insistent presence as a balm, a support. Cereno feels faint, and
Delano observes, time and again, that 'his servant sustained him' (p. 43),
physically propping him up. 'As master and man stood before him', the
narrator says, 'the black upholding the white, Captain Delano could not
but bethink him of the beauty of that relationship which could present
such a spectacle of fidelity on the one hand and confidence on the other'
(p. 45). While, through Delano's eyes, we see an increasingly sinister
relationship between Cereno and Babo – a relationship in which Babo's
support for Cereno exhibits the characteristics of a kind of forced restraint –
Delano remains blind to the possibility that Babo is exercising anything
other than faithful service to his master.

It is in the novella's famous shaving scene, in which the power relations
between master and slave are again pictured in a series of tense, symbolically overdetermined tableaux, that this menace, together with Delano's
blindness to it, reaches its greatest intensity. Babo prepares Cereno for his
daily shave while Delano looks on, Babo catching an echo of the hatchet
polishers on deck as he gives his razor 'an additional edge by expertly
stropping it on the firm, smooth, oily skin of his open palm'. Babo 'then
made a gesture as if to begin', the narrator says, 'but midway stood
suspended for an instant, one hand elevating the razor, the other profes-
sionally dabbling among the bubbling suds on the Spaniard's lank neck'
(p. 72). As he pauses in this attitude, all of the currents that are passing
through the novella – the peculiar and unreadable relations between master
and slave, the black and the white, the powerful and powerless – are held in
trembling suspense. 'Altogether', Delano thinks to himself, 'the scene was
somewhat peculiar', and even Delano entertains the idea that, 'thus pos-
tured', Babo appears as an executioner, that 'in the black he saw
a headsman, and in the white a man at the block' (p. 72). Such is
Delano's fixed conception of the racially embodied mechanics of power,
however, that he cannot sustain this thought, and the idea of Babo as
executioner seems to him one of those 'antic conceits' from which even 'the
best regulated mind is not always free'. Instead, he watches as Babo runs his
razor over Cereno's stretched throat – as the 'razor drew drops of blood,
spots of which stained the creamy lather under the throat' (p. 73), and as
Cereno, 'this unstrung, sick man' (p. 73), shakes in abject terror beneath
the 'gleaming steel' of Babo's blade – and sees only Babo's practiced
devotion, reflecting that 'there is something about the negro which, in

a peculiar way, fits him for avocations about one's person', that 'most negroes are natural valets' (p. 70). Delano acknowledges, in Babo's barbering expertise, a certain kind of mastery; 'smoothing a curl here', Delano thinks, 'clipping an unruly whisker-hair there', Babo is 'evincing the hand of a master' (p. 74). But Delano can only see the power of Babo's hand insofar as it works to sustain the myth of white supremacy; the work of black hands, as Toni Morrison suggests in a reading of 'whiteness' in Melville's fiction that I shall come to later in this book, is only thinkable as an invisible supplement to the spectacle of white power.[73] As Babo goes about his work, Delano thinks to himself that 'the negro seemed a Nubian sculptor finishing off a white statue-head' (p. 74). 'Backing off a little space' as he contemplates his shaved and barbered master, 'and pausing with an expression of subdued self-complacency, the servant for a moment surveyed his master, as, in toilet at least, the creature of his own tasteful hands' (p. 74).

Even as he is presented, then, with the spectacle of Babo holding a knife to the throat of Cereno, in the plainest of sights, Delano cannot shake his conviction that Cereno is in power. He sees the mastery of Babo's hand but can only conceptualise such mastery in terms of the process by which white power relies on the exploitation of the mute hand of slave labour. If Cereno is the 'creature' of Babo, he is so, Delano thinks, only to the extent that white bodies rely on the masterful work of black hands to achieve their self-ownership. But, of course, the real story of *Benito Cereno*, the under-narrative that thrills through all of those tense tableaux, and that builds colossally beneath the thick skin of Delano's racism, is the story of Babo's revolt, the rising up of the African slaves and the overthrow of their white masters, in what Michael Rogin calls 'the only successful mutiny in all of Melville's fiction'.[74] It is at the climax of the story, as its 'hidden energies' are 'let loose' (p. 56), that this under-narrative comes to the surface, and all of the counter-energies that are suspended in the novella's frozen tableaux are suddenly released. Delano is finally leaving Cereno's ship to return to his own vessel; as he prepares to disembark, standing at the threshold between the outside world and the tense interior of the San Dominick, there ensues a strange, slow-motion struggle between one frame of under-standing and another, a struggle conducted at the level of bodily gesture, as if the bonds that hold the Melvillian body together are being restrung, in front of our eyes. Cereno approaches Delano as if to detain him, and Delano, noticing a faint urgency in the gesture, moves to return towards Cereno's ship. As he does so, the narrator says, 'The Spaniard's nervous eagerness increased, but his vital energy failed; so that, the better to support him, the servant, placing his master's hand on his naked shoulder, and gently holding it there, formed himself into a sort of crutch' (p. 83). Even at this late moment, as Delano prepares to leave Cereno to the ministrations of Babo, he cannot understand the meaning of Babo's hold on Cereno – cannot understand Cereno's deadly nervousness or read the torqued contact of hand on shoulder. For Delano here, Babo is still a 'sort of crutch', the black prosthetic that allows for the sustenance of white power. Babo is 'anxious to terminate' this extended farewell, Delano thinks, because he is 'fearful that the continuance of the scene might unstring his master'. But then, as Cereno 'tears his hand loose' from Delano, and Delano clambers into the boat that will take him from the ship, everything accelerates, in a sudden intensification of action that is accompanied by a 'clattering hubbub in the ship, above which rang the tocsin of the hatchet-polishers' (p. 84). Cereno leaps from his ship into Delano's boat, and Babo leaps after him, so that the three men, Cereno, Babo and Delano, enter into a battle to the death: 'The left hand of Captain Delano, on one side, again clutched the half-reclined Don Benito, heedless that he was in a speechless faint, while his right foot, on the other side, ground the prostrate negro' (p. 85). In this attitude of locked struggle – which mimics the tableaux that have appeared through the story and captures the very gesture that is carved into the stern piece of the San Dominick – Babo manages to free a hand, with which, 'snakishly writhing up from the boat's bottom', he aims a blow 'at the heart of his master, his countenance lividly vindictive, expressing the centred purpose of his soul' (p. 85); with this act of naked violence, Delano suddenly understands the events that he has just witnessed. 'That moment', the narrator says, 'across the long-benighted mind of Captain Delano, a flash of revelation swept, illuminating in unanticipated clearness, his host's whole mysterious demeanour, with every enigmatic event of the day, as well as the entire past voyage of the San Dominick' (p. 85).

This is the moment for which *Benito Cereno* is written, the moment that the under-narrative, plainly discernable to all but the credulous Delano, erupts into visibility. 'Now', the narrator says, 'with scales dropped from his eyes', Delano 'saw the negroes, not in misrule, not in tumult, not as if frantically concerned for Don Benito, but with mask torn away, flourishing hatchets and knives, in ferocious piratical revolt' (p. 85). All of those mute tableaux that presented such an opaque spectacle to the benighted Delano suddenly resolve into sense. The oakum pickers are planted to surveil the sailors, to maintain the silent rule of the Africans over the Spaniards; the hatchet polishers are the armed guard enforcing the new piratical balance of power; the sailor tying the intricate knot and urgently imploring Delano to 'cut it' is warning Delano that the Spanish sailors are bound by the Africans; the Spanish sailor with his hand blackened by pitch is the victim of torture, as Babo's men have poured heated tar on his hands. And then, as a cable is cut in the final struggle between Cereno and Babo, the canvas shrouding the figurehead is whipped away to reveal the bleached white skeleton of the murdered slave owner Alexandro Aranda – 'chalky comment on the chalked words below, *"Follow Your Leader"'*. The sense, captured in each of the novella's tableaux, that the energies on board the San Dominick were 'unstrung', the sense that the power exercised by Cereno has entered into a kind of calm, in which the semantic and political structure of the ship's community had gone slack, is suddenly recalibrated, to reveal not a temporary weakening of white power but a total African overthrow of it. Babo, in this recalibration, is not Cereno's crutch – he is not the black prosthetic to white power. Rather, it is Cereno himself who is the prosthetic – the white mask behind which, throughout Delano's stay on board the San Dominick, an emergent, insurrectionary black power had disguised itself.

This is the moment, as I say, for which *Benito Cereno* is written – the moment at which an understory, an 'Inside Narrative', comes to light. As the scales drop from Delano's eyes, and as the novella concludes with Benito Cereno's 'Deposition', detailing the events that occurred during the rebellion, we finally see the 'interior' of the story that, the narrator says in the opening pages of the story, is 'till the last moment . . . hoard[ed] from view' (p. 38). 'If [Cereno's] deposition have served as the key to fit into the lock of the complications which preceded it', the narrator says at the close of the novella, 'then, as a vault whose door has been flung back, the San Dominick's hull lies open to-day' (p. 100). In bringing this hidden interior into the light, *Benito Cereno* performs the exposure of the internal mechanics of being that is the particular art of the novel form, as it develops over the nineteenth century. Melville's novella harbours a picture of what is called in Cereno's deposition the 'true state of affairs' (p. 98), which grows beneath Delano's ignorance, as the truth of Emma's love for Mr Knightley gestates beneath the mantle of her unknowing in Austen's *Emma*. When Emma finally discovers her devotion to Mr Knightley, Austen's narrator says that 'she saw it all with a clearness which had never blessed her before' (p. 335). 'With all the wonderful velocity of thought', Emma thinks, she 'had been able . . . to catch and comprehend the truth of the whole' (p. 353). It is just this peculiar narrative speed, this sudden unmasking, that is given to Cereno, as the scales fall from his eyes, and the 'flash of revelation' sweeps over him, revealing the truth of the whole. Cereno reviews the portents he has been given with Emma's 'wonderful velocity of thought', reseeing the events of the day in 'in images far swifter than these sentences'. As Babo leaps into the boat with Cereno and Delano, and the truth of the slave rebellion breaks through the artificial husk of Cereno's power, the revolution in Delano's seeing 'occur [s] with such involutions of rapidity, that past, present, and future seemed one' (p. 85). The interior of the story reveals itself with this suddenness, in the dawning of a new kind of narrative time; what we see as we adjust ourselves to the time of this inside narrative, like adjusting to brightness after gloom, is the inward junction between mind and material, the inside space of the prosthetic imagination, the secret place where we are knotted to ourselves and to each other with the most intricate of knots. The lightening flash of revelation exposes the knot by which Cereno is bound to Babo, as the will to power is bound to the body, both of the master and of the slave. Cereno is bound to Babo, as Dickens' Leicester Dedlock is bound to George Rouncewell, as Eliot's Mordecai is bound to Deronda, or as Melville's despotic captain Ahab is bound to the black cabin boy Pip in *Moby Dick*. Pip, devoted servant that he is, longs to act as a prosthetic for Ahab. 'Ye have not a whole body, sir', he says to the 'unstrung' Ahab; 'do ye but use poor me for your one lost leg; only tread upon me, sir; I ask no more, so I remain a part of ye.'[75] It is this act of prosthetic substitution that Babo refuses to perform for Cereno, and it is this refusal, this cleaving apart of prosthetic material from a naked will to power, that allows us to see deep inside the interior of being, that inside narrative that comes to light as the hull of the San Dominick flies open.

Benito Cereno, then, is an exemplary model of the nineteenth-century prosthetic imagination, as I have been exploring it through the phases of this long chapter. The Spanish sailor, whose hand is covered in tar, is one of the crowded examples of dead-handedness that recur throughout the novel of the period. His blackened hand 'seemed not naturally allied to his face' (p. 59), as the dead hand seems remote from animating mind in Dickens, Eliot, Zola, Wollstonecraft. *Benito Cereno* crafts this disjuncture between hand and face and then shapes an inside narrative, an interior form that allows us to approach the hidden junction between mind and matter to knit, from the sinews of prose narrative itself, a new novel body. Eliot writes that her fiction is devoted to articulating 'those vital elements which bind men together', and her novel *Middlemarch* ends, like Austen's *Emma*, with a picture of joined, living hands that is directly opposed to the dead hand that Casaubon lays upon Dorothea – a picture that arises at the moment that Ladislaw and Dorothea are finally united, against the prohibition in Casaubon's will, as Will 'laid his hand on hers, which turned itself upward to be clasped' (pp. 810–11). As Delano stands, regarding the Spanish knotter's intricate knot, it is this binding that he seeks to understand. Delano 'stood in silence surveying the knot', the narrator says, 'his mind, by a not uncongenial transition, passing from its own entanglements to those of the hemp' (p. 63). Standing, 'knot in hand, and knot in head' (p. 63), Delano registers the 'unstrung' state of affairs on board the San Dominick and prepares the frame through which the narrative, its hull finally lying open, might produce a new kind of knot, a new relation between mind and hand. But if *Benito Cereno* offers to undertake this binding, to gather an understory that refashions a new conjunction between mind and hand, what is so striking about Melville's novella – what makes it such a powerful witness to the nineteenth-century emergence of prosthetic life – is that the inside narrative it contains does not and cannot account for the radical distribution of life in material that it brings to thought. The enduring effect of Melville's novella is not to bind, not to humanise, but only to presage a kind of knotting, a poetics of prosthetic relation, that remains beyond the power of his narrative to realise or materialise. The 'flash of revelation' that is granted to Delano allows him to see the slave rebellion on board the ship. It shows him that Cereno's power is artificial – that the 'slender sword' which 'hung from a knot in his sash' (p. 45), the 'apparent symbol of despotic command' (p. 102), was 'not, indeed, a sword, but the ghost of one'. The phallic source of Cereno's power is prosthetic, as 'the scabbard, artificially stiffened, was empty' (p. 102). Cereno's relation to his body is overseen by the 'ghost' of his own 'flesh and blood' phallus, as Ishmael's binding to himself is haunted by the spectral hand of his childhood imaginings. But if the understory reveals the prosthetic nature of Cereno's power, what it does not express, what it can only contain in a fictional body that remains latent in the story, a bond between mind and hand that remains untied, is the revolutionary figure of the emancipated slave, the slave who takes ownership of his or her own laboring body. Everywhere in this novella one can detect the political desire for such revolution; everywhere one can see the burgeoning of a different story altogether, the story of barbarously imprisoned slaves who have risen up against their servitude, only to have their bid for freedom frustrated by the bumbling intervention of Delano. What burns at the heart of the narrative is Babo's livid countenance, expressing the 'centred purpose of his soul' (p. 85), as he struggles to overthrow his master. But this counter story, this inside narrative, remains untold, not because it is untellable, but because the logic of Melville's fiction suggests that the revolution that the novella calls for requires an overthrow too of the very narrative terms in which we have conceived of the human – the human as a construct indistinguishable from the artifice of white power with which Cereno stiffens his empty scabbard. As Morrison puts it, in her luminous reading, Melville seeks to anatomise the 'ideology' of 'whiteness' (p. 141) but in so doing is led to a kind of inarticulacy, to the requirement, as she puts it, that he must 'say something unsayable' ('It was the whiteness of the whale that above all things appalled me', Ahab says, 'I almost despair of putting it in a comprehensive form').[76] Babo's revolt lives on in *Benito Cereno*, not as the realised fiction of a successful slave rebellion but as a kind of shadow, an undertow that attends and disrupts the narrative construction of the human, and that calls for a distribution of life, power and meaning that might overcome the political and imperial ties that bind the experience of humanity to the grotesqueries of white supremacy. At the close of the narrative, in a passage that Ralph Ellison takes as an epigraph to *Invisible Man* – his own prose examination of the visibility of blackness[77] – Delano asks why it is that Cereno cannot recover his good humour, now that the 'malign machinations and deceptions' of Babo have been defeated: '"You are saved," cried Captain Delano, more and more astonished and pained; "you are saved; what has cast such a shadow upon you"' (p. 101). Cereno's answer, which is missing from Ellison's epigraph, is 'The negro'. It is negritude that stands as the shadow of the conjoined assemblage of whiteness and of humanity manifest in Cereno, and that calls for a different ordering of embodied being. 'The negro' who, Matthew Rebhorn argues, 'is an *embodied presence* whose *shadow* white antebellum culture wanted to misread only as an *absence*'.[78] Delano, oblivious as ever, tries to cheer up his gloomy friend; he should just forget about Babo, now that he is vanquished, as the 'bright sun has forgotten it all, and the blue sea, and the blue sky'. Cereno's reply is pregnant. The sea and the sky have forgotten Babo's revolt, 'because they have no memory', 'because they are not human' (p. 101). It is the fate of the humanity shared by Delano and Cereno, of humanity as it relies at once on the exploitation and the exclusion of those beings that it declares to be inhuman, to be haunted by the shadow of negritude, negritude as mode of living that exceeds those 'vital elements' which, for Eliot, 'bind men together'.

Melville's response to the demand that we attend to the shadow of those whom we exclude from the sovereignty of human being is to imagine a mode of art that fashions a new continuity between the human and the inhuman, the living and the dead, even if that continuity eludes the expressive power of prose fiction, remaining as an inside narrative that is unilluminated by any flash of revelation. It is the task of Melville's realism, both in *Benito Cereno* and across his oeuvre, to give aesthetic form to this subterranean continuity. As Michael Jonik has recently argued, Melville's 'political ontology' is 'dramatized not in exclusion of, but through inhuman material processes and relations'; and as David Alworth has suggested, Melville is a 'keen analyst of social interaction whose fiction is especially attuned to the role of the nonhuman'.[79] To respond to the call of Babo's insurrection – to understand the final image of the story, which shows Babo's decapitated head, 'that hive of subtlety' (p. 102), fixed on a spike – is to reconceive the means by which mind moves in material. The reality of slavery requires a material political response – one that is still unfolding as I write now, at the close of the second decade of the twenty-first century. But Melville's fiction suggests that the response to slavery is a narrative as well as a materially political task, one which involves the reshaping of the forces which bind the discursive construction of the human to the living material of the body. Babo's 'slight frame' the narrator says, in the closest that the narrative gets to explicit sympathy with the rebellion, is 'inadequate to that which it held'; the force of his revolutionary consciousness exceeds the bounds of any material frame. As Emily Dickinson put it in 1863,

> The Brain – is wider than the Sky –
> For – put them side by side –
> The one the other will contain
> With ease.[80]

For Melville, as for Dickinson, a poetic understanding of the way that thought materialises itself requires us to break the frame that shapes the relations between consciousness and the forms in which it extends into the world; it requires us to work against the protocols of life which align humanity with whiteness, the narrowly understood conception of 'vitality' which binds us into a human shape built on the exclusion of all that does not conform to a white colonial epistemology.

To that extent, then, Melville's realism moves in the opposite direction to Dickens' and Eliot's. Where Eliot is committed to binding, Melville's aesthetic, like Dickinson's, is a poetics of unravelling. Dickens produces a narrative frame which allows us to humanise an unruly body, and to give shape to an unruly time – to allow the spirits of past, present and future which strive within us to yield themselves to the lucidity of narrative sequence. Melville's narrative movement, in contrast, points to a kind of material time which cannot fit itself within narrative tense, which is much closer to Dickinson's 'Sequence raveled out of sound', a time in which, as the narrator of *Benito Cereno* puts it, 'past, present, and future seemed one'.[81] But if this is the case, it is true also that the realism of Dickens, Eliot, Austen, Zola – the form of realism that emerges with the development of the nineteenth-century novel – can only give the material of life a bound form by bringing mind into contact with a mode of prosthetic embodiment which continually exceeds the rhetorical forms which vitalise it. Life, in Dickens as in Melville, is close on death; death is close on life. Eliot's other side of silence is found in the intimate midst of the junction between Dickinson's syllable and sound. Melville shows us a dead hand, a hand whose blackness cannot be allied to the white face or to any existing protocols of living being. This is the dead hand that recurs throughout the nineteenth-century novel – and further back through the longer history of the form – like the conscious sign of an unconscious compulsion surfacing in a dream; the dream that Ishmael has, perhaps, which puzzles him to this day. Realism is the name given to the process by which we seek to bring that dead hand into the sphere of life. Eliot and Dickens seek do so by humanising the inhuman, Melville by inhumanising the human. But for all three writers, it is the gift of the novel – its beauty as well as its power – to enter into the spaces where living thought brushes against dead material, and to bring such spaces, such inside narratives, into the clair-obscure arena of discursive possibility.

CHAPTER 5

Strange Affinity: Gothic Prosthetics from Shelley to Stoker

My spirit will sleep in peace; or if it thinks, it will not surely think thus.

Mary Shelley, Frankenstein¹

It's ill to loose the bands that God decreed to bind.

Robert Louis Stevenson, The Strange Case of Dr Jekyll
and Mr Hyde²

If thought could exercise its influence upon a living organism, might not thought exercise an influence upon dead and inorganic things? Nay, without thought or conscious desire, might not things external to ourselves vibrate in unison with our moods and passions, atom calling to atom in secret love or strange affinity?

Oscar Wilde, The Picture of Dorian Gray³

I have been discussing the recurring figure of the dead hand in the nineteenth-century novel, to this point, as a central node in the development of prose realism. The history of realism, I have argued, is the history of an encounter with extraneous, intransigent material that resists the conjoined imprimatur of the living and of the human, while nevertheless leaving its mark on the narrative form it resists.

To have conducted this discussion, this far, as a sober reflection on the functions and contradictions of realism has been to repress a rather unquiet spirit that has moved through everything I have said so far, to overlook a rather sinister elephant in the room (if elephants can be sinister). That is, of course, the fact that dead-handedness might stand, in the critical and readerly imagination, as the central figure not of the realist novel but of the Gothic novel, not of the strand in the novel that seeks to make accurate pictures of the world we live in but of that other strand, that dark twin, that makes pictures of the world as it is not and could never be. Caroline Levine observed that 'Many critics would broadly agree' on the defining traits of realism, even if the subtler definitions can become technical or contradictory. 'Realist writers', she argues, 'rejected allegory and symbol, romantic and sensational plots, supernatural explanations and idealized characters, and opted instead for the literal, credible, observable world of lived experience'.[4] Levine goes on to offer a nuanced account of what is at stake in the urge to Victorian realism; but her bald opening points never- theless to a generic convention that draws a distinction between realist works which seek to capture a 'credible' world of 'lived experience' and those which do not, those which yield to the temptations of the 'sensa- tional' or the 'supernatural'.

If we accept, for the time being, that there is a reality to this distinction, then it quickly becomes apparent that the fascination with the dead hand that I have traced in Austen, Dickens, Eliot, Zola and Melville is shadowed by a Gothic dead hand, one that is more difficult to fit within the nine- teenth-century realist tradition. As Robert Miles has argued, the Gothic novel 'begins' with an image of a dead hand – the 'vision of a "gigantic hand in armour"' that is the impetus behind Horace Walpole's *Castle of Otranto* – and the 'metaphor' (as Miles calls it) remains at the 'centre of the genre's symbolic constitution'.[5] From Walpole's dead hand, the image recurs repeatedly, as if the Gothic cannot operate without it; and repeat- edly, perhaps necessarily, the image of the dead hand is bound up with an encounter with material that exceeds or blurs the taxonomic boundary between the living and the non-living – an encounter with that 'unwel- come state', first novelised by Cervantes in *Don Quixote*, 'that mingles life and death' (p. 908). Mary Shelley's *Frankenstein*, for example, which is a more certain origin of the mode of Gothic prosthetics I will be discussing here than Walpole's *Otranto*, generates its persistently uncanny effect by opening a difficult ground between living being and dead material – the unthinkable, abject ground that is the homeland of the nineteenth-century Gothic. It is Victor Frankenstein's driving ambition, he explains to Walton early in Shelley's novel, to fashion this new relation between life and death – to manufacture a prosthetic bio-machine that will be composed of dead material that partakes of the energies of life. 'Life and death', he says, 'appeared to me ideal bounds, which I should first break through, and pour a torrent of light into our dark world'.[6] But, of course, once Frankenstein has achieved this breaking through, once he has managed to 'bestow animation on lifeless matter' (p. 54), he finds that this creation of a living prosthetic does not lead to illumination, does not overcome the darkness of death, but rather opens some horrible, manufactured hinter- land between living and dying which threatens to unbalance the terms in which we have conceived of both life and death, both light and dark. The

enduring fascination of *Frankenstein* resides in its capacity to approach this
hinterland, to generate the spectacle of a dead body that, in all its deadness,
is nevertheless infused with life, making of the relation between the dead
and the living what Agamben would call an inclusive exclusion.[7] The
moment when the 'dull yellow eye of the creature opened' and
a 'convulsive motion agitated its limbs' (p. 57) is one of those moments,
described recently in a very different context by Amitav Ghosh, at which
'something that seems to be inanimate turns out to be vitally, even
dangerously alive', a moment when we are faced with the prospect of
what Frankenstein calls a 'filthy mass that moved and talked' (p. 147).[8]
And, almost inevitably, the first form taken by this inanimate animation
(or perhaps what David Wills calls this 'inanimation'[9]) is that of the dead
hand. The relationship between Frankenstein and his monster opens and
closes with the reaching of the monster's hand towards the hand of Victor
himself, the 'cursed' hand of the creator. Victor first encounters the
monster when he awakes to find him standing awfully at his bedside,
with 'one hand stretched out, seemingly to detain me' (p. 58), and this
pose is repeated at the end of the novel, as the monster stands over Victor's
death bed, with 'one vast hand extended . . . in colour and apparent texture
like that of a mummy' (p. 218). Victor is lying finally vanquished in the
shadow of the monstrous dead hand, returned, himself, to the inanimate
biomaterial that he shares with the creature whom he refers to, repeatedly,
as the 'work of my hands' (p. 164).

   Across the century, one can see the massing of such images of deadened
limbs brought to uncanny life by a dissident imagination. One has only to
think of the truly bizarre story by Silas Weir Mitchell, entitled 'The Case of
George Dedlow', which tells the story of Dedlow, a soldier who is injured
in combat and has all four limbs amputated, only to end the story by
gaining possession of his excruciatingly painful phantom limbs under
a mesmeric trance, enabling him to caper about, half comically, on invisible legs.[10] Or one might think of Poe's equally strange story, 'The Facts in
the Case of M. Valdemar', in which Valdemar is reanimated after his death,
like Apuleius' Thelyphron, so that he is able to speak from the very
province of death, again under a mesmeric trance, with a blackened,
dead tongue.[11] But is in Bram Stoker's 1897 work *Dracula* that this
transgression of the boundary between the living and the dead reaches its
definitive expression. It seems entirely appropriate – again somehow
inevitable – that the first encounter between Jonathan Harker and the
count, when Harker travels to Transylvania at the opening of the novel,
should involve the appearance of mortmain, of the dead hand. Harker

notes that the hand of the coach driver who drives him to Castle Dracula –
Dracula himself, of course, in scant disguise – has an inhuman quality. The
driver, he writes in his journal, greets him with 'a hand which caught my
arm in a grip of steel';[12] when Dracula meets Harker for the first time in his
own person, it is this inhuman grasp that Harker notices. 'His hand
grasped mine with a strength which made me wince', Harker writes, 'an
effect which was not lessened by the fact that it seemed as cold as ice – more
like the hand of a dead than a living man' (p. 26). This encounter with the
dead hand, as the signature of the vampire, recurs throughout the novel:
the ship that brings Dracula to the shore of Whitby is steered by 'the hand
of a dead man' (p. 105) in a mirror image of Harker's coach. Arthur
Holmwood, entranced by the beauty of Lucy Westenra's undead corpse,
is led to 'take her dead hand in his' to kiss (p. 219). The dead hand repeats
throughout the novel; when it does so, it calls always to the terrain that
Dracula calls to thought – the terrain that is proper to what Stoker calls the
undead. As Shelley's *Frankenstein* imagines a hybrid being, made of both
dead and living material, so Stoker's novel is dedicated to producing the
imaginative possibility of a differently distributed life, a life that reaches
out tendrils not only into dead biomaterial but also into earth, into stone.
Some of the most memorable passages in the novel, in which Harker and
his allies penetrate into the tombs of the undead, both of Lucy and of
Dracula – produce extraordinarily vivid pictures of such redistributed life.
Dracula lies in his coffin, partly buried in the ancient soil that is as much
part of his being as his bodily frame, shrouded in a 'deathly, sickly odour,
the odour of newly turned earth' (p. 66). His body has a continuity with
this foul-smelling earth that even now troubles thought, and there remains
something exorbitantly horrific about the sight that greets Harker when he
first finds him lying, in his undead state, composed at once of figure and
ground, of animate and inanimate, of person and thing. 'He was either
dead or asleep', Harker writes as he finds himself drawn into a face-to-face
relation with this aberration, 'I could not say which – for the eyes were
open and stony, but without the glassiness of death – and the cheeks had
the warmth of life through all their pallor, and the lips were as red as ever'
(p. 67). The count, lying in a condition of unbeing, looks at Harker with
'dead eyes' which, 'dead though they were', are animated by 'a look of hate'
(p. 67); it is this same sight that greets Harker and his team when they
disinter Lucy (or 'the thing that was Lucy because it bore her shape'
(p. 271)), to find her 'more radiantly beautiful than ever' (p. 258) and
dangerously, giddyingly desirable. 'Here', Van Helsing says to Harker, as
he gazes on Lucy's sumptuous form, 'is one thing which is different from

all recorded: here is some dual life'. 'In trance', he goes on, 'she died, and in trance she is un-Dead, too' (p. 258).

So, the nineteenth-century Gothic tradition is haunted by a ghoulish dead hand and by an erotically charged transgression of the boundary between the living and the dead that works against the dead hand of realism, that allows the space of that disjuncture between animate and inanimate that lies at the generative ground of realism to tumble into the darkly desirous unmeaning that always threatens to unbind the realist mode – the unmeaning that the imaginative energy of Dickens, of Eliot, of Melville is unevenly marshalled to contain, to sublimate into form. But if this is the case, it is nevertheless also true that the Gothic mode itself is closely related to the realism that it mirrors and distorts; it is true too that one cannot understand the prosthetic charge either of nineteenth-century realism or of the nineteenth-century Gothic without attending to this mutually entwined relationship, without responding to the ways in which realism is inhabited by a Gothicism that works as its repressed unconscious, while the Gothic itself can only come to consciousness through its own intense mode of realism.

It is this mutual entanglement between realism and the Gothic – and the ways in which both modes oversee and police the boundary line between them – that determines our understanding of the prosthetic force of the Gothic imagination. There is, of course, a strain of the Gothic that runs throughout the realist novel of the century, and which it is in part the task of realism itself to contain, to quarantine. It is obvious, for example, to all readers of Dickens that his realism, his extraordinary capacity to produce vivid pictures of a 'credible world of lived experience', is inhabited at all times by a Gothic urge. The picture of Jo the crossing sweeper in *Bleak House* is an excoriation of the relentless reality of poverty, rather than an indulgence of more unreal evils, but the 'wonderful strangeness' of his 'material and immaterial life' partakes too of the uncanny substance of the Gothic. Describing Jo's unthinkably abhorrent lodgings, Dickens' narrator says that 'Jo lives' in a 'ruinous place known by the name of Tom all alones', but he interrupts to correct himself. 'Jo lives', he writes, ' – that is to say that Jo has not yet died' (p. 235). Jo's living is a kind of deferred dying, and in attaching Jo to his undead body, to his bare life, Dickens calls forward, quite clearly, to Stoker's host of the undead. And those moments in Dickens' work when his characters undergo a kind of stupefaction, a kind of temporary death, always shimmer with a Gothic gleam. Lady Dedlock, when Guppy tells her that her daughter Esther is still alive, suffers a temporary death that has a rich genealogy reaching back through the

history of the realist novel. She sits apparently unmoved as she learns of her
daughter's continued existence, but 'she is, for the moment, dead' (p. 430).
She is overcome by a 'dead condition' that echoes all those moments of
suspension that I have traced in the novel so far, from Oroonoko's passing
death (in which his body 'knew not that it had being'),[13] to the moment
that Moll Flanders 'degenerates into stone' in Newgate ('I had no Tongue
to speak', she thinks, 'or Eyes to look up either to God or to Man'),[14] to
Pamela's falling, at the moment of her ravishment, into a 'deplorable state
of death' in Richardson's *Pamela*,[15] to Mary's insensibility on being given
away in marriage in Wollstonecraft's *Mary* (an insensibility in which her
'eyes' were 'no longer a sense; they conveyed no ideas to the brain').[16] All of
these moments of novelistic living death echo at this point in *Bleak House*
as Lady Dedlock absorbs the fact that her daughter is *not* dead; but also,
what thrills through the moment is a Gothic charge that calls to this twin
tradition. Death passes over Lady Dedlock 'like a ripple over water', but
her self-control is such that this dead condition seems to 'pass away like the
features of those long-preserved dead bodies sometimes opened up in
tombs, which, struck by the air like lightning, vanish in a breath'. Death
ripples and then passes in the midst of Lady Dedlock's majestic impassiv-
ity, in a fashion that echoes all those moments of sudden decomposition
that flow through the Gothic tradition, like that which emerges at the end
of Poe's 'Case of M. Valdemar', when Valdemar's uncannily suspended
living-death is brought to an end, and his 'whole frame at once – within the
space of a single minute, or even less, shrunk – crumbled – absolutely
rotted away beneath my hands' (p. 105); or that which is reprised at the end
of Stoker's masterpiece, as Dracula is impaled by Harker's knife, and, 'like
a miracle', 'almost in the drawing of a breath', his 'whole body crumbled
into dust and passed from our sight' (p. 484).

   The realist tradition, then, is shot through with these moments of
Gothic horror, these stirrings of an unreality that shadows its commitment
to mimesis, and the Gothic tradition itself cleaves closely to a realist mode.
Indeed, for all its fascination with the unregulated, with the unruly, with
the unstable, the Gothic mode often functions as a conservative form,
a mode which, even as it bears witness to the exorbitant energies of a life
that is not contained within the taxonomies of a properly living being,
seeks to bring such exorbitancy back into the regulated economy of the real
(the economy of Amaso Delano's 'well regulated mind', in Melville's
Benito Cereno (p. 72)). From this perspective – the perspective most
famously theorised by Stephen Greenblatt as the 'subversion containment'
model – the Gothic mode allows itself to abandon its mimetic function, to

spin off into an abyss of uncontained eroticism and radical intersubjectivity only to bring such transgressive desires into the realm of the regulated, of the orderly. As Greenblatt writes of Shakespeare's plays that the 'constant production' of 'radical subversion' effects the 'powerful containment of that subversion',[17] so the Gothic tradition can appear to approach that unhallowed ground between the living and the dead, that junction that lies at the heart of the prosthetic condition, only to banish it from the scene of our self-fashioning. The wilder, the more unfettered the Gothic approach to this region is, the more effectively it works to contain it, to colonise and tame the energies that it seems to release.

One can trace the passage of this relation between the transgressive and the contained as it develops over the course of the nineteenth century; in doing so, one can discern the outlines of a trajectory in which the Gothic novel deploys the shifting historical resources of realism against the subversive energies that it at once releases and contains. In Mary Shelley's early century novel *Frankenstein*, for example, it is easy to see that the narrative's fascination with Victor's subversive thinking – his strange alliance with the monster that he so despises – is contained within a realism that is shaped by Shelley's reception of the eighteenth-century novel, and particularly by her relationship with Goethe (as this is filtered through a romanticised version of Milton's cosmology). Frankenstein's horrified response to the monster he has created is determined, from the beginning, by his conception of the organic, and of the relationship between the organic and the aesthetic that Shelley finds in Goethe (a conception that the monster himself forms too, as he sits studiously in his hut reading first Milton's *Paradise Lost* and then Goethe's *Sorrows of Young Werther*). Victor is closely modelled on Goethe's Werther (as, oddly, is the monster, who declares improbably that 'I found myself similar' to the protagonist of Goethe's novel (p. 128)); like Werther, Victor has a passionate affinity with nature, and like him this affinity produces a sense of the dangerous promiscuity of life, a sense that the sheer profusion of life exceeds any human frame within which we might contain it. Werther's death drive, his capacity to enter into that peculiar, suspended state between life and death – the space, in Goethe's novel, that is as close as we can come to the space of suicide – is closely bound up with his sensitivity to the abundance of a sublime noumenal nature that cannot come to any phenomenal form. When, Werther writes, 'immense mountains surrounded me, chasms yawned at my feet, streams swollen by rain tumbled headlong, rivers flowed below me and the forests and mountains resounded' (p. 65), then he is able to divine something of the 'glorious forms of infinite creation', something of the 'inmost, sacred warmth of the life of nature' (p. 65). For Werther, in a passage that I quoted earlier, a sublime feeling for nature reveals that 'every speck of dust is alive' (p. 65) – a sense of the dispersal of life that is closely allied, paradoxically, to his deathly infatuation with the limits of the human. It is the non-taxonomised nature of life that leads Werther to that suicidal region where his 'entire self trembles on the edge of being and not-being' (p. 99), and it is this same sensitivity that drives Shelley's Victor, that takes him to the inmost junction between being and non-being that is materialised in the Gothic form of the monster. Victor is channeling Werther when he enthuses about the natural beauty of his native Switzerland. Walking in the 'Alpine valleys', he writes, surrounded by 'the immense mountains and the precipices that overhung me on every side – the sound of the river raging among the rocks, and the dashing of the waterfalls around', he divines a 'power mighty as Omnipotence' (p. 94). And, like Werther, this feeling for the power of nature leads him to 'examine the causes of life' (p. 51), to 'penetrate into the recesses of nature' to 'show how she works in her hiding places' (p. 47).

Both Werther and Victor, then, enter into an unregulated space, composed of a difficult meeting of the living and the non-living, through a sensitivity to the nonhuman vitality of nature; but if this is so, for both Shelley and Goethe, this approach to a diffused vitalism, to a mode of life radically dispersed in material, is conducted in the name of an organic wholeness, a wholeness that the form of the realist novel itself is shaped to guarantee. For both writers, this organicism is structured by an examined barrier, a barrier that the sublime feel for life leads both protagonists to exceed, but which it is the task of fiction to formalise. Werther, separated from the woman with whom he is infatuated, believes that he is condemned to live in unequalled misery; 'Ah', he thinks, 'have ever men before me been so miserable?' (p. 101). He lives in the solitude of his misery, unable to connect with the world around him, because, he says, the outside world is 'like a barrier my soul has come up against' (p. 101). Frankenstein and the monster that he has contrived feel that same combination of a boundless solitary misery with the imposition of a barrier that contains and deflects their dangerous energies, even as the tendency of their desires is to 'burst all bounds', to exceed any limits that are placed upon them. 'No creature', Victor thinks, again paraphrasing Werther, 'had ever been so miserable as I was' (p. 197); his misery resides, above all else, in the experience of the barrier, the sense that the intellectual activity that takes him across the boundary between the living and the dead should condemn him to self-alienation, to an ejection from the community of rules and taxonomies that he longs to rejoin. As he is locked into his pact with his monster, he thinks that 'an insuperable barrier' had been placed 'between me and my fellow creatures' (p. 169); earlier, as he reflects on his unwilling complicity with the monster's murder of his family, he says that 'I saw an insurmountable barrier placed between me and my fellow men', a 'barrier sealed with the blood of William and Justine' (p. 158); and earlier still, the monster has the same thought, rails against the same barrier that he feels reasserts the natural and organic proprieties that his very existence denies. He longs for loving contact with others of the human race, but he recognises, to his intense anguish, that such communion 'cannot be', that 'the human senses are barriers to our union' (p. 145). As Victor himself says to his monster, despite the difficult bond that joins him to his creature, the species barrier must remain intact; 'we are enemies', he tells him, 'there can be no community between you and me' (p. 100).

The delicate balance, then, in Shelley's novel, between its relation with realism and its Gothic tendencies, is struck in part to allow for the germination of a kind of alienated vitalism, a kind of prosthetic being, that the contracts of realism itself continually thwart. If the prosthetic junction is the repressed nursery of the realist imagination, then the Gothic body of the monster is the form that this junction takes when it comes out of hiding. The concentric shape of the novel – in which Walton's frame narrative on its icy outer ring yields to the inner story of Frankenstein's creation of his monster, which gives way in turn, at the very heart of the novel, to the monster's own narrative – allows Shelley, in a giddyingly high-risk experiment, to give a narrative voice to inhuman material, to let the unspeakable speak. The monster's description of the process by which his consciousness develops from an early formlessness ('no distinct ideas occupied my mind', the monster says, 'all was confused' (p. 103)), to the bright lucidity of language, remains to this day remarkably powerful. 'It was', the monster says to his creator, 'a long time before I learned to distinguish between the operations of my various senses' (p. 102), and longer still before 'my eyes became accustomed to the light, and to perceive objects in their right forms' (p. 104); as the monster gives us this first-hand account of the genesis of his mind, Shelley's narrative retraces not only Genesis but also the opening of Hobbes' *Leviathan*, giving us birth into a different kind of state, a different kind of sovereignty, one in which the distinction between the human and machine, the begotten and the created, the real and the artificial, is redrawn, reimagined. But as the novel sets out to contain this undifferentiated vitalism in its inner ring, it brings all those resources of organic aesthetics that I traced earlier in this book, inherited from Goethe, from Coleridge, to bear on this radioactive core, asserting its own organic form as the humanising solution to its discomposed radical-ism. As Goethe's oeuvre balances its fascination with distributed life against a trenchant humanism (as in Ottilie's Popish assertion, in *Elective Affinities*, that the 'proper study of mankind is man') so Shelley's novel seeks to contain its own energies within what Coleridge calls, in a passage I have already quoted, an 'organic form' which 'shapes ... itself from within'.[18] Shelley's creation of a hybrid being, part dead and part alive, D. H. Lawrence suggests in his later Coleridgeian remarks on the novel, does not pose a challenge to the humanising work of realism but rather maintains the distinction between the artificial and the real (or in Lawrence's terms between 'mechanical force and life itself') by performing its own organicism.[19] *Frankenstein* helps us 'accept', Lawrence writes, that it is 'one of the terms of our being' that 'no man has power over the creative mystery' (p. 34). 'Frankenstein's monster', he writes, tells us that 'the thing we can make of our own natures, by our own will, is at the most a pure mechanism, an automaton' (p. 35). The monster is marked, Lawrence suggests, by his deviation from our own organic wholeness, the wholeness that requires, as he puts it in 1915, that a man 'must have a nose, and his own nose too', or as he puts it in in 1925, that 'every tiny bit of my hands is alive, every little freckle and hair and fold of skin.'[20] Shelley's novel lets the voice of the monster speak from inside its delicate narrative structure, but it does so, at least from Lawrence's perspective, only to demonstrate the living organicism of that structure itself, to perform, by the evidence of the monster's empty mechanicism, the indissoluble bond between what Lawrence calls the 'living body of the universe' and the 'living soul of man' as it is diffused 'in the fingers and lips and eyes and feet' (p. 37). In a late twist in Shelley's novel – which is revealed without fanfare but which is nevertheless devastating in its implications – Frankenstein himself asserts this bond, defending that very 'barrier' between the living voice and the dead against which both he and his creature rail. 'Frankenstein discovered that I made notes concerning his history', Walton writes, in the hours before Frankenstein's death:

> he asked to see them, and then himself corrected and augmented them in many places; but principally in giving the life and the spirit to the conversa-tions he held with his enemy. 'Since you have preserved my narration', said he, 'I would not that a mutilated one should go down to posterity'. (p. 210)

Organic form, Coleridge writes, shapes itself from within; and here, Frankenstein works to shape his own narrative from within, to cleanse the monster's voice of its 'mutilated' quality, to cast out of the narrative those elements that seemed most to dehumanise it. We had thought that, at the heart of this narrative, we heard the voice of the creature, the subaltern voice of an inhuman consciousness speaking from outside the created realm; but here Frankenstein, in his dying act, denies such a prospect, asserting his creative ownership of the voice of his creature as much as of his mutilated prosthetic body, declaring that if the monster's voice has 'life' and Hegelian 'spirit', then it does so only to the extent that the properly living Frankenstein himself granted it these qualities, through his acts of correction and augmentation. The work of realism, Frankenstein here suggests, of recreating unmutilated life and spirit in prose, involves the banishment, the editing out, of that which strays beyond the barrier of human being, that which looses the Lawrentian bonds between 'living body of the universe' and the 'living soul of man'.

In Shelley's novel, then, the relations between its realist and its Gothic tendencies are shaped by the legacies of the eighteenth-century novel – both Goethe's sublime romanticism and the vivid immediacy that Shelley takes from the eighteenth-century epistolary form, from Richardson, Burney, Wollstonecraft and Rousseau. But as the Gothic form develops over the nineteenth century, one can see that the realist bulwarks that the Gothic imagination employs to contain its own subversive tendencies evolve too, in tandem with the evolution of realism itself, under the shifted technological and biopolitical conditions of nineteenth-century modernity. The production of an artificial lifeworld over the course of the century – manifest in the spread of the railway, the advent of electricity, the emergence of prosthetic technologies for storing sound and image – is reflected, as I have argued, in the development of nineteenth-century realism. In the fiction of Austen, Dickens, Eliot, Melville, Hardy, one can see that the balance between the real and the artificial – the very texture of fictionality itself – is shaped by those technological and political forces that are producing a manufactured body and a manufactured environment. As Friedrich Kittler has demonstrated, one can see the history of the century as a process by which 'machines take over the functions of the central nervous system', and 'essence escapes into apparatus.'[21] The 'telegraph', he writes, 'is an artificial mouth, the telephone is an artificial ear' ('artificial mouths and ears' which serve as 'technological implementations of the central nervous system' (p. 28)); with the development of these prostheses, Kittler argues, we enter into what he calls a 'new schematism of perceptibility' (p. xli) – the schematism that we find traced in Eliot's fascination with the microscope as a new means of gaining access to the fine grain of reality, or in Dickens' depiction of the railway as the frame-work of a new national consciousness, an iron central nervous system.

The realist novel registers, in its inmost formal structures, this prosthe-tisation, this mechanisation and technologisation of the culture; as the Gothic novel develops alongside it, as I have said, one finds that the relationship between its Gothic and realist urges is shaped by these same processes. The intense burst of Gothic fictions at the end of the century is fuelled by the energies that these processes release. Robert Louis Stevenson's *Jekyll and Hyde* is driven by a peculiar amalgam of new forms of chemistry and the emerging epistemologies associated with psy-choanalysis; Oscar Wilde's *Picture of Dorian Gray* frames the adaptability of matter, the new affinities between science and the body, in terms of an emergent aestheticism. And in *Dracula*, this shifted contest between Gothicism and realism is seen most clearly in the earnest (but nearly comic) exploitation of new media as a means of containing the subversive threat of vampirism. The central question that Stoker's novel asks is where and how true human knowledge and experience are stored, and how we are to combat those agents that work to derange the proper procedures for such storage. Madness, unreason, infection, illicit desire, these are the vampiric forces that disrupt our proper forms of being and knowing. The bond between Dracula and the zoophagic madman Renfield at the heart of Stoker's novel rests on their joint experience of a differently constituted mode of knowing and being – a different way of thinking about how we accumulate the stuff of life in our bodies (by the sucking of another's blood, by the ingestion of flies and spiders) – and it is the task of Jonathan Harker, Mina Murray, Van Helsing and the rest of the novel's crew to assert the sane protocols of living beings against these derange-ments, what Renfield gleefully calls Dracula's 'distribution of good things' (p. 135). It is necessary, Van Helsing remarks to the psychiatrist Dr Seward, to listen to Renfield's ravings – to risk contact with the dangerous derange-ment of his mind – because such ravings give us insight into the darkness of Dracula's mode of thinking (as later in the novel Mina Murray enters into a mesmeric trance that joins her intimately to the deathly life of the count); but even as Seward learns from madmen, Van Helsing remarks, it is crucial that he should 'deal discreetly' with them, that he should 'tell them not what you think', because it is only through such discretion, such self-protection, that 'you shall keep knowledge in its place, where it may rest – where it may gather its kind around it and breed' (p. 156).

The battle against Dracula, then, is a battle to 'keep knowledge in its place', and the means of achieving this hemming in, this gathering of one's being safely in the proper confines of one's own living body, is through narration, through the various technologies of notation that the novel explores. Jonathan Harker, when he is first exposed to the horrors of the count, alone in Dracula's vast Transylvanian castle, finds that it is only recording, only writing, that allows him to hold on to his sanity. Empathising with Hamlet's (misquoted) desire for diarising ('My tablets! quick, my tablets! / 'Tis meet that I put it down'), Harker writes that 'feeling as though my brain were unhinged … I turn to my diary for repose. The habit of entering accurately must help to soothe me' (p. 52).[22] Diarising, as Defoe's Crusoe finds when he is cast adrift on his island, is both a way of keeping oneself company and a prosthetic means of giving an ordered permanence to one's being. Harker presents Mina with the book that contains his dreadful (and embarrassingly erotic) experiences in the castle as a means of containing and sealing off that terrible knowledge (with hilarious literalism, Mina writes that she 'wrapped [the diary] in white paper, and tied it with a little bit of pale blue ribbon which was round my neck, and sealed it over the knot with sealing wax' (p. 139)); then each member of the team turns to their own diarising as a means of ordering experience. Mina writes in her journal that 'it soothes me to express myself here; it is like whispering to one's self and listening at the same time' (pp. 96–97); Arthur Seward notes that 'I was too excited to sleep, but this diary has quieted me' (p. 136). Journalising, as it is for Crusoe, and for Richardson's Pamela, and for Burney's Evelina, is for Harker's colleagues a way of regulating and archiving experience. But, of course, what drives and enables the mania for keeping knowledge in its place in *Dracula* is the discovery of new technologies and systems for the recording and transmitting of information. As Kittler wryly notes, one can read *Dracula* as a 'heroic epic of the final victory of technological media over the blood-sucking despots of old Europe'.[23] Mina is excited by her use of shorthand, perhaps partly because her shorthand is curiously allied to the darkly erotic art of mesmerism, to the hypnotic bond that she shares with Dracula (Harker notes, when Mina ventriloquises the count's voice during her mesmeric trances, that 'I have heard her use the same tone when reading her shorthand notes' (p. 402)). Shorthand is allied to mesmerism, and the power of the written journal as a means of fixing knowledge and thought is combined with all those other technologies that aid storage and transmission in the novel – the telegrams that allow the team to join forces against Dracula, the typewriter, the stenograph, and most strikingly the phonograph that allows Seward and Mina to take a wax impression of the voice of the journaliser (a wax impression that catches an echo of the wax with

which Mina seals the pages of her husband's journal). There is an odd
flirtatious charge to the moment that Mina discovers that Seward keeps his
diary not in writing but by recording his voice on a phonograph. 'I felt
quite excited over it', Mina writes, 'and blurted out: – "Why this beats even
shorthand"' (p. 283). The phonograph, as a means of capturing information, far exceeds anything that can be achieved by writing, or by typing. It
is a refrain of the epistolary form that the written record lacks something of
the completeness of experience: Burney's Evelina regrets that 'this cold,
this inanimate letter . . . will but ill express the feelings of the heart which
indites it' (p. 300); Shelley's Walton has much the same thought when he
reflects, in the frame narrative of *Frankenstein*, that though 'I shall commit
my thoughts to paper', the written journal is nevertheless a 'poor medium
for the communication of feeling' (p. 19). Walton and Evelina both regret
that paper cannot capture voice – Frankenstein's 'full-toned voice' which
Walton says, 'swells in my ears' as he writes (p. 31) – but it is precisely this
full tone that the phonograph can preserve and reproduce – voice in its
fullness and in its presence.[24] This is why Mina is so excited by the device.
'That is a wonderful machine', she says to Seward, 'but it is cruelly true. It
told me, in its very tones, the anguish of your heart' (p. 285). George Eliot,
in *Middlemarch*, writes of the necessary limits to narration, the sense that
narrating is always editing, selecting what material to include and what to
leave out. If we were exposed to an unedited version of reality, she writes, 'it
would be like hearing the grass grow and the squirrel's heart beat' (p. 194).
Narrative must edit out this noise to generate a signal, but the phonograph
allows no such editing. Listening to the recording of his diary, Mina says to
Seward that in the reproduction of his voice she was able to 'hear your heart
beat' (p. 286).

It is the exploitation of these prosthetic devices – the massively increased
capacity for information storage that they afford – that allows the team to
defend themselves against the various subversions of the count. None of
them could provide such protection on their own; the phonograph is
a 'cruelly true' means of capturing sound, but it is next to useless as
a narrative device, because, like the Internet before the advent of Google,
it is not searchable. Because of the sheer profusion of material it captures, it
does not store its data in an ordered and indexable way, but sounds instead
as a raw Eliotian 'roar' of information (as Seward himself recognises, 'I do
not know how to pick out any particular part of the diary. . . . It never once
struck me how I was going to find any particular part in case I wanted to
look it up' (p. 284)). It is only by combining Harker's written journal with
Mina's shorthand and stenography, with the phonograph diary that Mina

transcribes on her typewriter, that the team is able to produce a stable account of the dead life of the count. It is this gathering together that allows the team, and by extension the splintered authorial voice of Stoker's novel, to 'show a whole connected narrative' (p. 289). The various forms of notation that the novel exploits allow for a moment of clear seeing, a moment, as Van Helsing puts it, when our knowledge of the ways of the vampire will be 'whole and complete', and when we will 'understand as though the sunlight himself shone through' (p. 220). This is the moment at which a Victorian *fin de siècle* realism triumphs over pre-modernity, over myth and darkness – the moment at which a set of prosthetic technologies is employed to shore up the condition of whole, non-prosthetic being, the condition of human life as opposed to vampiric undeath. The realism that Stoker develops here works to combat the Gothicism that it nevertheless preserves in its transgressive erotic undertow, as the newly technologised resources of mimesis, of the mechanical reproduction of life, allow prose narrative to manipulate information with a new kind of power, and so to bring what Eliot calls the 'other side of silence' into the narrative realm, and to banish the living-dead count from the arena of properly living beings.

From Shelley to Stoker, then, we can see a dialogue between realism and Gothicism, as the Gothic novel shares the techniques with which realism asserts its own organic unities. But if this is the case, if the relation in the Gothic novel between the regulated and the unregulated can be indexed to the naturalising capacities of realism, then it is central to everything that I am arguing in this book that this conspiracy between realism and the Gothic opens onto a difficult region, outside of the terms in which we have characterised living being – the region that I have characterised here as the unmapped homeland of the prosthetic imagination. It is not just that the Gothic imagination refuses or exceeds the models of regulation that it seeks at the same time to accept – it is not just, in Greenblatt's terms, that the containment of subversion threatens always to yield an image of 'containment subverted';[25] rather, what makes the Gothic treatment of the prosthetic junction so compelling is that, as it conjoins with the realist techniques for securing the distinction between the living and the dead, so it resonates with that same unregulated material, that living death and dead life, that glimmers, like a dark energy, at the hidden centre of realism itself. As Nancy Armstrong has argued, the Gothic novel does not simply expel the threat to the possibility of integrated subjecthood; it also rehearses 'our extinction as liberal individuals' – it is deeply invested in the material it 'deliberately abjects as antagonistic to the very terms in which it negotiates the fraught relation of self to society'.[26] *Frankenstein* draws on Goethe's *Werther* to contain its urge towards unregulated being, as Stoker's *Dracula* exploits a technologised version of the epistolary and journal forms to keep knowledge in its place, within the envelope of a properly living body; but in doing so, these Gothic fictions do not deploy realist techniques to contain their own transgressions so much as they unearth a zone of non-knowledge, of unmeaning, that is common both to realism and to the Gothic, a zone composed of being and not-being that lies at the heart of Werther's suicidal imagination, and that I have mapped through the history of the novel, back through the eighteenth-century epistolary form, and further back, to Cervantes' depiction of a 'state' that 'mingles life and death', and to More's foundational invention of a utopian mode that is composed of an unstable, twisty amalgam of the real and the fictional. Van Helsing insists to Harker and his team, as I have said, that their struggle against the count will lead to a new way of ordering knowledge, a new way of seeing; 'the time will come', he says, 'when your trust shall be whole and complete in me, and when you shall understand as though the sunlight himself shone through' (p. 220). This is the dawning of a knowledge that might rest in its place, where it 'may gather its kind around it and breed' (p. 156) – the knowledge of one's true organic state that it is the task of realism to capture in form. But, as the Gothic dash in Van Helsing's image of a knowledge that 'breeds' with its own 'kind' might suggest, this generation of a true, sunlit mode of seeing involves precisely the kinds of dangerous artifice, the kinds of midnight necromancy, that Harker's courageous heroes pit themselves against. In Van Helsing's promise to his comrades that they will one day see as he sees, one can hear a distinct echo of Dracula's early warning to Harker that things in Transylvania will withstand Harker's powers of seeing, will require him to learn to see as Dracula sees, to see and think as an inhuman being. 'Our ways are not your ways', Dracula tells Harker on his arrival at his castle, 'and there shall be many strange things'. It will be difficult for Harker to acclimatise to this strangeness, he suggests, but 'there is reason that all things are as they are, and did you see with my eyes and know with my knowledge, you would perhaps better understand' (p. 32). Stoker's novel rests on this troubling resonance between Van Helsing's way of seeing and Dracula's, between the reparative and the toxic, this difficult sense that the production of organically stable taxonomies of living is itself a prosthetic operation from beginning to end. The team encrypt and guard over their assembled journals – which contain their 'whole connected narrative' – so that they might not fall into enemy hands (and so they can present to us, the readers, a version of the real which is cleansed of the demonic, mesmeric influence of the count). Van Helsing says of Lucy's papers that he has stowed them away, 'so that no strange hand might touch them – no strange eye might look through words into her soul' (p. 221). Van Helsing has in mind, no doubt, the strange, dead hand of the count, the strange, dead eye that Harker meets as he stands over Dracula's grave. But, of course, the narrative is itself composed by a strange hand – the hand of the stenographer, as well as of the typewriter; it is heard by a strange ear, the artificial ear of Kittler's phonograph; and it is read by a strange eye, the eye attuned to the shorthand symbols that Mina decodes in the very voice that she adopts when she speaks with the estranged voice of the count. The exploitation of new technological forms of recording and reproducing life might be the means by which Harker's team defeats the count – chief representative of Kittler's 'blood-sucking despots of old Europe' – but this necessarily lends their own experience a machinic quality, making knowledge partake of that very technological inhumanity that Van Helsing is most concerned to overcome.

This close weaving of the strange into the proper, as a function of the bonding between the realist and the Gothic, can be seen throughout the Gothic fictions of the nineteenth century. Underneath the historical trajectory I have traced here, from Shelley's Goethean realism to the technologised, mediatised forms that shape Stoker's narrative, one can see another kind of gathering, the subliminal, sub-noumenal development of a strange continuity between the living and the dead, between the organic and the prosthetic, that lies at the heart of both the realist and the Gothic traditions, and that comes, only now, to a kind of thinkability. From *Frankenstein* to *Dracula*, the forces that seek to regulate life, to distinguish between the living eye and the dead eye, yield to a recognition that life is distributed strangely, that it clings to material in ways that do not accord with any given way of seeing or of knowing. At the heart of *Dracula* is the recognition that true seeing involves artificial seeing, that to see with the quick eyes of Van Helsing is to see with the undead eyes of Dracula himself; and, at the heart of *Frankenstein* one can see the same reluctant, counterfactual recognition. The moment, as I have said, that the monster opens his 'dull yellow eyes' – his 'watery eyes, that seemed almost of the same colour as the dun white sockets in which they were set' (p. 57) – is a horrifying moment of animate inanimation that the resources of the novel are marshalled against; this is a moment when we are asked to set up a Goethean barrier between the dead eye and the living eye. As Aristotle has it, in a phrase I quoted earlier, 'a thing really is itself when it can perform its function; an eye for instance when it can see. When a thing cannot do so it is that thing only in name, like a dead eye or one made of stone.'[27] The monster's eye, like Dracula's 'open and stony eye', is an eye of stone – a glass eye, a prosthetic eye – that is also a seeing eye of flesh, and this is a perversity, an impropriety, that is an affront to the Aristotelian order of nature; but even if this is so, the real fascination of *Frankenstein*, and of the nineteenth-century Gothic mode, is the recognition that seeing, thinking, knowing belong not just to human but also to inhuman forms. 'Of what a strange nature is knowledge', Frankenstein's monster cries, as he struggles to understand the unaccountable tenacity of his being, his failure, despite his misery, to 'shake off all thought and feeling'; 'Of what a strange nature is knowledge', he says, in an early intuition of what Drew Milne calls 'lichenisation';[28] 'it clings to the mind, when it has once seized on it, like a lichen on the rock' (p. 120). Knowledge, in *Frankenstein* and in *Dracula*, clings like an alien, fungal life form to the undead mind, the monstrous mind that does not belong to the Aristotelian order of nature. Even as Shelley's monster prepares for death, even as the monster himself seeks to reassert the order of nature by returning his strange hand and strange eye to the undifferentiated dead material from whence it came, it is this unclassifiable clinging of life to death that the novel leaves us with. 'I long for the moment', the monster says, when his body will no longer be animated by a consciousness that has no right to encounter itself; 'I long for the moment when these hands will meet my eyes, when that imagination will haunt my thoughts no more' (p. 222), when the flesh of hand and the flesh of the eye are no longer differentiated by a prosthetic imagination, no longer separated by that bottomless gap that is conjured in the operation of Jaquet-Droz's 'Writing Boy', or given wriggling expression in Rembrandt's 'Anatomy Lesson of Dr Tulp'. But even as he expresses this longing, the logic that animates the strange, inhuman centre of this novel compels us to acknowledge a current of prosthetic life that cannot be extinguished by the monster's Wertherian suicidal urge. As the monster heads to his death, he ponders on whether there is, even now, 'some mode unknown to me' which 'hadst not ceased to think and feel'. At one of the most haunting moments in the history of the Gothic novel, the monster looks on suicide as only the overture to a kind of living death, a kind of unthinkable thought that is the very condition of the prosthetic imagination. 'Soon', he says, 'I shall die, and what I now feel will be no longer felt.' 'My spirit', he goes on, 'will sleep in peace'. This is a conventional enough welcoming of the death to come; but it is the qualification that is so devastating, that calls to a mode of dead thinking that thrills through this novel, and that stands as the legacy of the nineteenth-century Gothic – a dead thinking that raises goose bumps, even now: 'My spirit will sleep in peace; or if it thinks, it will not surely think thus' (p. 223).

***

Over the history of the nineteenth-century novel, then, one can see the passage of two trajectories, distinct but interwoven: the development of an expressive mode that seeks to contain the raging energies of life within a human biopolitical form and the growth of a subterranean form of alienated life that clings, in strange and frightening ways, to dead material. These two modes, or structures of feeling, correspond to the twin impera- tives of the prosthetic imagination – on the one hand to produce a mimetic form which most closely captures and regulates the experience of animated life, and on the other to recognise that life itself is an unstable and unevenly distributed amalgam *composed* of artifice. These imperatives find themselves expressed across the nineteenth-century novel in part as the tension between realism and Gothicism. This is a tension that one can see between two distinct traditions – between say, Dickens, Collins and Eliot on the one hand, and Shelley, Maturin and Stoker on the other; it is also a tension at work within a given novel itself, within Shelley's *Frankenstein* or Stoker's *Dracula* as much as within Dickens' *Bleak House*, or Melville's *Moby Dick*, or Hawthorne's *Blithedale Romance*, or Collins' *The Woman in White*. The possibility of realism itself is driven by a submerged Gothic affinity for a material that does not abide by the laws of living being; just as the Gothic novel works with and against the proprieties of realism to test and to reshape the terms in which the experience of living is mapped on to the co-ordinates of the human. The very possibility of the novel, over the course of the century, is shaped by this tectonic relation, this struggle between the regulated and the unregulated, between the compliant and the transgressive, between revealed surface and hidden depth; but it is at the end of the century, and with the publication of Oscar Wilde's 1890 novel *The Picture of Dorian Gray* that these twin imperatives enter into a new relation, in a fashion that marks a shift in the structure of the novel imagination, and that presages the stirring of an emergent modernism (expressed in Wilde's novel as a decadent aestheticism) that will be the subject of the next move- ment in this book.[29]

Wilde's story – the archetypal myth of the man who seeks to preserve his beauty by swapping places with his painted portrait – offers itself, from the beginning, as a work in the Gothic mode. The hook of the novel consists of a stroke of strange and impossible magic, which exhibits the tendency of the Gothic that I have been exploring here, the tendency to redirect or

discompose the proper relations between the living and the dead. What
'lends to Gothic art its enduring vitality', Dorian thinks, is its capacity to
produce artificial pictures that are 'instinct with . . . vivid life', that conjure
'phantoms more terrible than reality itself'; it is this capacity, this displaced
vitality, that lies at the heart of Wilde's novel.³⁰ The process by which Basil
Hallward's portrait of Dorian comes to life is one which turns around what
Gray thinks of as a 'strange affinity' between the living and the non-living,
that same affinity that we find in Shelley's *Frankenstein* and in Stoker's
Dracula – the affinity that the lichen feels for the rock, or that the mind
feels for its prosthetic extensions. 'If thought could exercise its influence
upon a living organism', Gray reasons, as he tries to fathom the nature of
the bond between himself and his portrait, 'might not thought exercise an
influence upon dead or inorganic things': 'Nay, without thought or conscious desire, might not things external to ourselves vibrate in unison with
our moods and passions, atom calling to atom in secret love or strange
affinity?' (p. 136). This secret love, this strange affinity, courses through
Wilde's novel, speaking at once of a homoerotic desire that is banished
from the sphere of the proper and of a subversive distribution of the
sensible, a radical anatomy of Gothic inanimation, what Leo Bersani
would call a new 'relationality' between 'thoughts' and 'things'.³¹ But if
this places *The Picture of Dorian Gray* firmly in the Gothic tradition, what
is so striking about Wilde's novel, what positions it at a tipping point both
of the Gothic and of the history of prose realism, is that this Gothicism is
not opposed to the realist urge in the novel but part of the very same
movement, an operation of the same aesthetic desire; the Gothic allure of
the novel emerges not from its transgression of the proprieties of realism
but as an effect of realism itself, a *symptom* of the super-real capacities of
a perfected, late-historical mimetic form. Dorian Gray, like Frankenstein's
monster, is an artificial being, a man-made creation, one of those aberra-
tions that, in Lawrence's view, can only attain to the status of 'a pure
mechanism, an automaton'.³² He is the creature both of the portraitist
Basil Hallward and of the novel's decadent, Wildean aphorist, Henry
Wotton. Basil believes, in Frankensteinian mode, that his painting has
given birth to Dorian, that the portrait is proof that he can 're-create life in
a way that was hidden from me before' (p. 32); Henry, conscious of his
influence on Dorian, thinks to himself that 'to a large extent the lad was his
own creation' (p. 83) (much as Harriet is the creation of Emma in Austen's
Emma). But if Dorian (both in art and in 'life') can be thought of, in this
way, as a Gothic monster, as a version of Lawrence's automaton, the central
proposal of *Dorian Gray* is that Dorian's being manifests not a *corruption* of

proper forms either of living or of representing life but the most intense form that both life and representation can take. Hallward does not regard the life that he instills in his painting as a monstrosity, as a perversion or misconception of the ways in which life and consciousness relate to material. On the contrary, Basil regards his astonishingly lifelike portrait of Dorian as the key example of what he calls an 'entirely new manner in art, an entirely new mode of style' (p. 32), a mode which does not separate art from life or mind from matter, as one would separate a representation from the thing represented, but which produces an absolute identity between the two, an 'absolute harmony', as Basil puts it, between 'soul and body' – a Ricoeurean mode in which art no longer refers to the world but *is* that world itself. 'We in our madness', he says, 'have separated the two' – separated soul from body, meaning from matter, signifier from signified; in so doing, we have 'invented a realism that is vulgar, an ideality that is void' (p. 33). One of the marks of this 'separation' is the disjunction I have mapped here between realism and Gothicism, as it turns around the disjunction between the living and the dead. But Basil, in his discovery of a new style, considers that he has overcome this disjunction, as Henry Wotton, in his own Wildean crafting of a new dandyish 'manner' of living, claims too to have overcome the distinction between art and life. Basil makes a painting of Dorian that becomes more real than the original, turning life into art; Henry creates Dorian as a living being who is himself a work of poetry, turning art into life. Dorian is, for Henry, 'a real work of art': 'Life having its elaborate masterpieces, just as poetry has, or sculpture, or painting' (p. 83). And for both Basil and Henry (who each speak as different aspects of Wilde's own sensibility), this coming together of art and life allows for a new era in the history of art to emerge.[33] 'The separation of spirit from matter was a mystery', Henry thinks to himself, 'and the union of spirit with matter was a mystery also'; but the aestheticist discovery of a mode of 'Life itself [that] was the first, the greatest, of the arts' allows him to solve that mystery, so that 'each little spring of life would be revealed to us' (p. 84).

The sign of this discovery, in Wilde's novel, is the conception of an art that is all surface. As Henry puts it, in an aphoristic denunciation of George Eliot's investment in that 'invisible history' that it is the task of the 'narrator of human actions' to trace,[34] 'it is only shallow people who do not judge by appearances. The true mystery of the world is the visible, not the invisible' (p. 45). The artwork that Henry and Basil between them conceive is an artwork that knows no differences, an artwork in which there are no hidden depths, no gaps between hand and eye, no oppositions between mind and body, an artwork in which everything is brought out of hiding and lies on the quivering surface of the canvas, or the page. It is this desire that takes Wilde's novel to the very edge of the relation between the Gothic and the realist traditions as I have traced them here – to the point where the tension between the drive to eradicate the artificial from the sphere of the truly living and the opposite drive towards a prosthetic life that is itself composed of artifice has been magically resolved. But, of course, what one can detect on every page of Wilde's novel is the recognition that such an art has not yet arrived, that Henry's announcement of the birth of an art that is life, of a life that is art, is premature. As Dorian Gray, in one of the ghoulish climaxes to the novel, reveals his now horribly defaced portrait to Basil Hallward, this recognition takes on a material form. Basil approaches the painting in the gloom of Dorian's attic and holds a flickering candle to the canvas:

> The surface seemed to be quite undisturbed, and as he had left it. It was from within, apparently, that the foulness and horror had come. Through some strange quickening of inner life the leprosies of sin were slowly eating the thing away. The rotting of a corpse was not so fearful. (p. 191)

There is no room on the undisturbed surface of the painting or on the surface of the page for the 'strange affinity' that exists between Dorian and his likeness, between the natural body and the prosthetic. However quick the aphoristic energies are that turn depths into surfaces in *Dorian Gray*, this affinity remains submerged in 'inner life', unattached to surface, hidden in the Gothic murk that clouds the brightness of Wilde's prose.

This persistence of the Gothic in Wilde's novel is the sign of a failure (both aesthetic and ethical) to overcome the distinction between the real and the artificial – the generic marker of a gulf between mind and its material extensions that cannot come to expression, or that can only be expressed in spectral from. As the pressure of Wilde's aestheticism seeks to bring the invisible depths that have powered prose realism throughout the nineteenth century onto the art surface, the continued dissonance between surface and depth, between mind and material, manifests itself as a late Gothicism, to which Wilde's aestheticism is awkwardly bound. The desire for a reordering of the relation between surface and depth, between art and life, that can be everywhere felt in Wilde would take another kind of technological and aesthetic revolution to find itself realised; the technological revolutions of twentieth-century modernity and the aesthetic revolutions of literary modernism, to which I will now turn.

PART IV

The Modernist Body: From James to Beckett

CHAPTER 6

A Duplication of Consciousness: Realism, Modernism and Prosthetic Self-Fashioning

We try to look in upon ourself, and ourself beats back upon ourself.

Olive Schreiner, *The Story of an African Farm*[1]

She seemed a stranger to herself, or rather there were two selves in her, the one she had always known, and a new abhorrent being to which it found itself chained.

Edith Wharton, *The House of Mirth*[2]

One stands over oneself with a whip; one flays oneself at the slightest opposition.

Frank Kafka, 'Report to an Academy'[3]

6.1 Modernism and the *Fin de Siècle*

From the earliest stirrings of prose narrative, the work of fiction has expressed itself in terms of a mirrored encounter with the self – an encounter in which fiction itself serves as the connecting ground, the meeting place. In this book so far, I have traced this encounter, as it has recurred in prose fiction, from More onwards, and as it is mapped on to the concealed junction between mind and biomaterial, between thought and the thingly stuff of the extended self. When the fictional Thomas More, in More's *Utopia*, meets with his fantastical alter ego Raphael, More's text brings together a series of shaped oppositions, between England as it is and England as it ought to be, between Thomas More as he is and Thomas More as he wishes to be, between pragmatism and idealism, between the familiar and the strange. More's text brings these oppositions together in an unstable alloy of the factual and the invented; as it does so, it exploits (perhaps to an extent inaugurates) the power of fiction itself to gain a certain critical access to the bond which attaches mind to the world. We are in the world, 'plunged in it', as Samuel Beckett's Moran has it, 'beyond recall';[4] we are *made of* world, objects among other objects, nameless things among nameless things. But we are also *not* in the world or of the world, not quite immersed in the stuff through which we recognise ourselves. It is this partiality – the immersion in the world combined with the separation from it that is the fundamental experience of consciousness – that has given rise to fiction as a phenomenon, and that fiction allows us to conceptualise, to convert into the very possibility of literary thinking, of narrative becoming. The work of fiction in More enacts the insistent, wriggling difference of mind from enworlded self that is the movement of thought; we are never quite identical with the object that we become when we are enworlded, and this difference, however catastrophic it might be for the instantiation of being, is also what allows us to intervene in our becoming, and in the becoming of the world, what allows us to interweave pictures of possible worlds and possible selves into the picturing mechanism through which we encounter our own true self.

I have traced this restless operation of fiction at the intimate junction between inner self and outer self, between self and world, as it has developed from More onwards. One can see it at work as Cervantes' Quixano finds himself transformed into the valorous Don Quixote, and as the imaginative struggle between Quixano and Quixote takes place across the contested ground of early modern Spain (that 'reality' which, for Auerbach, has become 'difficult to survey').' One can see this same mirrored struggle between self and self in operation across the eighteenth-century European novel, as Swift's Gulliver furiously resists identification with his own reflection, either in the mirror or in the spectacle of the hideous Yahoos; as Goethe's Werther crafts a dark, suicidal gap between inner being and its outer manifestations; as Burney's Evelina seeks to produce a mode of self-fashioning that frees her from the condition of the automaton foisted upon the society woman. And then, across the nineteenth century, the novel form responds to the accelerated emergence of an artificial lifeworld by developing an increasingly nuanced access to the interior movement of mind. From Shelley and Austen; to Melville, Dickens and Eliot; to Stoker, Stevenson and Wilde, the novel form reflects the production of manufactured environments and manufactured selves. It offers a narrative history of the emergence of artificial life, at the same time as it develops narrative strategies which allow for a reflective distance from such artificiality – which allow for the production of imagined spaces, vibrating between the inner mind and the external, artificial self, in which the possibility of a true becoming might be shadowed forth, in the disappearing medium of a self-conscious fiction.

I have, as I say, traced this trajectory up to this point – up to end of the nineteenth century. But, as I suggested at the close of the last chapter, the coming together of a set of forces, both political and aesthetic, at the Victorian *fin de siècle*, conspires to shift the terms in which the novel form has represented this struggle between self and self – to transform the ways in which prose fiction acts as a bridge between the unextended and the extended self. The political and aesthetic forces that lead to modernism on the one hand and twentieth-century modernity on the other also lead to the production of a new experience of surface, in which the opposition between self and counter-self that has allowed for the development of prose fiction from More to Wilde is squeezed into an increasingly narrow space – in which the opposition between the machinic and the organic, between the natural and the artificial, becomes compressed into a form of expression and of experience that fuses these oppositions. If something happens to the prosthetic imagination at the turn of the century – if there is a transformation in the terms in which narrative oversees the processes which allow mind to extend itself into matter – then this transformation has to do with the ways in which a duplicated consciousness is represented on the surface of the artwork, the way in which the vibrating difference that allows for self-recognition is recast as sameness, the compressed identity between life and art that one can see emerging under the sign of a Wildean aestheticism.

Take for example Charlotte Perkins Gilman's *The Yellow Wallpaper* (1892) and Edward Bellamy's *Looking Backward* (1888), both late-century works which focus on a meeting between two versions of the same consciousness, divided by the threshold of the fiction which brings them into contact with each other. Gilman's novella famously tells the story of an unnamed woman who is imprisoned by her husband John in a remote colonial mansion, where she is subjected to a version of Silas Weir Mitchell's brutal 'rest cure', ostensibly to help her recover from an unspecified nervous ailment, a 'slight hysterical tendency' brought about, it is implied, by recent childbirth.[6] The narrator-protagonist is forbidden contact with any stimulating friends and prohibited from any intellectual activity that might excite her nerves, but she manages, like Richardson's Pamela, to disobey such prohibition by secretly committing her thoughts to a diary ('this is dead paper', she says, 'and a great relief to my mind' (p. 10)). The diary that she writes, which becomes the text of *The Yellow Wallpaper*, offers itself in one sense as a record of her developing mental illness – as both the collapse of her sense of self beneath the crushing weight of a tyrannical patriarchal order and an implicit protest against the rank injustice that such an order represents. As the novella continues, the narrator becomes increasingly obsessed with the wallpaper in the room to which she is confined, developing a conviction that there is a 'figure' confined behind the wallpaper, whose movements she can just make out within the intricacies of the pattern. She starts stripping stretches of the wallpaper off the walls, in an attempt to free the figure from behind the pattern, and the story ends with the narrator creeping beast-like around the room declaring, 'I've got out at last', and 'I've pulled off the paper, so you can't put me back' (p. 36).

In one sense, as I say, we are invited to read this story as the record of mental illness, to substitute, for the narrator's deranged sense of her triumphant release from imprisonment, our own sane understanding that she has been unknowingly driven mad by maltreatment and forced confinement. The power of the text, its impact as a protest against late Victorian misogyny, rests to an extent on this interpretation; but even as we are led to read in this direction, against the flow of the narrator's sense of bestial liberation, the novella also offers another kind of story and opens another expressive plane, one which yields a darkly utopian model of fictional self-recognition. Even as we read the story, from beginning to end, as a descent into mental illness, we are also invited to read the story – to read our Yellow Wallpaper, as the narrator-protagonist reads hers – from front to back, as a play of aesthetic surface, rather than an unfolding of sequential narrative. The narrator gives an eloquent account of the difficulties of reading the yellow wallpaper (and *The Yellow Wallpaper*) in a consecutive fashion. She sets out 'for the thousandth time', she writes, like a dutiful close reader, to 'follow that pointless pattern to some kind of a conclusion' (p. 19). Even though she knows that the wallpaper, like the pages of her own diary, is 'dead paper', she feels certain that it contains some kind of living message; 'I never saw so much expression', she says, 'in an inanimate thing' (p. 16). But she realises early in the story that she cannot access this meaning, cannot interpret this living expression, by reading in sequence, by following the pattern to a conclusion. Rather, she understands that she has to read *through* the wallpaper, to find secreted in the pattern an animate version of herself which does not succumb to the compulsory condition of hysterical femininity prescribed by her husband. 'This wallpaper', she writes,

> has a kind of sub-pattern in a different shade, a particularly irritating one, for you can only see it in certain lights, and not clearly then.

But in the places where it isn't faded and where the sun is just so – I can
see a strange, provoking, formless sort of figure, that seems to skulk about
behind that silly and conspicuous front design. (p. 18)

This is the moment in the novella when the consecutive sense of the story –
the one which follows the submission of the narrator to the pitiless
demands of wifehood and motherhood – is counterposed to another
form of becoming, a mode of negatively utopian mirroring, in which the
woman is confronted with the image of a latent, 'formless' version of
herself, one which is not bound by the materiality of either language or
the body as these are shaped by a dominant hetero-patriarchal culture. This
is a version of selfhood which, in its formlessness, does *not* submit, which
resists those repressive Victorian myths of female embodiment that cast the
woman's body as the empty prosthetic receptacle of desiring men and
unborn babies. As the story continues, as the sequential narrative progresses towards its hysterical conclusion, so this encounter with another
form of selfhood, another model of consciousness, vibrating at the surface
of the page, gains strength also. The woman's conception of her own
language as a kind of constraint, a kind of imprisonment, becomes ever
clearer: 'At night', she writes, 'in any kind of light, in twilight, candle light,
lamplight, and worst of all by moonlight [the] outside pattern' of the
wallpaper (and by extension the consecutive narrative of *The Yellow
Wallpaper* itself) 'becomes bars'. Narrative reveals itself to be the wall of
a cage (what Fredric Jameson later calls the 'prison-house of language') and
as it does so, the narrator can discern 'the woman behind it as plain as can
be'.[7] 'I didn't realize for a long time', she says, 'what the thing was that
showed behind that dim sub-pattern, but now I am quite sure it is
a woman' (p. 26). The language of the text, the 'outside pattern' of the
wallpaper, remains a deadly form of constraint; it will lead only to the
madness and death which are conformity to John's version of tyrannical
sanity. But as the narrative reveals its deep complicity with the logic that
confines the narrator to the 'nursery', that 'cures' her by ruthlessly identifying her with her passive role as wife and mother, so it gives expression, too,
to a form of counter-identification, one which is registered in the very
mobility of the narrative, its capacity to oppose its oppressive consecutive
sense with a poetics of liberation conducted at the surface of the text itself.
'I have really discovered something at last', the narrator writes in the final
pages of the text, 'the front pattern *does* move – and no wonder! The
woman behind shakes it'; 'in the very shady spots she just takes hold of the

bars and shakes them hard' (pp. 29, 30). The 'formless figure', figment in
a dark mirror, shorn of body and of language, nevertheless makes an
impact on the novella's language, causing the surface of the text itself to
tremble, as she moves behind the paper which at once confines her and
gives her expression, offering the possibility of another mode of becoming
to the narrator who finds herself immersed in her own patriarchally
inscribed body, interred in the material of maternal unfreedom.

The Yellow Wallpaper, then, discovers, in the constriction to aesthetic
surface, the slim persistence of the kind of duplication of self that has been
the province of prose fiction since More. The novella registers the incapacity of existing political and narrative forms to represent a mode of female
experience that is gathering force in the 1890s – that is driving the 'new
woman' movement, and that will lead, by 1928, to full suffrage. Gilman
demonstrates, with great eloquence, how difficult it is to give form to this
dawning revolutionary consciousness; but her crafting of a trembling fictional membrane, which registers the movement of a formless, unextended
self in the ripples that self makes on the surface of the prose, is her poetic
response to that difficulty, her conjuring of a duplication of consciousness
from the very forces that are driving her narrator towards immurement in
the stuff of her own being. The fate of the woman, at the level of the
sequential plot, is to find herself chained to a prosthetic version of herself,
to the materiality of a body that is not animated by her own consciousness,
but which has been suborned by a misogynistic culture, to be exploited as
an instrument for the propagation of the species; but this fate is balanced
against an opposite kind of prosthetic logic, in which the narrator glimpses
a utopian version of self moving on the other side of the paper, attached to
her only by the most delicate of fictional bridges – a self that has not yet
come to form but which offers the nearly imperceptible promise of
a liberatory rather than oppressive extension into the world. Gilman offers
a glimpse of a revolutionary relation to the self, from the depiction of its
impossibility.

In Edward Bellamy's novel *Looking Backward*, we find a similar effect,
a similar persistence of a utopian duplication of self, won from the flattening of the aesthetic surface, in which self and counter-self are squeezed into
an increasingly tight space. Bellamy's 1888 novel offers a picture of a future
utopian state (Boston in the year 2000), in which all of the contradictions
of late nineteenth-century society have been magically resolved through
the military enforcement of an equal distribution of wealth. Like More's
Utopia, and so many utopian fictions that have been written since, Bellamy
reveals this transformation through the conceit of a duplication of self – in

which the novel brings the self as it is into contact with that same self as it might be, once it is freed from the disfiguring effects of capital. But while More's text (like the utopian ventures of Voltaire's Candide and Swift's Gulliver) involves the discovery of new and distant geographical worlds, Bellamy's novel (like Wells' *Time Machine*) founds its utopia not in another space but in another time, a future time that is tightly woven into the seams of Bellamy's *fin de siècle* present. *Looking Backward* encounters this future time through a somewhat clunky plot device, in which the protagonist, Julian West, falls into a prolonged sleep, like Washington Irving's Rip Van Winkle, waking up, after one hundred and thirteen years, on September 10, 2000. On his return to consciousness, West is treated, by his utopian guide Dr Leete, to a patient elaboration of the principles of Bellamy's perfect state (which involve a compulsory socialist militarism that is pretty obnoxious, I imagine, to most of us). This vision of Boston in the year 2000 has arguably not survived the test of time and has severely limited use as a utopian blueprint; but what remains intriguing about Bellamy's novel is the device itself – the means by which the West of 1887 is brought into contact with his doppelgänger, the West of 2000. The conceit of the long sleep allows Bellamy to annihilate the time that has passed between 1887 and 2000, to bring these two versions of Boston and of West into the same compacted space. Early in the novel, this takes the form of West's bewildered awakening, in a prevision of Marcel's disorientation at the opening of Proust's *A la recherche*, in the city of the future. His coming to consciousness produces an oddly suspended relation with his own self: 'I was no more able', he says, 'to distinguish myself from pure being during those moments [on first awakening] than we may suppose a soul in the rough to be before it has received the ear marks, the individualising touches which make it a person'.[8] West experiences the same release from the apparatuses of selfhood here that Proust's Marcel feels when waking in the middle of the night to find that 'I could not even be sure at first who I was; I had only the most rudimentary sense of existence, such as may lurk and flicker in the depths of an animal's consciousness.'[9] West's out of timeness grants him a release from self, and it produces a suspended relation, too, to the city, a kind of remove which allows him to discern two cities at once – the Boston of 1887 and the perfected city of 2000 – a suspended relation in which both images vibrate against one another, occupying the same perceptual frame. 'The mental image', he writes,

> of the old city was so fresh and strong that it did not yield to the impression
> of the actual city, but contended with it, so that it was first one and then the

other which seemed more real. There was nothing I saw which was not blurred in this way, like the faces of a composite photograph. (p. 38)

This scene of awakening in the new city comes early in the novel, and then the narrative closes with an opposite kind of awakening, one in which West imagines that his projection into the future has been a dream, and that he is in fact still materially confined to the space and time of 1887; in this latter vision, we experience that same vibrating, composite doubleness, but the other way around. Now, as West walks the late Victorian city, and as he sees the marks of poverty and disease everywhere about him, he feels he can see the outlines of a just future written as a kind of latent possibility in the stupefied faces of passersby. The inhabitants of late nineteenth-century Boston, West thinks, are as cruelly bound to dead prosthetic flesh as Gilman's narrator is bound to her maternal body. 'I perceived', he says, 'that they were all quite dead. Their bodies were so many living sepulchers' (pp. 157–58). It is only West's dream of futurity, the vision he is granted of what the city might become, that allows him to see counter-selves moving within that mass of dead material. 'As I looked, horror struck, from one death's head to another', he goes on, 'I was affected by a singular hallucina-tion. Like a wavering translucent spirit face superimposed on each of these brutish masks I saw the ideal, the possible face that would have been the actual if mind and soul had lived' (p. 158).

For both Gilman and Bellamy, then – as for so many novelists of the *fin de siècle* – the approach of twentieth-century modernity gives rise to two directly contradictory drives. On the one hand, they both register, like Wilde, the possibility that modernity produces an aesthetic flattening, a rising of depth to the photographic surface. As, in *The Picture of Dorian Gray*, the dialectical opposition between art and life is narrowed until it becomes a function of the living artwork itself, a vibrating play of difference on the art surface, so in Bellamy and Gilman the oppositions that drive their work – between the real and the ideal, the oppressive and the liberatory – are squeezed onto the imagistic surface of the work, Gilman's yellow wallpaper or Bellamy's composite photograph. But on the other hand, they give expression to a great gulf between experience and representation, between the dawning of female emancipation and a patriarchal language that cannot countenance or fathom it or between the spectre of a communist or Marxist state and the narrative principles of nineteenth-century realism. Across the utopian, anti-utopian, dystopian and Gothic fiction of the late nineteenth century, this contradiction is bound up with the persistence of the figure of the double, as a principle of novelistic becoming. The work of fiction expresses itself here in the prosthetic bridge that it makes between self and counter-self, between mind and world, as it does in More, in Cervantes, in Swift and in Eliot; but even as it does so, it is possible to see a shift in the ways in which that bridge operates, a transformation in the means by which fiction brings the interior self into contact with its avatars, with the forms in which it recognises itself. In one sense, this contact becomes close – too close, as in Dorian's becoming one with his portrait or in West's peculiar identity with himself -and in another it opens too great a distance, as self folds into the picture of self, and the world to which the fictional imagination calls – the world in which the formless figure in Gilman's novella might come to form – falls away from possibility.

For the mode of realism within which these writers work, this shifting of the terms in which fiction establishes a meeting ground between mind and self presents something of a problem. Bellamy employs a utopian form inherited from More and Bacon to bring an idealised city into contact with an imperfect one; but the form itself has become too unstable to effect the kind of dialogue that has characterised realist utopias to this point, so we are left with a rather dry political tome concerning the (questionable!) desirability of military socialism that does not quite fit within the more inventive formal conceit that frames it. Similarly, while Gilman's novella produces a powerful encounter with the 'formless sort of figure' that is the closest it can come to a picture of utopian feminism, the work cannot sustain the kind of contact between self and self that yields a utopian literary politics; instead, when Gilman comes to elaborate a feminist utopia in her 1915 novel *Herland*, she offers a conventionally realist depiction of an all-female state that lacks the poetic power of *The Yellow Wallpaper*. It is as if, in these texts, the transformation produced by the technological and the political revolutions of the *fin de siècle* mean that the forms of realism developed over the nineteenth century can no longer gain a transformative purchase on reality itself. It takes a revolution in aesthetic form, as deep and far reaching as the technological and intellectual revolutions of the period, to address this new reality, to craft a different kind of fictional bridge between self and counter-self, between mind and world – the aesthetic revolution that we know as modernism.

The first stirrings of this aesthetic revolution can be traced, I would suggest, to Gustave Flaubert, who Auerbach suggests is 'in many respects a precursor' to the modernists, and whom Scarlett Baron reads as prefiguring Joyce's modernism ('Flaubert envisions his own work', Baron writes, in a phrase that will become resonant as this book continues, 'as a cord hurled forward, showing somebody the way');[10] it first arises in Flaubert's recognition of a shift in the texture of the art surface, and in the nature of the representational bond between art and reality. In a famous and much quoted letter to Louise Colet, written on the Friday night of 16 January 1852, Flaubert seeks to formulate this aesthetic shift that he observes around him, and that he is trying to express in *Madame Bovary*. 'What seems beautiful to me', he writes to Colet, is an art that has no connection with what he calls its 'external attachments'. 'What I should like to write', he says, 'is a book about nothing, a book dependent on nothing external for its support; a book which would have almost no subject, or at least in which the subject would be invisible, if such a thing is possible'.[11] He seeks, here, an art that has freed itself from prosthetic attachments, from any need to extend into the world. 'The finest works', he goes on, 'are those that contain the least matter; the closer expression comes to thought, the closer language comes to coinciding and merging with it, the finer the result. I believe the future of Art lies in this direction' (p. 131).

   This is a remarkably prophetic statement – in which Flaubert predicts the tendency towards abstraction, and the weakening of the mimetic relation between art and reality that one can see unfolding across the literary and visual arts of the end of the nineteenth century and the first decades of the twentieth.[12] In calling, in 1852, for an 'emancipation from matter' (in both art and politics), he anticipates some of the manifestos that mark the history of modernism, from Marinetti's assertion that art should 'detach itself from reality' to Pound's demand that we 'make it new'.[13] 'From the standpoint of Pure Art', he writes to Colet, 'one might almost establish the axiom that there is no such thing as subject, style in itself being an absolute manner of seeing things' (p. 131). Form must free itself from content; style must become its own language; and art must become self-referring, unattached to anything outside itself, anything that extends into the world; but if Flaubert's letter to Colet is a powerful precursor to modernism, then it is so because it offers an early account of a central contradiction that runs throughout the history of modernist aesthetics. Flaubert's letter opens with an acknowledgement of this contradiction, an acknowledgement grounded in his own experience of a duplication of consciousness. 'There are in me', he writes, 'literally speaking, two distinct persons' (p. 131). There is the stylist, the one dedicated to an art free of material, an art of pure, unextended thought; and then there is another kind of artist, one who 'digs and burrows in to the truth as deeply as he can, who likes to treat a humble fact as respectfully as a big one, who would like to make you feel almost *physically* the things he reproduces' (p. 131, Flaubert's emphasis). For Flaubert, in 1852, the desire for an abstract art, a non-prosthetic art that frees itself from external attachments, is bound, in contradictory ways, to the persistent need for a material art, for an art that burrows into the stuff of being, that has physical weight and heft. And it is this combination, rather than simply its appeal to abstraction, that makes this letter so prescient, that suggests the 'direction' that will be taken by the 'future of Art'. If the emergence of modernist aesthetics offers a response to the problem that I have traced in the *fin de siècle* novel, in Bellamy, Gilman, Wilde and others, then it does so not because it frees the artwork from the appurtenances of matter, but because it refigures the ways in which a non-referential art is bound to the physical things it reproduces, the ways in which surface is attached to depth, the way that self is bound to counter-self, and that Flaubert's 'two distinct persons' are bound to each other.

This contradiction that Flaubert discovers in his own commitments as an artist runs throughout the passage of modernist fiction, from James to Stein to Woolf to Joyce to Beckett. On the one hand, modernism is an art of abstraction. It is an art that responds to Flaubert's 'emancipation from matter' – to the sense that the tendency of modernity is towards disappearance, towards virtuality. As late nineteenth- and early twentieth-century technologies produce an increasingly manipulable reality – the dematerialising of space and time produced by the telegraph, the telephone, the camera, the cinema, the gathering speed of motor travel and air travel – so the artwork tends towards abstraction, crafting a style that floats free of its attachment to a world that it seeks to mimic or represent.[14] If, as Gerald Stanley Lee suggests in his 1913 work *Crowds*, 'the telephone changes the structure of the brain', contributing to a transformation which will 'give us in an incredible degree the mastery of the spirit over matter', so the structure of the modernist artwork too changes to register this freedom from the material demands of space and time.[15] This is the burden of Auerbach's classic account of the anti-mimetic tendencies of the modernist novel, and of Georg Lukács' equally classic lament on its failure to carry out its representational duties. For Auerbach, modernist fiction is a response to the perception that 'exterior events' have 'lost their hegemony'.[16] 'Goethe or Keller', Auerbach writes, 'Dickens or Meredith, Balzac or Zola' belonged to a world of shared assumptions about the nature of reality (p. 535). 'As recently as the nineteenth century, and even at the beginning of the twentieth', he argues, 'so much clearly formulable and recognized community of thought and feeling remained . . . that a writer engaged in representing reality had reliable criteria at hand by which to organize it' (p. 550). For modernist writers, however, this is no longer the case. There is no shared agreement on the nature of 'exterior events', as 'the writer as narrator of objective facts has almost completely vanished' (p. 534). In place of the supposedly objective description of Dickens and Balzac, the modernists developed a 'method which dissolves reality into multiple and multivalent reflections of consciousness' (p. 551). As Georg Lukács puts it (in a more negative vein), modernist fiction constitutes an abandonment of the 'great realist writer's' vocation to 'grasp and portray trends and phenomena truthfully in their historical development'.[17] 'The modernist writer', Lukács declares, 'identifies what is necessarily a subjective experience with reality as such, thus giving a distorted picture of reality as a whole' (p. 51). Lukács and Auerbach, from rather different perspectives, agree that modernist fiction involves the discovery that the novel form can no longer gain access to a reality that is tending towards formlessness (which is why, in T. S. Eliot's grave estimation, the novel as a form 'ended with Flaubert and with James'[18]). As Henry James himself puts it, in a 1915 interview, as European history moves increasingly towards dematerialising technologies, and towards the violence of world war, so the novelist's words are 'voided of the happy semblance'.[19] Words have lost their mimetic power, he says, 'they have weakened, they have deteriorated like motor car tires' (p. 144). 'We are now confronted', he concludes, 'with a depreciation of all our terms, or, otherwise speaking, with a loss of expression through increase of limpness, that may well make us wonder what ghosts will be left to walk' (pp. 144–45).

Modernism, then, is an art of abstraction, an art which sees a growing gap between representation and reality.[20] But if this is so, what characterises the art and fiction of modernism, as surely and as fully as its abstraction, is the opposite tendency towards a material becoming, its condition as the apotheosis of the physical, the material, the thingly, its capacity not merely to represent the world but also to be the world represented. Representation falls away from a world tending towards virtuality, James suggests, as words lose their power of 'semblance'; but even as this happens, the process by which the world itself becomes manufactured, becomes manipulable and editable, leads the environment itself to *become* a kind of representation, to partake of the logic of representation. As the world becomes artifice, as the world becomes the product of the machine, of the man-made, the gap between an increasingly artificial lifeworld and the modes of artifice which depict it might appear not to grow, but rather to shrink. Wyndham Lewis declares, in the first issue of his modernist magazine *Tyro*, that 'we are the creatures of a new state of human life, as different from nineteenth-century England, say, as the Renaissance was from the middle ages'.[21] To live in the early twentieth century, after the Great War, Lewis asserts, is to belong to a different order of being, to be a member of a machinised species, and to live in an artificial prosthetic environment. 'All that distinguishes externally our time', Lewis writes, 'is machinery, trains, steam ships'.[22] 'Machinery', he writes, 'sweeps away the doctrines of a narrow and pedantic Realism at a stroke'.[23] The twentieth century is a prosthetic age, and it requires a prosthetic art to represent it, an art, like Lewis' own angular, metallic, disturbingly inhuman portraits or the portraits of retooled bodies from Frida Kahlo to Hans Bellmer, that becomes itself machinic.[24] This is not an art that represents, but an art that embodies – the machinised art of the futurists, of the vorticists and surrealists, but also the plastic art of the modernist novel, the hard surfaces of Gertrude Stein's prose (in which, Tim Armstrong writes, the 'depth model (the occult word as metaphor, hidden truth) is supplanted by a stress on metonymy') or the densely somatic work of James Joyce, which, Beckett writes, 'is not *about* something; *it is that something itself*'.[25] As Tim Armstrong argues, because 'the prosthesis . . . is bound up with the dynamics of modernity', we see in 'a range of modernist writers a fascination with organ extension, organ-replacement, sensory extension; with the interface between the body and the machine' (p. 78). Or as Spyros Papapetros has more recently demonstrated, the entire range of modernist art and architecture (from Dali's 'My Wife Nude' to Ludwig Mies van der Rohe's Friedrichstrasse skyscraper project) stages a process whereby aesthetic desire is prosthetised in the inorganic structures of our environment, and in which art becomes what he calls a 'transspecies communication with other forms of matter, whether vegetal, animal or mineral'.[26]

From Flaubert's 1852 letter to Colet onwards, then, one can see these two opposite drives in modernist aesthetics, towards abstraction on the one hand and materiality – Papapetros's 'inorganic animation' – on the other; if one is to understand the ways in which modernism transforms the encounter that fiction stages with the self – that encounter that I have traced from More to Bellamy and Gilman – it is necessary to respond to both of these drives. It is not, I would suggest, that modernism stages quite the dismantling of the mimetic apparatus that Auerbach sees in the passage from Dickens and Balzac to Woolf and Joyce. Neither is it the case that modernism discovers a representational form that becomes purely prosthetic, a form, in Beckett's overheated reading of Joyce, in which the artwork is no longer about something but becomes that something itself.

Rather, the aesthetic revolution that is brought about by modernism – that responds to the technological revolutions of modernity itself, and that helps us move beyond the impasse that realism reaches in Wilde, Gilman and Bellamy – involves the production of an art surface that is able to register, in its own shimmering expressive mode, the irresolvable tension between the material and the abstract, between an art that frees itself from the world and an art that becomes that world. The modernist novel does not escape the prosthetic logic that I have traced so far in this book, in which fiction works at the difficult meeting ground between mind and world, acting as a bridge between the unextended and the extended self; it is released neither into pure abstraction nor into pure material. Rather, modernist fiction offers an intensification of this logic, as the development of the prosthetic condition – the insistent emergence of the artificial lifeworld of modernity – forces the prosthetic junction that has always lain at the secret heart of the novel and always served as the unstable foundations of prose realism, onto the surface of the artwork itself. A young Samuel Beckett, writing on 9 July 1937 to his friend Axel Kaun, gives a description of what this kind of art surface might look like, in terms that recall the tension that Flaubert establishes, more than eighty years earlier, between an artwork devoted to nothingness and one devoted to materiality. 'More and more', Beckett writes, 'my own language appears to me like a veil that must be torn apart to get at the things (or the Nothingness) behind it.'[27] As Flaubert wants to write a 'book about nothing' – as Gilman's narrator tears at the surface of her own text to get at the formless figure behind it – so Beckett longs to destroy his own representational apparatus to enter into a negatively utopian formlessness. But, as Beckett embarks on his own writing career, and with the work of Proust, Joyce, Stein, Woolf and Kafka behind him, he recognises that this discovery of unextended being is a function of the art surface itself, 'this coloured plane', as he puts it elsewhere, 'that was not there before'.[28] 'Is there any reason', he asks in his letter to Kaun,

> why that terrible materiality of the word surface should not be capable of being dissolved, like for example the sound surface, torn by enormous pauses, of Beethoven's seventh symphony, so that through whole pages we can perceive nothing but a path of sounds suspended in giddy heights, linking unfathomable abysses of silence?[29]

Beckett does not reply to his own rhetorical question; but the response, I think, is the passage of his own writing, from the 1930s to the 1980s, which lives out the prosthetic logic of the modernist novel by capturing, in the terrible materiality of its own surface, an endless play between the extended and unextended self. 'Skewered on the ferocious dilemma of expression', as he puts it in his conversation with Georges Duthuit, he 'continues to wriggle'.[30] The surface of the modernist artwork becomes, in Beckett's writing, the space occupied, in one of his most forbidding works, by the narrator of *The Unnamable*. 'Perhaps that's what I feel', the narrator writes:

> perhaps that's what I am, the thing that divides the world in two, on the one hand the outside, on the other the inside, that can be as thin as foil, I'm neither one side nor the other, I'm in the middle, I'm the partition, I've two surfaces and no thickness, perhaps that's what I feel, myself vibrating, I'm the tympanum, on the one hand the mind, on the other the world, I don't belong to either.[31]

6.2   Art and Embodiment in James and Wharton

Over the course of the modernist novel, one can trace a trajectory, in which this condition, this orginary struggle between mind and world that becomes so excruciating in Beckett's *The Unnamable*, is increasingly exposed. It is not, I think, that realism increasingly gives way to abstraction – it is not, as Ludovic Janvier suggests at an early stage in the development of modernist studies, that 'reality is dissolving as though an anchor were raised, permitting the work to set out slowly toward its own myth';[32] rather, the tendency in modernist fiction is towards an increasingly naked encounter with the simultaneously contractive and expansive movement that I have characterised as the signature of the prosthetic imagination – the struggle, at the epistemological and aesthetic heart of the novel as a form, to unearth and to give narrative expression to the vanishing point where mind meets with matter, a struggle which is at once a laying bare and a dressing up, at once a paring back and an adding on.

It is in the society novels of the turn of the twentieth century – and particularly in the fiction of Henry James and Edith Wharton – that one can see the beginnings of this trajectory, the emergence of a modernist sensibility and style in the very midst of a realism that is reaching its own formal limits. And it is in the insistent recurrence, in both writers, of the predicament of the duplicated self that this emergence announces itself most clearly. Consider, in the case of James, works from his middle and late period, such as *The Middle Years* (1893), *The Figure in the Carpet* (1896), *The Jolly Corner* (1908) or *What Maisie Knew* (1897). All of these works turn around an encounter with an avatar of the self, with a self that has been divided from itself. *What Maisie Knew* begins and ends with an act of division, the divide in being that the young Maisie suffers as a result of her parents' brutal divorce, and of their ruthlessly selfish schemes to parcel her out between them, as if her person were an estate to be broken up. The outcome of the divorce settlement between Beale and Ida Farange, the narrator says on the opening page of the novel, was that the 'little girl' should be 'disposed of in a manner worthy of the judgement-seat of Solomon'. That is, 'she was divided in two and the proportions tossed impartially to the disputants.'[33] Maisie is divided, like spoils, between her warring parents at the opening of the novel, and then she finds herself, at the novel's close, still cloven in two. After the exhausting struggles between Ida and Beale, and then between her stepfather Sir Claude and her step-mother Mrs Beale – the struggles which are the object of the novel's forensic scrutiny – Maisie finds herself once again divided between two opposing parties, and belonging to neither. As her stepfather and step-mother give up their claim to the child in the final scene, the narrator says that 'the child stood there again dropped and divided' (p. 261), now between the claims of her step-parents on the one hand and her governess Mrs Wix on the other. *What Maisie Knew* is centrally about this experience of a divide in the conscious subject and so too is James' later novella *The Jolly Corner*. This story concerns the obsession of its protagonist, Spencer Brydon, with his childhood home in New York, located at the 'jolly corner' of the novella's title. Brydon, who has spent the past thirty-three years of his adult life as an aesthete in Europe, is obsessed with the house because, he says, it contains the spirit or ghost of his alter ego, of the self that he would have become if he had pursued his possible life as a New York real estate mogul, and if he had been nourished by what he calls the 'communities of knowledge' that such a life would have entailed.[34] As the story continues, Brydon becomes increasingly convinced that the house is haunted by this other self, this latent, unlived version of himself, that there is a 'strange *alter ego* deep down somewhere within me' (p. 349), who might be accosted in physical form, who might be 'run to earth' (p. 356) in the house in which both ego and alter ego had first come to consciousness.

What Maisie Knew and *The Jolly Corner* both turn around this experience of division; both works are involved in the search for a mode of art which might give expression to the self, both in the condition of its division and in the phantasmal wholeness to which the divided self implicitly calls. *The Jolly Corner*, like Bellamy's *Looking Backward* (to which James' novella surely refers), brings two versions of its protagonist, living in two different communities of knowledge, into the same compacted space; but where, for

Bellamy, the formal implications of this compaction is a problem to be overcome, for James, this meeting, in a single figure of a doubled being, of what he calls in this story a 'duplication of consciousness' (p. 356), is the central preoccupation of the work. How, James asks in *The Jolly Corner* and *What Maisie Knew*, can a single integrated literary subject accommodate this sense that being involves the immersion in more than one community of knowledge – the communities of knowledge presided over by Beale Farange, Sir Claude and Mrs Wix in *What Maisie Knew*, and by Europe and New York, the art world and the real estate market, in *The Jolly Corner*. In Bellamy's novel, as I have said, we are brought up against the spectacle of an undifferentiated state prior to individuation, what Bellamy calls the 'soul in the rough', 'before it has received the ear marks, the individualizing touches which make it a person' (p. 37). This is the undivided being, the naked, non-prosthetised consciousness which has not yet taken on the external attachments of form, and which Bellamy rushes to immerse in its twin communities of knowledge – the Boston of 1887 and that of 2000. For James, though, the central question is how this fleeting experience of undivided being might find itself enshrined in form, whether it is possible to capture, in the artwork itself, a version of Brydon that is not split between Europe and New York, or a version of Maisie that is not split between the various guardians that take possession of her. And for James the response to this question involves the manipulation of the art surface itself, the development of a word surface that might bring opposing ways of knowing and seeing into the force field of its own highly polished signification, without doing violence either to their difference or to their unity.

In both *The Jolly Corner* and *What Maisie Knew*, this fascination with surface as the site of a joining and separating of the self manifests itself in a concern with corrective lenses (a concern which is explored most fully in James' intriguing 1896 short story 'Glasses', and which is at the centre of his famous Preface to *The Portrait of a Lady*).[35] In *The Jolly Corner*, this takes the form of a monocle that is worn by Spencer's alter ego, and that stands as an odd clear-reflective surface that joins and separates the two versions of self when they finally encounter each other in the darkened New York mansion house. In *Maisie*, it appears as a pair of spectacles belonging to the kindly governess Mrs Wix, the only one of Maisie's guardians to have her best interests at heart. Mrs Wix, the narrator remarks, 'wore glasses which, in humble reference to a divergent obliquity of vision, she called her straighteners' (p. 49). These straighteners recur throughout the narrative, where they serve always to bring the various fields of vision, the various conflicting interests which gather around the slim being of Maisie, into some kind of focus. Suffering early in the novel from one of her first extended absences from her mother, and finding herself under the protection not of the soft and matronly Mrs Wix but of the sharply beautiful Miss Overmore (the governess hired by her father, soon to become his wife and Maisie's stepmother), Maisie finds herself bewilderedly longing for the security that only Mrs Wix can offer her, a longing which fixes itself on the straighteners. Miss Overmore forbids Mrs Wix to contact Maisie, so Maisie can only commune with her by tuning herself to her absence. Mrs Wix's 'very silence', Maisie thinks, became

> one of the largest elements of Maisie's consciousness; it proved a warm and habitable air, into which the child penetrated further than she dared ever to mention to her companions [her father and Miss Overmore]. Somewhere in the depths of it the dim straighteners were fixed upon her; somewhere out of the troubled little current Mrs Wix intensely waited. (p. 60)

Maisie, suffering from the self-alienation that her objectification as a marital asset has caused, can only encounter herself as she appears in the corrected vision of Mrs Wix. Where everyone around her offers her skewed pictures of herself generated by their own interests – Sir Claude, for example, whose 'eyes remained bent', is 'anything but straight' (p. 242) – Mrs Wix's straighteners offer a visual field in which Maisie may recognise her own image. James himself suggests that the central interest of *Maisie* is the kind of seeing that Maisie's predicament entails – the kind of seeing that would be developed by a character who has not a property in her own person, a character who has to learn to become – to think and to know, to develop an 'inner self' – as the disputed property of others, and without the epistemological apparatus necessary to understand that dispute. This kind of seeing, James writes in the Preface to *Maisie*, would require 'another scale, another perspective, another horizon' (p. 28), and Mrs Wix's straighteners, like the glasses that Swift's Gulliver keeps secreted in his pocket on his trip to Lilliput, are the prosthetic devices that allow us to see at such a scale (as the readers of *Portrait*, James tells us in the Preface to that novel, have to learn to adapt their readerly apparatuses of vision, 'one seeing more where the other sees less, one seeing black where the other sees white, one seeing big where the other sees small, one seeing coarse where the other sees fine' (p. 8)). The straighteners offer to refocus, to rescale; but what *Maisie* discovers, what *Maisie* knows, is that the deep focal field in which Maisie's 'inner self' might coincide fully with her external surfaces is not available, or at least is only available *as* surface. James lovingly describes Maisie, in his

Preface to the novel, as 'my light vessel of consciousness, swaying in a draught' (p. 26); one of the most striking and beautiful achievements of the work is its capacity to picture a young and innocent consciousness striving to fashion itself into a container for its own being, against the influence her parents and guardians, who seek to exploit her for their own purposes (a work of self-fashioning undergone too by Isabel Archer in *Portrait*, who is tasked, with the 'mere slim shade' of her fine intelligence, to discover the 'scale of her relation to herself' (p. 12)). Maisie's struggle is how to take ownership of the contents of what the narrator calls her 'light little brain'; she is a fragile cup in which the distilled liquid of her self is contained, but which is also a tragically 'ready vessel' for the bitterness of her parents, a 'deep little porcelain cup in which biting acids could be mixed' (p. 36). The depths of Mrs Wix's straighteners offer the only field in which Maisie might come to that knowledge of self, while being guided by the care of another; but the depth of field that the straighteners offer is always illusory, as they are always, after all, a hard surface not a deep pool. Growing up as the disputed property of her parents, Maisie thinks, has led her to become accustomed to seeing herself not as her own property – precisely not as a container filled with her own being – but as the dumb object of her parents' battles (and then, later, as the 'pretext' that 'brings' her stepmother and stepfather 'together'). Such a relation to self gives her, she thinks, a 'sharpened sense of spectatorship': 'It gave her often an odd air of being present at her history in as separate a manner as if she could only get at experience by flattening her nose against a pane of glass' (p. 101). If *What Masie Knew* is chiefly about what Maisie thinks of winningly as 'her personal relation to her knowledge', then here such knowledge is not secreted inside her being but is projected outside of her, onto the surfaces presented by her parents and step-parents, those that her own external being, like a tough, insensible integument, either separates or brings together (a projection which so often in James (in *The Jolly Corner*, in *Portrait*, in *The Turn of the Screw*) turns around the space of the window, of the doorway, of the threshold). 'She was to feel', she later thinks, as she struggles to forge a closer, more proprietorial relationship with her own inner self, with the content of her own understanding, 'as if she were flattening her nose upon the hard window-pane of the sweetshop of knowledge' (p. 120).

Mrs Wix's straighteners are a particular version of this widow pane – a glass surface which stands between Maisie and her 'knowledge'. Their special property, though, is that, like the hard surface of James' prose itself, they act not only as a barrier but also as an optical tool that conjures depths from surface. The spectacles offer a thin glass that is also a deep container – a surface which opens onto an inner dwelling where Mrs Wix and Maisie might enter into a union with themselves and with each other. On an occasion when both Maisie and Mrs Wix realise that Sir Claude loves neither of them, Maisie sees her own grief reflected in Mrs Wix's. 'Then she saw', the narrator says, 'the straighteners all blurred with tears which after a little seemed to have sprung from her own eyes' (p. 217). This is a moment of looking which is also a moment of communion; a moment when the straighteners join the epistemological worlds that they divide, when they stand not between Maisie and Mrs Wix but surround their conjoined grief like a bubble; a moment for both Maisie and Mrs Wix, in a striking phrase that appears both in *What Maisie Knew* and *The Jolly Corner*, when their 'eyes were in each other's eyes'.[36] But even as the surface of Mrs Wix's spectacles, and the glassy surface of James' prose, open themselves in this way to depths – allowing for the junction of one person to another, and also the junction of the undivided soul to the various communities of knowledge that clothe it and enworld it – the force of this junction is won from its absolute commitment to surface; the glass surface of the straighteners, the limpid surface of the page, which capture what James calls the 'residuum of truth', the delicate truth of Maisie's 'small expanding consciousness', only as it 'become[s] presentable as a register of impressions' (p. 24), only as it wriggles on the terrible materiality of the word surface.

Henry James' work is dedicated to producing this surface-depth assemblage, this vibrating merging and separating of the self which is the beginnings of a prosthetic modernism, of a modernism which works at the junction between mind and matter, and which brings that junction onto the word surface itself. As James puts it, his work seeks to 'write this history of the growth of one's imagination', so that we can approach that revealed junction at which the imagination is able to take on 'such and such a constituted, animated figure or form'.[37] But it is in the work of Edith Wharton – less highly polished that that of James, less obviously devoted to the crafting of a modernist style – that one can see most clearly the shift from a realist to a modernist sensibility, in the approach to the literary surface that both divides self from self and brings it into a new conjunction. Wharton and James were friends whose extensive correspondence suggests a shared literary vocation, but whatever the resonance between their work, it is often possible to detect a distance between them, a difference in emphasis that turns around their relationship with realism.[38] Wharton recalls, in her 1933 memoir *A Backward Glance*, a particular discussion between them at which this difference rose to the surface. 'I was naturally much interested in James's technical theories and experiments', she writes, 'though I thought, and still think, that he tends to sacrifice to them that spontaneity which is the life of fiction'.[39] For Wharton, James' fascination with 'technical theories', his longing for what Flaubert calls a work which is 'held together by the strength of its style',[40] leads him to technical prose lacking in 'life', and she expressed this misgiving to the morbidly sensitive James in person: 'The characters in *The Wings of the Dove* and *The Golden Bowl* seemed to me more and more lacking in atmosphere, more and more severed from that thick nourishing human air in which we all live and move' (p. 190). Wharton continues,

> Preoccupied by this, I one day said to him: 'what was your idea in suspend-ing the four principal characters in *The Golden Bowl* in the void? What sort of life did they lead when they were not watching each other, and fencing with each other? Why have you stripped them of all the *human fringes* we necessarily trail after us through life?' (p. 191)

James' response, Wharton remembers, was a rejection of the terms of the question ('after a pause of reflection he answered in a disturbed voice: "My dear – I didn't know I had!"' (p. 191)). Her objection to James' late infatuation with 'the void', however, remains suggestive for a reading of Wharton's own work – for framing her sense of the capacity and duty of fiction to capture 'life', and for understanding the means by which she tests the limits of the realism she inherited from her nineteenth-century pre-cursors in approaching the experience of alienated female consciousness at the turn of the twentieth century. In a novel such as *The House of Mirth*, for example – the compelling tale of an impoverished society woman strug-gling to exploit her beauty to achieve a financially advantageous marriage – it is easy to see that Wharton is working in a tradition that is deeply rooted in the development of prose realism, from Burney to Austen. It is true, from the beginning, that the novel registers a certain artificiality that is central to early twentieth-century New York society – an artificiality which erodes the cohesion of its fictional characters and worlds and troubles its realism. The protagonist of the novel, Lily Bart, is one of those characters, multiplying throughout the fiction of the *fin de siècle*, who lives at a remove from herself, who experiences, like Gilman's narrator, a 'duplication of consciousness'. It is a refrain in the novel that Lily feels thus divorced from herself: 'There were in her' she thinks early in the novel, 'two beings, one drawing deep breaths of freedom and exhilaration, the other gasping for air in a little black prison-house of fears';[41] or later, she thinks that 'the frightened self in her was dragging the other down' (p. 143); or later that 'there were two selves in her, the one she had always known, and a new abhorrent being to which it found itself chained' (p. 145); or later still she thinks that 'it was as though a great blaze of electric light had been turned on in her head, and her poor little anguished self shrank and cowered in it, without knowing where to take refuge' (p. 313).

This divide in the self is the central predicament that the novel explores – the distance from self that a woman experiences when she enters the world as an ornament, when she finds herself put up for sale in a marriage market that prizes her material being itself as her chief (perhaps sole) commodity. Lily's experience of herself as at once divided and commodified produces in her an overwhelming sense of her own artificiality, a conviction that the person she is attached to, the person she *is*, has been manufactured, a prosthetic being fashioned for the pleasure of others, as Maisie regards herself as existing solely to satisfy the vengeful demands of her various guardians. Lawrence Selden – the detached observer and cool critic of the superficial society to which Lily belongs – notes this quality in Lily in the novel's opening scene, as he is simultaneously drawn to and sceptical of her beauty. 'He had a confused sense', the narrator says, 'that she must have cost a great deal to make, that a great many dull and ugly people must have been sacrificed to produce her', that in some busy Promethean factory a 'fine glaze of beauty and fastidiousness had been applied to vulgar clay' (p. 7). Lily cost a great deal to make, like Richardson's Pamela before her who is informed by her parents that she 'did not make herself',[42] or like May Welland in Wharton's later novel *The Age of Innocence* whose 'frankness and innocence', the protagonist Newland Archer thinks to himself, is in fact 'an artificial product', 'cunningly manufactured by a conspiracy of mothers and aunts';[43] and Lily's task in life, she understands, is to stand guard over this objectified beauty, to protect it as the asset that will eventually yield the economic and social capital she needs to enter into a more secure relationship with her own being. 'Her beauty itself', she thinks, 'her skill in enhancing it, the care she took of it, the use she made of it' (p. 50) is a constant work of artifice that requires equally constant vigilance. To regard herself is to encounter this finely made mask. To look in the mirror is to examine the product for flaws; 'the white oval of her face' she thinks, as she frets that her face is beginning to show the wrinkles that come with age, 'swam out waveringly from a background of shadows; but the two lines about the mouth remained' (p. 29). Every moment of self-congress in *The House of Mirth* partakes of this artificiality, a late and heightened version of that self-alienation that Dickens' Esther Summerson feels as she looks at her disfigured face in the mirror in *Bleak House* (p. 528);

but even if this is the case, Wharton adopts a richly nuanced realism with which to give expression to this artificiality, a realism that owes something to Dickens, and a great deal to Jane Austen, particularly to Austen's *Emma* (which Wharton beautifully calls the 'most perfect example in English fiction of a novel in which character shapes events quietly but irresistibly, as a stream nibbles away its banks').[44] The great achievement of *Emma*, I argued earlier, is the crafting of a narrative voice that can depict a set of artificial social relations – between Emma and Harriet, between Emma and Frank Churchill, between Emma and herself – while incubating, in the narrative spaces made by its own tonal mobility, the fragile body of a true self, which enters into true relations with others. Austen's startlingly innovative use of narrative irony allows her to exploit a language which always means doubly to show a mind at odds with itself, a mind mired in error and falsity, while crafting an ironic undertow that leads that mind back to a proper, unified relation to its embodied self – a self fully at home in Wharton's 'thick nourishing human air in which we all live and move'. The apparent agent of this recovery of self in *Emma* is, of course, a man; it is Emma's slowly germinating love for Mr Knightley that leads her to an eventual appreciation of what Knightley primly calls 'the beauty of truth and sincerity in all of our doings with each other' (p. 365), even if the quietly dissident joy of Austen's novel is the recognition that truth and sincerity, even in the most intimate and earnest of relations, consist in the mobility, the forms of untruth, that Austenian irony continually deploys.

As many readers of *The House of Mirth* have noted, Wharton adapts a version of this Austenian mode to oversee Lily's artificial relation with herself; in doing so, she too suggests that it is a relationship with a man that might allow an alienated female consciousness to catch a glimpse of a non-prosthetic version of herself. Emma comes to self-knowledge, to a sudden 'development of self', through her relationship with Mr Knightley; Lily Bart encounters a version of self that is not a mirror image through the medium of Lawrence Selden, the only man with whom she has a spontaneous affinity. Wharton's novel turns around the opening gap between the artificial self that Lily is forced to adopt to maintain her precarious position in a morally bankrupt society and another self – shy, uncertain, unformed – that she discovers only as it is conjured by her relations with Selden. His critical distance from society – his ability to retreat from the public sphere to the private intellectual freedom of the book-lined room in which he and Lily meet in the novel's opening scene – allows him to offer her a space in which she too might escape from the prosthetic self that society has fashioned for her. The central scenes in the novel, and the most powerful, are those in which Selden and Lily glimpse the possibility of what they both call a 'republic of the spirit', a 'world apart' in which they might share a relation that is stripped of its artificial skin, its 'fine glaze', where they are no longer separated from each other by the hard, bright surfaces of the social world. In bringing such a space to possibility, Wharton employs the narrative realism she has inherited from Austen, and from Wollstonecraft before her, and Burney before her, and Behn before her. The narrative dynamics of *The House of Mirth* – its breathtaking capacity to conjure the intimacy of inner being from a language attuned to and shaped by artificiality – would not be possible without *Emma*, without *Evelina*, without *Mary* or *Oroonoko*; but in Wharton's prose, these dynamics achieve a kind of precision, a kind of painful vividness, that was not yet possible for Austen, as if Wharton is inheriting a mimetic technology that has gone through an evolution, from black and white to colour, from mono to stereo. In all of the scenes in which Lily and Selden meet – from their first hillside walk when they jointly found their republic of the spirit, to their last meeting in the shadow of Lily's death, at which she leaves her 'self' in Selden's care ('I have kept her with me all this time', she says, 'but now we are going to part, and I have brought her back to you – I am going to leave her here' (p. 300)) – Wharton traces an extraordinarily precise oscillation between the artificial and the real, the dead and the living, the prosthetic and the non-prosthetic, as it is set into motion by the relations between them. Just as Emma's relations with Mr Knightley partake at once of an overt language founded in error and of an implied one, structured as irony, in which a true relation might grow, so Lily's relations with Selden are conducted in two languages at once – the public language of the artificial social world and a private language, expressed in the same words, but pertaining to a different world, the real one they share, in which it would be possible for them both to live as full and free subjects. The movement of Wharton's prose, its balletic precision, is dedicated to achieving the constant shift between the former and the latter, conducting a push and pull, a contraction and expansion, in which an artificial language yields moments of reality, of 'life', those moments of being when the formless figure of political freedom that moves in Gilman's *Yellow Wallpaper* rises to the surface of the prose.

One can see this movement in almost every discussion the two have. 'Why', Lily asks Selden, at the climax of their hillside walk, 'do you make the things I have chosen seem hateful to me, if you have nothing to give me instead?' (p. 71). The question, grounded in the impossibility, the unreality of their relation, gives rise to one of those sudden rushes of real feeling that recur in the novel, which are always hedged about by insincerity, but which are nevertheless charged with intense political and emotional possibility. 'It was one of those moments', the narrator says, 'when neither seemed to speak deliberately, when an indwelling voice in each called to the other across unsounded depths of feeling'. Selden agrees with Lily that poor as he is, he cannot offer her anything in place of the social world they both know to be manufactured, artificial. 'I have nothing to give you instead', he agrees, 'If I had, it should be yours, you know' (p. 72). This declaration, this sudden, unpremeditated recognition that they share an understanding that is intimate and 'indwelling' to the same extent that it is latent and unrealisable, draws Selden and Lily into the unified being that is the shimmering promise at the heart of this novel – that is as real an experience of intimacy as it is possible for narrative to produce, as if the novel is here activating our own internal apparatus of loving openness to self and to the other. This sudden proximity leads Lily, accustomed as she is to distance in all her encounters, to an involuntary somatic response – one that recalls the moment when Emma's unacknowledged love for Mr Knightley takes the form of tears, unbidden and unaccountable, running down her cheeks. Lily 'received this abrupt declaration', the narrator says, 'in a way even stranger than the manner of its making: she dropped her face on her hands and he saw for a moment that she wept' (p. 72). Her weeping carries the romantic freight of a moment of truth, but it is the nature of Lily's and Selden's relations always to draw back from such revelation, always to find the true, the intimate, woven tightly into the staged, the artificial. Selden 'leaned nearer' to the weeping Lily and, 'draw[ing] down her hands' to reveal 'a face softened but not disfigured by emotion', 'he said to himself, somewhat cruelly, that even her weeping was an art' (p. 72).

Wharton's prose draws on the mobility of Austenian realism to choreograph this narrative movement between social artificiality and an underlying, indwelling emotional truth. Her depiction of the relation between Lily and Selden is pitched in such a way that it draws attention, at all times, to the artificiality of their encounter – the sense that they speak to each other always across a socially engineered divide – while also allowing it to nourish Lily's other self, 'this real self of hers' as the narrator puts it (echoing, as it happens, the terms in which Wharton describes her own relation with Henry James), 'which [Selden] had the faculty of drawing out of the depths' (p. 94).[45] But if Wharton's narrative skill allows her to develop Austen's technique, to penetrate more deeply than Austen could into the condition of prosthetic alienation suffered both by Emma and by Lily, it is also the case that this technique – indeed the possibility of realism itself – reaches a kind of vanishing point in Wharton's prose, a limit where the logic of realism starts to yield to the logic of modernism. This is not at all because there is any lessening of mimetic power – not, in James' phrase, that Wharton's words have 'weakened', or 'deteriorated like motor car tires'.[46] On the contrary, Wharton's powers of description – her ability to capture the texture of a social world of high artifice – allow her to develop an inside narrative of alienated femininity that is arguably finer grained than anything by Austen, and more embodied than James' portraits, from *The Portrait of a Lady* to *The Golden Bowl*. Rather, it is the mimetic power of the prose itself – the precision with which it traces the passage between the exterior and the interior of the ornamental self – that brings the narrative up against a kind of limit. Where, in Austen's work, the bridge that attaches the artificial to the real, the interior of being to its external attachments, remains implicit, woven out of the fabric of narrative irony, Wharton's prose takes us too far into that connective tissue itself to allow it to remain in hiding, to remain wrapped in the doubleness of Austenian narrative voice. It opens such a clear passage to the ground that it stakes out between the artificial world of New York society and the republic of the spirit for which it longs – the world where Lily might encounter both Selden and herself truly, the world in which her 'real self' might be preserved – that it brings that ground itself to the illuminated surface, forces it to *become*, itself, surface.

One can see this effect throughout the novel, whenever the narrative sets one version of self against another, the brightly lit world of twentieth-century modernity against the 'twilight world' which Lily and Selden share. One can see it everywhere in the dialogue between Lily and Selden, in the sense that the very terms in which they reach to each other 'across unsounded depths' are composed of the forms of artifice, of duplicity, that they seek to overcome. The real genius of Wharton's novel lies here – in its capacity to capture the artificial, public structures that support Lily's most frictionless moments of self-congress, as if Lily has no access to an internal thought that does not pass through the external, glazed surfaces of the self, no screen onto which to project such thought that does not belong to the social world that she has learned to despise, that has converted her into the property of others. Selden's presence has a somatic effect on Lily, as if her body is a biological register of the reality of their love for each other. She is aware of the 'quicker beat of life that his nearness always produced' (p. 135), 'the stir of the pulses which his nearness always caused' (p. 93), and the moments when he comes closest to declaring his love for her are always registered first in her body – as the 'slow colour [rises] to her cheek', in a blush 'drawn from the deep wells of feeling', 'as if the effort of her spirit had produced it' (p. 71). But even this involuntary response – a descendent of the 'blush of sensibility' that marks Emma's acceptance of Mr Knightley's love – becomes part of the artifice of their relation – not a sign on the bodily surface of hidden depths, but a sign that the glazed surface itself is the true province of the deep, of the real – a sign, as Selden thinks cruelly to himself in response to Lily's brightening and darkening face, that she has learned 'the art of blushing at the right time' (p. 8). One can see it too in the dreadful conversation that Lily has with herself, as she heads towards death, as she despairs of finding a form in which she might give expression to that formless self that struggles within her. 'That was the feeling that possessed her', she thinks, 'the feeling of being something rootless and ephemeral, mere spin-drift of the whirling surface of existence, without anything to which the poor little tentacles of self could cling' (p. 310). Exhaustion and despair have the effect of flooding her mind with unforgiving light – with the artificial light that ushered in the new illumination of twentieth-century modernity – a light which leaves no narrative fold or wrinkle in which one might hide. 'It was as though', she thinks, 'a great blaze of electric light had been turned on in her head, and her poor little anguished self shrank and cowered in it, without knowing where to take refuge' (p 313). But one can see this effect, this cleaving of surface to depth, most clearly of all in the dazzling central scene of the novel – the scene in which the yielding of a realist to a modernist sensibility is most evident – that is, in the scene of the *tableau vivant*, in which Lily becomes herself a living picture, what Wharton calls a 'speaking portrait', by taking on the appearance of Joshua Reynold's 'Mrs Lloyd'.[47]

This is a moment at which Lily comes closest to accepting and embracing her artificiality, her existence not as a mind attached to a body, as an emotional or intellectual depth moving beneath a somatic covering, but as pure aesthetic surface, hard, bright, specular. The spectacle presented by *tableaux vivant*, the novel's artist Paul Morpeth thinks to himself, is one which allows 'the fugitive curves of living flesh' to be 'subdued to plastic harmony without losing the charm of life' (p. 131) (as 'nature' is 'subdued', in Shakespeare and Dickens, 'to what it works in'[48]). In using her own body as an art form, in bringing about a strange duplication of being, like that composite photograph imagined in Bellamy's *Looking Backward*, Lily finds a means of triumphantly imaging forth her condition – the sense that she *is* the surface that she resists, that her life consists in the artificial prosthetic forms that seem to constrain it. The tableau affords precisely the coming together of art and life – the 'strange affinity' between living flesh and painterly representation – that is imagined by Wilde in *The Picture of Dorian Gray*. Lily 'had shown her artistic intelligence', she thinks as she stands on the stage, in the frozen aspect of a living picture, 'in selecting a type so like her own that she could embody the person represented without ceasing to be herself'. 'It was as though' she goes on, again catching an echo of Dorian's merging with his portrait, 'she had stepped, not out of, but into, Reynold's canvas, banishing the phantom of his dead beauty by the beams of her living grace' (p. 132). The tableau allows living body and dead representation to become one thing, a composite of prosthetic supplement and 'real flesh and blood', and Selden, standing in the crowd, recognises this coming together, sees in the public transformation of life into art the apotheosis of her private self, 'the real Lily' as his cousin Gerty Farrish puts it – 'the Lily I know' (p. 133). 'It was as though', Selden thinks, moved by the spectacle, 'her beauty, thus detached from all that cheapened and vulgarized it, had held out suppliant hands to him from the world in which he and she had once met for a moment, and where he felt an overmastering longing to be with her again' (p. 133).

This is a peculiar moment, one which has acted as the pivot in many critical approaches to the novel. Nancy Bentley offers a familiar condemnation of the tableau as a vehicle for the subjection of women when she argues that 'rather than secure her real identity and value, the staged appearance subjects Lily to the speculations of a group of wealthy men'; in appearing as Mrs Lloyd, Lily is 'caught and framed, as it were, by the forces of social speculation'.[49] As Michael Gorra suggests, the tableau is an 'auction' which only underlines the terms in which Lily is sold on the marriage market, so Selden's enthusiasm, his sense that he sees the 'real Lily' on the stage, might seem perplexing, might suggest that Selden himself has no more access to a non-prosthetic Lily – to Lily's 'real identity and value' – than the odious men, the Trenors and the Rosedales, who barter for their portion of her beauty.[50] But even if this is so, even if the tableau presents a set of socio-economic relations in the plainest of sights, this moment reaches deep into the imaginary mechanics of the novel and touches on the delicate boundary that it establishes between a realism working at the limits of its capacities and an incipient modernism that emerges from the testing of those limits. To understand *The House of Mirth*, I think, one has to understand that this moment is not simply a capitulation to the forces that produce being as prosthetic commodity but is rather an aesthetic climax, at which Wharton draws on the expressive power of the *tableau vivant* to imagine a new and potentially emancipatory set of relations between surface and depth, between the real and the artificial, that are only coming to literary possibility at the turn of the twentieth century. As Hannah Jordan has recently shown, the *tableau vivant* itself as an art practice is much more deeply entwined with the political and aesthetic radicalism of the later nineteenth century than has been acknowledged in the dominant critical accounts of the period, and emerges from the same networks and practices that sustain aestheticism and the other layered forms of experiment that lead to modernism in literature and the visual arts.[51] When Lily stands, posing at once as herself (as 'a picture that was simply and undisguisedly the portrait of Miss Bart' (p. 132)) and as a Reynolds painting, when she allows self and representation of self to exist at the same composite moment, she is living out the birth of a new art form, one grounded in the highest of artifice, but one which touches, Selden thinks, on the latent space of their true relation – one which opens a passage to their republic of the spirit. This is an art form that is driven by the recognition that with the emergence of photography, of electric lighting, of the other new technologies for the reproduction of reality that define twentieth-century modernity, the terms in which the artwork conducts the relations between the internal and the external self enter too into a transformation. When Selden sees, in the image of Mrs Lloyd, 'the real Lily Bart, divested of the trivialities of her little world' (p. 133), he is not mistaking commodified beauty for the reality of the self – or at least not simply so. His response to Lily as spectacle, it is true, is part of the political problem that the novel addresses; it is one of its great achievements that it gives such a powerful and moving indictment of the commodification of female experience – as powerful in its way as Gilman's picture of maternal unfreedom in *The Yellow Wallpaper*. But even as the tableau scene offers a culmination of this experience – capturing the same inside-out sense of self as other experienced by James' Maisie – it gives expression also to the persistence of a kind of *region* of literary and political emancipation, the space of the prosthetic imagination that I have traced throughout the history of the novel, and that is brought here to the very surface of the page, and of the skin. Selden thinks to himself, as he settles down to watch the performance, that 'to unfurnished minds', *tableaux vivants* are 'only a superior kind of wax-works' (p. 131). But the form of seeing that he seeks to develop finds in these frozen images a combination of the stilled and the moving, of mind and matter, that brings art into a new kind of transformative contact with life, that allows Gilman's 'formless figure' to move within the revealed pictorial lineaments of the plastic self. To some spectators, tableaux look like waxworks, but 'to the responsive fancy', Selden thinks, in a phrase that Jordan takes as the title of her rethinking of the emancipatory possibilities of *tableaux vivants*, 'they may give magic glimpses of the boundary world between fact and imagination' (p. 131).

It is this boundary world that Wharton opens, I think, not only between the real and the imaginary, between mind and matter, but also between realism and modernism. In Selden's appreciation of the *tableau vivant*, one can hear a faint echo of the terms in which Nathaniel Hawthorne describes the utopian possibilities of his mode of literary realism. His depiction of Brook Farm in *The Blithedale Romance*, Hawthorne writes in a passage I quoted earlier, offers him an 'available foothold between fiction and reality' (p. 2), the foothold that lies at the heart of the nineteenth-century novel, and that acts as a bridge or junction between the extended and the unextended self. The tableau in *The House of Mirth* offers a related kind of foothold, but here, the combination of political, technological and aesthetic forces operating at the turn of the twentieth century brings this boundary region out of hiding, making it appear on the vibrating surface of the artwork itself. Where, in Wilde's *Doran Gray*, the pressure that brings art and life into the same sphere is released by the generic return of the Gothic – the Gothic as the province of an 'inner life' that cannot come to the aesthetic surface[52] – in Wharton Wilde's Gothicism is replaced by a nascent modernism, that same modernist amalgam of depth and surface that is the medium of Henry James' prosthetic imagination. Of course, the forces that bring the internal self, Lily's 'real self', into identity with her prosthetic self, that ornamental self which is experienced always as the property of others, condemn Lily to a tragic fate – a fate that she shares with Gilman's protagonist in *The Yellow Wallpaper*. The triumphant moment that Lily experiences in the tableau leads, inexorably, to the closing scenes of the novel, in which Lily finds herself bound to an artificial version of herself, unable to find any hidden retreat in which her 'poor little anguished self' might find refuge. As Selden thinks, when he stands by her deathbed, looking at her dead face 'which seemed to lie like a delicate impalpable mask over the living lineaments that he had known' (p. 317), death eventually hardens the surface that had always separated them – the surface that had always yielded, in the play of their relations with each other, to those sudden unsounded depths, the painterly surface onto which she projected her own self in the *tableau vivant*. 'The tenuity of the barrier between them', he thinks,

> mocked him with a sense of helplessness. There had never been more than a little impalpable barrier between them – and yet he had suffered it to keep them apart! And now, though it seemed slighter and frailer than ever, it had

suddenly hardened to adamant, and he might beat his life out against it in vain. (p. 317)

Where, in Austen's *Emma*, the prose gestates an imagined space in which Emma and Mr Knightley might come together, a space where Emma might preserve a 'real self' woven out of latent irony, whilst becoming, as Mr Knightley puts it, his 'own Emma, by hand and word', this space is not available in *The House of Mirth*. The moment of marriage – the joining of hands with which *Emma* ends – marks the conjunction of the external, socially manufactured self, with the private self of the novel, the replacing of the dead hand of alienation and artificiality with the living hand of the fully realised self that it is the work of realist fiction to accomplish. Lily, though, remains estranged by that adamantine barrier which – like the pane of glass against which James' Maisie flattens her nose – both divides her from her self and offers the only terms in which she might achieve any kind of self-congress. The nineteenth-century happy ending is sacrificed here to the bleakest expression of unfreedom – a sacrifice which Maureen Howard sees as a symptom of Wharton's modernism ('I read Wharton's novel', Howard writes, 'as a modernist work which denies the comforts of the genre'[53]). The consolations of Austenian realism give way to an expression of female alienation which, as in Gilman, has no social or narrative cure. But if this is the case, it is also true that the modernist mode that Wharton fashions in *The House of Mirth* – the mode that she achieves by pushing the logic of realism past the threshold at which it can reabsorb and domesticate the dissonance, the ironic self-difference which drives it – produces its own emancipatory poetics, an emancipatory poetics that remains beyond the expressive power of Gilman, Bellamy or Wilde. Lily, as character, can achieve no redemption; there is no moment at which the unrelenting estrangement from self caused by the political commodification of female beauty is falsely reconciled, just as there is no figure available, no narrative or somatic blush, in which the republic of the spirit might find itself embodied or instantiated. But what the novel generates, in the expression of this impossibility, is a new kind of art surface, one which reveals, in its capacity to bring the private self and the ornamental self into the same shining frame, the fractures in the composition of selfhood that point towards a radical mode of being yet to be fully conceived – one which unearths the 'boundary world' between inner self and its prosthetic manifestations which is the only province in this novel of spirit, and which appears on the expressive plane itself as a flaw in the terrible materiality of the word surface.

This creation, in both Wharton and James, of a new aesthetic relation between surface and depth, is integral to development of modernist fiction over the following decades of the twentieth century, from Proust, Stein and Woolf to Joyce, Kafka and Beckett. The surface and depth assemblage that they jointly fashion accommodates both of those imperatives that Flaubert describes in his 1852 letter to Colet – the urge towards abstraction on the one hand and towards materiality on the other. In both James and Wharton, the highly evolved intricacy of their realism results in the failure of its capacity to bind mind into world, a failure which leads James' prose, in Wharton's estimation, into an infatuation with 'the void'. Wharton insists, in opposition to James' abstractions, that it is the task of the writer to capture the 'human fringes' that give 'life' to fiction, but in her work, nearly as much as in James', the relation between 'real self' and prosthetic supplement has become abstracted. It is easy to see how the failure to fashion a form in which Lily's mental life can find itself embodied leads to the abstracted consciousnesses that emerge in Woolf, Joyce, Faulkner, Kafka, the dissolution of the bonds which hold mental life in objectively shared worlds. The failure of Wharton's Lily and of James' Maisie to find a bodily container for their selves, a ready vessel in which they might preserve their consciousness intact, is the first stage in a Kafkan metamorphosis, in which consciousness becomes altogether alienated from world and from species, from the hard shell and wriggling legs of a dehumanised body that has no relation to mind. But equally the surfaces that James and Wharton invent produce the most materialised of aesthetics, a form of modernist expression in which the gap between signifier and signified is vanishingly small, in which fiction seeks not to be '*about* something', but that '*something itself*'.

Both of these urges, towards the material and the abstract, are captured in *The House of Mirth*, in the form of a 'word', that most modernist of things. In the moments before her death, Lily feels that 'there was something that she must tell Selden, some word she had found that should make life clear between them. She tried to repeat the word, which lingered vague and luminous in the far edge of thought' (p. 314). Selden, sitting by her bed after her death, 'draining their last moment to the lees', imagines that he has spoken that word, that 'in the silence there passed between them the word which made all clear' (p. 320). This word sounds silently in that space that opens in the novel at the turn of the twentieth century, between mind and matter, between art and life. This is the space, at once too wide and too narrow, that runs through the fiction of the *fin de siècle*, that is sandwiched between 1887 and 2000 in *Looking Backward*, that vibrates between the front and back pattern of Gilman's yellow wallpaper. In bringing this word to thought, in imagining the word that might 'make life clear', Wharton oversees a shift in the way that language gives expression to mind at a remove from its own 'external attachments'. The word that Wharton imagines in *The House of Mirth* clears the way for the 'revolution of the word', leading to Joyce's 'hundredletter thunderwords' in *Finnegans Wake*, or to that elusive word, 'afaint' and 'afar away', that haunts Beckett's late prose poem 'What is the Word'.[54] The word, of course, remains unspoken in Wharton's novel. The central concern of that work is the lack of a bridge that can bring a duplicated consciousness into unity, the lack of a form in which objectified being might come to knowledge of itself. But if the novel is a devastating political protest against this lack, it is also a witness to the emergence of a new aesthetic, which at once responds to the imposition of artificiality into the very heartland of the real and produces a means of bringing the real and the artificial into a new expressive conjunction – the conjunction forged by the material abstractions of a prosthetic modernism.

CHAPTER 7

All Twined Together: Prosthetic Modernism from Proust to Beckett

> I'm in my arms, I'm holding myself in my arms, without much tenderness, but faithfully, faithfully.
>
> Samuel Beckett, *Texts for Nothing*[1]

7.1 Survival and Annihilation Entwined within Me: Gathering and Dispersal in the Modernist Novel

The aesthetic conjunction between the artificial and the real that is forged by the early modernist imagination – the fashioning of a surface which brings self and counter-self, material and abstract, into the same vibrating frame – has a long afterlife. The forms that one can see emerging in James and Wharton, that make of the artificial extension of the self the ground of a new kind of reality, are developed by the modernist novelists of the following decades, in the modes of prosthetic self-fashioning that are crafted by Proust, Joyce, Kafka, Woolf, Stein, Faulkner, Barnes and others. The production, in early modernist prose, of a kind of art surface that is the province too of a sequestered depth yields a rhythm of gathering and dispersal that grows richer as modernism develops, a twining together of being, won from its dismantlement, that is the keynote of a prosthetic modernism.

One can see this rhythm everywhere in the modernist novel as it reaches its maturity. Consider, for example, the division of William Faulkner's 1929 *The Sound and the Fury* into four distinct narratives – a division which recognises that narrative life is a matter of discomposure, a fracturing into broken shards of seeing, but which offers, at the same time, a gathering together of seeing, a kind of composite whole, what Faulkner himself calls a 'complete picture' that paradoxically owes its integrity to its separateness.[2] Or consider Virginia Woolf's *The Waves* (1931), a novel which manifests the multiple variousness of being in the six viewpoints from which it is narrated. The switching of narrative from person to person is part of a Woolfian disassembly of *dasein*, a recognition that we are never entire, that we never saturate our extended selves with our own concentrated life. Woolf's novel, Louis writes, 'makes us aware that these attempts to say, "I am this, I am that", which we make, coming together like separated parts of one body and soul, are false'.[3] The narrative lives in the midst of this awareness, in what Louis calls the 'desire to be separate' (p. 80) from oneself and from others, and much of the novel's poetry is found in the gaps such disaggregation opens. There is a certain joy in Louis' perception that 'I am not single and entire', his sense that he is a Frankensteinian rag bag of old parts, antique artefacts dug up out of the ground with which to fashion an artificial man. 'Every day', he says, 'I unbury – I dig up. I find relics of myself in the sand that women made thousands of years ago' (p. 74). But even so, even as the novel opens such differences in the heartlands of being, it also works to produce new forms of wholeness. 'We have tried to accentuate differences', Louis thinks, 'But there is a chain whirling round, round, in a steel-blue circle beneath' (p. 80). There is a circle, bluish, steely, that spins at the heart of this novel, that makes a ring of lit being, that exerts a gathering, twining, centrifugal force. 'My imagination is the body's', Jinny says. 'My body goes before me, like a lantern down a dark lane, bringing one thing after another out of darkness into a ring of light' (p. 75). The body throws a ring of light, making of itself a gathered thing, like the body that Clarissa imagines in *Mrs Dalloway*, that body that gets heavier as one ages, fuller of years and of self. Clarissa shares Louis' conviction that he is not entire. 'She would not say of herself', she thinks, echoing Louis, that 'I am this, I am that';[4] but a central image of *Mrs Dalloway* concerns the possibility of enshrining oneself in one's own memory, of holding oneself complete in one's arms. 'For she was a child', Clarissa thinks,

> throwing bread to the ducks, between her parents, and at the same time a grown woman coming to her parents who stood by the lake, holding her life in her arms which, as she neared them, grew larger and larger in her arms until it become a whole life, a complete life, which she put down by them and said, 'This is what I have made of it! This!' (p. 46)

Even as Clarissa and Louis recognise their separateness, Woolf's prose makes of such separateness this growing unity, this new completion. As the six friends come together in *The Waves*, 'drawn', Bernard says, 'into this communion by some deep, some common emotion' (p. 74), they forge a kind of poetic ring, a ring which is drawn to itself just as the parts of a single body are knitted together in the ring of light cast by consciousness. Louis imagines the friends sitting in a ring, 'with our arms binding our knees', holding themselves, holding each other, and he suggests that this ring of gathered being might 'hint at some other order, and better'. 'This I see for a second', he says, 'and shall try tonight to fix in words, to forge in a ring of steel' (p. 24).

This conjunction between gathering and dispersal runs, as I say, throughout the modernist novel, this sense that the forging of a poetic unity can only come about as a result of a form of steely prosthetic distance. But it is, I think, in the work of Samuel Beckett that the logic of prosthetic modernism is given both its most exhaustive and most protracted expression.[5] There is something nearly perverse about the single-mindedness with which Beckett devotes his fiction to an exposure of the prosthetic condition, to a painstaking anatomisation of the fold which joins unextended mind to its prosthetic extensions, that hidden hinge where the possibility of a complete being is conjured from the experience of disunity, from the insurgence of an alloyed, technologised, machinised being into the most intimate spaces of the inward self. This anatomy reaches a climax of a kind at the close of *The Unnamable*, in that vibrating moment I discussed earlier, at which the narrative scenario is folded back to reveal a naked voice oscillating between the mind on the one hand and the world on the other, pinned to the buried junction that lies at the heart of the prosthetic condition. But if *The Unnamable* reaches a kind of climax, Beckett continues to work at this revealed seam over the following thirty years, in a series of fictions, from *How It Is* to *The Lost Ones* and *Stirrings Still,* that extend this climax decades past the once commonly agreed boundaries of modernism – that live out what Madelyn Detloff calls 'the persistence of modernism', and Alys Moody has more recently called the 'afterlives of Modernism'.[6]

In Beckett's late novella *Company,* for example, published first in English in 1980, one can see Beckett continuing to explore that predicament that surfaces with such violent intensity in his fiction of the post-war. This story depicts an archetypal Beckettian scenario in which the narrative scene is reduced to its bare essentials, to a naked fictional body housed in a featureless fictional space. The body is addressed by a 'voice' – 'A voice comes to one in the dark', to 'one on his back in the dark'[7] – which belongs in some limited sense to that body, but which is also divorced from it, as Beckett's late theatrical works experiment with the prosthetic media forms (television, radio, the tape recorder) that estrange the voice from the body.[8] The vocation of *Company,* its central concern, is to find a means of establishing a conjunction between the narrative voice and the body on its back in the dark – a means of establishing a kind of unified living being that is composed at once of mind and matter, of voice and flesh. The voice tells a story to the body, the story of a life, and the narrative desire is in part for the body to own that story, to accept it as the story of its own life. The voice speaks to the body in the dark, the narrator says, 'as if willing him by this dint to make it his. To confess, Yes I remember' (p. 12), just as the narrative voice in Beckett's novel *How It Is*, which was once 'without on all sides' is finally found 'in me'.[9] The narrator of *Company* longs for this coming together of voice and body, but even as it does so, even as the narrative current flows towards such unification, so it encounters just as powerful a pull in the other direction, staging again that rhythm of gathering and dispersal that we find in Faulkner, and in Woolf. The voice in *Company*, like the voice in *The Unnamable*, wants to witness itself in its truest, most naked, most unadulterated state. This is partly why the scenarios that both voices depict are so stony, so elemental. The voice can only stop, the unnamable narrator says, when it has encountered itself in this way; it can only 'go silent' when it has depicted 'myself, in my own land for a brief space'.[10] And yet, as soon as the voice grants itself even the most fleeting appurtenances of being, the barest apparatus through which it might transmit itself, it experiences such apparatus as a prosthetic extension, an addition to mind that does not properly belong to the narrative identity that the voice is seeking to create. The body on its back in the dark is the home that the voice seeks to prepare for itself; but as soon as it tries to live there, it finds that it is not the home that it hoped it would be, that, in giving a ground to the self it becomes something extraneous to the self, becomes, as the title of one of Beckett's later works for the theatre has it, 'not I'.[11] Prosthetic extension of being is necessary for the voice, but only to grant it an occasion and an apparatus with which to express its own rejection of prosthetic extension, just as the fictional scenario is depicted only to give the voice a being with which to dismiss these unnecessary fictions, these prosthetic figments, from the field of its true becoming. As the narrator of Beckett's later novella *Worstward Ho* puts it, in a passage I quoted earlier, the voice is thus condemned to say and to unsay its being at the same time and in the same movement, to 'Say a body. Where none', 'A place. Where none. For the body. To be in'.[12]

To conduct this forensic examination of the prosthetics of narrative over such an extended period of time, and in such a narrow fictional ambit, can seem almost perverse; and it can give Beckett's fiction, too, a somewhat untimely feel, as if in his writing the logic of modernist narrative, the modernist rhythm that I have suggested one can find in Woolf and that

Beckett himself anatomised so clearly in his early essays on Proust and Joyce, has stalled, frozen over, become reduced to stuttering, fizzling repetitions. But if this is so, I think that one can nevertheless see, in this extended aftermath to a prosthetic modernism, a kind of working through of what David James has called the legacies of modernism, a working through that brings the Woolfian, Proustian, Joycean examinations of the prosthetic condition, of the means by which mind is twined together with matter, to a kind of conclusion.[13] Beckett might appear, from his essays on Joyce and Proust in 1929 and 1931 to his 1980s novellas, to be simply repeating a blankly stalled modernist predicament; but I think that attention to the ways in which Beckett's fiction works at the prosthetic junction between mind and world allows us to see a long dialogue that Beckett has sustained with Proust and with Joyce, a dialogue through which he develops the fullest critical account we have of the terms in which a prosthetic modernism allows us to articulate our relations with a later twentieth-century technological lifeworld.

Indeed, one can see this dialogue at work in the frozen movement of *Company*, in the broken relations that novella stages between voice and body. *Company* appears to be in keeping with Beckett's other late prose works – *The Lost Ones, Ping, Imagination Dead Imagine* – in its depiction of bare narrative scenarios. But if this is so, *Company* also marks a departure from the unremitting sparseness of the post *Unnamable* fiction – a departure in which we can see a reaching back to Proust and Joyce, a careful reworking of their apparatuses for self-fashioning. The bare passages, in *Company*, which stage an abstract narrative encounter between voice and body, are interspersed with scenes of vividly realised life, scenes which appear as moments of sudden powerful remembrance, of Proustian involuntary memory. The voice tells the body of its present situation – 'You are on your back in the dark' – but it also tells stories of past lives, also in the second person, and it is these stories that come to us as memories flooding in from another world. The voice tells of its subject's birth ('You first saw the light on such and such a day' (p. 5), 'You first saw the light in the room you most likely were conceived in' (pp. 9–10)) and of its relations with its parents. There is a memory of a mother and father, leaning lovingly over their baby, the disembodied narrative voice becoming the voice of the parent, 'a mother's stooping over the cradle from behind. She moves aside to let the father look. In his turn he murmurs to the newborn' (p. 38). There is a memory of a walk with a mother on a summer's day ('looking up at the blue sky and then at your mother's face you break the silence asking her if it is not in reality much more distant than it appears. The sky that is. The blue sky' (p. 8)), and a diving lesson with a father ('You stand at the tip of the high board. High above the sea. In it your father's upturned face. Upturned to you. You look down to the loved trusted face. He calls to you to jump. He calls, Be a brave boy' (p. 14)). And there is a story, too, of a young love affair, which again stages that same insistent relation between faces, in which the one on his back looks up at a face which looks down upon him. 'You are on your back at the foot of an aspen', the voice says:

> In its trembling shade. She at right angles propped on her elbows head between her hands. Your eyes opened and closed have looked in hers looking in yours. In your dark you look in them again. Still. You feel on your face the fringe of her long black hair stirring in the still air. Within the tent of hair your faces are hidden from view. She murmurs, Listen to the leaves. Eyes in each other's eyes you listen to the leaves. In their trembling shade. (p. 39)

Company sketches these scenes and others (a hedgehog disastrously saved in a box, a walk in the snow with the father's ghost), offering them as stages in a remembered life that cannot coincide with the decommissioned body that lies, in the story's present, on its back in the dark, in the non-space of the abstracted imagination. And in so doing, in staging a kind of disjunct relation between a set of (partly autobiographical) memories, and the characteristically late Beckettian scene of emptied-out narration, the novella reanimates a series of thoughtforms that have preoccupied Beckett throughout his writing life, and that reach back to his early engagements with Proust and with Joyce (and, in this passage, to Henry James, to the echo of that phrase 'eyes in each other's eyes' in *The Jolly Corner* (p. 367) and in *What Maisie Knew* (p. 188)). If all of these scenes in *Company* are concerned primarily with the possibility of twining – of twining oneself to oneself, of twining oneself to another, as Woolf's Louis binds his knees in his arms – then it is Joyce's imagery, Joyce's literary thinking that offers one of the forms in which Beckett undertakes such twining. The process by which a voice seeks to remember itself and give birth to itself at the same time – the predicament, as the narrator of *Company* puts it, in which a 'devised deviser' is compelled to 'devise himself for company' (p. 20), 'devising figments to temper his nothingness' (p. 37) – this is surely a late reflection of Joyce's experiment in literary self-fashioning, Joyce's attempt to devise his own deviser in the figure of Stephen Dedalus (distant relative of Homer's 'old artificer', who soars sunward on prosthetic wings).[14] Beckett's narrator's struggle to create himself in the full knowledge of the artificiality of his creation reaches right back to Dedalus' creation of something from nothing, of life from dead material, his commitment to 'forging anew in his workshop out of the sluggish matter of the earth a new soaring impalpable imperishable being'.[15] As Beckett's narrator struggles to weave his own being out of disappearing stuff, to fashion the body of the creature in the dark from the impalpability of second person narrative voice, so Dedalus gives birth to himself, acts as his own foetus, attached to himself by a narrative umbilical cord. 'Yes!' Dedalus thinks (in an early echo of Molly Bloom's orgasmic climax to *Ulysses*), 'Yes! Yes! Yes! He would create proudly out of the freedom and power of his soul, as the great artificer whose name he bore, a living thing, new and soaring and beautiful, impalpable, imperishable.'[16]

   Beckett sets out to create a living thing in *Company* – to create himself as a living thing – as Dedalus sets out to create himself in *Portrait*, in *Ulysses*; as he does so, his literary landscape is woven into Joyce's, twined together, as Beckett has it in a late homage to Joyce, like the 'two arms' of the river Seine, which, meeting 'in joyous eddies', 'conflowed and flowed united on'.[17] One of the remembered passages in *Company* sees the character standing on a strip of beach – 'A strand. Evening. Light dying' – a scene which calls, insistently, to the young Dedalus 'walking into eternity along Sandymount Strand' in an early episode of *Ulysses*.[18] Beckett's character finds himself standing at the shoreline:

> You stand with your back to the wash. No sound but its. Ever fainter as it slowly ebbs. Till it flows again. You lean on a long staff. Your hands rest on the knob and on them your head. Were your eyes to open they would first see far below in the last rays the skirt of your greatcoat and the uppers of your boots emerging from the sand. (p. 44)

He stands, leaning on his staff, his boots sinking into the wet sand of the strand, just as Dedalus stands on Sandymount Strand, resting on his famous ashplant, coming 'nearer to the edge of the sea', where the 'wet sand slapped his boots', his 'feet beginning to sink slowly in the quaking soil';[19] as both characters stand, sinking into the ground like Beckett's Winnie in *Happy Days*, they reflect on the matter they are made of, the tension between the weighty stuff of the world and the weightless stuff of the narrative voice. What weaves us into ourselves, Dedalus asks; the '*lex eterna*' of narrative voice? Or the 'strandentwining cable of all flesh' (p. 32)?[20] This is cable as telegraph wire – the cable that summons Dedalus home before the opening of *Ulysses* with the mistranscribed telegram 'Nother dying come home father' (p. 35). It is also the strandentwining cable that attaches us to a material being outside of ourselves, to the sandy strand into which both Beckett's and Joyce's characters sink, as well as to those 'accursed progenitors' who beget us (Beckett),[21] those who 'lug us squealing into life' (Joyce),[22] as the 'gravedigger puts on the forceps' (Beckett)[23] – umbilical cord as telephone wire to presymbolic being, 'Hello! Kinch here. Put me on to Edenville. Aleph, alpha: nought, nought, one' (p. 32). Beckett summons Joyce in his balancing of the creative power of voice against the creative power of progeneration – conception as idea versus conception as procreation – in his enactment of the drama of self-fashioning; he calls to Joyce, too, to shape his imagining of the weaving together of one person with another. The delicate set of face-to-face encounters that *Company* stages – parent to child, lover to lover, voice to character – these encounters are alive with Joycean glimmers and shadows. In contraposing the face of the father to the face of the son – the father looks down on the son as he lies in his cot, the son looks down on the upturned face of the father as he floats in the sea – *Company* grafts these faces together, the face of the father becoming the face of the son becoming the face of the father again, just as Joyce imagines a 'consubstantiality' between father and son, a weaving together of different generations and histories, in *Ulysses,* in *Finnegans Wake.* Dedalus famously expounds his theory of the consubstantiality of father and son in *Ulysses*, where he argues that Shakespeare's *Hamlet* allows for a form of self-creation in which the son gives birth to the father (that 'old mole'), in which father and son are woven together in the space of the artwork.[24] 'As we', Stephen says,

> weave and unweave our bodies from day to day, their molecules shuttled to and fro, so does the artist weave and unweave his image. And as the mole on my right breast is where it was when I was born, though all my body has been woven of new stuff time after time, so through the ghost of the unquiet father the image of the unliving son looks forth. (pp. 159–60)

As *Company* merges the face of the father with that of the son, so too does *Ulysses* – an entwining of generations that, Beckett argues in his early essay on Joyce, is also the central achievement of *Finnegans Wake.* The *Wake*, Beckett writes, is an 'interior intertwining' of the life stages that it witnesses – a development of the 'consciousness that there is a great deal of the unborn infant in the lifeless octogenarian, and a great deal of both in the man at the apogee of his life's curve'.[25]

Beckett's recreation of life in *Company* – his discovery of a twined relation between voice and body that might bring a new kind of being to life – is infested, in this way, with the spectres of Joyce. But if this is so, it is the case, too, that the novella is involved in an equally intense dialogue with Proust.[26] The folding together of discrete moments in a life in *Company* might call to Beckett's reading of *Finnegans Wake*, but it resonates too, and perhaps even more richly, with the Proustian schema of remembrance. 'None of us', Marcel writes in the 'Overture' to *A la recherche*, 'can be said to constitute a material whole, which is identical for everyone, and need only be turned up like a page in an account-book or the record of a will'.[27] We are not identical with ourselves (we are not, as Woolf's Louis intuits, 'entire') but are instead composed of a number of different versions of ourselves, 'as though', Marcel writes, 'one's life were a picture gallery in which all the portraits of any one period had a family likeness' (p. 21). To live a life is to inhabit each of these successive versions or portraits of ourself, which remain quite distinct from one another, and which no act of voluntary memory can weave together or shape into a unity. As Beckett writes, in his early essay on Proust, 'we are not merely more weary because of yesterday, we are other, no longer what we were before the calamity of yesterday.'[28] 'The aspirations of yesterday's ego', Beckett goes on, 'were valid for yesterday's ego, not for today's', so the idea that the self of yesterday might coincide with the self of today, or of tomorrow, is 'as illogical as to expect one's hunger to be dissipated by the spectacle of Uncle eating his dinner' (p. 14).

The depiction of various versions of self in *Company* is, in part, a reflection of this Proustian condition. The forms of disjuncture that it conjures – the means by which the face-to-face encounters that recur throughout the novella call to but fail to establish a unity, a twined togetherness – come back, insistently, to Proust's great novel. *Company* merges the narrative voice, as it comes to the one on his back on the dark, with the voice of the parent as it bends over the cot, with the voice of the mother looking down on the son from the arced pale of the distant sky, and in doing so it recalls with some intensity the primal scene of Proust's novel, the broken relation that sets the whole machinery of narration in train – that is, Marcel's prohibited desire for his mother. The drama of Marcel's childhood is his desire to be with his mother at night, his longing for her to kiss him goodnight, against the wishes of his father. Every evening the desire grows in him, until it is too strong to be resisted: 'For what I wanted now', Marcel writes, 'was Mamma, to say good night to her. I had gone too far along the road which led to fulfillment of this desire to be able to retrace my steps'.[29] This passage might recall the opening of Beckett's *Molloy*, where Molloy is overcome by a similar urge ('I resolved to go and see my mother', Molloy declares, with a resolution which began to 'fill my mind until it was rid of all other preoccupations and I seized with a trembling at the mere idea of being hindered from going

there, I mean to my mother, there and then'.[30]) But it calls, too, to the
longing for the mother in *Company*, the promise of a filial relation to that
face as it hovers over the one on his back in the dark, a face that, like the sky,
is in reality more distant than it appears. It is this face that Marcel longs for –
lying in bed at night he can think only of the moment 'when she had bent
her loving face down over my bed, and held it out to me like a host for an act
of peacegiving communion in which my lips might imbibe her real presence,
and with it the power to sleep'.[31] But, for Marcel, as for the figure in Beckett's
Company, this face remains elusive, remains at a distance from the self, in the
same way that the self remains at a distance from its own being, failing
repeatedly to comprise Proust's 'material whole', to constitute 'real presence'.
In both Beckett and Proust, the longing for a meeting with another, with
a parent or a lover, is entwined with the desire for communion with self,
a desire that is continually thwarted, as the self becomes prosthetised, fixed in
stiffened attitudes of alienation. *Company* is built around this Proustian fault
line, this rift in being. As the character is summoned to consciousness, as he
first finds himself lying in the dark, it is this distance from self that asserts
itself. He is 'on his back in the dark', the character learns, but this perception
is not drawn from any continuous sense of self in the world, but from an odd
groping towards a body that is thrown clear from voice and from mind. He is
'on his back in the dark': 'This he can tell by the pressure on his hind parts
and by how the dark changes when he shuts his eyes and again when he
opens them again' (p. 5). The character's body here is no nearer to him than
the face of the mother or the face of the father. His 'hind parts' (as
dehumanised and discomposed as the body of Kafka's Gregor Samsa when
he wakes to find himself transformed into an insect 'lying on his hard, as it
were armor-plated, back')[32] communicate to him across a great lapse in
being – one which is built on that same gulf that greets Marcel, as he wakes in
his bedroom at the opening of *A la recherche*. Beckett's character has no
identity with the body parts that he occupies when he wakes in the dark, no
conception of what Rancière calls a 'common sensorium';[33] Marcel similarly
seeks to recompose himself after sleep by reaching into the darkness that
surrounds him, reaching towards a body that is not his. In the opening
paragraph of Proust's novel, Marcel finds that he, too, is lying on his back in
the dark. Waking, Marcel writes, 'I would be astonished to find myself in
a state of darkness, pleasant and restful enough for my eyes, but even more,
perhaps, for my mind, to which it appeared incomprehensible, without
a cause, something dark indeed.'[34] The dark that Marcel wakes into opens
a gap between mind and eye, a gap which he seeks to close, like Beckett's
character, by a feeling of mind towards distant body. 'It always happened',

Marcel writes, 'when I woke like this' that 'my mind struggled in an unsuccessful attempt to discover where I was' (p. 6). 'My body would attempt to construe' the 'position of its various limbs, in order to deduce therefrom the direction of the wall, the location of the furniture':

> Its memory, the composite memory of its ribs, its knees, its shoulder-blades, offered it a whole series of rooms in which it had at one time or another slept, while the unseen walls, shifting and adapting themselves to the shape of each successive room that I remembered, whirled around it in the dark. (p. 6)

The entirety of the Proustian experience emerges from this experience of distance between mind and the bodies in which mind finds itself briefly and successively embedded – a gulf between the sense of emplacement generated by a body and the possibility of an extended, continuous self generated by mind. In narrating the distance between the successive moments of embodied being in time on the one hand and the possibility of a consciousness that might gather those discrete moments into a unity on the other, Proust brings both the material experience of prosthetic extension and the abstract experience of intellection to expression, in a manner which demonstrates, again and again, their mutual incompatibility, their contradictory refusal of each other. The 'dark region' that lies at the heart of Proust's novel – the vaporous ground that, in an expression I have used at analogous moments throughout this book, comes out of hiding here – is the region between mind and extended self, a region which, in Proust's rendering, enters into a continual collapse. Drinking his famous tea, Marcel writes, has called a past into being, a past body, a past self, and Proust's novel enters into and springs from this gap between self and self that the drink has at once opened and closed. 'What an abyss of uncertainty' is summoned, Marcel thinks,

> whenever the mind feels overtaken by itself; when it, the seeker, is at the same time the dark region through which it must go seeking and where all its equipment will avail it nothing. Seek? More than that: create. It is face to face with something which does not yet exist, to which it along can give reality and substance, which it alone can bring into the light of day.[35]

As the voice in *Company* creates the subject in which it might find itself realised, so Proust's narrator enters into a drama of self-creation, reaching towards a future moment when he might be able to accommodate these past bodies which appear various and separate into some organically unified being, when he might be able to say, in Beckett's words, 'In the end', 'Yes I remember. That was I. That was I then.'[36] And the central contradiction, in Proust as in Beckett, is that the process which allows for such self-creation is bound with the utmost intimacy into the experience of self-loss, with the loss of being that attends every moment of self-communion, the death that lies on the underside of every act of life, what Marcel calls the 'abyss of not-being'.[37] As Marcel puts it much later, in 'The Intermittencies of the Heart', the recovery of self, like the memory of a loved one who has died, is also the recognition that the recovered self is irretrievably lost, that between the self who recovers and the self recovered there is a bottomless ocean of death. To mourn his grandmother, Marcel realises, is to live in this contradiction, this region of gathered dispersal, to 'endure the anguish of this contradiction'; 'on the one hand', to feel 'an existence, a tenderness surviving in me as I had known them', and 'on the other', to feel the 'certainty, throbbing like a recurrent pain, of an annihilation that had effaced my image of that tenderness, had destroyed that existence' (p. 785). The encounter with the reality of the dead grandmother, Beckett writes, amounts for Marcel to an encounter with 'the reality of his lost self'; to a discovery, as Marcel beautifully puts it, that the 'contradiction of survival and annihilation' is 'so strangely intertwined within me' (p. 786).

7.2 An Unintelligible Landscape of Atoms: Untwining Proust and Joyce

> From impenetrable self to impenetrable unself by way of neither.
> Samuel Beckett, 'Neither'[38]

When these Proustian and Joycean echoes resurface in Beckett's *Company*, then, one can sense the persistence of a modernist rhythm, the living on of a twined relation between survival and annihilation, long after the moment for that relation has passed. But if Beckett's work sustains the afterlife of a prosthetic modernism, if the spirits of Proust and Joyce live on in him in this way, belated, anachronistic, out of time, it is also the case that Beckett's prose is a historical development, a 'work in progress' which extends Proustian and Joycean rhythms, rather than merely repeating them. If the spectres of both writers move in the static images of *Company*, and if the rhythm of gathering and dispersal that drives Beckett's novella originates in part with them, this is not simple homage, not the merging of the unquiet father with the unliving son, but the incremental unfolding of a Beckettian adaptation of Proustian and Joycean dynamics, one which is driven by Beckett's determination to rid the experience of joining and separating, twining and untwining, of anything extraneous to it, anything which might allow twining to overcome untwining, gathering to overcome dispersal – a determination which stands as a radicalisation of a prosthetic modernism, and a driving of its logic to the limits of possibility.

For both Joyce and Proust, as Beckett reads them in the late 1920s and early 1930s, the encounter with a self at a remove from itself is counteracted by the possibility of a kind of unity that is offered by the artwork, by the aesthetic image. This is what is at stake in Dedalus' discussion of aesthetics in *Portrait*, his assertion that the 'esthetic image' is achieved 'when the vitality which has flowed and eddied around each person fills every person with such vital force that he or she assumes a proper and intangible esthetic life'; the 'esthetic image' is 'life purified in and re-projected from the human imagination'.[39] The accomplishment of Joyce's work, from *Portrait* to *Finnegans Wake*, Beckett writes, is the discovery of a form which can apprehend this wholeness, a form that can bring the play between being and not-being into a complete expression. 'The beauty' of *Finnegans Wake*, Beckett writes, is its capacity to 'apprehend' what he calls 'a temporal as well as a spatial unity'.[40] And similarly, Proust's immersion in the 'abyss of not-being' is a calculated risk, a casting of oneself away to find oneself recovered by an artwork which can draw being and not-being into a spatial and temporal unity. This is the burden of Marcel's closing reflections on the task of his own art. 'The idea of death took up permanent residence within me', Marcel writes towards the close of the novel, 'the way love sometimes does'.[41] Death is bound to his love for himself and for others, as survival and annihilation are so strangely twined together within him. But the close of the novel sees an extraordinary moment of literary becoming, when that death is transformed, as at the close of Cervantes' *Don Quixote*, from the opposite of love to its apotheosis, when the buried 'region' that I have traced through the history of the novel as it lies between self and self is brought into the ambit of a lit art surface. The pealing of a bell sounding in the final pages across the gulf that the novel maps, the 'dark region' through which it goes seeking, joins the Marcel of the novel's present to the Marcel of childhood, the lovesick child who finds himself 'no longer able to bear the prospect of waiting till morning to place my lips upon my mother's face' (p. 1103). He hears again the ringing of the bell on a gate at his childhood home, 'hears those very sounds, situated though they were in the remote past' and he realises that

> this could only be because its peal has always been there, inside me, and not this sound only but also, between that distant moment and the present one,

unrolled in all its vast length, the whole of that past which I was not aware
that I carried about within me. (p. 1105)

The pealing of the bell allows Marcel to say, 'Yes, I remember. That was
I. That was I then'; it leads him not only to the end of the novel but, as in
Joyce's *Wake*, to its beginning, to the recognition that his artistic vocation
is the creation of a chamber, a vessel, what Henry James calls the 'great
glazed tank of art', in which those gathered years might be contained.[42]
'This moment of Time embodied, of years past but not separated from us',
Marcel writes in the closing pages of *A la recherche*, 'it was now my
intention to emphasise as strongly as possible in my work' (p. 1105) – the
work that we must now, the implication is, reread. The pealing of the bell
triggers a revelation that takes Proust, Beckett writes, past the limits of
a realism which is 'content to transcribe the surface, the façade, beneath
which the Idea is prisoner'.[43] It opens, Beckett goes on, to an art which
might fuse surface and depth, might achieve what he calls, after Baudelaire,
'the adequate union of subject and object' (p. 76), the union of mind and
matter. It is in the 'brightness of art' (p. 76), Beckett writes, that it is
possible to achieve the 'identification of immediate with past experience,
the recurrence of past action or reaction in the present', the 'participation
between the real and the ideal, imagination and direct apprehension,
symbol and substance' (p. 74).

Proust achieves this union, Beckett thinks, this fusing together of mind
and matter into a unity; but his own prose, from his first novel *Dream of
Fair to Middling Women*, to *Company* and *Stirrings Still*, involves
a persistent critique of the terms in which such a fusion might be effected,
an exhaustive rehearsing of the ways in which dispersal continues to resist
the work of gathering, as untwining is twined into the work of twining, as
face remains at a distance from the call of mind. One can see this effect in
process from the beginning, in Beckett's near obsession, in his early prose,
with disassembly. As I argued earlier, when the narrator of *Dream* dwells on
the 'reluctance of our refractory constituents to bind together', it is perhaps
Beckett's dialogue with Goethe, and with the chemical binding of *Elective
Affinities*, that is closest to the surface.[44] When Beckett's narrator says that
the 'bodies' in his narrative are 'based on a principle of repulsion', that they
tend 'not only to shrink from all that is not they, from all that is without
and in its turn shrinks from them but also to strain away from themselves
(p. 119), one can hear a refutation of Goethe's Captain, who asserts rather
grandly that 'the first thing we notice about all the substances we encounter
in Nature is that each is always drawn to itself' (p. 30). The bodies in *Dream*

are closer to those imagined by Edith Wharton than to Goethe's organi-cally bound entities. There is a perhaps surprising resonance between Beckett's Belacqua and Wharton's Lily Bart, who finds herself dismem-bered by a modernity which allows for no form of unity, which condemns her, in a passage I quoted earlier, to be the 'mere spin-drift of the whirling surface of existence, without anything to which the poor little tentacles of self could cling'.[45] If Beckett's bodies 'strain away' from others, and from themselves, then Lily too finds that 'all the men and women she knew were like atoms whirling away from each other in some wild centrifugal dance' (p. 311). But while Beckett opposes the experience of modern self-alienation to a Goethean conception of organic unity, one can hear also the begin-nings of his long dialogue with Proust and Joyce, in which Beckett picks away at the terms in which his modernist forebears conceived of the role of the artwork in reconstituting the unity of a self which the technological and political forces of modernity have scattered, prosthetised.

This dialogue, as I have suggested, stretches across Beckett's fiction, but it is perhaps in the three novels of his postwar trilogy, *Molloy*, *Malone Dies* and *The Unnamable*, that one can trace its progress most clearly. These novels, to a degree, follow the trajectory towards unity and self-recovery that Beckett finds in Joyce and in Proust. Some such passage is captured in an odd echo that sounds, across the 'dark region' of the prose, between the opening of the trilogy of novels and its close. A few thousand words into *Molloy*, Molloy bemoans the artificiality of his being – the gap between his embodied self and the narrative spirit that inhabits him – in terms that draw metafictional attention to the status of his narrative as the first in a series of three. 'The fact is', Molloy says, 'that the most you can hope is to be a little less, in the end, the creature you were in the beginning, and the middle' (p. 32). The narrative journey towards becoming, Molloy thinks, is a matter of subtraction, of lessening. We chip away at the artificial husk of being, those clumsy prosthetic selves in which we are temporarily housed, so that we might come steadily closer to the core of our being, where we might find ourselves unadulterated by anything extraneous to mind. This is the process that Beckett finds in Proust, where becoming involves what Beckett calls 'a contraction of the spirit' (a somewhat eccentric, tenden-tious reading of Proust which, Shane Weller has wittily suggested, threa-tens to 'turn something into nothing').[46] 'The artist is active', Beckett goes on, in terms that echo Belacqua's 'shrinking' from objects in *Dream*, 'but negatively, shrinking from the nullity of extracircumferential phenomena, drawn in to the core of the eddy' (pp. 65–66). To become is to shrug off the selves that weigh us down, those thingly bodies that stiffen, atrophy, reify –

as Molloy's legs gradually stiffen over the course of his wanderings towards his mother, as Malone's legs stiffen as he lies on his deathbed. And, as if magically, a few thousand words from the end of *The Unnamable*, one can hear the faint strains of a naked narrative voice that has arrived at this moment of becoming, has finally divested himself of all that is not him. Molloy wants to depart from himself towards a voice that inhabits him, a narrative agency that, Malone says later in *Malone Dies*, feels like 'a blind and tired hand delving feebly in my particles and letting them trickle between its fingers', a puppeting, ravishing hand that 'I feel', Malone says, 'plunged in me up to the elbow', that 'fondles, clutches, ransacks, ravages, avenging its failure to scatter me with one sweep' (p. 225). But the voice that starts to announce itself towards the close of the *Unnamable* shapes to have crossed a threshold between world and mind, between puppet and ghostly puppeteer, between extracircumferential phenomena and the core of the eddy, so the task of this voice is no longer to leave itself but to cleave to itself. 'I should have liked', it says, 'in the end to be a little as I always was and never could be' (p. 400).

This journey towards self, achieved through a process of denudation, through an abrasive sandpapering away of the apparatuses of self-extension, this is the formal principle of the trilogy, and its plot. It re-enacts the self-recovery undertaken by Proust, replacing the elegiac Proustian tone with one of comic vituperativeness, and insisting on an equation between self-destruction and self-recovery that Beckett knows is not simple in Proust, even if he wants to find it so. But if this is true – if the trilogy's journey towards a naked narrative voice is mapped onto the journey in *A la recherche* towards the moment in the library when Marcel hears the distant music of that pealing bell – it is also the case that Beckett's trilogy is engaged, at every moment, in a dismantling of the forms of unity, of recovery, that he finds in Proust and in Joyce, a dismantling which radically transforms the means by which voice negotiates between mind and body. In *Molloy*, this drama of dismantlement is laid out in the encounter that this two-part novel stages between Molloy (the protagonist of part one) and his doppelgänger and superego Moran (the protagonist of part two). The first part of the novel follows Molloy as he struggles through a vast and alien 'region' towards his mother and towards the mother's room in which he writes his story ('I am in my mother's room', he writes in the opening sentence, 'It's I who live there now' (p. 7)). The second part concerns Moran's attempt to track down Molloy, in obedience to the command of an agency which has employed him, as some kind of private detective, for the purpose. Both parts of the novel turn around the failure of the quests that they depict – Molloy never makes it to his mother's room (and hence to the scene of narration), ending up lying in a ditch, thinking to himself that 'Molloy could stay, where he happened to be' (p. 91); Moran suffers a gradual disintegration during his long trek to the 'Molloy country', metamorphosing from an upright bourgeois to a disabled vagrant with stiffening legs who comes to resemble his quarry rather than capture him. But if both narratives are organised around these failures, the central territory that the novel stakes out, its real locus of failure and dismantlement, lies between the two narrators and narratives, in the cloven region that joins and separates Moran and Malone – the region that acts as a kind of counterweight to the Proustian movement towards the negative unity of the self. When Moran is given his instructions to pursue Molloy, Moran's first detective act is to stage an enquiry into the ontological and epistemological nature and texture of this region. He retires to his bed, like Marcel, to reflect on the instructions that he has received from his employer – 'I took off my coat and shoes', he says, 'opened my trousers, and got in between the sheets' – because, he thinks, it is in this kind of slumberous peace (lying on his back in the dark) that 'I best pierce the outer turmoil's veil, discern my quarry, sense what course to follow' (p. 111). It was only by retiring into this meditative state, 'by transferring', he says, 'to this atmosphere, how shall I say, of finality without end, why not', that 'I could venture to consider the work I had on hand' (p. 112). It is only in this withdrawn, immaterial space, only 'where Molloy could not be, nor Moran for that matter', that 'Moran could bend over Molloy' (p. 112). To hunt down Molloy is an arduous matter, as Moran soon discovers, of crossing inhospitable terrain, of dragging himself on crutches through forests in the snow, as his sense of able self is worn down to nothing; but it also requires him to look inside himself, to discover Molloy as a principle of his own becoming, to 'find' Molloy, as Moran puts it, 'ready-made in my head' (p. 112). It requires him, he says, to 'establish a kind of connection' (p. 112) with Molloy, both by trekking through the Molloy country, the rough terrain that separates them, and by penetrating into some other kind of twining principle, entering into the withdrawn space that connects mind to matter, and that connects him to himself.

The Proustian journey that *Molloy* stages, and that is undertaken by the trilogy more broadly, is determined by the texture of this region, its material and abstract qualities, its susceptibility to the lessening work of Proustian-Beckettian narrative. The ground that lies between Molloy and Moran is the ground that the contractive journey towards the naked narrative voice seeks to overcome, to dissolve, as voice frees itself from body, from ground; but even as this is so, the novel discovers that this ground, and the 'kind of connection' that it allows between one person and another, between mind and matter, insistently returns as a function of the very attempt to erase it. At the opening of his narrative, for example, Molloy recounts a story concerning two characters, named A and C, whom he sees walking along a country road at evening to illustrate his gnomic assertion that 'people pass' who are 'hard to distinguish from yourself' (p. 9). The focus of this vignette is on the landscape that distinguishes and separates – not only that separates A and C from Molloy but also that separates A and C from each other. Molloy is perched on some high eminence and so can see them approach each other from a distance. 'At first', Molloy says, 'a wide space lay between them. They couldn't have seen each other, even had they raised their heads and looked about, because of this wide space, and then because of the undulating land, which caused the road to be in waves, not high, but high enough, high enough' (p. 9). Molloy watches A and C pass by and is overcome by a desire to go to A or to C (interchangeable as they are (and by the way, where's B?)), 'perhaps even to catch up with him one day, so as to know him better, to be myself less lonely'; but the space that separates them defeats him. 'In spite of my soul's leap out to him' Molloy writes, 'at the end of its elastic, I saw him only darkly, because of the dark and then because of the terrain, in the folds of which he disappeared' (p. 11). The folded terrain separates Molloy from A or C, even as he stretches himself out towards him; and Molloy enters into that same estranged relation with his own body, which feels distant from him, with the same distance that separates him from Moran as he lies with his trousers open in his bourgeois bedroom. He longs for contact with A or C, Molloy says, but he is drawn too (in an echo of Belacqua's tendency to 'strain away' from himself) to the 'other things calling me and towards which too one after another my soul was straining, wildly':

> I mean of course the fields, whitening under the dew, and the animals, ceasing from wandering and settling for the night, and the sea, of which nothing, and the sharpening line of crests, and the sky where without seeing them I felt the first stars tremble, and my hand on my knee and above all the other wayfarer, A or C, I don't remember, going resignedly home. (p. 11)

This is an extraordinary moment in the novel – the moment that Molloy conceives of his own hand as one of those objects, like the whitening fields, the animals, the stars and the sea, towards which his lonely soul is straining. Indeed, it is so striking that it leads him to pause, to clarify. 'Yes', he says, 'towards my hand also, which my knee felt tremble and of which my eyes saw the wrist only, the heavily veined back, the pallid row of knuckles' (p. 11). Molloy's hand is no more part of his being than the 'hind parts' that appear at the opening of *Company* belong to the narrative voice, and his relation to his peculiarly cropped hand is conducted across that distance that separates Moran from Molloy, A from C. His hand is trembling not as the sign of a fearfulness that resides in him, or an exhaustion or a longing (indeed he can 'feel' the trembling of the sublimely distant stars more intimately than he can the trembling of his own hand); rather, he registers that trembling when he sees his hand with his eyes, when he detects its distant trembling with his distant knees. His being is an assemblage of discrete prostheses (hand, eye, knee) which are held together by a kind of elastic – the elastic at the end of which Molloy's soul strains but also the elastic ties and twines that come back repeatedly in the novel, forming a kind of Joycean weave, a 'strandentwining cable'. The elastic that binds Molloy's soul to his body is layered over the elastic that binds his hat to his coat. In homage to the hat belonging to Swift's radically alienated Gulliver (which is fastened by a 'cord' which passes through 'two holes bored in the brim'),[47] Molloy, Moran and Malone all attach themselves to their hats, 'by means of a string or an elastic' (p. 14). Molloy remarks that his hat 'is fastened, it has always been fastened, to my buttonhole, always the same buttonhole, at all seasons, by a long lace. I am still alive, then' (p. 14); Moran says of his hat, channelling Gulliver, that 'two holes were bored in the brim, one on either side of course, I had bored them myself with my little gimlet. And in these holes I had secured the ends of an elastic long enough to pass under my chin' (p. 127). The elastic that attaches Molloy to himself is also the elastic that attaches coat to hat, hat to head – that attaches him to what Gulliver calls the 'artificial covering' to his body, beneath which, he fears, he is an 'exact Yahoo in every part' (p. 264). And then, in a further extension, this elastic becomes the rope, or the chain, that attaches Moran to his son. 'I toyed briefly', Moran says, 'with the idea of attaching him to me by means of a long rope, its two ends tied about our waists', before realising that his son 'might have undone the knots in silence and escaped', whereupon, he says, 'I amused myself' by 'wondering how . . . I could chain my son to me in such a way as to prevent him from ever shaking me off again' (pp. 129–30).

Molloy is held together in this way by twine, as Mr Kelly is attached to his kite by a 'sagging soar of line' in *Murphy*;[48] the negative, contractive movement that Beckett finds in Proust, and that he himself seeks to enact in the trilogy, is set, to a degree, against this binding property, committed as it is to a process of unknotting, untwining. 'I am in my mother's room', Molloy writes, 'it is I who live there now'. We can measure here something like that distance from self that Molloy finds as he gazes on his 'heavily veined' hand. Surely, if Molloy is really in his mother's room, really present at the scene of his dwelling, the word should be 'here', not 'there' – it is I who live *here* now. In that opening sentence to the novel, in the distance it installs in the space of narration, one can see already gestating the failure of the narrative to meet up with itself, the process by which the narrative voice frees itself from the bodies with which it is only partly entwined. Molloy never makes it to the room in which he writes his narrative, and Moran's narrative ends famously with a moment of devastating negation, a dismantling of the 'report' that instantiates him. In a distorted mirror image of the circularity of Joyce's *Wake*, Moran's report begins with the line 'It is midnight. The rain is beating on the windows' and ends with Moran heading to his study to write his narrative, the narrative we have just read: 'Then I went back into the house and wrote, It is midnight. The rain is beating on the windows. It was not midnight. It was not raining' (p. 176). In living out a Beckettian version of the Proustian moment of recovery, the novel seeks to undo the bonds that hold us to our dead and dying selves, our prosthetic selves, to free us into what Marcel calls the 'abyss of not-being' (p. 6), and what Beckett's Malone calls the 'blessedness of absence' (p. 223), an absence in which the self achieves a kind of pyrrhic mastery over its own evacuated being. But if *Molloy* rehearses this strategy of Joycean circularity, of Proustian self-recovery, and if it does so by enacting a kind of untwining, a releasing of the self from its prosthetic apparatuses, what I want most centrally to argue here is that the *very process* by which Beckett seeks to free mind from world ends up restating the 'kind of connection' that Moran forges with Molloy, as he discovers that the dissolution of that prosthetic junction between extended and unextended being is bound to, almost equated with, its persistence. What one can see emerging from Beckett's dialogue with Proust and with Joyce, here in the first novel of the trilogy, is a scrupulous adjustment of the terms of recovery of self, as it is formulated as release from self – a recognition of a new kind of material limit to narrative reclamation, a new poetics of twining, which is already implicit in both Proust and Joyce, which is intrinsic to their rhythm of gathering and dispersal but which is nevertheless hidden, in *Ulysses* and *A la recherche*, beneath an investment in the mythic capacity of the artwork to overcome its own prosthetic distance from itself.

One can glimpse this limit, this shifted relation between twining and untwining, in the echo in Beckett's *Molloy* of that moment in Proust where the sound of a pealing bell recovers the lost unity of the self. The sound of the bell, Marcel writes, annihilates the gap between 'that distant moment and the present one', allowing him to discover that the 'moment from long ago still adhered to me and I could still find it again, could retrace my steps to it merely by descending to a greater depth within myself'.[49] This bell reappears in *Molloy*, where it is transformed into the more resonant sound of a 'gong' – a gong that makes an appearance in Marguerite Duras' Beckett-inflected novel *The Rapture of Lol V. Stein* (1964).[50] As an exhausted Molloy, coming to the end of his failed journey to his mother, finds himself marooned in the forest, he sets himself to listening for the celebrated 'forest murmurs'. 'It was in vain I listened', he says,

> I could hear nothing of the kind. But rather, with much goodwill and a little imagination, at long intervals a distant gong. A horn goes well with the forest, you expect it. It is the huntsman. But a gong! It was mortifying, to have been looking forward to the celebrated murmurs, and to succeed only in hearing, at long intervals, in the far distance, a gong. (p. 89)

Molloy hears (or imagines) a distant gong as he nears the end of his narrative, and, as in Proust, the reverberations of this gong, like the 'leaden circles' of Big Ben's bell that 'dissolve' in Woolf's modernist air, traverse the distance that the novel maps, suggesting that the broken parts of which the novel is made might still somehow 'adhere' to one another.[51] As Moran is 'bending over Molloy', trying to find Molloy ready made in his head, it is this same gong that he hears. 'It seemed as if the enquiry were about to start at last', Moran thinks, as he completes his shadowy contemplation of Molloy. 'It was then that the sound of a gong, struck with violence, filled the house' (p. 116).

The poetics of twining that is imagined in *Molloy*, and that unfolds over the trilogy as a whole, is shaped by the ringing of this gong, as it sounds across the region that separates Moran and Molloy. The pealing bell in Proust announces that moment when narrator and narrated meet, the moment when distance is absorbed into the unity of the work, the moment when we establish the 'adequate union of subject and object'. This is Proust's modernist version of the earlier meeting we find at the height of nineteenth-century realism, that moment when David Copperfield catches up with himself at the close of *David Copperfield*, and the character becomes one with the narrator. ('My lamp burns low', David writes in the penultimate paragraph, revealing the space of narration for the first time, 'and I have written far into the night'.[52]) But Beckett's gong does not achieve any such joining. It marks on the one hand the radicalisation of the Proustian descent – Marcel's 'descending to a greater depth within myself' – by opening an impassable gulf between depth and surface, self and self, enacting the failure of narrative to catch up with itself or to circle around itself. But even as it radicalises Proust, it produces on the other hand a kind of reaction against the Proustian equation, a dismantlement of it. As Beckett's narrative fails to feed into itself, the terrain that separates Molloy from Moran, rather than being dissolved or sublimated, asserts its resistance to the transformative power of narrative, a resistance whereby all of those modes of prosthetic connection, those ropes, twines, chains and elastic that stretch between mind and world, demonstrate their tensile strength, the irrefragability of the material that joins and separates self from self. This terrain, in refusing to be lessened by the work of Beckettian narrative, partakes of the nonhuman materiality that Beckett finds in Cézanne. Cézanne's painting, Beckett writes in a letter to Tom McGreevy in 1934, exemplifies what he calls 'the one bright spot in a mechanistic age – the deanthropomorphizations of the artist'.[53] What the Mont Sainte-Victoire shows us – what it discovers as a paradoxical complement to the prosthetisation of a mechanistic, 'man-made' environment – is that landscape will not be absorbed into the human coils of mind, that object will not be transformed into a function of the human subject.[54] 'Cézanne', Beckett writes, 'seems to have been the first to see landscape & state it as material of a strictly peculiar order, incommensurable with all human expressions whatsoever' (p. 222). Cézanne's painting shows us an 'atomistic landscape with no velleities of vitalism' (p. 222), a landscape 'by definition unapproachably alien', an 'unintelligible landscape of atoms' (p. 223); it is this landscape – inhuman, unintelligible, unsubornable to the cause of self-recovery – that intervenes at the heart of *Molloy*, that separates Molloy from Moran, and Molloy from his own trembling hand.

It is this principle – whereby the narrative dehiscence of self produces at once the radical dissolving of the prosthetic junction between mind and world and its equally radical, nonhuman materialisation – that is the outcome of Beckett's engagement with Proust and with Joyce in the trilogy. As we proceed from the beginning of the trilogy to the end, from *Molloy* to *Malone Dies* to *The Unnamable*, so we follow a process of denudation, a stripping back towards the narrative voice that one can almost hear in *Unnamable*, the voice which asks for nothing other than to be 'a little as I always was'. Malone tells a series of stories to himself as he lies on his deathbed, and he does so to allow those stories to discompose, as he too is discomposed, so that he might allow both his stories and himself to run out, and he might feel himself 'streaming and emptying away', as he puts it, 'as through a sluice' (p. 224). The 'business of Malone', he writes, and of those other imaginary creatures about whom he writes in his exercise book, is 'like the crumbling away of two little heaps of finest sand, or dust, or ashes, of unequal size, but diminishing together as it were in ratio, if that means anything, and leaving behind them, each in its own stead, the blessedness of absence' (p. 223). Malone's dying, like Moran's 'crumbling', his 'frenzied collapsing', is a strategy to allow the Unnamable to become what he/it always was in his/its own 'land', free of prosthetic addition; his 'dying' is equated with the process of writing itself, the material business of notation. For Malone, to die is to use up the pencil with which he writes both about himself and about his characters. As Defoe's Crusoe writes in his journal with his salvaged ink, 'which I eek'd out with Water a little and a little, till it was so pale it scarce left any Appearance of black upon the paper', so Malone is forced to husband his lead.[55] 'I write as lightly as I can', he says, but 'little by little my pencil dwindles, inevitably, and the day is fast approaching when nothing will remain but a fragment too tiny to hold' (p. 223). *Malone Dies* is written to witness this wearing away, this steady diminishing of the heap of existence; but what Malone discovers, like Moran before him and the Unnamable after him, is that his existence does not dwindle to nothing, to the empty freedom of literary absence. Rather, diminishment takes us towards the space of a junction, a threshold composed at once of the dead and the living, the animate and the inanimate, the ideal and the real – a junction that does not suffer itself to disappear, that does not erase itself in a Proustian moment of overcoming, but which rather asserts itself as the very non-taxonomised stuff of being, the stuff that overflows as it diminishes, that continues as it ceases, that unburies the junction between the living and the non-living even as it exposes its impossibility, its absolute resistance to expression. Malone watches as his hand writes his narrative in the exercise book that is the sole manifestation of his being ('this exercise book', he says, 'is my life' (p. 276)). 'My little finger', he says 'glides before my pencil across the page and gives warning, falling over the edge, that the end of the line is near' (p. 207); as he looks at his writing hand with such detached regard, we feel that same distance between hand and mind that Molloy feels as his hand lies trembling on his knee beneath the distant sky. This is the same distance, too, that Moran feels as he watches his hand write his abortive report. 'I wrote' the report, he says, 'with a firm hand weaving inexorably back and forth and devouring my page with the indifference of a shuttle' (p. 133). The hand weaves the life, as for Stephen Dedalus it is the task of artists to 'weave and unweave our bodies from day to day, their molecules shuttled to and fro'; but for Beckett's writers, weaving and unweaving do not enter into a transformative dialectic, into that aesthetic unity that Beckett finds in Proust and Joyce, but only to a confrontation with the space of the prosthetic junction itself, as it rises to the plane of the page, to the 'terrible materiality of the word surface'. 'I hear the noise of my little finger as it glides over the paper', Malone says, and as he does so he frees the voice from writing hand, frees the mind from the woven form in which it knows itself. With what hand, we are led to ask, are these words written? What kind of sound do they make? Are they written with a ghost hand, we wonder, like that 'supernatural hand' that Ishmael feels 'placed in mine' at the opening of *Moby Dick*, the hand that 'puzzles' him 'to this very hour' (p. 24)? Perhaps, but such freedom from the weaving hand exists in Beckett only for a fleeting moment, or better the very moment that such freedom stirs in the province of the artwork is the moment that it stills itself in the recognition that distance from the hand is only ever the work of the hand – in the recognition that mind can only rid itself of its prostheses by attaching itself, again and again, to those apparatuses it evades.

In the long aftermath of *The Unnamable*, in the prose works that Beckett writes from the early 1950s to the late 1980s, it is this condition that he interrogates in his extended reworking of the modernist forms of self-fashioning that he inherits from Proust and from Joyce. The stunted, evacuated prose fragments that Beckett writes immediately after *The Unnamable*, collected as *Texts for Nothing*, are already performing this interrogation. The *Texts*, for all their residual brevity, their devotion to nothing, evince a powerful longing for connection with self and with other. Text 1 imagines a relationship between father and son, which owes much to the merging of father and son that Joyce conjures in *Ulysses*. Recalling the ritual of bedtime storytelling, in which the father would read to the son every night a story 'about Joe Breem, or Breen, the son of a lighthouse keeper', the narrator takes the part both of the narrating father and the listening son.[56] 'Yes', he writes, 'I was my father and I was my son, I asked myself questions, and answered as best I could' (p. 102). As father and son lie together in bed, 'under that ancient lamp', descendant of the dim lamp under which David Copperfield writes out his own narrative parenting of himself, the narrator feels that he has gathered himself into himself, as Carissa Dalloway gathers her life in her own arms to present it as a gift to her parents. 'I'm in my arms', he writes, 'I'm holding myself in my arms, without much tenderness, but faithfully, faithfully' (p. 104). He longs to fall asleep in this embrace, to preserve such lovingness in suspended animation. 'Sleep now', he implores himself, father hushing a tired son, as he himself is hushed, a tired son in the arms of his father; 'sleep now, under that ancient lamp, all twined together, tired out with so much talking, so much listening, so much toil and play' (p. 104). But as powerful as this longing for entwinement is, the *Texts* know that twining is bound to untwining, that the relation to self and to loved one is overseen by the vanishing medium of voice, voice which at once materialises its abstractions and abstracts its materiality. This is a voice, like that which ends *The Unnamable*, that knows that it can neither stop nor continue, is neither dead nor alive, but that inhabits the space of the junction, the prosthetic join that is the most inward being of the novel form. 'It can't speak', the voice says, 'and it can't cease'; 'There is silence and there is not silence, there is no one and there is someone' (p. 154).

This is the intolerable, wriggling condition that emerges at the end of *The Unnamable* and that continues wriggling, until it re-emerges, pale for weariness, but with a new kind of lovingness, a kind of irreconciled reconciliation, in that late miracle *Company*. All the Joyce-haunted, Proust-haunted images that gather in that novella call to a form that might twine them together, so that face might be joined to back, parent joined to child, lover to lover, self to self. The narrative reanimates Proust and Joyce to summon the union between mind and matter that their work conjures, that union which I have traced as it reaches back and further back through the long history of the novel imagination. But here, in the flat, artificial light of the late twentieth century – in the 'great blaze of electric light' that floods Lily Bart's death-bound mind at the end of *The House of Mirth* (p. 313), and which renders the world of Beckett's *Lost Ones* 'uniformly luminous down to its least particle of ambient air'[57] – there is no hiding place for such a junction. The contradiction between twining and untwining, self and unself, can find no ground in which to bury itself and is forced to twitch and writhe on the very surface of the page, as the voice finds itself wedged in the ground between its poles, in a space which opens only to reveal its own impossibility. The narrative captures this contradictory movement most sharply when it dwells on its own mechanics, the process by which narrative voice generates a grammar of being:

> Use of the second person marks the voice. That of the third that cankerous other. Could he speak to and of whom the voice speaks there would be a first. But he cannot. He shall not. You cannot. You shall not (p. 6).

This is a wondrous short-circuit of a passage, which collapses and rebuilds at the same time, which contracts and expands, twines and untwines, as the voice teases out the various pronominal modes in which it might announce itself. In living out these contortions, the voice seeks to gather its dispersed self, to bring its multiplicity into a unity, to recognise at once that being involves the duplication, the triplication of voice, and that such triplication can be reabsorbed into singularity (into the orbit of the solitary I which refuses to name itself). But even as it establishes this simultaneous multiplication and division, this growing and shrinking, the voice opens up a kind of unnamable gulf in being, one that cannot find itself named either in its numerousness or in its solitude, the gulf in being that is the homeland of the prosthetic imagination as I have traced it across the history of the novel, and that now lies exposed, brought to the material surface, as Dr Tulp ushers the secret movement of mind into the renaissance light in Rembrandt's anatomy painting. 'Use of the second person marks the voice', the voice says, but what person, what mode of voice, is it that makes this declaration? Not the second, as the voice is not speaking now, the voice that comes to one on his back in the dark; not the third, as this voice is not located in the body that lies on its back in the dark or that looks longingly into the distant eyes of his lover; not the first, that I which is placed under a prohibition here, which sidles always out of view. The voice which speaks here, which gives us this guided tour of narrative grammar, does not belong to any of the pronouns which it names. Rather, it prises a gap in that scenario, an impossible, voiceless, groundless region, which opens just long enough to declare that it must shut, just long enough to discover that voice belongs necessarily to first, second or third person, that there is no neutral agency, no sovereign unself, in which being might be encountered in the abyss of its not being, in the blessedness of its absence.

It is this shut opening that Beckett bequeaths to us, this most naked rhythm of gathered dispersal that is the primordial movement of narrative being. It is here, in these stilled and moving images, that Beckett arrives at an encounter with the very possibility of life, as it is engendered in fiction. His prose brings us, as he puts it in his late work 'Neither', to a slim space 'between two lit refuges whose doors once neared gently close'; it shuttles us, ceaselessly, 'from impenetrable self to impenetrable unself by way of neither'.[58] It is this 'neither', lying at the disappearing ground of being, that is as close as we can come to the 'unspeakable home' of the novel form. Nother dying. Come home.

PART V

The Posthuman Body: From Orwell to Atwood

CHAPTER 8

Prosthetics and Simulacra: The Postmodern Novel

> Someday she might replace whatever of her had gone away by some
> prosthetic device, a dress of a certain colour, a phrase in a letter,
> another lover.
>
> Thomas Pynchon, The Crying of Lot 49[1]

8.1 The Limits of the Word

> I shall not let her get rid of me with words that recreate my shape.
>
> Christine Brooke-Rose, 'The Foot'[2]

Throughout the decades of the second half of the twentieth century, while
Beckett is occupying himself by stretching the boundaries of modernism –
crafting his particular forms of endless finitude, his shut openings –
a technological revolution is taking place which is to have a profound
and transformative effect on the ways in which we understand and experience the relation between mind and matter, between information and its
various embodiments. While Beckett's work cuts a side channel through
the later decades of the twentieth century, in which he extends a modernist
struggle to articulate the terms in which mind might both free itself from
and bind itself to its attachments, this revolution tends to produce the
perception that such a struggle has been resolved, that the tense relation
between thought and thing that has governed the production and representation of our lifeworlds over the history of modernity has yielded to
a new kind of accommodation, in which thing takes on the characteristics
and the texture of thought.

This revolution is brought about by two closely entangled developments, one material and technological, one cultural and discursive. That
is, the advent of computing (which Katherine Hayles dates to 1950 and to
the publication of Alan Turing's paper 'Computer Machinery and
Intelligence') and the emergence of a postmodern structure of feeling,

a set of discursive formations that can make of digital virtuality a new kind of reality.[3] As Jean François Lyotard puts it, in his seminal analysis of what he calls the 'postmodern condition', 'the status of knowledge is altered as societies enter into what is known as the postindustrial age and cultures enter what is known as the postmodern age'; the 'nature of knowledge', he goes on, 'cannot remain unchanged within this context of general trans-formation', a context generated by the 'hegemony of computers'.[4] The dematerialising power of the computer, in tandem with the deliquescing action of (late) capital, under whose hand, famously, 'all that is sold melts into air', gives rise to the perception that the material determinants of modernity have been overcome, succeeding to a new era overseen by a postmodern sensibility, and by its host of attendant 'posts' – posthuman-ism, post-feminism, postcolonialism and so on.[5] With this overcoming, the texture of the prosthetic condition itself, the quality of prosthetic materi-ality, enters too into a transition. At 'the inaugural moment of the com-puter age,' Hayles writes, we see the rebalancing of the relationship between information and material, a rebalancing in which the body – both the organic body, Freud's 'inch of nature', and the prosthetic or manufactured or augmented body – becomes itself informational. Computing, Hayles goes on, performs the 'erasure of embodiment' so that '"intelligence" becomes a property of the formal manipulation of symbols rather than enaction in the human life world' (p. xi). The forces that lead to the advent of posthumanism threaten a vanishing of the body as a materiality that is resistant to mind, a vanishing in which we encounter ourselves both as artificial and as endlessly editable and manipulable. It encourages us, Hayles writes, to 'regard the body as the original prosthesis we all learn to manipulate' (p. 3) and to enter into a fantasy in which 'because we are essentially information, we can do away with the body' (p. 12). Theories of posthumanism – to which Hayles seeks to offer a corrective – have tended to suggest that biopolitical being is always already a technologised addition, while characterising such prosthetic extension not as a material condition but an effect of language, a manifestation of information, which offers no form of material resistance to the discursive processes that produce it.

To trace the passage of the prosthetic imagination over this time – to understand the ways in which the novel articulates and critiques the emergence of a postmodern condition – requires us, I think, to attend to the ways that later twentieth-century fiction tests the boundary between the informational and the material, as technological, political and eco-nomic conditions tend towards the erasure of that boundary. If the emergence of the postmodern and the posthuman produce a scenario in which we are all led to recognise our own prosthetic artificiality, then how does the prosthetic relate to the real, or act, in a phrase from Ricoeur that I quoted in the Introduction, as 'a physical or mental replica of an absent thing'?[6] Or, to put the question slightly differently, what is the difference, under these conditions, between the prosthetic and the simulacral? If the emergence of a postmodern 'cultural dominant' is shaped, to a significant degree, by the arrival of the simulacrum as a replacement for the real – what Hayles describes, paraphrasing Jean Baudrillard, as a 'simulation that does not merely compete with but actually displaces the original' (p. 250) – then how far does our relation to our bodies as prosthetic fold into a perception that our bodies are simulacral?[7] How far does the prosthetic body become identical with the simulacral body, an empty representation of a biopolitical being that has no reality to which it might refer? And if the real is becoming itself simulacral, itself partaking of the structure of a fiction, then how does the novel as a form oversee the new relation between the prosthetic and the simulacral – how does this shift impact, or find itself bodied forth in, the mimetic texture of a postmodern prosthetic imagination?

Perhaps the most orthodox answer to that question would be to propose that the novel is the form most suited to articulating this shift, the form in which a postmodern condition might find its most natural expression. If, to return again to my earlier discussion of Ricoeur's narrative theory, it is the 'central paradox of fiction' that 'only the image which does not already have its referent in reality is able to display a world', then fiction might find itself naturally allied to the lifeworlds of postmodernity, worlds which themselves have no referent in reality.[8] 'In the case of fiction', Ricoeur says, 'there is no given model, in the sense of an original already there, to which it could be referred' (p. 120); it is easy to see that what came to be known as postmodern fiction, through the second half of the twentieth century, thrives on this perception that the novel, like postmodernism itself, is a discursive structure that is self-referring, that does not reach out towards a reality that precedes it or to which it must seek to be faithful. Think, for example, of Don DeLillo's 1984 novel *White Noise*, a novel that coincides, in many accounts, with the arrival of what Fredric Jameson calls 'full postmodernism', and which is often cited as an exemplary, perhaps the exemplary, postmodern fiction.[9] The comedy of this text is generated by its wry depiction of the ease with which the real is absorbed into the representational and the simulacral under later twentieth-century conditions. A famous early episode in the novel concerns the protagonist Jack Gladney's trip to see a local tourist attraction, known as 'the most photographed barn in America'. On the drive to the barn with his friend Murray, Jack says, 'the signs started appearing. THE MOST PHOTOGRAPHED BARN IN AMERICA. We counted five signs before we reached the site'.[10] The barn sits at the centre of a paraphernalia of signs advertising its status as a sign – 'a man in a booth sold postcards and slides – pictures of the barn taken from the elevated spot' (p. 12) – but, of course the barn itself is not described in the narrative and does not enter into this scene of celluloid representation. 'No one sees the barn', Jack's friend Murray says, 'Once you've seen the signs about the barn, it becomes impossible to see the barn.' 'What was the barn like before it was photographed?' he asks: 'What did it look like, how was it different from other barns, how was it similar to other barns? We can't answer these questions because we've read the signs, seen the people snapping the pictures. We can't get outside the aura' (p. 12).

The barn becomes the representation of the barn; then, later in the novel, we are given an account of a man-made disaster – the 'Airborne Toxic Event' – which requires Jack and his family to be evacuated from their small college town. The family hears on the car radio of the symptoms of exposure to the toxin – vomiting; sweaty palms; and, deliciously, *déjà vu* – and, naturally, they start exhibiting these symptoms, not because they have been poisoned, but, in some bottomless *mise en abyme*, because the disaster has become equated with its representation, its mediatisation, its symptomology. This is exposure not to the Badiouan event (which, like the photographed barn, recedes in its eventhood from view) but to the reporting of the event.[11] Jack's daughter Steffie and his wife Babette duly start experiencing *déjà vu* – that archetypal experience of the loss of origin, the sense that we are remembering an event which has no basis in reality, an event which is impossible to separate from the false memory of the event, its spectral, groundless genesis in misfiring synapses. 'I saw all this before', Steffie says, as she tries to situate herself in relation to the disaster unfolding around her, the toxic event, 'This happened once before. Just like this' (p. 125). And Babette, discussing Steffie's bouts of *déjà vu* with Jack, has the same feeling, at another remove, the feeling that her concerns about Steffie's *déjà vu* also have an origin elsewhere. 'This happened before', she says 'Eating yoghurt, sitting here, talking about *déjà vu*' (p. 133).

In *White Noise*, in 1984, the novel offers itself as the privileged form with which to articulate a simulacral condition, the form which seems to have been primed to open spiraling pathways into the regressing midst of those nested *déjà vu*s. No other form, perhaps, could give us such coloured, thought-laden access to a condition which is stripped of world, or capture the emptied world so vividly in the throes of its emptying out. But if this is the case, if the novel has a kind of affinity with what emerged in the mid-eighties as a simulacral postmodernism, I think that we cannot understand the relationship between postmodernism and prose fiction without accounting too for a kind of resistance to the simulacral that is inherent in the novel form, and that I will formulate here as an underlying tension between the simulacrum and the prosthetic. Throughout the passage of the novel from the post-war to the present day – and across the theoretical and critical languages with which we have sought to account for the vanishing effects of contemporary technicity – one can see *at once* the struggle to give expression to a simulacral condition, in which there is no outside to language and origin is subsumed into copy, and to account for a persistent materiality that is stubbornly irreducible to language, that it remains the task of language to describe or refer to, rather than invent. Even as the prosthetic becomes simulacral, becomes part of that virtual experience of artificial life that William Gibson captures so vividly in his 1984 novel *Neuromancer* – his proleptic fictional account of cyberspace – the task of literary thinking has been to account for a persistent difference between the prosthetic and the simulacral, to identify a material prosthetic residue that cannot be absorbed into the emerging simulacral logic of postmodernism, even if that logic makes it very difficult to find an outside to the linguistic structure of reality, to pass beyond the limits of the word. If, as Rosi Braidotti has argued in her Deleuzian account of the posthuman condition, 'the posthuman nomadic subject is materialist and vitalist, embodied and embedded' – if it is 'firmly located somewhere' – then the question is how we give narrative expression to that vitalism when the vanishing conditions of a simulacral postmodernism have made it so hard to actualise.[12]

One can see something of the difficulty of this task by attending to a slim difference of opinion that is discernable between Jacques Derrida and Bernard Stiegler concerning the relationship between the prosthetic and the simulacrum. At several moments in his work, Derrida accords a certain importance to the concepts of both the prosthetic and the simulacrum; in both cases this importance has to do with the ways in which each touches on the possibility of an origin, of a ground to being that might act as a foundation to discursive processes. In *Archive Fever*, in *The Monolingualism of the Other*, Derrida postulates that there is what he calls a 'prosthesis at the origin'.[13] The need for an archive, he suggests – our reliance for our very access to self on a technology of knowledge storage – is one manifestation of what Arthur Bradley calls our 'originary technicity', one sign of the inherence of Heideggerian techne at the very heart of the naked self.[14] The 'psychic apparatus', Derrida writes, is reliant for its becoming on 'all the technical mechanisms for archivization and for reproduction' that allow us to store knowledge and thought – reliant upon the 'prostheses of so called live memory'.[15] The prosthetic constitutes, in this way, a kind of supplement to being that is there at the origin of being; Derrida suggests too that the simulacrum serves a parallel kind of function. He argues, in *Dissemination* and elsewhere, that the simulacrum is an integral function of all representation, and of all discursive relations to truth. The disappearance of origin in the forms with which we represent it – dramatised in DeLillo's most photographed barn – is not for Derrida a failure or malfunction of our representational mechanisms but an intrinsic part of their operation. 'The disappearance of truth as presence, the withdrawal of the present origin of presence', Derrida writes, 'is the condition of all (manifestation of) truth'.[16] Just as the prosthesis is present at the origin, meaning that we are 'always already' divided between the living and the non-living, already technologised at the first breath of being, so the simulacrum is woven into the origin, as the experience of 'presence' itself is '*doubled* as soon as it appears, as soon as it presents itself'.[17] Presence 'appears', he argues, '*in its essence, as* the possibility of its own most proper non-truth, of its pseudo-truth, reflected in the icon, the phantasm, or the simulacrum' (p. 168).

Both the simulacrum, then, and the prosthetic are additions to being that are intrinsic to being, both features of the supplement which, in deconstructive thought, haunts or attends all experience of presence and thus empties presence of its presence to itself. 'Nontruth is truth', Derrida writes, 'Nonpresence is presence' (an echo of his declaration, elsewhere, that 'critique and non-critique are fundamentally the same').[18] In *Archive Fever*, Derrida makes explicit this proximity between the prosthetic and the simulacrum when he implies that they too are fundamentally the same. The prosthesis, as a technological extension or exteriorisation of being, also appears on the inside of being, as a feature of that being itself and as the relation itself between inside and outside enters into that collapse of oppositions that is a signature of Derrida's thinking. The prosthesis figures as an '*outside*', but also, by the same movement, as 'an *internal* substrate, surface, or space without which there is neither consignation or registration' – 'in sum', he writes, it appears as a '*prosthesis of the inside*' (p. 19), a doubling on the inside of being that performs the same putting of presence beside itself as the simulacrum. The 'psychic apparatus' is manifest, Derrida writes, through the operation at once of 'prostheses of so-called live memory' and as 'simulacrums of living things' (p. 15). It is central to the movement of

Derrida's thought to collapse these two things together; but the difference that one can detect between Derrida's and Stiegler's conception of prosthetics, and of technics, turns around Steigler's perception that the prosthetic, even under the conditions of later twentieth-century virtuality, stands in some kind of opposition to the simulacrum, that the prosthetic constitutes precisely the kind of materiality, the kind of thingly manifestation of being, that is the residue that the simulacrum denies in its reduction of origin to copy. For Stiegler, as Ben Roberts has demonstrated, a vanishing point in Derrida's conception of *différance* – the element of his work in which there is 'an indecision, a passage remaining to be thought' – is its incapacity to account for the difficult junction between the interior of being and its prosthetic exteriorisation – a junction that, for Stiegler, will not fold into the simulacrum but remains external to it.[19] However true it is that we can only conceive of the outside of being as it touches on and is transformed by some contact with a simulacral interiority – however inescapable Derrida's collapse of that opposition is – it remains the case, for Stiegler, that there is a category of what he calls in *Technics and Time* 'inorganic organized being' (p. 17) – that is, a mode of prosthetic materiality that will not become equated with the informational systems that animate it. It may be true, as Derrida has suggested, Stiegler writes, that 'the interior and the exterior are the same thing, the inside is the outside, since man (the interior) is essentially defined by the tool (the exterior)' (p. 142). But against the tendency towards the collapse of this opposition (outside/inside) into tautology, the thinking of the prosthetic requires us to understand that 'this double constitution' (whereby the interior constitutes the exterior, and vice versa) 'is also that of an opposition between the interior and the exterior' (p. 142) – the opposition that it has been the aim of this book to uncover, as it is reflected throughout the history of prose fiction. There is, Stiegler insists, a 'passage' from interior to exterior, what he beautifully calls the 'passage of the cortex into flint', which constitutes the 'paradoxical and aporetic beginning of "exteriorization"', the 'meeting of matter whereby the cortex reflects itself' (p. 141).

The dialogue between Derrida and Stiegler, then, turns around the difficulty of establishing a passage between the inside and the outside of being, of staking out a limit boundary between the informational and the real, under political, theoretical and technological conditions which are collapsing the distinction between inside and outside, between the real and the artificial. And if one can see the fugitive nature of this limit in the theoretical languages which have provided the philosophical foundation of the postmodern condition, then it is in the novel, from the post-war to the present day, that this limit-under-erasure is given its fullest critical expression. It may be that DeLillo's *White Noise* suggests a natural affinity between fiction and simulacra, but it is nevertheless the case that prose fiction has offered itself, from the first stirrings of a postmodern sensibility, as a means of expressing a resistance to a simulacral logic – a means of thinking, in words, towards the outside of the word. Indeed, it is in the novel form – in George Orwell's 1949 dystopia *Nineteen Eighty-Four* – that one can see the first articulation of a postmodern condition, long before the word came into use; if this is so, if *Nineteen Eighty-Four* can be thought of as a depiction of postmodernism *avant la lettre*, then this early encounter between fiction and postmodernism is one in which the resources of the novel do not conspire with postmodern logic but are rather deployed precisely to resist its stealthy and insidious allure. It is the enduring achievement of Orwell's novel – the outcome of what Thomas Pynchon calls its 'prophetic' capacity to see into the deeper structures that determine the passage of history – to recognise that the combination of globalisation with the emergence of new information technologies will lead to a diminishment of the real, the arrival of a simulacral lifeworld.[20] In the discussion that takes place at the heart of the novel in 'Room 101', between Winston Smith (the last human) and the party intellectual O'Brien (the agent of a new, posthuman epistemology), one can see the theoretical basis for this diminishment, this weakening of the real, being played out. In a torture scene that also reads as a first-year undergraduate seminar on Baudrillardian simulation, O'Brien explains to Winston that with the advance in the technologies of archiving and knowledge storage – with the wholesale prosthetisation of memory – the real itself becomes manipulable, no longer the ground of being to which our discursive structures refer but a flickering, groundless mirage conjured by those structures themselves. 'You believe', he says to Winston,

> that reality is something objective, external, existing in its own right. You also believe that the nature of reality is self-evident. When you delude yourself into thinking that you see something, you assume that everyone else sees the same thing as you. But I tell you, Winston, that reality is not external. . . . Whatever the Party holds to be truth, *is* truth. It is impossible to see reality except by looking through the eyes of the Party.[21]

The scenario that Orwell imagines in *Nineteen Eighty-Four* is one in which the political tendencies of the post-war lead to a failure of the limits of the word, a failure in which the word becomes all there is, in which there is no outside to the word. His invention of Newspeak is, of course, the most enduring form that this triumph of the word takes. As the philologist Syme explains to Winston early in the novel, the principles of Newspeak rely on the perception that the range of the possible is determined by the expressive range of language – that, as in Swift's Houyhnhnm land, the obliteration of the word for a thing amounts to the obliteration of that thing itself. 'It's a beautiful thing', Syme says to Winston, 'the destruction of words' (p. 54). 'The whole aim, of Newspeak', he says, 'is to narrow the rage of thought. In the end we shall make thoughtcrime impossible, because there will be no words in which to express it' (p. 55). 'Every year fewer and fewer words, and the range of consciousness always a little smaller': with the reduction of language and of consciousness to the minimum, 'the whole climate of thought will be different. In fact, there will *be* no thought, as we understand it now' (p. 56). In *Nineteen Eighty-Four*, in his invention of Newspeak, Orwell has already intuited that behind the pictures of the barn there is no barn, that the development of a specular society means that we cannot see the barn except through the mediatised forms in which it is represented to us, that we cannot 'get outside the aura'. But, of course, it is the desperate desire of Orwell's novel to find a means of resisting such a diminishment, of keeping faith with a conception both of realism and of reality, grounded in the idea that language refers to a world rather than acting as that world itself. Everything that happens in Orwell's novel turns around this desire, even if the recognition at the heart of the novel is that the technologies for the production and control of reality – the telescreen as well as the speakwrite – make it very difficult to realise such a desire, very difficult to maintain contact with the material ground to reality that the novel mourns. As if acknowledging that the task of thinking past the limits of the word is beyond the intellectual power both of Winston and of Orwell himself, the reaching for the real in *Nineteen Eighty-Four* remains crude, dogmatic, almost perversely blunt. Under intellectual and physical torture by O'Brien, Winston desperately strives to maintain his faith that there is some non-arbitrary relationship between language and the world, some tie between thoughts and things that might allow us to ground ourselves in a material reality through a speech act that is self-evidently true. Resisting O'Brien's proto-postmodernism involves Winston in repeating the mantra that '*Freedom is the freedom to say that two plus two make four. If that is granted all else follows*' (p. 84). 'The solid world exists', Winston tells himself, 'its laws do not change. Stones are hard, water is wet, objects unsupported fall towards the earth's centre' (p. 84). There are immutable laws that hold reality together, Winston thinks, a reality that is larger than us and indifferent to our concerns. 'The whole universe is outside us', he says to O'Brien, as he writhes under electrocution, 'Look at the stars! Some of them are a million light-years away. They are out of our reach for ever' (p. 278).

Winston's sense of self, the very possibility of his world, relies on his sense that reality is independent of the words with which we describe it, that two plus two will always make four, regardless of whether we say that they make five or three; but the final recognition of Orwell's novel is that the mechanism we have for holding on to that reality – the passage from word to world – has become inoperable with the advent of global capital and virtual information technology. There is a longing in *Nineteen Eighty-Four* for a kind of realism that can establish a contact with the real, together with a despairing sense that such a realism is unavailable; it is this longing for realism, combined with a sense of its unavailability, that drives a strand of post-war realism for which Orwell is a kind of origin, but which becomes increasingly sophisticated in its examination of the capacity of words to free themselves from self-reference. Realism, Orwell's novel tells us, cannot rely on a dogmatic insistence on the self-evident relation between word and world but has to experiment with new mimetic forms in which to couch its access to the real – a form of experimentation that is the vocation of a tradition in realist fiction after Orwell. From the variously experimental realisms of the 1940s and 1950s in works by Graham Greene, Henry Green, James Hanley, Patrick Hamilton, to the works stretching from the post-war to the mid-late century by writers such as Elizabeth Bowen, Iris Murdoch, Muriel Spark, Doris Lessing, Christine Brooke-Rose, Ann Quin, B. S. Johnson, Elizabeth Taylor and Paula Fox, a strand of the Anglophone novel form serves as a laboratory for testing the limits of the word – the terms in which word relates to world, and mind relates to body, under technological and political conditions which are dramatically transforming the production of the real.

Take, for example, Christine Brooke-Rose's extraordinary 1970 short fiction 'The Foot', a work that anatomises with extraordinary precision the logic of a later twentieth-century experimental realism. This story, in an odd inversion of Silas Weir Mitchell's 'The Case of George Dedlow', is told from the perspective of a phantom limb. Where Weir Mitchell brings the phantom limb into the narrative scene, in the bizarre picture of Dedlow walking around on his invisible amputated legs, Brooke-Rose gives primacy to the phantom limb itself, granting the phantom narrative jurisdiction over the fictional world. The unnamed female protagonist of the story has been involved in a car crash ('Why did I have to go with Denis in his crazy car?' [22]), and her leg, 'lacerated wrenched and crushed in all that twisted car metal' (p. 47), has been amputated above the knee. The voice that speaks in the story is the voice of the missing foot as it haunts the woman, a narrative agent which takes a great, sadistic pleasure in tormenting her, in subjecting her to a boundless pain that is distinct from 'real pain', the pain that she feels in her stump that 'aches in every neurone' (p. 45). 'The victim to be haunted', the voice says in the opening sentence, 'is female. And beautiful' (p. 43). 'Now she thinks about me', it says, 'giving me strength and existence, and creating my shape, her slim long phantom foot, her unendurable phantom pain'. 'She cries quietly', the voice continues, 'I find this very exciting' (p. 48).

In giving a voice to this phantom, the story gains a stunning, almost unthinkable proximity to the seam I have traced in this book as it runs through the history of the novel, the difficult boundary, buried in the nerve tissue exposed in Rembrandt's anatomy paintings, between unextended and extended being; it locates, too, and forensically anatomises that relation between the prosthetic and the simulacrum that is contested in the dialogue I have sketched here between Derrida and Stiegler. In giving narrative voice to the idea of the foot, its spectral presence, as opposed to the real foot – the bodily foot which, the woman insists, 'is an object. Outside myself. It exists' (p. 49) – the story lives out a Derridean logic of spectrality. There is, the story suggests, a phantom foot that shadows and supplements the thingly foot, and it is the gift of narrative to make this supplement, this simulacral prosthesis at the origin, audible, imaginable. This is a version of that spectral hand that Ishmael encounters at the opening of *Moby Dick*, or Ahab's 'crushed leg', of which, he says, 'I still feel the smart', 'though it be now so long dissolved' (p. 420). Narrative voice allows for the expression of the phantom supplement; but if this is so, what is so remarkable about Brooke-Rose's story is that the phantom limb that it depicts – the simulacrum of a limb, freed from an origin in the real – is given the most material of forms, living out what Stiegler calls the 'passage of the cortex into flint'. 'We phantoms', the voice says, 'infiltrate ourselves down the pathways of pain, down the spinothalamic tract to be precise' (p. 46). The pain that is the being of the voice is 'created', it says, in 'neuroblasts' that

> pass along the spinothalamic tract and the efferent fibres down to the neuroma in the stump where the axons of the severed nerves proliferate wildly and send back false messages to the cortical areas that will soon when the strong tranquiliser dies build up from them the central image of a limb no longer there. (p. 47)

The limb that is not there is registered as a function of biology not of mind, of nervous excitation not of imagination; the key image that the story yields to picture the relation between the voice and its victim, between the phantom and its body, is the umbilical cord, the strandentwining cable that I have traced, in its particular materiality, its particular diffused vitality, as it reaches through Beckett's late modernist imagination. 'The imitation neurones I am composed of', the voice says,

> agitate their dendrites like mad ganglia that arborise the system as the cell bodies dance along the axis cylinder within the fibres of the foot that isn't there, move backwards now, tugging away from the interlaced antennae as if trying to wrench themselves from some submicroscopic umbilical tie anchored in the soft tissue, caught into bone, straining, straining to freedom birth and terror of time and space as the impulses race down the fibrils and create me. (pp. 49–50)

The phantom limb, composed of 'imitation neurones', is attached to the body (of the woman, of the story) by this umbilical tie, the material conduit of life which is itself a peculiar amalgam of the vital and the inanimate, that both belongs to self and is extraneous to it (the 'umbilical tissue', the voice says, that opens 'pathways to the womb the tomb the cavern the ebb and flow of time' (p. 43)). And the task of the story is to test the nature of this umbilical attachment, to feel for the physical and ideational properties of the material that joins the phantom voice to its apparatuses, that attaches intelligence to material, word to world. In its phantomness, the voice declares its simulacral freedom from the material that instantiates it, from the words in which it speaks. 'Words', it says, 'are my enemies': 'The real danger of words is that they create thoughts which lead to other thoughts and these if stimulating and distracting and absorbing enough may smother me altogether or knock me out like a percussion mallet until my imitation unmyeleted nerve-fibres degenerate curl up and die' (p. 56). In declaring its hostility to words, the voice suggests, of course, that it does not itself speak in words, that the voice that speaks here is the voice of the unword, what Katherine Hayles might call the thought of the 'unthought'.[23] This is the phantom supplement to words that moves on the inside of words, Derrida's 'prosthesis of the inside'. But even as the voice declares, in this way, its unwordedness, its simulacral non-presence, it restates its condition as the most material of narrative forms, embedded in the biomaterial that is not there, the 'imitation unmyeleted nerve-fibres' that give it shape and substance. In becoming the amputated limb, in speaking *as* the unalive foot 'once in intimate touch with earth air water mother belly and bearing the whole weight of her existence in upright position on that structure of bone flesh fibre skin' (p. 57), the voice takes on the task of speaking as a thing.

'The Foot', then, sets this vibrating play in motion between a voice that enters into its own simulacral non-presence and a voice which embeds itself in the prosthetic material of thinghood – an opposition that is held together, overseen, by the vital materiality of the umbilical tie. But the real genius of the story, its punctum – the moment that captures with such precision the movement of a realism which seeks to gain material access to a real that is in the process of disappearing – comes towards its end, when it is revealed, strangely shockingly, that the voice that we are reading is authored by the woman herself, the beautiful victim to be haunted. 'She is thinking of me', the voice says, 'to write about in order to get me out of her system', 'out of her midbrain on to paper instead of aching there fifty-three and a half centimetres away from her stump' (p. 59). The speaking of the voice, we discover, is not after all the triumph of phantom pain, not the voice of a pain which is tormenting the woman; rather this very voice is the outcome of a process by which the woman is exorcising her pain, committing it to 'mere paper to be read by careless unsuffering millions vicariously and thus dispersed' (p. 60). 'I thought, perhaps, I could write', the woman says to her doctor, write the pain away. Not a love story, or a spy-thriller, or a literary masterpiece – 'no Proust she', this is not 'á la recherche du pied perdu' (p. 61) – but an act of therapeutic self-recreation. As Moran sits down to write the first words of the narrative that we are reading at the end of Beckett's *Molloy* – 'I went back into the house and wrote, It is midnight. The rain is beating on the windows' (p. 176) – so we see the woman sitting down, at the story's end, to write its beginning. Like Beckett's Malone, she is given an 'exercise book' (p. 61) ('this exercise book', Malone says, 'is my life'), and it is in this exercise book that she writes out the words of her phantom tormentor ('I write about myself', Malone says, 'with the same pencil and in the same exercise-book as about him' (p. 208)). She will 'formulate me anew within her brain along the spinothalamic tract', the voice says, 'and she opens meanwhile the small exercise book and in thin impersonal strokes she writes the words she hears like white sun swamping all other receptors in the brain so that the white page slowly engraves itself with the victim to be haunted is female. And beautiful' (p. 61).

This moment in Brooke-Rose's story is exemplary of the mode of realism that follows from Orwell's post-war testing of the limits of the word – a realism that seeks to work at the mined junction between the simulacral and the prosthetic, that seeks to reveal the ground, the passage that stretches between cortex and material – Swift's 'continuation of the brain' – just as the tendency of modernity is towards the disappearance, the erasure, of that ground. Brooke-Rose's protagonist here takes control of the narrative, wrests power from her torturer. This is a supercharged, feminist version of the moment that we see rehearsed in *David Copperfield*, in *Á la recherche*, in *Molloy*, where the narrative meets with itself, where it folds into itself. But, of course, as Beckett realises in *Molloy* and *Malone Dies*, this feeding of the narrative into itself is radically incomplete. It leaves a remainder, an umbilical residue, which constitutes the materiality of the prosthetic voice itself, a materiality which cannot be absorbed into the simulacral, the spectral – the materiality that is the residuum that emerges from Beckett's long testing of the prosthetic imagination. Even as the story shapes to come from the mind of the suffering woman, as it is engraved like white sun onto the mystic pad, the voice asserts its freedom from the involuting circuits of Proustian self-invention, demonstrating the failure of any story to swallow itself, to fully recover the lost foot, the *pied perdu*. 'I shall not let her get rid of me', the voice says, 'I shall not let her get rid of me with words that recreate my shape my galvanising atoms of agony' (p. 60). The voice asserts its refusal to be written, to be contained in the words that the woman is writing, and it does so in those very words that the woman writes to neutralise that refusal. In these written words – doubling themselves, trebling, overflowing their fields of signification – one can hear at once the reaching of the word to contain its own residue within its simulacral expressive power, and the refusal of that residue, of voice *as* residue, to come under that expressive regime. The limits of the word are imposed and exceeded at the same time, in the same compressed moment. It is the genius of Brooke-Rose's story that this prosthetic resistance to the simulacral is articulated as part of the movement of the simulacral itself – a prosthetic resistance to disappearance, in the process of disappearance, that is the keynote of a twentieth-century experimental realism.

8.2   Like-Lines: Simulacral Prosthetics in Morrison and Pynchon

> And the difference was all the difference there was.
>   Toni Morrison, *The Bluest Eye*[24]

It is against this strand of experimental realism, running through the second half of the twentieth century, that one can plot the emergence, and then the dominance, of the postmodern novel. Where Brooke-Rose and the group of novelists with which she has an affinity work, like Stiegler, to prise the prosthetic from the simulacral, it is the formal and philosophical principle of the postmodern novel, as it has often been understood, to oversee their collapse into identity, the identity that lies at the vanishing ground of Derrida's thought.

One can see the signs of this collapse – and its centrality to the explosion of literary and political possibility that is bound up with it – in a dialogue stretching from mid to late century between George Orwell and Salman Rushdie; between Orwell's despair, in the 1940s, at the loss of political agency occasioned by the emergence of an inchoate postmodern condition, and Rushdie's insistence, in 1984 (in the midst of the 'postmodern moment'), that political possibility lies in that very condition itself. This dialogue takes the form of Rushdie's counterblast, in his 1984 essay 'Outside the Whale', to Orwell's 1940 essay 'Inside the Whale'. In the latter, Orwell makes the argument, which he later fictionalises in *Nineteen Eighty-Four*, that the capacity for the novel to influence the world has expired, along with the end of a world view that Orwell associates with what he rather imprecisely calls 'liberalism'. Liberalism relies, for Orwell, on a set of shared consensuses about the nature of reality and of our place in it, consensuses which allowed the writer to take part in the narrating of a common, shared world. The emergence of the form of totalitarianism that Orwell imagines in *Nineteen Eighty-Four* as the coming political condition, however, means that it is no longer possible for literature to engage with the world in this way. 'The writer', he says, in a metaphor that has more purchase than he could have realised in 1940, 'is sitting on a melting iceberg'.[25] 'The literature of liberalism', he says, 'is coming to an end', as the 'autonomous individual' is 'stamped out of existence'. 'From now on', he concludes, 'the all-important fact for the creative writer is going to be that this is not a writer's world' (p. 131). The only option for the novelist, under these conditions, is to 'get inside the whale', to retreat like Jonah to the safety of the 'whale's belly', which is 'simply a womb big enough for an adult' (p. 127). 'There you are', he tells himself, 'in the dark, cushioned space that exactly fits you, with yards of blubber between you and reality, able to keep up an attitude of the completest indifference' (p. 127).

It is to express his horrified rejection of this indifference – this 'quietism' – that Rushdie writes 'Outside the Whale'. 'The truth is', Rushdie writes, 'there is no whale'.[26] We adults have to recognise, despite the post-partum trauma, that there is no womb available in which to isolate ourselves from the political realm, no Panglossian, Gulliverian garden to cultivate. 'We live', he says, 'in a world without hiding places' (p. 99). Literature and those who write it have no choice but to '*enter the political arena*' (p. 98); 'literature and politics', he says, 'are inextricably mixed' (p. 100). But what is so striking about the terms in which Rushdie insists on the necessarily political nature of the literary imagination is that they accord so closely with the diminishment of the consensuses about reality that Orwell sees as a consequence of the 'end of liberalism' in 'Inside the Whale', and that he describes with such force in *Nineteen Eighty-Four*. Orwell despairs because the technological and political forces that produce reality seem to him to have been overtaken by a compulsory artificiality, a diminishment of the real and the true, which leads, he says, to the '*impossibility* of any major literature' (p. 133). Rushdie sees much the same developments at work in post-war culture. There is, he writes in 'Outside the Whale', 'no consensus about reality' (p. 100). Reality, he says, has become simulacral, history unmoored from truth, as Orwell's Party, in Pynchon's phrase, is granted the power 'to debase history, trivialise truth and annihilate the past on a daily basis'.[27] As Rushdie puts it in his earlier essay 'Imaginary Homelands', and as his narrator puts it in his great novel *Midnight's Children* (an odd self-quotation which folds criticism into fiction), 'the illusion itself is reality' (p. 13).[28] While this development is the cause of despair for Orwell, for Rushdie it is the emergent condition that grants the literary imagination a new world-making power, a power that is particularly potent for those writing from the postcolonial margins. Where writers from Sam Selvon in *Lonely Londoners* to Chinua Achebe in *Things Fall Apart* seek to develop a form of realism in which to 'decolonise the mind',[29] in which to offer a counter-narrative of migrant experience to that which is disseminated by the ideologues of empire, Rushdie's conception of literary politics is founded on the conviction that the reality of shared experience is itself a mode of fiction – a conception that was given an influential articulation in the 1989 work by Linda Hutcheon, *The Politics of Postmodernism*.[30] Cultural identity, national communities and homelands, these, he argues, are imaginary, simulacral. The migrant experience itself affords a lesson in this fictionality. 'Those of us', he writes in 'Imaginary Homelands', who have experienced 'cultural displacement' have been 'forced to accept the provisional nature of all truths, all certainties' (p. 12). Migrancy opens a postcolonial perspective in which we recognise that there can be no Proustian recovery of a lost wholeness, and that when we seek to encounter ourselves in narrative, when we seek to 'reclaim the thing that was lost' (Brooke-Rose's '*pied perdu*'), we are led to 'create fictions, not actual cities or villages, but invisible ones, imaginary homelands, Indias of the mind' (p. 10). It is for this reason, he argues, in his fight with Orwell, that the writer must enter the fray. If our environments are simulacral, then it is only in imaginary forms, only in DeLillo's *déjà vu*, only in the production of narratives which have a simulacral origin, that we can reshape our worlds, or create new ones. It is the task of the novelist, he says, to 'draw new and better maps of reality, and to make new languages with which we can understand the world'. If the novel is to retreat from this task into Orwellian quietism, 'if writers leave the business of making pictures of the world to politicians, it will be one of history's greatest and most abject abdications' (p. 100).

It is this conviction, this sense that the political power of prose fiction rests on the simulacral nature of our own reality, that accords the post-modern novel, so called, such a central role in the production of imagined communities in the later twentieth century. With the virtualisation of every area of political life, with the discovery of the performative, discursive and informational element of our most material manifestations of identity and of history, one can see the emergence of an international generation of writers, from Rushdie, John Barth, Angela Carter, Kathy Acker, and J. G. Ballard to Gabriel Garcia Marquez, Italo Calvino and Don DeLillo, who generate a transformative political and poetic energy from this sudden alliance between a simulacral public sphere and a form of prose fiction that recognises its own world-making power.

One can see something of the range and the force of this coming together of postmodernism and simulacra by attending to a set of reso-nances between two of the most influential Anglophone novels of the second half of the century, gestated and written just as the elements of postmodern thinking were coming to possibility in the mid to late 1960s: Thomas Pynchon's *The Crying of Lot 49* and Toni Morrison's *The Bluest Eye*. Both of these novels turn around the perception that the real is a product of representation, that the outside of the word feeds into the involuted simulacral circuitry of its own insides; in both cases, this percep-tion has shaped their reception as exemplary of an emerging postmodern political aesthetic.[31] In Pynchon's novel, this takes the form, early on, of a reflection on the mutually generative relationship between a painting and the world that painting represents – the Ricoeurian question of a self-referring fictional image that I have returned to throughout the course of this book. The protagonist, Oedipa Maas, is taken by her then-lover, Pierce Inverarity, to Mexico, where she becomes fascinated by a Remedios Varo painting, 'Bordando el Manto Terrestre'.[32] This painting prepares Oedipa for a series of 'revelations' that she will experience when she is charged, after

Pierce's death, with the task of executing his will. Pierce leaves behind an elaborate system of clues that alerts her to the existence of a countercultural system of communication, known as the WASTE network, which harbours an entirely other mode of reality lying just beneath the skin of the one that we think we share. When he takes her to Mexico, Pierce has already begun this induction into an alternative reality. Oedipa believes, from the beginning of their relationship, that Pierce, as his name suggests, might help her pierce the sealed bubble of her aimless, mediatised life – a life in which, she thinks, 'she had noticed the absence of an intensity, as if watching a movie, just perceptibly out of focus, that the projectionist refused to fix' (p 10). Pierce promises a whirlwind escape from confinement in the bubble; however, the Varo painting suggests to her that Pierce is not after all freeing her from simulacral emptiness, but delivering her to it, to a much more intense experience of the groundlessness of representations, a more intense lack of intensity. Varo's painting, Oedipa says, shows

> a number of frail girls with heart-shaped faces, huge eyes, spun gold hair, prisoners in the top room of a circular tower, embroidering a kind of tapestry which spilled out of the slit windows and into a void, seeking hopelessly to fill the void: for all the other buildings and creatures, all the waves, ships and forests of the earth were contained in this tapestry, and the tapestry was the world. (p. 10)

The world is the representation of the world; this shattering realisation is the impetus behind everything that happens in *The Crying of Lot 49*, behind Oedipa's mad search for the locus of Pierce's simulacral power. It instructs Oedipa in the truth that 'all that had gone on between them', between herself and Pierce, 'had never really escaped the confinement of that tower' (p. 10). 'She had looked down at her feet', she says, as she stands in Mexico, 'and known, then, because of a painting, that what she stood on had only been woven together a couple thousand miles away in her own tower, was only by accident known as Mexico, and so Pierce had taken her away from nothing, there'd been no escape' (p. 11). Oedipa's response to this revelation is to stand in front of the painting, wearing her 'green bubble shades' as a disguise, and cry; this crying, the real crying of lot 49, prepares the medium for seeing in the novel, the index of its self-reference (as Maisie and Mrs Wix see each other through a medium of glassy tears in *What Maisie Knew*)[33]. 'For a moment', she says,

> she wondered if the seal around her sockets were tight enough to allow the tears simply to go on and fill up the entire lens space and never dry. She could carry the sadness of the moment with her that way forever, see the

world refracted through those tears, those specific tears, as if indices as yet
unfound varied in important ways from cry to cry. (p. 10)

Oedipa's crying here prepares the ground for the last sentence of the
novel – in which 'Oedipa settled back, to await the crying of lot 49'
(p. 142) – and it generates, in its relation with Varo's painting, a form of
closed self-reference, a field of meaning production in which the world is
drawn, relentlessly, into its own sealed sign system.

Pynchon's novel is fuelled by this sense that representations have overwhelmed the world represented; Morrison's novel, too, investigates this
condition, this sense, as Morrison herself has put it in an interview with Bill
Moyers, that 'history [is] a master fiction', that the truths by which we live
are generated by representations.[34] Just as *The Crying of Lot 49* opens with
Oedipa's incarceration in the tower of her own ego, so the opening of
Morrison's novel dwells on the experience of shattered, fragmented personal realities, each divided from the other. Oedipa's world is woven by
Varo's tapestry; in *The Bluest Eye*, the fragmentary effects of poverty and
racism incarcerate 'each member of the family in his own cell of consciousness, each making his own patchwork quilt of reality' (p. 32). Morrison
mirrors Pynchon here, and she also anticipates Rushdie's mode of historical
metafiction. Saleem, Rushdie's narrator in *Midnight's Children*, experiences
a certain pleasure in asserting the primacy of narrative over historical truth.
'The assassination of Mahatma Gandhi occurs', he says, 'in these pages, on
the wrong date'; but this does not trouble him, as he is perfectly content to
think that 'in my India, Gandhi will continue to die at the wrong time'
(p. 166). Morrison's narrator Claudia experiences much the same pleasure.
In telling her story, she says, 'my memory is uncertain; I recall a summer
storm in the town where we lived and imagine a summer my mother knew
in 1929.' Her own life is superimposed onto her mother's, their two
histories conflated; but Claudia, like Saleem, feels no concern. 'So much
for memory', she says, 'Public fact becomes private reality' (p. 186).

This ascendency of the representational over the real, of pictures over
things, can be felt at work throughout Morrison's novel, in a manner
which leads John Duvall to align Morrison with Hutcheon's postmodern
politics. 'In Hutcheon's scheme', Duvall writes, 'Morrison is
a postmodernist.'[35] But if Morrison draws on the same representational
dynamics that fuel Pynchon's imagination, Duvall suggests, it is also the
case that these dynamics register differently in a novel concerning
the politics of African American identity – that Morrison is alive to the
contradictions implicit in what bell hooks calls 'postmodern blackness'.[36]

One can see both the resonances between Morrison's simulacral imagination and Pynchon's and the disjunction between them, in two central
episodes in *The Bluest Eye* – episodes in which the comic lightness of
Pynchon's simulacra give way to something much more harrowing. The
first of these concerns Cholly Breedlove, the father of the novel's central
character Pecola Breedlove – the father who raped and impregnated Pecola
when she was herself a child. The narrator, as a means of investigating the
historical roots of the violence that Cholly commits against his daughter,
tells the story of an act of unspeakable racist violence that is visited on
Cholly himself when he was a teenager, an act of violence that estranges
Cholly from himself and prepares the ground for his own crimes. The
young Cholly is at his dead aunt's wake, where he meets a teenaged girl,
Darlene, and the two of them head off for a walk to a nearby wild vineyard
to pick and eat muscadine grapes. The scene quickly modulates into
a drama of mutual and consensual desire. Cholly tries to clean spilt grape
juice from Darlene's dress, and Darlene 'put her hands under his shirt and
rubbed the damp tight skin' (p. 144). The contact, unbidden, sudden, leads
to Cholly touching her in return: 'When he got his hand in her bloomers,
she suddenly stopped laughing and looked serious. Cholly, frightened, was
about to take his hand away, but she held his wrist so he couldn't move it'
(p. 145). Surprised in this way by the blooming of mutual desire, the two
begin to have sex – for Cholly for the first time. But their lovemaking is
interrupted by the brutal arrival of 'two white men', 'one with a spirit lamp,
the other with a flashlight' (p. 145). Cholly tries to escape the beam of the
torch – 'trying to kneel, stand, and get his pants up all in one motion'
(p. 145) – but the men, armed with guns as well as flashlights, force him to
continue, transforming the act from one born out of spontaneous embodied desire to an artificial show for the benefit of a white audience. The
men 'raced the flashlight all over Cholly and Darlene', the narrator says,
summoning them to visibility under this repellent gaze, and the two of
them are compelled to simulate sex. 'Darlene put her hands over her face',
the hands that moments before had been pressed to Cholly's skin, 'as
Cholly began to simulate what had gone on before. He could do no more
than make believe. The flashlight made a moon on his behind' (p. 146). As
he simulates sex with Darlene, and the torchlight brings him to
a representational regime violently at odds with his own sense of desiring
self, Cholly finds himself hating not the white men who subject him to this
probing light, but his own role in the event, and Darlene's – a hatred that
levers him away from himself and that leads, down the years, to his abuse of

Pecola. Cholly 'looked at Darlene', as she lay under him, in the light of the torch:

> He hated her. He almost wished he could do it – hard, long and painfully, he hated her so much. The flashlight wormed its way into his guts and turned the sweet taste of muscadine into rotten fetid bile. He stared at Darlene's hands covering her face in the moon and lamplight. They looked like baby claws. (p. 146)

The flashlight, carrier of a white representation of black desire, worms its way into the deep insides of the body here, replacing the embodied with the simulacral. And the other episode of simulation that lies at the heart of the novel – and that gives it its title – works similarly to enact the forces which make of the body not material owned by the self but representations generated by the 'master fictions' of history. This is the episode in which Pecola, who has learned to think of herself as ugly, and who has longed all her life to meet the criteria of beauty enforced by white America, is led to believe that she has been magically granted the blue eyes that are her dearest wish. In a powerful short circuit in Morrison's novel – which resonates with the sealed seeing that Oedipa reaches for in *Lot 49*, when she imagines she can see the world refracted through her own salvaged tears – Pecola imagines her dark eyes both as the objects that disfigure her, that confer blackness upon her, and as the means of her own seeing, the optics through which the world takes on its specular, simulacral shape. 'Each night, without fail', the narrator says, 'she prayed for blue eyes' (p. 44). Just as she longs for the ocular attributes of white beauty, she longs too to rid herself of her given body, the body that harbours 'the secret of the ugliness, the ugliness that made her ignored or despised at school' (p. 43). She finds she can imagine herself into disappearance: 'She squeezed her eyes shut. Little parts of her body faded away': 'Her fingers went, one by one; then her arms disappeared all the way to the elbow. Her feet now. Yes that was good. The legs all at once' (p. 43). She is able to imagine the disappearance of her body, but she can never, she thinks, manage to erase her eyes, because the eyes are themselves the organs of seeing, the containers of her specular sense of self, the pictured self which is the only identity to which she can aspire. 'Try as she might', she thinks, 'she could never get her eyes to disappear. So what was the point? They were everything. Everything was in there, in them. All of those pictures, all of those faces' (p. 43). If you are yourself a picture, rather than a thing, if your existence is conferred upon you as an image, rather than residing in you as a reality, then there is no escape from the specular. 'She would see', the narrator says, in a form of bound, near tautological locution that recurs at key moments through the novel, 'She would see only what there was to see: the eyes of other people' (p. 45). It is her immersion in this specular realm, her radical detachment from the reality of her body, that leads her, at the close of the novel, to accept the poisoned 'gift' of her blue eyes, to believe that her imaginary new eyes, objects and agents of seeing both, have transported her from 'blackness' that 'is static and dread' (p. 47) to a pure simulacrum of white beauty. It is this too that leads to the most devastating image of this devastating novel, the image of Pecola, happy in the secret of her blue eyes, 'walking up and down, up and down, her head jerking to the beat of a drummer so distant only she could hear':

> Elbows bent, hands on shoulders, she flailed her arms like a bird in an eternal grotesquely futile effort to fly. Beating the air, a winged but grounded bird, intent on the blue void it could not reach – could not even see – but which filled the valleys of the mind. (p. 202)

Both of these episodes turn around the central condition that the novel diagnoses, the condition in which the materiality of life is subsumed beneath its simulacra. We are joined to ourselves, they suggest, granted our being, by the work of representation – and this mode of attachment, this specular twining, is given, early in the novel, a form that resonates not only through *The Bluest Eye* but also through the later twentieth-century novel as I am seeking to characterise it here. It is in a discussion between Pecola and Maureen – one of the blue-eyed beautiful, of whom Pecola is in such awe – that this form emerges, a figure in which the specular attachment to self, to other, is cast in terms of the umbilical cord. Maureen and Pecola are sharing their recent experiences of 'mennistration', and Pecola asks what menstrual blood is 'for'. Maureen explains solemnly that it is 'for babies': 'Babies need blood when they are inside you, and if you are having a baby, then you don't menstrate. But when you're not having a baby, then you don't have to save the blood, so it comes out' (p. 68). Maureen's gynecological understanding is a little faulty here, as is her conception of the umbilical cord. Pecola asks how the baby 'gets' the menstrual blood that is 'saved' during pregnancy, and Maureen again offers an explanation:

> Through the like-line. You know. Where your belly button is. That is where the like-line grows from and pumps the blood to the baby (p. 68).

This is an extraordinary moment in the novel – a moment when Maureen's childish locutions and wayward understanding hit on a powerful means of imagining vital connection, under postmodern, simulacral conditions. Maureen, one assumes, is thinking here of the word 'lifeline', imagining the umbilical cord as a lifeline that transmits life from mother to baby. But in mistaking 'life' for 'like', in bringing the words 'life', 'like' and 'line' into this peculiar conjunction, she suggests the dissolution of life – the life that runs through the material vitalism of the umbilical cord – into 'likeness', the similitude that generates the image world for Pynchon, for DeLillo, for Rushdie. Where Brooke-Rose imagines the umbilical cord as tracing a material, Stieglerian passage from cortex into flint, where Orwell laments the late failure of the umbilical cord to separate us from the womb that we can no longer leave, Morrison here imagines an umbilical cord, a strandentwining cable, that is woven only out of airy likeness.

Like-lines, this moment in the novel might suggest, are the bonds that twine together the postmodern condition, that generate specular adhesion from the illusion of the similar. To be ourselves is to be *like* ourselves. But if this is so – if this is what Morrison is discovering at this oddly moving moment in *The Bluest Eye* – it is central to everything that I am arguing here that Morrison's exploration of likeness, of the simulacral, is shadowed by an investment in the prosthetic, in a material residue that will not go away, that will not vanish into likeness. There remains a Stieglerian disjunction here between the simulacral and the prosthetic that the early and influential formulation of a postmodern politics – shaped by critics from Hutcheon to Baudrillard to Jameson – has tended to obscure. It is not, I suggest, that prosthetic material, the vital materialism of the umbilical cord that runs through Beckett's imagination, has folded into the simulacral here, under emergent postmodern conditions; rather, what Morrison is bringing to expression, what Pynchon and DeLillo discover in their own narrative explorations of the simulacral, is that the processes that embed the *idea* of being in the *material* of being have become radically altered – so radically altered that one needs a new language, a new concept of vital distribution, to give form to our material relation to others and to ourselves, in the teeth of the political forces which are now determining our likenesses.

In Pynchon, in *The Crying of Lot 49*, this new distribution expresses itself as a tension between the material and the informational – a tension that is everywhere in the novel, but that cannot quite come to focus, like that absent intensity that Oedipa likens to watching a movie just perceptibly out of focus. The novel turns around the possibility that an informational system – here the WASTE postal network that has run through history as a latent counter-narrative – might give existence to another kind of reality, composed itself of information, of like-lines, might give rise to what Jesus Arrabal calls the 'anarchist miracle' of 'another world's intrusion into this one' (p. 91) (what appears, in *Gravity's Rainbow*, as 'another world laid down on the previous one', 'that identical looking Other World').[37] All of the elements of Oedipa's 'revelation', the revelation encoded in Pierce Inverarity's will, are organised around this miraculous entry into the simulacral world that Oedipa first intuits in Varo's painting. The novel turns around the multiplying associations among the slaughter of a company of American GIs in Europe in World War II, Inverarity's ubiquitous real estate developments in California, the historical secrets embedded in Pierce's stamp collection (soon to be auctioned as the 'Lot 49' of the title) and the events depicted in the (fictional) Jacobean play by Richard Wharfinger that lies at the heart of the novel, entitled *The Courier's Tragedy*. These associations come together in a set of resonances, which are focused through Oedipa's paranoid sensitivity, and which are embalmed, like a blueprint or code, in Wharfinger's play, the fiction within the fiction. At a climactic point in *The Courier's Tragedy*, the bones of a slaughtered unit of soldiers (the 'Lost Guard of Faggio', which are also the bones of the American GIs killed in Europe, which Inverarity has purchased to decorate the bottom of a lake in one of his Californian tourist attractions) are harnessed by the evil Duke Angelo and burned to make charcoal, which is in turn made into ink, the material from which, of course, words are made. This bony ink, Wharfinger tells us, has a magical quality, which means that any words written in that ink cannot lie but must reveal the truth of the world, hidden beneath its falsity. The coming together of slaughtered bodies with the ink that tells their story amounts, Angelo says, to

> A wedlock whose sole child is miracle:
> A life's base lie, rewritten into truth. (p. 54)

This is, of course, a version of Arrabal's anarchist miracle, and it is brought about by the triumph of language over history, of word over world. The machinations of the 'Trystero' that lie at the heart of the novel, that are the kernel of the WASTE network, are secreted in informational codes written in magic ink, codes that Oedipa feels she must reveal by stripping away the material of the world, as she strips off her multiple layers of clothing in a game of strip Botticelli with her lawyer/lover Metzger at the opening of the novel. It is 'as if', Oedipa thinks, the 'gowns, net bras, jeweled garters and G-strings of historical figuration that would fall away were layered as dense as Oedipa's own street-clothes in that game with Metzger', 'as if a plunge towards dawn indefinite black hours long would indeed be necessary before the Trystero could be revealed in its terrible nakedness'

(p. 37). To approach the truth of the Trystero is to strip away the surface, to discover a naked world, shorn of what Flaubert calls 'external attachments', made only of transparent, self-referring language;[38] but if this is the fantasy of a worldless word that drives the novel – a word that *becomes* its own world – what one can see everywhere in the novel is the movement of a counter-logic, which suggests that the shifting relation between word and world does not free information from material but rather delivers it to a different kind of materiality, a different relation between word, ink and bone, that is yet to be understood or mapped. The WASTE mail network is an acronym, of course, spelling out 'We Await Silently Trystero's Empire'; but it never stops suggesting the dead materiality of 'waste', that most substantial of substances that Julia Kristeva has theorised as the 'abject'.[39] To make subjects of ourselves, to transform our naked material being into animate personhood, requires us to engage with the waste product, requires us to oversee the distinction between that part of our bodies that we can accommodate within the economy of our live being and that part which we eject (excrement, vomit, nail clippings, hair), which we banish from the realm of proper being, as part of the effort of self-determination.

The discovery of the WASTE network, underlying our being in the world, offering another way of bringing it to thought, thus sits at a strange junction in the novel between sublimation and reification. WASTE offers to transform world into word, but only by bringing it into a new contact with the thing that is discarded (an odd, twisty proposition that is given its fullest articulation in DeLillo's great novel of waste management, *Underworld*); and the way that the novel imagines this junction between word and thing is as a fugitive tension, everywhere in discreet evidence, between the simulacrum and the prosthetic. Even in that first image of the novel, as Oedipa falls into the vertiginous swirls of Varo's painting, we can see the mark of this tension. The embroidered tapestry offers an escape from the tower of self, Oedipa thinks, only by recognising that the tower of the self *is* the world, that the inside of the whale is also its outside; but if this is so, if the means by which Pierce offers an escape from the tower are simulacral, then they are also prosthetic. Representations might offer freedom by making the world appear representational, but Pierce first offers Oedipa a more material means of escape. Oedipa casts herself in the 'Rapunzel-like role of a pensive girl somehow, magically, prisoner along the pines and salt fogs of Kinneret, looking for someone to say hey, let down your hair'. When that person 'turned out to be Pierce', she says, she'd happily pulled out the pins and curlers and down it had tumbled in its whispering, dainty avalanche, only when Pierce had got maybe halfway up, her lovely hair turned, through some sinister sorcery, into a great unanchored wig, and down he fell, on his ass (p. 10).

Escape into the simulacral void is counterpoised, at this opening, to the possibility of an escape through prosthetic extension, a letting down of one's hair so that a junction might open, a living/non-living lifeline that might lead from the tower of the self into the world. And from this opening onwards, one can see this difficult opposition, moving always beneath the play of surface, blurred always by the out of focus projection. Indeed, at the very disappearing heart of the narrative, as the director of Wharfinger's play, Ralph Driblette, provides us with the novel's central image of the informational nature of reality, Oedipa names the prosthetic as the obstinately non-identical twin of the simulacrum. On the last occasion that Oedipa sees Driblette before his suicide, when she visits him to ask him how his production of *The Courier's Tragedy* touches on the 'sinister blooming of the Trystero', Driblette insists that whatever meaning the Trystero has is representational, woven purely from mind. 'The reality' of the Trystero, in so far as it has any, he says to Oedipa, 'is in *this* head. Mine. I'm the projector at the planetarium, all the closed little universe visible in the circle of that stage is coming out of my mouth, eyes, sometimes other orifices also' (p. 58).

This image haunts Oedipa and comes to stand in for her relation to her revelation. If the Trystero is Pierce's legacy, if 'it was really Pierce's attempt to leave an organised something behind after his own annihilation', then she thinks 'it was part of her duty, wasn't it, to bestow life on what persisted, to try to be what Driblette was, the dark machine in the centre of the planetarium, to bring the estate into pulsing stelliferous Meaning' (p. 60). But for Oedipa who survives, unlike Driblette who dies, bestowing life, vitality, on the codes of the Trystero involves extension, involves prosthetic addition, rather than or as well as simulacral denudation. She worries as she tries to bring the Trystero to life that perhaps she will vanish into its non-being, rather than coaxing it to join her in presence. Reflecting on Driblette's suicide, she wonders whether 'some version of herself hadn't vanished with him' (p. 124). Perhaps, she thinks, echoing the beautiful woman in Brooke-Rose's story, it will be her fate from now on to be 'betrayed and mocked by a phantom self as the amputee is by a phantom limb' (p. 124). But if this phantomising of the self is the danger of contact with the Trystero, then, like Brooke-Rose's woman, Oedipa's response is to think of words themselves, narrative itself, as a kind of prosthetic material that will bring mind into contact with matter, that will effect an escape from the tower. 'Someday', she thinks, 'she might replace whatever of her had gone away by some prosthetic device, a dress of a certain colour, a phrase in a letter, another lover' (p. 124). It is through such a prosthetic (clothing, language, erotic or epistolary contact with another) that she will be able to 'reach out' from whatever informational signal was contained in Driblette's play to a shared lifeworld, to reach out from cortex to flint, 'the signal echoing down twisted miles of brain circuitry' (p. 125), down Brooke-Rose's spinothalamic tract.

It is not, then, that word has replaced world in *The Crying of Lot 49*; it is not, in terms of the discussion I staged earlier between Derrida and Stiegler, that the prosthetic has become identical to the simulacrum, both functioning as the nameless surplus, the groundless *différance*, that attends all acts of signification. Rather, Pynchon's novel suggests that word has entered, under the informational regimes of the later twentieth century, into a new relation with world, one which is very difficult to approach from within the closed circuits of literary language, but to which it is the task of the novel imagination nevertheless to bear witness. And if this shift, this emergent relation between language and matter, is registered in a delicate set of retunings in early Pynchon that are difficult to see and easy to mistake for the collapse of material into language *tout court*, then in Morrison's novel the expression of this shift, this redistribution, is its central concern, its political and poetic vocation. Even as Morrison traces the logic that collapses our lifeworlds into representational forms, life into likeness – and even as she generates a certain energy from that collapse – *The Bluest Eye* stands as a fierce rebuke to the organisation of the specular, as it tends to be associated with what she calls 'whiteness as ideology'.[40] The novel turns around the recognition that the cultural logic which leads Pecola to identify with an ideal of white beauty is part of a broader conjunction between a simulacral, self-referring lifeworld and a form of compulsory whiteness, one which cannot account for the 'participation' of what Morrison calls the 'black body' in the 'dominant cultural body'.[41] 'Black matter', she suggests, under this regime, becomes estranged, non-expressive, 'static', a form of 'disruptive darkness' which cannot find expression in the discursive forms in which subjects recognise themselves and the world.[42]

As so often in the history of the novel as I have traced it here, the central figure in which Morrison expresses this transformed relation between language and matter is that of the hand. The novel develops a fascination with the ways in which hands – as well as arms, legs, feet – achieve their agency in the world or sustain the pillar of being, as Brooke-Rose's woman thinks of her missing foot as 'bearing the whole weight of her existence in upright position on that structure of bone flesh fibre skin'. The hand in *The Bluest Eye* is divided always between two regimes – between the scopic, the simulacral on the one hand and the material, the embodied on the other – neither of which is able to give rise to fully animated selfhood, under conditions in which the relationship between discursive practices and material being has become inoperative. One can see this tension at work when Darlene's hands, in her lovemaking with Cholly, shift from their function as the bearer of a loving touch to alien prostheses in the beam of the white men's flashlight – as, 'covering her face in the moon and lamp-light', they come to resemble 'baby claws'. Or one can see this same shifting relation to the limb, to the appendage, as Cholly, in his youth, sets out to find the father he had never known. Cholly travels to the town in which he discovers his father is living; after making enquiries he is finally told that that his father is one of a huddle of men playing dice in the street. Regarding the group of strangers before him, Cholly tries to identify his father through some mode of likeness or sameness, through some kind of like-line. 'How would he know him?' he thinks, 'Would he look like a larger version of himself? At that moment Cholly could not remember what his own self looked like' (p. 152). To look for his parent is to search for some unknown version of his own being; then, as he understands that the man standing right in front of him is his father, the narrative offers an extraordinary twining together of father and son in which it is unclear whose being is whose, whose voice, whose hands are whose. 'There was his father', Cholly thinks, 'A man like any other man, but there indeed were his eyes, his mouth, his whole head. His shoulders lurked beneath that jacket, his voice, his hands – all real. They existed, really existed, some-where' (p. 153). As Cholly regards his father here, the possibility of a recovered familial relation seems at once to divide and to re-instantiate his personhood. His eyes, his voice, his hands – the 'his' names the astonishingly real attributes of the lost father, standing here in front of the transfigured son; it also, of course, names Cholly's own eyes, voice and hands, which, copied in his father's, prove the reality of the link between them (as Burney's Evelina proves her relation to her mother by bearing a perfect copy of her face)[43]. Standing before his father, Cholly sees his own hands, hears his own voice. These hands, like Christine Brooke-Rose's foot, miraculously 'existed' – 'an object. Outside myself' (p. 49). In seeing his own body materialised, reified, in that of another, Cholly can feel himself becoming, can feel the knitting of a bond between his own biomaterial and the transgenerational narrative that might account for it, might animate it. But the father's brutal response to his hesitant, devoted approach – 'get the fuck outta my face' – casts Cholly back into leaden estrangement from self, undoes that work of self-materialising that was shyly beginning as Cholly recognises his own hands in those of another. 'Cholly was a long time picking his foot up from the ground', the narrator says. 'He was trying to back up and walk away. Only with extreme effort could he get the first muscle to cooperate' (p. 154).

It is this failure to match, this continually opening gulf between the prosthetic matter of the black, labouring body and the scopic, simulacral forms in which it comes to visibility, that lies at the heart of Morrison's novel. The process of becoming involves an estrangement both from the material body that lurks somewhere beneath one's clothing and from the public forms of representation that might give that body form. This estrangement runs throughout the novel, but it comes to sharpest expression at an epiphanal moment in the narrative, one which again focuses on hands, hands as the extension of a self divided between incompatible regimes. It is one of the tragic consequences of alienated labour, the novel suggests, that the hands with which we conduct the most intimate offices are the same hands as those which are enlisted to work for others:

> The hands that felled trees also cut umbilical cords; the hands that wrung the necks of chickens and butchered hogs also nudged African violets into bloom; the arms that loaded sheaves, bales and sacks rocked babies into sleep. They patted biscuits into flaky ovals of innocence and shrouded the dead. They plowed all day and came home to nestle like plums under the limbs of their men. The legs that straddled a mule's back were the same ones that straddled their men's hips. And the difference was all the difference there was. (p. 136)

The currents that run through this novel that flow towards self-ownership, that give expression to an embodied presence, are here opposed directly to that counter-flow, leading to the alienated hand, the hand set aside from itself by the ideology of whiteness. But if this is so, what is so striking about this passage – about this novel as a whole – is that it refuses to offer a picture of a black body at one with itself, as an available antidote to the simulacral bodies that are imposed upon Pecloa, upon Cholly. This alienation, the loss of the real hand, cannot be resisted by the kind of dogmatic materialism that we find in Orwell – by insisting that two plus two equals four, or by a naïve faith in the capacity of language to mean what it says. Rather, the passage puts into motion a subtle opposition between likeness and difference that has a rich grounding in the history of the novel as I have traced it here, and that is Morrison's response to the broken relation between idea and material in the midst of which her subjects come to consciousness. 'The hands that felled trees also cut umbilical cords': the attachment between the hand and the hand – between the hand that labours for others and the hand that brings a new generation into the world – is sustained by a version of Maureen's 'like-line', but here materialised as the secret living tissue that holds us to ourselves and to others, a fugitive bond that cannot come to expression, that can only make itself felt as a prosthetic difference stubbornly at work in the expression of the simulacral, of the self-referring, of the tautological self-same. As Pecola finds that she 'would see only what there was to see' (p. 45), so the difference between the hand as it is owned by the self and the hand as it is owned by the abusive other falls into asymmetrical tautology, in which 'the difference was all the difference there was.' To give expression to this salvational difference, moving within the lines of likeness, requires us, Morrison suggests, to rise to the challenge that is posed earlier in the history of the novel by Herman Melville, in his own critique of the ideology of whiteness – requires us to undertake, like Melville, what Morrison calls the 'effort to say something unsayable'.[44] Morrison suggests that it is in *Moby Dick* that Melville works hardest to give this unspeakable difference a voice: 'It was the whiteness of the whale that above all things appalled me', Melville writes in Morrison's quotation, 'I almost despair of putting it in a comprehensive form' (p. 143). To capture the whiteness of the whale, Morrison suggests, is to approach an unspeakable, unpicturable 'whiteness' at work, like the beam of the torch that worms its way into Cholly's guts, in the very entrails of the culture – to approach the 'very concept of whiteness as an inhuman idea'.[45]

The terms in which Morrison embarks upon the effort to say the unsayable are, of course, different from those that shape Melville's encounter with the whiteness of the whale. Where Melville's prose seeks to lift the weight of an industrially produced nineteenth-century reality to open its glimmering inside narratives, Morrison's fiction, like Pynchon's, is a response to those forces – technological, political, cultural – which recreate Proust's 'real presence' as weightless simulacra.[46] But if this is so, it is also the case that Morrison's fiction still turns around that difficult limit-boundary where the sayable and the unsayable meet, where the word meets with something extrinsic to linguistic processes, that difficult passage that Stiegler traces from cortex to flint. There is a rich resonance between Morrison's differing hand here and the spectral hand in Melville, the ghostly hand that puzzles Ishmael in *Moby Dick*, the hand of black self-ownership that flickers, unsayably, in the hidden subtext of *Benito Cereno*.

Both Melville's hand and Morrison's reach towards the possibility of a differently constituted relation of representation to the biopolitical self – a mode of relation that is generated only in the novel form, only in the novel's capacity to embody what I have here called the prosthetic imagination. Morrison's novel demonstrates that in the later twentieth century as in the nineteenth, the simulacral is bound in a difficult relation to the prosthetic – even if the emergence of a postmodern cultural dominant makes such a relation extraordinarily difficult to see. It is the task of the novelist under these conditions to reach for the ways in which matter clings to narrative and counter-narrative, even if this can only become expressive in the play of difference and likeness, captured in that beautifully mirrored and self dismantling phrase, 'the difference was all the difference there was.' Difference, in that wrigglingly incomplete tautology, is insistently different from difference; no speech act can become completely self-referring, no prosthesis can become completely simulacral, no identity can be identical, or 'fundamentally the same'. As Beckett puts it, in his early essay on Proust, 'the most ideal tautology presupposes a relation, and the affirmation of equality involves only an approximate identification, and by asserting unity denies unity.'[47] There is always a residue, a material difference between the specular and the fleshly hand, and it is this residue, this unsublimated passage from mind to world, that is the substance of Morrison's fiction, the unspoken substrate of the unspeakable.

It is this prosthetic substance, at work in Morrison's engagement with the simulacrum, that stands as the corrective to our understanding of what we have called the 'postmodern novel'. The meaning of this term (which was always in any case uncertain) has become increasingly obscure in the first decades of the twenty-first century, as critical thinking, across the disciplines, has been preoccupied with theorising the end of postmodernism – with formulating the perception, everywhere felt, that postmodern forms no longer have the explanatory power that they exhibited through the last decades of the twentieth century. Much of the energy of this thinking has turned around the attempt to conceptualise an aftermath to postmodernism, to imagine how a movement that casts the question of origins and termini into such doubt can itself reach a conclusion. How do we imagine that the post, already bound up with the experience of supersession, can itself be superseded? Is it possible, in imagining such an aftermath, to avoid the preponderance, the multiplication of 'posts', which casts us into the reverse *déjà vu* of an endless postness – the post-postmodernism that threatens us with the spectre of infinite regress?[48] My response to this predicament – the response that is implied by the delicate but stubborn persistence of the difference between the simulacrum and the prosthetic in the later twentieth-century novel – is to suggest that the question of the aftermath to postmodernism is itself a false question, the wrong question to ask. It is not, I think, that postmodernism came and went, rose and fell. Rather, the moment of Jameson's 'full postmodernism', understood as the triumph of the simulacral over the material won by the joint operations of finance capital and information technology; this moment never came. The novel of the later twentieth century does not, I would suggest, yield to an informational world, a world where the image holds sway over the real. Rather, the novel, across its expressive range, from Orwell to Selvon to Brooke-Rose, from Morrison to Pynchon to DeLillo, turns around the junction between a world which has become like its representations, and one which remains different from them. It is this stubborn junction – native to the novel form as I have anatomised it here from More to the present – that the critical languages of postmodernism tended to obscure. It is the recovery of this junction that allows us to re-see the ways in which the legacies of modernism and realism play out across the last decades of the twentieth century and to reimagine the way that the novel has shaped the lifeworlds of modernity as they are transformed by contemporary technicity.

CHAPTER 9

Prosthetic Worlds in the Twenty-First-Century Novel

Only stones desire nothing. And who knows, perhaps in stones there are also holes we have never discovered.

J. M. Coetzee, *The Heart of the Country*[1]

Unless stones have being. Unless there's some profoundly mystical shift that places being in a stone.

Don DeLillo, *Point Omega*[2]

Is this the world as it truly looks?

Don DeLillo, *Zero K*[3]

9.1 World, Nature, Culture

How do we picture the world? What amalgam of abstract idea and thrown being, of fact and imagination, of blind circumstance and structured forethought, constitutes the experience of enworlding?

This question has been at stake in everything I have said in this book so far. The account of the novel that I have given here has traced the means by which what I have called the prosthetic imagination has acted as a connective structure that binds mind into world, that forges that amalgam between idea and material that is the condition of enworlding. From Thomas More's *Utopia* onwards, I have suggested, the novel imagination serves as a kind of bridge, attaching consciousness to material, joining the living and the dead, in such a way that we are able to house our being in the space of a shared world, a world animated by thought, a world made habitable for us and by us. More builds a delicate bridge between England and Utopia, a bridge woven out of the warp and weft of fact and fiction, a bridge that joins the fictional More to his counterpart Raphael, London to its shadow image Amaurot. This is a bridge that is modelled on the double helix at the heart of More's text – made at once of the real bridge that crosses the sixteenth-century Thames and the

imaginary bridge that crosses the fictional river in More's best of all
possible worlds – the river Anyder, which owes its utopian charge, its
capacity to enliven and purify the polluted waters of the sixteenth-century
Thames, to the waterlessness that is carried in its Greek compound name.
It is in doing so, in joining what is here – what Aphra Behn in *Oroonoko*
calls the 'little inch of the world' before us – to the possible worlds that
surround us in all their latency, that the novel partakes in the process of
world making.[4] From Thomas More's *Utopia* to Samuel Beckett's
Worstward Ho, I have traced the process by which the novel generates
emplacement from the picturing of no places, by exercising its particular
capacity to 'say' a 'place', as Beckett puts it, 'where none', 'a body. Where
none'.[5] The bridge in More's *Utopia*, the bridge in Cervantes' *Don Quixote*
that joins the living to the dead, the 'false bridge' of Tristram Shandy's
prosthetic nose at the opening of *Tristram Shandy* (p. 170) – these earlier
connective forms live on in Beckett as the thin sheet of skin or of paper that
brings mind into contact with world – the ear drum that the Unnamable
feels himself to be – a sheet of skin made of words stretched taut between
thought and thing. 'Perhaps that's what I feel', the unnamable narrator
says, 'I'm the tympanum, on the one hand the mind, on the other the
world.'[6] 'I'm in words, made of words'; but these are words that materialise
narrative being, enworld it. 'I'm made of words', the narrator says, 'the
place too, the air, the walls, the floor, the ceiling, all words, the whole world
is here with me' (p. 390).

The history of the novel as I have characterised it here is partly the
history of this model of world picturing, this capacity of a worded form to
bring the world into a human shape, to allow material to take on the
prosthetic forms that make it amenable to human activities. But if this is so,
we are living now at a time when the stakes of world picturing – and the
correspondence between word and world – have been suddenly, dramatically altered. The history of the novel has coincided with the history of
what Martin Heidegger calls 'The Age of the World Picture'.[7] 'The
fundamental event of the modern age', Heidegger writes in 1938, 'is the
conquest of the world as picture' (p. 134). In producing such a picture, such
a 'structured image', he goes on, 'man contends for the position in which
he can be that particular being who gives the measure and draws up the
guidelines for everything that is' (p. 134). It is this conception of the world
picture that underlies Heidegger's famous categorisation of being in terms
of human, animal and stone. In *The Fundamental Concepts of Metaphysics*,
he sets out to address the question 'what is world' – to 'delimit in
a provisional manner what we should understand by the term *world* in

general' – by advancing his thesis that 'the stone is worldless, the animal is poor in world, man is world-forming.'[8] It is 'his' forming of world as picture that places 'man in the midst of all that is'[9] – and that leads Heidegger to the later claim that 'man alone exists.' 'Rocks are', Heidegger writes, 'but they do not exist. Trees are, but they do not exist. Horses are, but they do not exist.'[10] It is easy to see that the novel has participated in this world-forming project, this anthropocentric organisation of being. One has only to consider the 'pregnant little fact' that an 'eminent philosopher among my friends' demonstrates to the narrator of George Eliot's *Middlemarch*. 'Your pier-glass', the narrator says,

> or extensive surface of polished steel made to be rubbed in all directions by a housemaid, will be minutely and multitudinously scratched in all directions; but place now against it a lighted candle as a centre of illumination, and lo! The scratches will seem to arrange themselves in a fine series of concentric circles round that little sun. (p. 264)

The human, in this analogy, is the sun, the 'egoism' that makes the world into a picture, that gives it its concentric shape. But, as I have said, our own time has seen the arrival of a differently constituted world – one that is shaped around a different centre, and in accordance with the logic of a new geological era, the era that we have come to call the Anthropocene. It has become apparent, in the first decades of the twenty-first century, that the processes that have allowed us to make the world into a picture have had an unanticipated and devastating effect on that world, an effect which we now recognise as climate change.

This eventuality, this transformation, is having a series of contradictory effects on our understanding both of the human and of the ways in which the human is related to the world. At the heart of these contradictions is the paradoxical predicament in which the dominance of humankind over the environment that is manifest in the phenomenon of climate change opens onto its opposite – the collapse of the very foundation upon which we have erected our conception of human agency. The age of the world picture, as Heidegger conceives of it, is an age in which human cultural operations unfold against the background of an environment – a nature – that is larger than the culture it sustained, and indifferent to it. When the stevedore Eugenio, in J. M. Coetzee's 2013 novel *The Childhood of Jesus*, opposes 'climate' to 'history', it is this magisterial indifference that he insists upon. 'Let us compare history with climate', he says, 'The climate we live in, we can agree, is greater than we. None of us can ordain what the climate shall be.'[11] It is this relation between climate and history that is at the heart of

Dipesh Chakrabarty's influential 2009 essay 'The Climate of History' (which is perhaps a quiet reference point for Coetzee's Eugenio). Throughout the history of modernity, Charkrabarty argues, humans have been able to dominate their environment precisely because human activity, human culture, has had no discernable impact on that environment itself. In an echo of Heidegger's denial that stones have world, or that rocks exist, Chakrabarty traces the process by which both the natural sciences and the humanities have accorded the environment meaning by absorbing it into an epistemological system from which it nevertheless remains detached. Reading the dialogue between the historian R. G. Collingwood and the philosopher Benedetto Croce, Chakrabarty suggests that these thinkers inherit and exemplify the long tendency for the relation between human and world to be mapped onto an unbroken boundary between an unhistorical nature and a historical culture. Just as for Collingwood it was necessary to distinguish between the natural body which is not historical and the social body which is ('only the history of the social construction of the body, not the history of the body as such, can be studied'), so Croce insists that the natural environment becomes historical only as it is converted by humans into social material.[12] For Croce, Chakrabarty writes, 'all material objects were subsumed into human thought. No rocks, for example, existed in themselves' (p. 203). Both Croce and Collingwood, Chakrabarty goes on, 'enfold nature' into 'purposive human action'. 'What exists beyond that' – beyond the realm of purposive human action – 'does not "exist" because it does not exist for humans in any meaningful sense' (p. 203). In a further paradox, it is thus the strict limits of the human's relation to nature that allows culture to dominate nature, human to form world. We can only frame the distinction between what is inert and what is purposive, what is living and what is dead, what is real and what is artificial, by reference to the human enfolding of nature into culture. Thus it is only when things become imbued with a human quality – only when we draw things as they are in the world into their role in human action – that we can recognise them as natural. Reality as it 'exists' is an effect of its relation with artifice, with 'human-made' culture, a relation overseen by a human assemblage that is itself an odd amalgam of thought and thing, itself part thingly body resistant to historicity and part rational being which partakes of the ideal.

The boundary between the cultural and the natural is what has granted culture its ascendancy over nature; but, Chakrabarty suggests, the arrival of the Anthropocene has put that boundary under erasure. It is the first of the 'four theses' he advances in 'The Climate of history' that climate change 'spell[s] the collapse of the age-old humanist distinction between natural history and human history' (p. 201). He quotes Naomi Oreskes' argument that while 'for centuries scientists thought that earth processes were so large and powerful that nothing we could do could change them' – that 'human chronologies were insignificant compared with the vastness of geological time' – we have lately come to recognise this is no longer the case: 'There are now so many of us cutting down so many trees and burning so many tons of fossil fuels that we have indeed become geological agents.'[13] We now act upon and transform the environment, rather than simply converting it into a form that makes it purposive for us, and with this shift we have broken through the dividing wall between the human and the natural – the dividing wall that granted us our world-forming power. 'Humans are a force of nature in the geological sense', Chakrabarty writes, 'A fundamental assumption of Western (and now universal) political thought has come undone in this crisis' (p. 207). The 'wall' that divided human from world has been 'breached' (p. 221); as a result, human has leaked into world, entered into a new material relation with it that does not obey the epistemological frames within which we have understood our relation to our environments – the terms of our dwelling.

This transformation, for Chakrabarty and for a new wave of environmental thought that has been influenced by him, requires us fundamentally to rethink the way that we understand our forms of representation and our conception of the political and discursive sphere. It has led, for theorists such as Wai Chee Dimock, Ursula Heise, Timothy Clark, Amy Elias, Timothy Morton and Christian Moraru, to what has been called a 'planetary turn' in critical thinking, which demands that we retune our sense of scale and our understanding of the ways in which political cultures are enworlded.[14] 'The discourse of planetarity', Elias and Moraru write in the introduction to their 2015 work *The Planetary Turn*, 'presents itself, in response to the twenty-first -century world and the decreasing ability of the postmodern theoretical apparatus to account for it, as a new *structure of awareness*, as a methodical receptivity to the *geothematics of planetariness*'.[15] 'In this emerging worldview', they go on, 'the planet as a living organism, as a shared ecology, and as an incrementally integrated system both embracing and rechanneling the currents of modernity is the axial dimension in which writers and artists perceive themselves, their histories, and their aesthetic practices' (p. xii). The breaching of the wall between human and nature opens onto a radically new set of networks and rhizomes, which require us to reorient, to recompose ourselves – and which call for us, Amitav Ghosh has recently argued, to reconceive the ways in which the novel imagination has figured the relationship between the living and the dead, the inert and the animate. Climate change, Ghosh writes, has led to a scenario, familiar from the Gothic tradition, in which 'something that seems inanimate turns out to be vitally, even dangerously alive.'[16] In his hybrid critical work *The Great Derangement*, which is in close dialogue with Chakrabarty, and with Timothy Clark's seminal 2013 essay 'Derangements of Sale', Ghosh suggests that Chakrabarty's breaching of the wall between human and environment has caused our capacity to delineate clearly between the inanimate and the animate to malfunction. It has become apparent, he writes, that the conception of the environment as an indifferent background to human affairs is a delusion, restricted to the period of modernity that coincides roughly with Heidegger's age of the world picture. 'The humans of the future will surely understand', Ghosh writes, 'that only in one, very brief era, lasting less than three centuries, did a significant number of their kind believe that planets and asteroids are inert' (p. 3). 'I do believe it to be true', Ghosh writes, 'that the land . . . is demonstrably alive; that it does not exist solely, or even incidentally, as a stage for the enactment of human history' (p. 6). The land is alive, not just the dwellers on the land; this, Ghosh suggests, requires us drastically to rethink the way we have understood the role of the novel as a bridge between the living and the non-living, between mind and world. What strikes Ghosh most forcibly in *The Great Derangement* is what he sees as the failure of the novel to address the enormity of climate change, as if the apparatus that the novel has developed to cast the relations between human and world cannot adapt to new environmental challenges, cannot accommodate the great derangement. There are, he suggests, 'peculiar forms of resistance that climate change presents to what is now regarded as serious fiction', as if the 'currents of global warming' are 'too wild to be navigated in the accustomed barques of narration'. 'If certain literary forms are unable to negotiate these torrents', Ghosh writes, 'then they will have failed, and their failures will have to be counted as an aspect of the broader imaginative and cultural failure that lies at the heart of the climate crisis' (p. 8). As the fictional writer Mia Erdmann puts it, in Richard Powers' modestly devastating short story 'The Seventh Event', climate change has revealed to us a 'basic lack in how we talk about literature, and a corresponding lack in how a good deal of literature talks about the world'.[17] Fiction, she says, has 'for two centuries wallowed in the bottomless vanity that promoted the individual self to be the measure of all things. . . . We have let our shot at self awareness be bought off with a bauble' (p. 62). 'The true scale of the world,' she says, 'may be too terrifying for even the largest acts of identification to grasp'. The real ground of the world is populated by 'superbugs [that] mass in a spoon of soil in concentrations beyond anyone's ability to number. What would a literature that knew all this look like?' (pp. 63–64).

Climate change has ushered in a form of enworlding that unsettles the terms in which we have imagined our environments, and which resists the narrative apparatuses of the novel; but if this is so, it is also the case that one can see, as a response to the shifting relations that Chakrabarty traces between climate and history, the emergence in the twenty-first century of a new kind of world novel that seeks to reinvent the terms of our world picturing. This phenomenon builds, in one sense, on the category of world literature that has its origins in Goethe, and that has become, since the later twentieth century, one of the modes in which the novel has been involved in producing pictures of a post-imperial global space.[18] Novels such as Roberto Bolaño's *2666*, Leslie Marmon Silko's *Almanac of the Dead*, Karen Tei Yamashita's *I Hotel*, or Ma Jian's *Beijing Coma* have invented what Kiron Ward has recently described as a new literary encyclopedism – which in turn reaches towards what Joel Evans has theorised as a new model of totality in the wake of the expired forms of gobalisation associated with postmodern paradigms.[19] Bolaño and Silko produce new imaginative political epistemologies, and across the global novel now, from W. G. Sebald's refiguring of cultural memory and landscape, to the reshaping of the legacies of European conflict from Jonathan Littell's *The Kindly Ones* to Daša Drndic's *Belladonna*, one can see the attempt to grasp the outlines of a world emerging newly from the shaping effects of European power.[20] But if this is so, the world that starts to come to thought in the twenty-first-century novel is one which witnesses Chakrabarty's collapse of the boundary between natural history and human history – one which is formed in the shifted relation between human historico-political action and the living world in which that action unfolds. At a moment late in his vast novel *2666*, Bolaño's Fascist General Entrescu gestures towards this shifted relation, in a speech he gives at a Nazi dinner party in the depths of World War II. 'Did Jesus Christ', he asks the assembled dinner guests,

> have what we today call an idea of the world? . . . And he answered himself, no, although of course in a way having an idea of the world is easy, everybody has one, generally an idea restricted to one's village, bound to the land, to the tangible and mediocre things before one's eyes, and this idea of the world, petty, limited, crusted with the grime of the familiar, tends to persist and acquire authority and eloquence with the passage of time.[21]

What drives Bolaño's gargantuan novel is the perception that the 'idea of the world' bequeathed to us by a Judeo-Christian political mythology has lapsed, and that as a result the environments in which we dwell, which we seek to convert into worlds, have become suddenly unmappable, suddenly mobile, animate, labile. To live in this new world space, Bolaño's novel suggests, is to live in the absence of an idea of the world, in matrices of shared life that, as the character Amalfitano puts it, 'don't exist or haven't yet had time to put themselves together' (p. 189). Under these circumstances, what is needed is a new kind of narrative imagination, one which is alert to the ways in which mind has been redistributed in world, after the breaching of the barrier between culture and nature. We are required to ask again, Amalfitano thinks, after the Wittgenstein of *On Certainty*, whether 'our hand is a hand', whether our hand is animated by mind or partakes of a material that eludes the world-forming power of consciousness.[22] We are required to think like the novel's artist Edwin Johns, whose work is built on a reframing of the relation between the living and the dead, between the mimetic and the prosthetic – between, in Ghosh's terms, the 'inanimate' and the 'vitally, even dangerously alive'. At the heart of *2666* is an artwork that attempts precisely this reframing – Edwin Johns' painterly response to Wittgenstein's question of whether a hand is a hand. His 'masterpiece', the narrator says, 'was an ellipsis of self-portraits, sometimes a spiral of self-portraits . . . in the center of which hung the painter's mummified right hand' (p. 53). If *2666* is interested, above all, in a redistribution of life in material, then this artwork is the talisman of this redistribution, a work in which – in a mirror image of the *tableau vivant* – the living artist has become the dead matter of the artwork. As the literary critic Morini discovers when he visits the painter in a mental asylum, Johns takes to wearing a prosthetic hand to replace his amputated painting hand, the amputated hand that has become the artwork. 'Where there should have only been emptiness', Morini observes, 'a hand emerged from Johns' jacket cuff, plastic of course, but so well made that only a careful and informed observer could tell it was artificial' (p. 89). Johns' hand here becomes prosthetic, 'lifelike', as life passes from the painter's hand to the painted, from the living hand to the aesthetic representation – as Bolaño's novel follows the migration of thought across the broken boundary between nature and culture.

9.2   Hand, Face, Wall

For Bolaño in *2666*, and for a wide range of writers working in the current century, it is this perception that the world is happening now in hybrid ecological spaces that do not obey our inherited conception of the distinction between the living and the dead, the real and the artificial, that is key to the task of contemporary enworlding. Take for example three of the writers who have been most influential in shifting our modes of world seeing from a twentieth- to a twenty-first-century frame – Margaret Atwood, Don DeLillo and J. M. Coetzee. All three writers are centrally concerned with the possibility that the task of building a bridge between mind and world has been fundamentally reconfigured under contemporary conditions. 'There is first of all the problem of the opening', Coetzee's narrator writes at the start of *Elizabeth Costello* (2003), 'namely, how to get us from where we are, which is, as yet, nowhere, to the far bank'.[23] 'It is a simple bridging problem, a problem of knocking together a bridge', the narrator goes on, catching an echo, perhaps, of Heidegger's seminal essay 'Building Dwelling Thinking'. 'The bridge', Heidegger says in that essay, 'does not just connect banks that are already there'. 'The banks emerge as banks only as the bridge crosses the stream'; 'it brings stream and bank and land into each other's neighbourhood. The bridge *gathers* the earth as landscape around the stream.'[24] For Heidegger, it is the built structure, the world-forming bridge, that gathers the earth into worldedness; but for Coetzee, as in different ways for DeLillo and Atwood, this capacity of the bridge to materialise the banks, to get us from the nowhere we are nevertheless in to the far bank, has lately faltered. The narrative voice that opens *Elizabeth Costello*, in reflecting on its own need to 'knock up a bridge' which brings voice into contact with word and world, has already, from that outset, cast itself into a certain disjunction, a certain nowhere discernable within the workings of voice itself. And with this failure, for all three writers, the mimetic apparatus of the novel – its capacity to penetrate into a subjective interiority while bringing that interiority into contact with shared external realities – has also failed, become inoperable.

In Atwood's dystopian fictions of the twenty-first century – *Oryx and Crake, Year of the Flood, Madaddam* – this failure turns around a series of collapsed boundaries that map onto Chakrabarty's broken distinction between nature and culture. *Oryx and Crake*, the first instalment of the *Madaddam* trilogy, dramatises this collapse by bringing together two of the forces that are shifting the terms in which we have understood the limit boundary between the natural and the cultural – that is biomedical genetic engineering on the one hand and ecological crisis on the other. The premise of Atwood's novel is that the emergence of artificially enhanced biomaterial will lead to the prosthetisation both of the human and of the environment. The novel imagines the process by which sophisticated gene-splicing techniques allow for the production of artificial life – both hybridised nonhuman animal life and enhanced human life. It traces the logic whereby the production of these prosthetic versions of ourselves leads, inexorably, to the creation of entirely artificial humans – here a race of perfectly adapted posthumans named 'Crakers'. And its imaginative proposition is that with the artificiality of the human, the environment itself becomes prosthetised, takes on an untaxonomised materiality that is the result of the failed distinction between nature and culture, the real and the artificial. The novel opens with an image of this prosthetic world – an afterimage of Beckett's *Imagination Dead Imagine*, which also seeks to picture a world that persists after the faculty of human world picturing has died. 'Islands, waters, azure, verdure, one glimpse and vanished, endlessly, omit', Beckett's text reads;[25] and Atwood's novel opens with a rhymed picture of the world as an environment that no longer fits within a human frame, that has outlasted the death of the imagination. 'The sea is hot metal', the narrator says, 'the sky a bleached blue, except for the hole burnt in it by the sun. Everything is so empty. Water, sand, sky, trees, fragments of past time'.[26] This is a world which we should not be here to see, a world which no longer accords to the chronologies, the histories, of the human agent that has despoiled it. The putative last human being, the novel's protagonist 'Snowman', is an anomaly left behind to witness this spectacle of a shorn world, in accordance with the tradition of apocalyptic dystopias since Mary Shelley's 1826 novel *The Last Man*. Just as the father in Cormac McCarthy's *The Road* is granted a bare vision of the 'absolute truth of the world', the 'cold relentless circling of the intestate earth', so Atwood's Snowman is able to see a world revealed, because drained of human meaning. Both Atwood's Snowman and McCarthy's father are faced with the prospect that, as McCarthy's narrator puts it, 'in the world's destruction it would be possible at last to see how it was made.'[27]

Oryx and Crake opens with a depiction of a denuded, revealed planet; but the way that the novel tests its capacity to picture this 'extraterrestrial' landscape is by interleaving the picture of a posthuman environment after the catastrophe with the story of the human, political events leading up to it. The perspective of the post-apocalyptic protagonist – Snowman – is entwined with that of his younger self – Jimmy – whose life is bound up with Crake's, the deranged genius who is responsible for the apocalypse. In accordance, again, with established dystopian traditions, it is this gap between before and after, human and posthuman, that grants the novel its critical purchase, a purchase that stands also as a verdict on the lapsing of the narrative forms that might allow us to conceive of eco-catastrophe – what

Ghosh thinks of as the peculiar inadequacy of prose fiction to the critical demands of climate change. A central preoccupation of the chapters describing 'before' that follow the progress towards catastrophe is the condition of Jimmy's 'interiority', the drama of the private life that it has been the central vocation of the novel to reveal. In a peculiar but familiar derangement of scale, the story of the end of the world doubles as the story of the protagonist's personal moral failings, a story which begins at the micro level with a family estrangement. Jimmy's relation to his inner life, the narrative suggests, is thwarted by the failure, when he was a child, of his parents' marriage. In a trope that recurs in variations throughout the novel, Jimmy feels that there is a person inside him, a version of self that his warring parents could not see. 'They knew nothing about him', Jimmy thinks of his parents, 'what he liked, what he hated, what he longed for. They thought he was only what they could see. . . . About the different, secret person living inside of him they knew nothing at all' (p. 91). This secret being lies buried beneath the forms in which it pictures itself and as a result becomes corrupted, perverse. It is this hidden, thwarted, desiring self that the title character Oryx recognises in Jimmy, that she can see into even as Jimmy first encounters her online – when he watches her as a young child acting in a pornographic film. 'She smiled a hard little smile', Jimmy thinks, as he watches on his computer, spellbound, 'and wiped the whipped cream from her mouth. Then she looked over her shoulder and into the eyes of the viewer – right into Jimmy's eyes, into the secret person inside him' (p. 104).

The question of Jimmy's self-relation – his fear that there might be a monster inside him, a 'fanged animal gazing out from the shadowy cave inside his own skull' (p. 307) – returns throughout the novel. But the novelistic structure that allows us to calibrate this relation, that pitches inside against outside, before against after, that makes these distinctions purposive, is precisely that which the novel's thought experiment brings to the brink of collapse. The plot of the novel, its propulsive logic, leads us to the narrative fold where before meets with after, where Jimmy meets with Snowman; but when we get there, we realise that it is precisely this continuity between past and future, and between the inside and the outside of being, that is dismantled by eco-catastrophe, and by the emergence of artificial life. 'The discipline of history', Chakrabarty writes, 'exists on the assumption that our past, present, and future are connected by a certain continuity of human experience. We normally envisage the future with the help of the same faculty that allows us to picture the past.' Eco-crisis, though, he argues, has 'precipitated a sense of the present that disconnects the future from the past by putting the future beyond the grasp of historical sensibility' (p. 197); it is precisely this present, no longer bridging the gap between past and future but falling into unspatialised ahistoricity, that is the ground of Atwood's novel – a prosthetised ground which does not conform to the rhetoric of before and after, inside and outside. As we arrive at the generic plot point at which Crake's experiment lays waste to the human population, the narrative dwells on the failure of the forms (both material and rhetorical) that allow us to demarcate the interior from the exterior. The post-apocalyptic terrain is teeming with a variegated life, a proliferating flora and fauna in which the artificial and the natural are entirely indistinguishable, and which is contained by no human building, dwelling or thinking. This is an environment in which, the narrator says, 'doors and windows have ceased to have meaning' (p. 412), an environment before which the novel's secreting of private selves in shadowy caves becomes suddenly irrelevant. Jimmy associates doors and thresholds with his parents' failed marriage – the slamming of the door indicating the climax of an argument. 'There was always a wind when the door got slammed', the young Jimmy thinks, 'a small puff – whuff! – right in his ears' (p. 19). But the only door that remains, when Jimmy becomes Snowman, is the 'airlock' that seals the laboratory ('Paradice') in which the Crakers are preserved in their Edenic state. The airlock, Jimmy notes nervously as he first enters Paradice, 'closed with a whuff behind them' (p. 351) ('Whuff, goes the wind in his ear, a door closing' (p. 325)). The airlock is the residue of Jimmy's parents' marriage; it is also the sealed space in which, on the day of the disaster, Oryx and Crake are left to die, and which stands as a last testament to the barrier between nature and culture that has enabled the history of the human, the history of the novel. The skin of the laboratory dome, the only surviving boundary in the prosthetic world, is itself alive – 'made of a new mussel-adhesive/silicon/dendrite formation alloy' that 'had the capacity to both filter and breathe' (pp. 350–51) – itself partakes of the distributed mixture of the animate and inanimate that has characterised the prosthetic as I have described it throughout this book. And the posthumans that it harbours have no secret interiority, observe no distinction between the inside and outside of being. They have no hidden desire, no mythology, no history, but merge seam-lessly with the environment, their skins enacting the continuity of artificial consciousness with artificial world, rather than imposing any kind of barrier between them. They will inherit no cultural memory and occupy a future that has no historical connection with present or past. Snowman is like a castaway in this futurity – *Oryx and Crake* a species of Robinsonade – but a castaway who has no posterity to which to bequeath his experience.

'Even a castaway assumes a future reader', he thinks, 'someone who'll come along later and find his bones and his ledger'. Snowman, though, will 'have no future reader, because the Crakers can't read' (pp. 45–46).

Atwood draws on the utopian and dystopian traditions, reaching from Mary Shelley, to Charlotte Perkins Gilman, to Yevgeny Zamyatin, Aldous Huxley and George Orwell, to give expression to this collapse of the relation between culture and nature – to imagine the kind of world such a collapse would inaugurate. The later work of Coetzee and DeLillo responds, too, to this same phenomenon, this arrival to thought of a prosthetic world that results from the folding of culture into nature; but they do so by drawing on a different tradition, by extending the legacies of prose realism past that threshold that is marked by Beckett's stretched finitudes, and by bringing the dismantled modernist apparatus bequeathed to them by Beckett into contact with a world that is moving beyond the grasp of the novel imagination.

Coetzee's cryptic, estranged late novels, *The Childhood of Jesus* and *The Schooldays of Jesus*, for example, are a response to the question posed at the opening of *Elizabeth Costello* – how to build a bridge out of prose, how to bring the banks of a human sensorium into being through an act of the imagination, when the relation between human and world has become unthinkable. Where *Costello* ends with the Kafkan parable 'At the Gate', in which Elizabeth Costello finds herself in some kind of post-mortem purgatory, waiting to pass from this world to the next, the *Jesus* novels are set in their entirety in this limbo, this disjunct, untuned world, amalgam of the living and the dead, an in-between space, some kind of median or meridian. The people of this world – the protagonist Simón, his child or Godson David, David's adoptive mother Inés – find themselves 'washed clean' of their former lives, having to orient themselves to a new life, without history, without culture, without mythology. This limbo life, like the life of Atwood's artificial Crakers, is incompatible with the secret interiority in which we have preserved our sense of the human – humanity shaped by desire, by a future time still to come, by the missing element that inhabits all acts of reflection, of signification, of becoming. This is a world, in a late-Wittgensteinian phrase that recurs throughout the *Jesus* novels, in which 'nothing is missing.' Simón's friend Elena tells him that everyone in this new land – a land named 'Novilla' in part for its newness – 'has put together a new life, a life from which she claims – with justice? – that nothing is missing'.[28] This is a world, Simón is repeatedly told, in which he will have to overcome his infatuation with thought, passion, longing, hope, and adapt himself to the passive regime of what is called 'the thing itself'

(p. 113). Passion, Elena tells Simón (quietly quoting Wittgenstein's preface to the *Philosophical Investigations*), 'is an old way of thinking':[29]

> In the old way of thinking, no matter how much you may have, there is always something missing. The name you choose to give this *something-more* that is missing is passion. ... This endless dissatisfaction, this yearning for the some-thing more that is missing, is a way of thinking we are well rid of, in my opinion. *Nothing is missing.* (p. 63)

The *Jesus* novels offer us a picture of this replete world, a world inert with its own fullness, a world in which consciousness has become immersed in material. This is the world presaged at the close of *Elizabeth Costello*, as Costello finds herself 'at the gate', preparing the confession that might allow her to pass to the other side. Her confession consists of a picture of life distributed in the landscape, as if it is only this recognition of unbound being that will free her from her limbo state. There are frogs, she tells the guardians of the gate, that bury themselves in the mud of the Dulgannon river throughout the dry season, passing into a state of suspended animation in which they temporarily die – 'their heartbeat slows, their breathing stops, they turn the colour of mud' (p. 216) – waiting for the rains to come and revive them. When the rains do come, the frogs rejoice – 'the dead awake', and 'their voices resound again in joyous exaltation beneath the vault of the heavens' (p. 216). But the image that Costello dwells on is not this riotous reincarnation, but the silent diffusion of suspended animal life in the mud. 'She thinks of the frogs beneath the earth', Costello says, she thinks of 'the fingers of their hands, fingers that end in little balls, soft, wet, mucous':

> She thinks of the mud eating away at the tips of those fingers, trying to absorb them, to dissolve the soft tissue till no one can tell any longer (certainly not the frog itself, lost as it is in the cold sleep of hibernation) what is earth, what is flesh. Yes, that she can believe in. (p. 220)

Coetzee's late work is driven by this encounter with being radically distributed in world, outside the terms of human exceptionalism – a distribution powerfully captured in those frog's hands (is this hand a hand?) merging with the earth. And DeLillo's work, too, since his expansive 1997 work *Underworld*, has dedicated itself to crafting a spare imagery of strangely living material, of consciousness merged with the environment. *The Body Artist*, *Point Omega*, *Zero K*, these are novels which are built around an examined membrane, a filmy skin, that stands between a literary mind passing beyond the terms of its own self-congress and an environment that no longer submits to the forms in which we have pictured it. *Point Omega* opens and closes with set pieces staged in a gallery space in New York City showing Douglas Gordon's installation art work '24 Hour Psycho' – set pieces bracketing the main body of the narrative, set in the lost depths of the desert, which follows the relation between a film-maker Jim Finlay, an intellectual Elster and his daughter Jessie. All of the thinking in the novel is framed by this relation, between the city at the novel's margins and the desert at its centre, between film time and geological time. Gordon's installation consists of a free-standing screen positioned in the centre of the gallery space, upon which Hitchcock's *Psycho* is projected, stripped of a soundtrack, slowed to two frames per second and stretched over twenty-four hours. The opening and closing of DeLillo's novel – in seeing the installation through the eyes of an unnamed man who watches the film obsessively, standing against the far wall, hours a day – seeks to tune itself to the peculiar temporality and spatiality that the artwork affords, the possibility that it might initiate us into a world of pure film, a world made of slowed, lifted time spun from projected mindlight, shining on a translucent screen thinner than skin or page. The slowed film opens passages, the watching man thinks, into the weightless insides of things, into the seams where the world is bound together, the 'slightest camera movement' a 'profound shift in space and time'.[30] The film reveals, he thinks – as he watches Janet Leigh during the famous shower scene, icily ensnared in 'the detailed process of not knowing what is about to happen to her' (p. 12) – a kind of counter gravitational force that shapes pictured life, a specular capillary action that is normally hidden: 'the way the water dances in front of her face as she slides down the tiled wall', a 'kind of shimmy in the way the water falls from the shower-head, an illusion of waver or sway' (p. 16), a set of forces released, made real on the screen, 'approaching something near to elemental life' (p. 12). 'It takes work', the man thinks, 'pious effort, to see what you are looking at', and it is this seeing that the film grants, this seeing of seeing, this access to the 'depths that were possible in the slowing of motion, the things to see, the depths of things so easy to miss in the shallow habit of seeing' (pp. 16–17).

The bookends of the novel are animated by this stretched slowness, elemental life made weightless and projected onto a free-standing screen; but the central section of the novel is powered by an opposite kind of logic, an apparently contrary relation between space and time that Elster and Finlay together witness in the stunned heat of the desert. If *Point Omega* is to be read as a reflection on the transformation of the relation between world and picture occasioned by climate change, then it is this opposition between city time and desert time that frames that reflection – an opposition that seems to organise itself around Naomi Oreskes' distinction between human and nature, in which 'human chronologies' appear 'insignificant compared with the vastness of geological time'. The intellectual Elster – an ethically bankrupt theorist who advised the Bush administration during the Iraq War, whose task was to 'conceptualize' the conflict, to 'apply overarching ideas and principles to such matters as troop deployment and counter-insurgency' (pp. 23–24) – himself makes some such distinction. City time, he says, is 'embedded, the hours and minutes', the 'train stations, bus routes, taxi meters, surveillance cameras'. 'Cities', he goes on, 'were built to measure time, to remove time from nature' (p. 56). The desert, on the other hand, materialises a deeper, anti-horological chronology, what Finlay calls the 'force of geologic time, out there somewhere', time layered in the 'distances that enfolded every feature of the landscape' (p. 24). Gordon's installation slows time down, in the service of revealing a swaying emptiness in the seams of measured duration, the emptiness that inhabits a city time removed from nature; the desert, Elster thinks, offers a different kind of slowness, pre-human, posthuman, anti-human. 'Time slows down when I am here', he says, 'time becomes blind' (p. 56), 'time that precedes us and survives us' (p. 56). Stripping measured time from geological time grants, Finlay thinks, access to naked worldedness. Walking out into the heat, he has a vision of this denuded world, one which carries echoes of McCarthy's intestate earth. 'The sky was stretched taut between cliff edges', he says:

> The sky, right there, scale the rocks and you can touch it. I started walking again and came to the end of the tight passage and into an open space choked at ground level with brush and stony debris and I half crawled to the top of a high rubble mound and there was the whole scorched world. (p. 116)

City time and desert time are opposed, here, in ways that seem to reproduce that long-standing distinction that Chakrabarty and Oreskes make between nature and culture – the landscape as the inert ground upon which human dramas (and lately, here, the Iraq War) are played out. But if DeLillo's novel reproduces this rhetoric, this paradigm, it does so only to witness the failure of such a distinction, the realignment, sparely enacted but shattering in its implications, of human and environment as they are brought into unreadable contact by faltering representational forms – film, language, narrative. It is Elster who offers a hollow theoretical frame for this realignment. His failure to 'conceptualize' Iraq leads him to a broader speculation about the migration of ideation from the political to the environmental. 'War creates a closed world', Elster says, and in trying to conceptualise such a world the architects of the war are charged with a kind of reality control. 'We were devising entities beyond the agreed-upon limits of recognition or interpretation', he tells Finlay. 'We tried to create realities overnight. These were words that would yield pictures eventually and then become three dimensional' (p. 36). Elster's retreat to the desert is a response to the failure of words to become pictures, the expiry of a certain theoretical model of the relation between word and world that has one outcome in the failed US invasion of Iraq; as he adjusts himself to the geological time of the desert, he propounds a new theory of the relationship between conscious-ness and the environment, one which sees the same collapse between culture and nature that Chakrabarty proposes as the result of eco-crisis. Political exhaustion, environmental disaster, these have brought us to an 'omega point', an 'introversion', at which the barriers that allowed us to picture the world are breached, our species being collapses, and we are propelled towards a 'leap out of our biology' (p. 67). 'Consciousness is exhausted', Elster says, 'Back now to inorganic matter. This is what we want. We want to be stones in a field' (p. 67). The encounter with desert time, 'deep time, epochal time' (p. 91), does not sustain the distinction the novel sets up between culture and nature but collapses it, bringing the slow time of the film mind into a strange and unconceptualised contiguity with the slow time of the desert. Elster, again, tries to provide a grand theoretical account of this shift, this 'worldly convulsion' (p. 91), this 'paroxysm' (p. 92). 'We want it to happen', he tells Finlay, speaking in parodic DeLilloese: 'We pass completely out of being. Stones. Unless stones have being. Unless there's some profoundly mystical shift that places being in a stone' (p. 92). Elster theorises this paroxysm, this becoming living of the dead, this stony deadening of the living (with the aid of Teilhard de Chardin's concept of the omega point)[31]; but the finely grained texture of the novel, perhaps in a late reaction against DeLillian grandiloquence, carries a scepticism towards such 'overarching' theoretical vocabulary. Instead, it registers this shift novelisti-cally, as a failure of the forms, the thresholds between the interior and exterior of being, that have allowed us to make world pictures. Jessie, Elster's 'otherworldly' daughter, is the manifestation of this failure, this malfunction of the mechanism that separates consciousness from stone. Hers is an inward kind of being, a being wound into the interior of her own collapsing conception of herself, 'attentive', always, 'to some interior presence' (p. 50). In an oddly enclosed phrase which resonates across

DeLillo's late prose, Elster says that Jessie 'heard words from inside them' (p. 50), that for Jessie speaking, hearing, thinking take place in some involuted spiral which does not escape the circuitry of the word. 'Her look', Finlay thinks, 'had an abridged quality, it wasn't reaching the wall or window', as if she cannot transmit mind far from the inwardness of self, as if 'she was missing, fixed tightly within' (p. 76). 'When she was a child', Elster remembers, 'she had to touch her arm or face to know who she was'. 'She'd put her hand to her face. This is Jessica. Her body was not there until she touched it' (p. 89). Jessie feels the same gap between hand, face and mind that Beckett's Molloy feels as he sits on his rock;[32] Finlay too experiences this disjunction, as he climbs to the top of his rock at the close of the novel to look upon the 'whole, scorched world'. Standing in the punishing heat, Finlay places his hand on the cliff wall, feeling the 'tiered rock, horizontal cracks or shifts that made me think of huge upheavals'; with this touch of hand on ancient sun-heated stone, he feels that same exposed inwardness coming into contact with the dry air, that same skinless distance that Jessie feels between her hand and face, as if here, at the crux of the narrative, all of the barriers and conjunctions that the novel holds to the light are in abeyance. 'Could I forget my name in this silence?' he thinks. 'I took my hand off the wall and put it to my face' (p. 118). Hand, face, wall: how to bring these things into relation with one another, and with mind, with name, when the screens, the representational forms, that have allowed us to cast such relations have faltered, as the distinction between nature and culture, between consciousness and stone, has faltered? To bring hand into relation with face and with wall requires, perhaps, a screen, a film, a membrane, a means of projecting mind onto matter; but the screen has lost its epidermal quality, as that free-standing screen in New York no longer stands as a barrier or limit but has become permeable, walk-roundable, stretched thinly in the midst of world.

Finlay is in the desert with Elster, and with Jessie, because he wants to make a film in which Elster stands against a wall and confesses to his involvement in Iraq. 'Up against the wall, motherfucker', as Elster wryly puts it. Film, Finlay thinks, might serve as a means of establishing that wall, of making it world forming. 'Film is the barricade', he says, 'The one we erect, you and I. The one where somebody stands and tells the truth' (p. 58). But Finlay's film remains unmade, as the relation between body and wall becomes unmappable, as the capacity for a surface to become a screen upon which we project a relation to the world yields to a new unbounded immersion of consciousness in the environment. As, in Atwood's post-apocalyptic landscape, 'doors and windows have ceased to have meaning', so, in this post-conflict desert, as Elster puts it, 'the sixties are long gone and there are no more barricades' (p. 58).

9.3   Mind, Body, World

In *Point Omega*, then, one can see the convergence of a set of forces that are operating across the twenty-first-century novel and are released by the passage of human history past a far threshold, into a model of worlding that resists our picturing, measuring capacities – our forms of building, dwelling and thinking – and that places the future at an unreachable remove from the past. But it is in DeLillo's 2016 novel *Zero K* – his generically insecure fantasy of endlessly extended, cryogenically preserved life – that these convergences are given their most developed form. As if by an irresistible cultural logic, this novel uncovers the fold which joins the political and environmental transformations that shape *Point Omega* with the biomedical prosthetisation of the body to which they are subliminally related – the fold between artificial life and environmental catastrophe that lies at the ground of the contemporary imagination. Where Coetzee's twenty-first-century novels are fascinated with a purgatorial condition, a kind of suspended animation, and where Atwood suggests that the artificial extension and augmentation of life are paired with the dehumanisation of the planet, *Zero K* responds to the prosthetisation of body and of world by imagining a biomedical installation (named the 'Convergence'), in which humans lie encased underground in the desert in pods, like Coetzee's frogs, extending an abstracted deathly life endlessly into an unpictured future. Like *Point Omega*, *Zero K* balances a portrayal of city life – life embedded in minutes and hours, the life of crossing at the green light, hailing taxis, checking our pockets for wallet and keys, the life of everyday striving – against a picture of abstracted, emptied, extended life deep in the desert, where the Convergence is buried in the barren landscape. The vivid pictures of city life – of people struggling to cope with damage and difficulty, of a schoolgirl, 'a natural blush on her face, an intent look, tiny hands', who 'could not take a step without sensing some premeditated danger' (p. 191) – are measured against and by desert space, as if the quality and texture of our striving are determined in some sense by this limit condition, the extreme place where human merges with world, where consciousness becomes stone. But here, the omega point, the leap out of our biology, is a leap not only into undifferentiated materiality but also into the altered state of a life that no longer ends, an artificial life unbounded by death. City life is skirted, endorsed, cancelled, at once by a landscape that absorbs and neutralises it and by a technology that erases its limits, so that all of the novel's lived moments are doubled, undermined by the technologised, prosthetised, earthen bodies that we all already are, the 'lives in abeyance' that flicker at the edges of our technologised life-worlds, 'the empty framework of lives beyond retrieval' (p. 141).

In offering this picture of limitlessly extended life, *Zero K*, like *Oryx and Crake*, like the *Jesus* novels, seems to enact the failure of a certain kind of novel imagination. The Convergence is at once a high-tech laboratory and an installation artwork, and the art that is imagined there works at the limits of expression, an art on the very threshold of disappearance, where consciousness merges with stone. 'This is the future', one of the Convergence artists says, 'this remoteness, this sunken dimension. . . . And one of our objectives is to establish a consciousness that blends with our environment' (p. 64). The human story at the heart of the novel – turning around the protagonist Jeff Lockhart's scepticism about the decision of his father, Ross, and his stepmother, Artis, to undergo the cryogenic procedure – struggles to survive this contact with radically redistributed life. The family drama, the primal scene, is projected onto these bodies at the edge of time and space – the blank bodies in glass cases, 'humans stripped of adornment, spliced back to fetushood' (p. 144), no longer 'man or woman alive on the earth', but 'laboratory life-forms shaved naked in pods' (p. 142) – and in the process it becomes difficult to gain any readerly purchase, either on the human plot or on the austere beauty of its post-human antithesis. The borderline artwork that Jeff sees as he wanders the corridors of the Convergence – the imagery of natural or human-made disasters projected onto free-standing screens or stilled bodies frozen in stylised poses, flickering on the edge of the real and the artificial – eludes his capacity to read it, to accord to it a scale. 'I wanted to see beauty in these stilled figures', he thinks of the living dead in the pods, as well as of the statues and tableaux that decorate the installation, 'an imposing design not of clockwork bodies but of the simple human structure and its extensions, inward and out' (p. 146). But it is precisely this human structure that is unavailable, that it is the purpose of the artwork here to depict in its unavailability. The built environment itself has lost its capacity to gather the landscape into Heideggerian worldedness; doors, windows, thresholds have lost their ability to mean. The presence in the installation of deathless bodies, of suspended consciousness blending with the environment, makes the room itself uninhabitable, so Jeff can no longer calibrate himself to its dimensions, as Jessie's inward look cannot quite reach the wall or the window. He views a gallery space in the Convergence, a room which is at once a room and a representation of a room, at once art and life (an after-image of the 'impossible room' imagined in J. G. Ballard's *Atrocity Exhibition*)[33]. 'I was taken', he says, 'to a room in which all four walls were covered with a continuous painted image of the room itself', a room in which he struggles to adjust to the 'fact of four plane surfaces being a likeness of themselves' (p. 252). This is a space where the wall abdicates its role as a barrier – the cliff wall that Finlay touches with his hand, the wall against which he wants to shoot Elster, firing squad as well as movie director – becoming instead a form of Reimann surface that collapses into itself. And his own room in the Convergence remains similarly impervious to his attempts to live in it, a place whose likeness to itself makes it unavailable as a dwelling place, bound into the non-space of tautological utterance. 'The room was small and featureless', he says, 'It was generic to the point of being a thing with walls. The ceiling was low, the bed was bedlike, the chair was a chair' (p. 20). The room is shrunk into its representations, becoming, he thinks, 'small and tight', but 'embodying an odd totalness' (p. 146), inside spaces absorbing the totality into themselves; by the same logic, the external environment becomes fashioned, artificial, machine tooled. Jeff sees an exit to the Convergence and walks through it to 'earth, air and sky', finding himself in a walled English garden, as Edenic as Atwood's Paradice. It takes him a while to realise that 'tree bark, blades of grass, every sort of flower' were 'all seemingly coated or enameled, bearing a faint glaze', like that 'fine glaze of beauty' that is applied to Lily Bart's 'vulgar clay'.[34] 'None of this was natural', he realises, 'all of it unruffled by the breeze' (p. 122).

Zero K is part of a body of contemporary fiction that traces this leakage between nature and culture, between consciousness and environment; in so doing, it offers one of the clearest renditions we have of the late prosthetisation of the world. In the image of the artificial garden, foliage 'clean and smooth to the touch, some kind of plastic or fiberglass, museum quality' (p. 122), one can see the expression of the prosthetic logic unearthed by climate change; but this is also the apotheosis of a prosthetic logic that is inherent to the novel form, that I have traced here across the history of prose fiction. Jeff reflects, towards the end of *Zero K*, on the 'Convergence, the name itself, the word itself'. 'Two distinct forces', he thinks, 'approaching a point of intersection'. The Convergence is a manifestation of 'what happens to a single human body when the forces of death and life join' (p. 255) – the joining of life and death that is the engine of the novel imagination, of the prosthetic imagination. This is the twined junction of life and death that powers Cervantes' great novel, that

Don Quixote sweetly laments as he returns to La Mancha, stripped of his prosthetic powers, his knightly armour. 'Living I die', Don Quixote sings, as the prospect of meeting his beloved but fantastical Dulcinea at last in the province of death brings him such joy that he is overcome, paradoxically, by the desire to live: 'Living I die, and as my breath / Dies, death recalls me to life again' (p. 908). This is the same conjoining of life and death that Mary Shelley's monster experiences in *Frankenstein*, as he struggles to understand how he is capable of such intense, Goethean desire for nature, when he is made of artificial stuff – how his dead being can be capable of such life, as a kind of inanimate thinking 'clings' to his mind, 'like a lichen on the rock' (p. 120). This is the same bleeding of thought into material that we find in the oozing gloom of the 'berrying ground' at the heart of Dickens' *Bleak House*, where one can see 'every villainy of life in action close on death, and every poisonous element of death in action close on life' (p. 165). The novel has always turned around this meeting, this exorbitantly dangerous 'point of intersection' between the living material that mind is able to animate – through which mind is able to know itself – and the dead material that resists such animation. But here, in the pictures of prosthetic worlds that recur in the twenty-first-century novel, the structures that allowed the novel to humanise this intersection, the distinctions that have allowed us to build fictional bridges from mind to world, to allow the banks of our lifeworlds to emerge as banks, have been swept away by rising sea levels, melting icebergs. The novel as a form has touched on the radical distribution of mind in material, partly as a means of bringing that material into a human shape, of conferring life on the living, inanimation on the inanimate. It is only this capacity of distinction, this ability to demarcate between human sound and what she calls the 'other side of silence', George Eliot says, that 'gives me the courage to write', that grants her a 'clearer conception' of 'those vital elements which bind men together and give a higher worthiness to their existence'.[35]

It is perhaps this apparent failure of the binding power of narrative that lends these late-world novels their death-bound hue. 'Everybody wants to own the end of the world' (p. 3), DeLillo's narrator says in the opening line of *Zero K*, as if the technological overcoming of death opens not onto life extension but also onto a zone of non-being, an undifferentiation in which persistence is only the dead after-image of global finitude, the end of the world (as Teilhard de Chardin puts it, in his theorisation of the 'omega point', we 'will reach collectively [our] point of convergence – at the "end of the world"'[36]). But if this is the case – if these novels oversee a failure of narrative to humanise the world – it is central to everything that I have argued in this book that such a failure is not inimical to the operations of the prosthetic imagination, not a late malfunctioning of its apparatuses, but a component of it, an unbinding that has attended its binding operations from the beginning. What would a literature that knows a non-human world look like, Powers' Erdmann asks; the answer is that it would look like the novel, but the novel re-seen, rethought, reread. The novel as a form constitutes an archive of knowledge about the prosthetic condition because its operations require an intimacy with that historically determined place where the living meets with the dead, where the living strives to bring the dead under its signifying power, to give it human form. This intimacy is the price of Eliot's binding, but it also always means that the novel partakes of that merging of the living with the dead that, for Chakrabarty, for Ghosh, is the signature effect of eco-crisis. As Coetzee's Magda puts it, in *The Heart of the Country*, it is the fate of the novel to occupy the space of the 'conjunction', DeLillo's 'point of intersection'. 'The medium', Magda says, 'the median – that is what I wanted to be! Neither master nor slave, neither parent nor child, but the bridge between so that in me the contraries should be reconciled'.[37] The bridge that fiction makes occupies the space of the 'neither', passing, as Beckett puts it, 'from impenetrable self to impenetrable unself by way of neither'; in doing so, it collapses continually into that unnamable ground, between 'two lit refuges', belonging neither to culture nor to nature, but partaking of both.[38] So when these late novels find themselves in a posthuman ground, where the distinctions that have allowed us to make pictures of the world are in abeyance, they register the terminus of the novel form, the exhaustion of its binding power, at the same time as they extend its expressive logic, its capacity to conjure the movement of living thought from its contact with the stasis of dead matter – life in action close on death, death in action close on life.

It is for this reason that the world novels I have been discussing – by Atwood, Coetzee, DeLillo – even as they oversee the failure of the novel form, of the world picture, draw deeply on the history of the novel as I have traced it here, finding in the imagery it preserves a means of seeing the world anew, after the bursting of the dam that separates culture from nature. *Oryx and Crake* is suffused with such imagery. Snowman appears as a late descendent of Robinson Crusoe, striving, as he did, to convert the terminus of an old world into the threshold of a new one. The final image of Atwood's novel reprises one of the most pregnant moments in Defoe's *Crusoe*, the moment when the eighteenth-century novel encounters its own capacity for the refashioning of the reality it describes. It is Crusoe's discovery of a footprint on the sand of his desert island – 'exactly the very Print of a foot, Toes, Heel and every part of a Foot' (p. 154) – that heralds the arrival of others on his island, and Crusoe's consequent passage from isolation to the founding of a new civitas over which he is sovereign, a civitas that is founded on 'Print', on the capacity of a print or an impression to fashion the bodily forms which such sovereignty might take. Snowman's discovery, at the close of the novel, of a 'human footprint, in the sand' (p. 431) carries an echo of Crusoe's, as both mark a coming paradigm shift, a new epistemology. Defoe's footprint captures the coming together of fictionality and print culture in the process of world forming; Atwood's image suggests that world fashioning is now entangled with the carbon footprint, the transformation in scale and nature of the relation between human and planet. Snowman leaves his own mark bedside the footprint that he finds on the shore – 'he stamps his own foot into the wet sand . . . a signature of a kind. As soon as he lifts his foot away the imprint fills with water' (p. 431).

Defoe lives on in *Oryx and Crake*, as Atwood strives for a form in which to make a new lifeworld expressive, one in which the relation between foot and sand, between body and print, has become transformed, in which figure is flooded, drowned by ground; in Coetzee and DeLillo, too, it is the movement beneath the skin of a novel imagination, the still stirring of a literary thinking that has become estranged from its own forms, that points towards a new model of enworlding after the failure of the distinction between culture and nature. In *The Childhood of Jesus* and *The Schooldays of Jesus*, this intuition of the future is drawn from the presence, woven into every line, of Cervantes' *Don Quixote*. Cervantes' novel appears as a prop in the *Jesus* novels, in the form of a tattered, abridged copy of the text with which Simón teaches David to read. For Simón, the novel has a kind of historical power, as a relic of the old world which has been erased, a container for memories, for desires, that were lost when Simón and David were 'washed clean'. The archetypal story of Don Quixote's struggle with reality, his testing of the boundary between fantasy and the way things are, serves as a lesson, Simón thinks, not only in how to read, how to understand the ways in which language makes meaning, but also in the ways in which humans interact with others and with the world – how we relate to others from whom we nevertheless remain distinct. Simón and David read from the text together, Simón pointing out how letters form words to construct stories as he reads: 'Now, Don Quixote and his friend Sancho – you see, *Don Quixote* with the curly *Q* and *Sancho* again – had not ridden far when they beheld, standing by the roadside, a towering giant' (p. 152). And then, later, David now reading to Simón:

'God knows whether there is a Dulcinea in this world or
   not,' reads the boy, 'whether she is fatansical or not
   fatansical.'
'fantastical. Go on.'   (p. 217)

This reanimation of Cervantes' novel in Coetzee's in the scene of lovingly
shared reading – the staging of those same passages I discussed at the
opening of this book, in which the workings of fiction in the boundary
space between mind and world are most exposed – preserves for Simón
a model of language and reality that he wants to pass on in turn to David.
The novel helps us distinguish between Quixote's fantasy and the reality of
seventeenth-century Spain (between giants and windmills, between a poor
woman from the local village and the 'peerless Dulcinea'), as it helps us see
how language and subjectivity are constructed. 'A story is made up of
words', Simón tells David, 'and words are made up of letters. Without
letters there would be no story, no Don Quixote. You have to know the
letters' (pp. 160–61). Language shapes the human relation between mind
and matter, between ourselves and others – allows for the conception,
Simón says, 'of the human being' as 'the pinnacle of creation' (p. 109).
Simón reads from the episode of the 'Cave of Montesinos', in which
Sancho lowers Don Quixote on a rope into a hole in the earth, to give
David a lesson on the nature of cracks and gaps in the surface of things, and
how to navigate them, how to incorporate them into a picture of the world.
It is the 'way of nature', Simón says, for there to be gaps between things,
like the gap in the ground into which Sancho lowers his master. 'Think of
lovers', Simón says to David,

> If lovers were tight up against each other all the time they would no longer
> need to love each other. They would be one. There would be nothing for
> them to want. That is why nature has gaps. If everything were packed tightly
> together, everything in the universe, then there would be no you or me or
> Inés. You and I would not be talking to each other right now, there would
> just be silence – oneness and silence. (p. 176)

This is the heart of Simón's rejection of Elena's insistence that 'nothing is
missing' – his discovery in Cervantes of the preservation of those distances
between people, the loving distance between Sancho and Don Quixote
that is measured by the rope with which Sancho lowers his master into the
ground, staking the living force of their relationship against the suspended
animation of live burial. Don Quixote and Sancho are separated and joined
by that rope, as David is joined to the memory of his mother by the
(umbilical) string that was tied to him when he began his voyage to

Novilla, the string that was attached to the letter revealing her true identity, the string that broke so the letter 'fell in the sea', David remembers, where 'the fishes ate it' (p. 27). Simón's mission is to recover that tie, to induct David into a model of reading and thinking that might allow him to establish a relation between people and things that turns around a lack, that is fuelled by the Blochian insistence that 'something is missing'.[39] But if this is how Simón wants to read Cervantes, David himself, source as he is of a quasi-theological revolution in seeing and thinking, insists on a completely different model of reading and relating, one which emerges not from the salvaging of distinctions between people and world, but from the intuition of their merging, their becoming one. David does not want to read words by recognising individual letters – by breaking meaning into a small set of separate signifying units; instead, he wants to read words whole. 'There are two ways of learning to read', Simón explains to David with strained patience, 'one way is to learn the words one by one, as you are doing. The other way, which is quicker, is to learn the letters that make up the words. There are only twenty-seven of them' (p. 161). Simón takes a dim view of David's method; but, at a critical moment in the novel, a seismic moment when one can feel the shift from one epistemology to another, Simón recognises that David is not simply wrong, not simply a stubborn child refusing to learn a system, but a mind belonging to a different order, one which is attuned to the new world in which they find themselves, in which everything in the universe is, indeed, 'packed tightly together', distributed according to a different, nonhuman logic, to a different conception of desire, of passion, of parturition. What David finds in Cervantes is not a series of oppositions – reality and fantasy, self and world, Don Quixote and Sancho – organised by the binding power of a human intelligence, but a new way of ordering thinking that turns around an anti-human continuity between such oppositions, the glimmering continuity between life and death that Don Quixote himself divines, on his sweetly melancholy ride home with Sancho to La Mancha and death. This is a kind of thinking that does not separate human from nonhuman, nature from culture, that does not enworld us according to a human picture, but which turns around an expanded mechanism of likeness, a new, nonhuman adhesion between things in the universe – a kind of thinking for which David invents a new language, a new sign system. Language, Simón says to David, has to mean according to a set of shared rules, to which everyone, including Cervantes, must submit. There's no such thing, he says, as 'one's own language'; but at this transformative moment in the novel, Simón begins to realise that David might indeed embody another language, another mode of signifying, one that he finds ready made in *Don Quixote*, and that lies outside of the paradigms that structure Simón's universe of thought. Simón 'looks into David's eyes':

> For the briefest of moments he sees something there. He has no name for it. *It is like* – that is what occurs to him in the moment. Like a fish that wriggles loose as you try to grasp it. But not like a fish – no, like *like a fish*. Or like *like like a fish*. On and on. (p. 187)

What Simón sees here – what I have traced in this book as it shimmers in *Don Quixote*, and as it runs like a twisting seam through the history of the novel – is the prosthetic mechanism of likeness itself, a mechanism that lies at the heart of the binding power that George Eliot finds in her own fiction, but which reaches far beyond such bonds, towards a universe of meanings, of relations, that exceeds the terms of the world picture. Our sense of the world, mimetised in narrative, relies on that mechanism. Without such a mechanism we cannot picture, for example, a fish (close your eyes, see it now). We cannot picture the fish that eats the string that attached David to his memory of his mother; we cannot picture Simón when he falls, at one point in the novel, into the quay, like Don Quixote falling into the Cave of Montesinos, and finds himself flapping in the oily water, he says, 'like a fish' (p. 235). To render a world that contains fishes, among other things thinkable and scalable, we are led to shape that mechanism of likeness around a human centre; as Eliot puts it, most famously, in *Middlemarch*, we have to limit the scope of likeness. We are required to 'walk about well wadded with stupidity', protected from the variousness of reality, because 'our frames could hardly bear much of it' (p. 194). We are led to a certain kind of deafness and blindness that preserves us, Eliot writes, from 'hearing the grass grow and the squirrel's heart beat' (p. 194), from the dizzying enormity of things that Erdmann finds in a spoonful of soil. But the mechanism of likeness – the worlding machine that has allowed the novel to conduct this casting of world into a human picture – is the same one that shows us, in Eliot's characteristically thought-tormented aesthetic, an unthinkable, anti-human contiguity between the visible and the invisible, that contiguity we find in Dickens' 'berrying ground' between life and death, the exorbitant contiguity that the novel conjures as the price of its signifying power; it is this power that leads Coetzee's David away from a picture of a fish towards the likeness of a fish, the 'like, like, like a fish' in which language opens onto a different relation with world, a relation held in that unthought 'something' that Simón sees moving in David's eyes, that takes us, like Crusoe's shipwreck at the episteme-shifting opening of *Robinson Crusoe*, 'quite out of our Knowledge'.[40]

For Coetzee, to enter into this new kind of thinking, the thinking that he associates with purgatory, with the suspended space between life and death, one has to think like an animal. In a late essay on Beckett, from which this picture of David's thinking is partly drawn, Coetzee wonders what the species limit of Beckett's thinking is. Are Beckett's 'selves' locked in their 'white cells', Coetzee asks, 'all white in the whiteness', removed from all contact with that which lies beyond them?[41] Or can they enter into a relation with an animal other in which, as in the look that Simón shares with David, 'something opens and then almost immediately closes again' (p. 212), some mode of extra-human thinking that lies at the vanishing edge of our imaginative capacity? Can Beckett's intelligences 'pierce the white wall' that is also the white wall of flesh behind which is secreted the seething mind of Melville's Moby Dick, the 'great scheming animal brain' that 'comes from another universe of discourse, thinking thoughts according to its own nature, thoughts inconceivable, incommensurate with human thought' (p. 208)? The *Jesus* novels are one answer to this question – one way of following the passage that Beckett's late work opens to a different model of worlding. Another answer, and that with which I will bring this book to a close, is offered by DeLillo's late work, from *The Body Artist* to *Zero K*. These pared, austere works, I have suggested, seem in one sense to stage the failure of the novel imagination, the exhaustion of the certain kind of novel thinking so brilliantly anatomised in Nancy Armstrong's *How Novels Think*. Where Beckett's intelligences are imprisoned in their white cells – body in box, the barest residual scenario that remains when everything extraneous has been stripped away – then the sealed spaces in DeLillo's late works can seem simply to extend the Beckettian predicament into the twenty-first century. Jeff's room in the Convergence, the 'introspective box', is drawn straight from Beckett's late works for television – *Ghost Trio*, . . . *but the clouds* . . . – works which map the limits of thinking onto the limits of the room, the limits of the built space. To think one's way to the far edge of artificially extended life, to think one's way to the collapsing junction where city time meets with desert time, measured time with unmeasured time, the manufactured with the organic, is to find oneself touching the place where thinking stops, where we fall into the emptiness of tautology that we find at the expressive limits of language. 'The bed was bedlike', Jeff thinks, 'the chair was a chair' (p. 20). Or, as Mr Tuttle says to Lauren in *The Body*

Artist, 'The word for moonlight is moonlight' (a formulation, Lauren thinks, that is 'logically complex and oddly moving and circularly beautiful and true' (p. 82)); or as the 'Scholar' says in DeLillo's eerie late play *The Word for Snow*, 'the word for snow will be the snow.'[42] But if these late works reprise a certain Beckettian exhaustion, their clair-obscure beauty lies in their capacity to find, in the very experience of such a limit, a passage beyond it, a release into another world that is implicit, already, in Beckett's thinking of the limit, a passage that has lain, imperceptibly passable, in the seams of the novel imagination, since More forged his utopian bond between fiction and non-fiction in 1516, his collapsing bridge. 'How can the prisoner reach outside', Melville's Ahab demands, in a passage Coetzee quotes in his essay on Beckett, 'except by thrusting through the wall? To me, the white whale is that wall, shoved near to me'.[43] Beckett's late intelligences, DeLillo's late intelligences, do not thrust through the wall; they entertain none of Ahab's fierce metaphysics, his crazed determination to scrape away the numb surface of things until he reaches the quick essence. But what they do find is that at the far limit of novel thinking, the boundary itself, the wall that allows us to build, to dwell, to think, reveals its porousness – the porousness that Melville, too, finds in the barrier between the human and the nonhuman, at the limit of his own thinking. We do not need to claw at the door of our cells, to tear our fingernails against the grain, because, as Beckett puts it in a deliciously impractical stage direction in *Ghost Trio*, the door that hems us in is already 'imperceptibly ajar', is already a kind of shut opening, a barrier that opens as it closes, and what is required to pass through it is not Ahab's passion, but a new kind of perception.[44]

It is this new perception that DeLillo seeks to capture in narrative in his late work, and that allows him to see beyond the limits of human thinking, towards the merged ground of nature and culture, human and nonhuman, that has been prepared by climate change and by the biotechnology of artificial life. At the heart of his late work, as he crafts new, extraterrestrial contiguities between city time and geological time, as he shapes screens and surfaces that bring the opposition between life and death into a trembling identity, one can glimpse the outlines of a world, a world outside the frame of Heidegger's world picture. At the slowed, sharply lit opening of *The Body Artist*, as the prose edges into the stalled time of mourning, Lauren looks out of the kitchen window and into the bright eyes of a blue jay, standing on the feeder. The gaze she shares with the bird effects a stripping away of picturing to yield a naked, unworlded seeing. 'When birds look into houses', she thinks, 'what impossible worlds they see. What a shedding of every knowable surface and process' (p. 22). To see the jay, to see with the jay, 'must be what it means to see if you've been near blind all your life' (p. 22). It is this same seeing that is afforded to Artis, in *Zero K*, as she prepares to enter into cryogenic suspension, as the prose here, too, edges its way into the living-dead hinterland in which we are all now required to dwell. Her approach to death, to suspended life, opens onto a space in which 'everything looked different' (p. 44). She sees only the naked room, the Beckettian chamber, that which is in plain sight. 'I was seeing what is always there', she says, 'the bed, the windows, the walls, the floor'. But the stripping back, the elemental tautology, lends the minimalism of the prose a radiance, an expansion into totality won from contraction, from unpicturing. 'And the windows', she says, 'what did I see? A sky of the sheerest wildest blue', 'the window frame, white, simply white, but I had never seen white such as this . . . a white of enormous depth, white without contrast, I didn't need contrast, white as it is' (p. 46). This is the white that shines in late Beckett, as the imagination survives its own death – 'all white in the whiteness the rotunda' – the bone white that Coetzee associates with the cells in which Beckett's intelligences are encased. But this white without contrast opens not only onto the redundancy of the tautology, white is white, snow is snow, the wall is a wall, but onto a world that exists beyond the limits of the human, the world that lies between life and death, between human mind and the 'scheming animal brain' on the other side of the white wall, the world that comes to thought when we place being in a stone. 'Is this the world as it truly looks?' Artis thinks, 'Is this the world only animals are capable of seeing?' (p. 46).

For DeLillo, as for Coetzee, to imagine this seeing requires us to imagine a new language, a private language that inhabits the English that we share, or the Spanish, that ripples under the skin of the prose like muscle under fur, like a current under water. Coetzee's David finds the source of his new language in Cervantes, finds that the vision of the world as a unity beyond the signifying power of English, or of Spanish, is already contained in the fantastical real of *Don Quixote*. And DeLillo, too, finds that access to the world as it truly looks – to world after the expiry of the distinction between the human and the nonhuman, the real and the artificial, natural and cultural – is granted by the novel form, by the prosthetic thinking that the novel allows. The work of the Convergence, its invention of life beyond death, of consciousness blended with the environment, requires the invention of 'a language that will enable us to express things we can't express now, see things we can't see now, see ourselves and others in ways that unite us' (p. 33). This is a language, like David's in *The Childhood of Jesus*, that withholds itself from the word, and from the world; the name of the Convergence language, we are told, 'will be accessible only to those who speak it' (p. 25). But when we come to hear a far echo of this language – in the middle section of the *Zero K*, composed of the brain hum that persists as Artis' prosthetic consciousness – we find it is the language of the novel, the language that Beckett inherits from Joyce and Proust, from Eliot, Dickens and Austen, from Melville, Swift and Cervantes, the language that Beckett strips and replenishes and opens to post-Heideggerian world-ing. Artis, shorn and suspended in her pod, prosthetised, extended, unbound, thinks in flurried, closed near tautologies, a mix of first person and third person, speech acts that close in on themselves. 'I am somebody inside this thing I am in' (p. 159); 'She is living within the grim limits of the self'; 'all I am is what I am saying'; 'It is only when I say something that I know that I am here' (p. 161). This is language eked out, the aftershocks of being, 'the residue', Artis thinks, 'all that is left of an identity', a language which, in sharing its sparsity with Jeff's tautological room, also embodies its 'odd totalness'. As Coetzee's David sees words whole, so Artis 'tries to see words. Not the letters in the words but the words themselves' (p. 162). But even as these words wheel into themselves, as they become at once empty and full, inert with their own fullness, they open great gaps, great gulfs that DeLillo finds in the bleached endlands of late Beckett, gulfs that open onto the space of Coetzee's 'like', the meaning mechanism of a language that is enfolded in world, that is blended with the environment. 'I am somebody inside this thing I am in'; this is a speech act that carries something of that phrase from *Point Omega*, 'she heard words from inside them' (p. 50), something of that tendency for the inside of the word to cast itself to the outside, for the inward engine of the word and of the sentence, the something missing that drives it, the 'like', to be materialised and externalised as its own prosthetic, even as it is reabsorbed within the grim limits of the self. 'It is only when I say something that I know that I am here'; hear how this sentence, in narrowing its transmission of consciousness, of thought, to the closed moment of its own utterance, moves through the scant impetus of reading insistently beyond that moment, beyond the straits of that consciousness, into an outside, into a world, that is conjured but unpictured, the world that is the residuum of the world picture, what is left when culture collapses into nature. 'I only hear what is me', Artis thinks, and we can hear the voice of *How It Is*, the voice of the bound self that Beckett's narrator quotes as he crawls through the mud, body merging with the earth like Coetzee's frogs, mumbling into the mud, 'I say it as I hear it.'[45] 'I am made of words', Artis thinks, and we hear the voice of Beckett's *Unnamable*, the voice which also insists that 'I'm made of words', 'the place too, the air, the walls, the floor, the ceiling, all words' (p. 390). 'She is first person and third person with no way to join them together', Artis thinks, and we can hear the voice of Beckett's *Company*, divided between second person and third person ('could he speak to and of whom the voice speaks there would be a first. But he cannot, he shall not, you cannot, you shall not' (p. 6)). This is the voice that it has been the task of the novel to produce, the voice partly bound by first person, by third person, but which reaches always into the space of the join, the bridge, between me and you, between I and she, the leap out of our own skin into the unmade space outside us, where we meet with a world that remains always beyond our power truly to see.

It is this entry, finally, into a world beyond the reach of any world picture, that these novels leave us with, that they craft from their own inheritance of the resources of the novel form. In the section of *Zero K* set in the heart of the city, Jeff visits a gallery (mirror image of those empty galleries in the Convergence), which has only one object on display, 'a large rock, one rock', 'officially designated an interior rock sculpture'. As he looks upon the rock, Jeff finds himself thinking about Heidegger: 'Man alone exists', he says, 'Rocks are, but they do not exist. Trees are, but they do not exist. Horses are, but they do not exist' (p. 213).[46] The presence of the alien rock, transported from some far flung place and resituated in the middle of the city, lives out the curatorial process by which 'man' assembles the world around his practices of seeing and thinking and knowing. But everything that drives *Zero K*, everything that drives the long history of the novel as I have characterised it here, argues against the proposition that the human is that 'particular being who gives the measure and draws up the guidelines for everything that is'.[47] Jeff's dimly remembered Heidegger is balanced by another moment from Heidegger that drifts into the novel's middle section, as Artis works her way into the residual language of the convergence. 'The only here is where I am', Artis thinks; another of her bound, enclosed speech acts, but even as she denies extension, insists on inward singularity, we can hear a dialogue with Heidegger, a response to his assertion, in 'Building, Dwelling, Thinking', that 'I am never here only, as this encapsulated body; rather, I am there, that is, I already pervade the room.'[48] It is surely true that we are always here and there, surely true that in order to 'pervade the room', in order for our 'abridged look' to make it to the wall or window, we have to cast ourselves beyond ourselves. We have to duplicate ourselves, as Wharton's Lily duplicates herself in *tableau vivant*, like Eliot's Gwendolen before her, and Goethe's Ottilie before her – all women whose corporeal projection into the world involves entering into the stilled gestural force field of represented bodies. But if this is so, what Artis discovers, encapsulated body that she is, is that the picturing mechanism that allows her to negotiate between here and there – that brings the world of there under the jurisdiction of here, the bridge that summons the banks into worlded-ness – is missing, has collapsed, as consciousness blends with environment, and the 'whole scorched world', the 'intestate earth', reveals its utter indifference to the human attempt to picture it. As Jeff thinks to himself, looking at the frozen bodies in pods, 'lit from within' (p. 258), 'Tableau vivant, except that the actors were dead, and their costumes were super-insulated plastic tubes' (p. 140). The art that comes to thought in the convergence, the art at the limits of mind and world, is one that can no longer picture, one that enters into a mode of likeness that has become one with that which is pictured, and so takes itself out of the realm of Heideggerian dasein; art that is but that does not exist.

It is Artis, again, who captures this particular kind of non-existence in a wriggling, self-cancelling phrase. 'I feel artificially myself', she says, 'I'm someone who is supposed to be me' (p. 52). This is surely a condition we can all recognise, this sense that the terms of our being – 'I am', 'I feel' – are bound up with, threaded through, the forms of artifice, of 'suppose', of 'like', that cancel them out. As we all find that technologised, extended, prosthetised life is irrevocably entangled with our forms of being and feeling; as we all look upon a despoiled, intestate world that is no longer a dwelling place, a world whose contact with the human has made it irretrievably incompatible with human life; we (if there is a 'we') surely feel the artificiality of our own most intimate self-congress. Hand, face, wall; mind, body, world: what junction can we imagine that holds these matrices of being together? The novel form has offered one such junction, but it is perhaps the expiry of this kind of adhesion, this kind of bridging, that is at work in DeLillo's late prose, and that determines his under-standing of the future of the novel. I wrote to DeLillo in 2016, on the publication of *Zero K*, to ask him what he thought his novel suggested about the future, both of prose fiction and of a technologised and ecolo-gically destitute lifeworld. His response, coming in the form of seven typewritten pages, a writer's voice from an earlier stage in the history of mechanical reproduction, eerily recreated the pattern of Artis' pod-bound speech, the involutions, the tautologies. 'What about the novel?' he wrote, 'The novel in the embrace of new technologies will be the novel that writes itself.'[49] The novel will be the novel, and in this collapse into tautology, this sparsening that is a doubling up, the novel becomes itself prosthetic, itself an artificial form, looping back on itself, detached from the human mind that might find itself realised in the narratives it creates. 'It may be', DeLillo went on, 'that the fragile state of the planet will summon a new kind of novel with a language that alters our perceptions' (p. 164). But if there is to be a new kind of novel, it may require too a new kind of consciousness. 'A final question lingers', he wrote, 'beyond the man or woman seated at the writer's desk. Will advancing technology revitalize human consciousness or drown it forever?' (p. 164).

The world novels of the twenty-first century bring us to the brink of this new kind of consciousness, the consciousness that comes to the edge of expression when mind bleeds into world and into screen, when to be is to be artificially oneself. They bring us to the point when the novel passes beyond its own conditions of possibility, when Eliot's 'vital elements that bind men together' disperse into the landscape, when being is placed in a stone. But if this feels like an ongoing end to the novel, the uncertain lingering of a final question, it is the argument of this book, its most profound conviction, that the novel has always touched on the place where the artificial meets with the real, the human with the nonhuman, where the self-same is shot through with difference, the difference that is all the difference there is. The novel, as I have read it here, has come into being as an encounter with artificial life – with More's recreation of himself as Raphael; with Don Quixote's invention of himself as 'the light and mirror of knight errantry' through the simple addition of his rusty armour; with the 'feigned distances' that enable scientific world-fashioning in Bacon's *New Atlantis* and Cavendish's *Blazing World*; with Aphra Behn's picture of the numb, alienated body of the slave; with the arduously fashioned life-world that Defoe's Crusoe whittles out of island rock; with the artificial assemblages that glimmer at the heart of Swift's *Gulliver*, its odd continuations of the brain; with the clockwork automatism foisted upon Burney's Evelina; with the artificiality moving at the heart of the purest sincerity that causes Austen's Emma to suffer her delicious 'blush of sensibility'; with the stony undeath we find in Shelley and Stoker; with the artifice of manu-factured life in Dickens and Eliot; with the heaving, seething forces of inanimate animation that storm so intemperately in Melville; with the machinic artifice of modernism from James and Wharton to Stein and Woolf, Proust, Joyce and Beckett; with the specular artifice of Pynchon, Rushdie and Morrison. In crafting this history of artificial life, the novel has known itself, always, as a prosthetic, has written itself always in an artificial hand, the automatic hand of Jaquet-Droz's 'writing boy' moving in empty tandem with his automatic eye, the biomechanical hand that lies exposed on the dissecting table in Rembrandt's 'Anatomy Lesson of Dr Tulp'. I have followed the process, here, by which the novel has encountered prosthetic material to humanise it, to invent the means by which artifice is ironised into truth. The novel as a form has traced and produced the historical forces that allow us to transform the dead hand into the living, the nonhuman into the human. But at every moment that the novel has been conducting this alchemy, performing a kind of mimesis that is also a prosthetic fashioning of the world, it has known something about the world that has exceeded its own expressive capacities, has known something of how the world exists outside our picturing mechanisms, has known that the condition of being artificially ourselves opens onto a consciousness that blends with the environment. To revitalise human consciousness is also, I would say in answer to DeLillo's question, to drown it forever; the vitality of thought and of being has always, throughout the history of the novel, shaded into extinction, been powered by extinction. This combination of survival and annihilation as it is so strangely entwined within the novel form – a twining in which death takes up permanent residence with us as love also does – assumes a new urgency, now, at the dawn of a new epistemology, a new geological era. The stage that we have reached in world history is one in which we are required to make a leap, to take a step – like DeLillo's fearful girl with the natural blush, the intent look, the tiny hands – towards a future that is not organised in relation to our past, towards a world which does not accord to the human forms of seeing that have destroyed it. It requires us to produce a way of thinking and seeing that takes us beyond the contradictions of human being, that uneasy Augustinian mean between beasts and angels. This is a daunting task, perhaps an immeasurably daunting task, as severe a challenge to thinking, to our powers of world forming, as we have ever faced. 'Will there be', DeLillo wrote to me in 2016, 'the lone individual seated in a room trying to create a narrative that is equal to the advancing realities of the world around us?' (p. 164). If the answer to this question is no, if those advancing realities require an imaginative leap that takes us beyond the man or woman seated at the desk, lost in thought and in the boundless pleasure of private imagining, then the novel, as I have read it here, has already taken that leap, already orients us in relation to the world that comes to view when the edges of the chiselled sentence give way to something beyond them, when the mechanics of likeness lead us to a different universe of thought.

'Why are you so melancholy?' Captain Delano asks Benito Cereno at the end of Melville's *Benito Cereno*; 'you are saved': 'See, yon bright sun has forgotten it all, and the blue sea, and the blue sky'. Why? Cereno replies, why am I melancholy when the sea and the sky are not? 'Because they have no memory, because they are not human' (p. 101). If we are to think our way into the unpictured world to come, and if the novel is to help us do so – if we are to know what it is to be saved rather than drowned – then we must listen to the ways in which the novel imagines unthought conjunctions between human memory and the blue sea, the blue sky, our planet of the sheerest, wildest blue.

Notes

Introduction

1. Apuleius, *The Golden Ass* (Oxford: Oxford University Press, 1994), trans. P. G. Walsh, p. 1.
2. Sigmund Freud, *Civilization and Its Discontents*, in Sigmund Freud, *Civilization, Society and Religion, Pelican Freud Library*, Vol. 12 (London: Penguin, 1985), trans. James Strachey, p. 280.
3. Virginia Woolf, *To The Lighthouse* (London: Grafton, 1977), p. 151
4. H. G. Wells, *The Time Machine*, in H. G. Wells, *Selected Short Stories* (London: Penguin, 1958), p. 9.
5. For a reflection on Hawking's prosthetic voice, see Allucquère Rosanne Stone, *The War of Desire and Technology at the Close of the Mechanical Age* (Cambridge, MA: MIT Press, 1995), pp. 4–5. For a critical response to Stone that offers a different account of Hawking's prosthesis, see Sara S. Jain, 'The Prosthetic Imagination: Enabling and Disabling the Prosthesis Trope', *Science, Technology, & Human Values*, vol. 24, no. 1 (1999), pp. 31–54, pp. 40–42.
6. David Wills, *Prosthesis* (Stanford: Stanford University Press, 1995), p. 26. See also Wills' two other books to explore the status of technological life, *Dorsality: Thinking Back through Technology and Politics* (Minneapolis: University of Minnesota Press, 2008), and *Inanimation: Theories of Inorganic Life* (Minneapolis: University of Minnesota Press, 2016).
7. For an account of developing 3D facial prosthetic research, see Faraedon M. Zardawi et al., 'Mechanical Properties of 3D Printed Facial Prostheses Compared to Handmade Silicone Polymer Prostheses', *European Scientific Journal*, vol. 11, no. 12 (2015), pp. 1–10.
8. Alison Landsberg, *Prosthetic Memory: The Transformation of American Remembrance in the Age of Mass Culture* (New York: Columbia University Press, 2004), p. 3.
9. Young-Joon Seol et al., '3D Bioprinted Biomask for Facial Skin Reconstruction', *Bioprinting*, vol. 10 (2018), np.

10. For an account of the evolution of Crispr technology, see Jim Kozubek, *Modern Prometheus: Editing the Human Genome with Crispr-Cas9* (Cambridge: Cambridge University Press, 2018).

11. Robert Mitchell and Phillip Thurtle, eds., *Data Made Flesh: Embodying Information* (New York: Routledge, 2004), p. 2.

12. N. Katherine Hayles, *How We Became Posthuman: Virtual Bodies in Cybernetics, Literature, and Informatics* (Chicago: University of Chicago Press, 1999), p. 3.

13. Jacques Derrida, *Archive Fever* (Chicago: University of Chicago Press, 1995), trans. Eric Prenowitz, p. 92.

14. Freud, *Civilization and Its Discontents*, pp. 279, 280.

15. For a reading of the relationship between Freud's conception of the prosthetic and the artificial self as it is developed in modernist forms of expression, see Hal Foster, *Prosthetic Gods* (Cambridge, MA: MIT Press, 2004).

16. Erich Auerbach, *Mimesis: The Representation of Reality in Western Literature* (Princeton: Princeton University Press, 2003), trans. Willard R. Trask, p. 6. Lukács makes a parallel argument in *The Theory of the Novel: A Historico-Philosophical Essay on the Forms of Great Epic Literature* (London: Merlin, 1971), trans. Anna Bostock, where he argues that in the age of the Homeric epic, 'the soul does not yet know any abyss within itself' (p. 30).

17. James Joyce, *Ulysses* (London: Penguin, 1986), p. 6.

18. For Lukács on the anti-realistic tendencies of modernism, see Georg Lukács, *The Meaning of Contemporary Realism* (London: Merlin, 2006), trans. John and Necke Mander, where he attacks the 'dogmas of modernist anti-realism' (p. 17).

19. Auerbach, *Mimesis*, p. 552.

20. Paul Ricoeur, 'The Function of Fiction in Shaping Reality', in Mario J. Valdés, ed., *A Ricoeur Reader: Reflection and Imagination* (New York: Harvester, 1991), p. 118.

21. For a recent reading of Ricoeur's work in relation to the ekphrastic image in contemporary fiction, see Leonid Bilmes, 'Prose Pictures: Memory, Narrative and Ekphrasis in Nabokov, Sebald and Lerner' (PhD Thesis: London: Queen Mary, University of London, 2018).

22. Paul Ricoeur, 'Mimesis and Representation', in Valdés, ed., *A Ricoeur Reader*, p. 137.

23. Ricoeur wrote his major works of literary criticism between 1976 (with the publication of *Interpretation Theory: Discourse and the Surplus of Meaning* (Fort Worth: Texas Christian University Press, 1976)) and 1985 (*Time and Narrative* (Chicago: Chicago University Press, 1990), 3 vols., trans. Kathleen McLaughlin and David Pellauer).

24. Jacques Derrida, *Speech and Phenomena and Other Essays on Husserl's Theory of Signs* (Evanston: Northwestern University Press, 1973), trans. David B. Allison, p. 156.

25. Derrida, *Speech and Phenomena*, p. 156.

26. Jacques Derrida, *Of Grammatology* (Baltimore: Johns Hopkins University Press, 1976), trans. Gayatri Chakravorty Spivak, p. 158.

27. Derrida, *Of Grammatology*, p. 159.

28. Part 1 of Don DeLillo's *White Noise* (London: Picador, 1999) is entitled 'Waves and Radiation'.

29. See Jacques Derrida, *Monolingualism of the Other: Or the Prosthesis of Origin* (Stanford: Stanford University Press, 1998), trans. Patrick Mensah.

30. Wills, *Prosthesis*, p. 10.

31. See Fredric Jameson, *Postmodernism: Or the Cultural Logic of Late Capitalism* (London: Verso, 1991).

32. See Donna J. Haraway, *Simians, Cyborgs, and Women: The Reinvention of Nature* (London: Free Association Books, 1991) and William Gibson, *Neuromancer* (London: Gollancz, 1984).

33. See Paul Virilio, *The Aesthetics of Disappearance* (Los Angeles: Semiotext(e), 2009), trans. Philip Beitchman.

34. See Catherine Belsey, *Culture and the Real* (London: Routledge, 2005).

35. Claire Colebrook, 'All Life Is Artificial Life', *Textual Practice*, vol. 33, no. 1 (2019), p. 2.

36. See Leo Bersani, *Thoughts and Things* (Chicago: University of Chicago Press, 2015) and Roberto Esposito, *Persons and Things: From the Body's Point of View* (Cambridge: Polity, 2015), trans. Zakiya Hanafi.

37. See Jane Bennett, *Vibrant Matter: A Political Ecology of Things* (Durham: Duke University Press, 2010).

38. For her fullest account of haptic criticism, see Laura U. Marks, *Touch: Sensuous Theory and Multisensory Media* (Minneapolis: University of Minnesota Press, 2002).

39. Margaret Anne Doody, *The True Story of the Novel* (London: HarperCollins, 1997), pp. 106–24.

40. Apuleius, *The Golden Ass*, p. 221.

41. Mikhail Bakhtin, *The Dialogic Imagination: Four Essays* (Austin: University of Texas Press, 1981), trans. Caryl Emerson and Michael Holquist, p. 119.

42. Bakhtin, *The Dialogic Imagination*, p. 121.

43. See Fredric Jameson, *The Antinomies of Realism* (London: Verso, 2013).

44. Samuel Beckett, *Dream of Fair to Middling Women* (London: Calder, 1993), p. 119.

45. See George Levine et al., '*Novel Politics*: Four Responses and a Reply from the Author', *Textual Practice*, vol. 32, no. 7 (2018), pp. 1049–93, p. 1050.

46. Victor Hugo, *Les Misérables* (London: Penguin, 1982), trans. Norman Denny, p. 619.

Fiction, the Body and the State

1. Thomas Hobbes, *Leviathan: Or the Matter, Forme, & Power of a Commonwealth Ecclesiasticall and Civill* (New Haven: Yale University Press, 2010), ed. Ian Shapiro, p. 9.
2. Isaac Asimov, *The Bicentennial Man and Other Stories* (London: Victor Gollancz, 2000), p. 155.
3. Giorgio Agamben, *Homo Sacer: Sovereign Power and Bare Life* (Stanford: Stanford University Press, 1998), trans. Daniel Heller-Roazen, pp. 163, 164.
4. See Muireann Quigley, *Self-Ownership, Property Rights and the Human Body* (Cambridge: Cambridge University Press, 2018).
5. See Rebecca Skloot, *The Immortal Life of Henrietta Lacks* (London: Pan, 2010).
6. See Jeremy Rifkin, *The Biotech Century: Harnessing the Gene and Remaking the World* (London: Victor Gollancz, 1998), pp. 60–61.
7. Andrew Norris, 'Giorgio Agamben and the Politics of the Living Dead', in Andrew Norris, ed., *Politics, Metaphysics and Death: Essays on Giorgio Agamben's* Homo Sacer (Durham: Duke University Press, 2005), p. 1.
8. John Locke, *Second Treatise of Government* (Oxford: Oxford University Press, 2016), p. 15.
9. For an analysis of Leonardo's anatomical drawings, in the context of the history of both science and art, see Michael and Stephen Farthing, *Leonardo da Vinci: Under the Skin* (London: Royal Academy of Arts, 2019).
10. Michel Foucault, *The Birth of Biopolitics: Lectures at the Collège de France, 1978–79* (Basingstoke: Palgrave, 2008), trans. Graham Burchell, p. 226
11. Roy Porter, *Blood & Guts: A Short History of Medicine* (London: Penguin, 2003), p. 59.
12. Jonathan Sawday, *The Body Emblazoned: Dissection and the Human Body in Renaissance Culture* (London: Routledge, 1995), p. viii.
13. Paula Findlen, 'Anatomy Theaters, Botanical Gardens, and Natural History Collections', in Katharine Park and Lorraine Daston, eds., *The Cambridge History of Science*, Vol. 3: *Early Modern Science* (Cambridge: Cambridge University Press, 2006), pp. 272–89, p. 276.
14. Quoted in Cynthia Klestinec, *Theaters of Anatomy: Students, Teachers and Traditions of Dissection in Renaissance Venice* (Baltimore: Johns Hopkins University Press, 2011), p. 37.

15. Katherine Bootle Attie, 'Re-Membering the Body Politic: Hobbes and the Construction of Civic Immortality', in *ELH*, vol. 75, no. 3 (2008), pp. 497–530, p. 502.

16. For a helpful discussion of the nature of Hobbes' objections to Descartes, see Marcus P. Adams, 'The Wax and the Mechanical Mind: Reexamining Hobbes's Objections to Descartes's *Meditations*', *British Journal for the History of Philosophy*, vol. 22, no. 3 (2014), pp. 403–24.

17. René Descartes, 'The Third Set of Objections & Replies containing the Controversy between Hobbes and Descartes', in Elizabeth Anscombe and Peter Thomas Geach, eds. and trans., *Descartes: Philosophical Writings* (New York: Macmillan, 1971), p. 133.

18. René Descartes, *A Discourse on the Method of Correctly Conducting One's Reason and Seeing Truth in the Sciences* (Oxford: Oxford University Press, 2006), trans. Ian Maclean, p. 29.

19. René Descartes, *The Philosophical Writings of Descartes*, Vol. 3: *The Correspondence* (Cambridge: Cambridge University Press, 1991), p. 134.

20. For a comprehensive discussion of the Vesalian references in Rembrandt's painting, and for the sources that have identified these references, see J. Bruyn et al., *A Corpus of Rembrandt Paintings II: 1631–1634* (Dordrecht: Martinus Nijhoff, 1986), pp. 172–89.

21. Simon Schama, *Rembrandt's Eyes* (London: Penguin, 1999), p. 353.

22. John Berger, *The Shape of a Pocket* (London: Bloomsbury, 2001), p. 109.

23. Joanna Woodall, 'Introduction: Facing the Subject', in Joanna Woodall, ed., *Portraiture: Facing the Subject* (Manchester: Manchester University Press, 1997), p. 10.

24. Johann Wolfgang von Goethe, *The Sorrows of Young Werther* (London: Penguin, 1989), trans. Michael Hulse, p. 60.

25. David Foster Wallace, *The Pale King* (London: Hamish Hamilton, 2011), p. 401.

26. Margaret Cavendish, *The Blazing World and Other Writings* (London: Penguin, 2004), p. 180.

27. Bernard Stiegler, 'Derrida and Technology: Fidelity at the Limits of Deconstruction and the Prosthesis of Faith', in Tom Cohen, ed., *Jacques Derrida and the Humanities* (Cambridge: Cambridge University Press, 2001), p. 249.

28. For an account of the treatment of classical and Renaissance political philosophy in *Utopia*, see George M. Logan, *The Meaning of More's Utopia* (Princeton: Princeton University Press, 1983). See also Quentin Skinner, 'Sir Thomas More's *Utopia* and the Language of Renaissance Humanism', in Anthony Pagden, ed., *The Languages of Political Theory in Early-Modern Europe* (Cambridge: Cambridge University Press, 1987), pp. 123–57.

29. Thomas More, *Utopia* (Cambridge: Cambridge University Press, 2002), trans. Robert M. Adams, p. 8.
30. Francis Bacon, *New Atlantis*, in Susan Bruce, ed., *Three Early Modern Utopias: Thomas More*, Utopia, *Francis Bacon*, New Atlantis, *Henry Neville*, The Isle of Pines (Oxford: Oxford University Press, 1999), p. 156.
31. Cavendish, *The Blazing World*, p. 126.
32. Thomas More, *Epigrams*, in Thomas More, *The Complete Works of Thomas More*, Vol. 3, part 2 (New Haven: Yale University Press, 1984), eds. Clarence H. Miller et al., p. 165.
33. See Thomas Healy, 'Playing Seriously in Renaissance Writing', in Margaret Healy and Thomas Healy, *Renaissance Transformations: The Making of English Writing (1500–1650)* (Edinburgh: Edinburgh University Press, 2009), pp. 15–31.
34. More, *Epigrams*, p. 165.
35. Stephen Greenblatt, *Renaissance Self-Fashioning from More to Shakespeare* (Chicago: University of Chicago Press, 2005), p. 57.
36. Don DeLillo, *The Body Artist* (London: Picador, 2001), p. 39.
37. Ricoeur, 'The Function of Fiction in Shaping Reality', pp. 119, 123.
38. Samuel Beckett, *Worstward Ho*, in Samuel Beckett, *Nohow On: Company, Ill Seen Ill Said, Worstward Ho* (London: Calder, 1992), p. 101.
39. Descartes, *Discourse on the Method*, p. 29.
40. Samuel Beckett, *Watt* (London: Calder, 1976), p. 247.
41. For a range of scholarship on the early novel form, see Andrew Hadfield, ed., *The Oxford Handbook of English Prose 1500–1640* (Oxford: Oxford University Press, 2013).
42. Catherine Gallagher, 'The Rise of Fictionality', in Franco Moretti, ed., *The Novel*: Vol. 1, *History, Geography and Culture* (Princeton: Princeton University Press, 2006), pp. 336–63. See also Catherine Gallagher, *Nobody's Story: The Vanishing Acts of Women Writers in the Marketplace, 1670–1820* (Berkeley: University of California Press, 1994).
43. Cervantes, *The Adventures of Don Quixote* (London: Penguin, 1950), trans. J. M. Cohen, p. 31.
44. Aphra Behn, *Oroonoko* (London: Penguin, 2003), p. 5.
45. Daniel Defoe, *The Life and Strange Surprising Adventures of Robinson Crusoe of York, Mariner* (Oxford: Oxford University Press, 1998), p. 1.
46. Michael McKeon, *The Origins of the English Novel 1600–1740* (Baltimore: Johns Hopkins University Press, 2002), p. 414.
47. José Ortega y Gasset, *Meditations on Quixote* (New York: Norton, 1961), trans. Evelyn Rugg and Diego Marín, p. 162.
48. Auerbach, *Mimesis*, p. 358; McKeon, *Origins,* pp. 273–94.
49. Hobbes, *Leviathan*, p. 11.

50. Thomas Hobbes, *The Elements of Law Natural and Politic* (London: Frank Cass, 1969), p. 52.

51. McKeon, *Origins,* p. 291.

52. Jorge Luis Borges, *Labyrinths: Selected Stories & Other Writings* (New York: New Directions, 2007), p. 242.

53. Mario Vargas Llosa, 'A Novel for the Twenty-First Century', *Harvard Review*, no. 28 (2005), pp. 125–36, p. 126.

54. Harold Bloom, *Where Shall Wisdom Be Found?* (New York: Riverhead, 2004), p. 85.

55. For an account of Cervantes' participation in the battle and his extensive wounds, see Donald P. McCrory, *No Ordinary Man: The Life and Times of Miguel de Cervantes* (London: Peter Owen, 2002), pp. 55–62, and William Byron, *Cervantes: A Biography* (London: Cassell, 1979), pp. 124–39.

56. See Ludwig Wittgenstein, *Philosophical Investigations* (Oxford: Blackwell, 2001), trans. G. E. M. Anscombe, p. 13, where Wittgenstein reflects on the process by which 'the shape of a chessman corresponds . . . to the sound or shape of a word.'

57. For a classic account of Cervantes' relationship with Aristotle (the discovery of whom was 'the great aesthetic experience of his life' (p. 3)), see Alban K. Forcione, *Cervantes, Aristotle, and the 'Persiles'* (Princeton: Princeton University Press, 1970).

58. Aristotle, *Meteorologica*, in Aristotle, *The Works of Aristotle*, Vol. 3 (Oxford: Clarendon, 1931), trans. W. D. Ross, p. 390.

Economies of Scale from Aphra Behn to Sarah Scott

1. Henry Fielding, *Tom Jones* (Oxford: Oxford University Press, 1998), p. 194.

2. Timothy Clark, 'Derangements of Scale', in Tom Cohen, ed., *Telemorphosis: Theory in the Era of Climate Change* (London: Open Humanities Press, 2012), online at https://quod.lib.umich.edu/o/ohp/10539563.0001.001/1:8/–telemor phosis-theory-in- the-era-of-climate-change-vol-1?rgn=div1;view=fulltext, np.

3. Frances Ferguson, *Solitude and the Sublime* (London: Routledge, 1992), p. 31.

4. Jonathan Swift, *Gulliver's Travels* (Oxford: Oxford University Press, 1998), p. 244.

5. Ian Watt, *The Rise of the Novel: Studies in Defoe, Richardson and Fielding* (London: Pimlico, 2000), p. 96.

6. Gallagher, 'The Rise of Fictionality', p. 361.

7. Samuel Beckett, *Proust, and Three Dialogues with Georges Duthuit* (London: Calder, 1965), p. 65.

8. For Rousseau's depiction of man in the state of nature, see Jean-Jacques Rousseau, *A Discourse on the Origin of Inequality*, in Jean-Jacques Rousseau, *The Social Contract and Discourses* (London: Everyman, 1993).

9. David Hume, *A Treatise of Human Nature* (Oxford: Oxford University Press, 2000), eds. David Fate Norton and Mary J. Norton, p. 165.

10. For a helpful summary of critical responses to *Oroonoko*, from its publication to the present, see Gallagher, *Nobody's Story*, pp. 54–55, n. 12.

11. See Janet Todd, *The Secret Life of Aphra Behn* (London: André Deutsch, 1996), pp. 35–45.

12. Behn's novel is included as Item 253, in John Harrison and Peter Laslett, *The Library of John Locke* (Oxford: Oxford University Press, 1965), p. 83.

13. Behn, *Oroonoko*, p. 5.

14. Rousseau, *Origin of Inequality*, p. 51.

15. See Olaudah Equiano, *The Interesting Narrative and Other Writings* (London: Penguin, 1995), and Frederick Douglass, *Narrative of the Life of Frederick Douglass, An American Slave: Written by Himself* (New York: Anchor, 1973). For a recent compelling reading of African American self-narration, see Lloyd Pratt, *The Strangers Book: The Human of African American Literature* (Philadelphia: University of Pennsylvania Press, 2016), particularly pp. 44–62.

16. Gallagher, *Nobody's Story*, p. 73.

17. Benjamin Schmidt, *Inventing Exoticism: Geography, Globalism and Europe's Early Modern World* (Philadelphia: University of Pennsylvania Press, 2015), p. 224.

18. See Susan B. Iwanisziw, 'Behn's Novel Investment in *Oroonoko*: Kingship, Slavery and Tobacco in English Colonialism', *South Atlantic Review*, vol. 63, no. 2 (1998), pp. 75–98.

19. See Wallace's story 'Incarnations of Burned Children', in which a child who suffers terrible burns grows up in an alienated condition: 'The child's body expanded and walked about a drew pay and lived its life untenanted, a thing among things' (David Foster Wallace, *Oblivion* (London: Abacus, 2005), p. 116).

20. Daniel Defoe, *The Life and Strange Surprizing Adventures of Robinson Crusoe, of York, Mariner* (Oxford: Oxford University Press, 1998), p. 5.

21. Freud, *Civilization and Its Discontents*, p. 280.

22. Karl Marx, *Capital: A Critique of Political Economy*, Vol. 1 (London: Penguin 1978), trans. David Fernbach, p. 170.

23. Watt, *Rise of the Novel*, p. 92.

24. McKeon, *Origins of the Novel*, p. 335.

25. Hume, *A Treatise of Human Nature*, p. 165.

26. Daniel Defoe, *Moll Flanders* (London: Penguin, 1989), p. 363.

27. Nathaniel Hawthorne, *The Blithedale Romance* (Oxford: Oxford University Press, 1998), p. 61.

28. Jean-Luc Nancy, *Being Singular Plural* (Stanford: Stanford University Press, 2000), trans. Robert D. Richardson and Anne E. O'Byrne, p. 18.

29. Descartes, *Discourse on the Method*, p. 47.

30. Jacques Derrida, *The Beast & the Sovereign*, Vol. 2 (Chicago: University of Chicago Press, 2011), trans. Geoffrey Bennington, p. 86.

31. Aristotle, *Meteorologica*, p. 390.

32. Derrida, *Beast*, p. 49.

33. Denise Schaeffer, 'The Utility of Ink: Rousseau and Robinson Crusoe', *The Review of Politics*, vol. 64, no. 1 (2002), pp. 121–48.

34. Heather Keenleyside, *Animals and Other People: Forms and Living Beings in the Long Eighteenth Century* (Philadelphia: University of Pennsylvania Press, 2016), p. 60.

35. For a classic account of the errors in *Robinson Crusoe*, see William T. Hastings, 'Errors and Inconsistencies in Defoe's *Robinson Crusoe*', *Modern Language Notes*, vol. 27, no. 6 (1912), pp. 161–66.

36. See Martin Heidegger, 'Building, Dwelling, Thinking', in Martin Heidegger, *Poetry, Language, Thought* (New York: HarperCollins, 2001), trans. Albert Hofstadter, pp. 143–59.

37. See, for example, Charlotte Perkins Gilman, *Herland* (London: Penguin, 2009), Marge Piercy, *Woman on the Edge of Time* (London: Penguin, 2016), and Margaret Atwood, *A Handmaid's Tale* (London: Vintage, 1996).

38. There is, however, a colonial dimension to the novel. For a reading of the role of colonial wealth in Scott's novel, see Nicolle Jordan, 'A Creole Contagion: Narratives of Slavery and Tainted Wealth in *Millenium Hall*', *Tulsa Studies in Women's Literature*, vol. 30, no. 1 (2011), pp. 57–70.

39. Sarah Scott, *Millenium Hall* (London: Penguin, 1986), p. 112.

40. For two readings of the way that Scott's novel regulates sexuality, monstrosity, sociality, see Bryan Mangano, 'Institutions of Friendship in Sarah Scott's *Millenium Hall*, *Texas Studies in Literature and Language*, vol. 57, no. 4 (2015), pp. 464–90, and Dorice Williams Elliott, 'Sarah Scott's *Millenium Hall* and Female Philanthropy', *Studies in English Literature, 1500–1900*, vol. 35, no. 3 (1995), pp. 535–53.

41. Laurence Sterne, *The Life and Opinions of Tristram Shandy, Gentleman* (Oxford: Oxford University Press, 2009), p. 170.

42. Voltaire, *Candide* (London: Penguin, 2001), p. 1. For Leibniz's philosophy of possible worlds, see Gottfried Wilhelm Leibniz, *Theodicy* (Dumfries and Galloway: Anodos, 2019).

43. Swift, *Gulliver's Travels*, p. xxxv.

44. See Gallagher, 'The Rise of Fictionality'.

45. J. M. Coetzee, *Elizabeth Costello* (New York: Viking, 2003), p. 103.

46. William C. Mottolese, 'Tristram Cyborg and Toby Toolmaker: Body, Tools, and Hobbyhorse in *Tristram Shandy*', *Studies in English Literature, 1500–1900*, vol. 47, no. 3 (2007), pp. 679–701, p. 694.

47. Jonathan Swift, 'A Discourse Concerning the Mechanical Operation of the Spirit', in Jonathan Swift, *A Tale of a Tub and Other Works* (Cambridge: Cambridge University Press, 2010), p. 173.

Organic Aesthetics from Richardson to Goethe

1. Samuel Richardson, *Pamela* (Oxford: Oxford University Press, 2001), p. 9.

2. Johann Wolfgang von Goethe, *Elective Affinities* (Oxford: Oxford University Press, 1999), trans. David Constantine, p. 30.

3. Samuel Beckett, *Dream of Fair to Middling Women* (London: Calder, 1993), p. 119.

4. Cervantes, *Don Quixote*, p. 425.

5. Swift, *Gulliver's Travels*, p. 176.

6. Scott, *Millenium Hall*, p. 23.

7. See Julie Park, 'Pains and Pleasures of the Automaton: Frances Burney's Mechanics of Coming Out', *Eighteenth Century Studies*, vol. 40, no. 1 (2006), pp. 23–49.

8. George Savile, *The Lady's New-year's Gift: Or, Advice to a Daughter* (London: Randal Taylor, 1688), p. 142, qtd. in Park, 'Pains and Pleasures', p. 24.

9. Julien Offray De La Mettrie, *Machine Man and Other Writings* (Cambridge: Cambridge University Press, 1996), p. 26.

10. Aram Vartanian, *La Mattrie's L'Homme Machine: A Study in the Origins of an Idea* (Princeton: Princeton University Press, 1960), p. 13.

11. Joseph Rykwert, 'Organic and Mechanical', *RES: Anthropology and Aesthetics*, vol. 20 (1992), p. 13.

12. Edgar Allan Poe, 'Maelzel's Chess-Player', in Edgar Allan Poe, *The Complete Works of Edgar Allan Poe*, Vol. 14: *Essays, Miscellanies* (New York: AMS Press, 1965), pp. 8, 9.

13. Poe, 'Maelzel's Chess-Player', pp. 13–14.

14. Walter Benjamin, 'Theses on the Philosophy of History', in Walter Benjamin, *Illuminations* (London: Pimlico, 1999), p. 245.

15. Heinrich von Kleist, 'On the Marionette Theatre', in Idris Parry, *Hand to Mouth and Other Essays* (Manchester: Carcanet, 1981), trans. Idris Parry, pp. 14–15.

16. Guido Mazzoni, *Theory of the Novel* (Cambridge, MA: Harvard University Press, 2017), trans. Zakiya Hanafi, p. 179.

17. Goethe, *Werther*, p. 32.

18. See Johann Wolfgang von Goethe, *The Metamorphosis of Plants* (Cambridge, MA: MIT Press, 2009), trans. Douglas Miller.

19. Samuel Taylor Coleridge, *The Complete Works of Samuel Taylor Coleridge*, Vol. 4: *Lectures Upon Shakespeare* (New York: Harper, 1854), p. 53.

20. D. H. Lawrence, *The Letters of D. H. Lawrence*, Vol. 2: *June 1913–October 1916* (Cambridge: Cambridge University Press, 1981), eds. George J. Zytaruk and James T. Boulton, p. 327.
21. Frances Burney, *Evelina* (London: Penguin, 2012), p. 8.
22. Park, 'Pains and Pleasures', p. 37.
23. See Julia Epstein, *The Iron Pen: Frances Burney and the Politics of Women's Writing* (Madison: University of Wisconsin Press, 1989).
24. Johann Wolfgang von Goethe, *Elective Affinities* (Oxford: Oxford University Press, 1999), trans. David Constantine, p. 152.
25. J. M. Coetzee, *Late Essays* (London: Harvill Secker, 2017), p. 59.
26. Coleridge, *Complete Works*, p. 53.
27. Woolf, *To the Lighthouse*, p. 151.
28. Bennett, *Vibrant Matter*, p. 122.
29. For a penetrating reading of Goethe's engagement with the *tableau vivant*, see Hannah Jordan, *Between Fact and Imagination: Victorian Tableaux Vivantes in Nineteenth-Century Britain* (PhD Thesis: Sussex: Sussex University, 2020).
30. Alexander Pope, *Essay on Man* (Princeton: Princeton University Press, 2016), p. 28.
31. Johann Wolfgang von Goethe, *Die Leiden Des Jungen Werther*, in Goethe, *Goethes Werke: Band VI* (Hamburg: Christian Wegner Verlag, 1951), p. 21.
32. Samuel Beckett, *Molloy*, in Samuel Beckett, *Molloy, Malone Dies, The Unnamable* (London: Calder, 1994), p. 36.
33. Fielding, *Tom Jones*, p. 194.
34. Andrew Bennett, *Suicide Century: Literature and Suicide from James Joyce to David Foster Wallace* (Cambridge: Cambridge University Press, 2017), p. 17.

The Dead Hand: Realism and Biomaterial in the Nineteenth-Century Novel

1. William Shakespeare, 'Sonnet 111', in William Shakespeare, *The Complete Works* (Oxford: Clarendon, 1988), p. 764.
2. Frederick Engels, 'The Part Played by Labour in the Transition from Ape to Man', in *Karl Marx and Frederick Engels: Selected Works* (London: Lawrence and Wishart, 1970), p. 355.
3. Mary Wollstonecraft, *Mary*, in Mary Wollstonecraft, *Mary* and *The Wrongs of Woman* (Oxford: Oxford University Press, 2007), p. 62.
4. Jane Austen, *Emma* (London: Penguin, 1996), p. 354.
5. Martin Heidegger, 'The Hand and the Typewriter', reprinted in Friedrich Kittler, *Gramophone, Film, Typewriter* (Stanford: Stanford University Press, 1999), trans. Geoffrey Winthrop-Young and Michael Wutz, p. 198.

6. Martin Heidegger, *What Is Called Thinking* (New York: Harper and Row, 1968), trans. Fred D. Weick and J. Glenn Gray, p. 16.

7. Elaine Scarry, *The Body in Pain: The Making and Unmaking of the World* (New York: Oxford University Press, 1985), p. 253.

8. For Hobsbawm's history of industrialisation and its relation to culture and politics, see Eric Hobsbawm, *The Age of Revolution: Europe 1789–1848* (London: Phoenix Press, 2000); for Raymond Williams' classic accounts of the dialectical materialist relation between literature and historical change, see *The Country and the City* (New York: Oxford University Press, 1973), and *The English Novel from Dickens to Lawrence*; for an account of the relation, at the end of the century, between literature, railways and the emergence of cinema and psychoanalysis, see Laura Marcus, *Dreams of Modernity: Psychoanalysis, Literature, Cinema* (Cambridge: Cambridge University Press, 2014); for two classic accounts of the spread of new communications technologies, from the nineteenth to the twentieth centuries, see Kittler, *Gramophone, Film, Typewriter*, and Marshall McLuhan, *Understanding Media: The Extensions of Man* (Cambridge, MA: MIT Press, 1994).

9. Freud, *Civilization*, p. 279.

10. See Landsberg, *Prosthetic Memory*.

11. Freud, *Civilization*, p. 279.

12. Heidegger, *What Is Called Thinking*, p. 16.

13. Raymond Williams, *The English Novel from Dickens to Lawrence* (London: Chatto and Windus, 1973), p. 192.

14. Émile Zola, *Thérèse Raquin* (London: Penguin, 1962), trans. Leonard Tancock, p. 109.

15. Mazzoni, *Theory of the Novel*, p. 179.

16. Wollstonecraft, *Mary*, p. 16.

17. See D. A. Miller, *Jane Austen, Or the Secret of Style* (Princeton: Princeton University Press, 2003), for a discussion of what Miller calls 'the unprecedented prominence of free indirect style in *Emma*' (p. 56).

18. Austen, *Emma*, p. 8.

19. Cavendish, *Blazing World*, p. 183.

20. For a reading of Quixotism in *Northanger Abbey*, see Jodi L. Wyett, 'Female Quixotism Refashioned: *Northanger Abbey*, The Engaged Reader, and the Woman Writer', *The Eighteenth Century*, vol. 56, no. 2 (2015), pp. 261–76.

21. Franco Moretti, 'Serious Century', in Franco Moretti, ed., *The Novel*, Vol. 1: *History, Geography, and Culture* (Princeton: Princeton University Press, 2006), p. 392.

22. For an astute reading of the blush in Austen (and Burney, as well as others), see Katie Halsey, 'The Blush of Modesty or the Blush of Shame? Reading Jane Austen's Blushes', *Modern Language Studies*, vol. 42, no. 3 (2006), pp. 226–38.

23. Wills, *Inanimation*, pp. 35, 34.
24. Tony Tanner, *Jane Austen* (Basingstoke: Palgrave, 2007), p. 16.
25. Eve Kosofsky Sedgwick, *Tendencies* (Durham: Duke University Press, 1993), p. 125.
26. Theodor Adorno, *Prisms* (Cambridge, MA: MIT Press, 1981), trans. Samuel and Shierry Weber, p. 262.
27. George Eliot, *Middlemarch* (London: Penguin, 1994), p. 455.
28. Charles Dickens, *Bleak House* (Oxford: Oxford University Press, 1998), p. 289.
29. Eliot, *Middlemarch*, p. 24.
30. George Eliot, *Daniel Deronda* (Oxford: Oxford University Press, 1998), p. 3. Goethe, *Werther*, p. 127.
31. Frank Kermode, *The Sense of an Ending: Studies in the Theory of Fiction* (Oxford: Oxford University Press, 2000), p. 67.
32. Thomas Hardy, *The Return of the Native* (Oxford: Oxford University Press, 2005), p. 56.
33. Eliot, *Middlemarch*, p. 24.
34. Thomas Pynchon, *The Crying of Lot 49* (London: Picador, 1979), p. 56.
35. Hawthorne, *Blithedale Romance*, p. 2.
36. Dickens, *Bleak House*, p. 235.
37. Goethe, *Elective Affinities*, p. 30.
38. Marshall McLuhan, *Understanding Media: The Extensions of Man* (London: Routledge, 2001), p. 98.
39. McLuhan, *Understanding Media*, p. 98.
40. See John Milton, *Paradise Lost* (Harlow: Pearson, 2007), p. 59, ll. 15–16, where the poet writes that he 'pursues / Things unattempted yet in prose or rhyme'.
41. Wollstonecraft, *Mary*, p. 3.
42. For two discussions of the relation between Eliot's fiction and the developments in nineteenth-century science and medicine, see Sally Shuttleworth, *George Eliot and Nineteenth-Century Science: The Make Believe of a Beginning* (Cambridge: Cambridge University Press, 1984), and Vanessa L. Ryan, *Thinking Without Thinking in the Victorian Novel* (Baltimore: Johns Hopkins University Press, 2012), pp. 3–7.
43. Gillian Beer, *Darwin's Plots: Evolutionary Narrative in Darwin, George Eliot, and Nineteenth-Century Fiction* (Cambridge: Cambridge University Press, 1983), p. 143.
44. Eliot, *Deronda*, p. 406.
45. Shakespeare, 'Sonnet iii', p. 764.
46. See Isobel Armstrong, *Novel Politics: Democratic Imaginations in Nineteenth-Century Fiction* (Oxford: Oxford University Press, 2016), pp. 91–92.

47. Giorgio Agamben, *The Use of Bodies* (Stanford: Stanford University Press, 2016), trans. Adam Kotsko, p. 263.

48. For a recent reading of Jo's relationship with dirt, in terms of Agamben's conception of 'bare life', see Sabine Schülting, *Dirt in Victorian Literature and Culture: Writing Materiality* (London: Routledge, 2016), particularly pp. 79–114.

49. John Ruskin, *The Works of John Ruskin*, Vol. 37: *The Letters of John Ruskin 1870–1889* (Cambridge: Cambridge University Press, 2009), p. 7.

50. Emily Dickinson, 'There's a certain Slant of light', in Emily Dickinson, *The Poems of Emily Dickinson* (Cambridge, MA: Harvard University Press, 1999), p. 143.

51. Thomas Hardy, *Return of the Native* (Oxford: Oxford University Press, 2005), p. 56.

52. For Hegel's account of the 'unhappy consciousness', see G. W. F. Hegel, *Phenomenology of Spirit* (Cambridge: Cambridge University Press, 2018), trans. Terry Pinkard, pp. 117–35.

53. Eliot's imagination is shaped, to a considerable degree, by her relationship with Feuerbach. See Eliot's translation of Feuerbach's *The Essence of Christianity*. See also Eliot's famous comment, in a letter to Sara Sophia Hennell that 'with the ideas of Feuerbach I everywhere agree' (George Eliot, *The George Eliot Letters*, Vol. 2 (New Haven: Yale University Press, 1955), ed. Gordon S. Haight, p. 153). For Feuerbach's influence on Marx, see Karl Marx, 'Theses on Feuerbach', in Karl Marx and Frederick Engels, *Selected Works*, Vol. 1 (Moscow: Progress Publishers, 1969), pp. 13–15. For a powerful recent discussion of Eliot's reception of Feuerbach that touches too on the relation between Eliot, Feuerbach and Marx, see Cristina Richieri Griffin, 'George Eliot's Feuerbach: Senses, Sympathy, Omniscience and Secularism', *ELH*, vol. 84, no. 2 (2017), pp. 475–502.

54. Alex Woloch, 'Partial Representation' in Robyn Warhol, ed., *The Work of Genre: Selected Essays from the English Institute* (Cambridge: English Institute, 2011), np.

55. Wollstonecraft, *Mary*, p. 39.

56. Hegel, *Phenomenology*, p. 123.

57. Kevin McLouhglin, 'Losing One's Place: Displacement and Domesticity in Dickens's *Bleak House*', *Modern Language Notes*, vol. 108 (1993), pp. 875–90, p. 234.

58. C. G. Jung, *The Symbolic Life: Miscellaneous Writings* (London: Routledge and Kegan Paul, 1977), trans. R. F. C. Hull, p. 95.

59. Beckett, *Proust*, p. 13.

60. Charles Dickens, *A Christmas Carol and Other Christmas Books* (Oxford: Oxford University Press, 2006), p. 77.

61. Caroline Levine, *Forms: Whole, Rhythm, Hierarchy, Network* (Princeton: Princeton University Press, 2015), p. 125.

62. Frantz Fanon, *Black Skin, White Masks* (London: Pluto Press, 1986), trans. Charles Lam Markmann, p. 10.

63. Agamben, *Use of Bodies*, p. 263.

64. Georg Lukács, *Studies in European Realism* (New York: Grosset and Dunlap, 1964), trans. Edith Bone, p. 8.

65. Agamben, *Use of Bodies*, pp. 263–64.

66. Jay Leyda, *The Melville Log: A Documentary Life of Herman Melville 1819–1891*, Vol. 2 (New York: Gordian Press, 1969), p. 703.

67. Herman Melville, *Moby Dick* (Oxford: Oxford University Press, 2008), p. 118.

68. George Eliot, *The George Eliot Letters*, Vol. 4 (New Haven: Yale University Press, 1955), ed. Gordon S. Haight, p. 472.

69. See Herman Melville, *Billy Budd, Sailor (An Inside Narrative)*, in Herman Melville, *Billy Budd, Sailor, and Selected Tales* (Oxford: Oxford University Press, 1997).

70. See Herman Melville, *Clarel* (Evanston: Northwestern University Press, 2008).

71. Melville, *Moby Dick*, p. 23.

72. Herman Melville, *Benito Cereno*, in Herman Melville, *Melville's Short Novels* (New York: Norton, 2002), ed. Dan McCall, p. 38.

73. See Toni Morrison, 'Unspeakable Things Unspoken: The Afro-American Presence in American Literature', online at https://tannerlectures.utah.edu/_documents/a-to-z/m/morrison90.pdf, pp. 123–63.

74. Michael Paul Rogin, *Subversive Genealogy: The Politics and Art of Herman Melville* (Berkeley: University of California Press, 1983), p. 209.

75. Melville, *Moby Dick*, p. 471.

76. Morrison, 'Unspeakable', p. 143; Melville, *Moby Dick*, p. 168.

77. See Ralph Ellison, *Invisible Man* (London: Penguin, 1965), p. 6.

78. Matthew Rebhorn, 'Minding the Body: "Benito Cereno" and Melville's Embodied Reading Practice', *Studies in the Novel*, vol. 41, no. 2 (2009), pp. 157–77, p. 173.

79. Michael Jonik, *Herman Melville and the Politics of the Inhuman* (Cambridge: Cambridge University Press, 2018), p. 129; David J. Alworth, 'Melville in the Asylum: Literature, Sociology, Reading', *American Literary History*, vol. 26, no. 2 (2014), pp. 234–61, p. 246.

80. Dickinson, *Poems*, p. 269.

81. Dickinson, *Poems*, p. 379.

Strange Affinity: Gothic Prosthetics from Shelley to Stoker

1. Mary Shelley, *Frankenstein, Or the Modern Prometheus* (Oxford: Oxford University Press, 2008), p. 223.

2. Robert Louis Stevenson, *The Strange Case of Dr Jekyll and Mr Hyde and Other Stories* (London: Penguin, 1979), p. 28.

3. Oscar Wilde, *The Picture of Dorian Gray* (London: Penguin, 1985), p. 136.

4. Caroline Levine, 'Victorian Realism', in Deirdre David, ed., *The Cambridge Companion to the Victorian Novel* (Cambridge: Cambridge University Press, 2012), p. 84.

5. Robert Miles, 'Political Gothic Fiction', in Angela Wright and Dale Townshend, eds., *Romantic Gothic* (Edinburgh: Edinburgh University Press, 2016), p. 133.

6. Shelley, *Frankenstein*, p. 54.

7. See Agamben, *The Use of Bodies*, p. 263. For an illuminating reading of the relationship between Shelley's novel and Agamben's thought, see Roberto del Valle Alcalá, 'Monstrous Contemplation: *Frankenstein*, Agamben, and the Politics of Life', *Textual Practice*, vol. 32, no. 4 (2018), pp. 611–28.

8. Amitav Ghosh, *The Great Derangement: Climate Change and the Unthinkable* (Chicago: University of Chicago Press, 2016), p. 3.

9. David Wills, *Inanimation: Theories of Inorganic Life* (Minneapolis: University of Minnesota Press, 2016).

10. Silas Weir Mitchell, 'The Case of George Dedlow', in David Seed et al., eds., *Life and Limb: Perspectives on the American Civil War* (Liverpool: Liverpool University Press, 2017), pp. 131–45. Thanks to Kameron Sanzo for drawing my attention to this story.

11. Edgar Allan Poe, 'The Facts in the Case of M. Valdemar', in Edgar Allan Poe, *The Complete Tales and Poems of Edgar Allan Poe* (New York: Castle Books, 2002), pp. 99–105.

12. Bram Stoker, *Dracula* (London: Penguin, 1993), p. 19.

13. Behn, *Oroonoko*, p. 46.

14. Defoe, *Moll Flanders*, p. 363.

15. Richardson, *Pamela*, p. 204.

16. Wollstonecraft, *Mary*, p. 16.

17. Stephen Greenblatt, *Shakespearean Negotiations: The Circulation of Social Energy in Renaissance England* (Berkeley: University of California Press, 1988), p. 41.

18. Coleridge, 'Lectures Upon Shakespeare', p. 53.

19. D. H. Lawrence, 'Benjamin Franklin', in D. H. Lawrence, *The Symbolic Meaning* (New York: The Viking Press, 1964), p. 41.

20. Lawrence, *Letters*, p. 327; D. H. Lawrence, 'Why the Novel Matters', in D. H. Lawrence, *Study of Thomas Hardy and Other Essays* (Cambridge: Cambridge University Press, 1985), ed. Bruce Steele, pp. 191–98, p. 193.

21. Friedrich Kittler, *Gramophone, Film, Typewriter*, p. 16.

22. The passage Stoker is thinking of is 'My tables, / My tables – meet it is I set it down', William Shakespeare, *Hamlet*, in Shakespeare, *Complete Works*, I, 5, 107–8, p. 662.

23. Kittler, *Gramophone, Film, Typewriter*, p. 86.

24. For a series of monographs that explores the technologies of presence, see Steven Connor, David Trotter and James Purdon, 'Technographies', online at www.openhumanitiespress.org/books/series/technographies/.

25. Greenblatt, *Shakespearean Negotiations*, p. 65.

26. Nancy Armstrong, *How Novels Think: The Limits of Individualism from 1719–1900* (New York: Columbia University Press, 2005), p. 152.

27. Aristotle, *Meteorologica*, p. 390.

28. See Drew Milne, 'Notes on Lichen', *Textual Practice*, online at www .tandfonline.com/doi/full/10.1080/0950236X.2019.1613828.

29. For a powerful reading of decadence and its relation to modernism, see Vincent Sherry, *Modernism and the Reinvention of Decadence* (Cambridge: Cambridge University Press, 2015).

30. Wilde, *The Picture of Dorian Gray*, p. 162.

31. For Bersani's theory of relationality, see *Thoughts and Things*. See also Leo Bersani, *Homos* (Cambridge, MA: Harvard University Press, 1995).

32. Lawrence, 'Benjamin Franklin', p. 35.

33. Wilde remarks, in a 12 February 1894 letter to Ralph Payne, that 'there is much of me' in *Dorian Gray*: 'Basil Hallward is what I think I am: Lord Henry is what the world thinks me: Dorian is what I would like to be – in other ages, perhaps.' Oscar Wilde, *The Complete Letters of Oscar Wilde* (London: Fourth Estate, 2000), eds. Merlin Holland and Rupert Hart-Davies, p. 585.

34. Eliot, *Deronda*, p. 164.

A Duplication of Consciousness: Realism, Modernism and Prosthetic Self-Fashioning

1. Olive Schreiner, *The Story of an African Farm* (Oxford: Oxford University Press, 2008), p. 103.

2. Edith Wharton, *The House of Mirth* (Oxford: Oxford University Press, 2008), p. 145.

3. Franz Kafka, 'Report to an Academy', in Kafka, *Complete* Stories, p. 258.

4. Beckett, *Molloy*, p. 111.

5. Auerbach, *Mimesis*, p. 358.

6. Charlotte Perkins Gilman, *The Yellow Wallpaper* (London: Virago, 1981), p. 10.

7. See Fredric Jameson, *The Prison-House of Language: A Critical Account of Structuralism and Russian Formalism* (Princeton: Princeton University Press, 1972).

8. Edward Bellamy, *Looking Backward* (New York: Dover Publications, 1996), p. 37.

9. Marcel Proust, *Remembrance of Things Past*, Vol. 1 (London: Penguin, 1983), 3 vols., trans. C. K. Scott Moncrieff and Terence Kilmartin, p. 5.

10. Auerbach, *Mimesis*, p. 547; Scarlett Baron, *Strandentwining Cable: Joyce, Flaubert and Intertextuality* (Oxford: Oxford University Press, 2012), p. 276.
11. Gustave Flaubert, *The Selected Letters of Gustave Flaubert* (London: Hamish Hamilton, 1954), trans. and ed. Francis Steegmuller, p. 131.
12. For a landmark study of the relation between modernism and movements in the visual arts, from Dada to Vorticism, see Peter Nicholls, *Modernisms: A Literary Guide*, 2nd ed. (Basingstoke: Palgrave, 2009).
13. Franco Marinetti et al., 'The Futurist Cinema', collected in Lawrence Rainey et al., eds., *Futurism: An Anthology* (New Haven: Yale University Press, 2009), p. 230; Ezra Pound, 'Canto LIII', in Ezra Pound, *The Cantos of Ezra Pound* (London: Faber and Faber, 1975), p. 265.
14. For an account of the relation between modernism and the twentieth-century technologies of motion, see David Bradshaw et al., eds., *Moving Modernisms: Motion, Technology and Modernity* (Oxford: Oxford University Press, 2016).
15. Gerald Stanley Lee, *Crowds* (London: Curtis Brown, 1913), p. 199. See Tim Armstrong, *Modernism, Technology and the Body: A Cultural Study* (Cambridge: Cambridge University Press, 1998), pp. 82–83, for a discussion of Lee's place in what Armstrong calls 'prosthetic modernism'.
16. Auerbach, *Mimesis*, p. 538.
17. Georg Lukács, *The Meaning of Contemporary Realism* (Monmouth: The Merlin Press, 2006), trans. John and Necke Mander, p. 56.
18. T. S. Eliot, '*Ulysses*, Order and Myth', collected in Lawrence Rainey, ed., *Modernism: An Anthology* (Oxford: Blackwell, 2005), p. 166.
19. Henry James, 'Henry James' First Interview', in Henry James, *Henry James on Culture: Collected Essays on Politics and the American Social Scene* (Lincoln: University of Nebraska Press, 1999), ed. Pierre A. Walker, p. 144.
20. For a theory of abstraction, as it stretches from modernism to the contemporary, see Rebecca Colesworthy and Peter Nicholls, eds., *How Abstract Is It? Thinking Capital Now* (London: Routledge, 2016).
21. Wyndham Lewis, 'The Children of the New Epoch', collected in Walter Michel and C. J. Fox, *Wyndham Lewis on Art: Collected Writings 1913–1956* (London: Thames and Hudson, 1969), p. 195.
22. Wyndham Lewis, 'Manifesto', in *Wyndham Lewis on Art*, p. 30.
23. Lewis, 'Manifesto', p. 30.
24. For reproductions and analysis of the work of Kahlo and Bellmer, see Emma Dexter and Tanya Barson, eds., *Frida Kahlo* (London: Tate, 2005); Claire Wilcox and Circe Henestrosa, *Frida Kahlo: Making Her Self Up* (London: V&A, 2018); Michael Semff and Anthony Spira, *Hans Bellmer* (Ostfildern: Hatje Cantz, 2006).
25. Armstrong, *Modernism, Technology, and the Body*, p. 201. Samuel Beckett, 'Dante . . . Bruno. Vico. Joyce', in Samuel Beckett et al., *Our Exagmination*

Round his Factification for Incamination of Work in Progress (London: Faber and Faber, 1972), p. 14.

26. Spyros Papapetros, *On the Animation of the Inorganic: Art, Architecture, and the Extension of Life* (Chicago: University of Chicago Press, 2012), p. 317.

27. Samuel Beckett, *Disjecta: Miscellaneous Writings and a Dramatic Fragment* (London: Calder, 1983), p. 171.

28. Samuel Beckett, *Proust and Three Dialogues with Georges Duthuit* (London: Calder, 1965), p. 126.

29. Beckett, *Disjecta*, p. 172.

30. Beckett, *Proust*, p. 110.

31. Samuel Beckett, *The Unnamable*, in Beckett, *Molloy, Malone Dies, The Unnamable*, p. 386.

32. Ludovic Janvier, 'Place of Narration / Narration of Place', in Ruby Cohn, ed., *Samuel Beckett: The Comic Gamut* (New Brunswick: Rutgers University Press, 1962), p. 101.

33. Henry James, *What Maisie Knew* (London: Penguin, 1985), p. 35. Thanks to Katherine Kruger for helping me to understand Maisie.

34. Henry James, *The Jolly Corner*, in Henry James, *Tales of Henry James* (New York: Norton, 2003), eds. Christof Wegelin and Henry B. Wonham, pp. 341–69, p. 344.

35. See Henry James, *Glasses*, in Henry James, *The Complete Tales of Henry James,* Vol. 9: *1892–1898* (London: Rupert Hart-Davis, 1964), ed. Leon Edel, pp. 317–70. For a reading of *Glasses*, see José A. Álvarez-Amorós, 'On Flora Saunt Being Vain: Aspectuality and the Social Construction of Identity in Henry James's "Glasses"', in *Textual Practice*, online at www.tandfonline.com/doi/full/10.1080/0950236X.2017.1422796. For James' interest in lenses in *Portrait of a Lady*, see his Preface to the novel, in which he says, of the many windows one finds in the 'house of fiction', that 'at each of them stands a figure with a pair of eyes, or at least with a field glass'. Henry James, 'Preface', in Henry James, *The Portrait of a Lady* (Oxford: Oxford University Press, 2009), p. 7.

36. The phrase is 'their eyes were in each other's eyes' in *What Maisie Knew* (p. 188), and 'her eyes were in his eyes' in *The Jolly Corner* (p. 367).

37. James, *Portrait*, p. 8.

38. For a collection of all existing correspondence between James and Wharton, see *Henry James and Edith Wharton Letters, 1900–1915* (London: Weidenfeld and Nicolson, 1990), ed. Lyall H. Powers.

39. Edith Wharton, *A Backward Glance* (New York: Charles Scribner's Sons, 1964), p. 190.

40. Flaubert, *Selected Letters*, p. 131.

41. Edith Wharton, *The House of Mirth* (Oxford: Oxford University Press, 2008), p. 64.

42. Richardson, *Pamela*, p. 20.
43. Edith Wharton, *The Age of Innocence* (London: Penguin, 1993), p. 42.
44. Edith Wharton, *The Writing of Fiction* (New York: Octagon Books, 1966), p. 129.
45. See Wharton, *A Backward Glance*, where she writes that Henry James 'used his magic faculty of drawing out his interlocutor's inmost self' (p. 173).
46. James, *Henry James on Culture*, p. 144.
47. Wharton, *The Writing of Fiction*, p.128. For a reproduction of Reynolds' *Mrs Lloyd Inscribing a Tree*, which is the basis of Lily's tableau, see Mark Hallett, *Reynolds: Portraiture in Action* (New Haven: Yale University Press, 2014), p. 263, plate 243.
48. Shakespeare, 'Sonnet III', p. 764; Dickens, *Bleak House*, p. 5.
49. Nancy Bentley, *The Ethnography of Manners: Hawthorne, James and Wharton* (Cambridge: Cambridge University Press, 1995), p. 190.
50. Michael Gorra, 'The Portrait of Miss Bart', *New York Review of Books*, online at www.nybooks.com/daily/2015/05/01/house-of-mirth-portrait-miss-bart/, np.
51. See Jordan, *Between Fact and Imagination*.
52. Wilde, *Dorian Gray*, p. 191.
53. Maureen Howard, 'The Bachelor and the Baby: *The House of Mirth*', in Millicent Bell, ed., *The Cambridge Companion to Edith Wharton* (Cambridge: Cambridge University Press, 1995), p. 142.
54. See James Joyce, *Finnegans Wake* (London: Minerva, 1992), p. 424; Samuel Beckett, 'What is the Word', in Samuel Beckett, *The Collected Poems of Samuel Beckett: A Critical Edition* (London: Faber, 2012), eds. Sean Lawlor and John Pilling, pp. 228–29.

All Twined Together: Prosthetic Modernism
from Proust to Beckett

1. Samuel Beckett, *Texts for Nothing*, in Samuel Beckett, *The Complete Short Prose, 1929–1989* (New York: Grove Press, 1995), pp. 100–154, p. 104.
2. Faulkner describes the process by which the duplication of narrative perspective produces a 'complete picture', in a public conversation held at the University of Virginia in 1957. An audio recording of the discussion, with a transcript, can be found at http://faulkner.lib.virginia.edu/display/wfaudio13.
3. Virginia Woolf, *The Waves* (Oxford: Oxford University Press, 2015), p. 80.
4. Virginia Woolf, *Mrs Dalloway* (New York: Alfred A. Knopf, 1993), p. 7.
5. For an extended analysis of Beckett's engagement with the prosthesis, see Yoshiki Tajiri, *Samuel Beckett and the Prosthetic Body: The Organs and Senses in Modernism* (Basingstoke: Palgrave, 2007). For a corpus of criticism that has turned its attention to the manufactured body in Beckett's work, see Laura Salisbury, *Samuel Beckett: Laughing Matters, Comic Timing* (Edinburgh: Edinburgh University Press, 2012), and Ulrika Maude, *Beckett, Technology and the Body* (Cambridge: Cambridge University Press, 2009).

6. See Madelyn Detloff, *The Persistence of Modernism: Loss and Mourning in the Twentieth Century* (Cambridge: Cambridge University Press, 2009); Alys Moody, *The Art of Hunger: Aesthetic Autonomy and the Afterlives of Modernism* (Oxford: Oxford University Press, 2018); Tyrus Miller, *Late Modernism: Politics, Fiction and the Arts between the World Wars* (Berkeley: University of California Press, 1999).

7. Samuel Beckett, *Company*, in Samuel Beckett, *Nohow On: Company, Ill Seen Ill Said, Worstward Ho* (London: Calder, 1992), p. 5.

8. For a range of Beckett's plays that offers critical reflections on prosthetic media, see for example, *Krapp's Last Tape, All that Fall, Eh Joe* and *Ghost Trio*, all collected in Samuel Beckett, *Complete Dramatic Works* (London: Faber, 2006).

9. Samuel Beckett, *How it Is* (London: Calder, 1996), p. 139.

10. Samuel Beckett, *The Unnamable*, in Samuel Beckett, *Molloy, Malone Dies, The Unnamable* (London: Calder, 1994), p. 400.

11. See Samuel Beckett, *Not I*, in Beckett, *Complete Dramatic Works*.

12. Samuel Beckett, *Worstward Ho*, in Beckett, *Nohow On*, p. 101.

13. See David James, ed., *The Legacies of Modernism: Historicising Postwar and Contemporary Fiction* (Cambridge: Cambridge University Press, 2012).

14. James Joyce, *A Portrait of the Artist as a Young Man* (London: Penguin, 1992), p. 276.

15. Joyce, *Portrait*, p. 183.

16. Joyce, *Portrait*, p. 184.

17. See Samuel Beckett, *Ohio Impromptu*, in Beckett, *Complete Dramatic Works*, p. 446. For an account of *Ohio Impromptu* as an homage to Joyce, see James Knowlson, *Damned to Fame: The Life of Samuel Beckett* (London: Bloomsbury, 1996), pp. 664–65.

18. Joyce, *Ulysses*, p. 31.

19. Joyce, *Ulysses*, p. 37.

20. See Baron, *Strandentwining Cable*, where Baron reads this image of umbilical connection as the manifestation of a series of intertextual connections binding Joyce's imagination to his precursors, and particularly to Flaubert.

21. Samuel Beckett, *Endgame*, in Beckett, *Complete Dramatic Works*, p. 96.

22. Joyce, *Ulysses*, p. 32.

23. Beckett, *Waiting for Godot*, in Beckett, *Complete Dramatic Works*, p. 84.

24. Shakespeare, *Hamlet*, I, 5, 164, p. 662.

25. Beckett, 'Dante . . . Bruno. Vico. Joyce', p. 8.

26. For two readings of Beckett's relation with Proust, see Nicholas Zurbrugg, *Beckett and Proust* (Gerrard's Cross: Colin Smythe, 1988) and James H. Reid, *Proust, Beckett and Narration* (Cambridge: Cambridge University Press, 2009).

27. Marcel Proust, *Remembrance of Things Past* (London: Penguin, 1983), 3 vols., Vol. 1, trans C. K. Scott Moncrieff and Terence Kilmartin, p. 20.

28. Beckett, *Proust*, p. 13.

29. Proust, *Remembrance*, Vol. 1, p. 36.

30. Beckett, *Molloy*, p. 16.

31. Proust, *Remembrance*, Vol. 1, p. 14.

32. Franz Kafka, *Metamorphosis*, in Franz Kafka, *The Complete Stories* (New York: Shocken, 1971), p. 89.

33. Jacques Rancière, 'The Aesthetic Revolution and Its Outcomes: Emplotments of Autonomy and Heteronomy', *New Left Review*, vol. 14 (2002), pp. 133–51, pp. 150–51.

34. Proust, *Remembrance*, Vol. 1, p. 3.

35. Proust, *Remembrance*, Vol. 1, p. 49.

36. Beckett, *Company*, p. 17.

37. Proust, *Remembrance*, Vol. 1, p. 6.

38. Samuel Beckett, 'Neither', in Beckett, *Complete Short Prose*, p. 258.

39. Joyce, *Portrait*, p. 233.

40. Beckett, 'Dante . . . Bruno. Vico. Joyce', p. 15.

41. Proust, *Remembrance*, Vol. 3, p. 1100.

42. Henry James, *The Middle Years*, in James, *Tales*, pp. 211–28, p. 213.

43. Beckett, *Proust*, p. 79.

44. Beckett, *Dream*, p. 119.

45. Wharton, *House of Mirth*, p. 310.

46. Beckett, *Proust*, p. 65. Shane Weller, *Beckett, Literature and the Ethics of Alterity* (Basingstoke: Palgrave, 2006), pp. 60–61.

47. Swift, *Gulliver's Travels*, p. 29.

48. Samuel Beckett, *Murphy* (London: Picador, 1973), p. 157.

49. Proust, *Remembrance*, vol. 3, pp. 1105, 1106.

50. See Marguerite Duras, *The Rapture of Lol V. Stein* (London: Hamish Hamilton, 1967), trans. Eileen Ellenbogen, p. 29, where an 'empty gong' stands in for what Duras' narrator calls a 'hole-word', an absent word that 'pollutes and contaminates all existing words'.

51. Woolf, *Mrs Dalloway*, p. 2.

52. Charles Dickens, *David Copperfield* (London: Penguin, 2004), p. 882.

53. Samuel Beckett, *The Letters of Samuel Beckett:* Vol. 1: *1929–1940* (Cambridge: Cambridge University Press, 2009), eds. Martha Dow Fehsenfeld and Lois More Overbeck, p. 223.

54. For reproductions of Cézanne's mountain paintings, see William Rubin, ed., *Cézanne: The Late Work* (New York: Museum of Modern Art, 1977).

55. Defoe, *Robinson Crusoe*, p. 133.

56. Beckett, *Texts for Nothing*, p. 103.

57. Samuel Beckett, *The Lost Ones*, in Beckett, *Complete Short Prose*, p. 215.

58. Beckett, 'Neither', p. 258.

Prosthetics and Simulacra: The Postmodern Novel

1. Thomas Pynchon, *The Crying of Lot 49* (London: Vintage, 2000), p. 124.
2. Christine Brooke-Rose, 'The Foot', in Christine Brooke-Rose, *Go When You See the Green Man Walking* (London: Michael Joseph, 1970), p. 60.
3. N. Katherine Hayles, *How We Became Posthuman: Virtual Bodies in Cybernetics, Literature and Informatics* (Chicago: University of Chicago Press, 1999), p. xi. Alan Turning, 'Computer Machinery and Intelligence', *Mind* 54 (1950), pp. 433–60.
4. Jean François Lyotard, *The Postmodern Condition: A Report on Knowledge* (Manchester: Manchester University Press, 1984), trans. Geoff Bennington and Brian Massumi, pp. 3, 4.
5. See Marshall Berman, *All That Is Solid Melts into Air: The Experience of Modernity* (London: Verso, 1983). The phrase is taken from Karl Marx and Friedrich Engels, *The Communist Manifesto* (New Haven: Yale University Press, 2012), p. 77.
6. Ricoeur, 'The Function of Fiction in Shaping Reality', p. 119.
7. For Baudrillard's seminal account of the simulacrum, see Jean Baudrillard, *Simulacra and Simulation* (Ann Arbor: University of Michigan Press, 1994), trans. Sheila Faria Glaser; and Jean Baudrillard, *Symbolic Exchange and Death* (London: Sage, 1993), trans. Iain Hamilton Grant.
8. Ricoeur, 'The Function of Fiction in Shaping Reality', p. 129.
9. Fredric Jameson, *Postmodernism: or, The Cultural Logic of Late Capitalism* (London: Verso, 1991), p. 297.
10. Don DeLillo, *White Noise* (London: Picador, 1999), p. 12. For an influential early reading of the relation between DeLillo and Baudrillard, see Leonard Wilcox, 'Baudrillard, DeLillo's *White Noise*, and the End of Heroic Narrative', *Contemporary Literature*, vol. 32, no. 3 (1991), pp. 346–65.
11. For his theory of the event, see Alain Badiou, *Being and Event* (London: Continuum, 2005), trans. Oliver Feltham.
12. Rosi Braidotti, *The Posthuman* (Cambridge: Polity, 2013), p. 188.
13. *The Prosthesis of Origin* is the subtitle to Jacques Derrida, *Monolingualism of the Other, Or The Prosthesis of Origin* (Stanford: Stanford University Press, 1998), trans. Patrick Mensah. See Derrida, *Archive Fever*, p. 18, for a discussion of prosthesis as 'originary threshold'.
14. See Arthur Bradley, *Originary Technicity: The Theory of Technology from Marx to Derrida* (Basingstoke: Palgrave, 2011).
15. Derrida, *Archive Fever*, p. 16.
16. Jacques Derrida, *Dissemination* (London: Athlone Press, 1981), trans. Barbara Johnson, p. 168.
17. Derrida, *Dissemination*, p. 168.

18. Derrida, *Dissemination*, p. 168; Jacques Derrida, 'Passions: An Oblique Offering', in David Wood, ed., *Derrida: A Critical Reader* (Oxford: Blackwell, 1992), trans. David Wood, pp. 5–35, p. 6.

19. Ben Roberts, 'Stiegler Reading Derrida: The Prosthesis of Deconstruction in Technics', *Postmodern Culture*, vol. 16, no. 1 (2005), online at http://pmc .iath.virginia.edu/issue.905/16.1roberts.html, np. Bernard Stiegler, *Technics and Time, 1: The Fault of Epimetheus* (Stanford: Stanford University Press, 1998), trans. Richard Beardsworth and George Collins, p. 139.

20. Thomas Pynchon, 'The Road to 1984', in *The Guardian*, 3 May 2003, online at www.scribd.com/doc/100899/Pynchon-s-Intro-to-Orwell-s-1984, np.

21. George Orwell, *Nineteen Eighty-Four* (London: Penguin, 1987), p. 261.

22. Christine Brooke-Rose, 'The Foot', p. 49.

23. See N. Katherine Hayles, *Unthought: The Power of the Cognitive Nonconscious* (Chicago: University of Chicago Press, 2017).

24. Toni Morrison, *The Bluest Eye* (London: Vintage, 2016), p. 136.

25. George Orwell, 'Inside the Whale', in George Orwell, *Inside the Whale And Other Essays* (London: Penguin, 1962), p. 48.

26. Salman Rushdie, 'Outside the Whale', in Salman Rushdie, *Imaginary Homelands: Essays in Criticism 1981–91* (London: Granta, 1992), p. 99.

27. Pynchon, 'The Road to 1984', np.

28. Salman Rushdie, 'Imaginary Homelands', in Rushdie, *Imaginary Homelands*, p. 13; Salman Rushdie, *Midnight's Children* (London: Vintage, 2006), p. 166.

29. For his critical decolonising of the mind, see Ngũgĩ wa Thiong'o, *Decolonising the Mind: The Politics of African Literature* (London: James Currey, 1986)

30. Linda Hutcheon, *The Politics of Postmodernism*, 2nd ed. (London: Routledge, 2002).

31. For a representative reading of Pynchon as postmodernist, see Shawn Smith, *Pynchon and History: Metahistorical Rhetoric and Postmodern Narrative Form in the Novels of Thomas Pynchon* (New York: Routledge 2005); for a reading of Morrison and postmodernism, see Susan Sniader Lanser, 'Unspeakable Voice: Toni Morrison's Postmodern Authority', in Susan Sniader Lanser *Fictions of Authority: Women Writers and Narrative Voice* (Ithaca: Cornell University Press, 1992), pp. 120–38.

32. For a reproduction and discussion of this painting, see Janet A. Kaplan, *Unexpected Journeys: The Art and Life of Remedios Varo* (London: Virago, 1988), p. 21.

33. James, *What Maisie Knew*, p. 217.

34. Toni Morrison's television interview with Bill Moyers, on 11 March 1990, is available online, with a transcript, at https://billmoyers.com/content/toni-morrison-part-1/.

35. John N. Duvall, *The Identifying Fictions of Toni Morrison: Modernist Authenticity and Postmodern Blackness* (Basingstoke: Palgrave, 2000), p. 17.

36. bell hooks, 'Postmodern Blackness', *Postmodern Culture*, vol. 1, no. 1 (1990), online at https://muse.jhu.edu/article/27283, np.

37. Thomas Pynchon, *Gravity's Rainbow* (New York: Viking, 1973), pp. 774, 262. For a reading of these doubling worlds in *Gravity's Rainbow*, see Leo Bersani, 'Pynchon, Paranoia, and Literature', *Representations*, vol. 25 (1989), pp. 99–118.

38. Flaubert, *Selected Letters*, p. 131.

39. See Julia Kristeva, *Powers of Horror: An Essay on Abjection* (New York: Columbia University Press, 1982).

40. Toni Morrison, 'Unspeakable Things Unspoken: The Afro-American Presence in American Literature', online at https://tannerlectures.utah.edu/_documents/a-to-z/m/morrison90.pdf, pp. 123–63, p. 142.

41. Toni Morrison, *Playing in the Dark: Whiteness and the Literary Imagination* (Cambridge, MA: Harvard University Press, 1992), p. 10.

42. Morrison, *Playing in the Dark*, p. 91.

43. Burney, *Evelina*, p. 442.

44. Morrison, 'Unspeakable Things Unspoken', p. 143.

45. Morrison, 'Unspeakable Things Unspoken', p. 143.

46. Proust, *Remembrance*, Vol. 1, p. 14.

47. Beckett, *Proust*, pp. 69–70.

48. There are many variations on the theme of the critical aftermath to postmodernism. See, for example, Jeffrey T. Nealon, *Post-Postmodernism, Or the Cultural Logic of Just in Time Capitalism* (Stanford: Stanford University Press, 2012); the 'new sincerity' proposed in David Foster Wallace, 'E Unibus Pluram: Television and U.S. Fiction', *Review of Contemporary Fiction*, vol. 13, no. 2 (1993), pp. 151–94; Adam Kelly, 'David Foster Wallace and the New Sincerity in American Fiction', in David Hering, ed., *Consider David Foster Wallace: Critical Essays* (Austin: Sideshow, 2010), pp. 131–46; and Timotheus Vermeulen and Robin van den Akker, 'Notes on Metamodernism', *Journal of Aesthetics & Culture*, vol. 2 (2010), pp. 1–14.

Prosthetic Worlds in the Twenty-First-Century Novel

1. J. M. Coetzee, *In the Heart of the Country* (London: Vintage, 2004), p. 142.

2. Don DeLillo, *Point Omega* (London: Picador, 2010), p. 92.

3. Don DeLillo, *Zero K* (London: Picador, 2017), p. 46.

4. Behn, *Oroonoko*, p. 46.

5. Beckett, *Worstward Ho*, p. 101.

6. Beckett, *The Unnamable*, p. 386.

7. Martin Heidegger, 'The Age of the World Picture', in Martin Heidegger, *The Question Concerning Technology and Other Essays* (New York: Harper, 1977), pp. 115–54.

8. Martin Heidegger, *The Fundamental Concepts of Metaphysics: World, Finitude, Solitude* (Bloomington: Indiana University Press, 1995), trans. William McNeill and Nicholas Walker, p. 185

9. Heidegger, 'World Picture', p. 134.

10. Martin Heidegger, 'Existence and Being', in Walter Kaufmann, *Existentialism from Dostoyevsky to Sartre* (Berkeley: New American Library, 1975), p. 378.

11. J. M. Coetzee, *The Childhood of Jesus* (London: Harvill Secker, 2013), p. 115.

12. Dipesh Chakrabarty, 'The Climate of History: Four Theses', *Critical Inquiry*, vol. 35, no. 2 (2009), pp. 197–222, p. 203.

13. Naomi Oreskes, 'The Scientific Consensus on Climate Change: How Do We Know We're Not Wrong?' in Joseph F. C. Dimento and Pamela Doughman, eds., *Climate Change: What It Means for Us, Our Children, and Our Grandchildren* (Cambridge, MA: MIT Press, 2007).

14. See for example Timothy Morton, *Ecology Without Nature: Rethinking Environmental Aesthetics* (Cambridge, MA: Harvard University Press, 2007); Wai Chee Dimock, *Through Other Continents: American Literature Across Deep Time* (Princeton: Princeton University Press, 2006); Ursula K. Heise, *Sense of Place and Sense of Planet: The Environmental Imagination of the Global* (Oxford: Oxford University Press, 2008).

15. Amy J. Elias and Christian Moraru, eds., *The Planetary Turn: Relationality and Geo-Aesthetics in the Twenty-First Century* (Evanston: Northwestern University Press, 2015), p. xi.

16. Amitav Ghosh, *The Great Derangement* (Chicago: University of Chicago Press, 2016), p. 3.

17. Richard Powers, 'The Seventh Event', *Granta*, vol. 90 (2005), pp. 58–74, p. 59.

18. For a classic account of Goethe's conception of world literature, see Fritz Strich, *Goethe and World Literature* (London: Routledge, 1949). See also Pascale Casanova, *The World Republic of Letters* (Cambridge, MA: Harvard University Press, 2004), trans. M. B. DeBevoise.

19. See Kiron Ward, 'Fictional Encyclopaedism in James Joyce, Leslie Marmon Silko, and Roberto Bolaño: Towards a Theory of Literary Totality' (PhD thesis: Sussex: University of Sussex, 2017); Joel Evans, *Conceptualising the Global in the Wake of the Postmodern: Literature, Culture, Theory* (Cambridge: Cambridge University Press, 2019).

20. For a reading of Drndić's fiction as a prosthetic response to political atrocity, see Merve Emre, 'Dismembered, Relocated, Rearranged', in *New York Review*

of Books, 6 June (2019), online at www.nybooks.com/articles/2019/06/06/da sa-drndic-dismembered/

21. Roberto Bolaño, *2666* (London: Picador, 2009), trans. Natasha Wimmer, p. 686.

22. Ludwig Wittgenstein, *On Certainty* (New York: Harper, 1972), trans. Denis Paul and G. E. M. Anscombe, p. 15e.

23. J. M. Coetzee, *Elizabeth Costello* (New York: Viking, 2003), p. 1.

24. Martin Heidegger, 'Building Dwelling Thinking', in Martin Heidegger, *Poetry, Language, Thought* (New York: Harper, 1975), trans. Albert Hofstadter, p. 152.

25. Samuel Beckett, *Imagination Dead Imagine*, in Beckett, *Complete Short Prose*, p. 182.

26. Margaret Atwood, *Oryx and Crake* (London: Virago, 2009), p. 13.

27. Cormac McCarthy, *The Road* (London: Picador, 2006), p. 293.

28. Coetzee, *Childhood*, p. 64.

29. See Ludwig Wittgenstein, *Philosophical Investigations* (London: Blackwell, 1967), trans G. E. M. Anscombe, where Wittgenstein suggests that the *Investigations* should be read against the mistaken thinking in the *Tractatus*. The *Investigations*, he writes, 'could be seen in the right light only by contrast with and against the background of my old way of thinking' (p. viii).

30. DeLillo, *Point Omega*, p. 5.

31. For his theory of the omega point, see Pierre Teilhard de Chardin, *The Phenomenon of Man* (London: Collins, 1959), trans. Bernard Wall, particularly pp. 254–72.

32. Beckett, *Molloy*, p. 11.

33. See J. G. Ballard, *The Atrocity Exhibition* (London: Fourth Estate, 2014), p. 44.

34. Wharton, *House of Mirth*, p. 7.

35. Eliot, *Middlemarch*, p. 194; Eliot, *Letters*, p. 472.

36. Chardin, *Phenomenon of Man*, p. 272.

37. Coetzee, *Heart of the Country*, p. 166.

38. Beckett, 'Neither', p. 258.

39. See Ernst Bloch and Theodor Adorno, 'Something's Missing', in Ernst Bloch, *The Utopian Function of Art and Literature: Selected Essays* (Cambridge, MA: MIT Press, 1988), trans. Jack Zipes and Frank Mecklenburg, pp. 1–17.

40. Defoe, *Robinson Crusoe*, p. 42.

41. Coetzee, *Late Essays*, p. 212.

42. Don DeLillo, *The Word for Snow* (New York: Karma Glenn Horowitz, 2014), p. 21.

43. Coetzee, *Late Essays*, p. 206.

44. Samuel Beckett, *Ghost Trio*, in Beckett, *Complete Dramatic Works*, p. 408.

45. Beckett, *How It Is*, p. 7.
46. Heidegger, 'Existence and Being', p. 378.
47. Heidegger, 'The Age of the World Picture', p. 134.
48. Heidegger, 'Building, Dwelling, Thinking', p. 157.
49. My conversation with DeLillo has been published in the form of an interview. See Don DeLillo and Peter Boxall, 'The Edge of the Future: A Conversation with Don DeLillo', in Katherine Da Cunha Lewin and Kiron Ward, eds., *Don DeLillo: Contemporary Critical Perspectives* (London: Bloomsbury, 2019), p. 164.

Bibliography

Achebe, Chinua, *Things Fall Apart* (London: Penguin, 2001).

Acker, Kathy, *Don Quixote: Which Was a Dream* (New York: Grove Press, 1986).

Adams, Marcus P., 'The Wax and the Mechanical Mind: Reexamining Hobbes's Objections to Descartes's *Meditations*', *British Journal for the History of Philosophy*, vol. 22, no. 3 (2014), pp. 403–24.

Adorno., Theodor, *Prisms* (Cambridge, MA: MIT Press, 1981), trans. Samuel and Shierry Weber.

Agamben, Giorgio, *Homo Sacer: Sovereign Power and Bare Life* (Stanford: Stanford University Press, 1998), trans. Daniel Heller-Roazen.

The Use of Bodies (Stanford: Stanford University Press, 2016), trans. Adam Kotsko.

Alcalá, Roberto del Valle, 'Monstrous Contemplation: *Frankenstein*, Agamben, and the Politics of Life', *Textual Practice*, vol. 32, no. 4 (2018), pp. 611–28.

Álvarez-Amorós, José A., 'On Flora Saunt Being Vain: Aspectuality and the Social Construction of Identity in Henry James's "Glasses"', *Textual Practice*, online at www.tandfonline.com/doi/full/10.1080/0950236X.2017.1422796

Alworth, David J., 'Melville in the Asylum: Literature, Sociology, Reading', *American Literary History*, vol. 26, no. 2 (2014), pp. 234–61.

Apuleius, *The Golden Ass* (Oxford: Oxford University Press, 1994), trans. P. G. Walsh.

Aristotle, *Meteorologica*, in *The Works of Aristotle*, Vol. 3 (Oxford: Clarendon, 1931), trans. W. D. Ross.

Armstrong, Isobel, *Novel Politics: Democratic Imaginations in Nineteenth-Century Fiction* (Oxford: Oxford University Press, 2016).

Armstrong, Nancy, *How Novels Think: The Limits of Individualism from 1719–1900* (New York: Columbia University Press, 2005).

Armstrong, Tim, *Modernism, Technology and the Body: A Cultural Study* (Cambridge: Cambridge University Press, 1998).

Arnold, Matthew, *Essays in Criticism* (London: Routledge, 1907).

Asimov, Isaac, *The Bicentennial Man and Other Stories* (London: Victor Gollancz, 2000).

Attie, Katherine Bootle, 'Re-Membering the Body Politic: Hobbes and the Construction of Civic Immortality', *ELH*, vol. 75, no. 3 (2008), pp. 497–530.

Atwood, Margaret, *A Handmaid's Tale* (London: Vintage, 1996).

Madaddam (London: Virago, 2014).

Oryx and Crake (London: Virago, 2009).

Year of the Flood (London: Virago, 2010).

Auerbach, Erich, *Mimesis: The Representation of Reality in Western Literature* (Princeton: Princeton University Press, 2003), trans. Willard R. Trask.

Augustine, *Confessions* (London: Penguin, 1961), trans. R. S. Pine-Coffin.

Austen, Jane, *Emma* (London: Penguin, 1996).

Northanger Abbey (Oxford: Oxford University Press, 2003).

Auster, Paul, *The New York Trilogy* (London: Penguin, 1990).

Bacon, Francis, *New Atlantis*, in Susan Bruce, ed., *Three Early Modern Utopias: Thomas More*, Utopia, *Francis Bacon*, New Atlantis, *Henry Neville*, The Isle of Pines (Oxford: Oxford University Press, 1999).

Badiou, Alain, *Being and Event* (London: Continuum, 2005), trans. Oliver Feltham.

Bakhtin, Mikhail, *The Dialogic Imagination: Four Essays* (Austin: University of Texas Press, 1981), trans. Caryl Emerson and Michael Holquist.

Baldwin, William, *Beware the Cat* (San Marino: Huntington Library, 1988).

Ballard, J. G., *The Atrocity Exhibition* (London: Fourth Estate, 2014).

Balzac, Honoré de, *Oeuvres Complètes* (Paris: Editions Louis Conard, 1948).

Baron, Scarlett, *Strandentwining Cable: Joyce, Flaubert and Intertextuality* (Oxford: Oxford University Press, 2012).

Baudrillard, Jean, *Simulacra and Simulation* (Ann Arbor: University of Michigan Press, 1994), trans. Sheila Faria Glaser.

Symbolic Exchange and Death (London: Sage, 1993), trans. Iain Hamilton Grant.

Beckett, Samuel, *The Collected Poems of Samuel Beckett: A Critical Edition* (London: Faber, 2012), eds. Sean Lawlor and John Pilling.

Company, in Samuel Beckett, *Nohow On: Company, Ill Seen Ill Said, Worstward Ho* (London: Calder, 1992).

Complete Dramatic Works (London: Faber, 2006).

The Complete Short Prose, 1929–1989 (New York: Grove Press, 1995).

'Dante . . . Bruno.. Vico. Joyce', in Samuel Beckett et al., *Our Exagmination Round His Factification for Incamination of Work in Progress* (London: Faber, 1972).

Disjecta: Miscellaneous Writings and a Dramatic Fragment (London: Calder, 1983).

Dream of Fair to Middling Women (London: Calder, 1993).

How It Is (London: Calder, 1996).

The Letters of Samuel Beckett: Vol. 1: *1929–1940* (Cambridge: Cambridge University Press, 2009), eds. Martha Dow Fehsenfeld and Lois More Overbeck.

The Lost Ones, in Samuel Beckett, *The Complete Short Prose, 1929–1989* (New York: Grove Press, 1995), pp. 202–23.

Molloy, Malone Dies, The Unnamable Molloy, Malone Dies, The Unnamable (London: Calder, 1994).

Murphy (London: Picador, 1973).

Proust, and Three Dialogues with Georges Duthuit (London: Calder, 1965).

Stirrings Still (Foxrock Books/Evergreen Review in association with OR Books, 2015).

The Unnamable, in Samuel Beckett, *Molloy, Malone Dies, The Unnamable* (London: Calder, 1994).

Watt (London: Calder, 1976).

Worstward Ho, in Samuel Beckett, *Nohow On: Company, Ill Seen Ill Said, Worstward Ho* (London: Calder, 1992).

Beer, Gillian, *Darwin's Plots: Evolutionary Narrative in Darwin, George Eliot, and Nineteenth-Century Fiction* (Cambridge: Cambridge University Press, 1983).

Behn, Aphra, *Oroonoko* (London: Penguin, 2003).

Bellamy, Edward, *Looking Backward* (New York: Dover Publications, 1996).

Belsey, Catherine, *Culture and the Real* (London: Routledge, 2005).

Benjamin, Walter, *Illuminations* (London: Pimlico, 1999).

Bennett, Andrew, *Suicide Century: Literature and Suicide from James Joyce to David Foster Wallace* (Cambridge: Cambridge University Press, 2017).

Bennett, Jane, *Vibrant Matter: A Political Ecology of Things* (Durham: Duke University Press, 2010).

Bentley, Nancy, *The Ethnography of Manners: Hawthorne, James and Wharton* (Cambridge: Cambridge University Press, 1995).

Berger, John, *The Shape of a Pocket* (London: Bloomsbury, 2001).

Berman, Marshall, *All That Is Solid Melts into Air: The Experience of Modernity* (London: Verso, 1983).

Bersani, Leo, *Homos* (Cambridge, MA: Harvard University Press, 1995).

'Pynchon, Paranoia, and Literature', *Representations*, vol. 25 (1989), pp. 99–118.

Thoughts and Things (Chicago: University of Chicago Press, 2015).

Bilmes, Leonid, 'Prose Pictures: Memory, Narrative and Ekphrasis in Nabokov, Sebald and Lerner (PhD Thesis: London: Queen Mary, University of London, 2018).

Bloch, Ernst, and Theodor Adorno., 'Something's Missing', in Ernst Bloch, *The Utopian Function of Art and Literature: Selected Essays* (Cambridge, MA: MIT Press, 1988), trans. Jack Zipes and Frank Mecklenburg, pp. 1–17.

Bloom, Harold, *Where Shall Wisdom Be Found?* (New York: Riverhead, 2004).

Bolaño, Roberto, *2666* (London: Picador, 2009), trans. Natasha Wimmer.

Borges, Jorge Luis, *Labyrinths: Selected Stories & Other Writings* (New York: New Directions, 2007).

Bradley, Arthur, *Originary Technicity: The Theory of Technology from Marx to Derrida* (Basingstoke: Palgrave, 2011).

Bradshaw, David, et al., eds., *Moving Modernisms: Motion, Technology and Modernity* (Oxford: Oxford University Press, 2016).

Braidotti, Rosi, *The Posthuman* (Cambridge: Polity, 2013).

Brooke-Rose, Christine, 'The Foot', in Christine Brooke-Rose, *Go When You See the Green Man Walking* (London: Michael Joseph, 1970).

Bruyn, J., et al., *A Corpus of Rembrandt Paintings II: 1631–1634* (Dordrecht: Martinus Nijhoff, 1986).

Bunyan, John, *The Pilgrim's Progress* (London: Penguin, 1965).

Burney, Frances, *Cecelia* (Oxford: Oxford University Press, 1988).

    Evelina (London: Penguin, 2012).

Byron, William, *Cervantes: A Biography* (London: Cassell, 1979).

Casanova, Pascale, *The World Republic of Letters* (Cambridge, MA: Harvard University Press, 2004), trans. M. B. DeBevoise.

Cavendish, Margaret, *The Blazing World and Other Writings* (London: Penguin, 2004).

Cervantes, Miguel de, *The Adventures of Don Quixote* (London: Penguin, 1950), trans. J. M. Cohen.

Chakrabarty, Dipesh, 'The Climate of History: Four Theses', *Critical Inquiry*, vol. 35, no. 2 (2009), pp. 197–222.

Clark, Timothy, 'Derangements of Scale', in Tom Cohen, ed., *Telemorphosis: Theory in the Era of Climate Change* (London: Open Humanities Press, 2012), online at https://quod.lib.umich.edu/o/ohp/10539563.0001.001/1:8/–telemor phosis-theory-in-the-era-of-climate-change-vol.-1?rgn=div1;view=fulltext

Coetzee, J. M., *The Childhood of Jesus* (London: Harvill Secker, 2013).

    Elizabeth Costello (New York: Viking, 2003).

    In the Heart of the Country (London: Vintage, 2004).

    Late Essays (London: Harvill Secker, 2017).

    The Schooldays of Jesus (London: Harvill Secker 2016).

Colebrook, Claire, 'All Life Is Artificial Life', *Textual Practice*, vol. 33, no. 1 (2019).

Coleridge, Samuel Taylor, *The Complete Works of Samuel Taylor Coleridge*, Vol. 4: *Lectures Upon Shakespeare* (New York: Harper, 1854).

Colesworthy, Rebecca, and Peter Nicholls, eds., *How Abstract Is It? Thinking Capital Now* (London: Routledge, 2016).

Collins, Wilkie, *The Woman in White* (London: Penguin, 1999).

David, Deirdre, ed., *The Cambridge Companion to the Victorian Novel* (Cambridge: Cambridge University Press, 2012).

Defoe, Daniel, *The Life and Strange Surprising Adventures of Robinson Crusoe of York, Mariner* (Oxford: Oxford University Press, 1998).

    Moll Flanders (London: Penguin, 1989).

DeLillo, Don, *The Body Artist* (London: Picador, 2001).

    Point Omega (London: Picador, 2010).

    Underworld (London: Picador, 1999).

    White Noise (London: Picador, 1999).

    The Word for Snow (New York: Karma Glenn Horowitz, 2014).

    Zero K (London: Picador, 2017).

DeLillo, Don, and Peter Boxall, 'The Edge of the Future: A Conversation with Don DeLillo', in Katherine Da Cunha Lewin and Kiron Ward, eds., *Don DeLillo: Contemporary Critical Perspectives* (London: Bloomsbury, 2019), pp. 159–64.

Derrida, Jacques, *Archive Fever* (Chicago: University of Chicago Press, 1995), trans. Eric Prenowitz.

    The Beast & the Sovereign, Vol. 2 (Chicago: University of Chicago Press, 2011), trans. Geoffrey Bennington.

Dissemination (London: Athlone Press, 1981), trans. Barbara Johnson.

Monolingualism of the Other: Or the Prosthesis of Origin (Stanford: Stanford University Press, 1998), trans. Patrick Mensah.

Of Grammatology (Baltimore: Johns Hopkins University Press, 1976), trans. Gayatri Chakravorty Spivak.

'Passions : An Oblique Offering', in David Wood, ed., *Derrida : A Critical Reader* (Oxford : Blackwell, 1992), trans. David Wood, pp. 5–35.

Speech and Phenomena and Other Essay's on Husserl's Theory of Signs (Evanston: Northwestern University Press, 1973), trans. David B. Allison.

Writing and Difference (Chicago: University of Chicago Press), trans. Alan Bass.

Descartes, René, *A Discourse on the Method of Correctly Conducting One's Reason and Seeing Truth in the Sciences* (Oxford: Oxford University Press, 2006), trans. Ian Maclean.

The Philosophical Writings of Descartes, Vol. 3: *The Correspondence* (Cambridge: Cambridge University Press, 1991).

'The Third Set of Objections & Replies containing the Controversy between Hobbes and Descartes', in Elizabeth Anscombe and Peter Thomas Geach, eds. and trans., *Descartes: Philosophical Writings* (New York: Macmillan, 1971).

Detloff, Madelyn, *The Persistence of Modernism: Loss and Mourning in the Twentieth Century* (Cambridge: Cambridge University Press, 2009).

Dexter, Emma, and Tanya Barson, eds., *Frida Kahlo* (London: Tate, 2005).

Dickens, Charles, *Bleak House* (Oxford: Oxford University Press, 1998).

A Christmas Carol and Other Christmas Books (Oxford: Oxford University Press, 2006).

David Copperfield (London: Penguin, 2004).

Great Expectations (London: Penguin, 1996).

Oliver Twist (New York: Vintage, 2012).

Dickinson, Emily, *The Poems of Emily Dickinson* (Cambridge, MA: Harvard University Press, 1999).

Dimock, Wai Chee, *Through Other Continents: American Literature across Deep Time* (Princeton: Princeton University Press, 2006).

Doody, Margaret Anne, *The True Story of the Novel* (London: HarperCollins, 1997).

Douglass, Frederick, *Narrative of the Life of Frederick Douglass, An American Slave: Written by Himself* (New York: Anchor, 1973).

Drndić, Daša, *Belladonna* (London: MacLehose Press, 2017), trans. Celia Hawkesworth.

Duras, Marguerite, *The Rapture of Lol V. Stein* (London: Hamish Hamilton, 1967), trans. Eileen Ellenbogen.

Duvall, John N., *The Identifying Fictions of Toni Morrison: Modernist Authenticity and Postmodern Blackness* (Basingstoke: Palgrave, 2000).

Edgeworth, Maria, *Belinda* (Oxford: Oxford University Press, 1999).

Elias, Amy J., and Christian Moraru, eds., *The Planetary Turn: Relationality and Geo-Aesthetics in the Twenty-First Century* (Evanston: Northwestern University Press, 2015).

Eliot, George, *Daniel Deronda* (Oxford: Oxford University Press, 1998).
   The George Eliot Letters (New Haven: Yale University Press, 1955), 7 vols., ed. Gordon S. Haight.
   Middlemarch (London: Penguin, 1994).
Eliot, T. S., '*Ulysses*, Order and Myth', collected in Lawrence Rainey, ed., *Modernism: An Anthology* (Oxford: Blackwell, 2005).
Elliott, Dorice Williams, 'Sarah Scott's *Millenium Hall* and Female Philanthropy', *Studies in English Literature, 1500–1900*, vol. 35, no. 3 (1995), pp. 535–53.
Ellison, Ralph, *Invisible Man* (London: Penguin, 1965).
Emre, Merve, 'Dismembered, Relocated, Rearranged', in *New York Review of Books*, 6 June (2019), online at www.nybooks.com/articles/2019/06/06/dasa-drndic-dismembered/
   Paraliterary: The Making of Bad Readers in Postwar America (Chicago: University of Chicago Press, 2017).
Engels, Frederick, 'The Part Played by Labour in the Transition from Ape to Man', in *Karl Marx and Frederick Engels: Selected Works* (London: Lawrence and Wishart, 1970).
Epstein, Julia, *The Iron Pen: Frances Burney and the Politics of Women's Writing* (Madison: University of Wisconsin Press, 1989).
Equiano, Olaudah, *The Interesting Narrative and Other Writings* (London: Penguin, 1995).
Esposito, Roberto, *Persons and Things: From the Body's Point of View* (Cambridge: Polity, 2015), trans. Zakiya Hanafi.
Fanon, Frantz, *Black Skin, White Masks* (London: Pluto Press, 1986), trans. Charles Lam Markmann.
Farthing, Michael and Stephen Farthing, *Leonardo da Vinci: Under the Skin* (London: Royal Academy of Arts, 2019).
Faulkner, William, *The Sound and the Fury* (New York: Norton, 1987).
Felski, Rita, *Uses of Literature* (Oxford: Blackwell, 2008).
Ferguson, Frances, *Solitude and the Sublime* (London: Routledge, 1992).
Fielding, Henry, *Joseph Andrews* (Oxford: Oxford University Press, 1999).
   Tom Jones (Oxford: Oxford University Press, 1998).
Findlen, Paula, 'Anatomy Theaters, Botanical Gardens, and Natural History Collections', in Katharine Park and Lorraine Daston, eds., *The Cambridge History of Science*, Vol. 3: *Early Modern Science* (Cambridge: Cambridge University Press, 2006), pp. 272–89.
Flaubert, Gustave, *Madame Bovary* (London: Penguin, 1992), trans. Geoffrey Wall.
   The Selected Letters of Gustave Flaubert (London: Hamish Hamilton, 1954), trans. and ed. Francis Steegmuller.
Forcione, Alban K., *Cervantes, Aristotle, and the 'Persiles'* (Princeton: Princeton University Press, 1970).
Foster, Hal, *Prosthetic Gods* (Cambridge, MA: MIT Press, 2004).
Foucault, Michel, *The Birth of Biopolitics: Lectures at the Collège de France, 1978–79* (Basingstoke: Palgrave, 2008), trans. Graham Burchell.

Freud, Sigmund, *Civilization and Its Discontents*, in Sigmund Freud, *Civilization, Society and Religion, Pelican Freud Library*, Vol. 12 (London: Penguin, 1985), trans. James Strachey.

Feuerbach, Ludwig, *The Essence of Christianity* (New York: Harper, 1957), trans. George Eliot.

Gallagher, Catherine, *The Industrial Reformation of English Fiction: Social Discourse and Narrative Form 1832–1867* (Chicago: University of Chicago Press, 1985).

  Nobody's Story: The Vanishing Acts of Women Writers in the Marketplace, 1670–1820 (Berkeley: University of California Press, 1994).

  'The Rise of Fictionality', in Franco Moretti, ed., *The Novel*, Vol. 1: *History, Geography and Culture* (Princeton: Princeton University Press, 2006).

Gasset, José Ortega y, *Meditations on Quixote* (New York: Norton, 1961), trans., Evelyn Rugg and Diego Marín.

Ghosh, Amitav, *The Great Derangement: Climate Change and the Unthinkable* (Chicago: University of Chicago Press, 2016).

Gibson, William, *Neuromancer* (London: Gollancz, 1984).

Gilman, Charlotte Perkins, *Herland* (London: Penguin, 2009).

  The Yellow Wallpaper (London: Virago, 1981).

Goethe, Johann Wolfgang von, *Elective Affinities* (Oxford: Oxford University Press, 1999), trans. David Constantine.

  Die Leiden Des Jungen Werther, in Goethe, *Goethes Werke: Band VI* (Hamburg: Christian Wegner Verlag, 1951).

  The Metamorphosis of Plants (Cambridge, MA: MIT Press, 2009), trans. Douglas Miller.

  The Sorrows of Young Werther (London: Penguin, 1989), trans. Michael Hulse.

  Wilhelm Meister's Apprenticeship (Princeton: Princeton University Press, 1995).

Gorra, Michael, 'The Portrait of Miss Bart', *New York Review of Books*, online at www.nybooks.com/daily/2015/05/01/house-of-mirth-portrait-miss-bart/, np.

Greenblatt, Stephen, *Renaissance Self-Fashioning from More to Shakespeare* (Chicago: University of Chicago Press, 2005).

  Shakespearean Negotiations: The Circulation of Social Energy in Renaissance England (Berkeley: University of California Press, 1988).

Griffin, Cristina Richieri, 'George Eliot's Feuerbach: Senses, Sympathy, Omniscience and Secularism', *ELH*, vol. 84, no. 2 (2017), pp. 475–502.

Hadfield, Andrew, ed., *The Oxford Handbook of English Prose 1500–1640* (Oxford: Oxford University Press, 2013).

Hallett, Mark, *Reynolds: Portraiture in Action* (New Haven: Yale University Press, 2014).

Halsey, Katie, 'The Blush of Modesty or the Blush of Shame? Reading Jane Austen's Blushes', *Modern Language Studies*, vol. 42, no. 3 (2006), pp. 226–38.

Haraway, Donna J., *Simians, Cyborgs, and Women: The Reinvention of Nature* (London: Free Association Books, 1991).

Hardy, Thomas, *The Return of the Native* (Oxford: Oxford University Press, 2005).

Harrison, John, and Peter Laslett, *The Library of John Locke* (Oxford: Oxford University Press, 1965).

Hastings, William T., 'Errors and Inconsistencies in Defoe's *Robinson Crusoe*', *Modern Language Notes*, vol. 27, no. 6 (1912), pp. 161–66.

Hawthorne, Nathaniel, *The Blithedale Romance* (Oxford: Oxford University Press, 1998).

Hayles, N. Katherine, *How We Became Posthuman: Virtual Bodies in Cybernetics, Literature, and Informatics* (Chicago: University of Chicago Press, 1999).

   Unthought: The Power of the Cognitive Nonconscious (Chicago: University of Chicago Press, 2017).

Healy, Thomas, 'Playing Seriously in Renaissance Writing', in Margaret Healy and Thomas Healy, eds., *Renaissance Transformations: The Making of English Writing (1500–1650)* (Edinburgh: Edinburgh University Press, 2009), pp. 15–31.

Hegel, G. W. F., *Phenomenology of Spirit* (Cambridge: Cambridge University Press, 2018), trans. Terry Pinkard.

Heidegger, Martin, 'Existence and Being', in Walter Kaufmann, ed., *Existentialism from Dostoyevsky to Sartre* (Berkeley: New American Library, 1975).

   The Fundamental Concepts of Metaphysics: World, Finitude, Solitude (Bloomington: Indiana University Press, 1995), trans. William McNeill and Nicholas Walker.

   'The Hand and the Typewriter', reprinted in Friedrich Kittler, *Gramophone, Film, Typewriter* (Stanford: Stanford University Press, 1999), trans. Geoffrey Winthrop-Young and Michael Wutz.

   Poetry, Language, Thought (New York: HarperCollins, 2001), trans. Albert Hofstadter.

   The Question Concerning Technology and Other Essays (New York: Harper, 1977).

   What Is Called Thinking (New York: Harper and Row, 1968), trans. Fred D. Weick and J. Glenn Gray.

Heise, Ursula K., *Sense of Place and Sense of Planet: The Environmental Imagination of the Global* (Oxford: Oxford University Press, 2008).

Hobbes, Thomas, *The Elements of Law Natural and Politic* (London: Frank Cass, 1969).

   Leviathan: Or the Matter, Forme, & Power of a Commonwealth Ecclesiasticall and Civill (New Haven: Yale University Press, 2010), ed. Ian Shapiro.

Hobsbawm, Eric, *The Age of Revolution: Europe 1789–1848* (London: Phoenix Press, 2000).

hooks, bell, 'Postmodern Blackness', *Postmodern Culture*, vol. 1, no. 1 (1990), online at https://muse.jhu.edu/article/27283, np.

Howard, Maureen, 'The Bachelor and the Baby: *The House of Mirth*', in Millicent Bell, ed., *The Cambridge Companion to Edith Wharton* (Cambridge: Cambridge University Press, 1995).

Hugo, Victor, *Les Misérables* (London: Penguin, 1982), trans. Norman Denny.

Hume, David, *A Treatise of Human Nature* (Oxford: Oxford University Press, 2000), eds. David Fate Norton and Mary J. Norton.

Hutcheon, Linda, *The Politics of Postmodernism*, 2nd ed. (London: Routledge, 2002).

Ishiguro, Kazuo, *Never Let Me Go* (London: Faber and Faber, 2006).

Iwanisziw, Susan B., 'Behn's Novel Investment in Oroonoko: Kingship, Slavery and Tobacco in English Colonialism', in *South Atlantic Review*, vol. 63, no. 2 (1998), pp. 75–98.

Jain, Sara S., 'The Prosthetic Imagination: Enabling and Disabling the Prosthesis Trope', *Science, Technology, & Human Values*, vol. 24, no. 1 (1999), pp. 31–54.

James, David, ed., *The Legacies of Modernism: Historicising Postwar and Contemporary Fiction* (Cambridge: Cambridge University Press, 2012).

James, Henry, *The Figure in the Carpet*, in Henry James, *The Figure in the Carpet and Other Stories* (London: Penguin, 1986), pp. 355–400.

Glasses, in Henry James, *The Complete Tales of Henry James,* Vol. 9: *1892–1898* (London: Rupert Hart-Davis, 1964), ed. Leon Edel, pp. 317–70.

The Golden Bowl (London: Penguin, 2009).

Henry James on Culture: Collected Essays on Politics and the American Social Scene (Lincoln: University of Nebraska Press, 1999), ed. Pierre A. Walker

The Jolly Corner, in Henry James, *Tales of Henry James* (New York: Norton, 2003), eds. Christof Wegelin and Henry B. Wonham, pp. 341–69.

The Middle Years, in Henry James, *Tales of Henry James* (New York: Norton, 2003), eds. Christof Wegelin and Henry B. Wonham, pp. 211–28.

The Portrait of a Lady (Oxford: Oxford University Press, 2009).

The Turn of the Screw and Other Stories (Oxford: Oxford University Press, 1992).

What Maisie Knew (London: Penguin, 1985).

The Wings of the Dove (London: Everyman, 1997).

Jameson, Fredric, *The Antinomies of Realism* (London: Verso, 2013).

The Political Unconscious: Narrative as a Socially Symbolic Act (London: Routledge, 1983).

Postmodernism: Or the Cultural Logic of Late Capitalism (London: Verso, 1991).

The Prison-House of Language: A Critical Account of Structuralism and Russian Formalism (Princeton: Princeton University Press, 1972).

Janvier, Ludovic, 'Place of Narration / Narration of Place', in Ruby Cohn, ed., *Samuel Beckett: The Comic Gamut* (New Brunswick: Rutgers University Press, 1962).

Jian, Ma, *Beijing Coma* (London: Vintage, 2009), trans. Flora Drew.

Jonik, Michael, *Herman Melville and the Politics of the Inhuman* (Cambridge: Cambridge University Press, 2018).

Jordan, Hannah, 'Between Fact and Imagination: Victorian Tableaux Vivantes in Nineteenth-Century Britain (PhD Thesis: Sussex: Sussex University, 2020).

Jordan, Nicolle, 'A Creole Contagion: Narratives of Slavery and Tainted Wealth in *Millenium Hall*', *Tulsa Studies in Women's Literature*, vol. 30, no. 1 (2011).

Joyce, James, *Finnegans Wake* (London: Minerva, 1992).
  A Portrait of the Artist as a Young Man (London: Penguin, 1992).
  Ulysses (London: Penguin, 1986).
Jung, C. G., *The Symbolic Life: Miscellaneous Writings* (London: Routledge and Kegan Paul, 1977), trans. R. F. C. Hull.
Kafka, Franz, *The Complete Stories* (New York : Schocken Books, 1971).
Kaplan, Janet A., *Unexpected Journeys: The Art and Life of Remedios Varo* (London: Virago, 1988).
Keenleyside, Heather, *Animals and Other People: Forms and Living Beings in the Long Eighteenth Century* (Philadelphia: University of Pennsylvania Press, 2016).
Kelly, Adam, 'David Foster Wallace and the New Sincerity in American Fiction', in David Hering, ed., *Consider David Foster Wallace: Critical Essays* (Austin: Sideshow, 2010), pp. 131–46.
Kermode, Frank, *The Sense of an Ending: Studies in the Theory of Fiction* (Oxford: Oxford University Press, 2000).
Kittler, Friedrich A., *Gramophone, Film, Typewriter* (Stanford: Stanford University Press, 1986), trans. Geoffrey Winthrop-Young and Michael Wutz.
Kleist, Heinrich von, 'On the Marionette Theatre', in Idris Parry, *Hand to Mouth and Other Essays* (Manchester: Carcanet, 1981), trans. Idris Parry.
Klestinec, Cynthia, *Theaters of Anatomy: Students, Teachers and Traditions of Dissection in Renaissance Venice* (Baltimore: Johns Hopkins University Press, 2011).
Knowlson, James, *Damned to Fame: The Life of Samuel Beckett* (London: Bloomsbury, 1996).
Kozubek, Jim, *Modern Prometheus: Editing the Human Genome with Crispr-Cas9* (Cambridge: Cambridge University Press, 2018).
Kristeva, Julia, *Powers of Horror: An Essay on Abjection* (New York: Columbia University Press, 1982).
Landsberg, Alison, *Prosthetic Memory: The Transformation of American Remembrance in the Age of Mass Culture* (New York: Columbia University Press, 2004).
Lanser, Susan Sniader, *Fictions of Authority: Women Writers and Narrative Voice* (Ithaca : Cornell University Press 1992).
Lawrence, D. H., *The Letters of D.H. Lawrence*, Vol. 2: *June 1913–October 1916* (Cambridge: Cambridge University Press, 1981), eds. George J. Zytaruk and James T. Boulton.
  The Symbolic Meaning (New York: The Viking Press, 1964).
  'Why the Novel Matters', in D. H. Lawrence, *Study of Thomas Hardy and Other Essays* (Cambridge: Cambridge University Press, 1985), ed. Bruce Steele, pp. 191–98.
Leavis, F. R., *The Great Tradition* (London: Faber, 2008).
Lee, Gerald Stanley, *Crowds* (London: Curtis Brown, 1913).
Leibniz, Gottfried Wilhelm, *Theodicy* (Dumfries and Galloway: Anodos, 2019).
Lennox, Charlotte, *The Female Quixote* (Oxford: Oxford University Press, 1998).

Levine, Caroline, *Forms: Whole, Rhythm, Hierarchy, Network* (Princeton: Princeton University Press, 2015).

'Victorian Realism', in Deirdre David, ed., *The Cambridge Companion to the Victorian Novel* (Cambridge: Cambridge University Press, 2012).

Levine, George, *The Realistic Imagination: English Fiction from Frankenstein to Lady Chatterley* (Chicago: University of Chicago Press, 1981).

Levine, George, et al., '*Novel Politics*: Four Responses and a Reply from the Author', *Textual Practice*, vol. 32, no. 7 (2018), pp. 1049–93.

Lewis, Wyndham, 'The Children of the New Epoch', collected in Walter Michel and C. J. Fox, eds., *Wyndham Lewis on Art: Collected Writings 1913–1956* (London: Thames and Hudson, 1969).

Leyda, Jay, *The Melville Log: A Documentary Life of Herman Melville 1819–1891*, Vol. 2 (New York: Gordian Press, 1969).

Littell, Jonathan, *The Kindly Ones* (London: Vintage, 2010), trans. Charlotte Mandell.

Llosa, Mario Vargas, 'A Novel for the Twenty-First Century', *Harvard Review*, no. 28 (2005), pp. 125–36.

Locke, John, *Second Treatise of Government* (Oxford: Oxford University Press, 2016).

Logan, George M., *The Meaning of More's Utopia* (Princeton: Princeton University Press, 1983).

Lukács, Georg, *The Meaning of Contemporary Realism* (London: Merlin, 2006), trans. John and Necke Mander.

Studies in European Realism (New York: Grosset and Dunlap, 1964), trans. Edith Bone.

The Theory of the Novel: A Historico-Philosophical Essay on the Forms of Great Epic Literature (London: Merlin, 1971), trans. Anna Bostock.

Lyotard, Jean François, *The Postmodern Condition: A Report on Knowledge* (Manchester: Manchester University Press, 1984), trans. Geoff Bennington and Brian Massumi.

McCarthy, Cormac, *The Road* (London: Picador, 2006).

McEwan, Ian, *Machines Like Me* (London: Jonathan Cape, 2019).

McKeon, Michael, *The Origins of the English Novel 1600–1740* (Baltimore: Johns Hopkins University Press, 2002).

McLouhglin, Kevin, 'Losing One's Place: Displacement and Domesticity in Dickens's *Bleak House*', *Modern Language Notes*, 108 (1993), pp. 875–90.

McLuhan, Marshall, *Understanding Media: The Extensions of Man* (Cambridge, MA: MIT Press, 1994).

McCrory, Donald P., *No Ordinary Man: The Life and Times of Miguel de Cervantes* (London: Peter Owen, 2002).

Mangano, Bryan, 'Institutions of Friendship in Sarah Scott's *Millenium Hall*', *Texas Studies in Literature and Language*, vol. 57, no. 4 (2015), pp. 464–90.

Marcus, Laura, *Dreams of Modernity: Psychoanalysis, Literature, Cinema* (Cambridge: Cambridge University Press, 2014).

Marinetti, Franco, et al., 'The Futurist Cinema', collected in Lawrence Rainey et al., eds., *Futurism: An Anthology* (New Haven: Yale University Press, 2009).

Marks, Laura U., *Touch: Sensuous Theory and Multisensory Media* (Minneapolis: University of Minnesota Press, 2002).

Marx, Karl, *Capital: A Critique of Political Economy*, Vol. 1 (London: Penguin 1978), trans. David Fernbach.

'Theses on Feuerbach', in Karl Marx and Frederick Engels, *Selected Works*, Vol. 1 (Moscow: Progress Publishers, 1969).

Marx, Karl, and Friedrich Engels, *The Communist Manifesto* (New Haven: Yale University Press, 2012).

Maude, Ulrika, *Beckett, Technology and the Body* (Cambridge: Cambridge University Press, 2009).

Mazzoni, Guido, *Theory of the Novel* (Cambridge, MA: Harvard University Press, 2017), trans. Zakiya Hanafi.

Melville, Herman, *Benito Cereno*, in Herman Melville, *Melville's Short Novels* (New York: Norton, 2002), ed. Dan McCall.

Billy Budd, Sailor, and Selected Tales (Oxford: Oxford University Press, 1997).

Clarel (Evanston: Northwestern University Press, 2008).

Moby Dick (Oxford: Oxford University Press, 2008).

Mettrie, Julien Offray De La, *Machine Man and Other Writings* (Cambridge: Cambridge University Press, 1996).

Miles, Robert, 'Political Gothic Fiction', in Angela Wright and Dale Townshend, eds., *Romantic Gothic* (Edinburgh: Edinburgh University Press, 2016), pp. 129–46.

Miller, D. A., *Jane Austen, Or the Secret of Style* (Princeton: Princeton University Press, 2003).

Miller, Tyrus, *Late Modernism: Politics, Fiction and the Arts between the World Wars* (Berkeley: University of California Press, 1999).

Milne, Drew, 'Notes on Lichen', *Textual Practice*, online at www.tandfonline.com /doi/full/10.1080/0950236X.2019.1613828

Milton, John, *Paradise Lost* (Harlow: Pearson, 2007).

Mitchell, Robert, and Phillip Thurtle, eds., *Data Made Flesh: Embodying Information* (New York: Routledge, 2004).

Mitchell, Silas Weir, 'The Case of George Dedlow', in David Seed et al., eds., *Life and Limb: Perspectives on the American Civil War* (Liverpool: Liverpool University Press, 2017), pp. 131–45.

Moody, Alys, *The Art of Hunger: Aesthetic Autonomy and the Afterlives of Modernism* (Oxford: Oxford University Press, 2018).

More, Thomas, *Epigrams*, in Thomas More, *The Complete Works of Thomas More*, Vol. 3, part 2 (New Haven: Yale University Press, 1984), eds. Clarence H. Miller et al.

Utopia (Cambridge: Cambridge University Press, 2002), trans. Robert M. Adams.

Moretti, Franco, ed. *The Novel*, Vol. 1: *History, Geography, and Culture* (Princeton: Princeton University Press, 2006).

Morrison, Toni, *The Bluest Eye* (London: Vintage, 2016).

    Playing in the Dark: Whiteness and the Literary Imagination (Cambridge, MA: Harvard University Press, 1992).

    'Unspeakable Things Unspoken: The Afro-American Presence in American Literature', online at https://tannerlectures.utah.edu/_documents/a-to-z/m/morrison90.pdf, pp. 123–63.

Morton, Timothy, *Ecology Without Nature: Rethinking Environmental Aesthetics* (Cambridge, MA: Harvard University Press, 2007).

Mottolese, William C., 'Tristram Cyborg and Toby Toolmaker: Body, Tools, and Hobbyhorse in *Tristram Shandy*', *Studies in English Literature, 1500–1900*, vol. 47, no. 3 (2007), pp. 679–701.

Nancy, Jean-Luc, *Being Singular Plural* (Stanford: Stanford University Press, 2000), trans. Robert D. Richardson and Anne E. O'Byrne.

Nashe, Thomas, *The Unfortunate Traveller* (London: Lehmann, 1848).

Nealon, Jeffrey T., *Post-Postmodernism, Or the Cultural Logic of Just in Time Capitalism* (Stanford: Stanford University Press, 2012).

Neville, Henry, *The Isle of Pines*, in Susan Bruce, ed., *Three Early Modern Utopias: Thomas More*, Utopia, *Francis Bacon*, New Atlantis, *Henry Neville*, The Isle of Pines (Oxford: Oxford University Press, 1999).

Ngai, Sianne, *Our Aesthetic Categories: Zany, Cute, Interesting* (Cambridge, MA: Harvard University Press, 2015).

Nicholls, Peter, *Modernisms: A Literary Guide*, 2nd ed. (Basingstoke: Palgrave, 2009).

Norris, Andrew, ed., *Politics, Metaphysics and Death: Essays on Giorgio Agamben's Homo Sacer* (Durham: Duke University Press, 2005).

Oreskes, Naomi, 'The Scientific Consensus on Climate Change: How Do We Know We're Not Wrong?' in Joseph F. C. Dimento and Pamela Doughman, eds., *Climate Change: What It Means for Us, Our Children, and Our Grandchildren* (Cambridge: MIT Press, 2007), pp. 105–48.

Orwell, George, 'Inside the Whale', in George Orwell, *Inside the Whale and Other Essays* (London: Penguin, 1962),

    Nineteen Eighty-Four (London: Penguin, 1987).

Ovid, *Metamorphoses* (Oxford: Oxford University Press, 1987), trans. A. D. Melville.

Papapetros, Spyros, *On the Animation of the Inorganic: Art, Architecture, and the Extension of Life* (Chicago: University of Chicago Press, 2012).

Park, Julie, 'Pains and Pleasures of the Automaton: Frances Burney's Mechanics of Coming Out', *Eighteenth Century Studies*, vol. 40, no. 1 (2006), pp. 23–49.

Piercy, Marge, *Woman on the Edge of Time* (London: Penguin, 2016).

Poe, Edgar Allan, *The Complete Tales and Poems of Edgar Allan Poe* (New York: Castle Books, 2002).

    The Complete Works of Edgar Allan Poe, Vol. 14: *Essays, Miscellanies* (New York: AMS Press, 1965).

Pope, Alexander, *Essay on Man* (Princeton: Princeton University Press, 2016).

Porter, Roy, *Blood & Guts: A Short History of Medicine* (London: Penguin, 2003).

Pound, Ezra, *The Cantos of Ezra Pound* (London: Faber and Faber, 1975).

Powers, Lyall H., ed., *Henry James and Edith Wharton Letters, 1900–1915* (London: Weidenfeld and Nicolson, 1990).

Powers, Richard, 'The Seventh Event', *Granta*, vol. 90 (2005), pp. 58–74.

Pratt, Lloyd, *Archives of American Time: Literature and Modernity in the Nineteenth Century* (Philadelphia: University of Pennsylvania Press, 2010).

The Strangers Book: The Human of African American Literature (Philadelphia: University of Pennsylvania Press, 2016).

Proust, Marcel, *Remembrance of Things Past* (London: Penguin, 1983), 3 vols. trans. C. K. Scott Moncrieff and Terence Kilmartin.

Pynchon, Thomas, *The Crying of Lot 49* (London: Vintage, 2000).

Gravity's Rainbow (New York: Viking, 1973).

'The Road to 1984', *The Guardian*, 3 May 2003, online at www.scribd.com/doc/100899/Pynchon-s-Intro-to-Orwell-s-1984, np.

Quigley, Muireann, *Self-Ownership, Property Rights and the Human Body* (Cambridge: Cambridge University Press, 2018).

Rancière, Jacques, 'The Aesthetic Revolution and Its Outcomes: Emplotments of Autonomy and Heteronomy' *New Left Review*, vol. 14 (2002), pp. 133–51.

Rebhorn, Matthew, 'Minding the Body: "Benito Cereno" and Melville's Embodied Reading Practice', *Studies in the Novel* vol. 41, no. 2 (2009), pp. 157–77.

Reid, James H., *Proust, Beckett and Narration* (Cambridge: Cambridge University Press, 2009).

Richardson, Samuel, *Clarissa: Or the History of a Young Lady* (London: Penguin, 1985).

Pamela (Oxford: Oxford University Press, 2001).

Ricoeur, Paul, 'The Function of Fiction in Shaping Reality', in Mario J. Valdés ed., *A Ricoeur Reader: Refection and Imagination* (New York: Harvester, 1991), pp. 117–36.

Interpretation Theory: Discourse and the Surplus of Meaning (Fort Worth: Texas Christian University Press, 1976).

'Mimesis and Representation', in Mario J. Valdés ed., *A Ricoeur Reader: Refection and Imagination* (New York: Harvester, 1991), pp. 137–56.

Time and Narrative (Chicago: Chicago University Press, 1990), 3 vols., trans. Kathleen McLaughlin and David Pellauer.

Rifkin, Jeremy, *The Biotech Century: Harnessing the Gene and Remaking the World* (London: Victor Gollancz, 1998).

Roberts, Ben, 'Stiegler Reading Derrida: The Prosthesis of Deconstruction in Technics', *Postmodern Culture*, vol. 16, no. 1 (2005), online at http://pmc.iath.virginia.edu/issue.905/16.1roberts.html, np.

Rogin, Michael Paul, *Subversive Genealogy: The Politics and Art of Herman Melville* (Berkeley: University of California Press, 1983).

Rousseau, Jean-Jacques, *A Discourse on the Origin of Inequality*, in Jean-Jacques Rousseau, *The Social Contract and Discourses* (London: Everyman, 1993).

La Nouvelle Héloïse (Paris : Garnier, 1960).

Rubin, William, ed., *Cézanne: The Late Work* (New York: Museum of Modern Art, 1977).

Ruskin, John, *The Works of John Ruskin*, Vol. 37: *The Letters of John Ruskin 1870–1889* (Cambridge: Cambridge University Press, 2009).

Rushdie, Salman, *Imaginary Homelands: Essays in Criticism 1981–91* (London: Granta, 1992).

Midnight's Children (London: Vintage, 2006).

Ryan, Vanessa L., *Thinking Without Thinking in the Victorian Novel* (Baltimore: Johns Hopkins University Press, 2012).

Rykwert, Joseph, 'Organic and Mechanical', *RES: Anthropology and Aesthetics*, vol. 20 (1992).

Salisbury, Laura, *Samuel Beckett: Laughing Matters, Comic Timing* (Edinburgh: Edinburgh University Press, 2012).

Savile, George, *The Lady's New-year's Gift: Or, Advice to a Daughter* (London: Randal Taylor, 1688).

Sawday, Jonathan, *The Body Emblazoned: Dissection and the Human Body in Renaissance Culture* (London: Routledge,1995).

Scarry, Elaine, *The Body in Pain: The Making and Unmaking of the World* (New York: Oxford University Press, 1985).

Schaeffer, Denise, 'The Utility of Ink: Rousseau and Robinson Crusoe', *The Review of Politics*, vol. 64, no. 1 (2002), pp. 121–48.

Schama, Simon, *Rembrandt's Eyes* (London: Penguin, 1999).

Schmidt, Benjamin, *Inventing Exoticism: Geography, Globalism and Europe's Early Modern World* (Philadelphia: University of Pennsylvania Press, 2015).

Schreiner, Olive, *The Story of an African Farm* (Oxford: Oxford University Press, 2008).

Schülting, Sabine, *Dirt in Victorian Literature and Culture: Writing Materiality* (London: Routledge, 2016)

Scott, Sarah, *Millenium Hall* (London: Penguin, 1986).

Sedgwick, Eve Kosofsky, *Between Men: English Literature and Male Homosocial Desire* (New York: Columbia University Press, 1985).

Tendencies (Durham: Duke University Press, 1993).

Seed, David, et al., eds., *Life and Limb: Perspectives on the American Civil War* (Liverpool: Liverpool University Press, 2017).

Selvon, Sam, *The Lonely Londoners* (London: Penguin, 2006).

Semff, Michael, and Anthony Spira, *Hans Bellmer* (Ostfildern: Hatje Cantz, 2006).

Seol, Young-Joon, et al., '3D Bioprinted Biomask for Facial Skin Reconstruction', *Bioprinting*, vol. 10 (2018).

Shakespeare, William, *The Complete Works* (Oxford: Clarendon, 1988).

Shelley, Mary, *Frankenstein, Or the Modern Prometheus* (Oxford: Oxford University Press, 2008).

The Last Man (Oxford: Oxford University Press, 1998).

Sherry, Vincent, *Modernism and the Reinvention of Decadence* (Cambridge: Cambridge University Press, 2015).

Showalter, Elaine, *A Literature of Their Own: British Women Novelists from Brontë to Lessing* (Princeton: Princeton University Press, 1977).

Shuttleworth, Sally, *George Eliot and Nineteenth-Century Science: The Make Believe of a Beginning* (Cambridge: Cambridge University Press, 1984).

Silko, Leslie Marmon, *Almanac of the Dead* (London: Penguin, 1992).

Skinner, Quentin, 'Sir Thomas More's *Utopia* and the Language of Renaissance Humanism', in Anthony Pagden, ed., *The Languages of Political Theory in Early-Modern Europe* (Cambridge: Cambridge University Press, 1987), pp. 123–57.

Skloot, Rebecca, *The Immortal Life of Henrietta Lacks* (London: Pan, 2010).

Smith, Shawn, *Pynchon and History: Metahistorical Rhetoric and Postmodern Narrative Form in the Novels of Thomas Pynchon* (New York: Routledge 2005).

Sterne, Laurence, *The Life and Opinions of Tristram Shandy, Gentleman* (Oxford: Oxford University Press, 2009).

Stevenson, Robert Louis, *The Strange Case of Dr Jekyll and Mr Hyde and Other Stories* (London: Penguin, 1979).

Stiegler, Bernard, 'Derrida and Technology: Fidelity at the Limits of Deconstruction and the Prosthesis of Faith', in Tom Cohen, ed., *Jacques Derrida and the Humanities* (Cambridge: Cambridge University Press, 2001), pp. 238–70.

 Technics and Time, 1: The Fault of Epimetheus (Stanford: Stanford University Press, 1998), trans. Richard Beardsworth and George Collins.

Stone, Allucquère Rosanne, *The War of Desire and Technology at the Close of the Mechanical Age* (Cambridge, MA: MIT Press, 1995).

Stoker, Bram, *Dracula* (London: Penguin, 1993).

Strich, Fritz, *Goethe and World Literature* (London: Routledge, 1949).

Swift, Jonathan, *Gulliver's Travels* (Oxford: Oxford University Press, 1998).

 A Tale of a Tub and Other Works (Cambridge: Cambridge University Press, 2010).

Tajiri, Yoshiki, *Samuel Beckett and the Prosthetic Body: The Organs and Senses in Modernism* (Basingstoke: Palgrave, 2007).

Tanner, Tony, *Jane Austen* (Basingstoke: Palgrave, 2007).

Todd, Janet, *The Secret Life of Aphra Behn* (London: André Deutsch, 1996).

Tolstoy, Leo, *War and Peace* (London: Penguin, 1982).

Turning, Alan, 'Computer Machinery and Intelligence', *Mind*, vol. 54 (1950), pp. 433–60.

Vartanian, Aram, *La Mattrie's L'Homme Machine: A Study in the Origins of an Idea* (Princeton: Princeton University Press, 1960).

Vermeulen, Timotheus, and Robin van den Akker, 'Notes on Metamodernism', *Journal of Aesthetics & Culture*, vol. 2 (2010), pp. 1–14.

Virilio, Paul, *The Aesthetics of Disappearance* (Los Angeles: Semiotext(e), 2009), trans. Philip Beitchman.

Voltaire, *Candide* (London: Penguin, 2001).

Wallace, David Foster, 'E Unibus Pluram: Television and U.S. Fiction', *Review of Contemporary Fiction*, vol. 13, no. 2 (1993), pp. 151–94.

Oblivion (London: Abacus, 2005).

The Pale King (London: Hamish Hamilton, 2011).

Walpole, Horace, *Castle of Otranto* (Oxford: Oxford University Press, 2014).

Ward, Kiron, 'Fictional Encyclopaedism in James Joyce, Leslie Marmon Silko, and Roberto Bolaño: Towards a Theory of Literary Totality' (PhD thesis: Sussex: University of Sussex, 2017).

Watt, Ian, *The Rise of the Novel: Studies in Defoe, Richardson and Fielding* (London: Pimlico, 2000).

Weller, Shane, *Beckett, Literature and the Ethics of Alterity* (Basingstoke: Palgrave, 2006).

Wells, H. G., *The Time Machine*, in H.G. Wells, *Selected Short Stories* (London: Penguin, 1958).

Wharton, Edith, *The Age of Innocence* (London: Penguin, 1993).

A Backward Glance (New York: Charles Scribner's Sons, 1964).

The House of Mirth (Oxford: Oxford University Press, 2008).

The Writing of Fiction (New York: Octagon Books, 1966).

Wilcox, Claire, and Circe Henestrosa, *Frida Kahlo: Making Her Self Up* (London: V&A, 2018).

Wilcox, Leonard, 'Baudrillard, DeLillo's *White Noise*, and the End of Heroic Narrative', *Contemporary Literature*, vol. 32, no. 3 (1991), pp. 346–65.

Wilde, Oscar, *The Complete Letters of Oscar Wilde* (London: Fourth Estate, 2000), eds. Merlin Holland and Rupert Hart-Davies.

The Picture of Dorian Gray (London: Penguin, 1985).

Williams, Raymond, *The Country and the City* (New York: Oxford University Press, 1973).

Culture and Society (London: Vintage, 2017).

The English Novel from Dickens to Lawrence (London: Chatto and Windus, 1973).

Wills, David, *Dorsality: Thinking Back through Technology and Politics* (Minneapolis: University of Minnesota Press, 2008).

Inanimation: Theories of Inorganic Life (Minneapolis: University of Minnesota Press, 2016).

Prosthesis (Stanford: Stanford University Press, 1995).

Wittgenstein, Ludwig, *On Certainty* (New York: Harper, 1972), trans. Denis Paul and G. E. M. Anscombe.

Philosophical Investigations (Oxford: Blackwell, 2001), trans. G. E. M. Anscombe.

Tractatus Logico-Philosophicus (London: Routledge 2001), trans. D. F. Pears and B. F. McGuinness.

Wollstonecraft, Mary, *Mary* and *The Wrongs of Woman* (Oxford: Oxford University Press, 2007).

Woloch, Alex, 'Partial Representation' in Robyn Warhol, ed., *The Work of Genre: Selected Essays from the English Institute* (Cambridge: English Institute, 2011), np.

Woodall, Joanna, ed., *Portraiture: Facing the Subject* (Manchester: Manchester University Press, 1997).

Woolf, Virginia, *Mrs Dalloway* (New York: Alfred A. Knopf, 1993).

　To the Lighthouse (London: Grafton, 1977).

　The Waves (Oxford: Oxford University Press, 2015).

Wyett, Jodi L., 'Female Quixotism Refashioned: *Northanger Abbey*, The Engaged Reader, and the Woman Writer', *The Eighteenth Century*, vol. 56, no. 2 (2015), pp. 261–76.

Yamashita, Karen Tei, *I Hotel* (Minneapolis: Coffee House Press, 2010).

Zardawi, Faraedon M., et al., 'Mechanical Properties of 3D Printed Facial Prostheses Compared to Handmade Silicone Polymer Prostheses', *European Scientific Journal*, vol. 11, no. 12 (2015), pp. 1–10.

Zola, Émile, *Thérèse Raquin* (London: Penguin, 1962), trans. Leonard Tancock.

Zurbrugg, Nicholas, *Beckett and Proust* (Gerrard's Cross: Colin Smythe, 1988).

Index